THE KITCHEN BOOK

THE KITCHEN BOOK

Terence Conran

Crown Publishers Inc., New York

Contributors
Charlotte Baden-Powell AA Dip. RIBA
Peter Collymore MA AA Dip. RIBA
Elizabeth David
Nicola Hemingway
Maerit Huldt
Dinah Morrison
Suzanne Slesin
Alexandra Towle
John Winter M Arch AA Dip. RIBA

Photographers
Clive Corless
Raeanne Giovanni
Roger Stowell

The Kitchen Book was edited and designed by
Mitchell Beazley Publishers Limited
Mill House, 87-89 Shaftesbury Avenue, London W1V 7AD

Editor	David MacFadyen
Art Editor	Peter Wrigley
Assistant Editors	Joanna Chisholm Susie Courtauld
Designer	Catherine Caufield
Picture Researcher	Jackie Webber
Art Assistant	Francis Morgan
Production	Barry Baker
Publisher	Bruce Marshall
Art Director	John Bigg
Executive Editor	Michael Bowers

First published in the USA in 1977 by
Crown Publishers Inc.,
One Park Avenue, New York N.Y. 10016

Typeset by The Vantage Group of Companies, London, England
Reproduced and printed by Smeets BV, Weert, Netherlands

Library of Congress Cataloging in Publication Data
Conran, Terence.
The kitchen book.
Includes index.
1. Kitchens. 2. Kitchen utensils. 3. Interior
decoration. I. Title.
NK2117.K5C66 643'.3 77-7059
ISBN 0-517-53131-3 (Hardback)
ISBN 0-517-55453-4 (Paperback)

To Caroline, *the best cook I know*

Introduction

The kitchen mirrors more effectively than any other room in the house the great social changes that have taken place in the last hundred years. In the early part of this century it would have been surprising to find a middle-class woman in her kitchen. Her servants guarded their domain as jealously as she and her family guarded theirs. Her sole contact with the kitchen would have been with the cook when she came upstairs to discuss the day's menus and with the butler to arrange the wines for dinner. But I think that many of the qualities of that below-stairs life should be studied again because, instead of being old-fashioned and inappropriate to the world today, they were simple, effective and efficient. Kitchens and pantries were well planned, cheerful places to work and often supported a contented work-force.

Kitchen design has altered dramatically in this century. The effects of two world wars and enormous advances on the technological front have made a woman's place in her home far different from that of her grandmother's. Many middle-class housewives in the 1920s and 1930s were ashamed that they could no longer afford the servants that once supported their life-styles. Their kitchens reflected this, being small, sad and dingy places where meals were prepared as quickly and surreptitiously as possible.

But now, thank goodness, we are returning to an almost medieval situation, where the kitchen is, once again, the hub of the home. It is not only the place where we cook, eat and entertain, it is also the place where we do our laundry and other household chores, and it is certainly the place where the children gather and play. It really ought to be renamed the "living room", because that is what it is.

We have also fallen in love with food again. The whole process of marketing, storing, preparing, cooking and serving, together with the quality of the equipment that we use to do it with, is again one of the great pleasures of life.

So, not surprisingly, the design and equipping of the kitchen is now the most important consideration when a home is being planned or altered. The purpose of this book is to help you design the right kitchen for your way of life. It discusses all the practical considerations and will help you decide what sort of style you would like to live and work in: it examines technical and aesthetic considerations: it may also cause you to question whether or not you need a dining-room or even a living-room.

It encourages you to begin your first kitchen in the simplest and most sensible way, only encouraging you into recherché refinements when your skill as a cook can justify them.

If you are a serious cook who loves the whole process then you probably spend more waking hours in your kitchen than any other room. I hope the ideas in this book will help to make those hours as happy as possible for you, your friends and your family.

Terence Conran.

Cave to microwave

When you study the history of cooking and kitchens you discover ideas, methods and equipment that have fallen into desuetude can be re-examined and adapted for contemporary use.

There is no better example than the Saxon home (circa AD 900), where the whole house was in effect one huge kitchen. Raw food was brought in at the front door and stored in cool larders insulated from the main room. This was dominated by an enormous open fire, which cooked the food and warmed the room. Tables on either side of the fireplace were used for food preparation and for eating, the family sitting on one side and servants on the other. The family and servants slept around the fire on raised ledges screened by curtains into compartments.

With a slight stretch of the imagination this might well describe a contemporary kitchen, bulk purchases of food being stored in larders or deep-freezers, big cooking ranges often heating the water as well as the room; large tables where family and friends gather to eat, talk and work. As yet we haven't abandoned the bedroom, but perhaps energy conservation will cause us to consider this too in the future—but as it was in Saxon times, a thousand years ago, the kitchen has once again become the real living-room, and the hub of the house.

Cave to microwave

The first kitchens

The first element that man learned to conquer was fire. Probably he used it first as a tool—and then some unknown genius discovered the marvel of cooked meat.

The first pots were made from the stomachs or hides of the slaughtered beasts. Filled with mixtures of meat, blood and wild grain, they were tied up and slung over the fire like primeval haggises. The bones were used for fuel—a neat, if smelly, form of waste-disposal.

As the last Ice Age retreated, the world's climate gradually improved and farming became possible. The first farmers built clusters of huts near streams and rivers, where wild grains flourished in the alluvial soil. Turning their attention from hunting to the sowing and harvesting of crops they domesticated the goat and then the sheep to provide meat, skins, milk, wool and fat for fuelling lamps.

The hut-dwellers developed grinding and cooking methods to cope with the new foods. One of the earliest known cooking pots is a large, very heavy stone with a hole in the centre, which sat permanently in the middle of the fire. Food was wrapped in leaves, placed in the hole with water and then "boiled" by adding hot stones to the pot. Another cooking method may have been baking, by surrounding food with clay and tucking it in the embers.

By 3500 BC centres of civilization were developing near the major rivers of Egypt and Persia, and later in India and China. A simple form of communication and barter began, with the exchange of skills, building materials and foodstuffs from nearby areas. In Britain, by about 3000 BC huts built with timber supports had a cooking area—a baked clay floor surrounded by layers of stone. People in other parts of northern Europe made a clay-covered patch in the floor—possibly the first oven.

Varieties of foods developed too, with the domestication of turkeys in the ancient Americas, geese, quail and duck in Egypt and chicken in India. The Egyptians knew how to make beer; bread was leavened by the sour-dough method, and fish and small birds were pickled and salted.

The influence of the Near Eastern civilizations gradually penetrated to what is now Europe. In the flowering of Crete, and later Greece, city-states developed whose houses contained a multiplicity of rooms including separate kitchens.

The diet of the early Greeks was simple—perhaps a slice of meat or game cooked over an open fire. But by the fifth century BC in Athens, the rich indulged in extravagant banquets, although their methods of cooking remained relatively basic. They enjoyed a fat goose or an overfed pig roasted or grilled over a slow fire.

Eating was an adored pastime of the Romans, who imported foodstuffs and spices, including the favourite black pepper, from throughout their empire. Liquamen or garum, made from salt and fermented fish in factories along the Mediterranean shores, was the essential ingredient of many dishes.

The kitchens of the wealthy were well equipped, staffed by many slaves and supervised by the lady of the house. Ovens were of two kinds, one heated from below, the other incorporating the fire. Food was also cooked on spits, or in pots balanced on tripods above charcoal fires. The sophisticated Roman recipes demanded a variety of utensils, which included doughnut pans and fish ladles. Kettles, pots, sieves, funnels, knives and spoons were in daily use.

Roman banquets were splendid and often lasted for many days. The ideal number of people at a dinner was said to be nine and they sat or reclined on couches around three sides of a low table. They used their fingers, which were cleaned with napkins and in fingerbowls.

The poor lived under very different conditions. They relied on a free grain ration and food brought from squalid cook-shops. Their tenements were too small to accommodate ovens for baking.

The Roman culinary influence, which spread far across their vast empire, declined with the recall of the legions during the fifth century AD. In the Dark Ages that followed, the quality of food deteriorated, as did the quality of life itself.

The cooking pit in a one-room dwelling at Skara Brae in the Orkney Islands (below). It is probably the most perfectly preserved Stone Age village in Europe.

A reconstruction of a Roman kitchen (above), as featured in the Museum of London. On the tables are the utensils and ingredients for cooking a lavish meal.

From the city of Pompeii stricken in AD 79 comes a bronze heating apparatus (below). Semicircular hollow walls of the cylinder contain liquids, heated by the enclosed hot ashes.

Exquisite terracotta figures were made in the Boetian city of Tanagra in the fifth century BC. Among them was this view of a housewife tending her oven (above).

Minoan art was among the most sophisticated of the Bronze Age civilizations. The beautifully decorated oil and wine jars (below) come from King Minos' Palace of Knossos.

Castles and abbeys

When the Roman legions were recalled in the fifth century AD, the province of Britain crumbled into tiny kingdoms and chiefdoms whose inhabitants clustered about the nearest overlord for protection. Communities grew up around timber halls that combined the functions of kitchen, barrack room and dormitory.

Dark Age cookery was more of a necessity than an art. That Roman refinement, the stove, was abandoned in favour of the spit, or a simple iron cauldron standing over indoor or outdoor fires. Only the great lords had separate kitchens, but these were no more than wooden shelters. Meat and ale were served upon boards balanced on trestles; family, guests, soldiers and servants ate much the same fare.

The nobility, according to finds in Saxon burial grounds, dined off bowls and dishes of silver; the lower orders used slabs of bread that were both plates and part of the meal. Embellishments such as salt cellars and tablecloths were not introduced until after the Norman Conquest of 1066.

Following that memorable date, stone fortresses gradually replaced wooden keeps, and kitchens of a kind were furnished with wood-fired ovens built into the walls. The peasantry, however, made do with culinary arrangements that had changed little in a thousand years. Open fires burned in central hearths, and the smoke found its way through holes in the roofs. But as stone and brick replaced wattle and daub, fires could be moved to side walls and equipped with hoods and flues. In the fifteenth century, these gradually evolved into the chimney, which, like the fireplace beneath, was built into the wall.

Above the late-medieval fireplace, chimney cranes with adjustable hooks supported cauldrons, and ingenious devices known as idlebacks permitted suspended kettles to be tilted. Skillets, saucepans and frying-pans rested on trivets near the fire, and upright wrought-iron stands with hooks and branches held the ends of the spits and cooking utensils such as the long-pronged implements with which cooks handled large chunks of cooking meat. Medieval cooks and their assistants were traditionally male as the heat and smoke in the kitchen and the weight of the cauldrons made the work very arduous.

Manorial and monastic life

The extensive kitchens of abbeys and manor-houses made these establishments almost self-sufficient. They incorporated bakeries and breweries and had access to fishponds and dovecots whose produce helped to feed sometimes as many as 900 inhabitants in an abbey and 300 in a private house. In castles and manor-houses a steward kept daily accounts of supplies ordered for the kitchen and supervised the enormous staff required to keep the establishment running. Under his charge were the buttery or wine store, the pantry or bread store, the scullery, saucery, spicery and many other specialized rooms, which in great houses were built around the kitchen.

A new age

At the end of the fifteenth century the discovery of the New World and of new routes to the Indies brought about an expansion and flowering of European trade to a degree hitherto unimagined.

Inspired by the atmosphere of the Renaissance, the new class of prosperous merchants built great houses filling them with beautiful furniture and paintings. The rebirth of cultural activity was accompanied by changes in the minor art of kitchen design, which became more complex to cope with the ever-increasing elaboration of dishes.

Kitchen fireplaces now had solid metal firebacks to reflect heat, bars in front to hold back the fuel and adjustable, more complicated pot-hooks equipped with all kinds of devices for hanging kettles and cauldrons over the fire. Spits, however, were still balanced on the hooks of firedogs and rotated by cook-boys sheltering behind fire screens. Ovens, built into the brickwork, continued to be pre-heated with wood fires.

Despite the luxuriousness of their existence, the mistresses of great sixteenth-century European households were far from idle and were expected to be skilled in all branches of the culinary arts. They preserved food for winter and supervised dairy, bakery, brewery, orchard and kitchen garden. No wonder a contemporary writer told his wife, "My fortune, sometime that thou shalt have so many thynges to do that thou shalt not well knowe where is best to begyn . . ."

12th-century ventilation for kitchen bonfires was a central hole (above right), as shown here in the monks' kitchen in Durham Cathedral.

Pies are shovelled into a wall oven (right) in an Italian painting of a 15th-century kitchen. The medieval oven, an alcove in the brick, was heated by bundles of burning faggots.

11th-century cooking scenes, including spit-roasting and grilling (above), are woven into the magnificently detailed Bayeux Tapestry

A domestic scene (above) from a 15th-century Italian manuscript, shows the turn-spit rotating meat by hand.

A huge hearth with side-ovens and assorted utensils (above) are remains of the 15th-century kitchen at Compton Castle, Devon.

Cooks prepare for a feast in this 16th-century engraving (below). The cauldron simmers on its adjustable pot-hook and ducks roast on a spit.

Kitchen renaissance

The prosperous merchant class that gradually developed in seventeenth-century Europe as overseas trade expanded enjoyed such imported luxuries as chocolate, sugar and fruits from the New World. The wealth of Restoration England was reflected in extravagant entertaining that demanded improved kitchen equipment. The Royal Society, under the patronage of Charles II, investigated various cooking methods and invented a device known as Papin's Digester. Although it was considered too dangerous for home use it was a forerunner of the modern pressure cooker.

Eighteenth-century European kitchens were the practical hub of self-sufficient households. In the grandest homes they included dairies, bakehouses, butteries and breweries. Coal replaced wood as the main fuel and, as coal needs a draught to burn properly, fire baskets were installed in grates. Meat, spit roasted by means of a chain drive or by dogs harnessed to a treadmill, was "done to a turn" as its dripping fell into an iron trough below. An improved roasting device was the Dutch oven, an open metal box, fitted with hooks and a dripping pan, that stood in front of the blazing fire.

An engraving (above right) from a book published in Germany in 1760 shows larger-than-life details of contemporary kitchenware.

A 17th-century artist interprets in naturalistic style (right) the preparations for the marriage feast at Cana.

A recurring theme in mid-18th-century genre painting in Europe (below) was the interpretation of the daily chores in humble households.

A cooking spit is powered by rising heat and smoke turning a smoke-jack in the chimney (above). From a book published in Nuremburg, Germany, in 1673.

The ceramic stove (below), wood-fired in its heyday, supports a cauldron and roasting spits among the tiles of the Amalienburg pavilion in the Nymphenburg Palace, Bavaria.

The great kitchens of Saltram House in Devon (above) were rebuilt after a fire in 1778. The wealth of cooking regalia acquired after the disaster remains on view today.

18th-century Italian painter Pietro Longhi specialized in scenes such as the Venetian banquet (below), whose preparation demanded massive kitchens and huge staffs.

Cave to microwave

The New World

Life for the first European immigrants in North America was exceptionally hard. The threefold threat of cold, starvation and hostile Indians stood constantly beside them as they carved their farms from the virgin wilderness and built their houses from the stones and timber gained in clearing the land. Many spent their first winters in single-room cabins and cooking was accomplished over an open fire or, at best, in an oven made of rocks and puddled clay. Though game was plentiful, the early colonial housewife was often hard put to it to feed her family through the long winter months. In intervals of working beside her husband, she salted and smoked meat and stored grain against the bitter days ahead.

Hard work, and the sheer fertility of the new land, however, soon brought success, so that long before the Revolution of 1776 the inhabitants of New England or Virginia, say, were in general far more prosperous than their relatives left behind in the Old World. Kitchen and dining-room furniture and fittings, for example, were no longer rough-hewn. Dressers, tables and chairs, carved from maple and other native woods in the simple but elegant style now known as Colonial, graced pleasant houses whose comfort rivalled all but the best that Europe had to offer.

But throughout the years after Independence the great hinterland beckoned to the adventurous, to the gold-seekers and the land-hungry alike. In the unrest that followed the Civil War, the covered wagon trains rolled west in their hundreds. On the journey, American housewives learned again to be pioneers. Each wagon was equipped with an iron bake oven, a cauldron and a spider—a frying-pan on legs—in which they prepared the simple meals that sustained the wanderers to the far horizons.

The old Kitchen of Shirley Plantation, Virginia (below), has a stepped chimney oven and crane, typical of an 18th-century colonial kitchen.

The long journeys between homesteads (above) in 18th-century Virginia made a well-equipped pantry a necessity to prepare for travellers.

An illustration (below) from a 19th-century history of America shows a family of self-sufficient pioneers gathering around their campfire.

Pioneers survived harsh North Dakota winters by building log cabins with sparse but cosy kitchens like the one reconstructed above.

Towards technology

The effects of the Industrial Revolution wrought significant changes in kitchen equipment, cooking and eating habits. Improved sea and rail routes meant better distribution of food. A new method of feeding animals throughout the winter months ensured a fresh meat supply all year.

Improvements on eighteenth-century cooking methods were slow. The first development was an oven separated by bricks from an open fire. The next step was to enclose the fire, first by putting a cover on top and then by putting a door in front, which was opened only when food was to be roasted. This machine, called the close range, dominated the kitchens of the 1850s. It was hailed as a boon, but could have been specifically invented to create a kitchen nightmare. Before lighting the fire for breakfast the cook had to clean out ashes, sweep flues, blacklead the case and polish the brass. It was hot, dirty and difficult to manage. In the hands of the inexperienced it would either not light at all or became so hot that the bars in front of the fire melted.

In 1841 black cast-iron gas-stoves were installed in the kitchen of London's Reform Club. Regarded with suspicion because people feared either an explosion, poisoning or gas-flavoured food, these new contraptions did not become popular until the end of the century, when gas companies promoted them and housewives better understood them.

In the mid-nineteenth century prosperous middle-class houses were staffed with a hierarchy of servants. If the popular Mrs Beeton is to be believed they all worked tirelessly to keep the establishment running. Her book of household management begins with the stirring words: "As with the Commander of an Army, or the leader of an enterprise, so is it with the mistress of a house." She counsels "Early Rising, Frugality and Economy, Good Temper and the Keeping of Accounts." It is hard to imagine how there was time for "visiting the Poor, Instructing them, in a pleasant and unobtrusive manner, in cleanliness, industry, cookery, good management, and the rules of health".

Not all kitchens were so large or so well equipped, however—many farms and cottages remained unmodernized and in some places ancient methods of cooking were still practised.

A sturdy 19th-century gas cooker (above) with two ovens and a water heater.

The apple peeler (far left) is a 19th-century notion of a labour-saving device.

Made in Birmingham, a 19th-century gas cooker (left) masquerades as a whatnot.

Country-house entertaining demanded big kitchens. The great 18th-century kitchen of Saltram House, Devon, witnessed the transition from the open to the closed range (right).

An ingenious early 20th-century carving table (above) with pulleys and plate warmers.

Plate warmer (above), a late 19th-century electrical appliance.

Depicted in a 1900 edition Le Petit Journal, *an army of Parisian chefs (above) prepare a gargantuan banquet for the mayors of France.*

The catalogue of the Great Exhibition of 1851 illustrated the very latest model of a complete kitchen range (below).

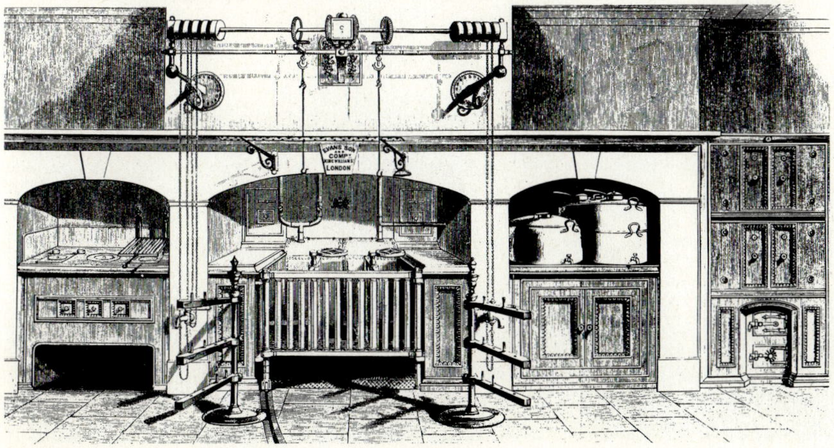

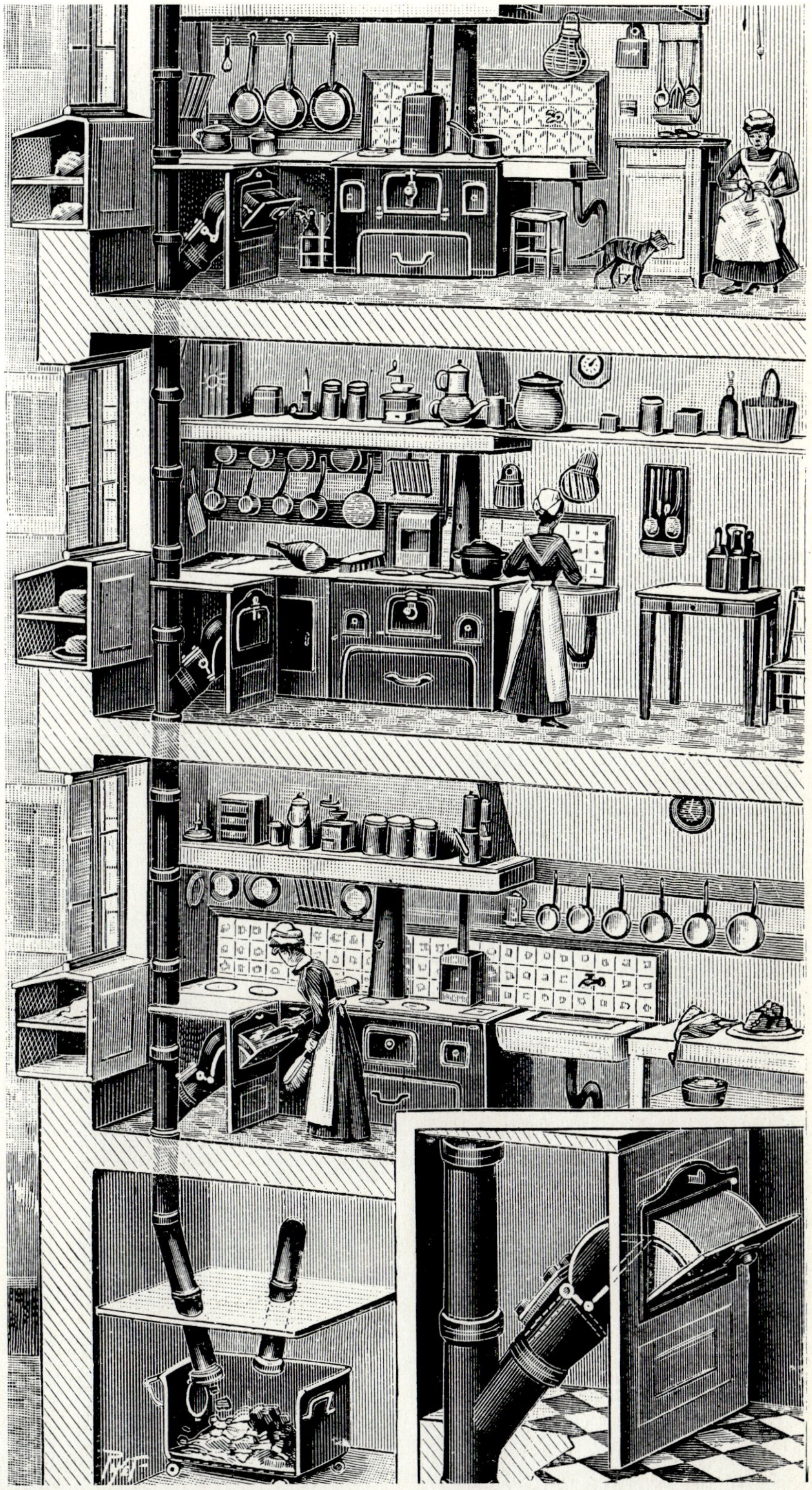

A slice of early 20th-century urban life, depicted in the cutaway above, demonstrates a primitive system of waste disposal. Refuse, thrown into the identical hatches of identical kitchens, cascades down the communal pipe into a mobile trough in the basement.

A century of contrasts

During the early twentieth century no one could foresee the enormous changes that would shortly take place. The Edwardian rich enjoyed their luxurious life and saw no reason why it should change. Large meals appeared regularly, well-staffed kitchens hummed with activity and larders were stuffed with food. Typical of an Edwardian kitchen was a large built-in dresser, loaded with china. Possible additions were a cast-iron gas cooker, acquired to help cook on a busy day, and a linoleum floor, which was more comfortable to walk on and easier to clean than hard stone. There was also the customary range of copper jelly moulds, although the copper saucepans might now be replaced with enamelled cast-iron. This agreeable life collapsed with the outbreak of the First World War. The supply of female servants dwindled as many found that working in a factory meant more money and independence. A late twenties building programme provided many of these women and their families with housing in new towns or estates. Now, for the first time, they had their own kitchens, even if provided with only a sink.

The middle classes, abandoned by their hordes of helpers, tried to manage by themselves. The large basement kitchen that had been suitable for an experienced cook and her team was a struggle for the single-handed, inexperienced housewife. New gadgets and equipment were welcomed, and gas and electric cookers gradually replaced the temperamental coal ranges. The first electric stoves, made of black cast-iron, were massive and were operated by switchboards on the wall above. By 1926 the cookers had a simpler control system and they were now enamelled, although they still stood high off the ground on legs.

During the 1930s well-insulated solid-fuel cookers such as the Aga and Esse came on the market. If electricity or gas was available it also became practical to have a refrigerator, especially for a small kitchen without room for a larder. Furniture manufacturers found a ready market for kitchen cabinets that were designed to hold almost everything the cook needed, including an extending table, flour bins and egg racks.

Food rationing and shortage of building materials during the Second World War inevitably brought hardship into the kitchen. Cooking without familiar ingredients was a matter of some difficulty, but with a lot of ingenuity the average civilian ate a balanced diet. Eating in the kitchen became a virtual necessity. It wasn't always comfortable because it hadn't been designed for family meals, but in times of fuel shortage it was often the warmest room in the house.

When building restrictions were lifted in the early 1950s there was a real chance at last to improve kitchens by adding new equipment and fittings. An American research team conducted a project on kitchen planning. They designed new types of refrigerators and cookers and for the first time built-in cabinets and work-tops were fitted around the walls of a kitchen at a convenient height, often with cupboards on the wall above. Popular colours, which were almost always cream and green in the 1930s, became pastel, then darker reds and blues and finally an almost unlimited choice was available. Plastic laminates for work-tops and new paint finishes made all these surfaces tough and easy to clean.

In the 1950s and 60s new architectural ideas for homes again included the complete redesign of kitchens inspired by the French architect Le Corbusier, who said that a house should be a machine for living. With the new formats and post-war technology electronic kitchens became a reality. However, modern equipment is not infallible and fuel supplies are not inexhaustible. In recent years, as a possible reaction to a cold and clinical kitchen environment, new pleasures are to be found in making bread, brewing beer and growing vegetables. Many people yearn to return to a self-sufficient life, but most want kitchens that combine efficient modern equipment with the old-fashioned virtues of a warm atmosphere and comfortable surroundings.

A gas-fired Stewart range (above) was the pride of a Canadian kitchen in 1926.

The kitchen of Mrs Leslie Howard, wife of the actor, was recreated as a centrepiece of the 1936 Ideal Home Exhibition (below). Even in the 1970s it would be up to date.

There were minimal kitchens (above) even in 1934. It was called a "compact kitchenette" when photographed at Dorland Hall, London.

August 1948. An evening meal in post-war Amsterdam (right) was taken in the kitchen, the warmest room in the house.

A 1946 exhibition, dubbed "Britain can't have it", displayed products for export. Housewives envied this kitchen of the future (left).

In 1900 an enterprising French chocolate-maker distributed cards in every box. This card (right) is a fantasy of the year 2000.

Robert Carrier

Perla Meyers

Michael Chow

George Lang

Prue Leith

Milton and Shirley Glaser

Werner Vögeli

Elizabeth David

Maschler

Gaston le Nôtr

mond Oliver

James Beard

The professionals

All the people in this chapter are professionally involved in the preparation of food. Some are great chefs in their own right, some are critics and restaurateurs, others teach cooking, and Elizabeth David, one of our greatest cookery writers, has altered a whole generation's attitude to food. What they all have in common are kitchens, either in their homes or at work, that have been designed in a most thoughtful way.

They have recognized that cooking is both an art and a craft, and that to carry out their work efficiently they must have surroundings that are a pleasure to be in and equipment that is efficient to use. From their examples I think it is possible to cull many ideas that can be applied to your own kitchen at home, even if you don't aspire to the culinary masterpieces created as a matter of course by these great cooks.

Michael Chow's restaurant

The expression "thinking on your feet" might have been designed expressly to fit Michael Chow. His mind moves swiftly and it rarely trips. Behind the elegant curved glass windows of his famous Knightsbridge restaurant lies a unique concept in eating; behind that watchful face with its lugubrious moustache is a quick wit.

Chow, in his late thirties, became a restaurateur only after a long march around some of the other arts. Born in Shanghai of a wealthy family of classical theatre actors, he was educated in England and attended St Martin's School of Art in 1955. In quick succession he studied architecture, acted in films, and tried his hand at painting and interior design. Then, for no other reason than that he thought London needed a sophisticated Chinese restaurant, he opened Mr Chow in 1968.

Even in the mercurial sixties it was something totally new, the first Chinese restaurant to refrain from chinoiserie, the first to aim its expensive classic Peking dishes at the *jeunesse d'orée* of London. It was a success and still is.

"Chinese food had never been important here because the Chinese and Europeans never communicated," says Chow. "Peking cooking is the most sophisticated in the world . . ." he pauses and relents, ". . . parallel to French haute cuisine. This restaurant is international: you could put it anywhere." To prove his point he opened Mr Chow L.A. in Hollywood in 1974.

The word sophistication means much to Chow, and crops up frequently in his conversation. His Knightsbridge restaurant reflects it with cool green tiles, panels of smoked glass and cane chairs. You can't eat sophistication, however, and Chow's staff feed up to a hundred diners at once. If you open the kitchen doors at the far end of the ground floor there is a step down into a glorious steamy contrast to the dining-room.

"Chinese food uses such a lot of grease," Chow says, surveying the kitchen's off-white walls. "We are continually cleaning and repainting." The premises were formerly an Indian restaurant. He didn't tamper with the basic structure of the kitchen, but the ventilation system was redesigned to cope with two steamers, a duck oven and a 2.4-m (8-ft) gas range. The scarlet canopies and extractor units fringing the high ceiling look dashing enough, but Chow still isn't satisfied: "I've done it two or three times, but I still haven't got it perfect," he admits. "To call in experts you have to be an expert."

Chow's perfectionist streak is not often thwarted. He found conventional ovens unsuitable for roasting ducks, so he designed a shoulder-high barrel-shaped oven that maintains a heat of 182°C (360°F) all around the hanging birds. Fresh ducks dangle from a steel rack above, in the same way that decorative silver ducks are suspended from the ceiling of one of the restaurant dining-rooms.

"Peking ducks are traditionally fed on sesame seed throughout their life. I have to use ordinary ducks, but at least I have now trained a supplier to gut them in the Chinese way for me."

Most of his provisions, including rice, flour, almonds, lychees, mushrooms, bean-shoots and shark's fin, come from Chinese emporiums, but he buys his fish at Billingsgate Market. "Lobster," he sighs, "so expensive, but I won't remove it from the menu."

Ten people work in the kitchen, seven chefs (three frying, two on pasta and two chopping) and three assistants. Chow explains that the "head chef in China is always the chief chopper. Chopping is most important; because the food cooks so quickly it must be evenly sliced." Some measure of how vital the chopping stage is in Chinese cooking can be gauged from the fact that the massive tree trunk that is used as a board is renewed yearly. The chopping knife is the size of a small axe. "Only Chinese can chop sideways and the weight of the knife must be right," says Chow, mimicking a ham-handed cook sawing through meat. One of the staff followed with an expert demonstration of slicing thin slivers at high speed.

The 1.5-m (5-ft) preparation table, which dominates the centre of the kitchen, is flanked by a wooden noodle board, where ropes of dough are made to dance in skilful

Hanging ducks are ready for the barrel-shaped duck oven (above), made to Chow's own design, so that birds are cooked evenly all around.

A shield prevents flour flying on to the main preparation table while the pasta is energetically worked at the wooden noodle bench (left).

Succulent dumplings are transferred straight from kitchen to table in these plaited bamboo steamers (right), which stack easily.

hands. A hand's breadth away is the dumpling steamer, where tiers of round bamboo steamers with plaited lids shroud their succulent contents. A neat way of resting the woks with their film of built-in oil is on a sheet of cardboard egg boxes ranged along a shelf above the gas range.

"The dishes I serve are all classic Pekinese except for a few Cantonese," Chow says firmly. "Classic Peking cooking hasn't really changed since it was perfected three thousand years ago. How can you improve it? You can't change Shakespeare. I do improvise the menu, though, that's important. If I get bored, the kitchen staff are bored, everyone gets bored. The customer is never right. I'm always right!"

If that seems cynical, it's said with a smile. Chow laughs at himself much too frequently to be dubbed arrogant. But he still thinks Europeans haven't quite mastered the art of eating his precious native dishes: "I try to give people what is good for them, like spinach. I know spare ribs are not particularly digestible so I take it off the menu, but always the customers want it, so back it comes. Not very sophisticated!" The sight of Europeans mismanaging chopsticks is painful to him, so he firmly discourages their use in the restaurant, where he is to be found every evening, including weekends. "If I don't come here all the time the continuity is lost."

Chinese food, Italian waiters, European decor might not major in continuity but Chow's art has been to weld them together with great imagination. Where does he go from here? "I could write a cookbook."

Oily woks rest on cardboard egg boxes above the gas range (above) when not in use. Small metal containers on lower shelf hold seasonings.

Michael Chow (above right) and Cheng Yim Chung, whose forté is frying. Ten staff work in the kitchen to feed up to 100 customers.

Restful white walls and green tiles in the upstairs dining-room (right) set off the clever use of tinted glass to give a sense of space.

The layout of the kitchen (below) allows food to progress from storage to preparation to cooking in a forward sweep.

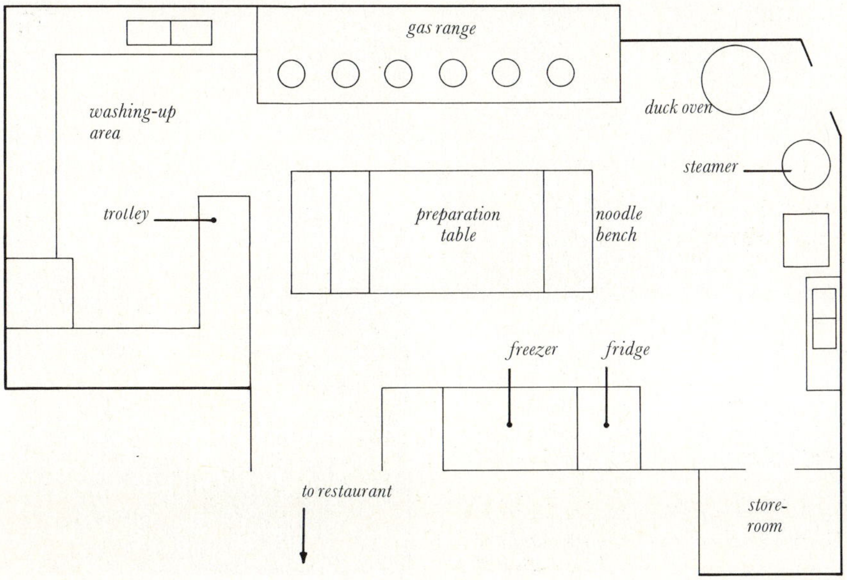

Michael Chow at home

The kitchen in Chow's house in Fulham is first seen framed by a dramatic circular window in the entrance hall. Then, on entering the kitchen, the eye is immediately drawn by another dramatic view through to an indoor swimming pool. What more exciting vista from the sink than the turquoise shimmer of water a few seconds' walk away?

The second surprise is the size of the actual working space: it is unexpectedly small and compact. An equal amount is provided for a seating area beyond it, where black leather sofas are arranged around a large glass table. On the other side of the work area, adjacent to the pool, is a dining area. The floor of plain cream tiles extends the entire length of the room, but two steps create a change of level between the kitchen and seating area. From a commanding position in the centre of the room the cook, either Michael or his wife Tina, is never far from the conversation of guests.

"The kitchen does take up a very small space, but I think it is very well designed," Chow remarks. "I don't believe in lots of cupboards; you should only have the minimum of what you need. People copy each other too much, think they have to have four sets of everything, but you can't have a relationship with an entire set of frying-pans."

The colour scheme is unobtrusive: natural wood for the built-in units, dining-table, mirror frames and the big high cupboard. The tiled work-surfaces are chocolate brown, the canopy over the hot-plates is white, and the walls have an ice-blue wash. An assortment of copper pans suspended above the work-surface adds warmth, and there's a splash of scarlet from the Aga cooker and from a plant positioned by the sliding glass doors to the swimming pool. Both refrigerator and freezer are built in and the dishwasher is smartly camouflaged as a cupboard.

"We eat simply here," Chow says. "Maybe a steak or veal for lunch, otherwise mostly roasts. Yes, the classic English roast—but the vegetables are cooked in the Chinese way, fried quickly with salt, pepper and a touch of sugar. Then, so that they come up slightly raw, sweet and very crisp, just a small quantity of water, or, for cauliflower, milk is added. You have to look at food as well as taste it. You should be able to tell just from looking if too much salt, say, has been used."

Tina is a good cook in her own right, but cheerfully admits that her husband sometimes comes in to supervise at the last minute. Chow will tell you with a grin that most good restaurateurs hate food, but he hasn't quite forgotten his arrival in England during rationing, and those school meals with a joint divided 50 ways and spoiled potatoes. It's something his delightful

Michael Chow and daughter China (above) in front of the Aga he favours for roasting.

A visitor to Chow's Fulham house first sees the tiled kitchen through a striking "porthole" (left) in the hall. Seating area has three leather sofas.

Spotlit work-space (right) leads past the dining area to a swimming pool. A canopy shields the cook-top and a sink splashback keeps guests dry.

daughter, China, is unlikely to have to endure. "To eat a bad meal is expensive, a waste," he concludes. "It's precision that counts. Anyone can cook one dish precisely, but a professional chef can do three hundred. The secret of a good chef is the number of dishes that he can cook well all the time."

So, given one last meal, what would Michael Chow select? "Spaghetti," he says innocently. "With truffle." "Black or white truffle?" He shrugs, smiles. "I'm not prejudiced."

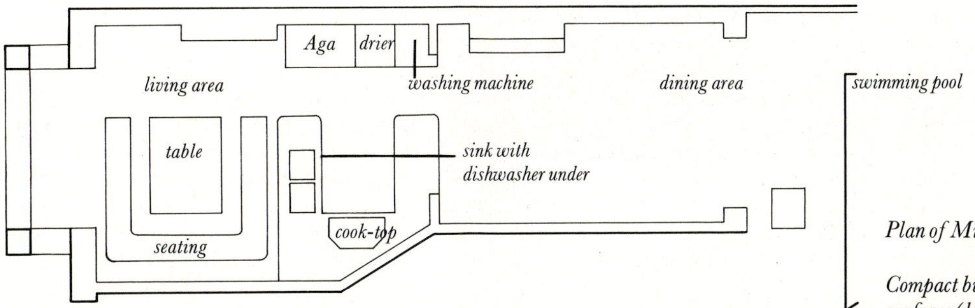

Plan of Michael Chow's kitchen (left).

Compact built-in units and well-placed work-surfaces (below) cut down travelling time for the cook, who can take part in guests' conversation.

Le Nôtre–haute cuisine to order

Sloping rails iron out the size differentials between big pans and little ones (above), to make them all equally accessible.

The massive central range in the "hot" kitchen (below) has gas burners for fast boiling and simmering rings for slow casseroles.

M. Gaston Le Nôtre is a "traiteur" by profession; "caterer" is the nearest English equivalent, but "catering" just does not evoke the right image. It does no justice to his perfect profiterôles, his astonishing cakes and confectionery, his exquisite ice-creams, his sensational charcuterie. He produces the most amazing food on a grand commercial scale from a factory bordering an industrial estate on the outskirts of Versailles. As fork-lift trucks roll off the assembly line of the engineering company next door, Le Nôtre's 500 chefs are kept busy, seven days a week, roasting sucking-pigs, decorating cakes with fantastical spun-sugar filigree and filling strawberry tarts and vol-au-vent cases.

The food is destined for six retail outlets and a very grand restaurant, the Pré Catalan, in the heart of the Bois de Boulogne. For a price, you can hire one of the sumptuously decorated reception rooms and invite friends or business acquaintances to feast upon the gastronomic masterpieces for which Le Nôtre is so justly famous: "I insist on only the best—the best ingredients, the best techniques—and I demand a high standard of cleanliness," says *le patron*. "We buy nothing but fresh ingredients, nothing we use is tinned or frozen unless we tin it or freeze it ourselves." He speaks very quickly, and he admits to finding difficulty in slowing down. "I always run at 200 kilometres an hour," and he hardly exaggerates—a tour around his premises is literally breathtaking. He races through the "hot" kitchen, where teams of chefs are preparing scores of stuffed ducks for the roasting ovens. A ratatouille for fifty simmers here, a huge vat of fish stock bubbles there. Wonderful smells enchant the nostrils and stimulate the palate. In the fish kitchen dozens of poached salmon are being skinned to make a massive mousse destined for a wedding reception. Le Nôtre stops to shake hands with the staff, smiles for the photographer and hurries on to the "cold" kitchen, where cocktail canapés and gargantuan salads are being prepared. Each mouthful, each lettuce leaf, gets individual attention. They are making ham sandwiches, but by a rather more elaborate method than is generally employed. There is the matter of raising and slaughtering the pigs on a Normandy farm; of curing the hams and boiling, boning and slicing them thinly. Then the bread must be made and baked, spread with a mixture of butter and mayonnaise made from the finest olive oil and fresh farm eggs. Then the sandwich is filled with fragrant ham, and given a final

A temperature check for the terrines (above). These enamelled cast-iron pâté dishes conduct heat evenly and efficiently.

garnish of freshly ground pepper and chopped gherkins.

M. Le Nôtre casts his expert eye over the scene, imparts a word of advice, pops a *bouchée* into his mouth and whisks around the corner, to emerge a split second later in the huge pâtisserie kitchens. "We use only butter here; in one week we use thousands of kilos of butter from my farm." Every busy team of chefs is engaged in making a different species of tart, cake or bread. Each team is self-contained around its own work-area, with its own supplies of flour and butter, its own refrigerators and ovens. "We cook here in much the same way as you do at home, not like a food manufacturer. When we need machinery, I generally have to invent it myself, because it is a unique idea to produce food of such quality in such large quantities. Industrial machinery does not produce good enough results. Some things can only be done by hand, and there is no mechanical substitute for the skill of a well-trained chef."

He pauses in the packaging department. The staff are putting cream cakes into boxes, wrapping them in cellophane and bedecking them with bows. The products leave the factory looking like so many delicious little gifts from Tiffany's.

In the pâtisserie kitchen, the sun glints on the eerie spectacle of nylon forcing bags drying out on a wire rack (above).

The huge tin-lined copper pans (above) will last a lifetime, even in "factory" conditions.

A batch of bread is wheeled out of the cavernous ovens (above). When cool they will be shuttled off to the "cold" kitchen and turned into magnificent double-decker sandwiches.

Le Nôtre has a special oven for everything. The cool ovens (above) produce trayful after trayful of meringue, 24 hours a day.

A preparation table in the "hot" kitchen (above). On the far wall adjustable industrial shelving houses trays of fresh vegetables.

In the fish department, le patron *(above) imparts a few encouraging words and checks the skinning of the poached salmon.*

The deft fingers of the pâtissiers (right) work in unison to produce hundreds of mouth-watering strawberry tarts.

Le Nôtre–cook extraordinary

The second stage of the tour begins in the cool, sterile environment of the ice-cream kitchen. Most large-scale food manufacturers use powdered milk to make ice-cream—but not Le Nôtre. Here, shining pasteurizing machinery processes about 500 litres (110 gals) of fresh milk every day. Cartons of farm eggs are piled on the table next to his patented egg-separating device—a dazzlingly simple chute that unfailingly deposits yolks in one bucket and whites in another.

Enticed by the tantalizing smell of roasting hams, he takes a quick look at progress in the charcuterie kitchen, where the day's quota of plump black puddings await a trial tasting. Close by, one chef opens an ovenful of roasting sucking-pigs, another is dexterously filling and twisting an endless sausage casing, which hangs garland-like on a metal frame. Yet another checks the recipe for a stuffing. Everything produced here has a standardized list of ingredients. A card-index system in every kitchen lists the dishes currently in production and the quantities of every ingredient to ensure that tomorrow's terrine will be every bit as good as today's.

Round the corner in the confectionery kitchen, preparations for Easter are in full swing. A parade of chocolate bunnies resignedly queue up for their ears behind a trolley of unfinished, beakless ducks.

In the controlled atmosphere of the cool-room, trays of handmade chocolates await the packers' attention. A quick mouthful of praline—and Le Nôtre whirls on to the decorating kitchen, the room where *pièces de résistance* are commonplace. Here the decorative potential of spun sugar is exploited to its limits. A life-size multi-coloured ostrich—a cancelled order—leans casually against the refrigerator. A sugary Cinderella awaits an invitation to the ball, and all around the room are piled the turrets of an immense wedding cake. With his *chef de décoration*, Le Nôtre discusses the sticky problem of a film director's birthday cake. They sketch rapidly on the back of an envelope and emerge with a design for a sugar-candy camera focused on a sugar-candy star—very Hollywood.

Le Nôtre appreciates and nurtures the skills of his staff. Apprentices are trained in the cookery school that forms part of the factory buildings. His chefs are "recycled" every year; the confectioners attend

The egg-separating chute in the ice-cream kitchen (above). Yolks and whites slither down into separate plastic bins.

Generous storage bins glide out from under the work-top in the ice-cream kitchen (above). Each bin holds a different type of sugar.

Hygiene is vital in the ice-cream kitchen, where alien bacteria could cause a disaster. The gleaming machinery (above) pasteurizes milk.

The ice-cream freezer (right) has four compartments so that the batch that is freezing is not disturbed by the opening of doors.

pâtisserie courses, the pâtissières learn the mysteries of charcuterie, and so on. Of course, the school is also a commercial venture; professional chefs come to learn new skills and brush up their old ones.

Le Nôtre started his career as a simple pâtisseur twenty years ago in Normandy. Since then, his formidable energies have created a vast family business, of which his wife is Commercial Director and his son Director General. One daughter researches and writes his cookery books and the other manages one of his Paris shops. Daughters and sons-in-law, brothers and sisters-in-law are all involved in this expanding gastronomic empire. "The most renowned restaurants in France buy my products," he says proudly, "because they are the best." And his boast is not entirely without foundation.

A giant recipe book (left). In every kitchen a clear card-index system lists all the ingredients for every dish in production.

An oven full of sucking-pigs in the charcuterie kitchen (above). Carcasses are placed directly on oiled racks; the fat drips through to the pan.

When dealing with gallons of lemon sorbet (above), the ice-cream chefs—chefs glaciers—*need sturdy mixers and giant-sized spoons.*

The tangible results of a seasonal burst of activity (above)—a year's supply of peaches, bottled when cheap and plentiful.

An Easter parade of unfinished ducks with jaunty marzipan bonnets (above) dry off in the cool of the chocolate kitchen.

Presenting the super-sausage—with a stuffing made from pork, herbs, plenty of garlic and a generous splosh of brandy (above).

Le Nôtre at Sennecy

Le Nôtre's country kitchen has windows on two sides. Traditional external shutters (above) screen out the direct glare of the sun.

Gaston Le Nôtre's farmhouse retreat, Les Bastes, lies in the flat, open country south of Orléans and the Loire valley. He goes there at weekends to relax with his family, though during the shooting season he also shares his country seat with about twenty paying guests, who come down for the pheasants. Weekend cooking, however, is left largely to Solange, his housekeeper.

The kitchen at Les Bastes is a large family room that can change into a mass catering establishment at the drop of a game bird. A tiled peninsular unit gracefully accommodates a large gas restaurant-range, two catering ovens and a massive, electrically driven, gas rôtisserie grill that could easily cope with a whole lamb or a dozen birds.

A discreet deep-freeze in an outside corridor augments the family-size refrigerator on busy days, and there is a lot of cupboard space—intelligently planned so that every centimetre is used and every utensil can be easily reached. But there is no aggressive display of cookery tools; the kitchen is above all a friendly room, well appointed for sunny Sunday breakfasts *en famille*. The Le Nôtre *famille* is pretty large, already half a dozen grandchildren have made an appearance, and Les Bastes is a house where one is more likely to find a toy car parked on the table than some esoteric item for the batterie de cuisine.

In the large cupboards, a great deal of space has been allocated to serving dishes, silverware and spoons. Le Nôtre is a stickler for good presentation of food both for his house guests and his family. He uses a lot of oven-proof earthenware and oval stainless-steel platters, both of which can take the heat of a fierce oven or grill so that food arrives on the table as hot and as appetizing as possible.

All around the house are tangible reminders of the shoot, from the gleaming leather gun cases in the hall to the game birds depicted appropriately on the dinner plates and coffee-cups, and the happy sound of unsuspecting quacks from the duck pond outside the kitchen window.

The marble work-top is set about 75 mm (3 in) higher than the sink, so nobody gets backache rolling out the pastry.

Inside the pan cupboard (below) space is intelligently organized for utensils of every shape and size.

The service cupboard (above) holds all the impressive dishes, silver spoons and salt cellars so necessary for sporting weekends.

Le Nôtre has chosen a catering range (below) because there is room to shuffle pans around and a central parking place to keep them warm.

The fearsome grill (above) can spit-roast a whole lamb. Heat and grease are sucked out through a duct in the tiled hood.

Drawers with wire-mesh bottoms (above) discreetly hide half-used heads of garlic and handfuls of shallots.

The drawer next to the sink (above) has plastic trays for soap and sponges that lift out for cleaning.

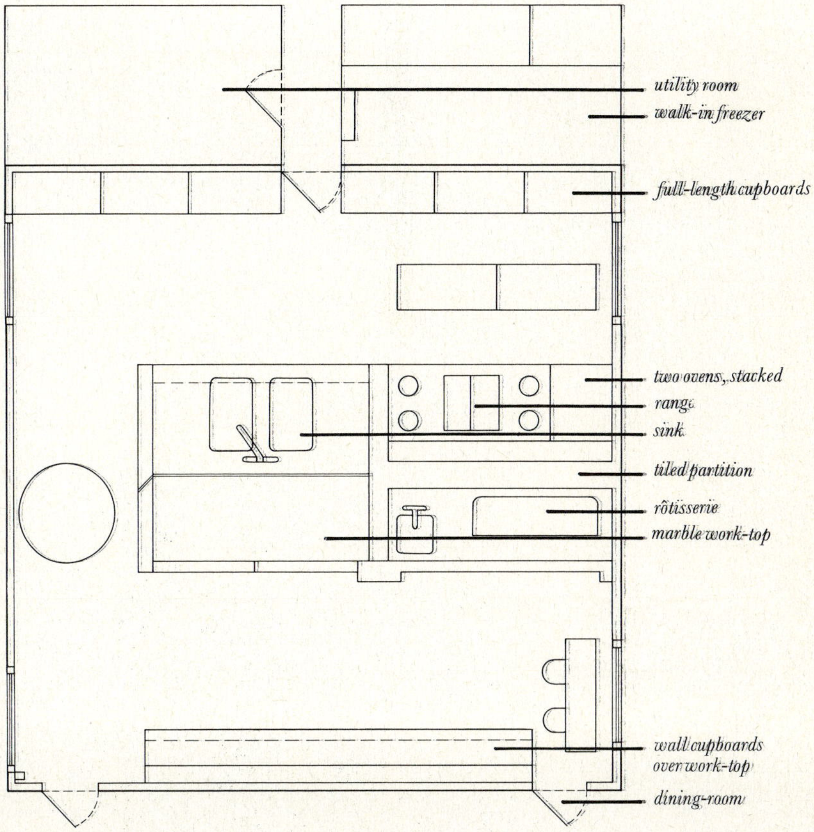

Plan of M. Le Nôtre's kitchen at his home near Orléans.

The enterprising Ms Leith

Prue Leith and Jean Reynaud, the restaurant manager (above), once a head chef himself.

Prue Leith is the girl who tried to storm Maxim's kitchens in Paris. "Women are on their way," she warned this all-male bastion. They shrugged and grudgingly allowed her to peel potatoes for an hour in the morning, until the chefs arrived; she didn't think she was learning much.

Prue Leith is also the restaurateur who, more recently, replied to an ecstatic letter about the food in her Notting Hill restaurant, Leith's, by saying: "Don't come again. You've had it once, it will never be so perfect another time."

Leith's was opened in 1969, nine years after she became interested in food while studying history at the Sorbonne in Paris. After Maxim's snub, she settled for another lowly start as an *au pair* with a French family to learn their cooking secrets. Then came a course at the Cordon Bleu School in England and a job cooking lunches for a London firm of solicitors. The success of the latter led to her own catering service run from a cramped Earl's Court bedsitter. "The other tenants complained bitterly. The bathroom was always full of lettuces. I had to hide my lobsters under the bed." Until she moved to bigger quarters and bought a mini van, the cooked food travelled by London's public transport.

In contrast to these makeshift beginnings, her restaurant, designed by an

Beyond the cook-tops, a hot cupboard forms a barrier between chefs and waiters in Prue Leith's restaurant kitchen (left).

Gas ovens and cook-tops are complemented by an electric deep-fryer (above). Fridges tuck under the stainless-steel work-surface; the door leads to a boiler room.

A charcoal grill in a tiled alcove adds heat to the kitchen, but the overhead extractor unit (above) is useful for utensils.

Magnets instead of a spike make pinning meal orders to the wall less dangerous (above).

American architect, has had ample facilities from its debut. It spreads across the ground floor of what were three terraced houses, and a rear basement courtyard was roofed to create an extensive kitchen. The shape of the kitchen was dictated by existing walls, but Prue had a free hand in deciding where things should go. "I was going to put the ovens against the wall, but the first chef who saw this plan said: 'Don't be silly, I wouldn't want to cook with my back to everything.' "

She also discovered that "nothing drives chefs madder than waiters charging through," so resolved to keep waiters away from them. This was achieved by locating the food preparation and cooking areas at the far end of the kitchen, leaving the space nearest to the restaurant free for serving. This section contains two fridges for chilled starters and cold puddings, a hot cupboard to warm plates and shelves to keep coffee-making equipment tidy. Leading off to one side is an extensive wash-up and crockery storage area. A bin for slops slides neatly underneath the counter so that dirty plates can be scraped off into it.

Moving farther into the kitchen, which combined orange paint with more practical white tiles, stainless-steel sinks and work-tables and yet more fridges dominate the long preparation area. Prue is pleased with the expensive two-gallon-capacity Hobart vertical slicer and shredder she invested in four years ago. "You get coleslaw from a cabbage in one second, soup in two." Other equipment includes a large professional mincer/mixer and knives of carbon steel. "They stain, but sharpen so easily."

Behind the preparation section is a cold-room with a deep-freeze and dry goods and vegetable storage areas. "We don't use any frozen food in the restaurant, but the staff will sometimes use it for themselves." Her staff, two girls and a junior chef working during the day (they don't serve lunches) and four chefs plus three washers-up at night, are pampered in other ways—good cloakrooms right by the kitchen and staff flats above the restaurant. Helpful, too, is an idea Prue stole from a Danish chef of using magnets instead of a dangerous spike to fix meal orders to the wall.

The cooking section of the kitchen next to the preparation area includes a gas oven, cook-top and grill, electric deep-fryers and a charcoal grill. Useful flat surfaces surround the cookers and an extractor unit was placed overhead. Saucepans of heavy copper were chosen because they won't burn food. "We couldn't afford these in the beginning, but bought them as soon as we could, she reveals."

Leith's reputation for good food has never faltered; passers-by get a tantalizing glimpse of discreetly-lit diners in the three restaurant dining-rooms, which accommodate ninety-five. "Like home cooking," Prue modestly describes the fare. "We'd rather serve fresh things simply than resort to truffles or asparagus out of a can. I hate bastard haute cuisine. But time is money.

Self-contained washing-up space adjacent to the service area (above) is designed to simplify the stacking of clean crockery.

Fresh peas and beans take too long to shell. We offer mange-tout or French beans."

She dines at the restaurant two or three times a week "to see it as a customer. If you work here all the time, in the end you don't notice things. When we opened we were dubbed fantastically trendy. I was worried. Fashions move on. I wanted solid middle-aged customers." Her eyes twinkle. "I haven't seen a rock star for years."

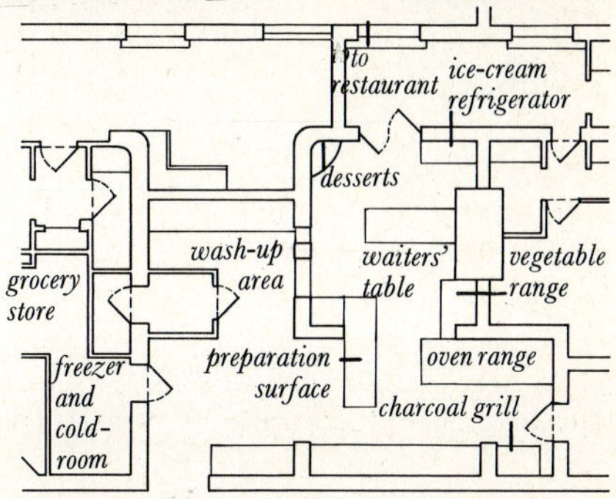

Plan of Leith's Restaurant.

Prue Leith in the Cotswolds

The superb work-table of fruitwood (left) was made especially for Prue Leith. On her cooking island is a microwave oven.

When she isn't demonstrating cooking abroad, or in London supervising her restaurant, her catering business or her own cookery school, started in 1975, Prue Leith has another commitment. This is a country house of Cotswold stone with Jacobean ancestry and twelve acres. Not all the restaurant's fresh vegetables come from Covent Garden: her acres are made to work. Here, too, are peaceful Gloucestershire views to admire between writing cookery articles and books. Finally, here is the kitchen space Prue always yearned for.

"It's a complete contrast to our London flat, where the kitchen is the small galley type," she explains. "I longed for plenty of cupboards so I had to have one of the largest rooms in the house. I chose this one because it is south-facing and next to the children's playroom. In summer I can look out and watch them on the lawn. It was a rather elegant dining-room before."

Like many professional cooks, she has divided the light, airy room into a working and an eating area by making a central island of the stoves. The planning stage produced a further refinement: with a trolley, which slides neatly out of the way next to the sink, she could move smoothly around the room collecting food from the preparation area, the fridge, then the cooker, finishing up at the dining-table. "It works in theory," she insists in mid-gallop.

The practical properties of a four-foot-diameter circular "table" in the centre of the kitchen area are immediately apparent. Solid fruitwood cupboards, shelves and drawers are recessed into the base, and on the top are tiered revolving shelves forming a central column, which leaves the surrounding surface free.

The tiers hold, in ascending order, herbs and flavourings, oil, vinegar and wine, a selection of knives and finally all kinds of wooden utensils. Prue pulls out a simple bulb baster which she finds indispensable: "It's marvellous for taking off stock from under fat," she points out. And those revolving tiers obviate "reaching continually to the backs of cupboards".

French walnut cupboards are installed around the room, but a judicious hand has kept their contents uncluttered. On shelves of the same wood are home-made preserves and a line of large glass storage jars containing flour, rice, pasta and pulses. Sapphire blue tiles form a backdrop to these shelves and the sink area, where white china ("reject—you go through such a lot of it with children") is displayed on a rack. But her sense of the absurd is never far away: a thick marble pastry slab resting on one of the beige work-surfaces over the built-in units has a familiar look... it's another reject, a tombstone she acquired from a local stonemason.

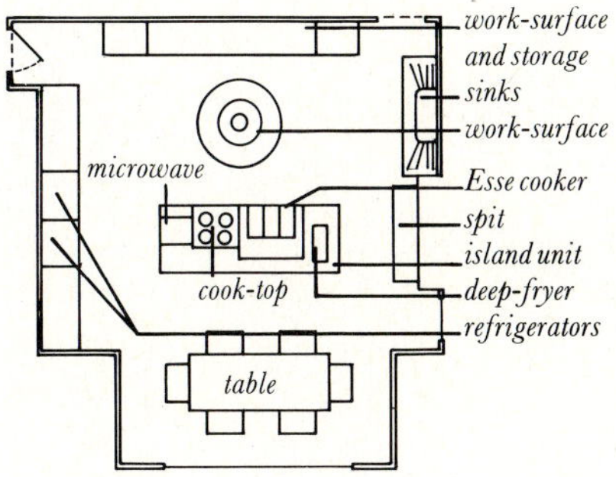

Prue Leith's home kitchen (above).

Food won't burn in copper saucepans, which rest on a rack above the stove (below). Earthenware saucepans can go into the oven.

She is dependent on Calor gas for the cooking work-top. An Esse stove and an electric deep-fryer are not unexpected on the cooking island, but there is also a microwave oven. "Marvellous for thawing if you forget to take a leg of lamb out of the freezer, and the children's suppers cook in three minutes," she explains. A charcoal grill and spit built into an outside wall gives her a further option. All cooking units have an "apron" of white tiles set into the wooden floor in front of them. Racks above hold her favourite saucepans.

When the garden is completed about two acres will be given over to fruit and vegetables. In the garage a pig lies salting. Next to the garage is an ample, north-facing tiled larder for bottled fruit and hanging hams. Two donkeys graze in the paddock. Two children and Rayne Kruger, her author husband, also need taking care of. Not to mention that fistful of professional commitments. "Maybe I'll open a pub next," she muses.

James Beard on kitchens

Framed by part of his collection of old confectionery lithographs, James Beard (above) proudly poses in his new kitchen.

Beard's kitchen (right) fills three important roles—part work-room, part school-room and as the place where he entertains his friends.

"I've been an 'electric' cook for over thirty years," says James Beard, who has been writing about food and drink for more than half a century. Beard has been called the "Dean of American Cookery", as well as "a Titan of the Table . . . a man whose vast culinary talents match his heroic proportions". He is author of some twenty books, was featured on the first food programme to be televised in the United States, and for five years ran his own radio cookery show.

Beard moved to New York from Portland, Oregon, in 1939. A year later he started a catering business called "Hors D'Oeuvre Inc." This led to the publication of his first book, *Hors D'Oeuvre and Canapés*, which is still in print to this day. In 1955 Beard opened his cooking school—one of the most successful in America.

Beard's kitchen requirements

In his Greenwich Village townhouse, Beard's kitchen has recently been redesigned by fellow Oregonian Jerry Lamb. It was planned to satisfy the three interrelated functions of Beard's culinary life—cooking, teaching and entertaining. "I want a kitchen that's roomy," said Beard. "I feel that there should be plenty of space to move around." So now, when his classes of twelve or more students are in session, they can all work together with room to spare.

Eye-catching

The first thing you notice in Beard's kitchen is the décor of a towering map of the world that covers both walls and ceiling. Once your eyes become accustomed, however, you will certainly pause to envy his three "cooking counters". There are twelve electric burners here in the main kitchen work-area, with four additional ones and two ovens in an adjoining pantry space—"no gas at all, and I don't miss it," adds Beard. "These cooking surfaces are perfect for simmering eighteen-hour broths and the only thing they can't do is deep-fry."

Double-duty work-areas

There are numerous electric sockets so that machines can be moved around easily. Separate work-areas help the kitchen to function more efficiently and different surfaces have been installed for different activities: marble for pastry-making; and a butcher's block for chopping and cutting. Work-areas double as serving areas. Therefore the sinks are kept out of the main kitchen area so that dirty dishes do not clutter the space when guests are being entertained. It also means that everything can be washed without disturbing the students.

Precious antiques

Despite the splendid array of equipment in Beard's kitchen, there is still a sense of openness. Every utensil has its special place. More than a dozen cleavers are stored in view, protected by a clear plastic shield; measuring cups of all sizes are hung on heavy-duty racks; wine racks are wall-hung within reach yet out of the way. Knives are kept in a circular wedge-shaped rack that fits neatly into a corner or in a mobile converted butter churner; and there are pots everywhere. "Somehow, whenever I have a party, I just can't get people out of the kitchen," says Beard. And no wonder. Among the room's many attractions is his exceptional collection of antique copper pots and moulds kept on permanent display. There is also an old wooden wall cabinet that holds glasses and herbs; racks to hold rolling pins; his collection of antique wine rinsers; and a charming series of turn-of-the-century lithographs depicting the grander works of German pastry- and marzipan-makers.

All this is displayed against the background of bright cartography. "The world is in eleven sheets," says Beard. "The metal fish sculpture is important here," he adds, referring to the work by a Californian artist prominently displayed in his kitchen. "I had to decide where to start the maps. So I thought that it would be most suitable for the fish to be hung in the Pacific Ocean and carry on from there."

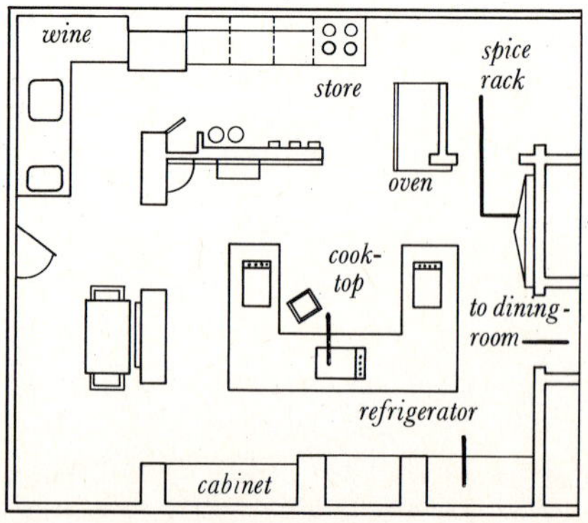

Plan of James Beard's kitchen.

Beard believes in copper both for cooking and decoration. Here (above) is part of his collection of antique utensils.

A converted butter churn (above), mounted on casters for easy movement, houses kitchen knives safely and conveniently.

Glasses, herbs and spices are displayed together in an old colonial cabinet (above) offset—startlingly—by the Pacific Ocean.

Another Beard passion is antique wine rinsers (above). Gems from his collection glow against a background of US government maps.

Twin sinks (right) discreetly dispose of the evening's dishwashing problems.

A craftsman's kitchen (above): Beard makes sure that his cooking area is brightly lit and that his principal working tools—as well as his favourite wines—are close at hand.

Equipment alcove with double oven (above).

Clever conversion makes the most of an old living area (left). The fireplace now provides storage for condiments and small kitchen tools and the wall is recessed to accommodate a large steel-faced refrigerator.

Elizabeth David's dream kitchen

So frequently do dream kitchens figure in the popular newspaper competitions, in the pages of shiny magazines and in department store advertising that one almost begins to believe women really do spend half their days dreaming about laminated work-tops, louvered cupboard doors and sheaves of gladioli standing on top of the dishwasher. Why of all rooms in the house does the kitchen have to be a dream? Is it because in the past kitchens have mostly been so underprivileged, so dingy and inconvenient? We don't, for example, hear much of dream drawing-rooms, dream bedrooms, dream garages, dream box-rooms (I could do with a couple of those). No. It's a dream kitchen or nothing. My own kitchen is rather more of a nightmare than a dream, but I'm stuck with it. However, I'll stretch a point and make it a good dream for a change. Here goes.

This fantasy kitchen will be large, very light, very airy, calm and warm. There will be the minimum of paraphernalia in sight. It will start off and will remain rigorously orderly. That takes care of just a few desirable attributes my present kitchen doesn't have. Naturally there'll be, as now, a few of those implements in constant use—ladles, a sieve or two, whisks, tasting spoons—hanging by the cooker, essential knives accessible in a rack, and wooden spoons in a jar. But half a dozen would be enough, not thirty-five as there are now. Cookery writers are particularly vulnerable to the acquisition of unnecessary clutter. I'd love to rid myself of it.

The sink will be a double one, with a solid wooden draining-board on each side. It will be (in fact, is) set 760 mm (30 in) from the ground, about 152 mm (6 in) higher than usual. I'm tall, and I didn't want to be prematurely bent double as a result of leaning over a knee-high sink. Along the wall above the sink I envisage a continuous wooden plate rack designed to hold serving dishes as well as plates, cups and other crockery in normal use. This saves a great deal of space, and much time spent getting out and putting away. Talking of space, suspended from the ceiling would be a wooden rack or slatted shelves—such as farmhouses and even quite small cottages in parts of Wales and the Midland counties used to have for storing bread or drying out oatcakes. Here would be the parking place for papers, notebooks, magazines—all the things that usually get piled on chairs when the table has to be cleared. The table itself is, of course, crucial. It's for writing at and for meals, as well as for kitchen tasks, so it has to have comfortable leg room. This time round I'd like it to be oval, one massive piece of scrubbable wood, on a central pedestal. Like the sink, it has to be a little higher than the average.

Outside the kitchen is my refrigerator and there it will stay. I keep it at the lowest temperature, about 4°C (40°F) I'm still amazed at the way so-called model kitchens have refrigerators next to the cooking stove. This seems to me almost as mad as having a wine rack above it. Then, failing a separate larder—in a crammed London house that's carrying optimism a bit too far—there would be a second and fairly large refrigerator to be used for the cool storage of a variety of commodities such as coffee beans, spices, butter, cheese and eggs, which benefit from a constant temperature of say 10°C (50°F).

All the colours in the dream kitchen would be much as they are now, but fresher and cleaner—cool silver, grey-blue, aluminium, with the various browns of earthenware pots and a lot of white provided by the perfectly plain china. I recoil from coloured tiles and beflowered surfaces and I don't want a lot of things coloured avocado and tangerine. I'll just settle for the avocados and tangerines in a bowl on the dresser. In other words, if the food and the cooking pots don't provide enough visual interest and create their own changing patterns in a kitchen, then there's something wrong. And too much equipment is if anything worse than too little. I don't a bit covet the exotic gear dangling from hooks, the riot of clanking ironmongery, the armouries of knives, or the serried ranks of sauté pans and all other carefully chosen symbols of culinary activity I see in so many photographs of chic kitchens. Pseuds corners, I'm afraid, many of them.

When it comes to the cooker I don't think I need anything very fancy. My cooking is mostly on a small scale and of the kind for intimate friends, so I'm happy enough with an ordinary four-burner gas stove. Its oven has to be a good size, though, and it has to have a drop-down door. Given the space I'd

Elizabeth David, doyenne of cookery writers, has inspired a whole generation of gourmets.

have a second, quite separate oven just for bread, and perhaps some sort of temperature-controlled cupboard for proving the dough. On the whole though it's probably best for cookery writers to use the same kind of domestic equipment as the majority of their readers. It doesn't do to get too far away from the problems of everyday household cooking or take the easy way out with expensive gadgetry.

What it all amounts to is that for me— and I stress that this is purely personal, because my requirements as a writing cook are rather different from those of one who cooks mainly for a succession of guests or for the daily meals of a big family—the perfect kitchen would really be more like a painter's studio furnished with cooking equipment than anything conventionally accepted as a kitchen.

The dining-table (right) is oval with a central pedestal base. Slim drawers for table cutlery allow ample space for knees.

The mixing centre (above). A cupboard opens on to the work-surface. The mixer, its accessories and the socket are inside.

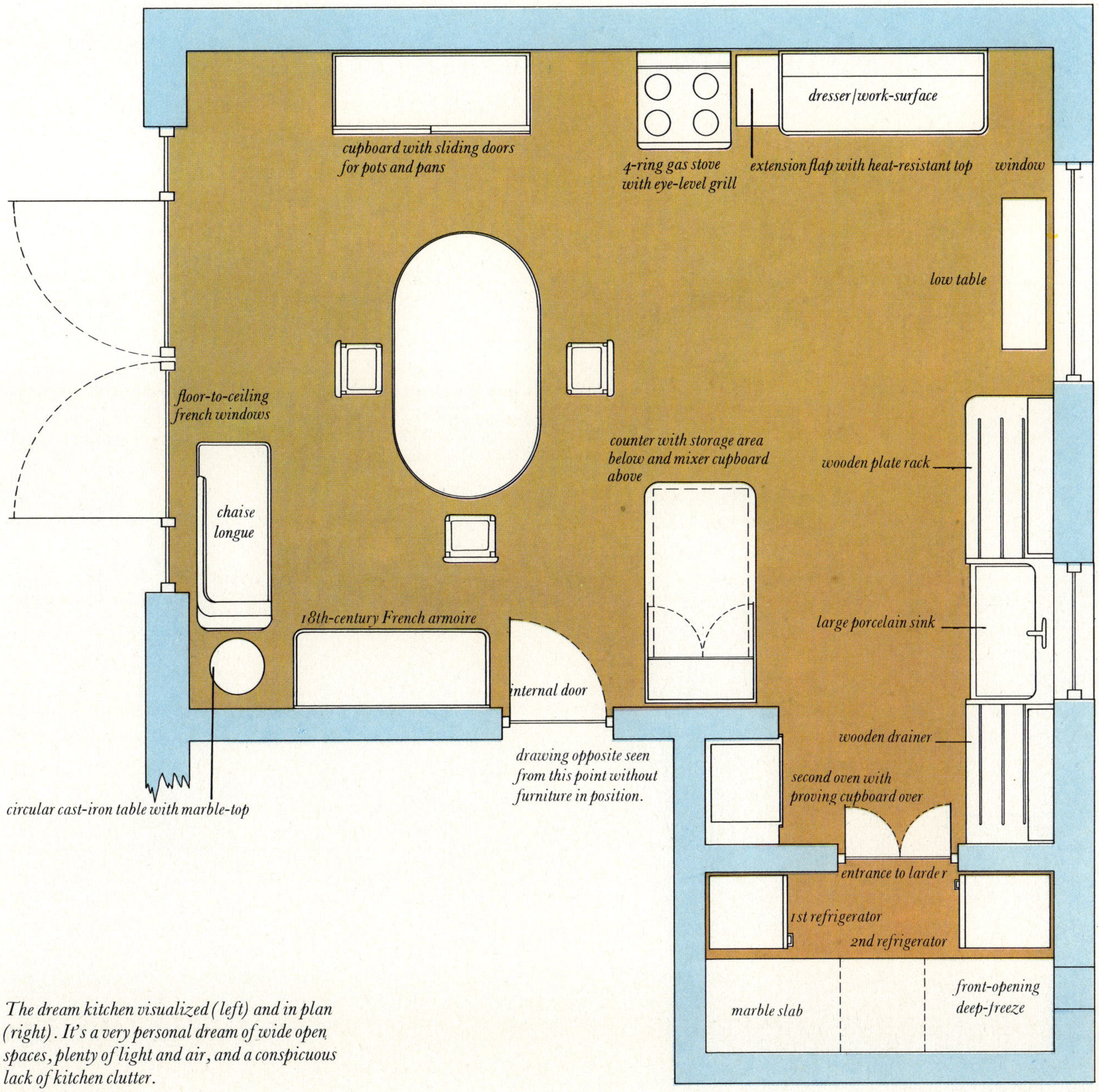

The dream kitchen visualized (left) and in plan (right). It's a very personal dream of wide open spaces, plenty of light and air, and a conspicuous lack of kitchen clutter.

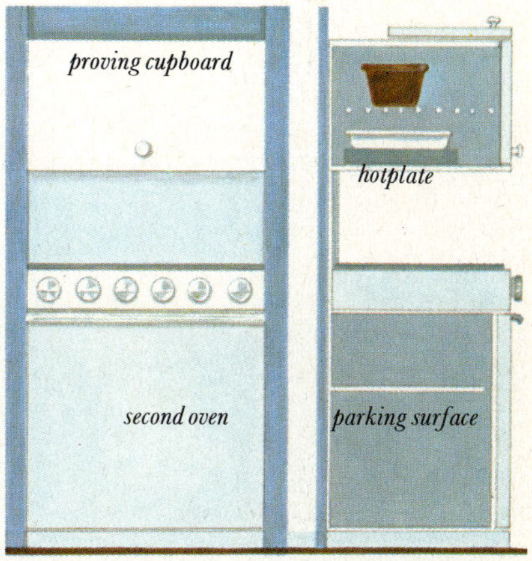

Proving cupboard, where bread dough rises, is kept warm and moist with a hotplate and dish of water. Cupboard door lifts up and over.

Above the mixing centre swings a "hammock" for tidying away all the papers and magazines that clutter up the dining-table.

The professionals

Fay Maschler—the critic's choice

"I don't like modern electrical equipment," says Fay Maschler, one of London's leading restaurant critics. "I much prefer a mandoline to a Magimix."

For one who must dine out three or four times a week, her own kitchen might easily be unimportant in her life, but the reverse is true. Children's toys, a telephone, a television set, even the dining-room are encompassed within its papered walls. It is very much the heart of the home.

"We didn't make any major changes when we moved in two years ago. The feeling then was American folksy," Fay explains. "Now it is English folksy. I like old things, not plastic-looking kitchens full of Formica and stainless steel."

Cream cornices hug the plain sage-coloured ceiling and bunches of dried flowers hang at the front bay windows. On one wall is what ominously appears to be a stuffed pike. The lighting, too, accents the period flavour: a stained-glass Art Nouveau lamp over the kitchen area, and a brass-framed shade of scalloped cream silk over the dining-table.

Kitchen equipment is in generous supply. Shelves run the width of the room, the top one packed with a mesmerizing array of earthenware dishes and casseroles, the lower with countless glass storage jars. Even the tiled surfaces around the cook-top are busy with crocks and caddies, biscuit tins and cooking wines. A time and motion expert would wince, but Fay says firmly that "cooking should be a relaxation, a pleasure. I like the look of many kitchen things; they can be very pretty."

Her oven is an electric Moffat and she has both electric and gas burners on the cook-top. "It is easier to simmer on electricity but gas cooks things quicker." Although machines don't particularly charm her, she concedes that "a fridge that size is a great joy", pointing to a vast fridge/freezer unit. On view, too, is a food mixer and an electric grinder, and discreetly tucked into one of the many built-in green and cream

cupboards is a dishwasher. Nevertheless, when she can, Fay deliberately chooses the old rather than the new. Wood, not stainless steel, draining boards surround her sink, and the solid pine work-table in the centre of the kitchen area has a traditional marble top and a deep drawer for implements.

Even more handsome is the pearwood sideboard flanking the dining-table. If all the objects on it were real, it might be described as groaning, but here appearances are deceptive. Various china and wax fruits are obvious fakes, a glossy cherry tart is actually a candle and the nut bowl masquerades as a stack of plates.

Whimsical objects dot the 6-m (20-ft) room. Even the stuffed pike is plaster of paris. Fay has a penchant for fish, both decorative and edible. They feature on wall plates and prints, as table plates and as an easy entrée for dinner parties.

"When we moved here I went through an anti-pattern phase and bought everything white, thinking food would look better on it," she recalls. But she soon succumbed to one, then another patterned serving dish. These are kept in a cream-painted dresser with coloured glass doors.

Fay has four shelves of cookery books in the hall—however, she clearly dislikes the pseudo-grandeur of much haute cuisine. Particular antipathies include "professional chef's sauce, aspic, piped potatoes, veal dishes drowned in Marsala and the school of cooking that thinks if you use lots of cream and brandy and garnish with lobster claws, you've arrived at a fantastic dish." She prefers to serve more simple food: "I tend to cook things I don't often find in restaurants, like boiled chicken or oxtail. I'm also fond of Indian vegetarian dishes. Their spices, like ginger and coriander, are so nice. And I can't bear to throw food away, it is so expensive. Sometimes we eat quite comical meals made from left-overs, such as odd bits of cheese."

Despite her squirrel instincts and the profuse detail that marks the contents of her kitchen-cum-dining-room, the final effect is surprisingly restful: nor does the gentle touch of fantasy stop at the front windows. At the end of the garden is an old-fashioned gas lamp; on the far side of the road a quaint chemist's shop recalls more leisurely days.

Fay, her publisher husband and their three children depart for a relaxing holiday at their cottage in Wales every summer. "We eat more elaborately in Wales. I have so much more time," she comments. "It's a twenty-mile round trip to the shops, so I take everything with me."

Everything? That, one suspects, must be quite a carful.

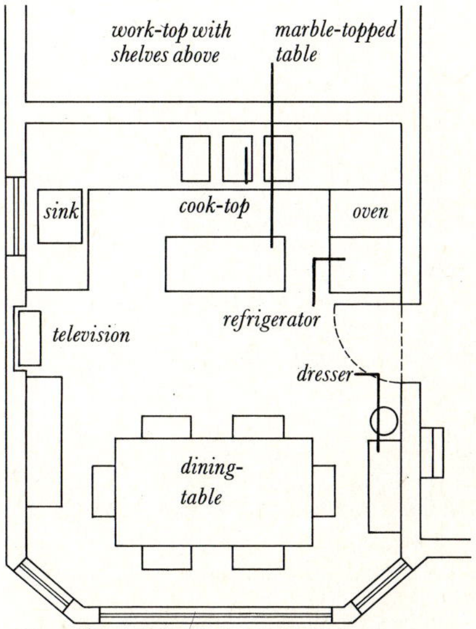

Plan of Fay Maschler's kitchen (above).

Despite her built-in cupboards, restaurant critic Fay Maschler (above) enjoys the display of ingredients that go into her cooking.

Much-loved ornaments on the antique sideboard bring a touch of humour to the Maschler's whimsical North London kitchen (left).

Traditional marble-topped pine work-table (right) is a boon for pastry-making, and the 1900's cream dresser houses attractive china.

George Lang – the experts' expert

Welcome to the world of George Lang and his extraordinary New York kitchen.

Restaurateur, calligrapher, concert violinist, author—George Lang, who heads the George Lang Corporation, "the only think tank in the food and beverage industry", has been called "the expert's expert", as well as the "Hottentot of Hospitality" and has been described as being able to combine the "head of a scientist with the heart of an artist, the ingenuity of a used-car salesman with the energy of a marathon runner."

So, when Lang and his wife Karen, working with architect Don Mallow, started the transformation of his New York apartment to accommodate "the kitchen where we can even cook", by tearing out the walls between an existing dining-room, a small study, a small kitchen and a bathroom, the result, as might be expected, was quite extraordinary—and Lang's kitchen, the room he calls "the emotional centre of the house"—is a unique experience.

According to Lang, "perhaps most important was the fact that we could afford the luxury of creating a kitchen that would have its own style." This attitude matches Lang's interior design theories—"I didn't want to copy any period," he explains, "and in general I feel that there has to be a good reason for designing anything and everything; but once you've done that, if a person who comes into the space is aware of it, then you have failed." So, Lang's kitchen incorporates many influences and ideas, but ends up by being unique. There are clues to its aesthetic style to be found: recollections of Lang's native Hungary, and the mirrors, reminiscent of Viennese coffee houses, as well as the white paint that Karen Lang admired in mid-nineteenth century New Orleans dining-rooms; Lang's experiences in the restaurant and hotel business, which made him an expert on the efficiency of all professional equipment; contemporary kitchen design; and, of course, all the ideas that Lang had always wanted to put into the "ideal" kitchen.

When did Lang start to put this kitchen together? "Before either Karen or I drew a single line, or started any of the actual planning, we made a list of some basic rules," explains Lang, "and included all the functions that may take place in the kitchen. Then, we treated the space available to us as a cube in which each single inch was examined to make sure it would be used to best advantage in relation

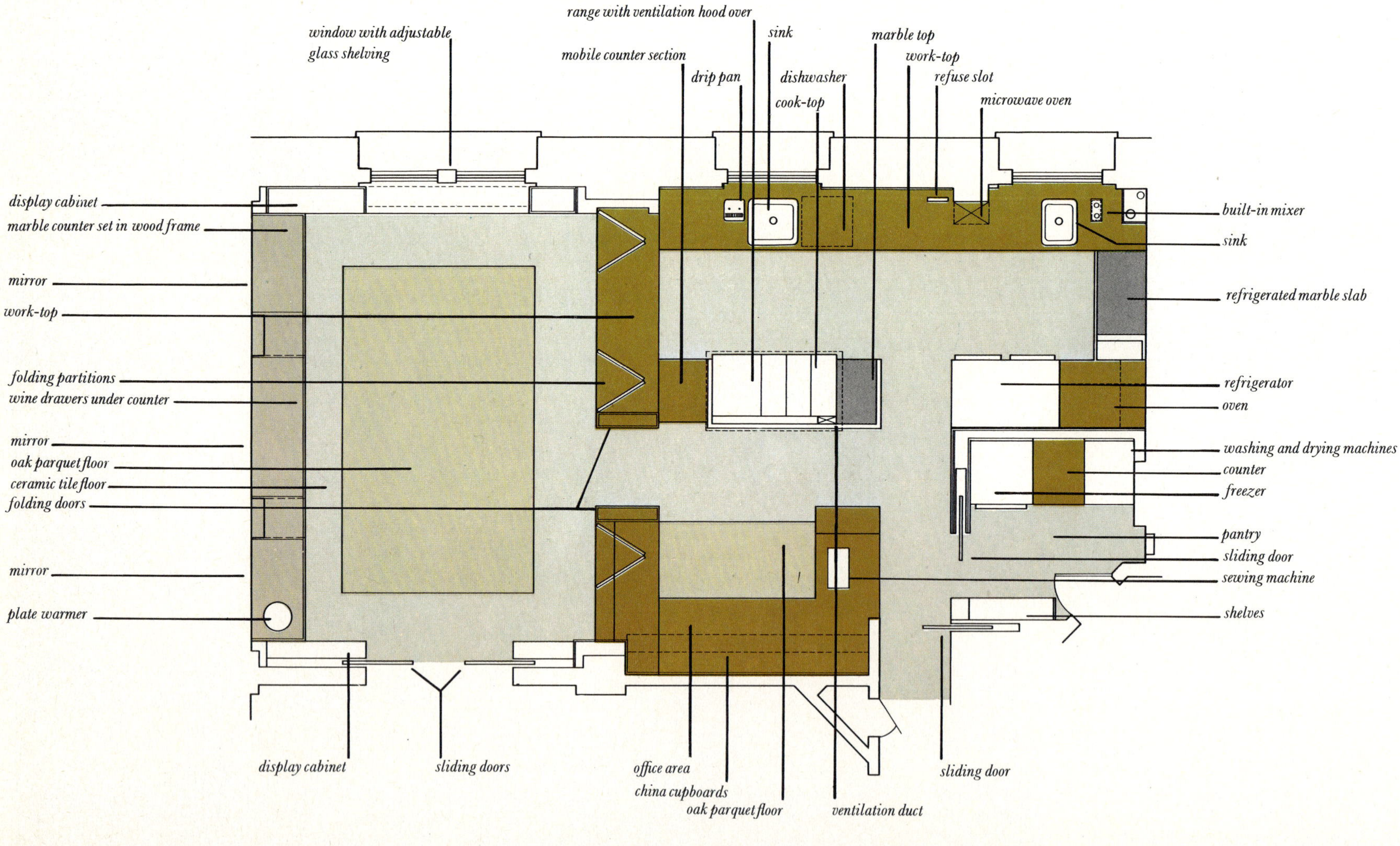

Plan of George and Karen Lang's kitchen.

to the whole plan." The Langs then made a list of all the equipment they would be needing, considered the kitchen's traffic patterns and sorted out the kitchen's functions. These were to include: formal and informal (sit-down) dining; buffet parties; desk and office work; sewing; canning; parties that might take place in the kitchen; Karen Lang's pastry kitchen—and space for classroom teaching; a test kitchen; and storage for all kinds of dishes, glassware, wine, food, teas, spices, coffees, pots and pans and machines.

Kataba (above), undoubtedly one of the best-fed cats in New York, casts a critical eye on the preparations for a cold buffet.

A large gas restaurant range is built into a plain of easy-to-clean tiles (right). It has two burners and two "hot tops" that will take a whole batterie of pans.

A view of the brass and stainless-steel oven housing unit (below) as seen from the office-cum-sewing-area.

China is kept in well-organized glass-fronted cupboards above the office area (below right).

The professionals

George Lang

After the removal of the walls, the space available for the Lang kitchen was approximately 20 feet wide and 40 feet long. There are two entrances to the kitchen: both from the living-room, one leading to the dining area, and the other to the cooking and work space. Because the living-room ceiling is 20 feet high, the ceiling in the eight-foot-high dining area has been mirrored and brilliantly lit to diminish the contrast in height between the two rooms. On the left side of the dining area, there is a buffet credenza that runs the length of the room. Lang has installed a device called a lowerator, to keep plates hot and accessible for a buffet. There are also two hot trays in the buffet, installed flush with the tiled surface to hold buffet foods and to keep serving dishes hot for second helpings. Underneath are Lang's "wine drawers"—thermostatically controlled pull-out layers for the storage of wine bottles. And there are also very organized drawers for linen, cutlery and silver that pertain to the dining area.

Throughout the kitchen and dining-room, the floor has been laid with 2-in-square white ceramic tiles. But, in the middle of the dining area, Lang has put in an inlaid dark parquet floor instead of carpeting. And in contrast to the kitchen's modernity is the dark, fathomless gleam of the dining-table and chairs, "ten rather curious mid-eighteenth-century variations on Queen Anne chairs."

Lang explains his choice by saying "I have always felt that to have two armchairs for the host and hostess while the other guests are all sitting on armless chairs was a ridiculous holdover from medieval times. So, we tried a set of chairs that were all armchairs and had them upholstered in red velvet to provide one of the few colours in the room."

The dining-room is separated from the kitchen by a central doorway and two side sections, with two folding panels (with bevelled glass inserts) that can, when shut, close off the dining area completely.

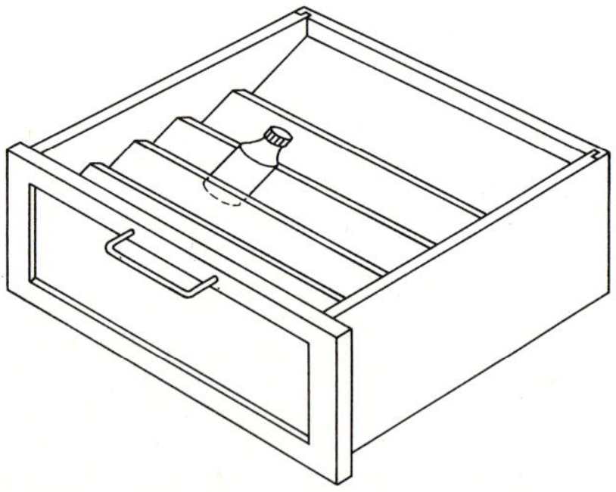

Tilted spice racks contained in a drawer (above) cut out the irritation of rummaging through shelves packed with jars.

The luxurious bulk of a sideboard, a treasure chest of silver and vintage wine, stretches along a wall of the dining-room (above) and is a tremendous boon when serving a buffet.

The democratic dining-room (right) of the "Hottentot of Hospitality", handsomely furnished with William and Mary table and antique armchairs for guests and hosts alike.

Discreet lighting is a keynote in the Lang dining area. Serried ranks of glasses sparkle a welcome from an illuminated cupboard (above).

For co-ordinated action, a multipurpose unit (above) combines marble slab, slide-out chopping board and orderly spice drawer.

Lang indulges his passion for good coffee with his own espresso machine, electric grinder and pull-out canisters of assorted roasts (above).

Chianti, Burgundy and brilliantly polished silver held in velvet-clad grooves await one of Lang's formal entertainments.

At the edge of the dining area (above), lovingly polished parquet gives way to the clinical check of the ceramic-tiled kitchen space.

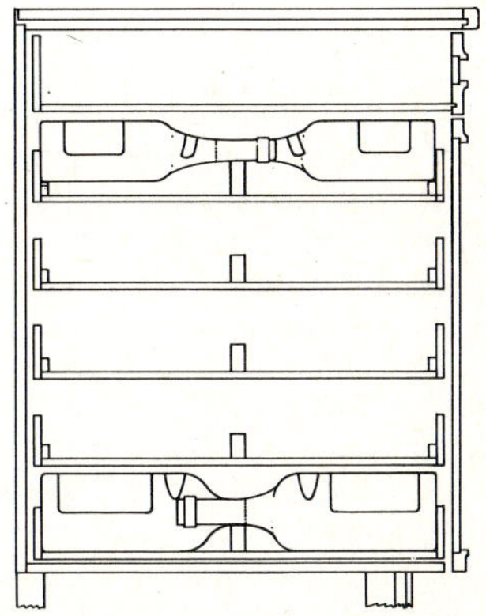

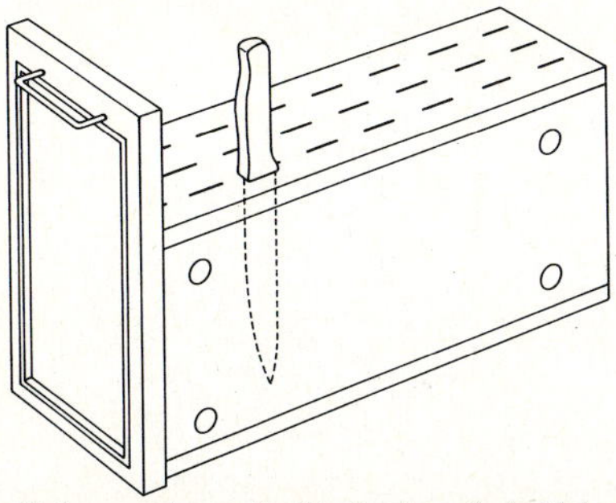

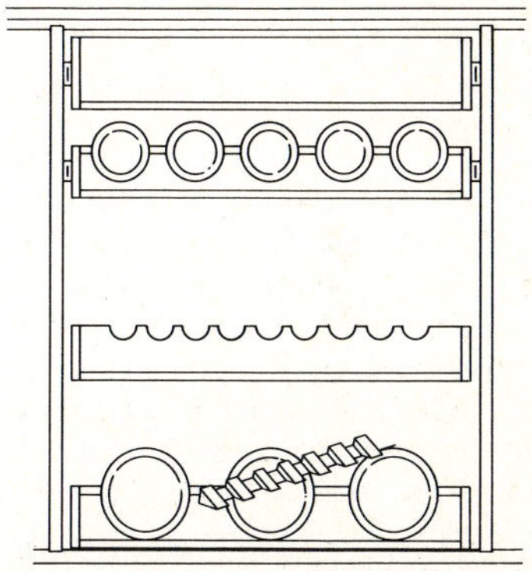

Knives stay keen-edged in the slots of a knife box-cum-drawer (above). Each slot has been designed to fit a specific blade.

Diagram of a wine-lover's chest of drawers (above), in which bottles lie neck and neck at an angle of nine degrees.

Awkward pots and casseroles, too heavy to be lifted high, are stored beneath the cook-top (above) in an easy-rolling drawer.

The marble-topped unit, part of a maze of storage systems, conceals a simple tray rack (above) behind its sumptuous copper door.

The master carver keeps his razor-edged knives in a slotted box that glides safely under the maple work-top (above).

Thermostatically controlled drawers (above) enable Lang's wines, after a suitable breathing space, to be brought straight to the table.

The professionals

George Lang

In what Lang calls the "kitchen work area", one section is a combination office-sewing centre, equipped with desk surfaces (that can be fitted with drawing boards), telephone stands, stationery cubbyholes, a typewriter, sewing machine, fitted drawers for pencils and paperclips as well as Lang's calligraphy pens.

The use of restaurant equipment is an essential part of this kitchen. Lang has a large dishwashing machine with a four-minute cycle, a glass-fronted four-door refrigerator large enough to hold "a case of oranges", plus a dozen bottles of wine, a large stockpot and an oversized platter of food at the same time. This section also has a convection oven. A restaurant stove manufacturer made Lang one with a white front and equipped the unit with a griddle-top salamander, a large oven, two open burners and two hot-tops. The whole gas unit is topped with a custom-built brass and stainless-steel hood.

The kitchen also has a soda fountain unit that dispenses chilled, bottled or carbonated water and a sink unit that makes instant boiling water (handy for scalding and peeling tomatoes). Every square inch of the kitchen has been planned to accommodate a maximum of storage space. Three functional divisions have been made: Karen Lang has a completely organized and equipped pastry kitchen: "She's the baker," says Lang, "and she learned to bake in a methodical way from her mother, also an excellent baker." Karen's pastry area has a white marble top with a recessed electric hot-top cooking surface (for caramelizing sugar, for example), underneath drawers for flour, sugar and every type of baking equipment, a corner swing-out storage cabinet for larger baking dishes and a built-in blender and food mixer. Secondly, there is a cold pantry, with a slot for waste, a pull-out knife drawer and storage for pots and pans, colanders and platters. Then, opposite the range is the hot-preparation area. On one side of the stove, Lang has installed a marble-topped unit that can take pots straight from the stove, a slide-out carving board, and a drawer where spices are stacked conveniently at hand, yet out of sight.

Lang has also planned storage space for coffee beans right under the counter where the espresso machine and the electric coffee grinder are situated.

Instant boiling water (above) at the push of a button is a time-saving device, especially for scalding and peeling tomatoes.

To save counter-top space, the blender (above) is installed near the pastry kitchen and fitted flush to the counter-top.

Working at his kitchen desk, which can be fitted with a drafting board, Lang (left) keeps his drawing quills close by.

A four-door refrigerator (right), which could service a small restaurant, is roomy enough to hold a case of champagne.

Children visiting the Lang kitchen make a beeline for this friendly monster (above), which creates delicious fizzy drinks to order

The maple-topped storage unit (above) has been put on wheels for Lang to push it out of the way during kitchen parties.

Karen Lang's pastry kitchen (right) is fitted out with all the equipment and ingredients needed to make pasta, cakes and bread.

A detail of the corner of the pastry kitchen shows how neatly the tile, wood and marble surfaces are co-ordinated (above).

Deep under the counter (above), bins hold a large supply of flour, ready to be scooped up on the marble pastry slab.

A revolving corner cabinet swings out to display an array of mixing bowls, rotary beaters and baking pans.

As in commercial kitchens, a slot for trash has been cut into the butcher-block counter. Wastes drop into a trash bin below.

Conveniently located under one of the sinks, the garbage can slides out and flips up when the cabinet door is pulled open.

George Lang and the Café des Artistes

Lighting the room was given special consideration. Architect Don Mallow designed the special light fixtures, which run the length of the kitchen/dining-room, but not in a straight line. He had over 40 additional invisible light sources put in so that each area could be controlled separately and so that the Langs could change the atmosphere of the kitchen/dining-room to suit the way in which they are entertaining. "The lighting enables us to transform the mood from casual to extremely formal, and from conservative to way-out," adds Lang.

This attitude suits Lang's thinking about food— "I don't have a speciality," he says. "When I entertain I establish the market, for example, 'who is coming to dinner?' Then I evaluate my capabilities (time, ingredients), I decide on the atmosphere (formal, casual), and then I choose my materials (basing the party theme on the season, the occasion, or a special food)."

Lang likes to cook "something very complicated, or something very simple—that's also an indication of my life," he says. Author of *The Cuisine of Hungary*, Lang is equally familiar with that of many other countries. "I have no prejudices, and no clock in my stomach," he adds, "and somehow I'm never full or tired of tasting a new food."

Lang prides himself on doing more than one thing at a time. He practises his music in the kitchen—"the space is perfect"—and remarks that both knife and bow are "natural extensions of my hand".

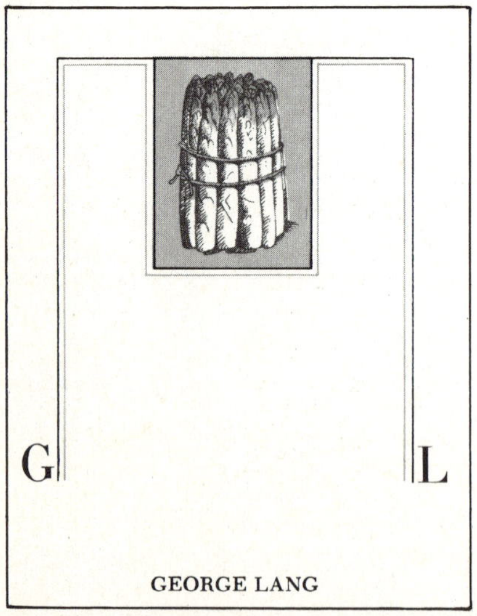

Illustrator Milton Glaser chose a bunch of asparagus to grace Lang's stationery (above).

Electric surfaces have been set into the tile counter (above) to keep casseroles hot for second helpings and buffet parties.

The lowerator (above), a device that is usually seen only in commercial kitchens, has a balance system to dispense warmed-up plates.

A sophisticated system of lights (below), designed by architect Don Mallow, is reflected in the dining-room's mirrored ceiling.

Music-lover Lang (above) finds musical inspiration among the cooking pots.

Just down the street from where he lives is the *Cafe des Artistes*, George Lang's restaurant, where he can try out some of the ideas he has on cooking, eating and the presentation of food on the public. "When I took over the restaurant I eliminated the obviously symbolistic dishes which stand for expensive restaurants and elegance," he explains, "such as lobster, crabmeat, foie gras, and caviar. I also eliminated all the cliché French foods that are fashionable and which include quenelles, quiches, anything encased in pastry, and all food covered in green peppercorns."

Lang decided to create a menu where virtually everything is in the kitchen's control, that is can be made on the premises and to his exact specifications. "I didn't want a stagnant menu," says Lang, so items change daily, based on the season, market availability, price and the previous day's speciality. For example, in the restaurant there is a different choice each day of pasta, vegetable and potato dishes. The Cafés desserts are baked at home by several local housewives using recipes handed down to Lang by his mother.

In terms of design, Lang believes that there are two ways to plan a restaurant. "One way is to create something from nothing," he explains, "the other is to take something and peel off the layers that were added by the decades." In the *Café des Artistes* Lang chose the second approach. The murals, by 1920s artist Howard Chandler Christy (depicting many of his girlfriends in a sylvan, romantic setting), have been cleaned and restored. So, too, was the remainder of the restaurant, but so carefully that no vestige of its bohemian flavour has been lost.

The Café des Artistes' staff (above) stand behind the restaurant's impressive display of favourite Lang hors d'oeuvre and cakes.

In his refurbished restaurant, the Café des Artistes, always-enthusiastic Lang (above) clowns with some painted ladies by 1920s artist Howard Chandler Christy.

Aluminium shelves, stacked with the day's luncheon specials and over a dozen skillets (right), frame the cooking area in the restaurant's basement kitchen.

The professionals

Milton Glaser—dining and designing

Milton and Shirley Glaser's Woodstock, New York, kitchen is housed in what used to be a separate shed, which was attached to their main house when they acquired it some fifteen years ago. "We just moved things around a little," explains Glaser, a dedicated writer on food topics and, until recently, Art Director of *New York Magazine*. A local craftsman "who was young when he started working here," rebuilt and reinstalled the original cabinets under a chestnut counter. "It's not practical but it is beautiful," says Shirley. "We hated our old electric stove so we had it replaced by a restaurant gas range and put some tiles on the floor—that's about all we did." In the Glaser kitchen the stove is the centre of attention; the tiles behind it were painted by the house's former owner, sculptor Bruno Zim.

"In the last 14 years, we may have eaten out 20 times," explains Shirley—a testimony to the cooking abilities of the Glasers. They both cook. Shirley alternates between "romantic and classical dishes"; Milton likes to work on "complex dishes that combine many ingredients, like stews, cassoulets and twenty-ingredient Chinese casseroles." Shirley only got seriously interested in cooking in 1958, when she lived in Italy and "wanted to know how to make everything I ate in restaurants." Bologna was Milton's inspiration, "the food was dazzling and I think it's the best city in Europe to eat in." He owes a great deal to his mother who, he says, was a "terrible cook." Also "like everyone else who grew up in the Bronx, I love Chinese food." He went on to study Chinese cooking at the China Institute in New York. "I have a long way to go," he adds, "but I love the cutting and preparation, the working out of a problem. It's just like designing." And he practises. Milton cooks a Chinese banquet every Saturday night he's in Woodstock. Adds Shirley, "I buy everything and do all the cleaning afterwards."

The Glaser kitchen is long and narrow, with a food-preparation and sink area two steps up from the cooking area. Shirley, who thinks this is a "nearly perfect kitchen", likes small kitchens and notes that its only imperfection is a "too-small sink".

Every corner of the Glaser kitchen reflects the professional flair of its owners. Shirley (above) expertly prepares a salad.

A new use for old candy-store jars—the bright rack of food containers, which graces the chestnut counter (below).

A Chinese banquet is a regular Saturday-night ritual at Woodstock—cooked by Milton Glaser himself. An array (below) of spices and utensils awaits the maestro's hand.

Twelve years ago, Glaser started co-authoring articles about food with Jerome Snyder—articles that grew to become best-selling books called *The Underground Gourmet*. Milton calls this experience, "the single most important perception of my life. We went all over New York reviewing cheap ethnic restaurants." The "landmark" piece was entitled "Yonah Schimmel and the Mock Knish." New York is still talking about it.

Since then design consultant Glaser has gone on to plan menus and themes for restaurateurs Joe Baum and George Lang and has gone into business and formed a company called Beard Glaser Wolf to produce and market kitchen equipment.

The Glasers' passion for edible fungi is proclaimed (above) by French schoolroom charts and a collection of wooden mushrooms.

Not dinner on the hoof, but Mr Hoffmann (above), an honoured family friend and fellow gourmet, who enjoys a complete run of the kitchen.

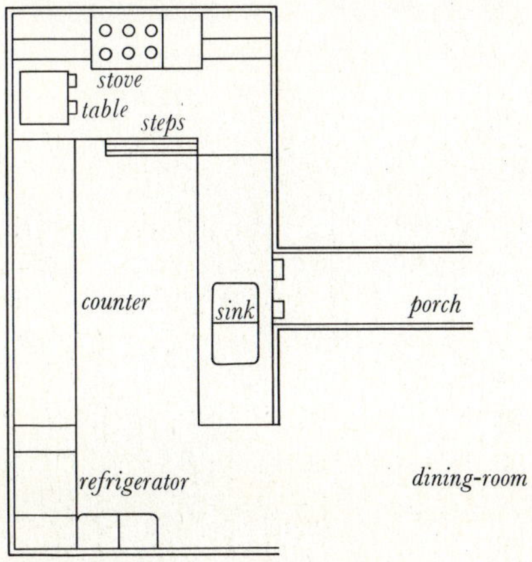

Kitchen of a writer-designer-gourmet.

Side-lamps and the warm glow of stained glass (above) do greater justice to the batterie de cuisine than any overhead lighting.

The Glasers proudly present an informal lunch (below). The plates are part of a series designed by Milton for a Canadian restaurant.

Perla Meyers—a fresh approach

"When I was young, we travelled to eat, not to visit museums," says Perla Meyers, author of *The Seasonal Kitchen* and *The Peasant Kitchen* and teacher of creative cooking at her own school in New York. Born in Vienna and raised in Barcelona, she has travelled extensively in England, France and Italy. Her father was Alsatian and had "an incredible interest in food. We went hundreds of miles for a meal at a special restaurant. He was also a mushroom fanatic, so we visited Bologna for white truffles and Marseilles for cèpes." With a Viennese mother and a Spanish cook in their Barcelona home, Perla learned early that different cuisines could mix happily. She studied at the Ecole Hôtelière in Lausanne, and later met Raymond Oliver of the Grand Véfour restaurant in Paris. He suggested that if she was serious about a career in food, she should study cooking by working in restaurants. "It's hard to realize now," she says, "but in Europe in the 1960s there was no real way for a woman to learn about food, unless her parents owned a restaurant."

Perla Meyers' tiny but highly professional kitchen perfectly illustrates her cooking philosophy—lack of clutter, good tools and plenty of vegetables.

Mrs Meyers went on to study confectionery at the Hotel Sacher in Vienna, French cuisine at the Cordon Bleu in Paris and now spends two months a year working in the kitchens of well-known European restaurants such as Giannino's in Milan, Demels in Vienna, and Paul Bocuse's restaurant near Lyons, as well as in many small regional restaurants in Italy, Spain and France. She speaks seven languages, and this enables her to keep in touch with the latest trends and innovations in European cooking. "When I see grande cuisine, I don't try to copy it," she says, "I simply try to learn and then to simplify."

In 1967, she opened her own cooking school in New York, The International Kitchen, to teach "creative cooking" and make "people feel more comfortable in moving from one type of ethnic cuisine to another". She explains that she grew up "selecting what was best from the different cuisines", and that this freedom is one of the most valuable contributions she can make to her students. "Once you understand the techniques of food preparation, and how ingredients work with one another, you can incorporate regional dishes into other parts of the menu and be happy doing it," she adds. Her students are taught to select the proper kitchen equipment; "a task sometimes ten times more confusing than mastering the preparation of a perfect soufflé." Her interest is less in "new" dishes than in teaching students to "put their own stamp on a dish, transforming it into something personal" by learning not only recipes but by understanding the philosophy behind the recipes.

Most weekends she commutes with her husband Robert and their young son Claude to their Washington Depot, Connecticut, country home, where most of their entertaining takes place. The house was recently remodelled and a new kitchen added. "Unlike most professional cooks", Perla says, "I do not like clutter. To me the most important aspect of a kitchen is the amount of working space available." She had noticed that in France "the most efficient kitchens were never cluttered", and proceeded to plan her own space in those terms. "I only want to work with the tools that are absolutely necessary." The small kitchen was converted from a bedroom, porch and bathroom, which overlooked beautiful woodlands and a pond, one of the features of the Meyers' land. "As we spend most of our time in this room, we gave it our prime spot," she explains. The kitchen is painted throughout in white, except for wooden work-tops and a butcher's-block table. "I want colour to come from the food," adds Mrs Meyers, "and I like the simplicity and freshness of an all-white kitchen."

All the pots and pans are put away when not in use. "You can take better care of them that way," she explains, so closed cupboards have been carefully planned both under the work-tops and hung on the only available large wall. One cupboard is reserved for casseroles, one for mixing equipment and one for the serving pieces. The cupboards are deep, so that everyday things are up front, and dishes and pots and pans used infrequently are stored at the rear. "A kitchen should have as many drawers as possible, and also a separate pantry with narrow shelves."

Perla Meyers' philosophy is based on using only fresh seasonal foods. "Freshness means peasant food. A countrywoman has to cook with what's available." She rarely uses canned vegetables, but makes only two exceptions: tomatoes and canned peas, "because a canned pea is really a totally different vegetable and doesn't compete

A herb cabinet laid on its side (above) makes a convenient ready-to-use store for fistfuls of kitchen equipment for all occasions.

with a fresh pea". This is the way she eliminates a huge variety of foods that commonly need storing.

Mrs Meyers grows her own vegetables in the country, but her kitchen does not have an especially large freezer. "I only freeze stocks, sauces, breads and ice-cream," she says, "I don't believe in advance freezing for parties—food just doesn't taste the same." She believes strongly in following the seasons and enjoys "looking forward from one season to another" and "of making the most of a particular vegetable at a certain time of the year", even if "you end up having it every day". All in all, her emphasis is on simplicity and freshness—"I tell my students to forget about copper pots and to limit themselves to five good knives. For ten years I was concerned with 'what was right and what was wrong' in cooking. Today I'm more interested in 'mood cooking'—doing what I feel like at a given time, incorporating all the influences of my training and background."

A cosmopolitan collection of cans is housed in an old broom cupboard (above). Shallow shelves allow the contents to be seen at a glance.

Simple tools for mood cooking—Perla Meyers' wood and wicker equipment (above) testifies to her love of natural materials.

No mess, no fuss—the crisp, neat dining area (below) is overlooked by the kitchen, but never encumbered by cooking paraphernalia.

The dining area (above) of Perla Meyers' home in Washington Depot, Connecticut. (Below), a plan of the kitchen and dining areas.

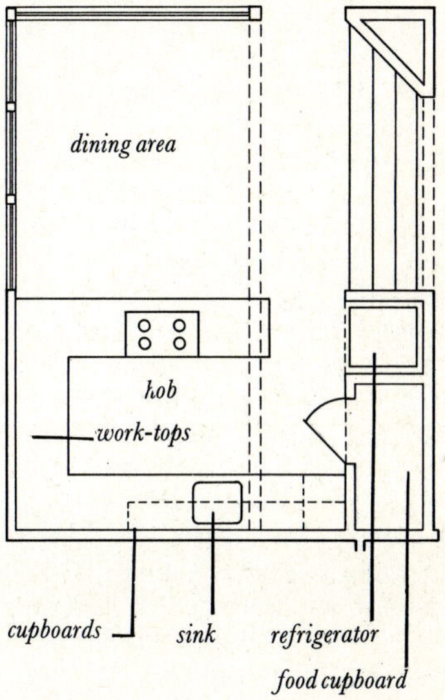

Robert Carrier's stately restaurant

Robert Carrier's vision transformed Hintlesham Hall (above) from stately home to England's most sumptuous restaurant.

Specially designed skylights (right) and a garden door help to dispel summer heat and cooking smells in the kitchen.

"It was going to be a hobby," reminisces master-restaurateur Robert Carrier: Hintlesham Hall in Suffolk was almost in ruins when he bought it as his country retreat six years ago. It bore the traces of a splendid past—a moulded plaster ceiling in the Carolean Room attributed to Grinling Gibbons and a twenty-four-foot-high two-storey saloon, formerly the Elizabethan Great Hall—but did it have a future?

Carrier bought Hintlesham Hall, unseen, because it sounded exactly what he'd always wanted. Sixty craftsmen laboured six months to restore it. "The main work was saving the ceiling and twenty dormer windows. I hadn't bargained on those."

It proved an expensive hobby, even for such a highly successful restaurant owner, cookery book writer and cookware merchandizer. Why not form a dining club? And why not revive the Hintlesham Music Festival? He did both, and offered an intrigued county, curious to see what this American-born dynamo would make of the splendid old house, literary lunches and art exhibitions as well. None of these, however, really offset the cost of restoration. Why not create a restaurant on the ground floor? His London restaurant in Islington, which opened in 1966—another snap decision—had been superbly successful.

Today, after admiring Hintlesham's Georgian façade, set in eighteen acres of parkland, customers enter between stately pillars and turn left down a long hall towards the panelled dining-rooms. What they don't see, behind the house, is the vegetable garden, which will provide much of their meal. Three years ago it was only bare space and a hedge. "It took me two years to get the dirt right and two months to lay out. I wanted symmetry. The crops are planted so that the colours complement each other." Who but Carrier and perhaps the gardeners of the Renaissance Château Villandry on the Loire would care whether the colour of turnips harmonized with that of courgettes? In the summer there are raspberries and strawberries and five varieties of lettuce; nine kinds of herbs grow in the borders. Now he's trying figs and aubergines. The severe drought of 1976 forced him to sink his own well.

The new restaurant kitchen was built of local brick on to the back of the house. To aid lighting and ventilation, pyramid fibre-glass skylights were let into the roof. "These are marvellous in summer when they are opened to let in fresh air," Carrier says.

His reverence for colour is reflected in the gleam of navy and white tiles behind wooden shelves holding glass storage jars of spices and herbs, but unnecessary aesthetics don't feature in this kitchen. Walls are plain white tiles, the floor is of quarry tiles and stainless-steel equipment predominates.

Two ovens and four cook-tops (run on bottled gas) make up the central cooking island under an extractor unit. At one end is a bain-marie, at the other a three-foot-high stock pot. The stock is used mainly for demi-glace and is changed every two days.

A salamander is employed to give the finishing touch to some dishes, though a large proportion of the meat is cooked on two charcoal grills set against a wall. Interestingly, Carrier's version of boeuf bourguignonne has slices of sirloin cooked quickly this way and added at the last minute to the rich sauce. He buys his meat in London, but uses local game, guinea-fowl, eels and Colchester oysters. "We hang our meat for ten to fourteen days. I learned that from Bocuse. There are two walk-in cold-rooms in the cellars, one for meat and game, the other for cheese and vegetables."

The kitchen also boasts several fridges and a special cold-surface unit for food taken from the fridge is something Carrier strongly recommends. "It's the reverse of the bain-marie; ideally every home kitchen should have one." So enamoured is he of good equipment that he'd like to see a salamander and a charcoal grill in every private kitchen, too—but then, he does tend to think in the grand manner.

A hot cupboard adjacent to the only wooden preparation surface warms plates, and utensils hang in a cluster over the cooking island: an electric mixer rests against one wall. The copper pans and the Le Creuset cookware are washed up in one recessed area, the plates in another, well out of the way.

Thirty-two staff keep Hintlesham going, seven working in the kitchen. There are two head chefs "so that we need never say a dish is unavailable if one chef is absent". It is that

Charcoal-grilled meat (above) helped the restaurant gain world-wide fame.

Washing-up is banished from the main kitchen into two separate areas, one for crockery (above) and the other for pots and pans.

White tiles and gleaming steel in Hintlesham's kitchens (below) strike a bright modern note in an ancient setting.

The cold-surface unit (above) keeps salads and hors d'oeuvre fresh and crisp.

sort of professional pride that has made cooking impresario Carrier so successful; he never cuts corners.

"The problem with food is that it follows fashions," he remarks. "I'm trying to look at old things with a new eye, delving back into seventeenth- and eighteenth-century recipes. The basic quest is for freshness. As you get more sophisticated in cooking, the techniques somehow become simpler."

Few restaurateurs can emulate the grandeur of Hintlesham. Not many have customers arriving by helicopter (he counted eight on the lawn one day). A hundred people can dine comfortably. After a drink in the Blue Room they move to the China Room, whose green panels are further enlivened with a multitude of blue-and-white-patterned plates, or, if they're a large party, to the two-storey Great Saloon, restored to its original magnificence with trompe-l'oeil marble. Then to coffee and liqueurs in the Red Room, also sometimes used as an extra dining-room.

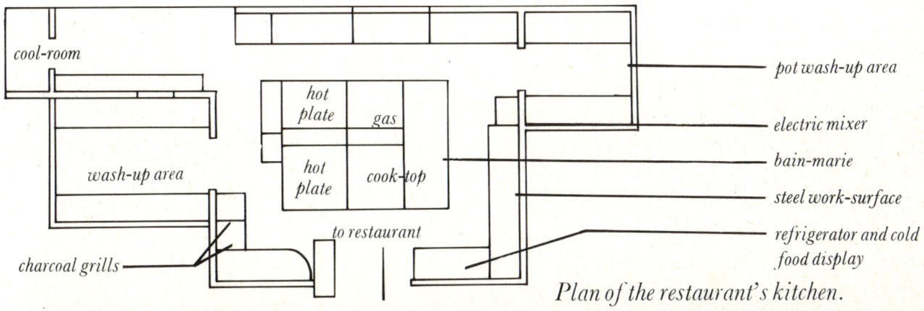

Plan of the restaurant's kitchen.

Sauces, made with fresh herbs from the garden, are kept at the correct temperature in the warm water of the bain-marie (above).

Willow pattern and chintz harmonize in the China Room (below), one of the principal dining-rooms at Hintlesham Hall.

Robert Carrier relaxes

Carrier's private kitchen at Hintlesham Hall, formerly the billiard-room, is reached through his library. Any temptation to linger there is offset by the joys that await next door in the kitchen-cum-living-room, where the host may well be cooking something delicious in his hidden oven.

"I don't like ovens staring at me," he explains. His solution was to build his oven into the wall, surround it with patterned tiles and cover it with a colourful Alsatian inn sign purchased twenty years ago.

Despite his pleasure in growing vegetables, he thinks that they too should be kept out of sight until it is time to prepare them. His chopping board is a log set into an iron table base from an old pub. There is a waste-disposal unit in the centre, plumbed into the floor. Knives and a steel slot into the wood. "An all-purpose cook's knife, a ham slice, a vegetable paring knife and a boning knife, that's all you really need," he ticks off.

One of his favourite aids is a simple mortar and pestle: "I can't do without it for crushing a handful of spices." The other is a table base from an old pub. There is a professional mixer/shredder called a Robot Coupé, big brother to the Magimix. "This is the first machine I've ever liked," he says. "The other day I made forty pints of pesto sauce in just a few seconds.

The Robot perches on a pine bench next to the gas cook-tops, which are set into a pine surface. There are drawers underneath, and on top rests a wok, cooking pans and a container for utensils. More copper and enamelled pans and storage jars are casually arranged on top of wall cupboard units facing this cooking island; moulds hook on to the tiles surrounding the oven. "I don't think kitchens should be too designered," says Carrier, taking a mild swipe at those whose kitchen equipment is arranged in precise ranks. His fridge and washing-area have been banished behind white louvered doors.

Fortunate in being able to locate his kitchen so pleasantly—it is surrounded on three sides by windows—he has also gone to tremendous pains to enhance its internal appearance. The walls, for example, panelled in a pale misty blue picked out in white, are not painted conventionally but "frescoed because I wanted them to match the Suffolk sky and only powder would do it". His floor demanded even more patience: he wanted to turn this into a copy of a thirteenth-century Arab ceiling. "The boards were painted, then coated with polyurethane, then walked on for six months before touching up the paint and recoating with polyurethane. This was done three times." It has the look of mellow tiles.

Carrier also takes his moments of relaxation seriously. Flanking the marble fireplace at one end of the room is a comfortable sofa and a long, low chaise-longue that he calls "my invalid's chair". Blue and white prints cover these and he has

Carrier hates rooms that are "too designered". The work-surfaces in his own kitchen are of solid, practical pine (above right).

The wooden floor (below right) is a copy of a 13th-century Islamic ceiling; the walls are frescoed "to match the pale Suffolk sky".

Robert Carrier cooks the meal while Hoover, his pug (below), deals with the crumbs.

used yet another print for curtains and window-seat covers.

Carrier's guests dine at a long seventeenth-century French game table, but there's also an African safari table of wood and rhino hide and a small Dutch card table where he writes his recipes. A Louis XV sacristan's cupboard displays china (blue and white patterned, inevitably), but he thought its doors fitted his bathroom better. Elephant-tusk candle holders contrast with the working area spotlights, and many paintings of dogs (he has over a hundred such paintings) stare round the room. The one genuine article is a pug called Hoover.

Carrier rarely eats alone: he is too busy professionally, too gregarious personally. But when he does he likes to tuck into "canned red salmon mixed with mayonnaise, onion and celery, chilled well and spread thickly on toast". The picture of this energetic, dazzlingly successful exponent of the art of good living quietly munching this homely snack while relaxing on his invalid's chair, guarded by a resigned Hoover, is one of charming incongruity.

The chopping block with its own built-in waste-disposal unit is boldly displayed on a pub table base (below). The oven, however, is discreetly hidden behind an inn sign.

An old French menu holder (right) brightens the wall of Robert Carrier's kitchen.

Blue and white patterned china is a Carrier favourite. He displays it here in a Louis XV sacristan's cupboard (above).

Robert Carrier's passionate involvement with food is reflected even in his collection of ceramic curiosities (above and left). Another abiding interest—dogs—shows in the portraits on Hintlesham's walls.

A plan of Robert Carrier's kitchen.

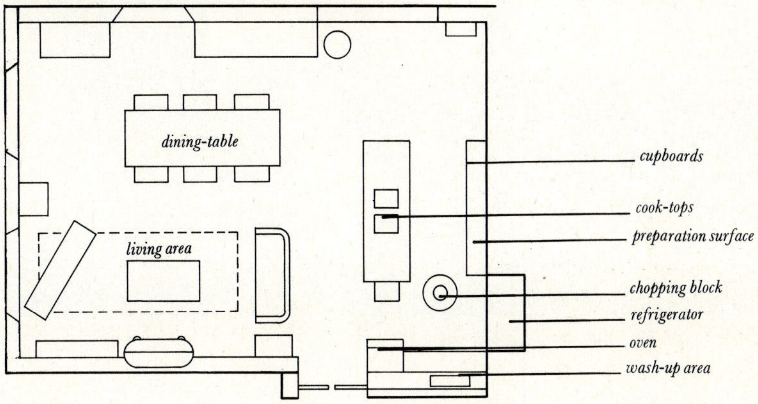

Raymond Oliver at the Grand Véfour

If you stand over the gratings in the Peristyle de Joinville, looking out over the gardens of the Palais Royal, the most wonderful smells waft up to greet you, for you are standing directly above the kitchens of the Grand Véfour, one of the most delightful restaurants in Paris. It belongs to Raymond Oliver, the "Grandfather of 'la nouvelle cuisine' ", or, more prosaically, the new way of cooking.

"The new cooking", explains M. Oliver, "is based on the use of the best and the freshest ingredients cooked with subtlety, very quickly and exactly. This is how we cook at the Grand Véfour. When the market is not open, this restaurant is closed."

M. Oliver is one of the fraternity of great chefs—he has cooked for royalty, for presidents and for television; he has opened a cookery school and interested his whole family in the business. "I grew up", he says, "in the Sauternes area of France only nine kilometres from Château d'Yquem—so it is not surprising if I have a taste for good things. I started learning to cook in the kitchens of my father's restaurant when I was only eight years old. My childish hands were put to work plucking and drawing small game birds and chickens. I have been cooking professionally for fifty years, but I am not a traditionalist. If you agree that cooking is a form of art, then you must also agree that it should move with the times; like music or painting, it cannot remain static. A musician has to learn his scales and arpeggios before he can improvise; in the same way, a good cook must first learn the basic skills. Like the musician, the cook has to add something of himself to the piece—cooking is making a gift of yourself. Women feel this more deeply than men, I think—a woman cooks with love for her family, her lover, her children, while a man, he cooks for himself—to prove to the world that he is a man of good taste."

M. Oliver has impeccable taste both in food and in restaurants. The splendid painted glass interior of the Grand Véfour has changed little since it was built in 1785. The restaurant's name derives from Jean Véfour, a cook from the royal household, who wisely bought the restaurant during the French Revolution, a period when working for royalty offered little future to an ambitious man. The present kitchens are squeezed into an eighteenth-century subterranean skittle alley. "It is a hot kitchen," admits M. Oliver, "but we've done our best with air conditioning to make the working conditions as favourable as possible. Anyway, the most important thing in any kitchen is not the layout, not the view, but the stove. There is no problem with fridges and freezers, they are cheap, and run steadily for years. It's the source of heat that is particularly important, especially for us, as we cook every dish to order, so we need a lot of space on the cook-top and in the ovens. Fourteen cooks work in these kitchens, three of them concerned with finishing—adding the last-minute touches that are vital to the success of the dish."

With such a troupe of chefs backstage (all personally trained by M. Oliver) and an impressive line-up of waiters tending the front of house, one might be forgiven for thinking the Grand Véfour was designed to feed five hundred, but there is room only for fifty people at most. The service is as impeccable as the food. M. Oliver, like the born restaurateur he is, paces around the room and is always in position to wish his customers *"Bienvenue"* and *"Au revoir"*.

Raymond Oliver looks young for his years and it is no surprise to hear that he is firmly on the side of all things modern.

"If there is something new, then I want to try it," he says. "We use gadgets in this restaurant because the time of a good chef is very expensive, and I don't believe that peeling potatoes is in some magic way good for the soul. If a machine can do the job, then we will use it." The kitchen of his Paris home bears out this philosophy; it is small, compact and full of sophisticated gadgetry. He is experimenting at the moment with a microwave oven. "This is a completely new way of cooking," he enthuses, "this is the only cooker that heats from the middle to the outside—imagine an egg cooked in this oven, it would have a hard-boiled yolk, and a raw white; one must experiment, keep an open mind to all the possibilities of the thing. It cooks fish and shellfish particularly well. Red mullet, cooked from raw with herbs, tastes wonderful, better than one cooked in a conventional oven. What this microwave permits you to do is to be

M. Raymond Oliver, distinguished restaurateur and author of several authoritative tomes on the art of cooking (right).

The waiters, wine waiters and head waiters of the famous Grand Véfour standing proudly in the gardens of the Palais Royal (above).

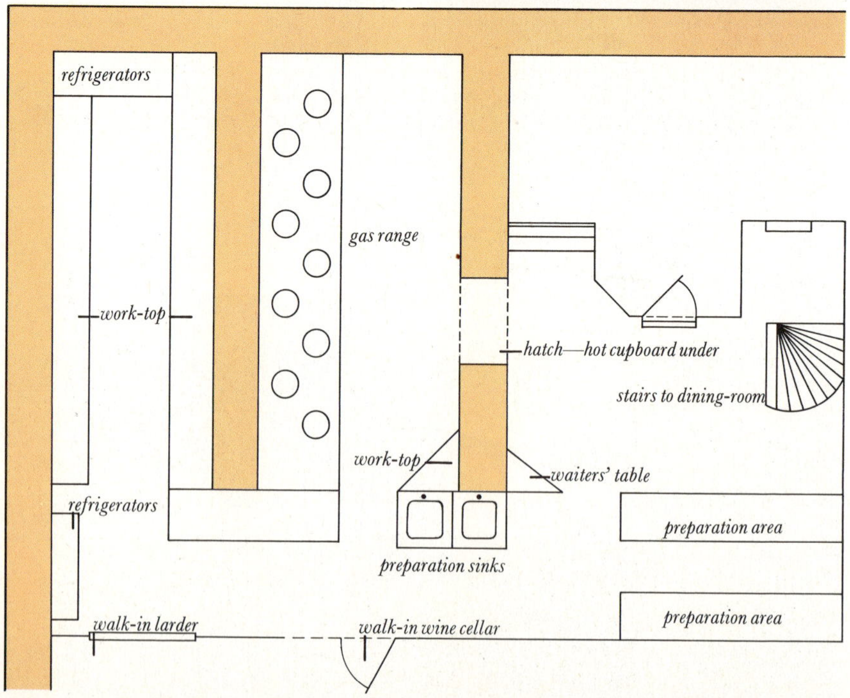

The Grand Véfour kitchens. Just before the Revolution these vaults were skittle alleys patronized by young aristocrats whose merriment was shortly to end beneath the guillotine.

precise, you can time a dish exactly, and this way it helps you to reach perfection."

M. Oliver is very enthusiastic about ovens. "In the slang of the French restaurant kitchen a stove is a 'piano'—the instrument on which a cook plays his tune. I learned to cook with solid-fuel ovens", he says, "and now I can do anything with any kind of oven. I can cook a soufflé in anything. I find that the new electric convection ovens give very good results, but I still prefer gas for the cook-top, because it is so much easier to control." He also waxes lyrical on the subject of kitchen knives. Every good chef, he says, at the beginning of his career will invest in, or inherit, a set that he will guard as jealously as he would guard his wife. "I have the knives of an old Japanese cook, who gave them to me on his retirement. They are wonderful knives, made in Japan a long, long time ago. The knife has a terrific importance to the Japanese cook—he even sleeps with them. But I don't imagine a Frenchman would feel quite like that about a knife. Personally I can't cook without a two-pronged fork—I use it to prod things with, turn them over, see if they are done—for me it's like a mascot. I promised to give my grandson a set of knives, but I gave him a set of forks instead—I hope they bring him luck."

The massive cooking range runs the length of one of the old skittle alleys (above). Serving dishes keep hot above the stove, and a massive ventilator duct keeps everybody cool.

A painless death for lobsters (below) on a polypropylene chopping board.

The splendid mirrored dining-room (above) has happily remained untouched by passing fashion since the days of Napoleon and Josephine.

The heated serving hatch through which the exquisitely prepared food is passed directly from the "finishing" chefs to the waiters (below).

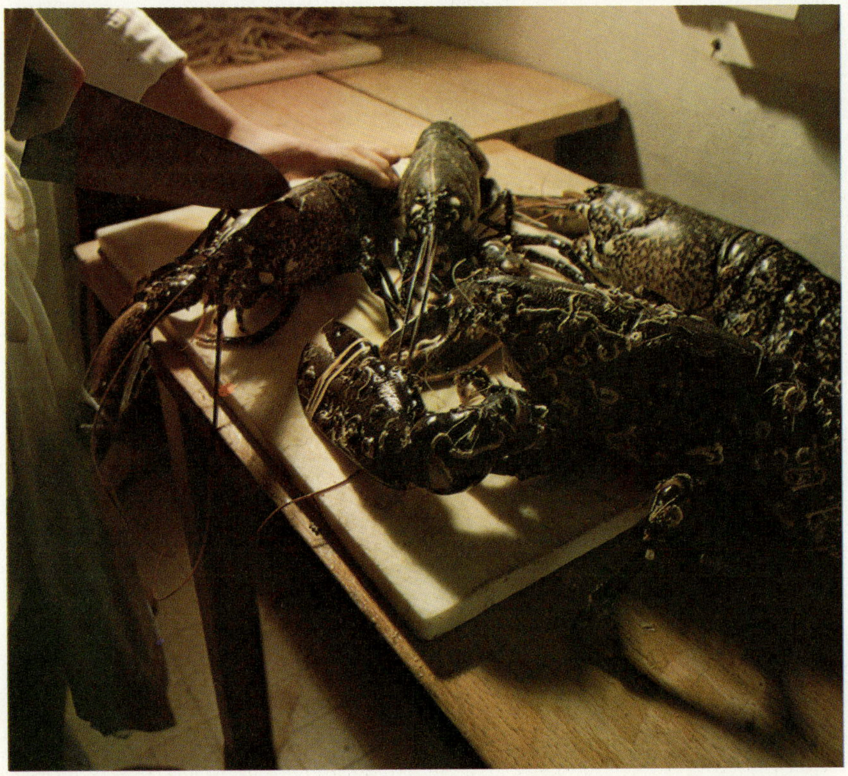

Stockholm's Operakällaren

The main kitchen at the Operakällaren is a warren of linked work-areas: from the fish kitchen (above) come many specialities.

The severe practicality of stainless steel is softened by blue and white tiles; but a Swedish love of hygiene rules (below).

A massive pleasure boat moored in a sea of rich carpet, the twenty-five-foot, double-decked smörgåsbord table dominates the dining-room of Stockholm's Operakällaren (Opera Cellar) restaurant. Surrounding it, the dark-panelled walls, the massive brass chandeliers and the tactfully separated tables breathe an air of elegant discretion.

For romantic as well as culinary reasons this, for generations of Swedes, has been the great restaurant. The setting, opposite the royal palace, is magnificent enough to move the most stoic Norseman to lyricism: an acquaintance in Stockholm wrote recently: "Go there one day in spring. Walk along the river, look at all the birds diving, flying and crying. Lots of them! Swans, wild ducks, seagulls! Enjoy seeing the white full-rigged sailing ship *af Chapman*, her lovely white lines against the light green of the budding trees."

The restaurant's founder was a Swedish king of great personal charm. While building the opera house in 1787, Gustav III decreed that its cellar should be a place of refreshment for performers. This philanthropic gesture seemed all the more poignant to Stockholm's citizens when the king was assassinated in the opera house five years later, and it has held a special place in their affections ever since.

In 1892, the Operakällaren was burnt out and rebuilt, and thereafter for the next half-century went through various changes of fortune. The restaurant s present fame really dates from 1955, when it was bought by Tore Wretman, a well-known Stockholm restaurateur.

Wretman set about making his new restaurant a byword for true Swedish cuisine. His first concern was to revive the smörgåsbord—Sweden's greatest contribution to global gastronomy. The word actually means "bread and butter board"—under normal circumstances a ridiculous understatement, but in 1955 an apt enough description. Wartime shortages, soaring post-war food prices and the amount of labour required to prepare a true smörgåsbord had reduced the magnificent array of pre-war days to a dismal shadow. Wretman spoke up for the smörgåsbord on radio and television; he also provided Operakällaren customers with one on a scale hitherto undreamed of. Intent on a true reincarnation, he banished the smörgåsbord's fussy, essentially nineteenth-century appendages—the furbelows of swans fashioned from ice and fruit sculpted into flower shapes. With a potter he designed serving plates, mostly square-cornered and rimless; not particularly decorative in themselves, but, when loaded with food and fitted together on a table, they form a sumptuous pattern.

Wretman's final stroke of genius was to hire a little-known Swiss cook, Werner Vögeli, as head chef. First, however, he gave him an open brief to renovate the Operakällaren kitchens.

In doing so, Vögeli echoed the combination of tradition and modernity that had taken place in the dining-room. Close co-operation with the architects produced a kitchen that was both technically superb and a delight to work in. The entire complex of four kitchens is linked by a universal storage system: trays and shelves are designed to a common size that will fit all refrigerators, cabinets and storage racks. Working surfaces are of hygienic stainless steel, the floor is non-slip and the air-conditioning is ultra-efficient. It has to be to conform with Sweden's high standards of hygiene and staff working conditions. Here the staff have well-equipped changing rooms and a pleasant rest room.

A modular storage system of standard-sized trays and shelving (left and above) permits vast quantities of food and tableware to journey about the busy kitchen complex from oven to freezer without a hitch.

Werner Vögeli's fame has spread across the water: Stockholm's Royal Palace, glimpsed through the window (left), borrows his services for banquets at home and abroad.

One of the thoughtful touches found at a top-flight restaurant is fresh flowers and polished silver gracing every table: the Operakällaren boasts its own cool flower room (above).

Stockholm's Operakällaren

Vögeli's kitchen discipline is firmly based on the great traditions of haute cuisine. The main kitchen produces 250 luncheons and dinners each day, as well as the smörgåsbord and the incomparable Operakällaren sausages. The separate chefs for soup, fish, meat and, king among princes, the *chef saucier*, work there at their own stoves with plenty of space between them. They use raw materials prepared ahead by lesser beings in the kitchen sub-departments. These are training areas for novice cooks: in the old days, it took three years for a boy to work his way up from chopping onions, via pastry-making (a world in itself) before being allowed to lay his hands on anything so sacred as meat. Things move faster in the Operakällaren now, but in the central theatre of operations there remains the classic atmosphere of dedication and well-organized discipline. As Werner Vögeli puts it, "no running around".

In addition to the main kitchen there is a small, highly efficient kitchen that serves the opera terrace and rotunda restaurant, which can cope with 400 guests. On one great occasion, to a burst of applause, 400 soufflés were produced almost at the same moment.

Next to Werner Vögeli's office is a small personal kitchen in which he tries out new dishes. A recent success, salmon quenelles in pastry with a wine and lobster sauce, was a special creation for the King of Sweden's marriage to Silvia Sommerlath—the dish was named after the new queen. This superb compliment was presented by Vögeli in his capacity as a royal chef— both he and his team are frequently summoned to the palace kitchen for state banquets. Occasionally, too, they travel with the royal household on state visits, rejoicing the hearts of overseas potentates with pickled salmon and other Swedish delicacies.

A proud moment for Werner Vögeli (above) was when 400 soufflés left this subsidiary kitchen almost simultaneously.

Ranks of ovens line the pastry kitchen and specially cooled work-surfaces make kneading the dough easier (below).

A shoal of soles stands by while Werner Vögeli briefs an assistant on last-minute details of lunchtime strategy (below).

Though Vögeli's hands keep a firm grip on the reins, the spirit in the kitchen is one of democracy. It is the staff, not he, who essentially decide what is to go into the menus, and it is they who do the marketing. As Vögeli puts it: "They must be given free hands." His sacred daily ritual is a visit to each chef, asking if he has any surprises for him—perhaps an unusual type of fish or a really good cut of meat.

"I like that so much," continues Vögeli. "I think that if I did not let them work in this way, I should deprive them of all their pleasure."

"I like so much to go to the head waiter telling him, 'Today the eels came living to us. We intend to prepare them grilled on straw.'"

Despite his enormously busy day, Vögeli finds his profession endlessly fascinating. "Even if I feel a little bit tired when I come home, after a while I think it would be nice to cook something for my family."

The inexpensive Hip Pocket (above) is the smallest star in the Operakällaren galaxy, but diners flock here daily.

Delicious take-away food ranging from soup to sausages has turned the shop from a sideline into a brisk business (below).

The maestro who never tires of cooking relaxes at home in a simple, sunny kitchen free of frills and commercial pressures (above).

Cooking to order

When I was very young I worked as a vegetable boy and washer-up in a restaurant in Paris. This experience taught me a great deal about life and the design and working of kitchens as well. I learnt that the layout should reflect the sequence of events in the preparation and cooking process—that equipment and raw materials should be close at hand when they are needed, and that a good professional cook not only produces good food but also maintains his equipment in first-rate order—his knives are always sharp, his pots and pans are always clean and polished and he never lets dirty equipment pile up behind him. He rules his kitchen with the authority of a general on the battlefield, and the people who work in his kitchen respect this discipline.

This chapter examines kitchens where food is being cooked on a large scale. Many of the problems that occur are similar to the ones that are encountered on a minuscule scale in our own domestic kitchens, and much is to be learnt from their solutions.

Caterers' kitchens

Plagiarism can seldom be so profitable as when the private kitchen-maker sets out to borrow ideas from professional establishments. Whether it's a restaurant, an institutional or industrial kitchen, the galley of an aircraft, submarine or train, there are always a few tips for the interested amateur to pick up.

Both private and professional cooks have, after all, the common object of producing good food on time and at a reasonable price. The only difference is in the scale of operations, but it is this very difference that makes the professional kitchen such a treasure-store of ideas.

The caterer's kitchen, which may cope with scores of leisurely gourmets or hundreds of hungry factory workers, must be organized to a high degree of efficiency—and this is reflected in its design. Planning is aimed at saving time, space and effort, which, in real terms, means money. These goals are achieved through the combination of hundreds of ingenious ideas, many of which can be adapted by the shrewd householder.

Efficiency

Professional kitchen engineers are responsible for providing the finest possible conditions in which good food can be created. Where several cooks, working in the same room, get under each other's feet, tempers and cookery deteriorate together. The kitchen layout must be so designed to permit each chef to get on with his task with a minimum of interference.

Professional kitchens are therefore deliberately zoned. The larger the *brigade de cuisine* the greater is the need for cooking stations that function as more or less self-contained units. The sauce-chef, the fish-chef, soup-chef, *rôtisseur*, *patissier* and others, each with attendant minions, has his own allotted department. Each chef has his own stove, surrounded by the glittering array of his batterie de cuisine, to keep cross-kitchen traffic to a minimum. The chef in charge, called the *gros bonnet*, since he is distinguished by wearing the tallest hat in the *brigade*, usually has an office close to the kitchen. He is responsible not only for the quality of the food but also for the administration of the kitchen and for the costings. He is part cook, part planner and part accountant, a condition only too familiar on the domestic front as well.

It is, in essence, the *gros bonnet*—often, of course, he is also the *patron* or owner of the restaurant—who, in conjunction with the architects and engineers, does the kitchen planning. Each projected menu will require different facilities for storage, refrigeration, preparation, cooking, heating, service and washing up. A kitchen that is not geared to the menus to be produced in it is doomed to inefficiency. Indeed, each new dish included in the restaurant's repertoire is analysed not only for its material costing but for the facilities it will require as well. In this way it will not upset the rhythm of the kitchen.

The most flexible type of restaurant kitchen revolves round a central island. This may be a stove with plenty of work-space around its edges, or one or more chefs' tables. The walls are lined with refrigerators, freezers, cookers and ovens. Also on the periphery are grills, broilers and steam-ovens; heated cupboards and bains-marie for keeping prepared food hot; chillers for keeping it cool; and the massive banks of sinks and dishwashers.

All this equipment is laid out to ensure an efficient flow of work. Setting-down places are created exactly where they are needed. Taps and sinks for washing vegetables and salads are next to the area where these foods are prepared. The siting of ovens is considered in relationship to the *rôtisseur's* and *patissier's* stations. Pots, pans and larger implements are often suspended from frames within easy reach of their users; larger items rest face down, on shelves slatted to permit the free circulation of air. These utensils, too, are sited close by the stations where they are most used. Where there is a central island made up of chefs' tables, the space under the work-tops is utilized: there, a tiered, slatted rack provides additional storage space and sometimes drawers are slung beneath the table-tops to hold the chefs' smaller implements. Knives receive special treatment and are never placed in drawers, where they get knocked against other cutlery and lose their fine edges. In some establishments, the tables themselves have slots to accommodate them; in others there are knife-racks or magnetic holders.

Whatever the kitchen layout—island, U-shape or galley—life is made easier by a carefully plotted water supply. Chefs' tables always have built-in sinks and taps.

The magnificent gas cooking range (left) in the kitchens of Simpson's-in-the-Strand, in 1928. Preparation areas line the walls.

In the well-planned preparation area (above), everything—from the batter tray to the brandy bottle—lies close to the chef's hand.

One inspired restaurateur even installed an extra tap by the cooker for topping-up saucepans—to the approval of his staff.

How can the masters' kitchens help us with our own planning? Few domestic kitchens are likely to be large enough to house central islands. No domestic kitchen will need such a variety of appliances, and since in our own establishments the *brigade* consists of ourselves, preparing one meal at a time, we shall hardly need an abundance of stations.

Yet, there are a number of useful lessons to be drawn. Storing the utensils by function, rather than by type, is one of them. To have a single storage place for, say, all the baking equipment, from sheets to cutters, makes more sense than to store the bowls with the basins, the larger metal items with the hardware and the cutters and other small tools in the backs of drawers, whence so often they mysteriously disappear.

Planned setting-down places make another most useful idea to copy. In a kitchen where work-tops are surfaced with laminated plastic, it is desirable to cover an area near the cooker with stainless steel for the setting down of hot pans. It is also useful to have various slabs and boards set right into the work-tops: marble for pastry, for example, and teak for chopping.

In some restaurant kitchens, the *garde manger* (the chef responsible for the larder and whose job also includes the preparation of salads and cold dishes) has his own sink inside the larder; an idea that might well be adapted to domestic kitchens. Another notion with domestic potential is to build or hang your spice and herb racks where they are needed most: by the cooker. Follow the professionals, too, in standing a wide-mouthed salt jar by the stove, for use at a moment's notice. To save constant marching about the room, establish a second jar in the preparation area as well.

In chefdom, the degree of eminence is indicated by the height of hat. A gros bonnet*—chief of chefs (above)—proudly towers among the stainless sparkle of his batterie de cuisine.*

Size isn't everything—about fifty freshly cooked lunches a day emerge from this minute open-plan kitchen in a Parisian restaurant (right).

Making use of space

It is in the smaller professional kitchens that the most ingenious space-saving arrangements are found. In the galleys of boats, trains and planes every cubic inch must earn its keep. Here, a vacuum is abhorrent, and space often does double duty: hinged boards, raised only when needed, create extra work-tops; so do lipped, laminated pull-out boards. Sinks may have purpose-built fitted tops, which serve as additional working surfaces as and when required. The virtues of hinged and pull-out boards are self-evident. Sink-covers might well appeal to those who have to entertain in a kitchen.

In a submarine, the galley may adjoin the messes, into which food is passed by lift or through a hatch. The latter may be fitted with infra-red heat to keep food warm while it awaits collection: an excessive refinement for a private house. However, the two-way locker beneath the hatch, through which dirty plates are returned to the galley, may well be an idea worth copying.

In cramped professional kitchens, door-knobs and handles are conspicuous by their absence. Drawers are lipped; cupboard doors slide sideways; projections are banned and corners are rounded.

Vertical space is as carefully husbanded as horizontal. Crockery sits in shelves in spaces not much higher than itself. These shelves are shallow; where the storage unit is inconveniently low down or shallow, pull-out racks are used. At the same time, the chance of wholesale breakage is minimized by fixing the racks so that they cannot be completely detached.

Appliances

Whenever possible, professional kitchens have both gas and electricity for cooking: gas cook-tops for instant heat; electric ovens for more even, stable heat. Convection ovens, powered by electricity, are highly favoured and considered quicker and therefore more economical to run than conventional electric ovens. Microwave ovens are beginning to make their mark, but professionals are so far using them for the most part to finish off par-cooked foods and to cook deep-frozen stores.

The true professional is no despiser of home-made equipment. One Japanese restaurant has a particularly impressive example of improvisation. They cook fish over volcanic rock heated by a gas burner. Above the rock is a platform of wire mesh on which the fish are placed.

Salamanders are standard equipment in most restaurant kitchens. They are small wall-mounted ovens, generally gas-heated, that give a fierce top-heat, so that dishes put into them are very quickly glazed or browned. Its domestic substitute is a circular iron plate on a long handle that is preheated and placed over, say, a pudding, to brown it. This is a much neglected implement, which gives the classic finishing touch to many dishes.

Professional refrigerators, unless they are of the walk-in variety, are essentially no different to the domestic version. In this connection, however, it is worth mentioning a practice that could be copied with a view to saving space in a very small kitchen: on submarines, a fridge containing the day's rations is placed not inside but outside the galley.

In professional kitchens, sinks are mostly of stainless steel and dishwashers are positioned close to the sink. Surprisingly, few establishments use waste-disposal units; and those that do tend to find them unreliable, probably because of the heavy workload imposed. It may be that only the private user is in a position to care properly for this sort of machinery. In some restaurant kitchens, a shower-head is fitted on to a tap—an admirable way of producing a stream of water at pressure sufficient to rinse surplus mess off plates prior to putting them in the dishwasher. Also very useful is a purpose-made board that partly covers the sink, allowing messy cleaning jobs—for instance, gutting fish—to be done with maximum convenience. Hot and cold taps may be mixed or independent, although it is thought generally that separate taps are more economical. Less hot water is wasted and the cold water runs cold quicker.

Gourmets maintain that mechanical aids to preparing food impair taste and texture and this explains why mechanical slicers and pulverizers tend to be absent from professional kitchens. In domestic situations they are more justified—saving time and labour. Contrarily a few appliances, such as potato chippers, are of value to professionals, but for most private kitchens they would be an unjustifiable expense.

Freshly made fettucine hanging up to dry emphasize the spotless gleam of equipment in a New York pasta restaurant (left).

A taste of luxury for Royal Navy submariners (above). Later in the voyage, the chefs must revert to opening the more traditional cans.

A separate depot for doing the dishes aids efficiency in a restaurant kitchen (above).

A convection oven in the London Hilton's pastry kitchen provides even heat, which browns all pies to the same degree (right).

A panel of instruments in a Boeing 707 first-class galley includes soup dispensers and electric ovens (above).

Hundreds of pounds of salmon pass through British Airways' chilled pools at Heathrow Airport, en route to first-class laps (above).

Reuters flash—front pages held as editors swoop on meals prepared in great news agency's London kitchen (right), where gadgetry is kept to austere minimum.

Practical considerations

Durability and ease of cleaning are the main criteria when choosing the materials for floors, walls and work-tops in professional kitchens. Heavy-duty quarry tiling, washable, non-slip and almost indestructible, is an admirable choice for floors, especially when laid in a gently sloping pattern towards a central drain. Sheer weight, however, makes this kind of flooring impractical above ground level, and caterers whose kitchens are situated on upper floors generally make do with linoleum instead.

But whatever the surface, the floors of all professional kitchens are thoroughly washed down each morning and sluiced and mopped at intervals during the course of the day. This constant wetting can damage even the toughest of surfaces and restaurateurs stress the importance of following manufacturers' recommendations when choosing detergents or other cleaning materials.

Walls in most professional kitchens are faced with white ceramic tiles. These may extend to the ceiling or, if they stop short, the wall above them is painted. Some establishments break up the expanse of white with a band of coloured tiles at head level to relieve the weary eyes of their staff. All walls are wiped or hosed down daily or even more frequently; in good kitchens, hygiene is a fetish. Care is taken in construction to eliminate all dirt-collecting gaps. Most professional kitchens have curved backplates, joining the floor to the skirting board and running round the bases of units. Others join unit tops to walls, producing a continuous surface.

Ceilings of professional kitchens are often covered with acoustic tiles, though these must also be fire-proof. The fire hazard is often further reduced by ceiling sprinklers and, by law, fire-fighting equipment must hang close to hand. The most important item is the asbestos blanket, the only safe means of tackling fat flare-ups and electrical fires. It is no less essential in domestic kitchens, where, rolled in its canister, it occupies remarkably little space.

Stainless steel is without doubt the best choice for professional work-tops. It is hygienic, easy to clean and looks good; but it is expensive and so laminated plastics are often used instead.

Lighting

Professionals always insist upon an even distribution of lighting in the kitchen, with the occasional boost over areas where intricate work is called for or where potentially dangerous equipment is used. Thus, lights are incorporated into the extractor hoods built above each cooker and into recesses over work-tops.

In the huge kitchens of British Airways, where travellers' meals are prepared and pre-cooked, care is taken to ensure that the light in the kitchen matches that in the aircraft, the idea being that the food will then appear as attractive to the consumer as it did to the cook. By the same token, might it be an idea to match your kitchen lighting to that in the dining-room?

A spick and span work-surface of stainless steel (above), allied to a bold arrangement of tiles, gives gloss to a sink unit.

Fluorescent lighting provides chefs with a brilliant view, and an ultraviolet ceiling insectocutor destroys flies (below).

Feather-light pâtisseries demand a cool hand and plenty of room to manoeuvre on the massive wooden pastry board (above).

Different tiled surfaces and a marble slab for pastry-making form a sleek work-area in an office kitchen (above).

Dinner for Presidential guests at the White House starts here in a kitchen strong in stainless steel and mighty pans (below).

Tradition takes a tumble in this chef's outfit, but his sabots ease his journey across the duckboard flooring (above).

I'm colourful, try me: aircraft lighting is simulated in an airport catering centre to ensure food will look appealing on board (below).

Cooking to order

Pots, pans and professionalism

By the turn of the eighteenth century, the batterie de cuisine at Saltram House—the home of a reasonably well-to-do Devonshire country gentleman—included six hundred copper pots, pans, kettles, moulds, vats and urns. For the next 150 years, until shortly after the Second World War, they were employed in the creation of myriad wedding breakfasts, children's parties, ball suppers, funeral meats and simple family dinners. Now, hanging still in their accustomed places, glowing as brightly as on the day they left the coppersmith's hands, they enchant thousands of tourists each year.

The moral they imply—and one that would be endorsed by all modern professional caterers—is that you should buy the very best of equipment, look after it well, and it will serve you for ever. Hard though the life of the Saltram batterie has been, it might easily be equated to a single year's wear in a professional kitchen. Cheap utensils, to serious cooks, are a false economy. To this day, copper pans are still probably the best buy, problems of weight, cleaning and initial expense notwithstanding. Durability, good looks and, above all, dependable heat distribution easily outweigh the disadvantages. All the same, for professional and domestic cooks alike, there is still something to be said for pots and pans made from more modern materials. In a busy kitchen, stainless-steel and aluminium pans are satisfactory alternatives: they are cheaper; they don't need polishing; and they are lighter to handle.

Cooks are less fussy, however, about the humbler kitchen utensils. Mixing bowls may be made of toughened glass, traditional crockery or stainless steel—though one chef expressed the opinion that the latter is too slippery for many kitchen tasks. Cooking tins should be seamless; they are easier to clean and therefore more hygienic. For those who have the energy and the skill, wire whisks and wooden spoons are still the best tools for beating by hand, though toughened plastic spoons are perfectly satisfactory for ordinary stirring. Chopping boards may be constructed of wood, hard laminates such as melamine, or compressed rubber.

Kitchen knives, kept razor-sharp by frequent use of a stone, are the chef's pride and joy and he will carry his own set with him throughout his professional life. Though the initial expense is high, it is well worth buying a set of chef's knives of your own. You will quickly appreciate how essential they are and will jealously guard them from the family, who may wish to use them for their own perfidious purposes.

Storing food

Obviously, professional kitchens require greater refrigeration facilities than do private houses. They must find space for freezers, bulk refrigerators for fats and the basic stocks for soups and sauces, and *mise-en-place* refrigerators that contain the food to be consumed within a day or so. These short-term stores are often paired: one for cooked foods, another for raw. This hygienic storage method should be translated to the domestic front by keeping cooked and uncooked foods covered and well apart in the same refrigerator. Care is taken in professional kitchens to enclose such things as fish or meat, so that their odours do not impregnate one another. Muslin or damp cloths are used for the purpose. Domestic cooks might use foil or cling-film.

Salad ingredients are stored in refrigerators, soft and delicate fruit—tomatoes, avocados—being first covered with cloth since they may become frostbitten. Ready-prepared raw food is always tightly wrapped to prevent it drying out.

All fats, if they are not kept under refrigeration, are stored in a cool, dark place. Dry goods are kept on racks, fixed an inch or so from the wall for easy cleaning. Huge, metal, mobile grundybins are used for flour, rice and other staples. Tight-closing containers—tins or glass jars—can perform the same function.

Root vegetables are stored in their wooden pallets or sacks in dark corners, sometimes on low racks. The closer they are to the floor the cooler they will be.

There is no denying that heating up can spoil good food. Though most kitchens bristle with equipment such as hot cupboards and bains-marie for keeping cooked food hot, many chefs have perfected a technique of par-cooking dishes, only finishing them when they are ordered. Some of the tricks of their trade can be used at home: if vegetables are blanched for a few minutes beforehand, they can quickly be brought to perfection when needed, instead of going soggy when dinner guests are late.

The chilled cupboards under the carpet of egg sandwich (right) are kept at the correct temperature for cheese—4° to 10°C (40° to 50°F).

No place for weight-watchers—a pâtisserie kitchen (right) with a central bank of spice drawers and a cool marble work-top.

If you do have to heat things up, do it gently, and over boiling water.

Separate washing-up rooms are to be found in few of our houses, but they are a feature of most professional kitchens, where washing-up is almost an art form. What professionals do is this: in the first compartment of the sink they leave all dirty but scraped dishes to soak in cold water, then the dishes get a violent shower-bath in very hot water. Where there is no dishwasher, the crockery then goes into the second compartment, filled with hot, soapy water. Rinsing water, too, is always very hot, because cold dishes are harder to dry.

For drying, many professionals like to use disposable rather than conventional tea-cloths, but the most hygienic, as well as the most time-saving way of all, is to let all the crockery drip itself dry. As domestic dishes are less likely to be speedily reused than restaurant crockery, it is here that the domestic sector has the edge on the professional.

The dishing-up area geared for action (above). The cloth on the stainless-steel work-top will stop plates sliding about.

Beyond the dishing-up area, the washing-up area (below), so the clean plates don't have far to travel back to the heated plate cupboard.

The round-bottomed Chinese pan—the wok—is an awkward thing to store. Here they repose on a bed of egg cartons (above).

Cake-making made easy (below). A mobile baker's rack stands by with all the prepared ingredients in little plastic bins.

Style

There are several ways that you can decide the style of your kitchen; the most obvious and usually the most satisfactory is to let the type of house or apartment have a very large say in the look of the room. The advantages to this approach of course are that the room itself already possesses a lot of the fundamental characteristics that you might otherwise have to acquire. For instance, a country cottage might already have brick or stone floors and exposed beams, which makes it a lot easier to decide that the kitchen you really want is what I have called "Farmhouse" style. However, people are perverse, and if you live all your life in the country perhaps the kitchen that you really covet is streamlined and glossy, the style that I have called "Urban".

More than likely, monetary considerations will play a large part in deciding what style of kitchen you can have. A room that reflects your own personal taste and is built or adapted with economy and ingenuity is often the most satisfying for you and the most interesting for your friends.

The most important consideration, however, is the life you lead. If you are extremely busy you will want a very efficient kitchen with the minimum amount of equipment to clean, whereas if you are really a dedicated cook with time to enjoy your art, you will want a large selection of equipment and a large friendly kitchen to go with it.

Style

The country-house

Almost the only characteristic the country-house kitchen has in common with its cosy neighbour, the farmhouse kitchen, is the amount of elbow-room. The lady of the house was never intended to cook in the functional, rambling and slightly old-fashioned kitchen of the large country estate. It is not a heart-warming, welcoming room piled high with the clutter of cookery where meals are eaten, but a preparation area—clean and glossy, with everything neatly stored in cupboards.

There is a scullery, where dishes are dealt with, and a big walk-in larder, well stocked with provisions. Fridges, ovens, toasters and mixers are on a large scale, to cope with fluctuating numbers of guests.

If you inherit such a kitchen, or wish to emulate one, keep the walls a glossy, pastel shade and virtually bare except for a clock and perhaps a sporting calendar. Work-surfaces should be sensibly wide and deep, covered with practical plastic laminate. The flooring is traditionally plain and hard-wearing enough to stand up to the muddy traffic flow through the back door.

A country squire of long ago looks down upon an oasis of comfort amid the gleaming laminate and stainless steel (below).

Wide work-tops, plenty of space, good lighting and a restful view create the typical country-house kitchen (above).

A cool, fully tiled kitchen with generous space for storage is ideal for the cook who entertains regularly and lavishly (right).

Style

The farmhouse

Whether because of nostalgia or a simple desire to create a haven of refuge, the farmhouse style has become almost as common in city and suburban houses as it once was in farmhouses, where the kitchen was undoubtedly the centre of the home.

Certainly the image is a warm and welcoming one, suggesting open hearths, fireside chairs and the soothing charm of a rural existence that most of us have never known and many of us might find less agreeable than we imagine.

The key to this style is simplicity and function: if it works well it probably looks good. Natural colours, the earthy shades of brick, slate, wood and tile, look best in this type of kitchen. Little decoration is needed; the natural activities of the kitchen will provide their own—perhaps a cluster of traditional cooking utensils, bunches of drying herbs and a string of onions or garlic.

Above all, the true farmhouse kitchen has plenty of space for everyone to eat, cook, make wines, bottle fruit or just relax in a warm and cosy atmosphere.

The details

Do not strive for effect; ideally, it should just happen. The mood, however, can be helped along by hiding up-to-date electronic gadgetry in simple wooden units. Display pretty plates and cups and home-made jams and pickles on narrow open shelves if there is no kitchen dresser.

Use the produce from the garden or the greengrocer for its decorative properties. Pile fruit and vegetables into trugs, baskets or earthenware bowls and leave them on the work-top or kitchen table to make an edible still life.

The sunny door-yard (right) leads into a typical farmhouse kitchen with an undulating brick floor, a beamed ceiling and a china-filled dresser.

Looking deceptively rural with its oak beams and flagstone floor, the compact and well-proportioned kitchen (below) is part of a London house.

Style

The family centre

The ideal family kitchen is all things to all the household. It is where babies learn to crawl—so the flooring must be warm to the touch as well as infinitely wipeable. It is where the cook spends most of the day—so it must be both functional and pleasant. It is probably the room in which pets are fed and cared for, and where urgent storage requirements include somewhere to keep teddy bears, train sets and half-finished paintings, as well as jelly moulds, cake tins and cans of food. It is the room where friends and family congregate, either because it is warm, because the cook is there or because it is the source of food and drink and of informal conversations over cups of coffee and glasses of wine.

A kitchen with pans on the boil, sharp knives and slippery floors is a potential death-trap for children, so the play area must be well defined. If the kitchen is not large enough, consider knocking through to an adjacent room. A row of units can replace the wall and a safety gate will keep the children out of harm's way.

If the kitchen is large, try to isolate the children's activities at one end. If they must pass close to the cooker, fix a guard around the cook-top and keep pan handles well tucked in.

This is an opportunity to plan a kitchen that will grow with the children and change in style as the family changes. While children are young, however, it must be practical and easy to work in.

Open shelves are far too tempting for children. Choose an efficient unit storage system flexible enough to house all the implements of a busy kitchen. Remember that the only safe place to keep bleaches and disinfectants is out of reach or in locked cupboards.

Catering for meals at different times of the day means a great deal of time spent at the kitchen sink unless you think ahead. Consider a freezer and a microwave oven to keep pace with quickly needed meals for your ever-demanding family.

A chair under the well-lit work-top creates a child's desk (above) at a sensible distance from the knives and stove.

Separate areas joined by generous floor space create a children's playground (right) without hampering kitchen activities.

Warm and welcoming with its mellow brick floor, the "cats' kitchen" (below) is the hub of a home in Highgate, London.

Style

The family centre

Cheerful splashes of colour liven up a basically sophisticated kitchen (left). A change of level keeps children out of the way.

A child's art gallery and the family snaps decorate this friendly eating area (right).

Deep drawers and wall cupboards provide extensive storage in this French kitchen (far right). The tiled floor and glossy walls are easy to clean—so there will be no recriminations if the pancake hits the deck.

A beautiful old table (below) visually divides this large and practical kitchen.

The cook's kitchen

The cook's kitchen is an efficient, hard-working room that must be planned and organized to the last detail. Work-surface heights and the relationship between the work-areas—its ergonomics—are very important.

A busy cook might finish her day with an aching back, tired feet and a very bad temper unless she is physically comfortable in her kitchen.

There must be plenty of imaginative storage space for fish kettles, couscousiers and copper-bottomed pots as well as for the basic utensils. All this impressive equipment must be within easy reach of the place where it is most needed. The collection of fine wire strainers, and strings of garlic and onions, are not there for show but for everyday use. If they are arranged intelligently, the cook can reach for a wooden spoon, a garlic press or a sharp knife as instinctively as a motorist changes gear.

The good cook carefully considers the quality of the surfaces, and the ideal kitchen will incorporate several slabs of different materials. Somewhere in the cook's kitchen, probably built into the work-top, will be a large chopping board made of end-grain hardwood, preferably sycamore or maple, that will endure years of chopping, slicing and scrubbing. A generous square of cool slate or marble is the perfect surface for rolling out pastry and next to the cook-top it is advisable to have an expanse of stainless steel, which will withstand the heat of the hottest pans.

The flooring must be practical, slow to show dirt and quick to clean. Plenty of work-space and a generous area around the sink are essential. Good cooks automatically clear up as they go along.

There must also be adequate space for foodstuffs and, ideally, room for a proper larder, where meat, fish, eggs and vegetables can be kept.

Ceiling storage space (right) is cunningly exploited by using a steel hoop. The spatulas, ladles and forks are quickly and easily accessible.

Witty details (below) belie the serious purpose here. A rack lettered T-O-A-S-T and a margarine slab for apples accompany an impressive batterie de cuisine and two fine chopping blocks.

The urban kitchen

The urban kitchen should be a sophisticated adult room, gleaming with practicality. Streamlined units protect food, china and electronic gadgetry from the polluted city air. Floors, walls, units and equipment are easy to clean.

Organization is the keynote. Except for kitchens in large townhouses, space tends to be limited, so every corner must be exploited to its full potential. All of the appliances should be built in, from the efficient dishwasher to the eye-level oven.

The details

The visual impact of the urban kitchen depends largely on the colour and texture of the fixtures and fittings. Experiment with the high gloss of stainless steel, the smoothness of ceramic tiles, the coved edges of a cupboard unit. When thinking in terms of colour, concentrate on the darker end of the spectrum.

The decoration of many kitchens suffers because of the natural side-effects of cooking. With a super-efficient ventilation and extraction system that eliminates grease build-up and condensation, the urban kitchen begins to have more decorative scope. Plastic work-surfaces and "kitchen" wallpapers become unnecessary—you can put up a smart wallcovering and perhaps your collection of paintings or prints. Roller blinds can be used to bring another texture to the room and lighting effects, if carefully handled, will complete the sophistication.

The sharp angle of the window (above) is visually sleek. A bland colour scheme unites the wall, floor and units. The accessories blend in with the streamlined effect.

The tiles in this kitchen (right), designed for an English family, strike the dominant decorative note. Sink, stove-top, kettle and extractor hood of stainless steel accent the scheme.

Toe-space under work-tops and a large window make this kitchen (above) seem wider than it actually is. When buying cupboards for a narrow area choose those with sliding doors.

An architect designed this starkly modern English kitchen (below) to fit within the shell of an earlier building. He retained the original ceiling to make an unusual contrast in texture and style.

The minimal kitchen

It is surprising how efficient a tiny kitchen can be. Many people much prefer an encapsulated galley because a meal can be prepared quickly, without interruption from chattering friends.

Equipment

Save space with a small cooker and a small fridge/freezer—indeed, all the appliances should be scaled to fit. Choose a small sink with one draining-board and, with floor space at a premium, use every inch of wall intelligently. Electrical gadgetry may well have to be omitted unless you are lucky enough to find a spare area of wall on which they can be hung. Buy dual-purpose equipment wherever possible. Choose flame-proof and oven-proof casseroles so they can be used both on the cook-top and in the oven. They can be utilized at other times for storing bread and vegetables. In a minimal kitchen, ingenuity gets full marks.

Decoration

The galley kitchen is a very simple, basic, cooking machine, and should be treated as such, but decoratively. Study the organization and "look" of galleys on yachts, in aeroplanes, even caravans, and learn how to recreate their best points.

Keep the kitchen clean, uncluttered and unfussy—especially if it is on show as part of a one-room flat. Above all, don't expect too much of a small kitchen—it's ideal for very tidy, precise cooks who live alone or for the type of people who don't much care for home cooking. If your life-style changes, or your cooking becomes more ambitious, then your kitchen must change, too.

Big windows counteract claustrophobia in the box-sized kitchen (left). Space restrictions mean that the cook can reach all surfaces at once.

The pull-out work-top is almost an essential in the very small space allotted to this gleaming stainless-steel kitchen-cum-launderette (below).

The doors are a mobile wall (right) to screen the cook and the neatly compressed "cupboard" kitchen from the adjacent sitting-room.

SIEMENS

Style

Towards the future

Is it a lunar module, a time machine, or does it belong in an operating theatre? The futuristic kitchen tends not to look like a kitchen at all. It breaks completely from tradition and becomes part of the general living environment.

The style is sculptural, the final outline of the conglomeration of units is the one that counts. The materials are hard, shiny,

Reflections of Andy Warhol's "Marilyn" create shimmers of colour in the chillingly polished art gallery of a kitchen (left).

mostly man-made—stainless steel, ceramics or injection-moulded plastics.

This is not a kitchen for the serious cook or the dedicated gourmet. It is for instant clean, odourless cooking, whose chief protagonists are the freezer and the microwave oven. There are miraculous waste-disposal systems that even eliminate the washing-up. Computer-like, the kitchen is programmed to help produce a meal efficiently and effortlessly whenever it is required.

The colours and decorations are as fantastical as the gadgetry. The futuristic kitchen has tamed technology to such a degree that, like a house-trained lion with no teeth, it can lie on a white carpet and the children can play with it in total safety.

Octagonal work-tops are brilliantly illuminated by an intricately woven honeycomb formation of fluorescent lights (below).

The kitchen as nightclub (right) with a midnight-blue tubular arch enclosing chrome units and an impressive array of drinks.

The cooking module (below) is bounded by hoops of dangling utensils. A sleek, plastic-coated niche encapsulates a shiny black stove.

Plastic slots together perfectly in the storage system (below). Circular shelves slide into grooves and curved doors fit around them.

A primitive revival

An ever-growing group of people is convinced that modern life is becoming overcomplicated by labour-saving devices. Gadgetry and processed foods, they feel, are destroying our souls and stomachs.

To them, the future contains not an ever-advancing technology but a return to the

Oil lighting, simple fare and a minimum of luxury in this American kitchen (left) recapture the brave life of the pioneers.

basic virtues and values of our ancestors. A batterie de cuisine consisting of knife, frying-pan, saucepan and mixing bowl, hardly requires a super-laminated-ventilated-cantilevered cupboard. Cooking and washing require only heat and running water.

The appeal of this Danish kitchen (below) is derived from a blending of new wood and old country furniture.

The ecology-conscious will want to make good use of natural resources—the sun and wind, and to recycle compost for the vegetable plot.

Homespun clothes will be washed with home-made soap. Simple meals will be eaten at hand-hewn tables. The children of this bright new dawn will make the delightful discovery that egg whites can be whisked without a food mixer, and that peas do not grow in freezer bags.

Hand-turned wooden utensils (above) are both decorative and hard-wearing. The designs have changed little since the Middle Ages.

Cooking on an open range (below) has its hazards, but enthusiasts swear by the flavours this method imparts.

Planning your kitchen

Planning a kitchen can seem almost as difficult as planning your life. Its success or failure can have such an influence on the happiness of the household that it really is worth while taking a great deal of care over the design of this room. You will spend a large part of your life in the kitchen, especially if you, and your family and friends, love food. Therefore, you must design an environment that everyone can enjoy and that works really well.

This chapter explores all the problems and possibilities open to you, and when you have read it you should be equipped to decide how you want your kitchen to be.

Do remember that the simpler things are the better they work. It is much easier to start with a well-planned simple layout, with all the basic equipment and services in the right place, than a complex installation, over-equipped with gadgetry, much of which will never be used and which will impede the daily work of the kitchen. Things can always be added; it is much more difficult to take them away when you discover that they are useless.

A kitchen for the life you lead

More than a fur coat or a hi-fi system, happiness is a modern, fitted kitchen—such was the conclusion of a consumer survey run by a London advertising agency in 1977. Evidently, looking forward to living in the kitchen of your dreams is a popular pastime, but try not to let the pleasure of anticipation cloud your judgement. If you rush for the first attractive option your affair with your kitchen could quickly turn sour.

It was only in the great old mansions and palaces that a kitchen was (and in a few instances still is) filled by servants and occasionally visited by the mistress of the house. It occupied that middle area in the pitiful housemaid's life-cycle, which Byron described as "Born in the garret, in the kitchen bred, promoted thence to deck her mistress' head." In the vast majority of households the kitchen always has been *the* room, the place for almost every activity of domestic life: cooking, preserving, eating, wine-making, shoe cleaning, flower arranging and entertaining; it is also the handyman's workshop and a playground for the children. With good planning, yours could be just as versatile. Although poor design may quickly lead to frayed tempers, what causes the greatest grief is no planning at all: that apparently easy compromise between the equipment you possess and what you find around you. It may well be summed up by the attitude, "If you have a cooker, start cooking", or "If there's a sink, what's the problem about doing the dishes?"

Of course, cynics will tell you that, no matter how well you plan, something will always be wrong with the result. Do not listen to them. Taste is personal, but comfort is a fact, and proper design can achieve it. There is no mystery about planning; it simply needs patience and thoroughness to sort out your requirements.

Your first step is to decide what type of kitchen will suit the life you lead.

Do you live in a single room? For most of us, studio or bed-sitter existence is transitory, and this should be borne in mind when planning kitchen space in a one-room apartment. Tiny ovens and miniature fridges allow you to maximize the effective use of available space, but this kind of doll's house furniture is expensive—and a waste of money if the premises are rented or you plan to move on. So, unless your bed-sitter is a long-term arrangement, your two priorities are, first, for a way to conceal the cooking area when not in use—with either doors, blinds or curtains—and, second, for an extractor fan to keep the atmosphere pleasant.

If you have young children, give yourself the best-equipped kitchen you can afford. But almost more important than labour-saving devices is adequate space. Children hang around their parents regardless of whether there is a separate playroom in the house, and this means they will be all but permanent fixtures in the kitchen. Equally, there will be times when you are working in the kitchen and actually want to supervise them there. The sort of room you need will therefore have sufficient floor and table space in which young children can play well away from the cooker, sink or your feet. As an alternative to buying your kitchen equipment on hire-purchase, remember that building societies are sometimes willing to increase your loan to cover the cost of kitchen improvements. And console yourself that children neither respect nor appreciate textured wall coverings and expensive tiled floors, so you can spend more on machinery and less on decorations with a clear conscience.

If you are near retirement or anticipate spending more time at home, you have good reason to make the kitchen especially attractive. Once the family has grown up and dispersed, the most sophisticated, high-capacity washing machine, stove and refrigerator may become redundant. Should your kitchen be large enough, it may well be the moment to convert half of it into a conveniently positioned dining area.

Eating in the kitchen makes serving meals altogether simpler, but elegance can still find a place (below).

The ideal family kitchen should permit the cook to keep an eye on the children, yet keeps them from under her feet (below).

But remember that a kitchen for two people requires gangways at least 1200 mm (4 ft) wide if people are to pass each other without standing back. Kitchens for the elderly or disabled need specialized planning and should not be attempted without experts.

How often are you going to eat in the kitchen? One statistician ventures that 80 per cent of European families eat three-quarters of their meals there. If you decide to use the kitchen only for breakfast, you will probably just need a place to keep stools out of the way when not pulled up to a work-top/table for eating. Should you want to have the majority of your meals in the kitchen, you must design a separate area for this away from the cooking and preparation areas. Is it sufficiently large to accommodate the size of table and number of chairs you would like?

Dirty dishes should be kept out of the sight of guests, and powerful ventilation is vital to ensure that cooking smells do not hang miasma-like around the table.

If you are likely to move again soon, do not plan a kitchen that requires expensive modification of standard units. You will not want to leave them behind, especially if the premises are rented.

The second stage in designing a kitchen is purely practical—allocating space. You need graph paper, pencil and a tape measure. Choose a convenient scale, e.g. 1:20, in which to draw up your plans; for instance, every inch on your graph paper can represent twenty inches in your kitchen. Having done this, measure and draw in the size of your kitchen and any permanent fixtures. Then plot the space taken up by every unit in position, first on a floor plan, then on a wall plan for each vertical surface.

The standard layout sequence for any kitchen should be: storage, preparation, sink, cooker, serving, eating. Dirty dishes return along this line. The sequence may become a triangle, which is perfectly acceptable as it complies with the basic principle that should be behind all kitchen layouts—to create the minimum of unnecessary journeys.

The kitchen for machine-age man is stripped of frills until only the bare essentials of catering remain (below).

Calculate how much storage space you will need. The ideal way to do this is to find units of a similar size to the ones you contemplate buying and experiment with fitting in your food stores and equipment, or their equivalent in size. Unit measurements fortunately have now been standardized internationally so there should be no problems about obtaining units of the correct height and depth for your reach.

Stove, refrigerator, sink and work-top should preferably be no more than a step from each other.

All equipment used regularly in cooking should ideally be within an arm's reach of the stove. The rest may be stored slightly farther away but still in a convenient location. Broom cupboard, cleaning materials, food reserves, freezer, ironing-board, etc., can all be rather more out of the way.

Professional help with kitchen planning can readily be obtained either from kitchen planning specialists or from many of the unit manufacturers themselves. However, one of the many advantages of designing your own kitchen is that you never need be depressed by lack of current funds. What you cannot afford now may well be within your financial reach at a later date. Simply check that the appliance or units of your choice are likely to be in production for several years ahead; then plan the necessary space for the coveted item, and meanwhile improvise with existing equipment.

There is one aspect of kitchen planning in which you are completely on your own: the nebulous one of personal taste. Nowadays, it really is possible to create any sort of kitchen. Your comfort is what matters, whether this is to be in an office kitchen with filing cabinets by the refrigerator, in a warm, friendly farmhouse kitchen or in an antiseptic angular kitchen that satisfies your desire for hygiene. If there is one drawback to modern fitted kitchens it is that the very convenience of their planning makes it too easy to create one that is efficient and nothing else—an impersonal, glossy wasteland.

Relating the kitchen to the house

A few fortunate people are in a position to design and build their own houses; a larger number undertake major conversion work. All of them share the agony of trying to resolve the competing claims of different rooms for the best positions on the site. Not least of the contenders is the kitchen, and planning its best position within the house is surprisingly complex.

Until at least 1930, better-off households contained a kitchen banished as far as possible from the living apartments. This is not to say that the general importance of kitchens was lost on those as practical and enlightened as Mrs Beeton. Her encyclopedical *Book of Household Management*, published in the mid-nineteenth century, recommended that the kitchen, that "great laboratory of every household", should have "convenience of distribution in its parts, with largeness of dimension . . . excellence of light, height of ceiling and good ventilation . . . easiness of access . . . plenty of fuel and water".

Contemporary architects sometimes begin designing houses by writing the names of living areas on a blank sheet of paper. Then they connect them with lines to represent the recurring need of the occupant to travel from one to the other. For example, a sitting-room would have at least two lines leading out of it, one to the hall and one to the garden. A bedroom would also have two, one to the bathroom and one to the landing.

The kitchen, of course, needs to connect with virtually every room in the house: the hall (answering the front door); the garden (picking a bunch of parsley); the dining-room (laying the table); the sitting-room (television supper); the larder and the laundry.

Without any doubt, the kitchen is the natural hub of any house, probably exceeding in status even the living-room. An American architect, determined to reflect this in his work, put the kitchen right in the centre of a bungalow, and made good the absence of an outside window by installing a large skylight. This turned out to be a sensible if somewhat claustrophobic arrangement.

Light is one of the key considerations in determining just where to position the kitchen in a house. With large, efficient refrigerators and freezers, it is no longer necessary for a kitchen to have an outside, north-facing wall to keep the larder cool. The importance of capitalizing on available sunlight most of the day—in other words to have a kitchen on the south side of the house—now weighs more heavily. Nevertheless, the larder is an excellent institution convenient for storing food at all stages of preparation, and it will prove well worth while to incorporate one if possible.

The view you would like to have from your kitchen will doubtless have some effect on its lighting, so consider both questions together. Obviously, you will want the best view possible, although there are differing schools of thought concerning exactly where this picture window should be. Some pundits say that time in the kitchen is largely work-time, spent in a head-down attitude so that the view from the eating area is more likely to be appreciated than that from the sink or stove.

Providing the best form of access from outside is the next problem. Animals and children gear their lives around constant toing and froing between the kitchen and the garden, via the back door, bringing with them the inevitable concomitants of dirt, mud and damp. One way of confining this mess while retaining heat in the house and ensuring that your kitchen is the soothing place you wish it to be is to provide a back-door lobby for the old coats and wellington boots and wet dog-towels.

It is important to be able to park your car near the kitchen door. After a frustrating morning in the supermarket it is doubly tiresome to have to carry heavy cartons all around the house. The position of the front door is not critical in relation to your kitchen unless it is on another level. If this is so, plan if possible for an entryphone connection in the kitchen—food can spoil while you answer the door.

The herb garden should be planted as close to the kitchen as possible—inspired cooking so often depends on an intuitive dash for a bay leaf or sprig of mint. The patch need only be very small, and should ideally be right by the back door. The vegetables can be planted a little farther off. Patios and barbecues also require easy entry to the kitchen, so, if there is no suitable door, make sure there is a convenient window through which food and drink can be passed.

Inside your house, the most direct access from kitchen to dining area is vital. Every extra metre between the kitchen and the dining-table works out at hundreds of unnecessary kilometres walked in a lifetime. Conservatories, beloved of Victorians, are coming back into fashion as relaxing or eating areas. Like any other room in the house where food is eaten, its position ought to be considered in relation to that of the kitchen.

A separate laundry, if you are lucky enough to have the space, should preferably adjoin the kitchen.

If the household employs living-in help then a whole range of planning problems arise. It may be sensible to provide a little staff flat next to the kitchen, although some kitchen appliances are noisy enough to make this impractical.

The installation of plumbing, electricity, gas and oil are matters for professionals, but it is as well to have a nodding acquaintance with the working of these mysteries. Should you have a solid-fuel boiler sited in the

A stream of fresh air makes the kitchen (left) a joy in summer, and herbs are provided without a hike across the garden.

kitchen, ensure that the fuel bunker is near at hand. Also remember not to have the dustbins too far away from the back door.

Cold water, gas and electricity can be piped by almost any route, however circuitous. But hot-water taps should be not too far from the hot water cylinder: it is irritating (and wasteful) to have to wait for water to run hot. Drainage can cause problems, especially if the waste pipe from the sink is some distance from the vertical stack. If you doubt your plumber's abilities, call in the local building inspector.

The final consideration, and possibly the most enjoyable factor in relating your kitchen to the rest of your house, is the matter of decorating.

There are two approaches to the interior decoration of houses. One is to consider the house as a single entity and to select a basic decorative theme which all rooms in the house follow in one way or another; the other is to allow the occupant of each bedroom to decide upon its colour and also to make all the communal rooms very different in mood.

The first approach is meant to give the basic beauty of the building itself a chance to shine without being upstaged by distracting decor. This idea was put into action in an apartment block on Chicago's Lake Shore Drive designed by Mies van der Rohe. Every tenant was obliged to use plain material for his curtains in order not to spoil the uniform effect of the glass façades with their projecting steel columns. Less surprisingly, similar instructions were issued to the inhabitants of the married quarters in Knightsbridge Army Barracks, London.

The second approach is less austere. But though it may be fun putting all your ideas into effect, it can also be disastrous. Interior designers have a reputation for putting their aesthetic principles before their clients' personal tastes, but when this alternative method of decoration is considered, they do have some justice on their side. The result of informal, democratic designing can end up looking chaotic.

Most houses fall somewhere between these extremes of vanity and diversity, and it is with the kitchen, bathrooms and lavatories that the problem of integration is most acute, since all these rooms require special wall and floor surfaces. There is something to be said for allowing them to look different; but remember that the kitchen door is often left open, and a glimpse through it should not give the impression of looking into a completely different house.

Ceilings and floors can assist integration if they flow in a uniform colour from one room to the next. There is no efficient method of joining two different floor finishes, so cut your losses and try to extend the living-room or hall carpet, for example, into the dining area of the kitchen. Similarly, if the kitchen floor is tiled, these might reach into the hall.

Plain wood and glossy tiles are continued beyond the kitchen into the eating area to pull the two together (below).

In a relaxed holiday home (above), an open-plan kitchen keeps the cook in the swim of things, and a tough carpet copes with wet feet.

The argument about who gets the view is clearly solved in this kitchen (below), where both cook and diners benefit.

The integrated kitchen

Garden, games-room, music-room and kitchen is a rare combination, but the partnership works with a restful colour scheme (above).

Separated eating and working areas blend smoothly together without forfeiting their own identity (below).

The modern version of the baronial hall (above) slips a kitchen into a recess and places the table against a wall.

A partition produces two rooms in one, but keeping walls and ceilings identical makes the division less pronounced (right).

A stairway wall can be sliced away to give an intriguing glimpse into the attractive kitchen beyond (above).

A sliding glass door is an easy way of linking two rooms together while preventing kitchen smells from escaping (left).

Two very different rooms coexist side by side but on different levels, separated by a frontier of pillars and shelves (above).

The open-plan house

Upstairs and downstairs reduced to homely proportions (left) is one way of rising above reduced circumstances.

A detail (above) of the kitchen photographed left shows how a dining area was included in the grand design.

An aura of tranquillity is arrived at by surrounding the kitchen with wide open spaces and choosing muted colours (above).

A recessed kitchen tucks elegantly into a broad room (below) without spoiling its proportions or eating up too much house space.

A clever play on a Romeo and Juliet set puts the kitchen downstage and surrounds it with bold furniture (above).

Planning with professionals

It is one thing to have a host of bright ideas on the style and layout of a kitchen, but quite another to turn those thoughts into reality. The building and redecorating process can be frustrating, expensive and aggravating, but intelligent forethought and planning can ease the strain. So can a little professional advice.

The building industry harbours a bewildering array of professions. There are surveyors and quantity surveyors, there are architects and scores of different engineers. However, in planning and constructing a domestic kitchen the architect is the only one who really matters. His advice will be unbiased, for the code of his profession does not permit him to receive any payment from builders or suppliers of equipment.

Not all architects are willing, or able, to design a domestic kitchen. The best way to find one who will is to follow up personal recommendations and see work that he has done. If this approach is not successful, consult a professional association of architects. (See useful addresses.) They will be able to provide information concerning architects in each part of the country, and members of the public can call and see photographs of their work to help make the choice on a sensible basis. Architect and would-be client have to have some measure of personal rapport as well as sharing similar tastes on matters of design.

Once appointed, the architect will measure up the space for the kitchen and produce a survey drawing showing the area as it exists. Then after a discussion between owner and architect a mutually agreed solution is found that satisfies the requirements in terms of style, function and cost. The architect will then turn this agreed design into production drawings—which show how the finished kitchen will look; and a specification, which not only describes how it is to be built but includes such details as when the work must start and finish, which parts of the house the builders may use and how and when payments are to be made. The architect sends the drawings to the various departments of the local authority to obtain their permission. If the house is leasehold or is mortgaged, or if the kitchen is against a party wall, then there may be other consents to be obtained as well. When any changes required by all these bodies have been incorporated into the drawings, then the architect obtains prices from builders. It is then his job to recommend a builder and a price, to supervise the work that the builder does, to certify payments to the builder and to agree the final account.

Some people bring in an architect for the early stages only, to get his design ideas, and then deal with the builder on their own. This will reduce the architect's fee, but would seem to be a poor bargain for the owner as there is no one on his side when technical or financial problems arise during or after the building work. For a full service an architect will charge a percentage, usually between 12 and 15 per cent of the cost of the building work. He should be able to save more than his fee by knowing how to spend money sensibly, by giving the builder clear instructions and by knowing where to go for competitive estimates.

Kitchen specialists

Some of the firms that sell kitchen equipment, and most of the manufacturers of kitchen cupboard units, offer a free design service. Because they spend their lives planning kitchens, and because they know intimately what their own firm's products can do, these specialists build up a considerable expertise and, if you have firmly decided to buy a range of fitments as opposed to having them made by a builder, and if you have already chosen which particular range of fitments is the right one, then the manufacturer's own designers can help to work out how to plan the kitchen. The disadvantage is that these specialists work for the supplier, not the consumer, so their advice is not likely to be impartial.

Builders

It is not easy to live with builders in the house, especially in the kitchen, which is the very heart of the home. It will not be easy for the builder or his workmen either. With so many potential sources of friction it is wise to consider how the situation can be alleviated. If you are buying the house, try to have the building work done before moving. Or if the replanned kitchen is to go in your present home, try to be on holiday

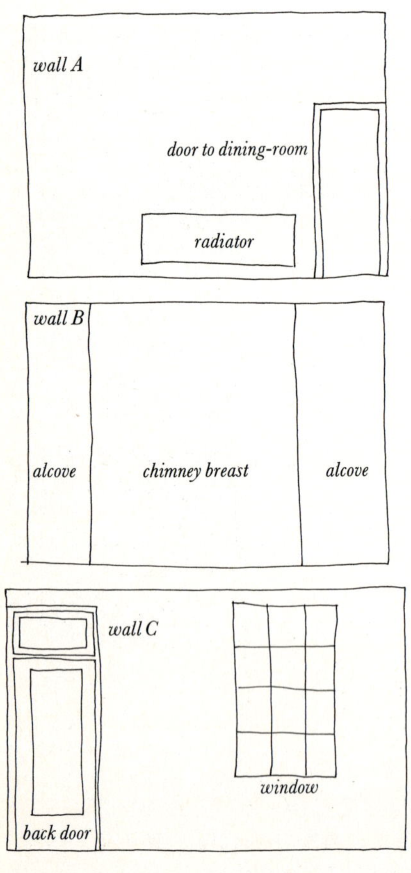

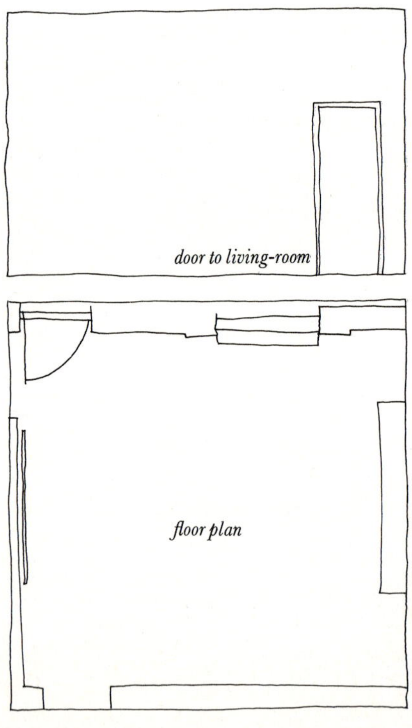

Stage one of drawing your own plan is to make rough freehand sketches of the four walls and the floor, showing the positions of fixed objects such as alcoves, doors, windows and radiators. Take measurements and add them to the sketches.

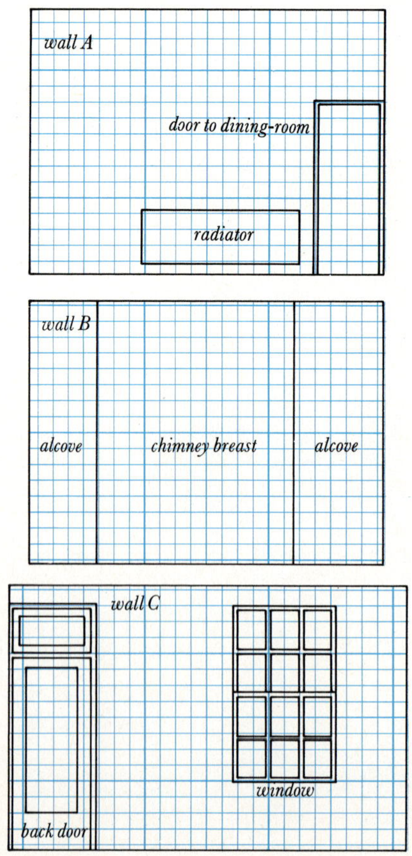

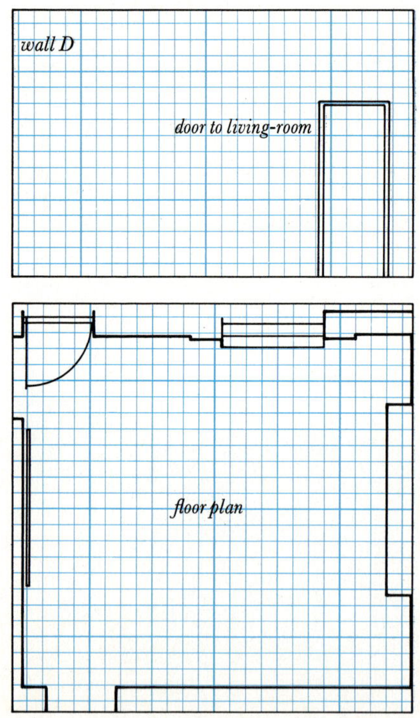

Stage two: using the information on your sketches draw the plan properly to scale on graph paper using your original sketch for reference. Choose a sensible scale to work to—twenty inches on the ground to one on paper is practical.

for a while to give the builders a time when they can disconnect plumbing and electrics without upsetting the household. Above all, remember that pre-planning saves time on site, so work everything out beforehand, give the builder time to obtain materials and fitments and then let him get on with it without changes. Any change to the agreed plan may cause delays, and delays are expensive. If your builder is under the control of an architect, make sure that all instructions go through the architect so he can keep control of time, quality and cost. If you are employing the builder direct, all instructions should go to the man running the job, not the individual craftsmen. If new instructions involve money or delay this should be agreed in writing at the time. The penalty for being slap-dash and indecisive is a frightening bill at the end of the job.

Choosing a builder

The right size of building firm is probably one that is just big enough to tackle the job, so that the boss takes a personal interest, yet is not so small that it cannot finance the job properly. Builders should be chosen carefully on the basis of their reputation and their previous work. In a kitchen requiring specially made joinery, it is important that the builder has a good joinery shop, or subcontracts that part of the work to a firm that has. No specification in the world is sufficiently watertight to save you from the builder who uses the wrong glue and then goes bankrupt just after he has been paid. If you are unable to find a suitable builder, contact the appropriate advisory body. (See useful addresses.)

Tradesmen

Be as tough as you like with your architect and your builder, but do be nice to the tradesmen! You will get better work if they feel their work is appreciated. If you lose your temper with the plumber, then you may find your water supply disconnected on a Friday night—and serves you right!

Doing it yourself

If you have the time and energy, remodelling your kitchen yourself can be an absorbing hobby and can save you a lot of money. But a not-too-skilled operator working only weekends and evenings may take a long time to finish the job, so see that the family does not suffer too much in the meanwhile. Hints on how to set about designing your own kitchen without the help of an expert are given below.

Once you have settled on the positioning of units, cooker, refrigerator and so on, add electric points and lights to your plan and note the floor and wall finishes you have chosen. The completed drawing must then be shown to the local building inspector. Finally, write a specification describing exactly how and when the work is to be done and give it and the drawing to the builders as a basis for discussing quotations.

There is no doubt that plastic waste pipes, melamine-faced chipboard and a host of new products and tools have made it much easier for the home handyman to work quickly and well, and there are some excellent instruction manuals in the bookshops to show how the amateur can tackle most simple building operations. It is unwise to do your own electric wiring, but if you do feel confident enough, get your electricity board to check before switching on.

Keep it legal

Regulations governing the simplest building operation have multiplied so dramatically in the last few years that even those who administer them have difficulty in understanding them. The only thing to do is to take your proposals directly to the people concerned. The planning department will want to know if you intend to add a room. If you live in a conservation area they will want to know if you are intending to alter any part of the exterior of your house. The building inspector has to be informed if you are altering any of the walls or windows in your house, if you are changing the drains or waste pipes, if you are putting inflammable surfaces, such as wood, on walls or ceiling or if you are changing a fireplace. In fact you should consult him even if you are doing little more than changing a few cupboards. All this may sound a bit daunting, and it is. If you have an architect it becomes his worry; if you don't then it is probably best to start with the building inspector and ask him to refer you to any other people whose permission may be required.

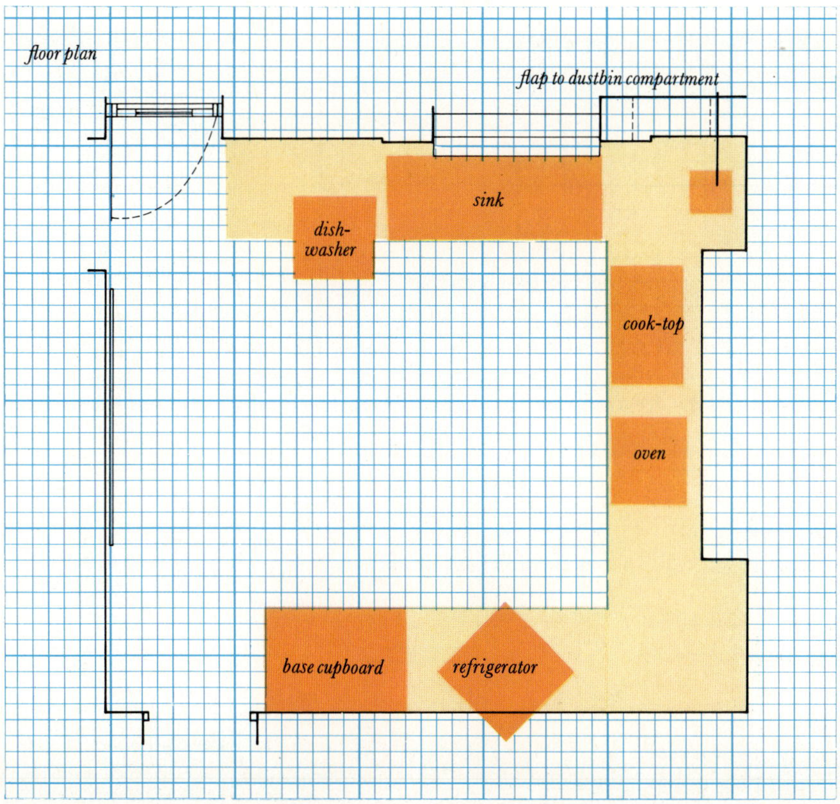

Stage three: cut out cardboard shapes to the same scale as the plan to represent all your equipment and units, and move them around until you reach a satisfactory arrangement.

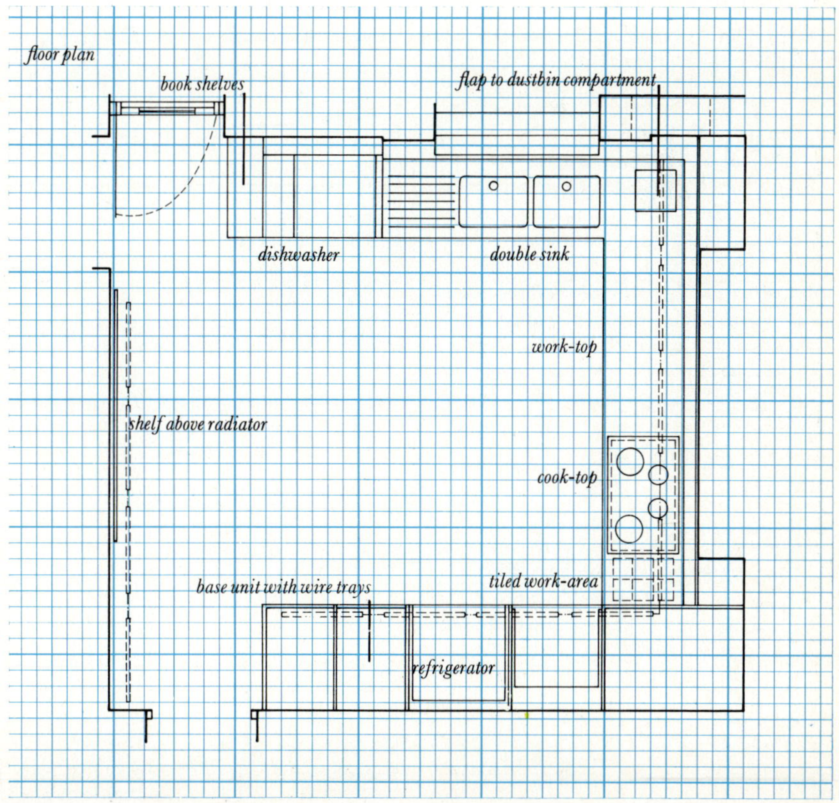

Stage four: the finished drawing, ready for the builder, shows everything in place. Mark on it all the power points you require and the wall and floor finishes you have chosen.

Ergonomics

The dictionary definition of ergonomics is "the study of man in relation to his working environment and the adaptation of machines and general conditions to fit the individual, so that he may work to maximum efficiency". The domestic workshop (sometimes called the kitchen) has been the object of much interest and study on the part of ergonomists. Research carried out at Cornell University in the early 1950s established the concepts of "work centres" and the "work triangle" that are the bases of kitchen planning to this day.

The work triangle

The Cornell studies revealed that it is not the size of the kitchen that affects efficiency so much as the disposition of the work areas, cupboard space and work-tops within it.

In most kitchens, activity centres around three principal areas—the food storage area (the refrigerator and larder); the sink; and, of course, the cooker. These key areas form the "work triangle", linked by the food-preparation area, a mixing zone and a serving area. Each activity, so far as is possible, should be self-contained.

Each trip from one area to the next will cause a break in the continuity of the meal-making process—so the idea is to relate the areas logically to one another. The small, compact kitchen is thus easier to work in than the traditional large farmhouse kitchen with yards to walk between range, scullery, sink and outside larder.

A good test for checking the effectiveness of your kitchen is to examine the steps involved in making a cup of tea. When spelled out in detail, what superficially appears to be a very ordinary, simple task is in fact a surprisingly complex manoeuvre.

Pick up a kettle from the cooker, take it to the sink and fill it with water, return kettle to cooker and turn on burner. Get teapot and put in a little hot water to warm the pot, then fill with tea from the tea caddy and place the pot next to the kettle. Get cups and saucers from the china cupboard, assemble teaspoons, sugar bowl, tea strainer and milk jug. Pour boiling water on to the tea, place pot on table.

This could be a tiring operation if the distances between centres are too great. A trip around the triangle should be no more than 7 m (22 ft).

Although the smaller kitchen is the more efficient to use there are certain minimum dimensions which must be observed. The passage between facing units in a galley kitchen should not be less than 1200 mm (4 ft). This space is needed for bending down to get dishes out of ovens and cupboards, and to allow someone carrying a tray to squeeze past. The minimum acceptable clearance between an inward-opening door and the front of a run of cupboards is 400 mm (16 in). If the cupboard has to be closer to the door, then the door must be changed to swing outwards or slide back on the outside wall.

The most basic layout of all is a simple sequence that follows the pattern—work-surface; cooker; work-surface; sink; work-surface. It is a simple and practical line-up enabling any room with a 3-m (10-ft) run of uninterrupted wall space to become an efficient kitchen. It is always desirable to have cooker and sink as near together as is practical, that is, both having work space on either side. Since the sink, with all its attendant plumbing, is the most expensive item to move around, it is best to take a "fix" from the present position of the sink and start plotting your layout from there. Neither the sink nor the cooker should be stuck in a corner of the room; they should be at least 400 mm (16 in) away from the corner to allow you to stand comfortably in front without banging elbows on a wall.

Do not interrupt the work sequence with tall units such as broom cupboards or oven-housing units. They should be grouped together at the end of a run of work-tops.

The floor plan is not the only consideration in designing the kitchen; the vertical dimensions are equally important. Cupboards, shelves and drawers should be designed to minimize bending down and stretching. Bending below the work-top is more tiring than stretching upwards, as well as requiring more space to do it in. Heights between 760 mm and 1520 mm

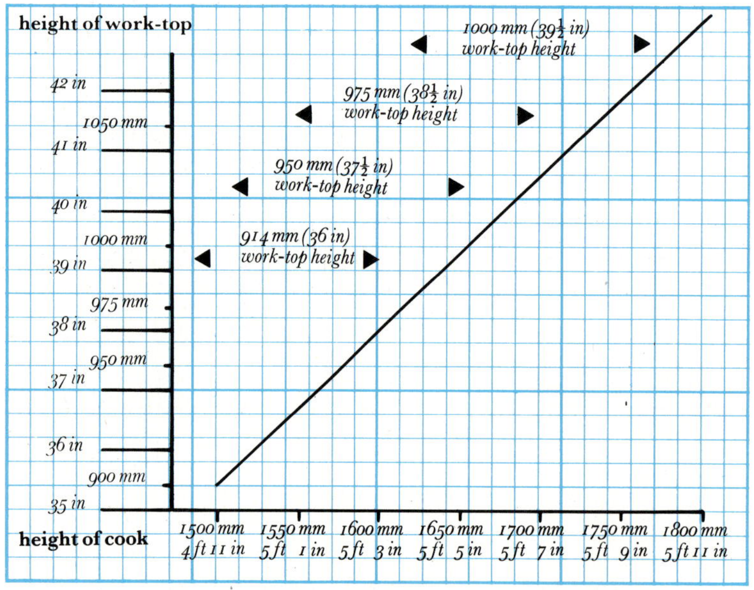

Graph showing ideal sink heights (work-tops should be 75 mm/3 in lower). Arrows indicate the range of stature for which standard heights are suitable.

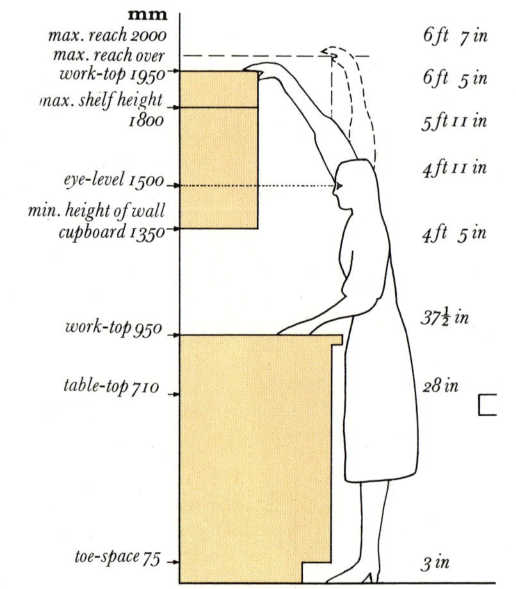

Diagram showing the critical heights and dimensions based on a person 1625 mm (5 ft 4 in) tall.

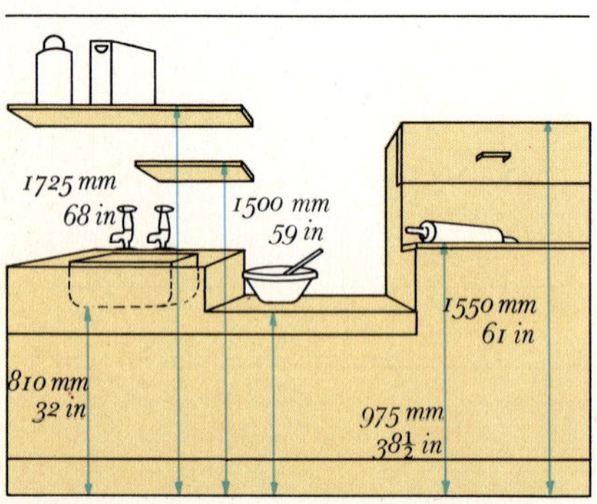

The Cornell researchers' perfect work-top for doing the dishes and most other kitchen tasks.

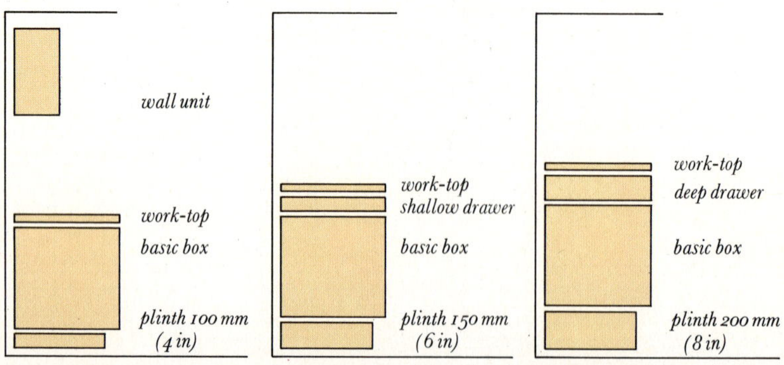

Adjusting the height of the work-top to suit the height of the cook. These "sandwich" units have a range of components that can be built up or down as required.

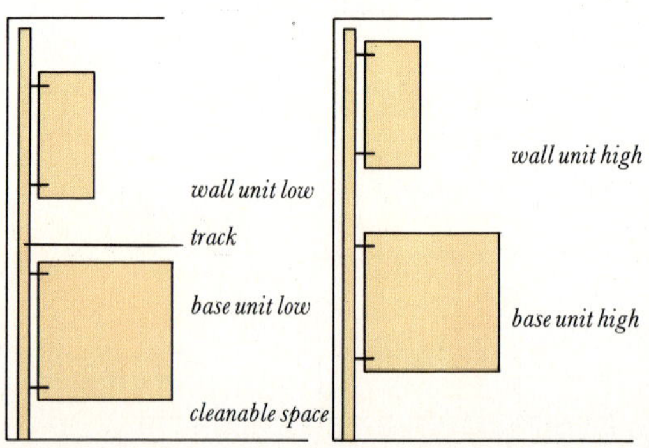

An adjustable system cantilevered out from wall-fixed track. Units can be moved up or down in 100-mm (4-in) intervals.

(2 ft 6 in and 5 ft) are comfortable to reach. The maximum comfortable upward reach when standing in front of a work-top is 1700 mm (5 ft 7 in); this increases to 1950 mm (6 ft 5 in) where there is no work-top to reach over. It will be difficult to see what is happening on shelves above 1550 mm (5 ft 1 in) and in drawers more than 1500 mm (4 ft 11 in) high.

Heights for work-tops

There is a great deal of controversy over the "ideal" height for the kitchen work-top. Most studies have been based on the average woman's height of 1625 mm (5 ft 4 in), failing to consider that tall husbands, sons and small daughters work in the kitchen too. The most recent studies suggest that the standard proprietary kitchen work-top height of 900 mm (2 ft 11½ in) is too low and that it should be increased to at least 950 or 975 mm (3 ft 1½ in or 3 ft 2½ in). The housewife works an average of four hours a day in the kitchen, of which as much as 70 minutes are spent standing at the sink. The height of the sink work-top is therefore of prime importance. As one tends to work more at the bottom of the sink than at the top, it is generally agreed that the sink work-top should be about 50 mm (2 in) higher than the general work-top. This is often unpopular, as a change in level can be awkward. So, all things considered, to prevent backache at the sink it is advisable to raise the levels of all the work-tops throughout the run. If one work-top height is preferred then a compromise of 950 mm (3 ft 1½ in) would suit most people. If you want the work-top on two levels, then the higher surface should extend into the corner, rather than the lower one.

Some tasks, like hand whisking or pea-podding, are better done sitting at the traditional table-top height of 710 mm (2 ft 4 in). Where there is no room for a table, a small pull-out work-top will do. It is worth remembering that, since the introduction of electric mixers, the amount of hand mixing has been considerably reduced. This means the operation can easily be carried out on the higher work-top levels.

If you are exceptionally short, say under 1.5 m (5 ft), and few other taller people will be using the kitchen, then you may need a lower work-top height of about 860 mm (2 ft 10 in). If you are not happy about the height of standard floor-based units then choose a system which can be wall-mounted at the height you choose. Some systems can be put together with shorter or taller plinths or drawers, giving two and three different work-top heights. Other systems, in which cabinets are cantilevered out from wall-fixed slotted racking, are also available. (All wall-hung systems require sturdy fixing to a solid, outside wall if they are to carry the considerable weight of full cupboards and support the pressure on work-tops.)

The height of the cooker is not critical, but it should always be level with the work-tops on both sides; one of these should have a heat-proof finish.

When planning kitchen cupboards, bear in mind that cupboards (and appliances) very often have side-hung doors and the direction of the door swing must be considered. Most fittings have a choice of hinges, enabling you to select the swing most suited to your needs. Most refrigerators, however, are still manufactured with right-hand hinges only; this means they will be inconvenient to use if positioned at the left-hand end of a work-top area.

Appliances such as refrigerators, dishwashers, washing machines and split-level ovens can all be mounted at a high level. This will reduce the amount of bending down and improve your view into the machines. Nevertheless, this must not be done at the expense of work-top space. If there is room for only one appliance to be wall mounted, then it should be the refrigerator, as it is most frequently used.

Wall cupboards should not be mounted lower than 400 mm (16 in) above the work-top, otherwise they will obscure the rear of the work area. In a small kitchen, cupboards fitted with sliding doors are preferable; side-hung doors left open are likely to bang passing heads. Wall cupboards should be installed only above a work-top, otherwise there is a danger of walking straight into them.

Base cupboards must have a continuous toe space along the bottom so that you can stand comfortably at the work-top. This space should be not less than 75 mm (3 in) high and 100 mm (4 in) deep. If knee-space is needed for sitting on a high stool at the work-top, either for working or eating, then the space should not be less than 460 mm (18 in) wide and 500 mm (1 ft 7½ in) deep and the height not lower than 150 mm (6 in) below the work-top. Work-tops should project at least 19 mm (¾ in) in front of base cupboards so that a receptacle can be held under the front edge when wiping the work-top clean.

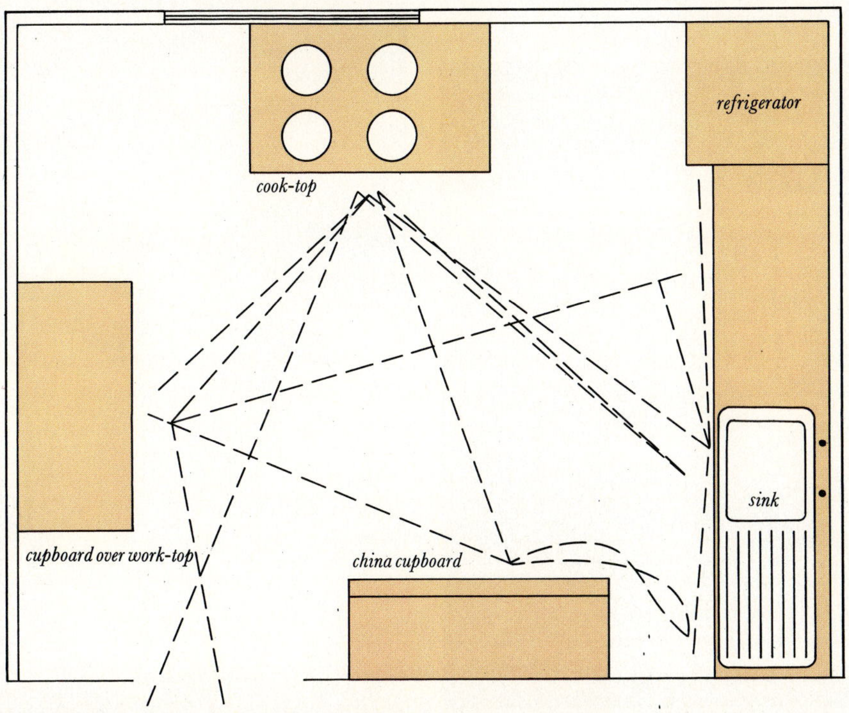

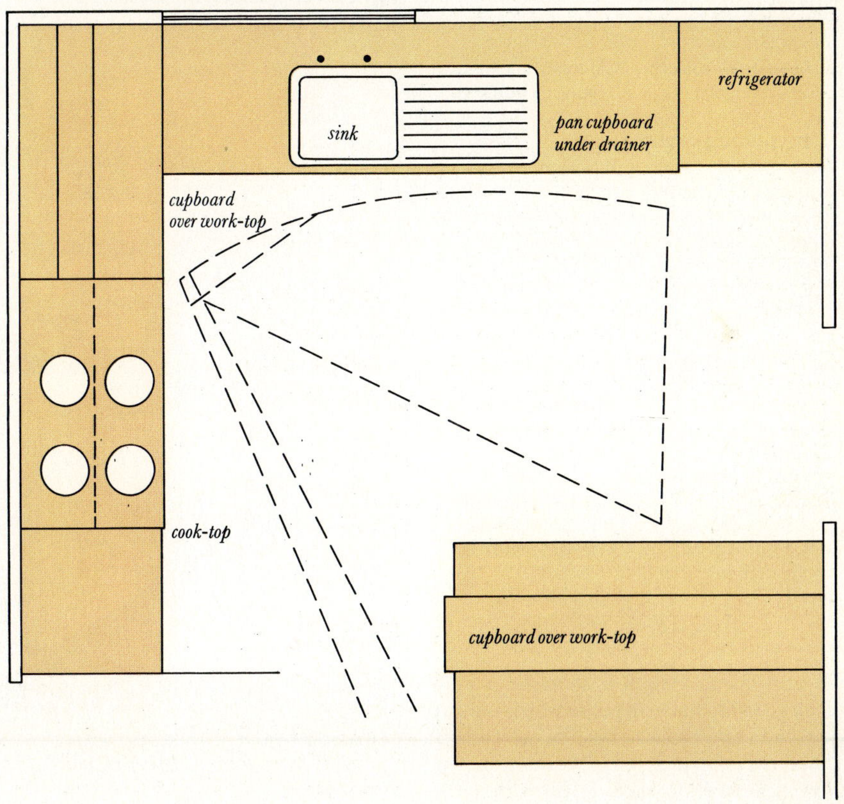

Two diagrams of the same kitchen, proving beyond doubt the advantages of a well-planned kitchen. In the haphazard arrangement (above) the dotted line traces the progress of a foot-sore tea-maker—the well-organized kitchen (right) more than halves walking distance.

he work sequence

"A place for everything, and everything in its place" should be the motto for the dream kitchen. In order to cut down walking distance between work centres, arrange for materials and utensils to be stored where they are first needed. For example:

The sink area (washing up and vegetable preparation)

Item	Position
Soap powders, mops, detergents, etc.; small vases and jars.	Wall cupboard over sink.
Draining racks.	Wall above sink.
Washing-up bowl, waste bucket/bag.	Cupboard under sink.
Dish cloths, hand towel.	Rail near sink.
Knives, peelers, etc.	Under drainer.
Colander, sieves, chopping boards, plastic rubbish bags.	Base or wall cupboard near the sink.

The work-top (food preparation and mixing)

Item	Position
Dry stores, e.g. flour, sugar, pulses, etc.	Wall cupboards over work surface.
Spice jars, knives.	Wall racks.
Pastry board, awkwardly shaped utensils like mouli-legumes, etc.	Hung inside base cupboard door.
Mixing bowls, baking tins, casseroles, mixer attachments, mincers, mashers, etc.	Deep pull-out drawers.
Scales, electric mixer/liquidizer/blender.	On counter or wall-hung on brackets.

The cooking centre

Item	Position
Seasonings and herbs.	Shelf next to cook-top.
Wooden spoons, fish slices, spatulas.	Rack next to cook-top.
Saucepans, frying-pans, pressure cookers.	Heavy pans in deep pull-out drawers, lightweight ones on overhead shelves.

The serving centre

Item	Position
China, glassware.	Wall cupboards.
Table cutlery, mats, napkins, tablecloths.	Drawers.
Trays.	Narrow vertical slot under work-top.
Salt, pepper, jams, cereals, butter dish.	Wall cupboards or shelves.
Bread.	Deep drawer or air-tight bin.

A well-planned kitchen should not only look good but make the cook who is using it feel content with his or her place of work. A handsome kitchen that is exhausting or uncomfortable to work in is, at best, an expensive mistake. It cannot be emphasized too often that there is no "ideal" kitchen. No magic formula exists that is automatically right for everyone. But there is no mystique either. Kitchen planning is simply a matter of common sense, and a great deal of sound research has narrowed the field of error considerably. Once work-centres and storage facilities are laid out in order, you have the beginnings of a workable plan.

It is tempting, especially to those unfamiliar with the techniques of kitchen planning, to see cooking as an industrial process with a clear throughput—purchased raw materials entering one end and passing through a succession of work-areas until hot meals emerge on the table at the other end. But a domestic kitchen is not an assembly line, it is more like a craftsman's workshop. If you were to plot the lines of movement between work-centres during the making of a turkey dinner, you would end up with a diagram of a spider's web. One clear fact, however, does emerge, and that is that most trips are made between the sink and the cooker, so there is everything to be said for placing them close together. As for the other journeys, the best that can reasonably be done is to keep them as short as possible. The other vital ingredient for the well-planned kitchen is the intelligent storage of key items so they can be reached without a route march in between.

Standard layouts

No one layout is more "ideal" than another, so it does not make sense to habour a fixed preference for a certain type of plan and then force it into a space that it does not want to go into. Let the room itself have a say in the design of the kitchen, and keep your eyes open for anything within the room that can add character to your kitchen—like an interesting fireplace or mantle. In order to create a workable kitchen it may be necessary to block up a door or knock down a wall. The cost of installing a well-fitted kitchen is considerable, so the extra expense of removing a couple of walls is worth contemplating, but first make sure they are non-structural.

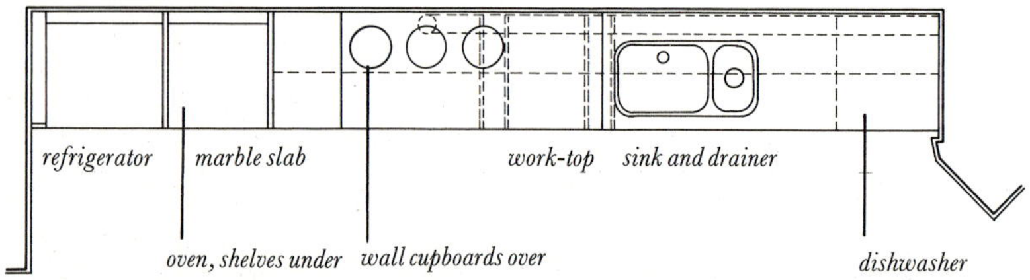

The single-line kitchen

A very basic layout that should be kept as compact as possible. In the plan above, the standard arrangement of work-top/cook-top/work-top/sink/work-top is sandwiched between an oven and a refrigerator that were built in at high level and linked across the top to high-level cupboards. Thus, the entire run of units is framed in and stands like a piece of furniture. Food is stored on the other side of the room. The overall length is only 4870 mm (16 ft).

The cook can keep an eye on her sauce while engaged on other tasks in the compact single-line kitchen (above).

Confining the work-centre to one wall with dry and cold storage close by accentuates the freedom of an open-plan room (right).

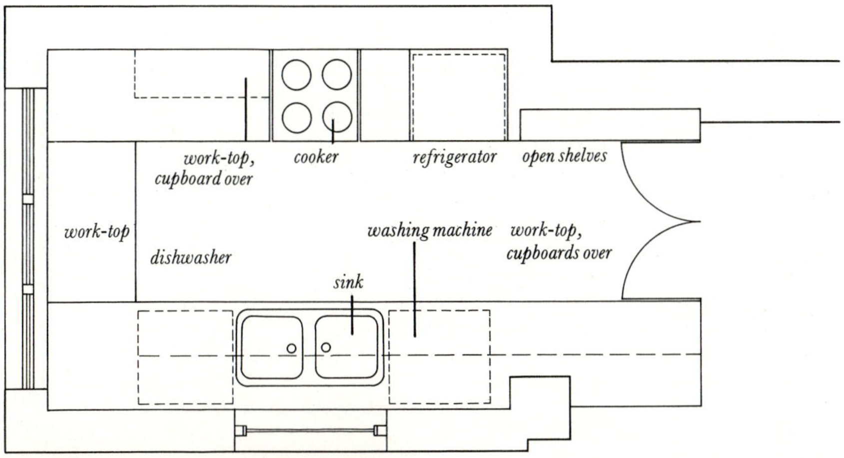

The galley kitchen
The plan on the left shows the back annexe to a London town house that opens on to a large family room. Though small, the annexe was just wide enough at 2400 mm (7 ft 9½ in) to give 600 mm (1 ft 11½ in) depth of unit on either side and a walkway of 1200 mm (3 ft 11 in). Galley kitchens in general have a more compact work triangle than any other arrangement, so are less tiring to use. This plan loses some of its advantages in having sink and cooker on opposite sides. On the other hand, since the room is more of a cul-de-sac than a through traffic route, it will pose no safety hazard. The work-top continues out into the dining area to form a breakfast bar/serving area.

In a narrow room with a view the galley style keeps equipment shipshape (above).

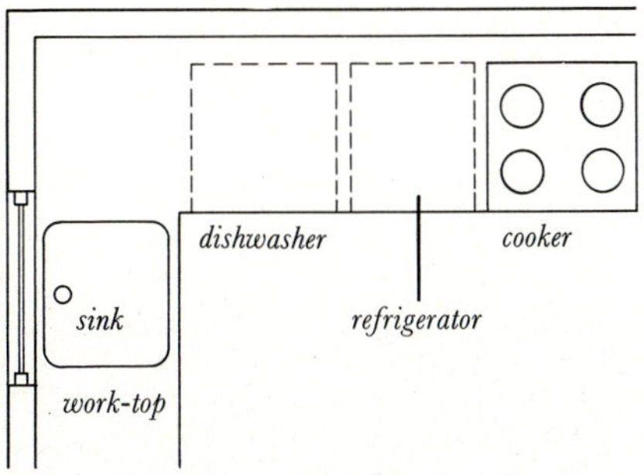

L-shaped layout
Here, the classic work sequence is run around two walls, so the work triangle is kept reasonably compact. In a very small room it may be difficult to avoid placing the refrigerator next to the cooker. This is not an ideal arrangement, as the refrigerator will use more electricity to keep its cool.

In a long L-shaped kitchen the cook can move forward to the cooker, leaving her preparation clutter out of sight and out of mind (left).

The small L-shaped kitchen requires a neat hand with dirty dishes, but leg-work is cut to a minimum (above).

The work sequence

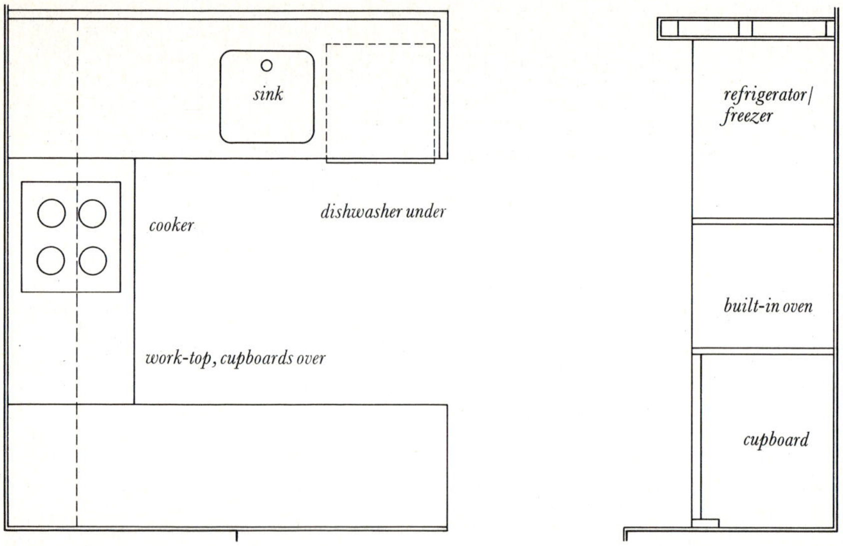

U-shaped layout
This adaptable layout is wrapped around three walls in an unbroken sequence. Tall units, in this case a wall oven and a refrigerator/freezer, are mounted on the fourth wall to keep the work triangle free. The example in the plan was built into the middle of the ground floor of an old town house. The layout provides a lot of work-top, but, because there are two corners to deal with, there will be some wasted space. Special attention must be given to low-level storage in the corner, and the counter space above it should not be included when calculating the amount of work-top that will be required.

Ancient and modern make a serene team in a traditional setting (above). Bringing the work centre out permits the walls to be splashed with colour rather than stains.

Despite its busy ceiling and hive-like appearance, a U-shaped work-centre this size (above) leaves room for two enthusiasts to exercise their culinary talents in reasonable harmony.

Escapist cooks are better able to shrug off kitchen bondage when their surroundings are carefully tailored to conceal the reproachful presence of machines (below).

A self-sufficient kitchen island takes the steam out of commuting between units and forms a pleasant natural barrier—and a shrewd division—between working and eating areas (above).

Soap opera addicts needn't miss a tear in this simplistic kitchen (above), which offers a dash oj drama as well as more practical appliances on the cooking island.

Stainless steel assumes a softer mien in a circular island unit (left) and overheads become assets when they include a shelf for seasonings and good lights to cook by.

Not all work centres are uniform; in the kitchen below the pièce de resistance is a separate preparation table with three surfaces—including the pastry-maker's favourite marble.

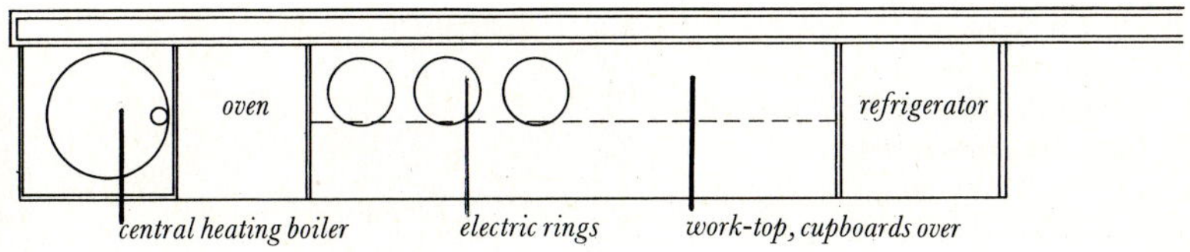

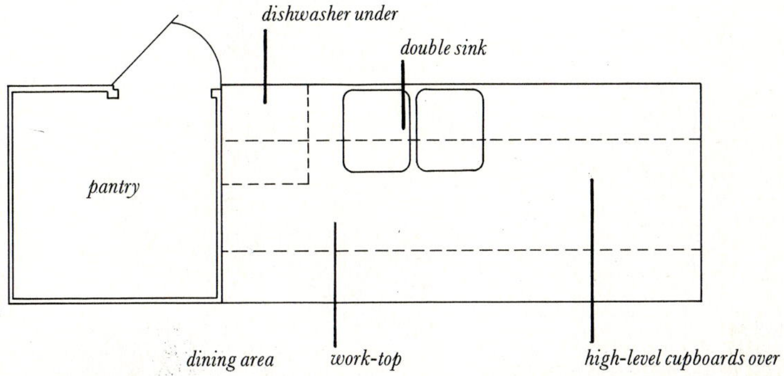

Island layout

The island kitchen should only be considered in rooms where space is plentiful, and care must be taken to see that the dimensions of the work triangle do not get out of hand. If the cooking process requires the cook to walk around the island, then the chances are the distances will be too great for comfort. This example uses one side of the island and the facing wall as a galley kitchen, so the journeys between work-areas are kept short.

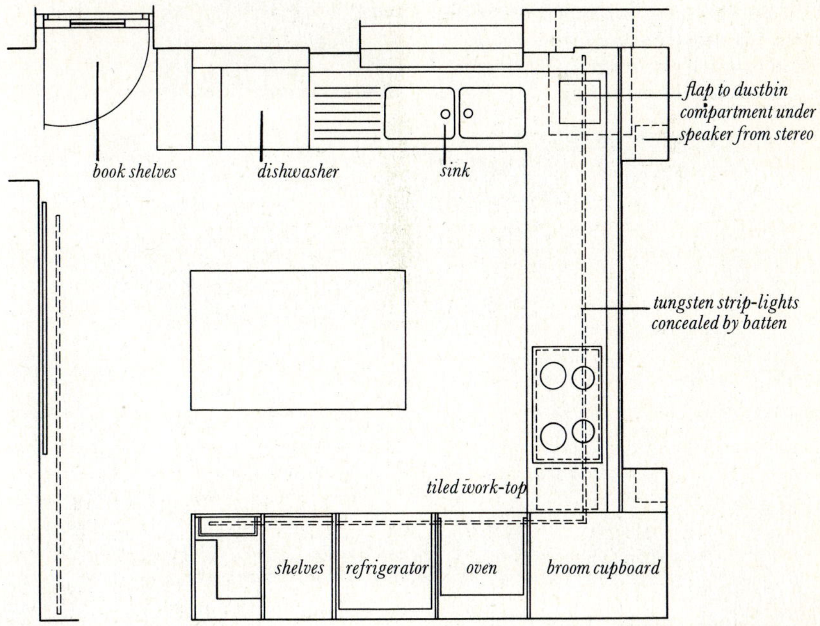

Central table layout

The classic farmhouse kitchen has a huge central table and the work-areas strung out around the walls. It may look very folksy and nostalgic, but as a working kitchen it could be punishing on the feet. In the example illustrated, an attempt has been made to reduce travel distances by concentrating work-areas on the right-hand side of the room. The central table is not used as a work-surface, only for eating. The counter around the edge is set at the right height for work and stools are provided for tiring jobs.

Planning your kitchen

Ideas for layouts

Few kitchens are clear-cut examples of one form of layout or another and the kitchen that will suit you will probably be more of a mongrel than a thoroughbred. Let your own preferences, and the space that you have available, dictate the layout that makes you feel confident.

A shallow, spice-packed cupboard is the thin end of the wedge-shaped sink unit (above), which, with its polygonal counterpart (right), channels the cook between sink and cook-top.

This Scandinavian kitchen (above) revolves around the chunky cooking axis. Economy of movement is assured, since each side is equipped for a different task.

Conveniently cornered by the compact, L-shaped unit, the cook may perch on the tall stool (right) with a stirring spoon in one hand and a tea towel in the other.

A three-cornered arrangement (above). The dexterous chef can supervise oven, sink and cook-top from the commanding position behind the bottle-green wall.

Splendid isolation is possible in big kitchens. The elongated tub (above) with its chopping board "lid" is ideal for a preparation sequence. The rounded corners make accidental knocks less painful.

In the one-track kitchen (right) you stick to a semicircular path. The sumptuous stretch of marble, and the floor's resemblance to pâté aux truffes, glamorize the straightforward line-up of appliances.

Planning for safety

The kitchen is the most dangerous room in the house—40 per cent of all home accidents happen there. The under-fives and the over sixty-fives are most vulnerable, but haste, carelessness and muddle might easily make painful statistics of us all.

Planning

The safest layout places cooker, work-top and sink in an unbroken line. This eliminates the potentially dangerous ferrying of hot pans and scalding kettles.

Cookers should not be installed near windows, where draughts may blow out gas flames and trailing curtains might catch fire. Neither should they be placed near inward-opening kitchen doors. A heat-resistant work-surface on either side of the cook-top makes a safe place to rest pots and pans and keeps the handles out of the reach of children. The risk of fire is considerably reduced by ensuring that no wall cupboard—or drying dishcloth—hangs above the hot-plate.

Insufficient storage room creates a potentially dangerous overcrowding of work-surfaces and floor space. Cupboards over 1800 mm (5 ft 11 in) high should be used only for long-term storage. Daily clambering to reach inaccessible shelves increases the risk of falls, particularly among the elderly.

A large number of accidents are due to inadequate lighting. Make sure that all work-surfaces, storage areas and floors are brightly lit.

Floors should be level, and any damaged places quickly repaired. Provide your kitchen with non-slip floors of the type that prevent skidding even when wet. Natural or synthetic resin polishes should be used rather than wax, which builds up a lethal shine. Always wipe up spills immediately, especially oil and grease, which are the most treacherous of all.

Children

Young children particularly are at risk in the kitchen. Never let them get "underfoot" while you are cooking—they should have a play area of their own, where a weather eye can be kept on them. Never let children play with polythene bags—they will suffocate if they put them over their heads. Ensure pan handles are turned towards the back of the cooker so that the pans cannot be pulled off the cooker top. It might well be worth investing in a cooker guard, which is a rail fixed round the cooker top. Gas cookers with automatic ignition are safer should the controls accidentally be turned on. Bleaches, caustic powders, weed killers, acid oven cleaners and all such poisons must be stored out of the reach of children, preferably under lock and key. Keep sharp knives and small portable electrical equipment well out of their way, and discourage toddlers from sharing the dog's dinner or vice versa.

Dummy plugs can be purchased to shield electric sockets from exploring fingers. A kitchen clock placed where children can read it prevents them clambering on to chairs to see the time and then discovering they have no head for heights.

Rounded corners on kitchen tables cut down the agony of playtime knocks and won't catch clothing as children rush past. Tables without tablecloths minimize the chance of small children pulling hot food, cutlery or china over themselves.

Since most accidents occur in the kitchen this is the best place for a first-aid cabinet. But make it a lockable one.

Disaster kitchen (right), strewn with potential and actual hazards, of which everyone should be aware.

Electricity

It is a fault common to us all that as we acquire more and more electrical gadgets in the kitchen—mixers, toasters, blenders, percolators and the like—we tend to buy ever-larger adaptors rather than going to the expense of installing additional sockets. This is highly dangerous. To prevent overloading and trailing flexes ensure you have at least four switched socket outlets behind the work-top for small free-standing appliances. Fixed machines should be professionally wired and controlled by spur switches with neon indicators. All switches and sockets must be installed well away from sinks and washing machines to minimize the risk of water splashes. Check regularly that the insulation round flexes has not worn thin.

It is dangerous to let the steam from a boiling electric kettle discharge on to a socket outlet and, before being poured, the kettle should always be switched off, unless it has a built-in automatic switch, and the plug should be pulled out at the back. Always read the manufacturer's instruc-

Keep highly inflammable clothes away from the heat.

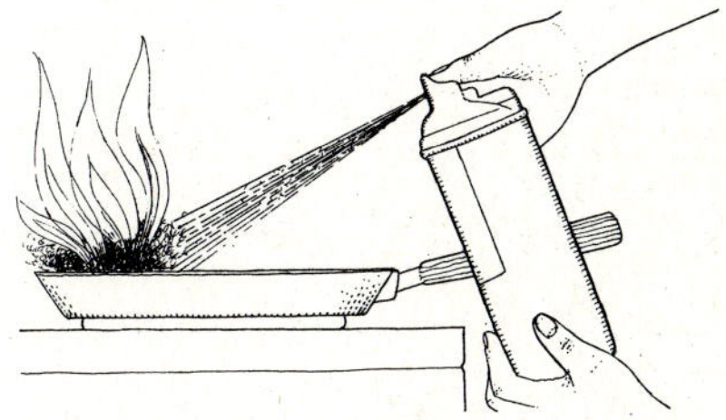

Fire extinguishers should always be aimed at the base of the fire. Never put water on to flaming fat, it will spread the blaze.

Smothering fires
Fires on the cooker should be smothered with a fire blanket to seal off air. If you are caught without one use a large lid or a damp cloth.

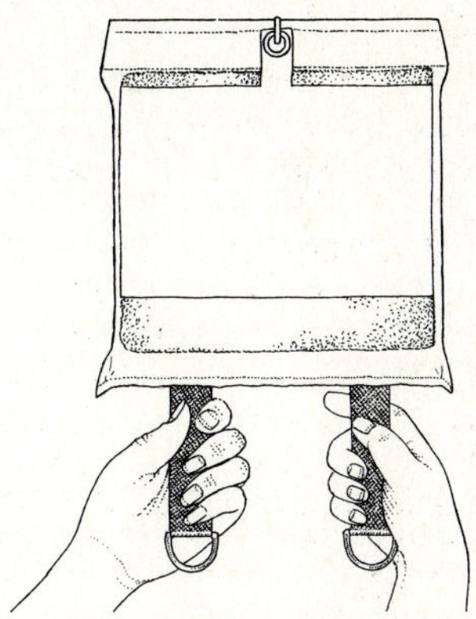

Take a release tape in each hand and pull downwards and outwards.

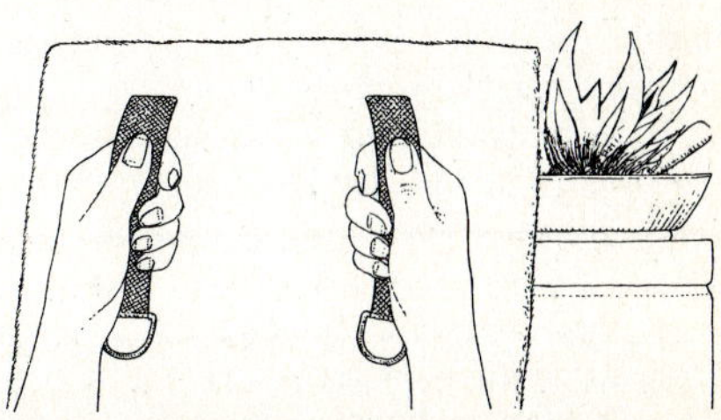

Drape the blanket over the flames to cut off the air. Switch off heat. Leave in position until cool. Refold blanket.

tions and follow them carefully. Major electrical appliances such as dishwashers and washing machines should be serviced regularly to lessen the risks of flooding or overheating.

Gas
If you smell gas never look for leaks with a naked flame. First, check that pilot lights have not been blown out. If the smell persists, check that cigarettes are extinguished, and all appliance controls are turned off. Then turn the gas off at the mains and get expert advice immediately. You must never try to repair gas leaks yourself. Once the leak has been repaired and the gas has been turned on again, remember to relight ALL the pilot lights in the house.

Fire
One of the greatest hazards in a kitchen is fire, so place a small fire extinguisher where it is easily accessible. Water must never be poured on a fat fire as this will spread the blaze; you should smother the flames with a lid, a damp cloth, an aerosol fire extinguisher or a fire blanket so that the air is cut off. Aerosol cans will explode if they get too hot, so they must be kept in a cool place.

Hygiene
In a kitchen as much as possible must be kept clean and tidy; food must be fresh. Dirty hands, insects, pets and rotting food are common causes of food poisoning, which is caused by harmful bacteria contaminating food. Meat, eggs, milk and vegetables are particularly vulnerable and should be stored in a cool place protected from flies. Make sure all equipment is washed thoroughly in hot water (65°C/150°F). On the whole it is more hygienic to let most things drain naturally rather than drying them with a cloth. Always wash hands before preparing food, keep pets off work-surfaces and mice out of doors. Don't leave dirty clothes on the work-top, and don't make up your face, comb your hair or smoke in the kitchen.

Kitchens for the disabled

There is no one blueprint for a disabled person's kitchen. Each must be specifically planned for the individual using it, who may be wheelchair-bound, on crutches or walking aids, one-armed, blind, elderly or infirm. Fortunately there are numerous special aids available to encourage both self-sufficiency and safety. Wheelchair users generally have most problems in a kitchen because of their lack of manoeuvrability and limited upward reach.

Planning

Preparation, sink, cooking and serving areas placed in an unbroken sequence are most suitable. "U"- or "L"-shaped plans are preferable to a corridor arrangement, where things have to be lifted from one side to the other rather than slid along. All work-tops should be at the same level, although the height will vary to suit individual requirements.

The standard wheelchair measures 1040 mm (3 ft 5 in) long x 635 mm (2 ft 1 in) wide x 965 mm (3 ft 2 in) high, with the seat height at 460 mm (1 ft 6 in). It needs a turning circle of 1500 mm (4 ft 11 in), which can be effectively reduced to 1400 mm (4 ft 7 in) if there is a good toe-recess beneath the kitchen furniture. Toe recesses should be 200 mm (8 in) high x 150 mm (6 in) deep to accommodate wheelchair footrests.

It is easier to have the dining-table in the kitchen so general movement and plate carrying can be kept to a minimum. If there is a separate dining-room, a trolley is easier to use than a serving hatch. Eliminate doors between dining, cooking and larder areas, and, if possible, level out steps and changes of floor height.

Cabinets

The standard base cupboard depths of 600 mm (1 ft 11½ in) and wall-cupboard depths of 300 mm (12 in) are suitable for most disabled people, but wheelchair users will have difficulty reaching to the back of the work-top. Therefore cooker controls, electric sockets and switches should be moved nearer the front, either along the return wall or fixed into work-top fascias.

It is inadvisable to fix cabinets above 1800 mm (5 ft 11 in), because climbing on to stools to reach above this height can cause accidents. Hinged cupboard doors must swing 180° for wheelchair users. Sliding doors may be preferred, but they can be difficult for weak hands to operate. "D" handles, lever handles and continuous drawer and door pulls are more suitable than knobs. Magnetic catches are easier to use than ball catches.

Wheelchair users and the elderly have difficulty in reaching the back of fixed shelves in base cupboards. Drawers, pull-out baskets, trays and corner swivel shelves overcome this problem. Although shallow open shelves collect dust, they are better than cupboards. For the blind a small upstand on the front edge of shelves will prevent things being knocked off.

Sinks

A continuous knee space 400 mm (16 in) deep x 650 mm (2 ft 2 in) high is needed for a wheelchair to fit under a sink. The knee space should also be continued under the preparation area alongside the sink. To achieve this height the sink bowl must be shallower than usual, about 150 mm (6 in) deep. Insulating the underside of the bowl protects knees from the heat of the water. The fascia to the sink work-top should be recessed 50 mm (2 in) immediately under the work-top to allow for the wheelchair armrests.

It is a good idea to position the mixer taps to one side of a single-bowl sink so that pans standing on the draining area can be filled without lifting them in and out of the sink. Remote-controlled lever taps positioned on the sink fascia are easier to operate for people with limited reach or arthritic hands. It will be difficult to fit a waste-disposal unit without impeding the wheelchair knee space. A front-loading dishwasher, however, will be welcomed, because working at the sink is a tiring and awkward task for someone in a wheelchair.

Cookers

A split-level cooker is a better choice than a low-level oven with high-level grill, as it is more accessible. Generally, electric models are safer than naked-flame gas appliances. The blind, however, run the risk of burning themselves with the residual heat of electric rings and prefer gas because they can hear it when it is turned on. Gas cookers should have automatic ignition and should reignite automatically when a burner is accidentally blown out by a draught. Gas ovens should have flame-failure devices to cut off the gas should the flame be extinguished. Gas and electric cookers fitted with specially adapted lever or cross-shaped handles are helpful for those with missing or arthritic fingers and thumbs.

High-level ovens should be set with the bottom shelf not lower than 400 mm (16 in) from the floor, and the centre shelf should be level with the adjoining work-top. Drop-down doors provide a surface for hot dishes, but a wheelchair can come closer to an oven with side-hung doors. Slide-out oven shelves should be fitted with a "stop" to prevent them being pulled out completely.

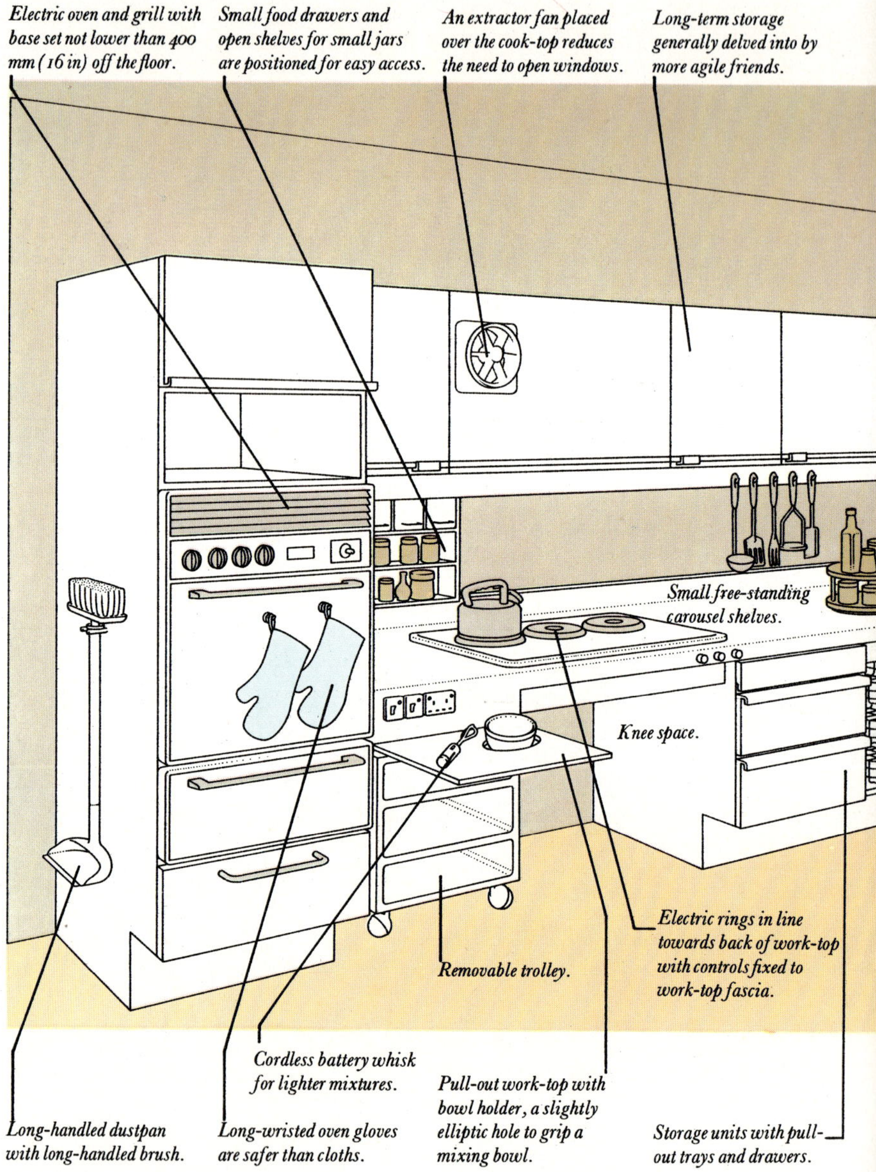

A kitchen designed specially for the wheelchair user (right).

	Wheelchair	Elderly	Ambulant disabled
Preferred work-top heights	800 mm (2 ft 7½ in)	850 mm (2 ft 9½ in)	900 mm (2 ft 11½ in)
Maximum upwards reach	1300 mm (4 ft 3½ in)	1700 mm (5 ft 7 in)	1800 mm (5 ft 11 in)
Maximum downwards reach	400 mm (16 in)	400 mm (16 in)	300 mm (12 in)

NB: These are approximate figures and should be used only as a general guide

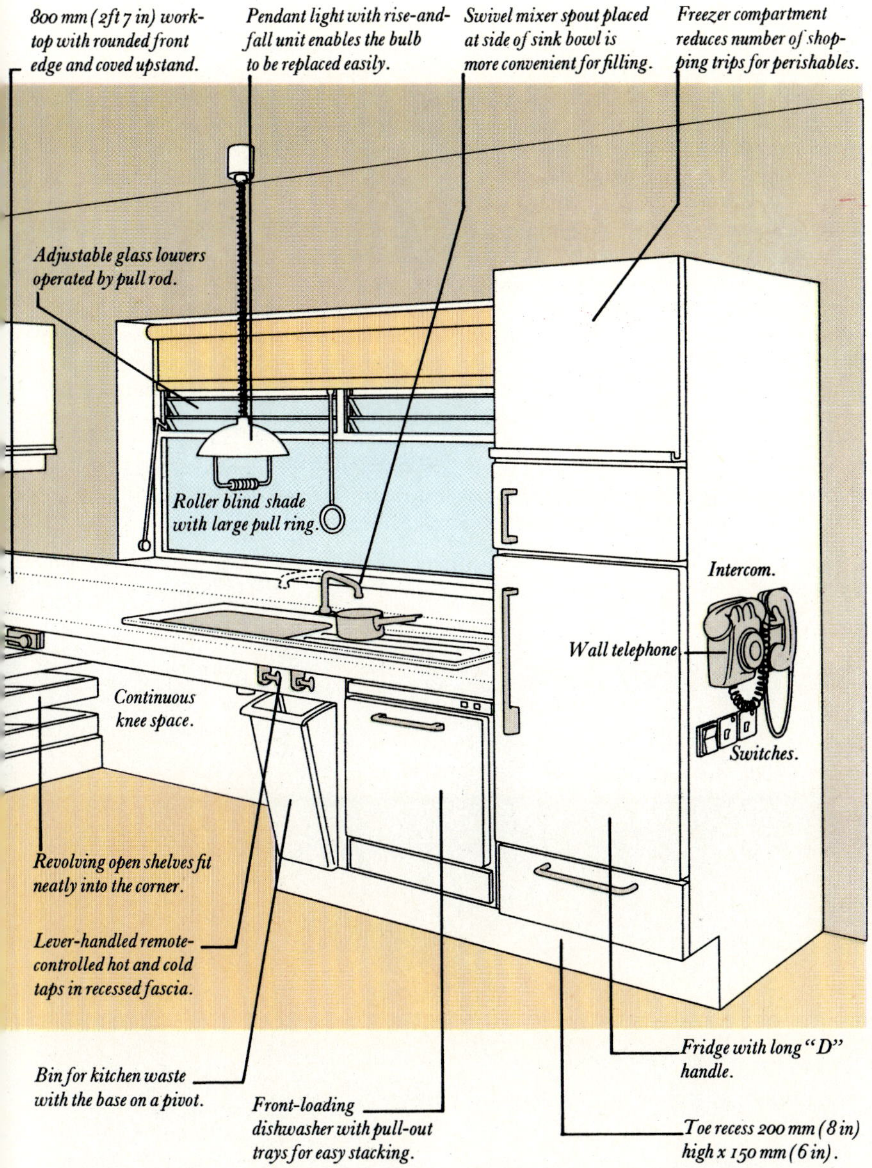

The main working areas in this kitchen (above) are easy to reach because there is room for a wheelchair to get close in to the work-top, which is set at a comfortable height.

To avoid possible arm burns, set hot-plate rings in a single line at the back of the work-top with a 250-mm (10-in) deep heat-proof parking space in front. However, for the wheelchair user knee space must be provided underneath the cook-top, controls should be brought forward, and fascias should be recessed.

Refrigerators

Fridges for wheelchair users should be mounted with the bottom shelf not lower than 400 mm (16 in) off the floor. A freezer compartment is very useful to cut down the number of shopping trips. Doors should have "D" handles and magnetic catches.

Windows

Check that windows can be opened easily. Top-hung fanlights are often out of reach and wheelchair users cannot open windows behind work-tops. Windows can be fitted with winding gear; lever-handled espagnolette bolts and glass louvers can be operated with a simple drop rod. Even with these devices, opening windows may still be difficult, so place an extractor fan over the cooker, controlled by an accessible switch or pull cord.

Helpful devices

Pull-out work-tops set at 660 mm (2 ft 2 in) high are invaluable for wheelchair users. A slightly elliptic hole 190 mm ($7\frac{1}{2}$ in) wide x 170 mm ($6\frac{1}{2}$ in) deep with a flexible PVC edge will grip mixing bowls well. Pull-out trolleys make an additional low-level work- or eating-surface, with open storage on the lower shelves. For the walking disabled, 35-mm ($1\frac{3}{8}$-in) diameter rails fixed along the length of the work-tops provide useful support. They should not project above the work-surface and must be very firmly fixed 35 mm ($1\frac{3}{8}$ in) from the working fascias. Carousels, or small revolving shelves, are convenient to store small items needed on the work-top. Stooping is avoided when a long-handled dustpan and brush are used. Wall telephones and a front-door or house intercom supply vital links with the family, neighbours or friends.

Electric aids

Light switches can be fixed with large rocker plates, which require little pressure, enabling them to be operated by an elbow or stick. Plug tops with plastic loops and ceiling pull switches with large pull rings are easy to use. Kettles are often unwieldy to lift, so wall-mounted water boilers with swivel spouts are much better in a kitchen. Small cooking devices such as electric frying-pans, deep-fryers, low-wattage stockpots and pop-up toasters may all be preferred to conventional cookers. Where hand strength or dexterity is limited, electric liquidizers, mixers, grinders, knife sharpeners, carving knives and can openers are invaluable as food-preparation aids, as are specially designed tools and utensils.

Choosing fuel

Is it to be gas or electricity, oil or solid fuel?

The two most popular fuels for cooking are gas and electricity. Gas has flexible controls, but is messier than electricity, which is versatile, clean but less economical. In Britain, most domestic gas is "natural" and is non-toxic. A smell has been added for safety reasons, to make it easier to discover if a gas burner has been turned on accidentally, and to assist the location of possible gas leaks. Being lighter than air, natural gas never collects in reservoirs that are likely to explode on chance ignition. The toxic town gas, manufactured from coal, has now been superseded in most areas by natural gas.

There is a higher fire risk with a naked gas flame than with an electric radiant ring. One other minor inconvenience of gas is having to light it, either by electric spark ignition or with a match, unless the gas ignites automatically when the control knob is switched on.

Only with gas is it possible to change the heat source instantly from a high to a low temperature, from a fast boil to a gentle simmer. Electricity is also controlled by turning a knob, but the burner is slower to respond. Even electricity enthusiasts will know how maddening it is waiting for an electric radiant ring or solid burner to heat up, or for its slow response to the control knob when more or less heat is required. Gas heats a pan quickly from the moment it is turned on, but electricity produces a more even heat slightly less speedily.

Electricity is therefore a more extravagant fuel, as heat is wasted when the radiant ring or ceramic cook-top cools down after use. Many electric stoves have at least one radiant ring that is dual controlled, allowing the small central coil to be heated separately. This is an economical way of heating small pans containing small quantities or for long, slow simmering. Black ceramic cook-tops utilize the principle of "magnetic induction" rather than conventional heating. Although expensive to buy, they minimize waste in cooking as the contents of the pan are warmed without the pan or cook-top rising much above body heat.

Auto-timers are also an economy and are a standard feature on most gas and electric ovens. They are not available with solid-fuel stoves.

The only undisputed advantage of electricity lies with convection ovens, which are quicker than radiant electric ovens, give a more even, stable heat than gas and allow dishes to brown properly wherever they are placed in the chamber. More sophisticated electric stoves have a separate smaller oven/grill compartment, which can save a considerable amount of money if used intelligently.

Some gas ovens provide "zones" of heat—the top of the oven being the hottest, descending to the bottom, which is the coolest part. It is therefore possible to cook a complete meal at the same time—an extremely efficient method of cooking as it saves time, money and valuable fuel. Other gas ovens have their flames at the side, not the back, and the oven temperatures are even throughout.

A choice of fuels for a London restaurant critic, who appreciates the virtues of both gas and electricity.

All gas stoves should be installed by authorized gas contractors, who will give advice on suitable positioning. There is likely to be an adequate supply for the stove if gas is already piped into your house for another purpose, such as firing the boiler. The stove is connected to the supply line either rigidly or, preferably, with a flexible hose. The latter method allows you to pull it out so you can clean behind it. In the absence of a mains supply, stoves can be converted to run on bottled gas. This, however, has the disadvantage of being heavier than air and is therefore more likely to collect in potentially explosive pockets.

Electricity is simple to install. There can be very few houses not lit by electricity, and the service cable will invariably be of an adequate size. Wiring a cooker control unit is not complex.

Solid-fuel stoves, which burn coke, coal, anthracite and wood, are heavy, semi-permanent fixtures that should be installed by experts. They are cheaper to run than gas or electricity and the entire unit is always hot—a gigantic radiator that heats the whole kitchen area. Most stoves have two solid-top burners (hot and simmering) and two ovens (also one hot, one for simmering). There are models available that have four ovens of graduated heat from fast-roast and bake to one for warming plates. On top there are two burners plus a flat aluminium plate to keep dishes hot. Solid-fuel stoves can be converted to gas or oil, which makes their heat control more flexible. Once mastered, many cooks declare that these stoves, with their constant heat, the option of truly slow cooking and their self-cleaning properties, are the finest of all.

Cleanliness could be the deciding factor in the choice of fuels. On balance, electricity probably has the edge in terms of cleaning convenience. Solid-fuel stoves tend to leave a film of dust around the kitchen, but their burners and ovens are "self-cleaning". You will need to remove and clean the metal grilles from a gas cook-top before tackling the cooked-on mess around the base of the burners. Most gas and electric ovens are fitted with linings that help to clean themselves while cooking. A few models of electric oven have a special control setting, which raises the oven to a very high temperature so that the stains and spills are carbonized and drop off. This is not completely efficient. Flat ceramic cook-tops have their electric heating elements concealed on the underside. The outside edges of the cook-top are sealed to prevent seepage of liquids, and so they are the ultimate in cleaning convenience.

For the most economical use of fuel, saucepans should match the size or be slightly larger than the ring or flame. You can also buy pans with two or more segments that allow cooking of more than one vegetable on the same ring. Any good-quality saucepan with a flat, preferably ground, base will perform well on any source of heat.

In practice there is no question of a dilemma between the two most popular forms of cooking. Apart from the obvious drawbacks, both systems are superb in their own right. An ideal arrangement, now widely enjoyed, is a gas cook-top complemented by a separate electric oven.

Microwave ovens are one of the recent technological advances in cooking. Their appeal is mainly for those who want to thaw or reheat food, as they greatly reduce cooking times. When cooking fresh food in a 600-watt microwave oven, poultry needs about five minutes to the pound, lamb about nine minutes and beef about eight.

Microwaves work by shaking up the food's constituent molecules so that they vibrate at great speed. The resulting friction creates heat so that cooking is from within. The container (which must not be metal) remains unaffected, but does grow warm as the food itself heats up.

This is a clean, simple way of preparing meals. The cook is never exposed to radiation: open the oven door and the microwaves cease instantly. The oven takes up very little space and can be housed on a working surface. Unfortunately, one of the limitations of a microwave oven is that it does not have browning facilities—thus cakes and pastries do not take on their familiar golden colour. However, there are available ovens that combine microwave and convection heating—the latter providing the browning facility.

Finally, there are the specialized cooking fuels, such as charcoal (for grills) and sawdust (used in smoking boxes). They are not in any way substitutes for other fuels, but serious cooks welcome them as antidotes to gas or electric spit-roasters. These, they feel, contradict the entire point of cooking outside an oven—which is to impregnate meat with the flavour of wood smoke.

A happy meeting of old and new—a modern electric cook-top set above a solid-fuel range preserved for its looks and its baking oven.

Water, gas and electricity

It is important to consult the building inspector and the water company before planning any new plumbing installations or major alterations to sinks, waste-disposal units, water softeners, dishwashers, washing machines, radiators, boilers, gas cookers, water heaters and so on. When designing a new kitchen, first decide on the maximum number of machines you are ever likely to need in that room. It is more economical and convenient to install all the supply and waste pipes in one operation than just to cater for your immediate requirements and subsequently have to arrange for someone to plumb in any later acquisitions you may make. Supply pipes for machines that have yet to be bought can be capped off until needed.

Water pressure

The correct level of water pressure is vital to the efficient working of instant gas water heaters and automatic dishwashers and washing machines. There must be at least 2.8 m (9 ft 1 in) between the water inlet of these machines and the underside of the cold-water tank—which may be difficult to achieve in high-rise buildings. The most satisfactory solution to this dilemma is for machinery that works from a cold-water feed only to be connected directly to the mains supply pipes. However, permission from the water company must be obtained before you do this.

Water pipes

A cold-water storage tank serves all the fittings in a house except the drinking-water taps, which should branch directly off the rising main.

The change-over from Imperial to metric pipe sizes can create problems with alterations to existing plumbing. Nevertheless, most pipe sizes are compatible and special connectors are available to adjust the old pipe bore to suit the new.

Supply and waste pipes are generally made of copper or plastics (PVC or polypropylene). Plastic is cheaper than copper and easier to handle should you decide to plumb it yourself, but it is not suitable for hot-water supplies due to its high rate of expansion and contraction. Copper pipes look neater and are less noisy, but they must never be connected direct to a galvanized steel cistern without a special connector, as the two metals are not compatible. Cold-water pipes on outside walls should be lagged to stop them freezing up in cold weather, and hot-water pipes should be insulated to conserve heat.

Mains services

The simplified house (right) shows how the location of a kitchen is dictated by the position of plumbing and drainage, which tend to be centred on one external wall.

cold-water pipes
hot-water pipes
electricity: power circuits
electricity: lighting circuits
drainage and waste pipes
gas pipes

Pipes from sinks and waste-disposal units must be fitted with a trap, or water seal. This stops smells coming back into the room from the drains, and provides a convenient access point from which to clear any blockages in the drain pipe.

Stopcocks should be fitted to the hot and cold supply pipes of dishwashers and washing machines so that the water can be turned off when the machinery needs an overhaul.

Water softeners

Hard water contains a high level of calcium and magnesium salts. It leaves scale in pipes and kettles, scum around the bath and sink, is unkind to the skin and more soap is needed than with soft water to create the same amount of lather. Soft water, on the other hand, can pick up trace metals from pipework, and this may eventually cause pipes to leak. Most people prefer the taste of hard water; soft water blends well with whisky, but it does not make a good cup of tea. Unless your water is exceptionally hard, or your skin particularly sensitive, the argument for water softeners is not very convincing.

The chemicals in water softeners immobilize hard minerals, which are then removed by a filter. Generally, the softeners have two parts: a resin tank and a brine tank. The most efficient and labour-saving models have an automatic cycle and only require periodic refilling with salt. Mains water softeners are connected to the rising main, leaving a branch to the kitchen for unsoftened drinking water. The softened water then passes into the main cold-water storage tank to feed the appliances in the rest of the house. Water softeners need a drain connection and some models will require an electric socket for a time-clock.

An alternative to installing a water softener is to use chemicals such as washing soda. However these products are often more harmful to sensitive skins than the original hard water.

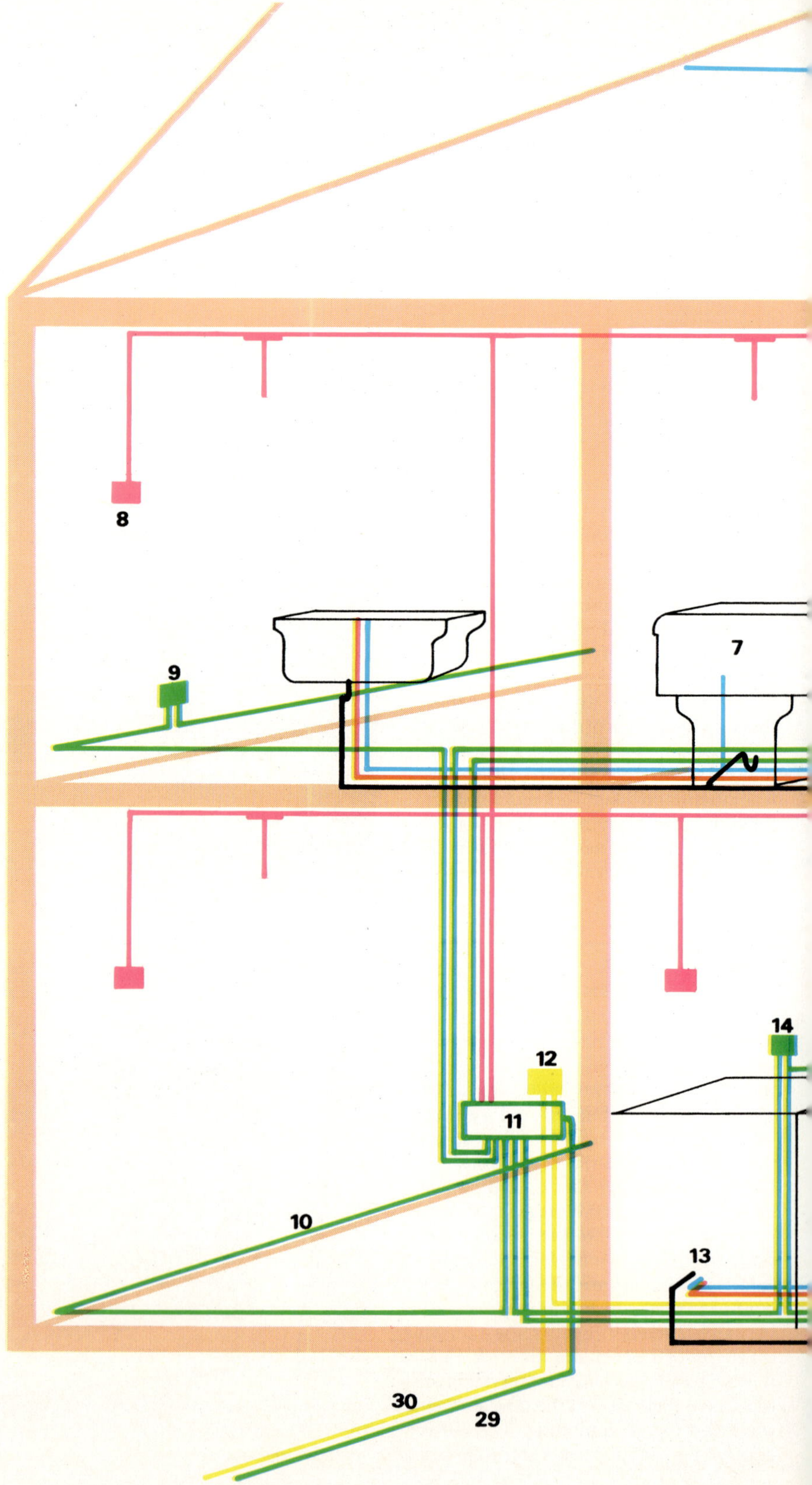

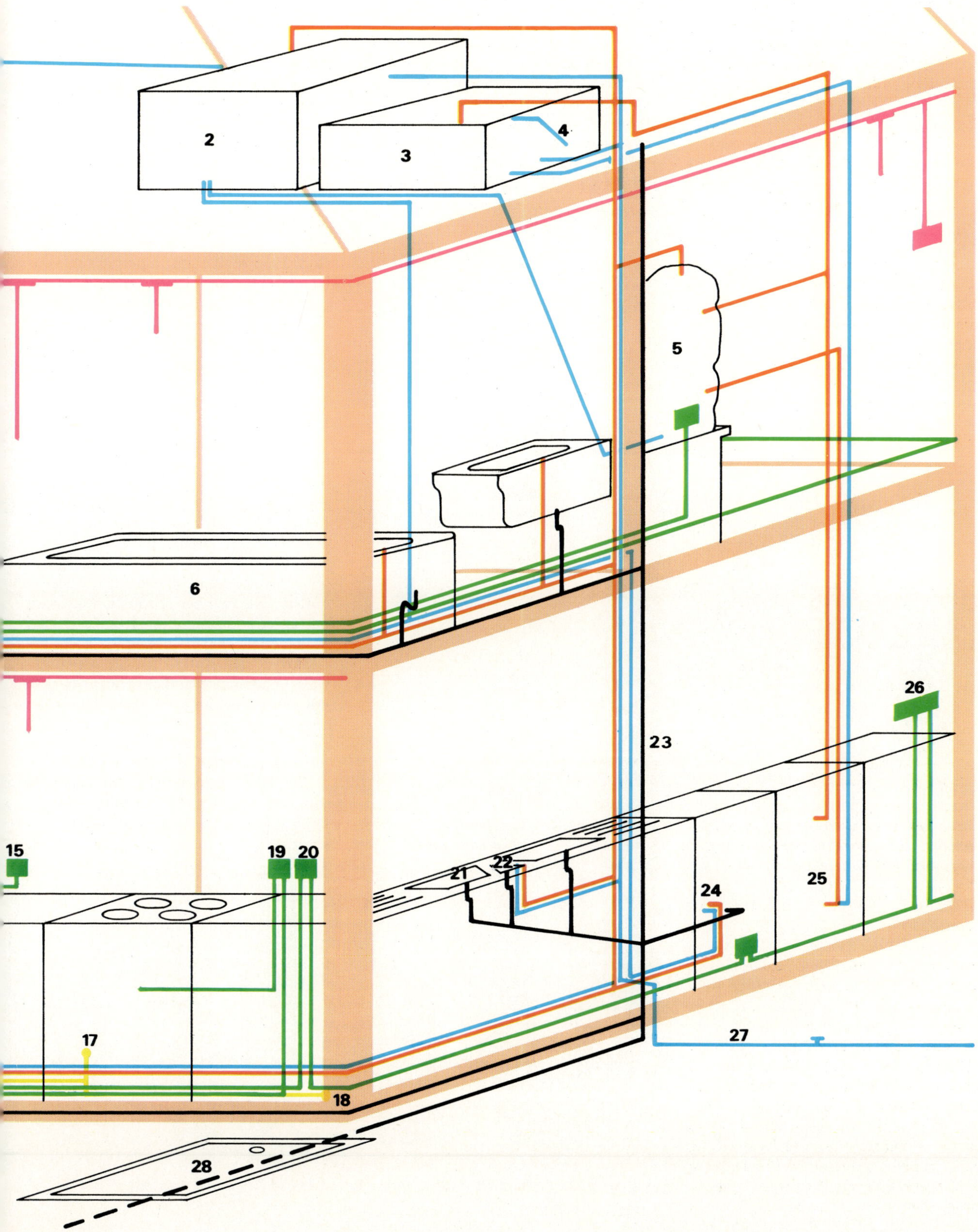

1 Cold-water overflow from main storage tank.
2 Cold-water storage cistern supplied direct from rising main.
3 Feed and expansion cistern for cold water.
4 Cold-water overflow from expansion cistern.
5 The well-lagged hot-water storage cylinder.
6 Bath supplied with hot and cold water and waste pipe.
7 Lavatory with soil branch pipe and cold-water supply.
8 Switch for overhead light.
9 Power socket outlet on ring main.
10 Ground-floor ring main circuit, continuing round at that level until it eventually returns to fusebox.
11 Electricity meter and combined master switch and consumer's fusebox (containing fuses for all circuits in house).
12 Mains gas meter.
13 Washing machine plumbed in for hot- and cold-water supply, with waste branch pipe.
14 Wall-mounted switched socket outlet, for washing machine.
15 Switched spur outlet, for spin-drier.
16 Spin-drier with waste outlet.
17 Gas supply pipe capped off, but convenient for possible gas cooker.
18 Gas supply capped off but ready to be extended into rest of house.
19 Separate fused socket for cooker.
20 Socket outlet for small appliances over work-top unit.
21 Double-bowled sink, served by a swivel mixer tap. The cold water is supplied direct from the rising main. Between the two bowls is a small waste sink (22) with plumbed-in waste-disposal unit.
23 Central waste pipe for house.
24 Dishwasher plumbed in with hot and cold water and fitted waste pipe.
25 Kitchen boiler.
26 Wall-mounted twin-socket outlet over work-top and cupboard.
27 Rising main with water authority's stopcock.
28 Airtight cover over sewage inspection chamber.
29 Mains cable supplying house with electricity.
30 Mains gas supply pipe.

Water, gas and electricity

Natural gas is found in oil deposit regions and is the type most commonly used. In Britain, it has now almost completely superseded "town" gas, which is manufactured from coal.

Mains gas

Due to the potentially explosive nature of gas, any installations or alterations must be undertaken by the gas company or one of their approved contractors; you should on no account attempt gas installations yourself.

However, a few details to bear in mind when planning your kitchen are that small gas pipes are generally made of copper and larger ones of wrought iron or mild steel. Sharp bends or angles in pipe-work reduces pressure, so pipes should rise steadily from the mains gas entry point in the house. The pipes should be accessible to facilitate leak detection and must not touch the wall surface. So ensure they are properly supported with metal clips and encased with a sleeve where they pass through walls. They should be kept well away from electric cables and hot-water pipes, and a stopcock must be provided for each appliance. If free-standing cookers are fitted with flexible metal hose connections, they can easily and conveniently be wheeled out for cleaning.

The fumes from natural gas are noxious only after combustion. Therefore, good ventilation is essential in a room with gas cookers and water heaters without flues, as these create fumes and water vapour. All appliances that require flues, such as central-heating boilers and multi-point water heaters, are safer with a "balanced" flue that takes in air for combustion from the outside, not from within the room, and is built into an outside wall directly behind the appliance. Where a "conventional" flue (i.e. pipe) is used, permanent ventilation by air brick must be provided. Should fumes persist in the house, turn off the mains gas tap, which is located next to the meter, before seeking expert advice about the cause of the fumes.

Bottled gas

Where piped gas is not available, cookers, refrigerators, water heaters, fires and lights can be supplied from bottled gas. This is normally Butane or Propane and has a high calorific value, which means that much smaller pipes and gas jets are used than for mains gas. The flame is easily affected by draught, so appliances should be positioned in a sheltered place otherwise the jets will become clogged up with soot.

The gas is stored under pressure in steel containers, which should be kept outside and not placed in cupboards or near heat sources. They can be linked together to provide the correct pressure for any number of appliances. Bottled gas is not poisonous, but can be explosive, so all pipe runs should be accessible for quick and easy leak detection.

Electrical installations

Remember that electricity can be dangerous if not correctly planned and installed. Water and steam are particularly hazardous if in contact with badly insulated wiring, so keep a vigilant check on all electrical installations, especially in your kitchen or laundry. When carrying out any electrical work, ensure that the supply is turned off at the mains or that the relevant appliance is unplugged from the socket outlet.

Wiring

Every household has a consumer unit (fuseboard) containing all the necessary fuses or miniature circuit breakers. A ring main consists of a continuous circuit that connects all the power-socket outlets, thereby spreading the electrical load evenly over the entire circuit. Each spur circuit, which is a branch off the ring main, can serve a maximum of two further socket outlets. The number of spur sockets must not exceed the number of power socket outlets on the ring main itself.

Stoves and water heaters are high-wattage appliances and must be run back to the consumer unit (fuseboard) on an entirely separate circuit to that of the main ring or rings, as there is a separate ring to serve the power sockets on each floor.

The ring main system has now generally superseded the British radial wiring system. Each power socket was wired direct to a separate fuse in the main fusebox and was

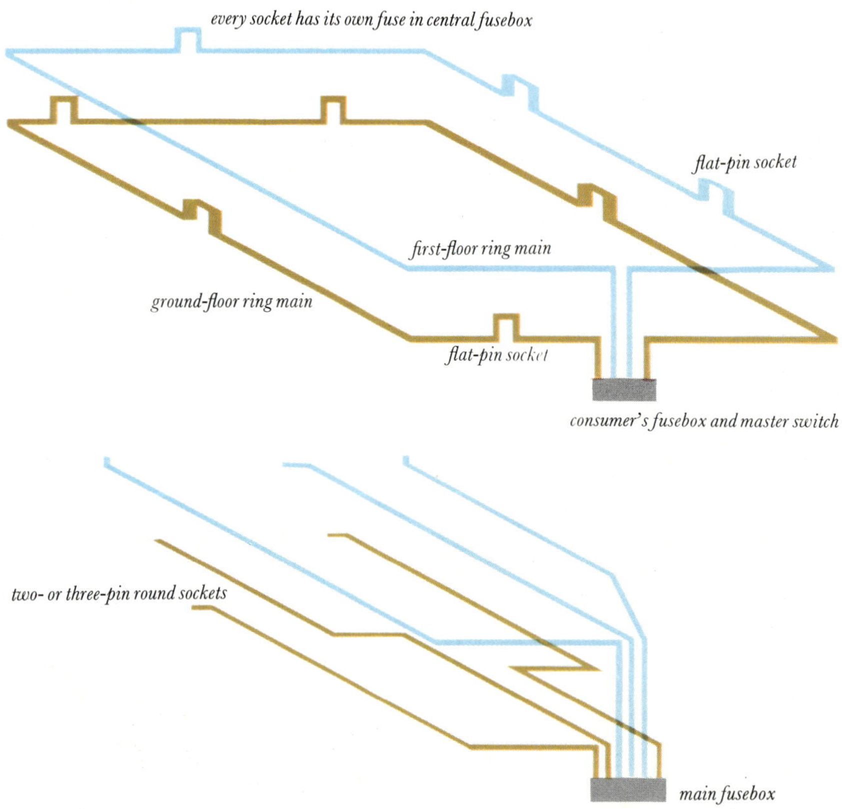

The old British radial wiring system (above) is now largely superseded by the ring main system (top), where the ring on each floor is fused separately and each plug is fused. In the radial system the power sockets have their individual fuses in the main fusebox.

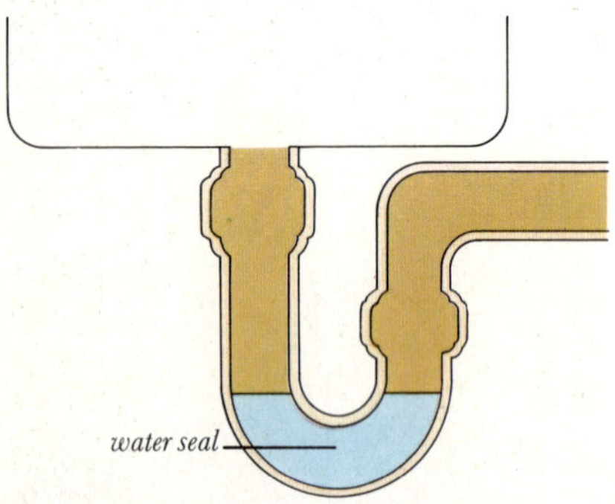

Cross-section of sink sealed with P-trap for horizontal waste outlet.

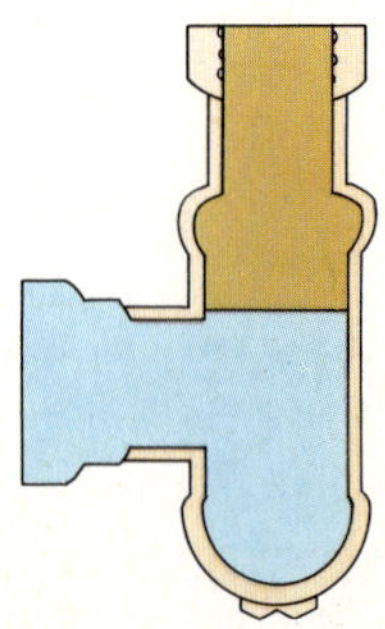

Bottle trap with cleaning eye at bottom for easy access.

A simple S-bend trap for vertical outlet, with cleaning eye at bottom.

Two-piece S-trap with detachable section for unblocking waste pipe.

rated to suit the socket it served. The power points had round holes to fit either two- or three-pin plugs.

This radiant method of wiring is still sometimes chosen for wiring an extension or an extra power point.

Electrical cables should be kept well away from water pipes, flues and other heat sources. In solid floors they must be run in conduits, and when chased into plastered walls they must be protected with metal channels.

Socket outlets

In the kitchen a minimum of four socket outlets should be provided for portable electric appliances such as food mixers and kettles. These sockets should be fixed to the wall about 150 mm (6 in) above the height of the work-top where the appliance is to be used. They must be kept well away from water sources, including possible steam from boiling pots on the stove. Twin-socket outlets are preferable to single ones, because they diminish the need for adaptors, which could put too much strain on the circuit and possibly cause a dangerous fire.

Switched spur outlets

Fixed electric appliances up to 3 kw rating, such as dishwashers, washing machines, tumble-driers, waste disposers and extractor fans, should be connected to a switched spur outlet by a flex sufficiently long to allow the machine to be pulled out for maintenance. Switches should be positioned above the counter-top level and away from water sources. They should be adjacent to but not obscured by the machine and should be readily accessible so that they can be quickly turned off in an emergency. Neon indicators in switchplates are helpful reminders that the power to the machine is switched on.

Plugs

Before fitting a plug to an appliance, first check that its voltage is the same as that in the rest of your house; if the voltage is different you will need a transformer. Also, you must ensure that the correct rating fuse is used so that the appliance will be protected from damage should a fault occur. When wiring the plug, remove only sufficient insulation from the cable to fit into the relevant terminal. Twist the wire ends so that stray wires cannot make contact with others and cause a short circuit; and always double check that you have connected the cables to their correct terminal.

Electrical assistance is carefully concealed yet readily available from these conveniently placed power sockets (above).

Gas rings on demand (below)—a flexible way to cope with a fluctuating cooking schedule, yet easily tidied away between times.

If gas or water pipes cannot easily be hidden, use them instead to concoct a dramatic and eye-catching display (above).

Planning your kitchen

Lighting

The kitchen is first and foremost a place of work: it needs good lighting at all times. Daylight must be supplemented by artificial light for both dark corners and dull days. The prime ingredient of good lighting is its quality, which is affected by the colours and textures of the various finishes surrounding the light sources. Pale colours reflect light and dark colours absorb it. Matt surfaces diffuse light and gloss surfaces cause reflections that can create glare. Glare tires the eyes and should be prevented by shielding light sources and avoiding too strong a contrast between light and dark areas. On the other hand, too bland or uniform lighting makes a room seem dull and formless, so a balance must be struck. The most effective kitchen lighting is where the light sources are not apparent but the work-areas are efficiently illuminated. The exception to this rule is a lamp fitting consciously used as a decorative object.

Different types of illumination are needed for work-areas, general background, dining-table, special displays, appliances and storage.

Work-surface lighting

The most efficient method is to fix strip lighting to the underside of wall cupboards or shelves directly above counters. The lamps should be fixed to the front edges of cupboards so that the counter is evenly lit. Shield the lamps with a batten or opal diffuser. Where there are no wall cupboards, recessed or surface lights can be positioned on the wall or ceiling immediately above the work-tops. Hoods for extractor fans over cooking areas are a good housing for lights directed down on to the stove. It is important to see what's going on in the oven and, sensibly, some cookers have their own interior lights. Storage cupboards should not be forgotten. If possible, fix lights inside operated by a simple door switch.

General lighting

Avoid a central ceiling light if it is the single source, because it throws shadows on the counters. Background light should always be subordinate to work-top lighting. Fully luminous ceilings can be created with suspended louvers, which conceal fluorescent lights. These lights can be wired with two or more circuits to achieve different lighting levels. Walls can be "washed" with lights recessed into ceilings, and ceilings lit by lights fixed on top of wall cupboards. Where individual ceiling fittings are used, several low-wattage lamps will give a more even light than a single large one.

Concealed lighting

When positioning concealed lighting, check that the bulbs are hidden from sitting as well as standing eye levels. Also ensure that they are not betrayed by mirrors or other reflective surfaces. Fittings should be reasonably accessible for cleaning and bulb replacement.

The dining-table

Use a low-hung pendant fitting over the eating area. The bulb should not be visible when sitting at the table. Rise-and-fall fittings can be easily adjusted to suit the varying eye levels of a growing family. A plug-in ceiling rose is useful for pendant lights, which might need to be moved if the table is taken away for a party. An alternative to a pendant light is a cylindrical "downlight", which can be surface mounted or recessed into the ceiling. Dining areas adjacent to large glass doors or windows can be dramatically lit at night by spotlights in the garden supplemented only by candles on the table.

A well-lit kitchen. From left to right: tungsten strip light over picture, light inside refrigerator, rise and fall pendant over dining-table, spot-light on garden, strip lighting over work-surface, and a light in the eye-level oven.

Strip lighting over work surfaces casts an even glow and a lamp in the extractor hood makes for brighter cooking (above).

A bold fluorescent tube enclosed in a perspex panel lights up a cook-top more efficiently than a hanging lamp (below).

A subtle combination of strip lighting and cylindrical downlighters (above) bring a dark kitchen out of the shadows without any headaching glare.

A pendant lamp with an opaque shade provides a pool of light over a table (above) but doesn't dazzle diners. The depth of the shade and the use of a rise and fall fitting control the exact area illuminated (below).

Clever lighting, thoughtful decor and an attractive arrangement of practical equipment lend charm to this inexpensive kitchen (above).

Concealed lighting behind a batten fixed to the underside of a high storage unit angles light on to a work-top (below left) and direct overhead lighting cuts out shadows over washing-up areas (below right).

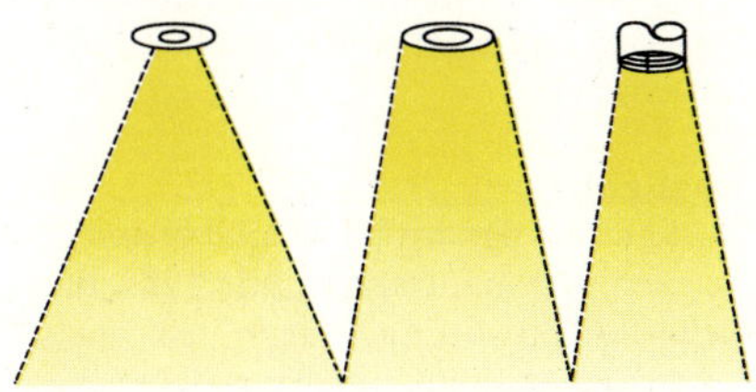

Downlighters give a different area of light according to the method of fitting. The diagram (above) shows the variations: fully recessed into the ceiling, semi-recessed or mounted on the ceiling surface.

Concealed strip lighting brightens up the work-surfaces and cheers the walls—but it is the warmly glowing ceiling that gives the room its character (above).

Even a small square of overhead lighting brings a gleam to china and turns a storage alcove into a decorative feature (above).

Light variations

Fluorescent bulbs use less electricity and last five times longer than tungsten. They are cool, which is good for kitchens already full of heat-generating equipment. The lamps have a slight flicker that can be disturbing and thus should be fitted with diffusing shades or concealed behind battens. Their lengths range from 450 mm to 2440 mm (18 in to 96 in) with miniature sizes from 150 to 530 mm (6 in to 21 in). Circular fluorescent tubes are also available, in two sizes, 300 mm and 400 mm (12 in and 16 in) diameter. Fluorescent lights need control gear that can be remote or incorporated within the fitting, such as the "batten" fittings, which are particularly suitable for mounting over work-tops. They can be "switchstarted" or "quickstarted", i.e., come on slowly or instantaneously. They also emit a slight hum, which can be reduced by mounting the fluorescent fittings on rubber washers. Fluorescent light appears colder than the yellow tones of tungsten. The best colour to use is "De Luxe Warm White", which blends better with the other house lighting.

Tungsten tubes are also available, in sizes ranging from 220 mm to 1200 mm (9 in to 48 in), but have a short life, are expensive to replace and emit a fair amount of heat. However, as they give an exceptionally mellow and sympathetic light, they may be preferred to fluorescent lighting with its flicker, hum and relatively cold tone.

There are many different shapes and sizes of tungsten bulbs. Most common in the UK are the GLS (General Lighting Service) lamps, 40-150 watts, which come clear, pearly or silica coated, the latter giving the most evenly diffused light.

Spotlights can be fitted with ISL (Internally Silvered Lamps), 40-150 watts, or PAR (Press Armourglass Reflectors), 35-300 watts, which are also suitable for external use. Crown-silvered lamps are used with parabolic reflectors to give a carefully controlled glareless beam. Spotlight lamps are more expensive and shorter lived than GLS lamps. Some fittings are suitable for either type of lamp, which allows more flexibility of use and the possibility of cheaper running costs. Tungsten lamps can shatter from thermal shock when splashed with water, so should be used in totally enclosed fittings if near steamy or wet places.

Heat lamps using a 300-watt tungsten infra-red hard-glass bulb can be used to keep freshly cooked food hot without the risk of overcooking or drying out. They should be mounted 330 mm to 450 mm (13 in 18 in) above the food surface, and will heat an area approximately 380 mm (15 in) in diameter.

Lighting track is an aluminium channel 1220 mm to 3660 mm (4 ft to 12 ft) long into which a wide variety of lights can be fixed anywhere along its length, giving great flexibility of position and easy adjustability to suit different tasks. The channel encloses continuous lengths of live conductors, which could be dangerous if accessible to children or positioned over wet areas. The tracks can be wall or ceiling mounted and are useful for low-powered kitchen tools, providing the total wattage of the track is not exceeded.

Gaslight

Gaslight fittings are still available and can be used with natural or bottled gas. Brass swan-necked fitting, single—or multi-armed, are manufactured as wall or ceiling lights with simple spherical bowls or mock Victorian shades. Each mantle gives about 30 to 40 watts. The light has an atmospheric greenish tinge, a slight hiss and a warm smell. Small-bore copper supply pipes can be chased into the walls. Gas lights need regular cleaning and the mantles have a shorter life than electric bulbs.

A large skylight and brilliant overhead lamps lend a bright, spacious air by day or night. But built-in units like the cook-top still need their own concealed lighting (above).

Switches and dimmers

Light switches should be of the "rocker" type, easily accessible and positioned at elbow height for easy action when hands are full. When the kitchen has more than one entrance there should be two-way switches. The different lighting areas such as work-surface, ceiling and dining-table should be separately switched to provide flexible lighting levels and economy of use.

Dimmer switches can be most effectively fitted to control tungsten lamps. To dim fluorescent lights requires special fittings with additional gear and wiring. Door switches are useful for interior cupboard lights. A door switch combined with an automatic door closer in the larder makes it easier to enter and leave with full hands.

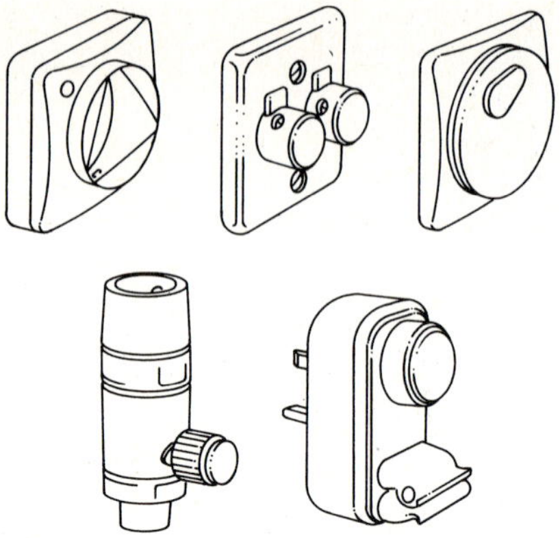

Dimmer switches combined with on/off switches (top line of sketch above) are easy to fit. Brightness is controlled by turning the knob. There are also bayonet-type adaptors to fix into bulb sockets and dimmer plugs to control one or two fittings (bottom line) which need no rewiring. However, these still use as much electricity when dimmed as when brightly lit.

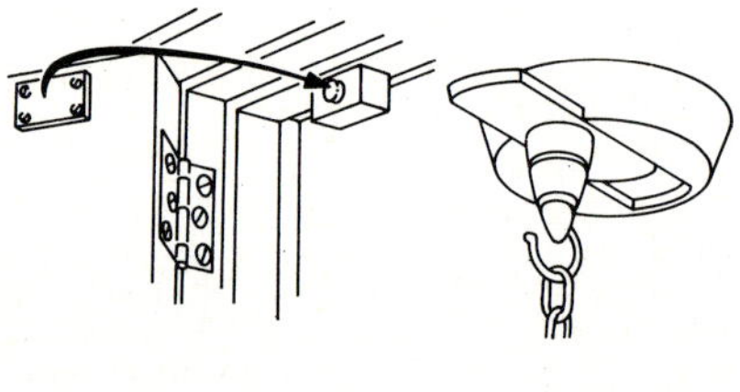

Door switches that come on automatically when cupboard doors are opened (above left) are operated by a button set in the door frame. Lamps are easier to clean with a detachable ceiling rose (above right). The lower part slides out; the upper part, connected to the mains, remains fixed in position on the ceiling.

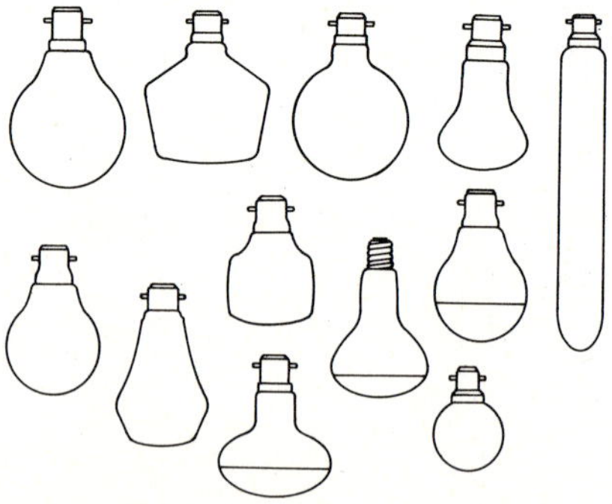

Incandescent light bulbs containing tungsten wire are available in many different shapes and colours, some silvered internally, others only at the crown. Fluorescent tubes can distort colour, but are particularly useful in kitchens because they reduce shadow.

Despite the relatively short life of the bulbs, the owner of this kitchen (above) prefers the warm glow of tungsten lamps.

A busy room crowded with equipment gains from lighting kept simple: these bold fluorescent panels (above) look cool and unfussy.

Not a cinema foyer, but a severely practical American kitchen given a gently welcoming touch by incandescent lighting (below).

Lifted from the shop floor, industrial lighting installed over the working area worked out well in this kitchen (above).

Heating and air conditioning

Though a kitchen generates a lot of heat, a back-up system is always welcome, especially in a large kitchen on a chilly winter morning. While it makes sense to relate the heating to the rest of the house, there are special considerations that apply to the kitchen. As wall space is often scarce, conventional radiators and storage heaters can be difficult to place. Remember, too, that good ventilation is vital.

Radiators

Radiators are usually hung 150 mm (6 in) above the floor, using up valuable wall space. Wall cupboards can be hung above a radiator, but not within 300 mm (12 in) or the heat will warp the unit and damage the goods inside. But in fact a radiator can be hung anywhere on the wall and in any position, as long as the pipework can supply it with water. Hung up high, it will not interfere with the layout at all. Long, thin radiators can be turned sideways, running from floor to ceiling, so that only a narrow width of wall is sacrificed.

Skirting heating units are very low, thin radiators about 228 mm (9 in) high. As they are so small, you will need several to generate sufficient heat. Units can be fitted above skirting heaters as the heat is not sufficiently concentrated to do any damage.

Fan convectors

Fan convectors are smaller and neater than radiators with a similar heat output. Fans can be thermostatically controlled, which is useful in kitchens, where intermittent heat is produced by cooking equipment.

Gas heaters

Individual gas heaters are small and compact, giving out a considerable amount of heat for their size. They must be sited on an outside wall as they require flue ventilators. If there is pipework already supplying gas to the cooker, then gas heating is an economical choice.

Electric heaters

Electric heaters, of which there are several types, are clean and easy to operate. Individual electric wall heaters should be fitted well above wall cupboards, and angled carefully to avoid misplaced draughts of hot air. Alternatively, free-standing electrically heated oil-filled radiators are efficient and fairly economical. Less suitable are night storage heaters because their bulkiness will preclude them from all but the largest kitchens.

Underfloor heating

Underfloor heating is ideal for ceramic tiles, slate, marble, stone or brick finishes as these materials are kinder to the feet when warmed. Sub-floors are heated by electric wiring or hot-water pipes embedded in the concrete or screed, and their temperature is thermostatically controlled. Pipes and wires must be deeply embedded to get an even spread of heat over the whole floor.

This method is well worth considering if a new kitchen is being built or if a timber sub-floor is being replaced with a concrete one. The snag is that underfloor heating is very slow, taking a day or two to warm up or cool down. This is very inconvenient where the weather changes rapidly, and it is unsuitable for week-end homes unless it can be turned on before you arrive.

Wall and ceiling heating

Electric wiring embedded in the plaster thickness of vacant walls or ceilings provides instant heat at the touch of the switch. Once the wires have been plastered in and painted over, it is important to remember where the wires run, otherwise putting up a shelf or nailing in a picture

A vertical radiator emphasizes the room's stark design. The floor-to-ceiling window is double glazed to prevent heat loss in winter.

hook could be dangerous. Kitchen units should not hang over the heating elements as this will reduce the heat output and also damage the units and their contents. If there is no free wall space, you could always wire up the ceiling, but heat from above is not always comfortable. Wall and ceiling heating is economical to install if incorporated into the original design of a house, but it is expensive to run.

Warm-air ducts

If the rest of the house is heated by this method then it is simple to run a duct into the kitchen and fit a grille in a convenient spot. Grilles are small and unobtrusive; their positioning will depend on the duct work. Warm-air systems must be properly designed so that the heater runs noiselessly and the warm air is pleasantly distributed.

Solar heating

Obtaining heat from the sun is one way of reducing other fuel and energy needs. Most houses that use solar energy have solar panels of copper, steel or aluminium with a glass cover incorporated into their roofs or south-facing walls. These collectors absorb the sun's direct and diffused energy and transfer it into a pumped circulating liquid, usually water with an anti-freeze additive for winter use.

How much hot water can be provided "free" varies enormously throughout the world, and even within a country, as it depends on the hours of sunshine. For example, in the United Kingdom roughly half (200 kWh) the average annual requirement for domestic hot water can be provided "free" by combining solar-heated water with the normal boiler immersion heater in a larger than usual (100 gal) well-insulated hot-water cylinder.

The trouble with solar energy for house heating is that there is least of it available when it is most required, but research shows that heavily insulated room-sized tanks of water, heated up in the summer excess period, can prove a useful reserve to the heating needs of a well-insulated house.

Back to the range

Not so long ago most kitchens had coke boilers or solid-fuel ranges, which warmed the room and cooked the food. Today that same warmth and comfort is provided without the attendant mess and fuss by cooker/boilers, which run on oil, gas or solid fuel. They can be adapted to heat domestic hot water, and some of the larger models will heat a number of radiators as well. All cooker/boilers need a proper flue for ventilation.

Air conditioning

The great advantage of an air-conditioned house is that it is cool in summer and warm in winter. The ideal system, with air cleaners, heaters, coolers and humidifiers, can automatically provide the perfect indoor climate all year round, and there is a wide range of equipment, of varying degrees of sophistication, to achieve this.

Dry air can irritate the skin, eyes and throat, so if you are thinking of having a warm-air system, try to build in a humidifier to counteract the dryness. In some systems only part of the warm air is extracted to the outside; the remainder is recirculated to preserve the required degree of heat or coolness.

Even if you have air conditioning in your kitchen, it is important that you have a separate extractor, preferably near the stove, to cope with the extra grease- and moisture-laden atmosphere that is endemic to all kitchens.

A solid-fuel range recollects kitchens that were warm and welcoming on winter nights, even if overpoweringly hot in summertime.

Ventilation

In a kitchen ventilation is vital. Cooking produces steam, fat-laden fumes and lingering smells. Good ventilation is not just for the personal comfort of the cook; heat and moisture cause condensation, which can rapidly play havoc with timberwork and ruin decorations.

Condensation

Warm, moisture-laden air condenses on contact with cold surfaces, and it is not only the kitchen walls that will suffer. If there is no specially designed ventilation system to whisk away the water vapour at source, then the warm air, pregnant with moisture vapour, will escape from the kitchen and drift around the house until it finds a cool place—such as a north-facing wall—where it will turn to condensation on the walls or furnishings of a nearby room. To avoid this problem, which is endemic in kitchens and bathrooms, water vapour must be extracted at source and walls and ceilings should be kept warm. Always insulate the ceilings of one-storey kitchens. If outside walls are also insulated, the kitchen will be cheaper to heat and less likely to stream with condensation—an economy well worth while despite the initial expense.

The reversible kitchen (below) has matching tubes and cubes on floor and ceiling. The box above the stove pipes fumes away.

Fans and hoods

To extract steamy air efficiently fans must be placed high up over the cooker. Kitchens, especially those with no windows, need constant ventilation. When all pans are furiously bubbling, an extra boost will be needed, so it is wise to choose a fan with a speed-control switch. Fans smaller than 225 mm (9 in) cannot cope with a sudden burst of steam.

Extractor fans should be fixed into an outside wall. Fans fitted into windows, although cheaper, are rarely satisfactory as the window must be shut for the fan to work and the noise level is irritatingly high. Shutters that open only when the fan is switched on eliminate possible draughts in the kitchen.

An extractor hood fitted over the cooker and sink will collect smoke and steam at source. There are two types of extractor hood: one kind cleans the air by passing it through a filter of charcoal, which must be changed at regular intervals; the other more efficient system removes smoke, steam and smells and a certain amount of heat via a vent pipe to the outside.

Pure, vivid colours stay that way with the help of a fierce extractor (below) that sucks up steam as it emerges from the kettle.

Ventilated equipment

There is a range of electric cook-tops with a variety of grills and glass-ceramic cooking plates, which have an air-extract grille on a level with the cooking surface. An internal fan whisks the smoke and steam down from the surface of the unit to an outside ventilator, either set in an outside wall or roof. With ducting adaptors below the floor or in the ceiling the unit could be placed on an island or peninsular unit. This system gets rid of smoke and fumes at source, although other ventilation should be provided for the rest of the kitchen.

Abstract sculpture or ventilation shaft? The hard-edge-style hood (above) keeps the yellow kitchen as bright as an art gallery.

A shining example of metallic chic (above). The lustrous, stainless-steel ventilation hood keeps the air sweet and the pans pristine.

The neat little grid extractor (above) swallows the greasy fumes before they have a chance to waft upwards or outwards.

The professional's choice (below)—an all-enveloping copper hood that throws light on the cooking and combats clouds of steam.

The monumental ventilation hood (above) provides light for the stove and acts as a hanging cupboard for spices and sauces.

Gourmet aromas from Clement Freud's oven and cook-top fly into the overarching Formica arm of the ventilator (below).

Vital item in the happy couple's three-piece kitchen suite, the hood (above) clears the air for meals eaten almost off the cook-top.

Waste-disposal

The main problem with waste is that there is far too much of it, even in the smallest household. How you get rid of it depends very much on where you live. Dwellers in high-rise apartments must rely on the waste-disposer, the chute, the compactor or incinerator. The garden-owner, however, can usefully recycle a good deal of general household rubbish via the compost heap or with a bonfire.

Second time around
Recycling waste is a justifiable obsession in our over-consuming Western World. Some local authorities already ask householders to separate waste into four broad categories: organic matter, paper, glass and metal—and many more are considering this policy. The good gardener conserves all vegetable waste and anything that is biodegradable, such as eggshells, tea leaves, newspapers and rags, for the compost heap. Clean dry paper neatly packed is generally welcomed by refuse collectors or charitable organizations. Glass jars and bottles should be returned or re-used wherever possible. Most plastic wrappings, sadly, have no foreseeable second use.

Waste bins and bags
Pedal, hinged- or swing-lid bins are generally made of plastic, which is colourful and cheap, or of stainless steel, which is more glamorous. But bins are rarely beautiful and are best concealed while still allowing quick and easy access. If there is no waste-disposal unit, site the bin near the sink. It should be lined with plastic or paper bags that can be sealed for removal. A waste bucket fitted inside a sink-unit door is a good kitchen notion, providing it does not collide with the plumbing.

Waste-disposal units
A waste-disposal unit devours a good deal of kitchen waste, including small bones, pips, paper, cardboard egg-boxes and waxed food cartons. But it will not digest metal, plastics, rubber, cloth, large bones, ceramics or string. In fact it disposes of only about 15 per cent of household rubbish, but for the flat-dweller it does eliminate the storing of rotting food waste. Waste-disposers multiply the amount of sludge in sewers and increase the household water consumption by 9 litres (2 gal) of water per head per day. This may cause problems in some rural areas, so local authorities should be consulted before you install one. A waste-disposer is possible for a household not connected to a sewerage system providing the capacity of the septic tank is no less than 2250 litres (500 gal).

Waste-disposers use little electricity and require little maintenance. But they are noisy, and the noise increases with age. All the same, the running time is so short it should not be too much of a problem. A waste unit should be installed by a plumber. Ideally it should be placed in the second sink, but if there is only one, install a separate waste outlet for use when the disposer is blocked. The disposer should be fitted with a rubber gasket to a suitable waste outlet, and the waste pipe, with a "P" or "S" trap, should have easy bends to prevent blockages. In a flat, a length of flexible waste pipe will reduce the amount of noise transmitted to the rest of the plumbing system. A fast-running cold-water tap should be installed over the bowl (hot water lines the pipes with melted grease). Position switches well away from water supplies for reasons of safety.

Choosing a waste-disposal unit
A waste-disposer consists of a fixed ring with rotating grinders operated by a small electric motor. Choose a model with reversible grinders, which help unjam blocked material and reduce wear on the machine. The motor should have a thermal overload device to prevent it from burning out when jammed. There are two basic types: the continuous feed, into which waste is fed while the grinder is running; and the batch feed, where the unit is loaded, the plug inserted, and the motor switched on. Continuous-feed models are more flexible, but batch-feed units are safer, especially when children are about, because the grinders cannot operate unless the plug is in position.

Dustbins
Dustbins should be placed near the kitchen on a firm, dry base. If you conceal them in a bunker or shed, make sure there is adequate access for the garbage collectors.

A hatch in the kitchen that discharges waste directly into dustbins outside the house obviates the need for an indoor bin.

Metal bins should be rust-proof, with rubber lids and feet to cut down noise during rubbish collection. Choose a size to suit the household and the number of collections made during the month. Plastic bins, which are not suitable for hot ashes, must be sufficiently heavy to prevent them being blown over and they must have a lid that locks on.

Incinerators
An incinerator will reduce about 90 per cent of household waste to ashes; this makes a great saving on storage and collection costs. But though the ash may be used on the garden, the opportunity for recycling waste will be lost and neighbours may find the smoke objectionable. Some central-heating boilers are designed to burn rubbish, a very real contribution to the household economy. Incinerators are fired by gas or electricity, but gas is more efficient and cheaper to run. Incinerators are not really cost-effective for the average household, and are better suited to multi-storey flats, where the opportunity to combine chutes and flues will offset high installation and running costs.

Compactors
Compacting machines reduce rubbish to less than one-quarter of its bulk and compress it into neat bundles wrapped in paper sacks. The domestic model is about the size of a small refrigerator and fits under a work-top. Compactors are very expensive to buy and eliminate any opportunities to recycle waste. Environmentalists look upon them as a threat to ecological balance, because of the very long time it takes for the bundles to decompose. It is important to check with the local authority that their own compactors are capable of handling the size and type of package that your machine produces.

The stainless-steel bin (below) is operated by the door-opening mechanism. But you have to stand well back from the sink to get at it, which could be inconvenient.

The front panel of the sink unit (below) is hinged to provide access to the rubbish area. Peelings go in one bag, en route to the compost heap; cans are destined for the dustbin.

A compactor (above) will accept virtually all household waste— glass, tin cans, light bulbs— even aerosols. Each bag holds a seven-day accumulation of rubbish for a household of four. But bundles decompose very slowly.

A built-in slatted bread board (above). Crusts and crumbs fall through into a pull-out drawer (see drawing below).

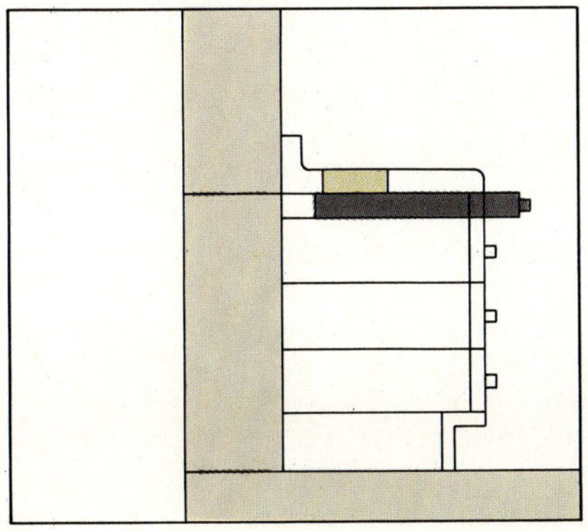

The steel hatch above the sink covers the opening of a chute that leads directly to a rubbish bag gripped in a metal frame (see drawing below).

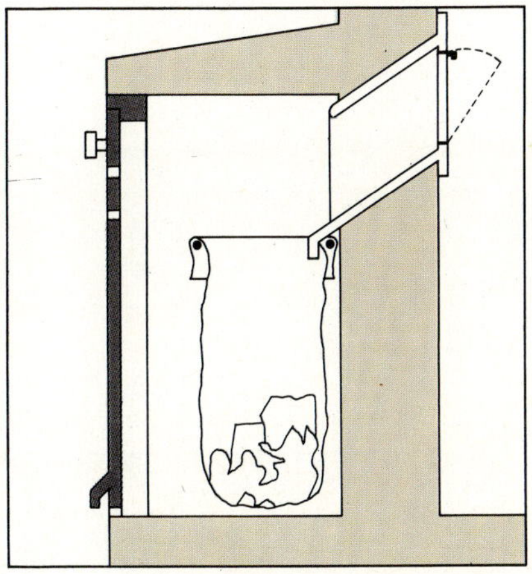

A counter-top hatch placed directly above an open dustbin (below). Smelly waste should first be wrapped or sealed in plastic bags.

Robert Carrier's chopping block (above) is plumbed for a small sink and waste-disposal unit that grinds up vegetable peelings.

A waste-disposal unit (below) plumbed into a small sink with a separate waste outlet for use in emergencies.

An ingenious use for old wine bottles (above). Cemented together in layers they make a colourful garden wall.

Doing the dishes

Washing up is hardly the most stimulating of kitchen tasks, but it must be done by someone. Since that someone is likely to be you, it is worth investing in decent equipment to speed the dishes back to the shelves. If the chore still does not appeal, draw comfort from the old definition of an intellectual—"one who believes you wash up before a meal".

Sinks

Sinks are made from glazed fireclay, enamelled steel, teak, acrylics or stainless steel. Old fireclay sinks look good, but they chip easily, and a chipped sink is unhygienic. Enamelled steel, too, is likely to chip and acrylics may succumb to sizzling hot pans and lighted cigarettes. Teak is traditionally used in restaurants because its resilience helps prevent chipping in plates that may be washed half a dozen times a day. However, teak sinks generally have to be custom-built and are therefore expensive. Stainless steel is hard to beat since it cannot chip and is resistant to rust, heat, abrasion, cigarette burns and even paint-stripper. Stainless steel sinks are not as colourful as those made from enamelled steel or acrylic and the draining-boards, which are liable to spotting, need constant wiping down. Metal sinks, too, can be noisy and should have a bituminous or rubber undercoating to prevent the Niagara-like roar each time you turn the water on.

Sinks are available in many different arrangements of bowls and drainers, and it makes no difference if they are arranged in a left- or right-hand sequence. Items have to be transferred from one hand to the other whichever way it is done, so it depends on which way you like to work. For most efficient use, sink bowls should be at least 180 mm (7 in) deep.

If the kitchen boasts a dishwasher the draining area need not be very large, but a double-bowl sink is always desirable in the family kitchen to cope with the varied activities of vegetable preparation, kettle-filling, cloth-soaking and so on. And, of course, china and glass should always be washed in detergent in one bowl and rinsed in hot water in the other before being put on the draining-board. Where space is tight, choose a sink with one large bowl plus a small rinser bowl, which can also house the waste-disposal unit. Alternatively, select the largest single bowl possible and place a small plastic bowl inside to make a rinsing area within the sink.

One-piece sinks and draining-boards are the most efficient, but if they will not fit into your particular design, fix a bowl with a flat flange under the counter-top. Do not fix bowls without drainers over rimmed counters as the join collects dirt. Inset bowls are best used in conjunction with counters made of solid materials such as teak, marble or terrazzo, which can be grooved and sloped as draining-boards. Bowls can also be set into a plastic, laminated counter-top, but it needs expert workmanship to achieve a watertight joint. Often, sink units are designed to fit over a base cupboard, but these, too, will create undesirable dirt-collecting joints with adjoining work-areas.

Taps

Thermostatically controlled mixer taps with swivel spouts are best for washing up and a spray/brush attachment to the mixer is very useful for rinsing dirty dishes. Taps can be fitted to the wall, to the sink, sink-top or draining-board. Wall fitting is preferable, since it makes for an uncluttered counter-top.

Wherever possible, tap handles should be inclined towards you when you are facing the sink. Most handles now available are encased, but the traditional cross-tops still have their advantages especially for the elderly or disabled. Lever handles are generally prohibited for domestic use in the United Kingdom, since they cause "hammering" and weakening in the pipes.

Draining-racks

Providing the sink is not set under a window, a plate rack can be housed in a bottomless wall cupboard so that plates drip directly into the drain. But if the sink is under the window, there must at least be sufficient space to hang a rack over the draining-board. A wall-fixed rack is preferable, since it helps to keep the draining-surface clear.

Plastic-covered steel racks are colourful, warp-free and hygienic, and accommodate more dishes that the traditional wooden racks. Some double sinks are equipped with a draining-rack that fits over one of the bowls, but it has to be stored somewhere else when not in use, and the sink is out of action while plates are drying.

Washing-up aids

Soaps, detergents, scouring powders and pads, disinfectants, rinse aids, water softeners, dishcloths and sponges all need a home. They should live in a cupboard or recess over the sink or on a shelf behind it, but never on the counter. Bleaches and caustic powders must be kept well away from children; nor should you handle them without wearing gloves. Keep cleaning powders in plastic containers rather than their original cardboard boxes; these tend to become soggy. Brushes and mops can look almost attractive in a pretty jar.

Drying the dishes

Contrary to general practice, crockery should be left to dry on the rack or within the dishwasher. Glasses and cutlery do need to be polished, however, prefereably with clean linen. Cloths should be hung up to dry in a place where air can circulate freely around them, either on rails, in rubber grippers or on heated towel driers—sited near the sink.

Dishwashers

If you can afford it, buy one. It doesn't mean the end of washing up, since delicate china and glass and heavily encrusted pots and pans will still need handwashing, but they do save time and effort even in the smallest household. To get the best out of a dishwasher it must be used economically. For example, the machine should be run only when full. After all the dishes have been washed and rinsed, it can then be used as an additional storage cupboard that is unloaded only when the time comes to lay the table for the next meal.

Check that your crockery and cutlery is dishwasher-proof. High temperatures and caustic detergents can craze the surface of

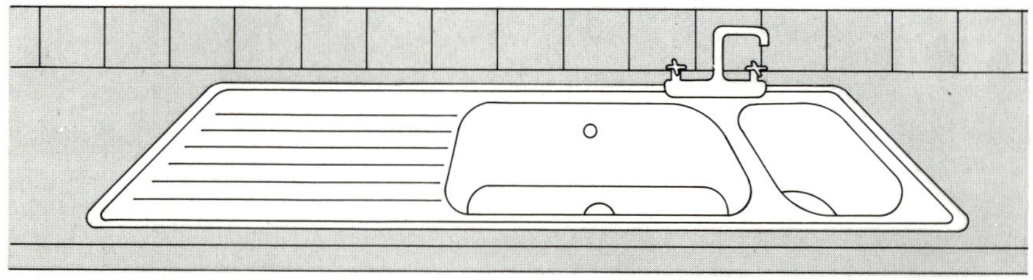

Inset sink-top (above) allows for unbroken work-top surfaces with a front edge and upstand at the back, preventing watery dirt traps.

A sink unit (below) designed to fit over a base cupboard creates dirt-collecting joints in the work-top, the fascia and the upstand.

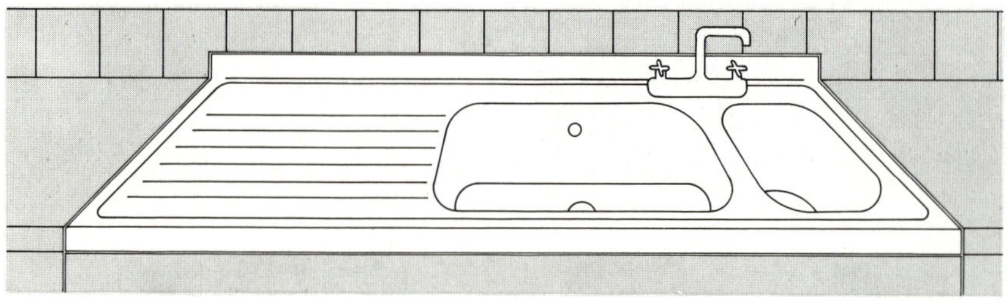

Fixing inset bowls

1 and 2. *Where the flange of an inset sink meets a counter-top of Formica, the join must be well sealed to prevent water reaching the plywood core material.*

3. *A drop-in sink bowl—the join is more cumbersome but is at least watertight.*

4. *A traditional fireclay sink set in beneath a solid work-top.*

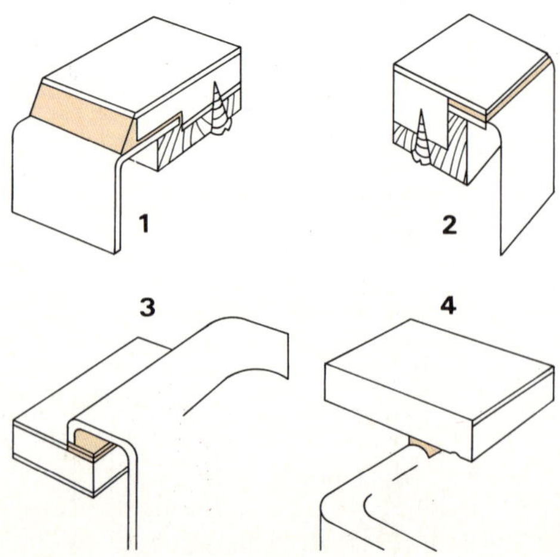

beautiful old china, tarnish silver, melt soft plastics, split wood and unglue handles.

Dishwashers are noisy and run from 40 to 90 minutes. Many people prefer to run them only at night or when out of the room, so bear this in mind when considering an open-plan kitchen/living-room. Site the dishwasher close to the sink, waste-disposer or bin, so that plates can be scraped before putting them in the machine.

Choosing a dishwasher

Dishwashers come in various sizes, designed to take between six and twelve complete place-settings. Most are intended to fit under counter-tops or to be mounted in high-level cabinets (which eliminate stooping and backache). The drop-front door should open at about 800 mm (31 in) above the ground. Avoid small table-top models with hose connections trailing into the sink; they are so inconvenient that it's easier and quicker to wash up by hand.

The programmes generally consist of pre-rinse, normal and intensive cycles. Prerinsing is a useful feature. It prevents food from drying on, as the pre-rinse programme can be run separately before the machine is fully loaded. Some have a plate-warming programme, which is useful only if the machine is not to be used as a store-cupboard. In hard-water areas, select a machine with a built-in water softener, or use a detergent combined with a water softener to prevent glass from "clouding". All machines have internal filters, which must be regularly cleared, so choose a machine with filters that are easily accessible. Machines must be mobile for ease of maintenance. Most models have wheels or castors and some have levelling feet, which are useful if the floors are uneven. Dishwashers are controlled by a programme-selector switch. A good machine also has an on/off switch and a rinse-aid indicator. Rinse aids lower the surface tension of the water and thus reduce streaking on plates and glasses. Last, but not least, choose a manufacturer with a good service record and contract for twice-yearly maintenance visits.

Disposable plates

Why not dispense with washing up altogether and use throw-away plastic or paper cups, plates and cutlery? Because it is a shameful waste of natural resources, expensive and inelegant. But there are occasions to which they are ideally suited, such as picnics and children's parties, when good china runs the risk of getting broken.

How not to put up a plate rack (above). Plates stacked in it will have to be first dried by hand or they will drip on the floor.

Delicate china and glass are washed in the face-to-face sinks (above) and tougher stuff goes in the dishwasher. This arrangement is ideal where more than one person uses the kitchen.

Beauty and utility—what might have been a chilly corner of the kitchen has been transformed by the imaginative use of old tiles (left).

In this workmanlike arrangement (below) the larger sink is used to wash the dishes, while the smaller provides hot water for rinsing.

The racks (above) allow the crockery to drip-dry into the sink while providing a display that changes at every washing up.

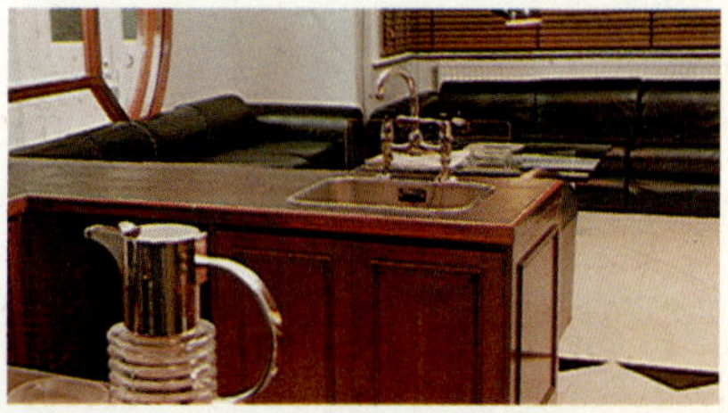

The sink in Mr Chow's kitchen-to-live-in (above) is fitted with a perspex shield to protect guests from random splashes.

Storage–behind closed doors

If you were to draw up a list of all the things in the kitchen that need to be stored you would probably never finish it. Finding the right place for all those diverse bits and pieces is a daunting but not insoluble problem. Efficient storage depends on having some kind of flexible master plan. It must be flexible because a plan that fits too tightly around your present possessions becomes obsolete as soon as you buy anything new.

The first thing to be done is to take out of the kitchen everything that does not deserve to be there—like carpet sweepers, dog baskets and carpentry tools. The storage space required for cooking equipment alone is too valuable to waste on extraneous items. Having got down to the essentials, sort out those items which get used in one part of the kitchen only, and store them within reach of that place; mops and detergents belong with the sink, the heat-resistant glove with the oven, tea and coffee near the electric kettle, a supply of cooking salt near the cook-top, and so on.

Narrow shelves inside the cupboard and on the doors make a cupboard of average depth twice as useful (below).

Utensils that fall into no one specific category, such as the ubiquitous cook's knife, should be stored where they are easily accessible, and, in order to decide where that is, the various work-centres should be examined.

Food-preparation and washing-up

These revolve around the kitchen sink and the adjacent work-surface. Refrigerator and larder should be reasonably near at hand and a rack for kitchen knives within easy reach. Around the sink there should be a place for washing-up materials, a rack for drying dishcloths, where air can circulate freely around them, and bins for rubbish and food waste.

The mixing area is likely to be a part of the food-preparation area. The mixer itself is probably the bulkiest item to store. Some kitchen-unit manufacturers make cunning hinged devices for storing mixers that pop up when in use, but mixers are getting more compact in design and they can easily be left parked on the counter. Apart from all the accessories for the mixer, space is needed for wooden spoons, baking tins, bowls and all the gear for pastry- and bread-making. Near by should be the dry foods such as sugar and spice and all things that will have their first use in the mixing bowl.

The cooking area is the hot-spot where items used during cooking should be within arm's reach. Storage will be needed for spatulas, stirrers, whisks and seasonings as well as saucepans, lids, frying-pans and roasting tins.

The serving area may not even be in the kitchen, but, however and wherever serving is done, the principle of "first use" should stand. This is the place for cutlery, crockery, table mats and linen, and perhaps those foods that go straight to the table without preparation, like cereals and jam.

Open shelves or closed cupboards

Having decided where to keep things, think next about how to arrange them from both the aesthetic and practical point of view. On the aesthetic side, you must decide whether you want a busy-looking kitchen with everything on show or a streamlined kitchen where all things kitcheny are firmly shut away behind cupboard doors. If you live in the clean air of the country or the rarefied atmosphere of an air-conditioned town house, you can surround yourself with good-looking utensils displayed on open shelves in a way that is warm, friendly and reminiscent of old farmhouse dressers—but the dust of an urban environment would turn such an exhibition into a greasy dirt trap. Narrow shelves are the most useful, as nothing lurks unseen at the back. Shelves 200 mm (8 in) wide are big enough for most items.

Storing knives, crockery and pans

Kitchen knives will be blunted if they rattle around in a drawer; they should be stored in racks, either wooden or magnetic. A simple alternative is to cut a slit through the back of the counter-top into which the blade is inserted, leaving the handle above board.

China manufacturers tell us that cups should be stored in cupboards, placed on their sides in nests of four. But if you are prepared to risk weakening the handles a little, cup hooks are much more convenient, especially for mugs and cups used every day. Plates are best stacked in piles of six on adjustable shelves—if the shelves are close together the plates will get less dusty. Everyday crockery doesn't need to be put away at all, it can live in the plate-rack.

Casseroles, saucepans and frying-pans are heavy, so they should be stored at a low

Keeping out the dust with cheerful PVC roller blinds (above). The blinds run in simple tracks to stop them flapping about.

level near the cooker and preparation areas. The best way of coping with their awkward bulk is to buy a range of sizes that nest inside each other, or store them in a deep, solid, low drawer, subdivided so that pans slot in like files in a filing cabinet with the handles sticking up. If there is a tall cupboard next to the cooker, the pans can be hung on hooks on the back of the door. If your pans are worth looking at then hang them on a butcher's rail above the stove.

A little chest of drawers, custom-built from old pinewood boarding (above), proves that drawer units can be attractive.

A text-book case—a food-preparation area that has everything (right)—work-top, sink and ingenious storage cupboards and trolleys.

Open to view

The drawer that holds all is a basket (above). A space beneath the work-top accommodates clean linen and cutlery—an economical idea, since wooden drawers are expensive.

A wall-hung canvas hold-all bulges with kitchen equipment (left), efficiently and attractively replacing conventional drawers, shelves and racks.

How to transform a jumble of mashers and fish slices into a kitchen feature—here a simple stoneware jar holds a utilitarian posy of kitchen equipment (above).

Plastic-coated wire drainers are, of course, very hygienic; but not so pretty as a wooden rack filled with simple plates (left).

Storing pans can be a real problem in a tiny kitchen. Pan racks are hardly à la mode *at the moment, but this one (above) has been used to good effect in a cluttered corner.*

Why hang pictures on the wall when you have a good-looking collection of utensils? The pans (right) are arranged according to frequency of use.

Shelve it

When your equipment is too pretty to hide, resort to a bold shelving system (above). Shelves don't have to be crammed full to look good.

A vertical maze of narrow shelves built to fit the jars, glasses and canisters that sit within it (left) transforms a blank kitchen wall into an ever-changing still life.

Glass shelves make a sparkling resting place for glasses (above)—but take care when putting them away—the rims are the weakest part.

A purpose-built shelving system has sensible low-level storage for heavy pans (left). Plates and spice boxes are within easy reach—for adults.

Row upon row of home-made jams, bottled fruits and pickles deserve a showing (below).

An antique wine bottle drying rack holds saucepans and skillets. Other equipment is displayed on lozenge-shaped wine bins (above).

Above the cook-top, all the necessary whisks and strainers, seasonings and spices fit neatly and precisely in their places (below).

A store of ideas

Pull-out vegetables (above) are kept fresh and firm on a three-tier wire rack in a ventilated cupboard.

Dexion Speedframe (below) looks like Meccano and could be assembled by a child.

A plastic-coated metal cage (above) standing in a cellar workshop holds an assortment of bottles and cans as well as fresh produce.

Big drawers set back beneath the cook-top (left), so that handles don't bump the cook, are an appropriate place to keep awkward pots.

Contents dictate shelving (right). Wicker baskets and pasta jars fit perfectly into hutches under the work-top.

Knives will blunt if they are scattered in a drawer. This grooved wedge of wood (above) protects them from each other.

An answer to otherwise inaccessible cupboards, the ladder (above) runs rails and wheels.

Choosing work-surfaces

A great deal is required of a kitchen work-top. It must withstand the heat of pots and pans, the sharp edge of a knife, frequent dousings with soapy water and the abrasive effects of scouring powder. In addition, it must be capable of being accurately cut to accommodate sinks, cook-tops, etc.

Not surprisingly, no one surface is ideal. The perfectionist's kitchen would have a different surface for every purpose—a heat-resistant ceramic or stainless-steel area near the cook-top, a cool marble or slate area for rolling out pastry, and a solid timber chopping board. Few manufactured kitchen units allow for such multiplicity so, unless you are building your own unit, compromise is inevitable.

Timber
Hardwood work-tops are very attractive and, with the wide range of seals available, are well worth considering. However, constant wear from hot and cold water and other fluids soon breaks down most seals. Only frequent cleaning and careful resealing will keep the timber in its pristine condition. Veneered boards can also be used, but with thicker-than-usual veneer.

The best chopping blocks for even wear are made from wood cut against the grain.

Marble
This cool surface is ideal for pastry-making, and is very beautiful but expensive. It can be cut to take sinks and worked to a rounded edge or in grooves. Marble is slightly porous and will stain with oil or harsh spirits. Sinks should be fixed below a marble slab.

Slate
A good alternative to marble, this is a traditional material for draining-boards (and roof tiles) because it is waterproof. It is a dense, non-porous stone in beautiful shades of blue and green, and for a work-top choose a sawn, polished finish. It is easily cut and very hard-wearing.

Terrazzo
A precast terrazzo work-top could be specially designed. It is hard-wearing and can have sinks let into it, but they must be fixed into the terrazzo slab on its underside.

Patent ceramics
Recent developments in ceramics have produced a material that is as cool and smooth as marble yet so heat-resistant it can be used as a cook-top. It is an expensive material, usually inlaid as a block into a general work-surface.

Corian
This material has a deep opalescent quality, and it can be cut and shaped accurately. It is tough, non-porous and easy to keep clean.

Polypropylene
As a chopping surface it is excellent as it has good resistance to liquid spills and marks, and is fairly cheap.

A surface for every purpose. Twin slabs of timber and marble inset in a stainless-steel cooking island (right).

A modern polypropylene chopping board in the preparation area of a traditional kitchen is given a border of antique ceramic tiles (below).

Sealed pinewood work-top (below) will keep its warm glow for years, as long as it is not used as a chopping block.

An unusual counter-top of lava from the mountains of central France (above). Its smooth surface is virtually indestructible.

This cool and simple Danish kitchen has a specially made timber work-top running the length of the sink wall (right). Heat-resistant ceramic tiles surround the enamelled steel cook-top unit.

An old pine marble-topped table enjoys a new lease of life as a work-surface (below). Marble is the perfect cool surface for pastry-making.

Corian (above) is a flexible plastic sheet material with the look of marble. It is tough and easy to care for as it is non-porous. Unlike the real thing it is warm to the touch.

Choosing work-surfaces

Plastic laminates
Laminates, such as Formica, are the best all-purpose surfaces for work-tops. They come in a wide range of colours and patterns, smooth or textured.

A laminate is stuck down with a special adhesive to a chipboard, blockboard or plywood base. It can be contoured in a special press to curve down over the front edge, and up to meet the wall at the back to eliminate dirt-harbouring joints and sharp edges. It is very easy to cut, simple to keep clean and withstands a certain amount of heat, knocks and scratches—though do not use it as a chopping board.

Tiles or mosaic
If you do not object to the joints, ceramic tiles make a very good-looking surface—hard-wearing, heat- and stain-resistant, but they tend to be a bit noisy as they echo sounds on the work-top.

Round-edged tiles can be fitted vertically to the front edge and coved tiles used at the back edge will sweep up to meet the wall surface.

Quarry tiles are acknowledged as a highly practical flooring material, and they make an attractive work-top too. Quarries are naturally water-proof and impervious to most household liquids.

Tiles or mosaic are best bedded into concrete, or stuck directly to a base board and grouted in. Use an insert-type sink with a good sealed rim clamped over the tiles.

Stainless steel
Very common as a sink and draining-board material, it can also be obtained in larger sizes to form a whole counter, including sink, drainer, work-top and cut-out for a cook-top unit. Stainless steel can be matt, polished or patterned. Its disadvantage is noise, which can be reduced by gluing insulation board to the undersides of the work-tops. Only good-quality stainless steel can truly be described as stainless. It is very hard-wearing and withstands extremes of heat, making a good surround for a cook-top unit. It is hygienic and easy to clean.

Copper and zinc
Polished copper makes a beautiful bar counter, but it does need a great deal of looking after. Although there are clear lacquers for keeping the shine on copper, it would not last long on a surface used daily as a work-top.

Both copper and zinc are susceptible to scratches from sharp knives and stains from acid fluids such as lemon juice. In the past zinc was quite widely used as a work-surface, but now there are misgivings as to its toxic effects on food.

A beautiful collection of antique ceramics from the famous faience works of Holland and Spain makes a work-top (right).

Plain ceramic tiles (below) are the ideal surround for a cooking recess because they are heat-resistant and easy to clean.

Plastic laminate is perhaps the best all-purpose work-surface (below), but it will scratch if used as a chopping board.

Shiny black glazed ceramic tiles on a low, wide larder shelf (above). Like slate and marble, tiles are cool to the touch.

Quarry tiles with inset electric radiant rings (below). These tiles are cheap, practical, and easy to clean.

Continuous counter-top of textured stainless steel with integral sinks (above). The choice of the professional, as it is tough, heat-resistant, hygienic and easy to maintain.

Honey-coloured hexagonal mosaic tiles are set into the top of a standard island cooking and preparation unit (above).

Wooden chopping blocks are an essential in the stainless-steel kitchen (right). A hard surface will blunt the keenest of knives.

loors–sheet materials

The choice of flooring for a kitchen will depend largely on the substructure. A concrete subfloor, which should have a damp-proof course under, within, or on top of it, can be finished with all types of flooring from timber boarding or vinyl sheeting to ceramic tiles and even marble slabs. However, a subfloor over timber joists would present problems if a ceramic or marble-tile floor was required, as timber deflects and moves, which would cause cracking of the tile joints or even of the tiles themselves.

It is important to consider the finished level of the floor. This must relate to adjoining rooms, as an abrupt change can be dangerous as well as aesthetically unacceptable. Floors laid to finish higher or lower than before may require doors to be rehung to clear the new level.

Finishes for a concrete subfloor

Ceramic tiles, marble, slate, brick paviors or stone can be bedded down with mortar directly on to the rough concrete surface. The thickness of the mortar bed will vary with the type of material used. For instance, uneven stone slabs will require a mortar bed of varying thickness to give a level floor finish, but for accurately made ceramic tiles a bed about 12 mm (½ in) thick will be adequate.

To lay timber successfully on a concrete subfloor, use 12-mm (½-in) felt-backed parquet-wood tiles laid on a level screed. Tongued-and-grooved wood strip flooring can be pinned through to wood battens buried in the screed or pinned into the concrete, or both. Wood-block flooring can be stuck directly to the screed.

Thin sheet material like vinyl, vinyl-asbestos, cork, linoleum or rubber is the most common finish, and is available in roll or tile form. It should be laid on a screed about 40 mm (1½ in) thick; if the screed is not smooth enough, then a latex screed about 3 mm (⅛ in) thick should be put down before the sheet material or tiles are stuck with an adhesive recommended by the manufacturers.

Finishes on a timber subfloor

Floor joists have to be spanned with boarding, which can either form the finished floor or be covered with another material such as sheet vinyl. Softwood, hardwood, chipboard or plywood are all possibilities for a finished floor if sealed with polyurethane lacquer. It is unlikely that a hardwood, like parquet tiles, would be covered with a further finish, but softwood boarding, plywood or chipboard often forms the base for a finishing layer of sheet material.

Where sheet materials such as vinyl are to be laid over floorboards the floor should first be covered with hardboard to prevent the joints showing through. Ceramic or marble tiles need sticking to a blockboard or particle-board base, about 25 mm (1 in) thick, to eliminate any problems caused by the movement of timber joists.

Maintenance

All kitchen flooring is subject to a great deal of scuffing, especially near the cooker and sink. If timber is chosen it should be resealed frequently to prevent the wood becoming bare. Wax polish is not recommended for kitchen floors because it stains when damp. The hardest-wearing materials are ceramic tiles, slate and marble; but they are also the hardest on the feet. The weak point of tiling is the grouted joints, which can, of course, be raked out and remade from time to time. Marble is somewhat porous and will stain if oil comes in contact with it.

Far cry from the gaudy patterns of old-fashioned vinyl, a mosaic of white vinyl tiles (above) suits the new look of chaste elegance.

Cushioned vinyl (right) is bouncier, warmer and quieter to walk on than the brightly glazed ceramic tiles which it imitates.

Cork

Cork tile is made from cork granules and natural or synthetic binders compressed and baked. It has excellent insulation characteristics and, although usually laid in tiles only 3-7 mm (⅛-¼ in) thick, it is resilient and feels warm to bare feet. But the tiles are fragile and may chip. Natural cork must be sealed with several coats of polyurethane and worn patches should be resealed immediately. Recent innovations include cork tiles with a clear, practically invisible, vinyl skin integral with the surface. This type should not be sealed, and only needs wiping down. Coloured and patterned cork is available.

Vinyl

Now the most popular kitchen flooring material, it is available in sheet or tile form in a vast range of plain colours and patterns. It is water-proof, resistant to oil, fat, grease and most domestic chemicals. It is resilient, easily cleaned and hard-wearing, and can be laid on hardboard over floorboards, chipboard or directly on to screed. Cushioned vinyl comes in sheet form and is extra warm and tough underfoot. A textured finish shows fewer marks and is slip-resistant.

Vinyl asbestos

Cheaper than pure vinyl, it comes in tile form. It is comparatively brittle and hard and is laid in the same way as pure vinyl tiles, except that tiles must be heated before they are laid on to a very smooth surface.

Linoleum

This, obtained in sheet or tile form, is hard-wearing and comes in a wide range of deep, dense colours. Stick it down on hardboard over floorboards, or on chipboard, or directly on to screed with a damp-proof course. Thicker qualities have a high resilience and are warm underfoot. Lino is susceptible to damage from alkalis. It should not be sealed, but can be polished with an emulsion polish.

Carpet

Carpet is resilient and easy to fit, but presents cleaning problems, as it will readily attract dirt if used in the kitchen. The only practical carpet for a kitchen is a synthetic fibre such as close-looped nylon backed with latex or foam. It is hard-wearing and washable, but it may prove difficult to remove all traces of dirt. Synthetic fibre is relatively cheap so it can be replaced fairly frequently.

Epoxy resin

Not strictly a sheet material, but rather a plasticized liquid either laid with a trowel as a 3-mm ($\frac{1}{8}$-in) screed or applied in a liquid self-levelling form finishing 2 to 5 mm ($\frac{1}{8}$ to $\frac{1}{16}$ in) thick. It is suitable only for concrete subfloors and is very hard-wearing and comes in a wide range of colours. It is expensive for a small area (it is mostly used for industrial floors), but may well gain wider acceptance. A sprinkling of carborundum dust on the surface, applied at the time of laying, will give epoxy resin a non-slip finish.

Rubber

This material is sold in a variety of colours, as tiles or in sheet form, plain, ribbed or studded, and is suitable for concrete or timber subfloors. The smell of rubber will always be faintly present, but rubber is resilient and very hard-wearing. Plain sheet rubber can be slippery, so choose studded or ribbed varieties for the kitchen.

Roll out an Italianate tiled floor (right). Made of tough vinyl sheeting, it is softer and quieter than the real thing.

Be rustic with plastic (above). Relief vinyl tiles, gently groovy underfoot, simulate the rough bricks of traditional farmhouse floors.

High polish gives toffee-coloured linoleum its caramelized look (right) and helps to protect it from the pernicious effects of damp.

Floors–natural finishes

Plywood and chipboard

These can be painted or stained and sealed, or simply sealed to reveal the natural colour. Again, seal and stain must be compatible. Ply and chipboard materials are comparatively cheap and are available in sheet form, or as tongued-and-grooved panels in manageable sizes that can be quickly laid directly over floor joists to form the finished floor, or as a base for sheet material. Worn areas will need frequent resealing.

Hardboard

Not really recommended as a kitchen-floor finish, but it is cheap. It can be sealed or painted, but it must be laid over floorboards or a base such as plywood or chipboard.

Ceramic tiles against richly coloured walls (above) make the kitchen look neat, clean and crisp while avoiding hygienic impersonality.

Softwood

This can be stained, painted in a wide range of colours or sealed to show its natural colour. After staining timber always use a seal compatible with the type of stain. There are special floor paints, which may be slightly better than conventional gloss paint, but scuffing will wear away any paint film fairly soon. A softwood floor needs constant attention to retain its pristine appearance, but it has considerable advantages in economy and ease of laying.

Hardwood

A polyurethane seal will bring out the colour and the grain. Waxing the floor will only make it slippery. Hardwood is available in strip or block form, prefabricated "mosaic" or parquet tiles. It is not a usual finish for a kitchen, and will need constant attention if its appearance is to be maintained. Bare patches must be resealed immediately.

A floor to play Japanese noughts and crosses on? Its grid-patterned surface is made of thousands of mosaic tiles (above).

Little girl plays peasant in a French country kitchen (left). The rough parquet floor is made of blocks of larch and strips of beech.

As traditional as English Stilton, the craggy old stone floor (right) looks ruggedly mellow, though it is chilly to bare feet.

Quarry tiles

Very hard-wearing, they come in a variety of sizes, thicknesses and colours. Tiles from the same batch may vary in size, which means that the joints must take up any variation. It is this irregularity and their natural colours that give quarries their charm. Quarries should be neither sealed nor polished, it is all too easy to build up a treacherously slippery surface. Wash them down with mild detergent, and apply a mixture of one part boiled linseed oil to four parts turpentine to bring up the colour (this will attract dust when first applied). Disadvantages to be considered are that quarry tiles are noisy, hard on the feet and cold if not warmed by underfloor heating.

Ceramic tiles

Accurately made ceramic tiles can be neatly laid with uniform narrow joints. Altogether crisper and smoother than quarries, they are also thinner. Plain colours and a wide variety of patterns and shapes are available. No sealing is required as tiles are normally vitrified or glazed.

Mosaic

Made in a wide variety of shapes, colours and materials ranging from glass silica to ceramic chips, they usually come in panels mounted on paper for ease of laying. No seal is required. Wash with mild detergent instead. Suitable where there is underfloor heating.

Bricks and clay pavers

Brick floors look good both indoors and out, and old bricks, if you can get them, look even better. When laid, clay pavers look just like bricks, but, as they are only 33 mm ($1\frac{1}{4}$ in) thick, they can be used in situations where the thickness of a brick may be unacceptable. Brick is hard and unresilient, but easy to care for and suitable for underfloor heating.

The pale floor made of filled travertine (below) is discreetly opulent and does not discredit its less luxurious surroundings.

Peninsular unit juts out into the polished sea of parquetry (above), a compound of teak, maple, oak and cherry.

Marble

Can be obtained in large slabs or tile size. It is expensive, hard, cold and beautiful. It can be washed or scrubbed, but not with an acid cleaner, and oil will stain it. Suitable where there is underfloor heating.

Terrazzo

An impervious material that should be professionally laid when wet and ground down when dry to produce a smooth, hard, waxable finish. It is made of marble chippings and cement and forms a surface approximately 20 mm ($\frac{3}{4}$ in) thick laid on a 16-mm ($\frac{5}{8}$-in) layer of screed. It is hard and cold and can be slippery. It is uneconomical for small areas. Terrazzo can also be cast in tile form and laid like other tiles.

Travertine

Ancient Rome was constructed of this honey-brown marble. It is fissured and requires special filling to make it suitable for flooring. If used for a kitchen floor it is best finished with "eggshell"—a mechanically worked finish applied by the suppliers.

The contemplative's kitchen (below); an austere, airy barn with a floor like sectioned ice made of white ceramic tiles.

Slate

It can be used in large slabs or in tile form, with a smooth or riven finish— the former is liable to be slippery. Although slate scratches easily, scratches can be concealed with a mixture of one part boiled linseed oil and four parts turpentine. It is hard, cold and expensive, but very durable and good-looking; it is only really suitable where there is underfloor heating.

Stone

Stone is cold and hard, but any disadvantages are outweighed by its mellow appearance. It can be sealed with a varnish or water-based sealer.

A multicoloured patchwork floor made of hexagonal quarry tiles (above). The hard, glassy surface is easy to clean.

Designs on the floor

Studded Pirelli rubber flooring (left) is tough, springy, quiet to walk on and easy to clean with warm, soapy water.

Linoleum (above), a conventional choice of flooring on account of its warmth and cheapness, is available in many strong colours.

Hard underfoot but hard-wearing, too, glazed ceramic tiles (below) echo the lean, cuboid look of the units and chairs.

Spanish terracotta tiles (above), hard, waterproof and easy to clean, are sealed with a coat of glossy polyurethane.

Wall finishes-tiles and boarding

Before planning your kitchen, discover what each wall is made of and how much strain it can take. An internal partition wall of lath and plaster is only suitable for pinning up shopping reminders and is not strong enough to take the weight of a cabinet or shelf laden with pots and pans.

If there is any dampness in the walls, this should be eliminated by a professional as soon as possible. No wall finish is sufficiently cosmetic to disguise a damp wall in really bad condition.

Condensation occurs when steam meets a cold surface. If condensation is a problem, consider having foam injected into the cavity wall for insulation. A warm, thick finish, such as cork or thick wallpaper, will also insulate walls against some heat loss.

Ceramic tiles

Walls, work-tops, floors and even ceilings can be faced with glazed ceramic or quarry tiles, which are tough and durable. Ceramic tiles are usually made in two sizes—105 mm ($4\frac{1}{4}$ in) and 152 mm (6 in) square and are available plain, textured, patterned, glazed or unglazed, machine- or hand-made. However, their grouted joints can pick up dirt, so they will need regular cleaning. Unless you can find a socket plate in the same module as the tiles, it may be difficult to put electric outlets exactly where you want them.

Timber boarding

Tongued-and-grooved timber boards help to insulate a kitchen against heat loss and noise and they do help to conceal uneven or crumbling walls. They are fixed either vertically, horizontally or diagonally to battens running at right angles to the direction of the boards. It is advisable to treat the battens with a preservative against possible damp. The narrow space between the boards and the actual wall may be used to channel wiring and pipes. Seal the outside surface of the wood with clear polyurethane.

Stainless steel and copper

Copper or stainless-steel tiles are an expensive luxury, which look very glamorous when clean. But since they dull easily they will need frequent polishing. Both materials are available in sheet or tile form and should be stuck directly on to smooth plaster or to a backing panel.

Lightly decorated, glazed ceramic tiles (above), reaching right up to the wooden ceiling, gaily highlight the kitchen units and the working collection of bottles and jars.

A mosaic splashback keeps the wet plates and cups away from the wall (above).

Break up a large expanse of monotone wall and floor with your own designs created from coloured and part-coloured ceramic tiles (right).

Frame the sink, preparation area and window frames with richly coloured mosaic tiles (above) to brighten up your working environment.

Individually designed tiles depicting kitchen scenes and food (below) are eye-catchingly contrasted with old wood.

Hand-painted tiles of pastoral scenes continue up the wall from the plainly decorated counter work-top (above).

Highly polished stainless-steel tiles (below) shine brightly in the glow of concealed lighting from beneath the cupboard.

Narrow striped tiles changing to plain with a small coloured dot, successfully break up this monotone kitchen (above).

Warm, comfortable wooden walls and ceiling (above) offset the stark angular units, cooker and refrigerator.

Fill your kitchen with vivid colour contrasts tempered by a haphazard but amusing mixture of wall-hung food and equipment (below).

Wall finishes

Cork
This is available either glued to a backing paper to hang like wallpaper, or unbacked in tiles or panels to glue to the wall, or in self-adhesive tiles. However, the first would be a bit delicate for use in a kitchen. Tiles sealed with PVC or polyurethane are the easiest to keep clean. Like timber boarding, cork is a good insulating material, which looks best in its natural colours—from very pale to dark brown.

Plastic laminate
The join between work-top and wall is often difficult to keep clean, so many of the new plastic laminate work-tops are moulded to a curve that travels a little way up the wall at the back. In fact, the whole wall can be covered with moulded panels faced with plastic laminate to provide a smooth, hard-wearing, continuous surface.

Vinyl or lino tiles
Vinyl tiles are often used on kitchen floors and can just as easily be stuck to the walls. However, they are not heat-resistant so keep them away from cooking areas.

Washable wallpapers
Vinyl wall coverings are made from PVC. They are water- and steam-proof, which means they are ideal for the kitchen. Because they are impermeable, they must be stuck down with a fungicidal adhesive so that mould does not form underneath.

Washable papers have a transparent, plastic coating, which makes them water-resistant rather than water-proof. They are not as tough as vinyl, but have a pleasant matt surface, unlike the sheen of vinyl.

Paint
Each year, industrial research provides us with paints that are ever tougher, more washable and easier to apply. Oil-based paints are more durable and washable than water-based emulsion ones. In general, the glossier the paint, the more hard-wearing it is. Gloss or satin finishes are available in myriad colours with a bewildering list of additives. "Vinyl" or "polyurethane" paint is extra tough; if it claims to be thixotropic, it does not drip or run. It is important to prepare a surface well beforehand by cleaning it thoroughly and sanding down all gloss areas. A kitchen wall may need three coats.

New brilliance was given to an old London flat by this startling colour scheme (right) devised by four students.

Not everyone's taste, but here's how to use metallic wallpaper and coloured strips to add character to a painted kitchen wall (above).

To please your bank manager—a cheerful inexpensive combination of wallpaper, plastic and stripped pine (right) enlivens an old room.

Easy-to-wash tiles behind the cooker (above) lend a touch of medieval grandeur even to a wall of new, raw brick.

Rough, painted plaster, old quarry tiles and pots and pans hung with careless artistry (above) enhance an old Irish farm kitchen.

New York cookery writer James Beard favours US government world maps as a background to his highly professional kitchen (above).

Sunlight pouring through the window (below) gives warmth and charm to a somewhat austere length of wall.

Partitions

Oddly enough, cleverly designed partitions can impart a greater sense of space to a room than is actually the case. Sir John Soane's ideals of "hazard and surprise" are some of the most appropriate to interior design and still some of the least used. He thought that life should be full of little surprises, and that every time you walk round a corner a fresh, interesting and unexpected vista should greet you.

A cheerfully painted partition (left and below) breaks up a long, thin kitchen and screens the cook from the diners—but the flow of conversation and hot food is unimpeded.

In a modest way, you might adapt Sir John's notion to the kitchen. If the room is suitable, try screening off the dining area from the cooking area, or the laundry from the food preparation area. Suddenly there may be a chance to introduce some much-needed storage shelves that are accessible from both sides, or for an extra work-top with a hatch above it. If the dining-table is to be placed up against the partition consider whether you want the partition level with the table at about 710 mm (2 ft 4 in), or level with your work-tops at about 1067 mm (3 ft 6 in) or even higher still, at eye-level.

Some cooks do not like to be watched while practising their craft. Roller or venetian blinds in timber, cotton, bamboo, plastic or metal can be lowered to shade bright light, or to shut off the work-area from the dining space if a more formal atmosphere is required. Blinds are available in many cheerful patterns, and you can paint your own designs on plain ones.

Sliding or folding doors, concertina PVC or timber doors, hardboard panelling or vertical blinds, make a partition more definite but are probably more expensive, and they do have to be parked safely out of the way when not in use.

Half a table pokes through into the kitchen for breakfast (above). For lunch or supper it glides obligingly into the dining-room.

Eye-level cupboards (below) are accessible from both sides and visually divide the kitchen from the formal dining-room.

Concealing the cooking pots in a one-room apartment (above). The partitions in this light and airy room are carefully positioned so that the windows are not obscured.

See-through shelves make an interesting and useful divider (left). Plates, pots and home-made wines are available to either side.

A folding louvered screen completely conceals or reveals this one-wall kitchen (right). The rooflight means that wall-space is given over to cupboards, not windows.

A gigantic serving hatch (far right) doubles as a breakfast bar. When the shutter rolls down, the counter becomes a sideboard.

Ceilings

For years ceilings have been the Cinderella of decoration. People who devote care and expense to floors and walls will thoughtlessly live with a ceiling of cracked plaster. Yet, because the ceiling is probably the only big empty surface in the kitchen, the scope for imagination is boundless.

Adding

If the kitchen is in an old townhouse that has been converted, then it may be too high for comfort. Remember that the Victorians with solid-fuel ranges and gas lamps needed height to give them air; given a good extractor fan we can manage happily with much lower ceilings.

If the ceiling is to be brought down it does not have to be another flat plaster one. There are a number of alternatives. The new ceiling can be lower in some parts than in others, and this change in level can be used to define areas—a cooking area or an eating area, for example; or it can be used arbitrarily to satisfy decorative whims.

Taking away

In some cases the kitchen can be improved by adding a false ceiling. In other cases a better approach would be to remove the existing ceiling and expose what is above it. It is satisfying to give character to a room by exploiting what is already there, by bringing out its hidden assets.

Above the ceiling of most kitchens is a wooden floor resting on roughly finished wooden joists. Those may look well uncovered, although sound-proofing will be needed if there is a bedroom above, and building regulations may require exposed timbers to be treated against fire.

Many terraced city houses have their kitchen in a single-storey annexe at the back. This annexe usually has a sloping roof over it. By removing the old ceiling the underside of this roof can be exposed.

Colour

Because the cost of kitchen fittings is so high, great care must be taken to make the right colour choice the first time. However, with ceilings bolder experiments can be made, and if the first doesn't seem right it is not too expensive to try another colour. Most surfaces in the kitchen must be tough and practical, but the ceiling, as long as it is cleanable and does not harbour too much dirt, can be treated much more freely.

As a rule, dark colours make a ceiling look lower and pale ones make it look higher, but there are enough exceptions to make an experiment worth while.

Texture

There are very good reasons why most surfaces in the kitchen need to be hard and smooth. So for a little relief, both for the eyes and the ears, there is much to be said for a soft, textured ceiling. Sealed wood boarding is very practical, and so is plywood. A wallpaper that can be washed gives a cheerful finish, and hessian or burlap is splendid so long as the cook doesn't splash fat on the ceiling.

Services

The ceiling may be a sensible place for lighting, ventilation and heating, if all the other surfaces are fully used. In a house with conventional central-heating radiators and a small kitchen, the ceiling may be the only surface left for the radiator. This is not ideal as hot air tends to settle at the top of the room, but there is probably enough air movement to prevent this from becoming a problem. If you decide to have a suspended ceiling, remember that by stopping it short of the wall or changing its level you make a good place for concealed lighting and for extractor ventilation.

Wall and ceiling are one (above). The curvaceous plastic form is a shield against harsh lighting and modifies the rectangular severity of the room.

The cook can see any activity in the lower room through angled windows along the counter-top (below). The ceiling is of stained pine board.

A contrast to the stark fittings, patterned wallpaper (above) extends across the ceiling to give the effect of an intimate box.

A jet-black ceiling (above), punctuated by chrome spotlights, emphasises the polished, hard-edge look of the kitchen.

The radiant kitchen (above) is lit by a large, circular dome light, recessed into a conventional ceiling of smooth white plaster.

More storage space is always valuable and the ceiling can help provide it. A shelf fixed to a bracket (above) is hung from boarding.

The matted ceiling (above) is a coarse-textured contrast to the hard, shiny finish of the Formica cupboards.

The suspended light system (above) defines the space of the "snack-bar" eating area.

A ceiling of rough-textured wide boards (right) is suitably rugged for a country kitchen.

View from the sink

Windows can make or break a kitchen. Light, ventilation and thermal and sound insulation depend upon them, so give them plenty of attention when making your kitchen plan.

Daylight and sunlight

In Britain, kitchens are required by law to have a clear glazing area of one-tenth of the floor area. This is a barely acceptable minimum, and yet it may be difficult to achieve, especially in basement rooms.

The daylight factor must not be confused with that of sunlight, which depends entirely on which way the window is facing. Too much sunlight causes glare, heat build-up and food deterioration, and for this reason the ideal kitchen window in the northern hemisphere will face east. South- and west-facing windows will need some form of solar control unless they are adequately screened by trees outside. A north-facing window will receive no direct sunlight, but will often look out on to pleasant sunny scenes lit from behind the house. Large kitchens need more than one window, preferably on different walls, to diffuse the light and reduce glare.

Ventilation

Kitchens in Britain must have a clear area of opening window equal to one-twentieth of the floor space. To achieve the maximum amount of fresh air, the top of the opening area should be at least 1.8 m (5 ft 9 in) from the floor, and in addition it is highly desirable to have an extractor fan that will dispel steam and smoke from the cooking area. It should not be set in the window, however. Not only is a window fan unsightly, it will also obscure the light, and unless the cooker is immediately adjacent to the window, the greasy vapour will be dragged across the room, fouling everything in its path.

View

Because the housewife must spend so much time at the sink, it has become traditional to position it under the window so that she can enjoy the view while working. However, there are certain disadvantages to this arrangement. It makes the placing of draining racks over the sink impossible, the panes are often splashed with dirty water, and it makes it difficult to open the window behind the sink. A good compromise is to place the sink at right angles to the window, near enough to take advantage of both the light and the view.

In some kitchens the view may leave a lot to be desired. Bleak basement area walls, for instance, may be improved by painting them white to reflect light into the room, or be enlivened with brightly painted murals and "trompe-l'oeil" effects. Where there is plenty of daylight but not much to look at, frame the view with climbing shrubs and window-boxes. If even this fails to add charm, the dreary outlook may be obscured by fixing well-lit glass shelves (removable

Making the most of daylight

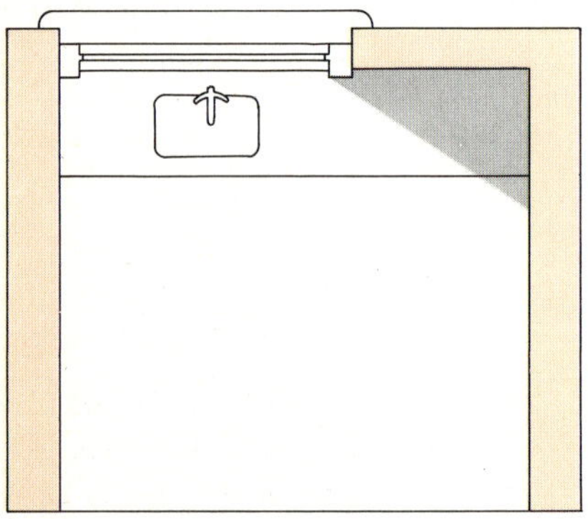

A corner window lights the adjacent wall.

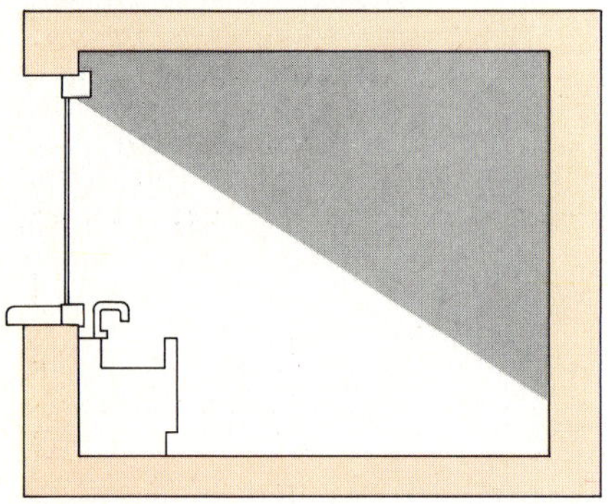

Here, a window with a high head throws light well back into the room.

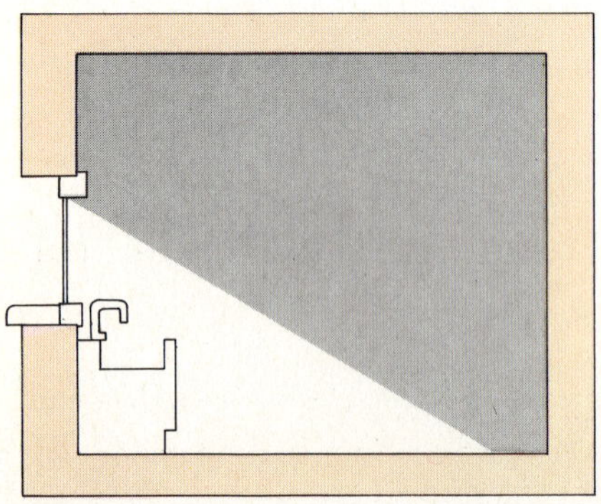

A window with a low head reduces daylight.

A sink with a view into a well-stocked pantry (above). While washing up after one meal you can be thinking about the next.

Dazzling white walls (above) reflect light into a formerly dingy basement, and a gaudy blind adds deliberately startling colour.

Window at right angles to the sink (left)—the glass stays unsplashed, the cook loses no light, and the garden is just a glance away.

The high-headed window (above) admits plenty of light and frames a wooded mountain view in the Adirondacks, New York.

for cleaning) inside the window to display plants and a collection of treasured possessions.

Installing windows and glazed doors

The position and shape of a window will make a tremendous difference to the amount of daylight entering a room. Windows built right into a corner provide a really good light along the return wall. The higher the top of the window, the more light is thrown into the room. Strip windows set between the counter and the wall cupboards or shelf units throw strong light on to work-surfaces. Clerestory lights over wall cupboards reflect sunlight on to the ceiling.

The position of the window in relation to the thickness of the wall is also important. If the window is set flush with the outside wall face, the resulting "reveal", or return wall, will give useful space for internal shelves, blinds or curtains. On the other hand, it might be set flush with the inside wall instead. The external sill would then be large enough for a window-box or some pots of fresh herbs.

If a glazed door is the only source of light and ventilation in your kitchen, you should, if possible, cut a window into another outside wall. Failing this, remake the door as a stable door with a separately opening top half. This will help to cut down chilly winter draughts. Timber-framed glazed doors can, of course, be fitted with cat flaps to give your pets access.

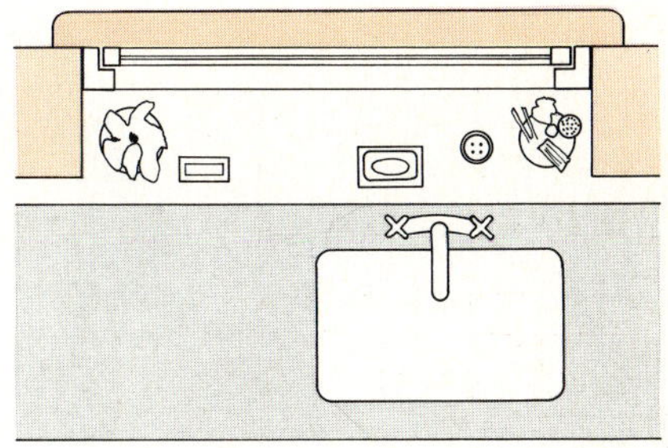

A window flush with the inside wall (right) provides outside sill space for growing herbs or pot plants.

A window flush with the outside wall (far right) makes space on the inside ledge for washing-up utensils. The sink unit may also be built level with the sill and taps sited on the ledge.

The wall pierced with brick-sized openings (above) lets in the light while concealing a dismal urban view.

Different types of opening windows

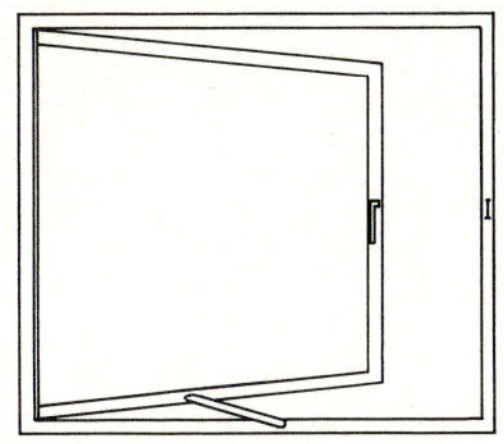

side-hung opening out

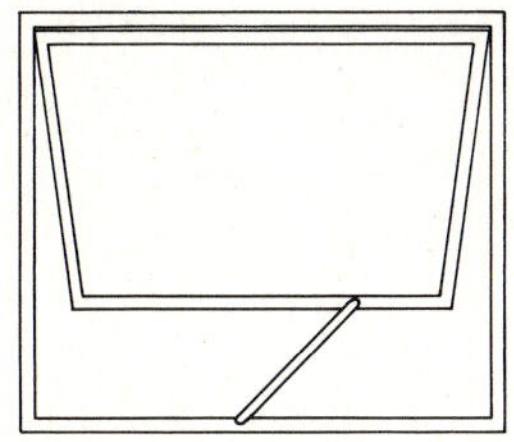

top-hung opening out

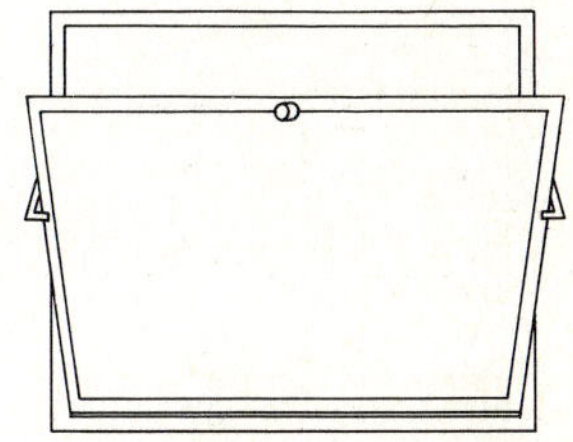

bottom-hung opening in

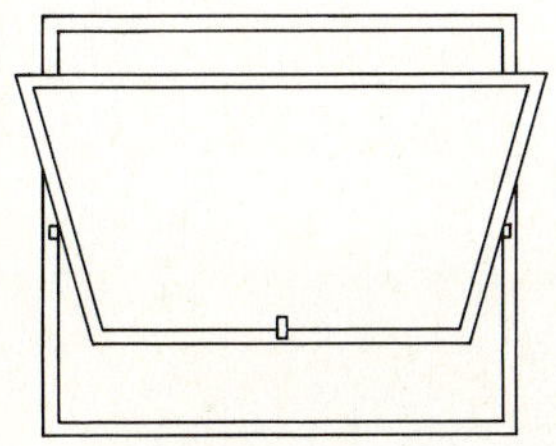

horizontal pivot

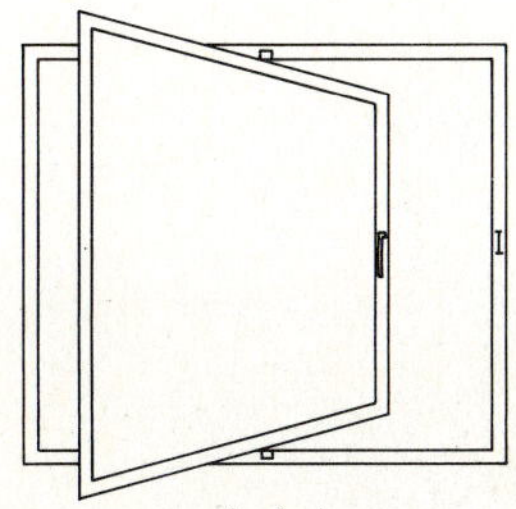

vertical pivot

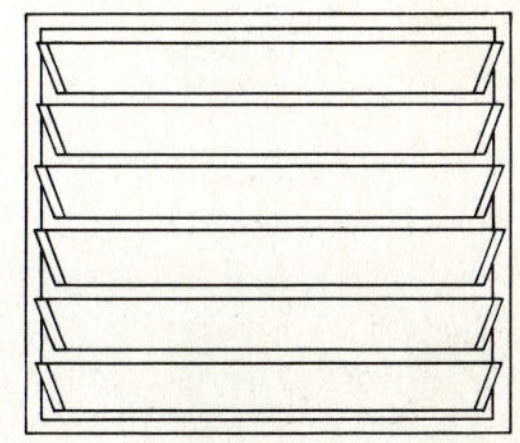

adjustable louvers

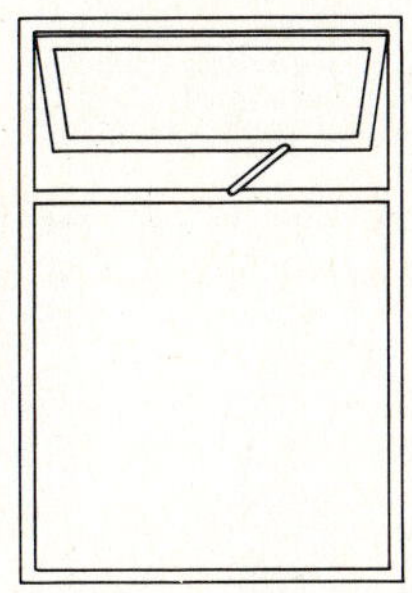

ventilator opening out over fixed pane

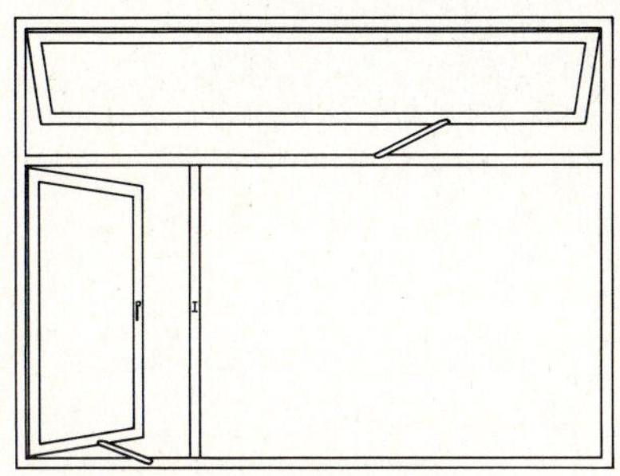

top-hung ventilator opening out, side-hung casement and fixed pane

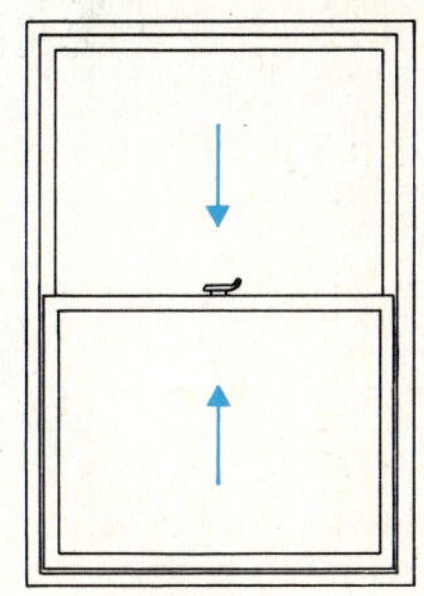

vertical sliding (double-hung sashes)

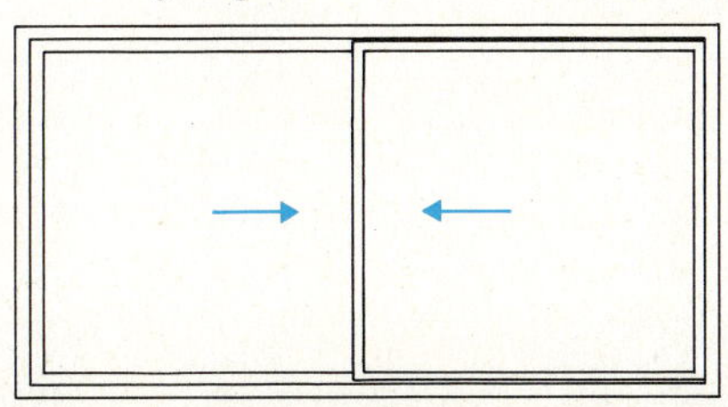

horizontal sliding

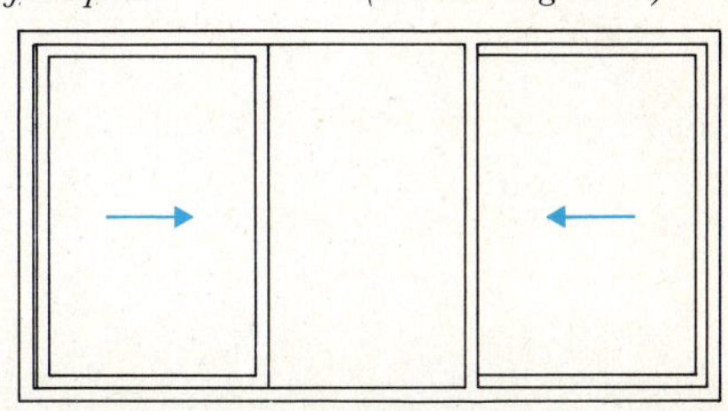

horizontal sliding with fixed centre pane

NB Windows that open inwards will catch on blinds and curtains.

In this kitchen (right), light and interest are provided by an interior window overlooking a glass-roofed rear extension.

Let the sun shine in

A kitchen solarium perhaps? A futuristic glass vault (top) highlights a décor based on the objets d'art of yesteryear.

The observatory-type kitchen with a wall of glass (left). An even intensity of light pours on to the flawless work-surfaces.

Rooflights

In a kitchen built under the roof, a skylight will help to illuminate dark corners and internal larders. Rooflights are made of glass, plastic or fibreglass and are sold in various styles such as domes, pyramids and barrel vaults, all of which can be singly or doubly glazed. There is a system for fully glazed sloping roofs called "Patent Glazing", which consists of metal glazing bars set 600 mm (2 ft) apart spanning up to 3 m (10 ft) without intermediate support. Wired glass should be fitted to rooflights where there is danger of falling tiles or vandalism—it also gives additional fire protection.

Existing windows

If you want to build a work-top across or in front of an existing window, make sure it can still be opened easily. Where the window is fitted with vertical sliding sashes the provision of extra sash lifts, pulleys, or a long-arm hook may be helpful. The addition of white-painted window reveals and glazing bars helps reflect more light.

Solar control

Solar control glass reduces heat build-up and minimizes glare. Though it is expensive, it helps to keep south-facing kitchens cool on hot sunny days and saves on air-conditioning costs. Solar control glass is made either surface-tinted (vulnerable to scratches) or body-tinted. The tints are bronze, green or grey; all colours will marginally affect the room's colour values, though perhaps bronze is the most sympathetic. The glass is available in 4- to 12-mm ($\frac{5}{32}$- to $\frac{1}{2}$-in) thicknesses, and while it can safely be incorporated in double-glazing units, it should not be used in conjunction with wired glass, as the heat differential between the glasses could cause cracking.

Window treatments

Apart from reducing sun glare, some windows—those facing into a neighbour's house, for example— may require screening. Patterned, textured, sand-blasted and acid-etched glass all give varying degrees of privacy, but will, of course, reduce the light. Blinds, drapes, louvers and curtains may be employed instead; the type of window reveal and wall space at either side will determine the most suitable covering.

Curtains, because they attract dirt and may become a fire hazard, should never be hung in kitchens, unless the window is well away from the cooking and sink areas. Even then they should be of flame-proof material that is easily washable.

Blinds and shutters fixed to the outside wall give good shade from sun, but have to be operated from outside; they must also be taken down in winter. Internal shutters require a deep sill space to allow for folding and unfolding.

Roller blinds that tuck neatly away at the top of the window, far from any work-surface, are particularly suitable for kitchens. They are made in a wide range of materials from the traditional holland to PVC-coated fabrics, stiffened cotton lace, linoleum and split cane.

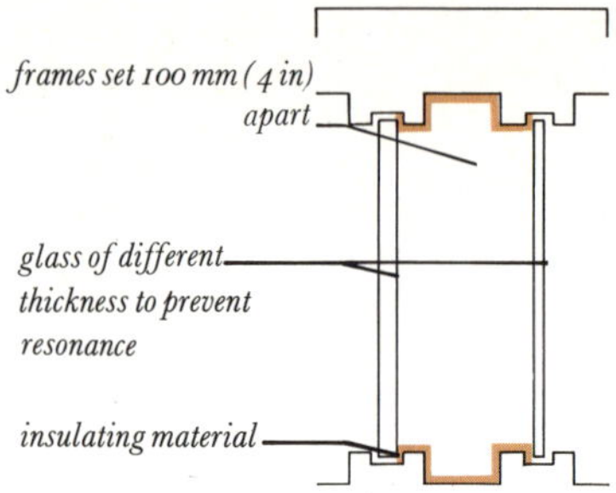

If you live close to a motorway or an airport, double glazing will help to cut down noise.

Insulation

Double glazing improves thermal insulation and helps to cut draughts, condensation and fuel bills. There are two methods of double glazing, in one of which two sheets of glass are set 6 to 12 mm ($\frac{1}{4}$ in to $\frac{1}{2}$ in) apart, hermetically sealed together and fixed to one sash. The other consists of two single-glazed windows, which are separately hinged on to the same frame.

Insulating against aircraft noise or that of heavy traffic is a much more complicated operation. It involves the construction of two completely separate windows at least 100 mm (4 in) apart; the space between the frames must then be lined at the sides and the top with insulating material. The glass of inner and outer panes must differ in thickness to prevent sympathetic resonance. While this method certainly helps to reduce the tumult outside, the snags are that the frames are cumbersome to operate and the insulation material is difficult to keep clean.

The work-top across the window (above) is a pleasant place to prepare a meal. Remember not to obstruct window handles with shelves.

For private lives—diagonal slats of timber, delicately suggesting Art Deco, screen the small kitchen (above).

The tall Georgian sash window (below), white-painted to make the most of light, is a perfect frame for an English country garden.

Lace curtains (below) soften the light and create an olde worlde atmosphere in the midst of a modern industrial complex.

Ribbed glass in the lower window panes (above) shields pyjama-clad breakfasters from the curious glances of neighbours.

Ssssh!

Truly sound-proofed, your kitchen would be nightmarish—a hushed tomb dedicated to an eternity of chores. Absolute quiet cocoons the nerves to a point where normal domestic noises, such as the ringing of a telephone, explode upon the consciousness like a fire-cracker. Extraordinarily, when office buildings are constructed with over-effective sound insulation, acoustic engineers are frequently obliged to introduce machines that produce low-pitched background sounds, known as "white noise", to restore an atmosphere of controlled quiet.

Fortunately, full sound-proofing is not the only method of achieving quiet. Unless you live in exceptionally noisy surroundings, perhaps close by an urban motorway or in the direct flight path to an airport, it is sound control, rather than sound-proofing, that will add comfort to your existence.

The reasons for this are curious and somewhat complex. Sound is transmitted from a vibrant source—say, your vocal chords or the door bell—by myriad perpetually dancing aerial molecules. Just as a ripple moves across a pool, crossing the water and returning from the far bank to the source of the original disturbance, so too do waves of sound reverberate from the surfaces that enclose them. Of course, some surfaces give rise to less reverberation than others: curtains, carpets and acoustic tiles, for example, soak up sound as a sponge soaks up water—because, like a sponge, these materials, too, are porous. The sound waves bounce in the air pockets contained in them until their energy is finally dissipated.

When trying to control the noise within a room, these characteristics of sound must be borne in mind. First, impose what control you can over the source of the sound and then cut reverberation. The first step involves reducing vibration: you might, for example, try mounting the washing machine on rubber pads, lagging the ventilator motor with a canvas sleeve, or eliminating water hammer by introducing air chambers into the water pipes.

The second step, that of cutting reverberation, is rather more difficult and calls for a compromise. Few materials reflect sound better than hard, tiled floors, steel work-tops and shiny kitchen units.

Carpet is the quietest floor covering—but is impractical in cooking areas. If you can bear to sacrifice the notion of ceramic tiles it is really better to put down cork tiles or foam-backed vinyl sheeting instead. Wood provides the quietest of all work-surfaces. Every kitchen should have a good-sized wooden chopping board and, if you can afford it, replace any laminated wall units you may have with wooden shelving.

Doorless cupboards also help to keep the noise down, since the exposed contents and the irregular wall behind present a surface less sympathetic to reverberations than a flat, closed door.

Wooden panelling on walls or ceilings reflects less sound than plaster or paper, but if you are truly noise-conscious it is best to install acoustic tiles or beams. These may be made of either fibre or perforated metal; fibre tiles are not usually recommended because they are not easily cleaned.

Two or three of these measures, harnessed together, will help you towards a calmer, more ordered kitchen; they are also relatively cheap to install.

Full sound insulation, however, either to prevent the escape of noise from your kitchen or its entry from the outside world, is much more complicated and expensive to achieve. It is probably only worth doing if you have a professional kitchen, as it will involve completely rebuilding floors, walls and ceilings with materials recommended by local authorities. It is possible to improve an existing wall by erecting a curtain of fibreglass quilt held in place by battens and an inner skin of special sound-absorbing board. But the exercise is pointless—as is any type of sound-proof partition, floor or ceiling—unless every single air leak is sealed. This may or may not be achieved with fibreglass lagging, but it is certainly not the end of your problems.

You must tackle doors as well as walls—a heavy solid-core door will be better than a light one. Sound flows in straight lines, so a baffle of any kind will achieve some results. The rebated meeting of door and frame can be improved by adding a cover batten screwed to the door edge on its opening side. Door threshold fittings can be fixed to the floor so that the door shuts against a rubber buffer, thus sealing the surround.

Double-glazing windows to exclude sound is not the same operation as that for thermal insulation. For sound-proofing the two panes of glass should ideally be 200 mm

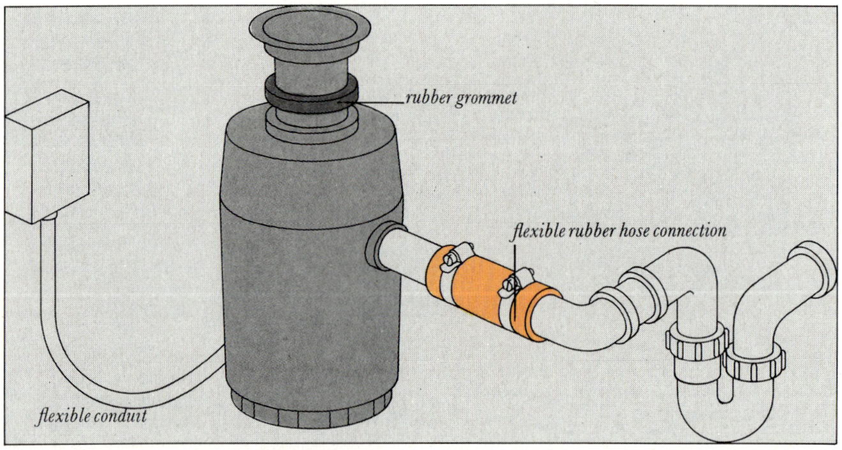

Rumbling waste-disposal units can be subdued by installing rubber connections and flexible pipes. These reduce noise and vibration (above).

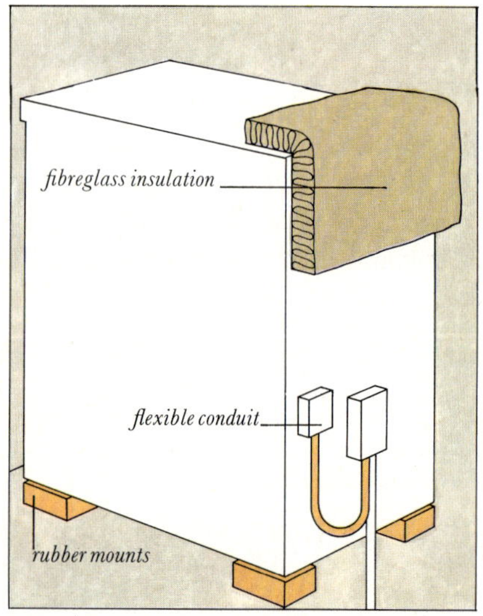

A dishwasher's cycle is not so obtrusive if the machine rests on rubber mounts, has a flexible conduit and is insulated from the work-top (right).

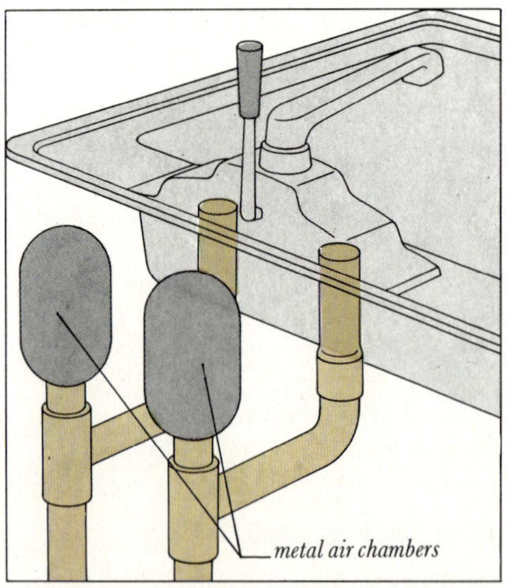

Even well-buried water pipes sometimes betray their presence with off-stage noises. To prevent "water hammer", fit hot and cold pipes with metal air chambers.

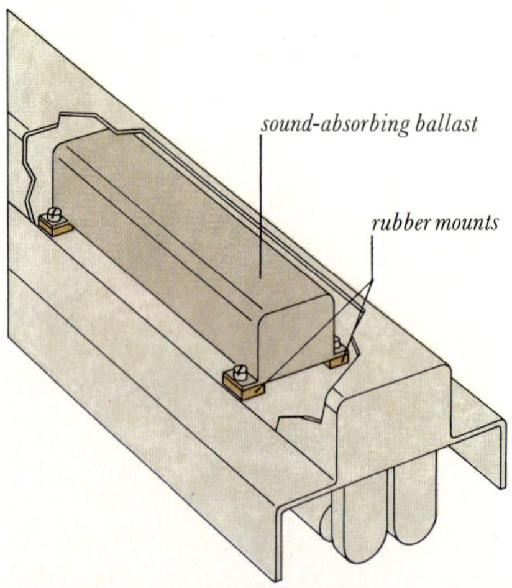

If the continuous hum of a flourescent light becomes too irritating, place some sound-absorbing ballast on rubber mounts over the top of the fitting.

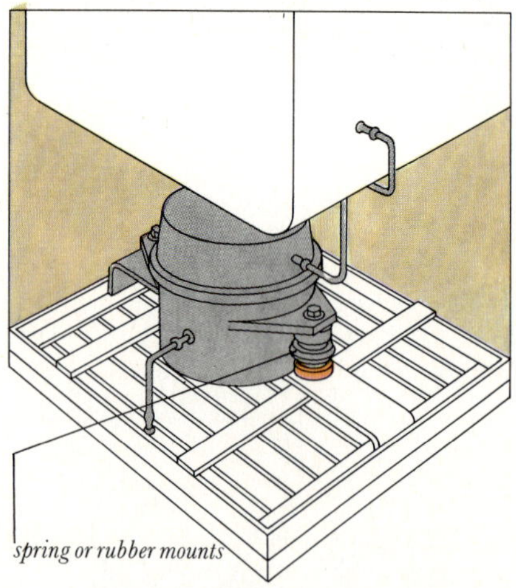

A vibrating refrigerator can be cured by fitting rubber or spring mounts and moving it to a level site. The latter also helps to ensure that the door will close automatically.

(8 in) apart, with the sides of the space between finished with sound-absorbent material.

Unless doors are close fitting and specially constructed, and windows double-glazed, the effect of your work will be spoilt. Also you must be wary of what acoustic engineers call the flanking elements—any unsound-proofed wall, floor or ceiling that adjoins the one you have soundproofed. It is a perverse characteristic of sound that if any flanking element is acoustically weak, sound will be transmitted through it (especially if it is a window), ignoring the presence of the sound-proof wall, and the noise will probably be at a greater volume than if there were no partition to avoid.

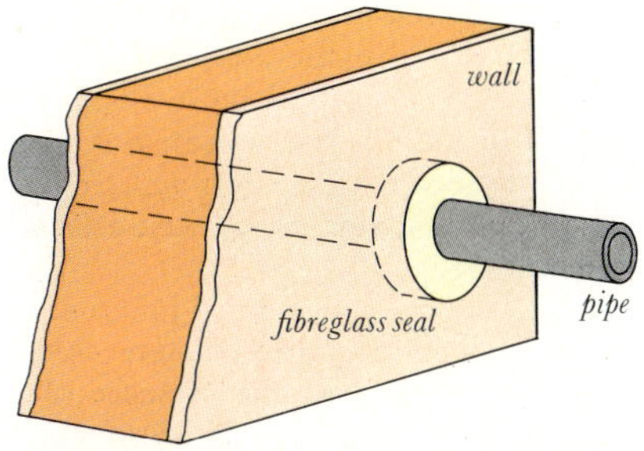

Seal holes cut through common walls for heating or water pipes with a resilient material to stop noise escaping (above).

Cork flooring and rubber mounts underneath machines cut down noise (below).

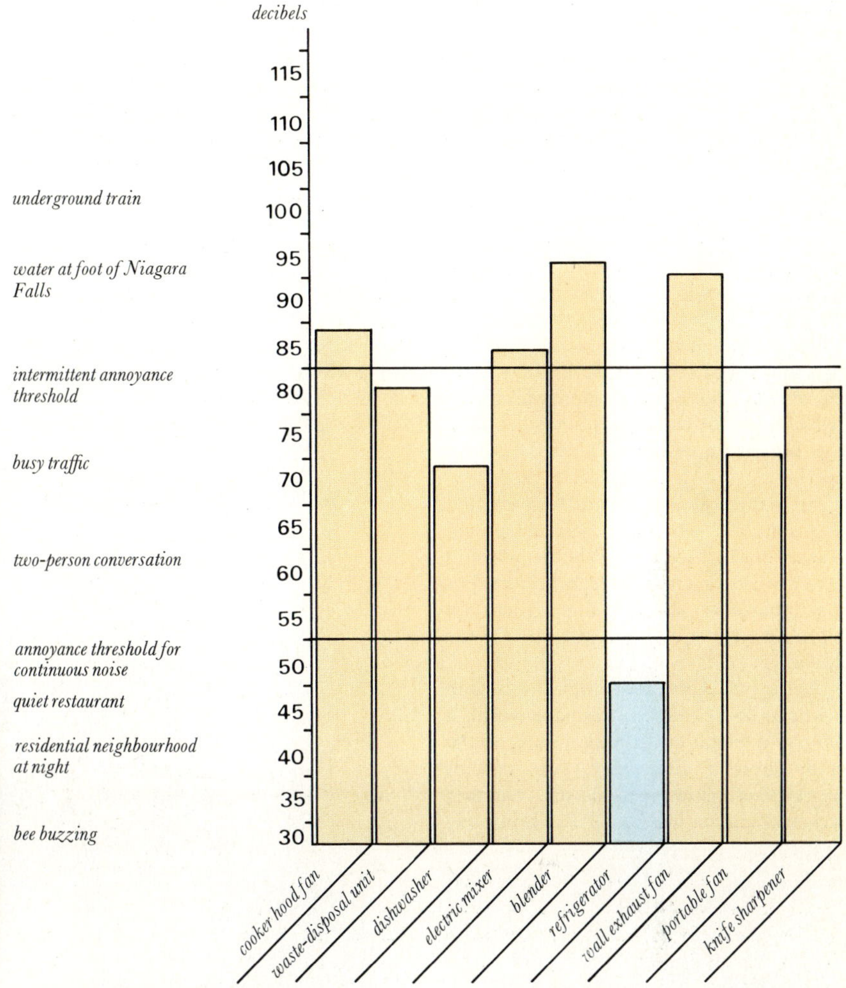

The table above demonstrates the noise levels of kitchen equipment. All but the refrigerator are above the continuous annoyance threshold.

However, kitchen machines that are switched on only intermittently can cause even more distress than continuous sound.

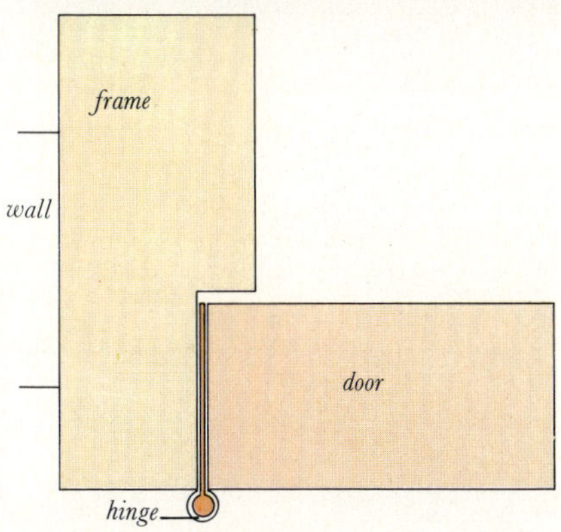

A cross-section of a standard door with a single rebate. The heavier and more solid the door—an old-fashioned panelled-pine one, for example—the better it will exclude sound.

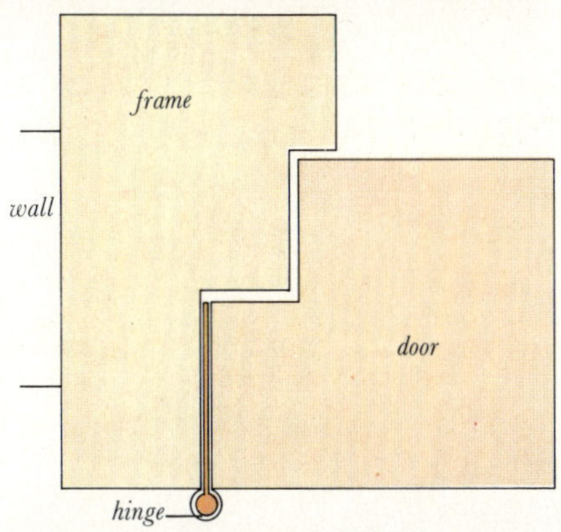

A door with a double rebate provides an even more effective barrier against noise. Sound travels in straight lines, so the extra corner acts as a further muffle.

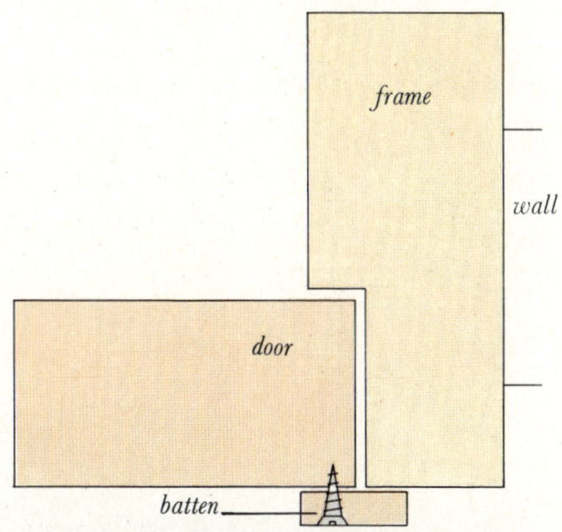

The sound-proofing of a single rebated door is improved by fitting a batten to the top. Remember to fit it to the side opposite the hinges so that the door can be opened.

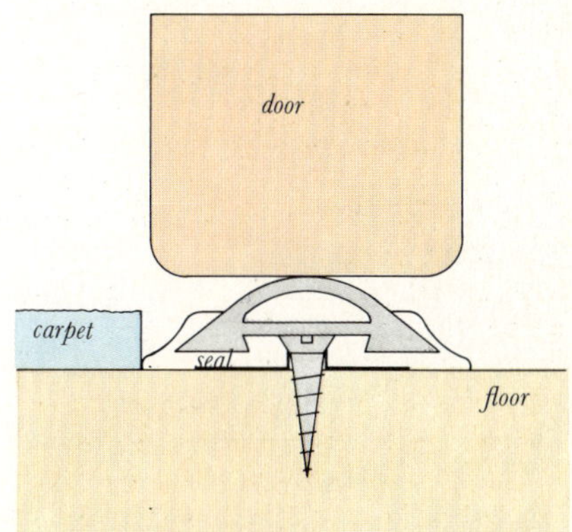

An end view of a kitchen threshold fitted with a seal to close the gap between the bottom of the door and the floor. The seal used in this case is a long metal strip.

Keeping in touch

With one neat stack of instruments in the kitchen, it is now possible, without taking any exercise, to check on all the activities of the house. Closed circuit TV can tell you that the children are not misbehaving in the swimming pool and keep an eye on the front door at the same time. Welcome callers can be admitted by pressing a button and an extra pint can be ordered from the milkman by intercom. You can pre-record a sharp message for your daughter when she comes in late from her date, operate the hi-fi, watch TV, listen to the radio, make a phone call and control the heating anywhere in the house. For good measure, there is an emergency button for summoning the police or fire brigade and wave detector in case humans or animals fall into the pool at odd hours.

An American electronics firm created this domestic communications command post to "make life easier". Whether it would actually do so is a matter for conjecture, but most people would agree that if there is a place for such equipment, then it is in the kitchen.

As the hub of the household, the kitchen ought to be linked to the outside world, if only by a telephone extension hung on the wall. Have a desk diary, note pad or blackboard within easy reach, together with writing implements. There is just one comfortable, efficient way to write during a telephone conversation: and that is on a flat surface. A desk or writing-top by your kitchen telephone, complete with a chair or stool, will encourage you to pay the household bills while waiting for something to boil—in the long term, this is probably as labour-efficient as any electronic command post.

Equally desirable is a doorbell within earshot of the kitchen and, if the front door is on a different floor, an Entryphone. If you have more than one entrance to the house, install doorbells with different tones, or a bell and a buzzer. A baby alarm, too, with a speaker installed in the kitchen, can save you many a climb to the nursery.

Occupying a humbler, but nevertheless important, niche is the noticeboard. It is useful for messages, price-lists and recipes, and fun for pinning up nursery art and photographs.

"Of all noises," said Samuel Johnson, "I think music is the least disagreeable." Countless people take the presence of a radio in the kitchen for granted. One has only to be a little less lukewarm about music than the great lexicographer to find the kitchen a natural place for extension speakers from the record or cassette player.

A complete lack of family communication caused by supper-time TV (above). For kitchen viewing a small portable set working from an indoor aerial is quite adequate.

Three coats of blackboard paint on the kitchen door (left) make memos unforgettable. Chalk and duster are provided in the little wooden box.

The intercom has graduated from raising the alarm in the nursery to summoning the children from far-flung corners of the house at meal times.

Next to the telephone extension is a door porter (above)—a saving of time and energy if your kitchen is in the basement and a ring at the doorbell necessitates a considerable climb.

The communication command post of the future (above), from which the lucky housewife can summon the police, keep an eye on the children or telephone her mother.

Speakers throughout the house are fed from this stereo equipment (right), which is sufficiently removed from the kitchen to be safe from damp and vibration yet near enough for convenience.

Colour sense

Living with a colour scheme

The choice of colour, pattern and texture is highly personal. It is also susceptible to fashion. This year's "avocado" may be ousted by next year's "eau-de-nil", and change for the sake of change is wasteful. Make your own decisions—do not be persuaded by your friends into a colour scheme you instinctively reject. Remember that the kitchen is a much used room; equipment and cabinets are too expensive to change on a colourful whim.

It is unfair to choose a colour actively disliked by other members of the family. After all, you will all have to live with it and the mood it creates, and you will have to live with it all year round. A vibrant, aggressive red and orange kitchen will certainly pep you up in the morning and keep you thinking warm thoughts all winter, but you could find yourself painting everything a cool shade of lime green by next summer.

When selecting colours, have a look at them in the daylight and in artificial light; and make up a patterns board, assembling small samples of the finishes and materials to be used, so you can see what effect they all have on each other.

Opinions vary enormously as to what effect colours have on people. It is generally acknowledged that, if used to excess, red can be unsettling, orange too stimulating, yellow too tiring on the eyes, green too restful, blue too cold, purple very off-putting and brown or black too mournful and depressing.

However, laying down rules about colour is a dangerous pastime, as often the most successful colour schemes consciously break all the rules at once.

The cosmetic effect of colour

Your choice of colour should take into consideration the size and orientation of the room. Blues tend to be cold and would be a chilling choice for a dark, north-facing room. Bright yellow is sunny and cheerful, but may be too overpowering in a kitchen streaming with afternoon sunshine. If the window area is inadequate, then pale colours will reflect more light into the room and on to work-surfaces. Light colours tend to make walls recede, thus making the room seem bigger. Conversely, dark colours have the effect of bringing surfaces nearer, so it is possible to visually lower a ceiling, or shorten a long, thin room. Kitchens with awkward nooks and crannies can be pulled together by painting walls, ceilings and even equipment all in the same colour.

Kitchen units

Kitchen cabinets are expensive, and as the work-tops and cabinet doors will probably be the most dominant feature in the room, the choice of finish is a most important colour decision. The natural colours of wood and tile are easy to live with, but need more attention than the intensely colourful plastic laminates and vinyls. On the practical side, dark surfaces show marks more readily than pale ones.

Colourful kitchen equipment

Most refrigerators, cookers, dishwashers and washing machines have a bright white enamel finish, which will shine out like a beacon in a line-up of smart dark units.

Choc-ice colour scheme (right). A dark-brown recess makes a delicious contrast to the creamy white rows of Formica cupboards.

What is colour? When light is refracted through a prism—or raindrops—the colours of the rainbow can be seen in an invariable sequence of red, orange, yellow, green, blue, indigo and violet. The full spectrum is made up of infinite gradations of these colours.

Colour schemes fall into three main categories:

Monochromatic where one colour only is used in all its varying shades from an intense, dark tone through to white. If handled with flair the effect can be dramatic, but all too easily it turns out dull and soporific.

Related colour schemes are built up from colours adjacent to one another in the spectrum, such as reds and oranges. A related scheme of varying tones is generally harmonious and restful. It's a tried and tested way of mixing colours and there's little risk that you'll go wrong.

Contrasting schemes use colours from opposite ends of the spectrum, but not necessarily of the same intensity. If handled judiciously a contrasting scheme is exciting and stamps personality on the dullest of rooms; badly interpreted, it creates a very unsettling atmosphere.

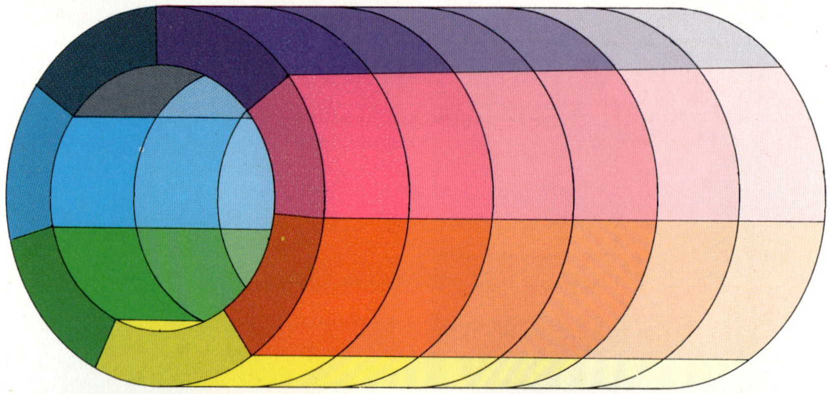

A prism splits light into the colours of the spectrum—red, orange, yellow, green, blue, indigo and violet. They are arranged (right) in their unalterable sequence with the pure tones of each hue progressing towards white.

Close tones of one colour can be soothing but monotonous (left), whereas contrasting tones (right) look livelier.

Complementary, or opposite, colours intensify each other (top) and may be overpowering unless you use a little tonal ingenuity (below).

Related colours (top) are inevitably harmonious, although tonal contrast is often more interesting (middle) than tonal equality (bottom).

Some manufacturers provide metal frames so you can slip in a door panel of whatever material you choose. It is possible to paint over enamel with specially formulated paints, but if you want coloured equipment, it is more satisfactory to buy it if you can. There is a range of very colourful acrylic sinks, and cooker/boilers come in lovely glossy primary colours. Even taps are colour-conscious now, but refrigerators and dishwashers tend to stick at white.

Extremes meet in the kitchen (above), where white units cut a dash against jet-black rubber. A dramatic scheme that is hard to better.

Trompe-l'oeil kitchen (below), painted with primary colours that ignore boundaries, helps lower an over-high ceiling.

Kitchen to munch violet creams in (above); sharp greens and dark blues help guard against a sickly surfeit of gentle mauve.

Illusion of infinity (left). The striped blind irradiated by glaring daylight seems to hover in a midnight-blue void.
Summer sunshine pours into the kitchen (below), where the green and white cloth is an extension of the bright, sun-bleached view.

Colour choice

Daffodil yellow and its chromatic relative, green, translates this kitchen (above) into an ode to spring.

As carefully composed as a Mondrian, areas of chrome-edged black and white create streamlined glamour around a sophisticat (above).

The cool school (above). White is restful, light, clean and obviously conducive to study as well as to calm cooking.

Natural and artificial colours are effectively juxtaposed (below). The tunnel of wood and brick is grafted on to a slickly painted alcove.

Thoughts of Red China in an English kitchen (above). Glossy paint and contrasting whiteness save the scarlet from being too overpowering.

Pastel without timidity (below). Stark white, slate grey, blue and brown echo the muted colours of the sombre seascape.

An Hellenic colour scheme of sparkling whiteness against a blue sea creates a look of airy freshness in the kitchen (above) at Saltaire, Fire Island, New York.

Maintenance

Cleaning equipment and materials
Your kitchen cleaning tackle will serve you better and last you longer if you follow the manufacturer's instructions. Remember to wash out dustpans and brushes regularly. Bristle brushes should be washed in pure soap rather than detergent and left to dry naturally. Squeezy mops occasionally need their sponges replaced, and dusters should be washed every week.

Machines
The modern kitchen contains a good deal of expensive equipment. Make sure you get the best out of your investment by using the machinery correctly and by instituting a regular maintenance programme.

When you have just bought a new machine it is very important to read the instruction book. It's surprising how many people don't. Ensure, too, that the plumber or electrician installing the machine is familiar with the make; each brand has a different set of foibles. When unpacking, institute a careful search for padding. Many a machine, on first being switched on, has burst into flame through its unhappy owner overlooking a piece of corrugated cardboard. Check that the electrical rating is suitable for the socket outlet and that the correct rated fuse is fitted in the plug.

Next, study the operating instructions and if in any doubt ask the supplier to give you a demonstration and make sure the whole family understands how the machine works. If your new purchase is a washing machine, use the detergents recommended by the manufacturers, otherwise they might refuse to honour the guarantee should problems arise.

Keep all instruction booklets in one place, together with the guarantees, which should show the name of the supplier, the date of purchase and the price paid. Receipts should also be kept throughout the period that the guarantees are in force.

Many manufacturers operate servicing contracts whose terms generally include periodic visits to check the machines as well as an emergency service. These contracts are generally good value so, when selecting a machine, you should take the manufacturer's record for prompt and efficient service into consideration.

It is also important to inspect flexes periodically for cracks in insulation.

Cookers
Catalytic linings in all modern ovens help to reduce the problems of keeping a cooker clean. Try to mop up spills as they occur and use caustic cleaners for the oven. Steel wool and abrasive cleaners will help deal with stubborn marks.

Refrigerators
Defrost regularly (unless defrosting is automatic). Wipe out periodically with mild bleach solution to disinfect, and with a weak solution of bicarbonate of soda to retard frost build-up.

Deep-freezers
Clear out every six months, wrapping up frozen food in newspaper for temporary insulation. Remove ice with special plastic

Kitchen—general

Brushes and sponges	
Scrubbing brush	for vegetables.
Bottlebrushes	large for flower vases; small for teapot spouts.
Suction plunger	for unblocking sink waste.
Washing-up liquid	
Scouring pads	
Steel-wool soap-pads	use only with rubber gloves.
Dishwasher powder	
Rinse aid	for dishwashers.
Water softener	for some dishwashers in hardwater areas.
Floor-cleaning detergent	
Silver dip	for removing the odd egg tarnish off silver cutlery.
Household soap	for washing hands and pure bristle brushes.
Dirty-hand cleaner	
Methylated spirit	for general grease and stain removing.
Ammonia	(as above)
White spirit (turps)	(as above)
Descaler	for descaling kettles in hardwater areas.
Caustic oven cleaner	take great care—will burn skin.
Spirits of salt	for unblocking wastes.
Non-scratch scouring cream	
Abrasive cleaner	
Laundry (if separate from kitchen sink)	
Soap flakes	for woollens and delicate fabrics.
Washing powders	for automatic machines, other machines and hand washing.
Bleach	for whitening clothes and disinfecting drains.
Fabric conditioner	
Broom cupboard	
Soft broom	for general sweeping of hard floors.
Hard broom	for outside yards.
Soft brush	for general use.
Hard brush	for carpet edges and stairs.
Dustpan	
Cobweb brush	long handle for tall rooms and stairwells.
Vacuum cleaner	
Hand vacuum cleaner	for stairs and motor car (with extension lead)
Electric floor polisher	only necessary for large polished floors.
Squeezy mop	for floors.
Long-handled squeezy mop	for windows.
Plastic bucket	
Scrubbing brush	for floors.
Kneeling pad	
Carpet shampoo	
Cleaning rags	for 'putting on".
Dusters	for 'taking off" and general dusting.
Chamois leather	for cleaning windows.
Silver brush	
Furniture cream	
Wax polish	
Non-slip floor polish	for kitchen and "wet" areas.
Graphite cream and fireplace brush	for blacking and polishing grates.
Spray cleaner	for all-purpose cleaning.

Finishes

Cabinet and wallfinishes

(WWD—Warm water and mild detergent)*

Finish	Care
Acrylic	*WWD—remove scratches with metal polish. Never use abrasive cleaners.
Glass and mirrors	Use proprietary cleaner, or wipe with linen cloth dipped in methylated spirit. Remove paint and stubborn marks with a razor blade. To avoid condensation droplets, rub over with a cloth dipped in equal parts of glycerine and methylated spirit.
Gloss paint	WWD. Methylated spirit is good for removing kitchen grease; rinse the paint well and polish with furniture cream to preserve finish.
Marble	Wipe with warm water and pure soap, not with strong detergents or abrasives. Oil and fruit juice spills should be wiped immediately or they will stain. Remove minor scratches with powdered tin oxide (putty powder), rinse and polish with a soft cloth. Marble can be sealed with a water-based sealer.
Melamine	WWD—no abrasives—liquid cleaner if necessary.
Plastic laminate	WWD—no abrasives—liquid cleaner if necessary.

scraper and wash in the same way as refrigerator. Replace frozen food only when freezer temperature has returned to its normal operating level.

Dishwashers
Clean filters after use. Have a contract maintenance check every six months.

Washing machines
Follow operating instructions carefully and do not overload. Ensure you use the correct washing powder for your type of machine. A regular maintenance contract is definitely worth while.

Tumble-driers
Clean filters after every use, otherwise elements will burn out from overheating.

Irons
Some steam irons can only be used with distilled water, otherwise they will fur-up. Others can be descaled by removing the central panel in the base. Materials burnt on to the base should not be scraped off. Depending on the metal, remove them with: metal polish (for chrome), steel wool (for aluminium) and a nylon mesh pad for non-stick bases. Do not iron over zips and metal fasteners or the base may become damaged.

Electric kettles
Before switching on, always make sure the element is covered with water to prevent it burning out. Fill only to water level mark to prevent the water bubbling over. If there is no automatic cut out, switch off the kettle before pouring. In hardwater areas, descale the inside periodically with a patent scaler, and keep the chrome or stainless-steel body clean with appropriate metal polishes. Plastic handles can be cleaned with furniture cream.

Electric toasters
Never try to remove jammed-in toast with a metal object while the toaster is switched on. Periodically remove crumbs from the underside, but check that the toaster is unplugged before doing so. Clean the case with metal polish for chrome and furniture cream for enamel and plastic parts.

Electric mixers and blenders
Do not strain the motor by running it for too long or using to stiff a mixture, otherwise it may burn out. Clean mixer bodies—when unplugged—with furniture cream.

Extractor fans
Grills and filters should be regularly dismantled and cleaned with methylated spirit or furniture cream. As with every other electrical appliance, water must never come in contact with the motor. A maintenance contract can often be arranged with the manufacturer.

Light fittings
Keep shades and lamps clean as dirt reduces the lighting levels. Switch off lights at the mains before removing any parts. Clean lamps with methylated spirit, and wash acrylic and glass shades in warm soapy water. Dry thoroughly.

Polyester paint	WWD—finish with furniture cream.
Polypropylene	WWD—finish with furniture cream.
Polyurethane	WWD—finish with furniture cream.
Stainless steel	Non-scratch scouring cream, then WWD. Never use silver dips as these will turn metal grey. Pitting can be caused by salts and acid if left in contact too long.
Tiles, ceramic	Normally only need wiping down. When necessary, clean with non-scratch scouring cream. Use liquid shoe whitener on dirty joints.
Vinyl wall covering	WWD.
Washable wallpapers	Wipe with WWD, but do not let surface get too wet.
Wood—french polished and clear cellulose	Remove heat marks with cloth dipped in 1:4 linseed oil/white spirit; leave overnight; wipe clean and polish.
Wood—sealed	WWD—rinse and dry thoroughly; rub with wax polish to preserve finish.
Wood—teak work-tops	WWD daily; periodically, when dry and bleached, apply boiled linseed oil, warmed in a double boiler, and rub with fine steel wool. Repeat two or three times, allowing a day between applications. Alternatively apply proprietary oil according to manufacturer's instructions.
Wood—wax polished	To remove stains, rub with cut cork or fine steel wool lubricated with white spirit, wipe with clean cloth and rewax.

Floor finishes

Finish	Care
Brick	Sweep and wash. Apply water-based seal if rquired.
Cork	Apply oleoresin or polyurethane sealer. Sweep, wash and occasionally emulsion polish.
Hardwood	Sweep and mop; occasionally emulsion polish if wood is sealed. Never use wax polishes in kitchen, as they are slippery when wet.
Lino	Sweep, wash, and wipe dry as water and oil rots lino. Finish with emulsion polish.
Marble	Sweep and wash, but not with acid cleaners; use water-based sealer occasionally.
Mosaic	Sweep and wash, but do not polish.
Plywood	Sweep and mop; occasionally use emulsion polish. Seal with oleoresin or polyurethane sealer.
Quarry tiles	After initial laying, seal with 1:4 linseed oil/white spirit. Cover with brown paper and leave unwalked on for two days. Normally sweep and wash. Apply water-based seal if required.
Rubber	Sweep and wash; occasionally use emulsion polish. Never use spirit solvents.
Slate	Sweep and wash—finish off with water-based seal if required. Rub with milk for a lighter finish. Can be polished, but make sure a non-slip polish is used.
Stone	Sweep and wash.
Terrazzo	Sweep and wash but do not polish. Do not use acid cleaners.
Vinyl	Sweep and wash; occasionally use emulsion polish.

Windows

Finish	Care
Pleatex blinds	Dust with vacuum cleaner attachment.
Roller blinds—PVC and cotton	Sponge with warm water—never immerse or scrub.
Roller blinds—holland	Dust only, unless treated with special finish that can be wiped with warm water and detergent.
Venetian blinds	Use venetian blind brush for ordinary dusting. Occasionally unhook and wash in bath with mild detergent.

Maintenance

Kitchen Utensils

Pots and pans

When buying a new pan, check whether the handles and knobs are oven-proof. Always wash them before use and remove labels with furniture cream to avoid scratches. Always follow the manufacturer's instructions about how to look after a pot or pan. New materials are constantly being developed and their performance and cleaning instructions may vary.

Flame-, fire- and oven-proof

Flame-proof pans may be used directly on gas flames or electric rings. However, for added safety it is wise to use a heat-diffusing mat, which spreads flames under the pot and reduces the shock of initial temperature change, or with electricity to place the pan on a cold ring, which can then be heated up. A flame-proof pan should always be heated up and cooled down slowly. Fire-proof and oven-proof dishes can be used in the oven, but not on the cook-top unless specifically marked flame-proof as well.

Pottery

Many glazed clay pots are serving dishes only, so check whether yours is oven-proof. Never try to warm empty pottery vessels in the oven and avoid subjecting them to sudden temperature changes. If the glaze becomes cracked pottery will pick up stains.

Stoneware

Stoneware is clay-fired to temperatures above 1200°C (2200°F); vessels made of this material are vitrified and non-porous. Stoneware is oven-proof and sometimes flame-proof, and will not stain if the glaze becomes cracked.

Patent ceramics and glassware

These are oven-proof and some are flame-proof. Although they will withstand temperature changes better than untreated ceramics, mats are still advisable.

Aluminium

Aluminium is light, easy to clean and does not tarnish or rust. Pitting can be caused by using sharp utensils or by storing food and water in them. Never use washing soda, which has a harmful chemical action. Hot frying-pans must not be immersed in cold water since they may buckle. Wash in hot water and detergent, using scouring pads and abrasives when necessary. Boiling acidic fruits will remove discoloration.

Stainless steel

These pans are expensive, but look good and are easy to clean. Most have copper or aluminium bases to improve heat conductivity. Wash with hot water and detergent using a nylon scourer.

Steel

It is normally sufficient to clean steel pans with kitchen paper. They are apt to rust if washed in water, unless they are thoroughly dried. Wipe over with oil.

Cast-iron

Cast-iron pans are usually finished with vitreous enamel (see below). Unfinished cast iron needs to be seasoned, so heat up a cup of olive oil and leave it to cool in the pan. Pour off the oil and wipe all round with kitchen paper. Clean the pans with hot water, detergent or a soda solution: dry thoroughly and re-oil before storing.

Enamel

Vitreous or porcelain enamel is glass-fired on to a metal base. Stove enamel is paint-fired on to metal and is more likely to become scratched than vitreous enamel. Wash with hot water using nylon scourers; if necessary, soak in a weak solution of bleach to remove stains. Avoid sudden temperature changes and hard knocks, which can chip the finish.

Copper

Use only wooden utensils in unlined copper pans and bowls. Remove tarnish by rubbing them with half a lemon dipped in salt and vinegar; rinse and dry before storing. Some copper pans are lined with tin; they should be relined when necessary.

Out, damned spot

The only efficient way to keep kitchen stains off your clothes is to cook in the nude; alternatively, having dressed for your guests, you can cover your finery with an all-enveloping apron. The first can be painful and the second is often impractical; for some reason of kitchen ballistics, grease always flies to that tiny portion of your clothing that the apron has failed to cover.

Greasy marks on washable materials should be rubbed with detergent and then rinsed thoroughly with hot water. Otherwise, use a grease solvent applied with a soft rag, first placing another piece of rag directly underneath the stain. Always work from outside the mark towards its centre to prevent leaving a ring around the original spot. If a yellow mark does persist, rub it with sodium perborate or chlorine bleach, or with hydrogen peroxide. Non-washable materials should also be sponged repeatedly with a cleaning fluid, allowing time to dry between applications.

In the case of non-greasy stains, immediately sponge or soak the materials in cool water. Then work undiluted liquid detergent into the mark and rinse. If spotting remains, take the garment to a dry cleaners, remembering to tell them the cause of the original stain.

For stains that are a mixture of greasy and non-greasy, such as white sauce or chocolate, treat the non-greasy element first, using cool water and detergent. Rinse thoroughly and let the material dry. Then dab the spot with cleaning fluid to remove the remaining grease.

Here are a few tips on dealing with the most common of household stains.

Beetroot	Soak in cool water. Then rub in undiluted detergent and rinse. Alternatively, spread an absorbent such as salt or talcum powder on the material and work it in gently. When the absorbent becomes caked up, brush it off and repeat applications as necessary.
Blood	Soak in cold water. On washable materials, apply a few drops of ammonia to old or stubborn stains, then wash again with detergent; non-washable materials should be sponged with a little hydrogen peroxide.
Butter	Washable fabrics should be laundered normally. Sponge non-washables with cleaning fluid.
Coffee and tea	Stretch fabric over a bowl, fasten it with a rubber band, and pour boiling water on the stain from a height of two or three feet. Wash the material afterwards. If traces of the stain remain, bleach fabric in the sun or use a diluted chemical bleach. If the drink contains cream, sponge in cool water and detergent. Rinse thoroughly and leave to dry. Then use a cleaning fluid to remove any grease.
Cream	Sponge non-washable materials with grease solvent. When dry, dab with cool water. Rinse washables with cool or lukewarm water; then wash them in soapy water and rinse thoroughly.
Egg	Scrape off as much as possible, then sponge with cold water. If washable, launder in usual way. Non-washable materials should be allowed to dry after sponging; then dab them with cleaning fluid.
Fruit and berry	Always sponge fresh stains promptly with cool water. Stretch the material over a bowl, secure it, and pour boiling water over it from a height of one to three feet. Never use soap on fruit stains.
Gravy	Soak washable fabrics in cold water to dissolve the starch; then launder. If spot persists, dab with cleaning fluid. Non-washable fabrics should be sponged in cool water, then dabbed with salt or a grease solvent.
Grease and oil	Treat fresh oil or grease stains promptly. Rub with detergent, then rinse thoroughly with hot water. For non-washables, use a cleaning fluid or cover with salt and leave until gummy. Brush off, and repeat application as necessary.
Heat marks	Rub lightly with cloth dampened with camphor oil, peppermint oil or turpentine.
Milk	Soak in cool water immediately, then work neat detergent into the stain and rinse. If spot persists, use a little bleach.
Mustard	On washable materials, apply liquid detergent to the dampened stain; then rinse. If the stain remains, soak in hot detergent solution overnight. Sponge

Tin
Tinned mild steel is used for baking tins, moulds, graters, whisks, etc. Abrasives may scratch tinned surfaces and expose the steel base to rust. Soak burned pans in detergent or washing soda; rinse before storing.

Non-stick
Non-stick pans should be handled with great care. Do not place on a fierce heat, and grease lightly before cooking sticky things, such as scrambled eggs, or cakes. Always remove food from non-stick pans with wooden, rather than metal, utensils. Wash the pans in hot water and detergent, leaving them to soak, if necessary, and avoid steel wool, scouring pads or abrasives.

Tableware

Crockery
Old china with fine glazes, gold patterns, etc., will be damaged by the high temperatures and washing powders in dishwashers. Wash them in a plastic bowl instead, using warm water, detergent and a bristle brush. Never use abrasives. Tea stains can be removed with salt on a damp cloth dipped in bicarbonate of soda. Chipped or cracked crockery may harbour bacteria and should be thrown away. Mugs and jugs with repaired handles are still liable to break in the hand.

Cutlery
All cutlery should be polished with a soft clean cloth immediately after washing to prevent possible staining or spotting by water. Cutlery with glued handles should never be placed in a dishwasher, since the high temperatures are likely to dissolve the glue. By the same token, you should never leave glued handles to soak, as this may cause discoloration and splitting. Clean stainless steel with metal polishes, never with silver dip.

Carbon-steel knives will rust unless dried immediately after washing. If not in constant use, lightly grease them with edible oil before storing.

Silver should be kept in baize-lined drawers to prevent scratching. If not in daily use, store in airtight boxes, or wrap the pieces individually in clinging polythene to prevent tarnishing. Clean periodically with silver polish and wash the pieces in warm water afterwards to remove the last traces of polish. Use a stiff brush to clean odd corners and intricate designs. Contact with salt, egg, vinegar, fruit juices, leaking gas or rubber will seriously tarnish silver. Remember, when using silver dip that it contains a strong corrosive acid, which can damage some brushes and leave silver lustreless; use it only for egg stains.

Silverplate is metal cutlery coated with a fine finish of pure silver. This is softer than sterling silver and therefore less durable.

Glass
Never subject glass to sudden temperature changes. When pouring hot drinks, put a spoon in the glass first then slowly pour in the hot liquid. The rim of a glass is the weakest part and glasses will break more easily if stored upside down. Wash glasses in hot (not boiling) water with detergent and a soft brush; rinse and dry immediately with a soft clean cloth for a sparkling finish. Decanters and narrow-necked vases can be cleaned by swilling with vinegar and salt. Alternatively, try soaking them overnight with one or two false teeth cleaning tablets. Rinse milky glasses in cold water first, as hot water simply smears milk fat on to the glass, making it more difficult to remove. To unstick stacked tumblers, stand the bottom glass in hot water and fill the top with cold.

Woodware
Wooden spoons and chopping boards in daily use are best kept where the air can circulate freely around them. Wash them in warm water and detergent, rinse well and let them dry naturally away from direct heat. Both sides of a board should be washed evenly, as warping can occur if one side is less wet than the other, or if it is left to soak in water. Lemon juice will whiten boards; stains can be removed with bleach but rinse the boards afterwards.

	marks on non-washable fabrics with spirit. Dilute with two parts water before using on acetate.
Soft drinks	Sponge immediately with cool water. Rub in liquid detergent, then rinse.
Vinegar	Rinse with cold water. Dab with ammonia (one tablespoon to one cup of water) or dissolved baking soda (one tablespoon per cup of water). Wash in clean water.
Wine	Stretch stained material over a bowl and secure. Sprinkle with salt and then pour boiling water over it from a height of one to three feet. Fresh stains on non-washables can sometimes be removed with salt. Alternatively, sponge with spirit. Dilute with two parts water for acetates.

Kitchen cleaning agents

Alcohol	Excellent for cleaning glass.
Ammonia	An alkaline gas dissolved in water that is sold for domestic use in strengths between 5 and 15 per cent. Household ammonia will dissolve grease, so add it to washing or rinsing water to make windows and glassware sparkle.
Borax	Dissolves grease, loosens dirt and halts the growth of many moulds and bacteria.
Carbon, activated	Comes from coconut shells and absorbs odours, so place a piece in the refrigerator, where it will kill any strong smells. Heat a piece in a frying-pan to dispel the odours it has absorbed.
Chlorine bleach	To remove stains from cleaned sinks, enamelware, tiles and woodwork, wipe or soak the spot with a solution (4 tablespoons bleach: 1 quart water).
Enzyme	Use enzyme soaking powders, e.g. Ariel and Radiant, at a moderate temperature for burnt-on food in saucepans, for cleaning blocked drains and for removing stains from teacups, vacuum flasks and flower vases. Never add to water that is above 60°C (140°F).
Lye	A very strong alkali for unblocking drains. Follow directions on the bottle exactly because lye is a dangerous caustic agent that must not come in contact with your skin.
Pumice	A good scourer and polisher that can be bought in powder form, in varying degrees of fineness, at hardware stores.
Silver polish	Apply a fine grade of whiting dampened with a little household ammonia or white spirit as a silver polish.
Sodium bicarbonate	Baking soda or bicarbonate of soda will remove stains from china, deodorize drains, help make cakes and biscuits, kill germs in refrigerators and, as a paste, will protect the interior lining of a stove. It will also clean glass, tiles and porcelain.
Sodium carbonate	An effective cleaner known as washing soda for cleaning drains, washing floors and degreasing pots and pans.
Sodium hydrate	A caustic soda sold as lye and used to unblock drains.
Stove polish	Mix finely powdered graphite with a little water. Otherwise buy a stove polish either as powder, liquid, paste, cake or stick. Avoid those containing inflammable liquids such as turpentine.
Turpentine	A resinous juice obtained from pine and fir trees. Will remove grease and will penetrate into wooden furniture to restore the original colour of the stain.
Vinegar	Cuts soap film, so useful cleaning agent.
Whiting	A very fine preparation of chalk used in cleaning powders, polishes, putty and oil-cloth. It can be bought by the pound at paint stores.

undries

It is far better to keep the laundry out of the kitchen altogether. A food preparation area is no place for dirty linen and the hot, damp atmosphere created by laundering it. It makes more sense to put the washing machine near the bathroom and bedrooms, but in many homes the kitchen is all too often the only available space with a water-resistant floor and sufficient plumbing. In these circumstances, try to keep the laundry area separate, and well away from the food and eating areas.

The laundry centre should be efficiently organized and fitted with reliable machinery. The list of equipment for an ideal laundry is long; an automatic washing machine, warm-air drier, spin-drier, sink and drainer, drip-dry rack, hanging rods, a work-top for sorting linen, baskets for clean and dirty linen, an airing cupboard, a safe place for washing powders, an ironing board, an efficient extractor fan and good lighting. Optional extras include an ironing machine and a sewing machine for running repairs.

Sinks and drying racks

In a mechanically equipped laundry where the sink is only for occasional hand-washing or soaking, a large deep, single bowl will suffice. Fix a rack over the draining-board for drying nylons and other hand-washed items. Hanging rods near the ironing area are useful for finished work.

Controls

Most washing and drying machines have child-proof doors, but switches are a temptation. Connect all machines to spur switches set in counter upstands well out of the reach of small children.

Washing machines

Sink-top and twin-tub washing machines have now been largely superseded by automatics. Sink-top models take up valuable work-top space and must be stored somewhere when not in use. Twin tubs need supervision and wet clothes have to be heaved from the wash tub to be rinsed in the spin-drier. Like sink-top models, twin tubs cannot be stored in the place in which they are to be used. However, they do spin well, and are cheap to buy and run.

Automatic machines combining washing, rinsing and drying programmes are obvious space savers, but there are disadvantages. Laundry time is long and inflexible, and in most models only half the wash can be dried at one time. Machines combining multiple activities are necessarily complex and are therefore likely to be less reliable.

An automatic washing machine and separate warm-air drier is the best but most expensive arrangement. A front-loading machine fits under a counter-top, stacks underneath a drier or builds into a high-level cabinet. Top-loading machines spin better, but break up the continuity of a work-surface. Most machines take a 4-kg (9-lb) load and have a variety of programmes, including pre-rinsing and a separate spin programme. Whichever model is chosen be sure there is enough space behind the machine for connecting pipes to waste and water supplies and sufficient flex for the machine to be pulled out for maintenance.

Spin-driers

A spin-drier is a useful adjunct to an automatic washing machine and tumble-drier. Vertical drums spin faster than the horizontal drums of front-loading automatics and therefore extract more water; expensive warm-air drying time is reduced, and they are ideal for hand-washed clothes, especially woollens.

Tumble-driers

An electric tumble-drier makes damp clothes completely dry, thus eliminating dripping clothes-lines. It can be stacked over the washing machine (if of the same make) or fitted alongside, under a counter-top. A drier must be ventilated. Up to 4.5 litres (1 gal) of water is evaporated during the drying programme and a ventilating kit is provided with most machines to get rid of this water vapour. It consists of a flexible hose fixed to the back or front of the machine to take the steamy air through the nearest window. Such Heath Robinson contraptions are better than nothing, but should be replaced by proper ducts built in behind the machine leading to an air brick

"Previous to the arrival of the electric washer, the housewife was faced with . . . sending clothes to the laundry to be washed along with everybody else's in a most drastic manner." Illustrated London News, *June, 1928 (right)*.

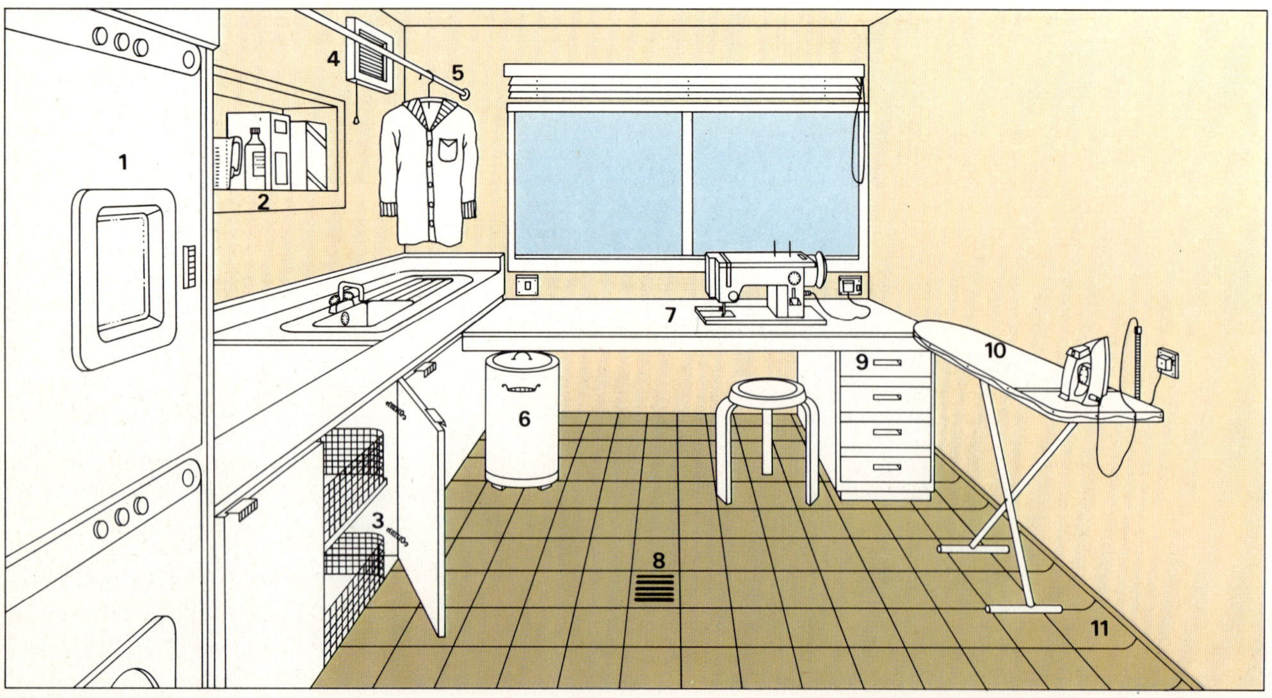

Plan of an ideal laundry (left). Commercial laundries would soon go out of business if we all had the space and the money to set up a utility room furnished like this.

1 *Built-in drier over washing machine with vent behind to outside wall.*
2 *Shelf for washing powders and bleaches over work-top.*
3 *Plastic-coated baskets that slide into the cupboard store dirty or clean clothes out of the way.*
4 *Extractor fan.*
5 *Rod for drip-dry clothes.*
6 *Separate spin-drier, for hand-washed clothes, can be plugged in to spur switch placed conveniently at back of work-top.*
7 *Lower level work-top for sewing machine.*
8 *Floor slopes gently towards central grating so any water will drain away naturally, and the floor is easily washed down.*
9 *Drawer for sewing accessories.*
10 *Free-standing ironing board with socket at high level.*
11 *Coved skirting protects walls against wet and is easy to clean.*

outside. Ideally a drier should be placed against an outside wall to save complicated duct-work. Some models vent through the doors, which is tolerable only if the room is large and well ventilated.

An alternative is the condenser type of machine, where moisture is recycled within the machine and this completely eliminates all humidity. Condenser machines are more expensive, drying time is slightly longer, and they need waste and water connections.

Good features to look for in a tumble-drier include a choice of heat settings, easily accessible filters, and an automatic reversing action, which reduces drying time and prevents creases. Some sophisticated models have moisture-content monitors that switch off when the required degree of dryness is reached.

Make sure the machine is placed on a solid floor, as it can set up considerable vibration and almost shake an old house to pieces. Be considerate of your neighbours, as the vibration can disturb them if the machine is placed next to a party wall or directly over their bedroom.

Wall driers

Fan-operated wall-mounted driers are cheaper than tumble-driers. They are basically electric fan heaters blowing hot air on to damp clothes hung on racks or lines that can be folded back against the wall when not in use.

Ironing boards

For efficient ironing one must stand over the work. The board should be mobile and adjustable from 575 mm to 1030 mm ($22\frac{1}{2}$ in to $40\frac{1}{2}$ in), it should have a finely tapered nose, a sleeve board and a flex support.

Hand irons

There are dry irons, steam irons and spray steam irons that dampen dry materials and make ironing quicker and easier. For easy manoeuvrability an iron should weigh about 1.2 kg (2 lb), with a flex at least 2.3 m (7 ft 6 in). Good features include a well-pointed toe, button grooves, easy descaling (for steam irons), indicator lights and clearly marked fabric and temperature guides.

Rotary and flat-bed irons

These machines claim to halve ironing time and enable you to sit down with both hands free to work. However, manual ironing will still be required for delicate and fiddly items, cuffs and collars, frills and seams. Unless there is a large amount of simple ironing, such as sheets and table cloths, ironers are not only of doubtful value but take up a lot of space.

Storage

Three large baskets or bins are needed for dirty clothes, clean clothes awaiting ironing and ironed clothes waiting to be put away. A high-level cupboard, out of the reach of young children, is required for bleaches, washing powders, conditioners, dyes, irons, starch, distilled water, spray bottle and damping cloths. Where space permits the ironing board is best left standing to avoid tiresome dismantling.

Floors

As washing machines will sometimes during their working life get blocked and overflow, make sure that the flooring material will not suffer if flooded. Ideally install a floor drain so that the water can be easily and safely swabbed down.

Top-loading machines break the continuity of a work-top (above)—but this one, well sited in a niche between sink and counter-top, does not interfere with the food-preparation area.

A well-ventilated condenser-type drier eliminates humidity and is therefore the best choice for a small kitchen (above).

A laundry in a cupboard is a neat kitchen compromise (left), but remember to leave sufficient room for maintaining the machines.

A front-loading duo of washing machine and warm-air drier (above)—the most practical combination for washday.

Work-rooms

The New York writer-cook George Lang insists upon a kitchen that combines his dual roles with the working requirements of his wife, Karen. Sewing machine and drawing-board, china cupboards and office equipment all have their allotted place in this recipe for a busy life (above).

In this Swedish marriage of living area and traditional bakery (left), a huge bread oven, polished wood, a few antiques and sheer professional know-how live together in amity.

Live-and-let-live is the spirit that animated this narrow kitchen (right), carved out of an old converted house by a husband-and-wife team. Despite the limited space they have found room for a highly efficient cooking area and a do-it-yourself work-bench, where every tool has its outlined place—an idea that might be adapted for kitchen utensils.

Bathing the offspring on the refrigerator top (above) alleviates backache and permits mother to keep a weather eye on the dinner.

A kitchen squeezed into a hall (above) leaves a well-lit space in the area beyond for a sewing bench.

A simple desk with adjustable shelving above is tucked into an alcove next to the oven (right), providing a working/relaxing area for the busy cook. The pinboard, made of chipboard covered with cheerful felt, is hung with memoranda, recipes and recent examples of child-art.

Tables and chairs

Kitchens often become the dumping ground for furniture too eccentric or worn to be appreciated elsewhere in the house. The result of this random selection is a junk yard, but a soulless over-regimented room can be just as unappealing.

Kitchen furniture needs to be robust, easily cleaned and mobile, so that it does not get in the way when the floor is being swept—nothing is more irritating than having to brush through a forest of legs.

A table is one of the most important pieces of furniture in the kitchen. A common dilemma is what sort fits best in a room full of plastic-finished units. Too sharp a contrast can jar, but simple pine tables and chairs are pleasant to look at and add much-needed warmth and humanity to the room. Although formal rooms gain distinction from matching chairs around an elegant outline, the kitchen isn't really the place for highly polished surfaces or Chippendale. Conversely, in an informal room, a stained, scarred surface riddled with cracks carries casualness too far.

Often a kitchen table has two functions: food preparation and eating. It can reflect this dual purpose by having a working surface such as marble, tiles or plastic at one end and timber at the eating end. Alternatively a table with just one overall surface may seem more practical. The old farmhouse table included a drawer each end—an invaluable idea to adopt where drawer space is at a premium.

If you decide to eat off a breakfast bar at counter height (900 mm to 1040 mm or 3 ft to 3 ft 5 in), you will need to sit on stools. Much safer for children are breakfast bars set at table height (710 mm or 2 ft 4 in) where ordinary chairs will suffice.

Chairs in a plain style without fussy mouldings are best for the kitchen. Bentwood ones with easily cleaned curves are very attractive, but any chair that can just be wiped down is practical. Upholstered chairs and cushions tend to pick up kitchen smells, so they must have washable loose covers. Light folding chairs make sense in smaller rooms.

Bench seats are a great boon in a kitchen: it is surprising how many people can be squeezed on to one for a meal if they don't mind a degree of discomfort. However, conventional benches are usually heavy and not easily moved for floor cleaning. One solution is to construct the bench as a fixture against the wall, cantilevered or otherwise supported so that no legs touch the ground. Another is to make the bench into a solid piece of furniture with lift-up seats on top of storage units, which can hold awkwardly shaped kitchen equipment or items such as jam jars not in constant use.

Trolleys are convenient and more stable than trays for ferrying food round the house. However, they tend to be bulky, measuring approximately 810 mm (2 ft 8 in) long, 480 mm (1 ft 7 in) wide and 710 mm (2 ft 4 in) high, so storage can be a headache. When not in use they should be parked near or in the kitchen, ideally under a work-top. Positioned there they can also be useful as extra shelves— temporary, of course—for table linen and cutlery.

Hang-ups propitiated—where better to keep your chairs but on the wall, where they can't make a nuisance of themselves (above).

The usefulness of a trolley depends on how easily it can be manoeuvred: some clever flooring (left) smooths its path.

Brilliant bentwood chairs will keep their good looks long after less hardy models are showing signs of age (above).

Tailored to suit its rustic surroundings, the sideboard fulfils a practical need as a serving centre (above).

The trolley that tucks away into its own cubby-hole is easy on the eye in off-duty hours, but it needn't stand idle (above).

Bar stools are hot favourites as the best seating for high-level breakfast counters (above) and storage presents no problems.

Sturdy wicker stools measure up attractively to the demands of casual living, yet don't obtrude when off duty (above).

The traditional farmhouse table with its wide drawers (above) still stands out as a treasure in a world where workmanship is all too often skimped or shoddy.

Light, easy-to-clean chairs cut down chores and a table like this offers sufficient room for preparation, serving and eating (left).

Serving and eating

Before the advent of sophisticated building techniques, it was the general practice, in run-of-the-brick houses, to maintain the same room pattern from one floor to the next, so that the interior walls acted as supports throughout the whole structure. On the ground floor, this imposed a format that always included a separate sitting-room, a dining-room and a kitchen.

But once construction methods were able to provide larger living areas and central heating made them comfortable to live in, a vogue developed for open-plan living. Like so many new notions, it was taken to excess in its early days, and architects designed areas of "flowing space" in which televisions blared, children gambolled, meals sizzled, all in one great cacophony, with nowhere to escape to except the bathroom.

When the novelty wore off, internal walls, partitions and privacy gradually returned, but somewhere along the line the separate formal dining-room seemed to have vanished.

In new houses there is often a living/dining-room with a separate kitchen, or a kitchen/dining-room with a separate living-room. Both arrangements have their protagonists and critics. Supporters of the living/dining-room argue that it brings together all aspects of formal entertaining, and that guests do not enjoy either cooking pots or cooking smells while they are eating.

Advocates of the kitchen/dining-room claim that as food is prepared in the kitchen, it is altogether more sensible to eat it there, and much friendlier, too, since in this way the cook isn't cut off from the company and the whole family can join in preparing the meal and washing the dishes. With proper ventilation, smells are not a problem; with imaginative lighting and intelligent planning no one's sensibilities need be offended by a sinkful of dirty pots.

If you decide to have a dining/kitchen you must play up the advantages and draw a discreet veil over the seamier side. First and foremost, the room must feel right. The cooking area will have to up-grade itself a bit, or it will let the dining area down—this is not the place for a chipped sink and hard fluorescent lighting. The dining area has to acknowledge its place in a working room—tables that mark when you put your drink down and delicate chairs swathed in velvet upholstery are inappropriate here. The cooking and eating areas may be separated by a partition, a screen or an island unit, but they should be clearly part of the same room—not look as if the dining-room furniture has somehow found its way to the far end of the kitchen.

Provide good ventilation for the cook-top and the oven, and try to position the table so that your guests have a pleasant view, rather than a vista of detergents and dishcloths. Get into the habit of concealing dirty pots and plates in a corner where they can't be seen; and install gentle tungsten lighting so that you can see to serve without intruding on the softly lit dining-table—separately switched dimmers are a help here. If there is an interesting view from the kitchen window, frame it with curtains, or illuminate it with a spotlight fixed to the outside wall, so the eye is attracted by sights other than domestic ones.

One way to hide the empties is to provide a special slot near the sink (below). Different floor levels help to add interest.

When storage space on the walls runs out the ceiling provides some extra mileage (right). Over the professional cooking range is an extractor unit to take away fumes.

The kitchen is given a big build-up when it is arranged all along one wall with units tailored to a perfect fit (above). Then, when the blinds are pulled down, the eating area assumes command and all the cooking equipment is neatly concealed from the diners (below).

Even in the narrowest kitchen a breakfast bar can be created by combining a simple work-top with some slender stools (below).

A table for two is always available in a crowded room with this type of flap-down design and some folding chairs (above).

Feeding the children is made easier by installing low work-tops between the cooking and eating area (below).

Serving and eating

Though the meal has been cooked to perfection, a good deal still remains to be done. Chief among the problems is to ensure that it reaches the table while still in the perfect state. Professionals can call upon bains-marie, infra-red heat lamps and an army of nimble waiters, but on the home front the cook so often juggles with a pile of hot dishes while putting the finishing touches to a temperamental sauce—and all for the lack of somewhere to put things down.

So at dishing-up time, make sure there is a clear area of heat-resistant work-top near the cooker, where hot food can be transferred into serving dishes or directly on to the plates.

Serving hatches

A communicating hatch between kitchen and dining-room cuts out a lot of running back and forth. The hatch will be more useful if the shelves around it are open on both sides so that glasses, cutlery and so on can be reached from either room.

A separate dining-room

If the dining-room is some way from the kitchen—all too often the case in old houses—then you will have to establish a serving area within the dining-room itself. A sideboard and an electric plate-warmer are all that is really necessary. The temptation to turn a serving area into a mini-kitchen with hot plates, sinks and bains-marie should be kept firmly in check as it only makes for more work and an expensive duplication of equipment.

A combined work-top, sink and breakfast bar makes for streamlined service in this forward-looking kitchen (left).

Take one: a zippy yellow panel brightens up a plain wall (below left). Take two: the panel slides across to reveal a serving hatch into the kitchen (below right).

Serving trolleys

To save time and temper in the early morning, keep a tray or trolley permanently loaded with salt pots, toast racks, syrups, jams and packets of cereals, which are likely to be needed at breakfast.

At lunch- or dinner-time, electrically heated food trolleys can be a help; but the truth is, apart from roasts, which do need ten or fifteen minutes in a warm place to "set" before carving, no food is improved by sitting about in a hot cupboard. If you do decide to use one, undercook everything slightly, because despite the makers' claims the contents of those hot metal shelves will keep on cooking.

The gregarious host or hostess who finds their show-piece dish requires last-minute touches should either change the menu or throw formality to the wind and entertain in the kitchen.

Apportioning the space

The traditional farmhouse kitchen, with its scrubbed pine table sitting squarely in the middle of the room with all the cooking activities going on around it, is a nostalgic image. It is not, however, the most

economical arrangement in terms of space. To be efficient, the cooking area should be concentrated in one part of the room with all equipment and stores readily accessible.

Some degree of separation from the dining area can be achieved by a thoughtful use of the kitchen units themselves. A 150-mm (6-in) upstand on the dining side of a peninsular work-top effectively screens the clutter from the people sitting down. Two-way high-level cupboards act as a screen that virtually turns one side of the kitchen into a long serving hatch. More drastic screens, such as louvers or sliding panels, are perfectly acceptable in a bed-sitting room where the kitchen should be out of sight and out of mind, but they defeat the object of the kitchen/dining-room by implying that cookery is something to be ashamed of.

People with flair disprove every rule, but, in general, the best kitchen/dining-rooms are the ones that accept their dual role with equanimity.

Breakfast bars, tables and chairs

If the kitchen is big enough, it may be possible to incorporate a bar counter as well as a fully fledged dining-table within the layout of kitchen units. Most breakfast bars are at work-top height (900 mm/33 in) so to be comfortable you will need bar stools. These are not very safe for young children and cannot be used at the dining-table. By lowering the bar counter to table height, dining chairs can do double duty, and the cook can sit in comfort to do some of her chores.

Bench seating around the table does mean that a lot of people can be squeezed into a small space (which is why benches are so popular in snack bars), but it is difficult to get in and out unless everyone moves at once. It is very important to sit comfortably while eating—it improves your appetite and your humour. It is also important to be able to talk to everybody, and for this reason the traditional rectangular table is hard to beat.

If space is really tight, there are clever fold-away tables that disappear completely when not in use, but you may find the lack of stability a little worrying. It may be better to make a permanent built-in table, even if it is an odd shape.

Cupboards and drawers that open either side overcome parking problems in the divided kitchen/dining-room (above). A warming plate stands by to cosset the food.

Drawers swing open easily and everything for a simple little repast is to hand (above); the blind gives an illusion of privacy.

A miniature Garden of Babylon creates an eccentric kitchen (left), though the exotic effect is balanced by practical drawers and an elegant table setting.

A plan of action

The work of building a new kitchen (or of improving an existing one) must be carefully co-ordinated, or the result will be a shambles. Workmen of various trades will be tripping over one another in their endeavours to get their particular work finished; sinks and dishwashers will arrive when the plumber has soldered his last joint, and, worst of all, you could find a tangle of pipes and wires snaking across your expensive wallpaper.

When the room has been measured and appraised, the existing structure must be surveyed to check on dry rot, faulty construction, insect attack, drainage, damp-proofing and so on. The measures needed to put any defect right may involve changes in the structure that will affect dimensions of the finished walls, floors and ceilings, and these in turn will affect the size of units and equipment.

Stage A

1 *Floor: Check damp-proof course, floor joists and floorboarding. Clean out blocked airbricks or provide new ones.*
2 *As a preventive measure against rot, spray the space under the floor with proprietary liquid before fixing floor finish. If rot is discovered, call in a specialist firm, who will cut out any affected timbers and inject nearby brickwork with rot-preventing fluid.*
3 *Threshold: Decide on finished floor levels.*
4 *Ceiling: Check that the horizontal timbers along the top of the walls and the ceiling joists jointed into them are sound. Put up temporary supports if required.*

Stage B

1 *Extractor fan: Cut hole in wall for fan, and grooves for the wiring.*
2 *Wood treatment: Expose timber where rot or fungicidal attack is suspected. Treatment by a specialist firm is recommended as their service includes a thorough examination and a guarantee of ten years or more.*
3 *Window: Insert new lintel after first propping up the load of the wall above. Cut out brickwork to form jambs and sill. Remember to build in vertical and horizontal damp-proof courses and to seal gaps with mastic gum.*
4 *Door: Create door opening, supporting the load above in much the same way as for windows.*
5 *Hatch: Form opening and support the wall over.*
6 *Wall boiler: Cut hole through external wall first to allow for balanced flue terminal. Also cut grooves for all pipes (i.e. gas and water).*

Stage C

1 *Floor: Complete all underfloor pipes and other services before fixing down floorboards.*
2 *Lay concrete screed in preparation for finish.*
3 *Detail threshold to accommodate junction of floor finishes.*
4 *Hatch: Line opening with board and fix grooved track to receive sliding panels. Fit moulding round both sides of lining.*
5 *Door: Fix door, complete with lining and architrave ironmongery, etc.*
6 *Patio door: Fix left- or right-hand opening panel and single or double glazing.*
7 *Wall lining: Consider first lining wall with recompressed polystyrene before applying wallpaper; this will inhibit condensation and increase the warm feel of the room.*
8 *Window: Fix window frame and glass.*
9 *Wiring: Wire for lighting electricity supply and fix mountings. Provide fused socket outlets for any appliances that are required under work-top with switches located in convenient position above work-top height, e.g. dishwasher, waste-disposal unit, washing machine, refrigerator. Wire for radiators. Wire for telephone.*
10 *Ceiling: If ceiling is badly cracked, fix new plasterboard into existing ceiling with galvanized clout nails. Finish with a thin coat of plaster and line with paper, polystyrene or other insulation.*
11 *Stopcocks: Place stopcocks in supply pipes to both cold and hot taps. This enables water supplies to the sinks to be disconnected without disabling remainder of the house.*

Stage D

1 *Floorboarding: Carefully fix down loose boarding and, if fixing hardboard or ply sheeting over to receive tiles, ensure that nails of right length are used (over-long nails will endanger pipes, wires, etc., underneath). Lay floor finish to go under units.*
2 *Skirting: Use stick-on plastic skirting where walls have been damp-proofed. If timber skirting is used, treat rearside against rot.*
3 *Plumbing: Install boiler for central heating and constant hot water. Pipes for gas and water should be chased or ducted in. Install gas pipes.*

Stage E

1 *Sink: Install sink with drinking-water tap fed from mains supply (other cold-water taps should be plumbed to the storage tank).*
2 *Service duct: Allow space at rear of cupboards for all service pipes.*
3 *Install units.*

Stage F

1 *Flooring: Lay vinyl tile or cork finish.*
2 *Walls: Fix wall-finish, and, if using wood boarding, wax or varnish it to prevent staining.*

Stage G

1 *Install electrical equipment.*
2 *Fix lights and telephone.*

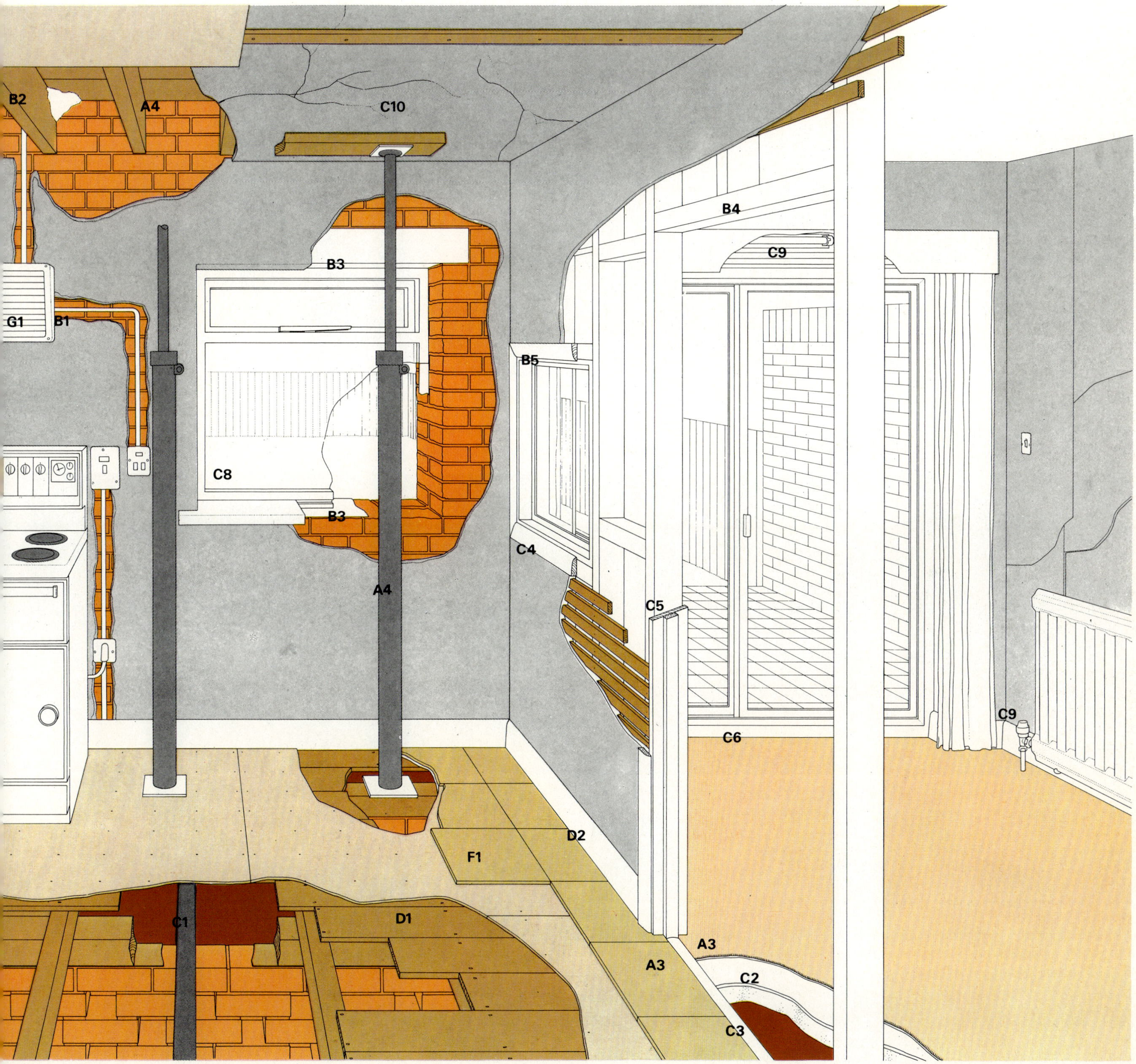
B2
A4
C10
G1
B1
B3
B4
C9
B5
C8
B3
C4
A4
C5
C9
C6
D2
F1
C1
D1
A3
A3
C2
C3

Cookers

Choosing a cooker is a matter for serious consideration. Having made the choice, you will probably have to live with it for years to come and the problem is how to make the right selection in a showroom full of disconcertingly similar machinery.

Buying a cooker

Your choice of cooker is principally governed by the type of fuel available in your area, or, more often, the type that is best suited to your cooking requirements. That settled, the next thing is to decide whether to cook on a traditional all-in-one stove or to opt for a split-level arrangement, which though about twice as expensive is undeniably convenient.

You must then judge the value of the attendant gadgetry—the rôtisserie and kebab motors, high-level grills, self-cleaning ovens, automatic timers, re-ignition devices and so on. Such gadgets, time-saving boons to one cook, are unnecessary and expensive complications to another. Much depends on your cooking style and, indeed, on the pace of your life.

Ceramic cook-top (above), expensive but beautiful, and as easy to clean as the surrounding work-surface. Slide-out magnetic switches help to prevent accidents.

A unit (above) that combines gas and electricity and the benefits of both. The sealed discs are easier to keep clean than radiant rings, but take longer to heat up.

The cooker/boiler (below) doubles as a room heater. Its warm and friendly presence is welcome in winter if a little overpowering in summer. Practical if you do a lot of cooking.

A smart all-in-one electric cooker (below) has two ovens with drop-down doors—very useful for parking scalding pots, but dangerously impractical in a narrow kitchen.

A barbecue grill (above), set at a convenient height, is built into a bricked-up chimney in Terence Conran's country house.

Two levels for two fuels (below). The gas cook-top is inset in a purpose-built cabinet. The electric eye-level oven doubles as a grill and broiler.

In a tiny kitchen (above) the chronic shortage of space is eased with a fold-down electric cook-top. Suitable for cooks whose repertoire extends no farther than coffee and scrambled eggs.

The stainless-steel gas cook-top (above) has plenty of parking space in the middle. The central push-button ignites a battery-powered spark to light the burners.

Ancient and modern both have their place in this Finnish kitchen (below). Quick meals are made on the electric cook-top and slow-simmered casseroles in the old solid-fuel stove.

Cookers

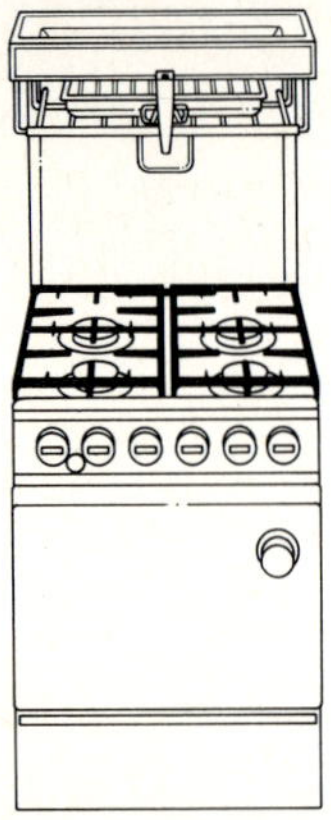

With a small family and a limited budget you need nothing more complicated than a simple gas cooker with eye-level grill and plate-warming rack. Model: Lincoln by Main.

A very sophisticated gas cooker with two ovens, a large grill, twin rôtisseries, four large burners with automatic ignition and reignition. Model: New World Spectrum.

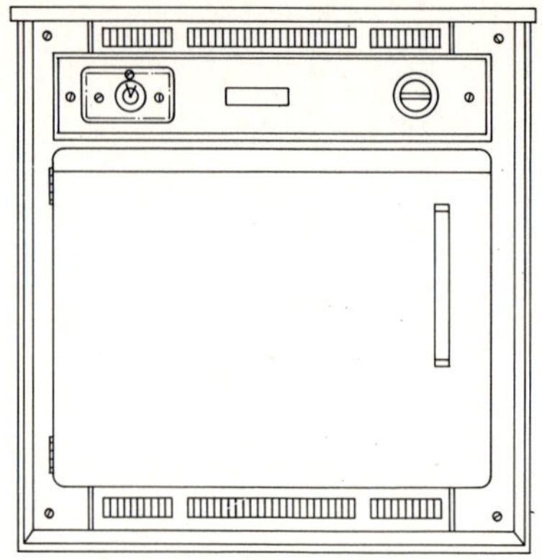

Built-in automatic gas oven with spark ignition and an approved flame failure protection device. Door can be hinged on the left or right to suit your layout. Model: Moffat 2000.

Compact family-sized cooker with automatic ignition and gas cut-off safety device in the oven. The eye-level grill gives an all-over, even heat. Model: New World Super Sola.

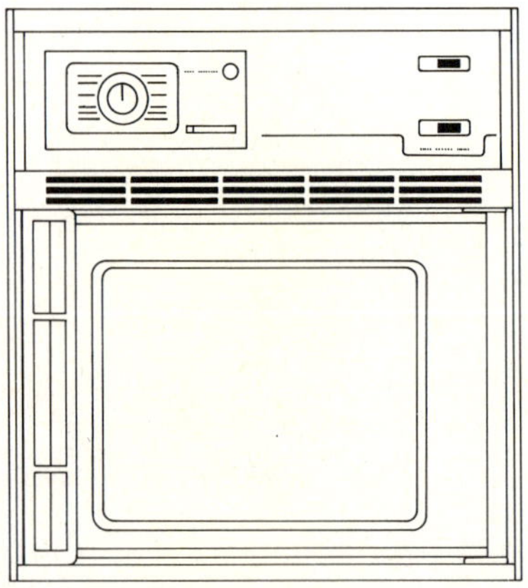

Full-size self-cleaning electric oven, complete with rôtisserie, interior lights and a finely graded temperature control for precise, even cooking. Model: Balay H2201.

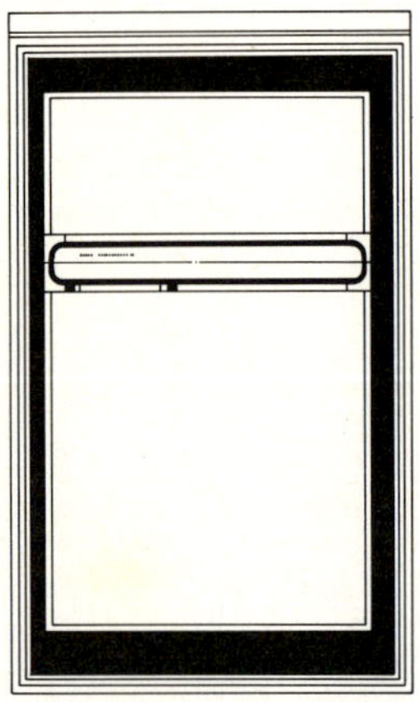

A built-in electric twin oven unit from a range of colour-co-ordinated kitchen appliances, all with the same exterior measurements that fit into matching housing units. Model: Tricity.

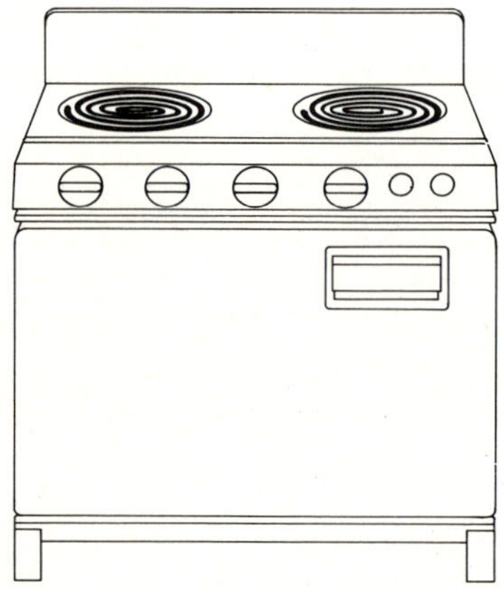

A miniature electric cooker with two boiling rings, a full-size grill and an oven big enough for roasting and baking. It runs from a standard power point. Model: Baby Belling 120.

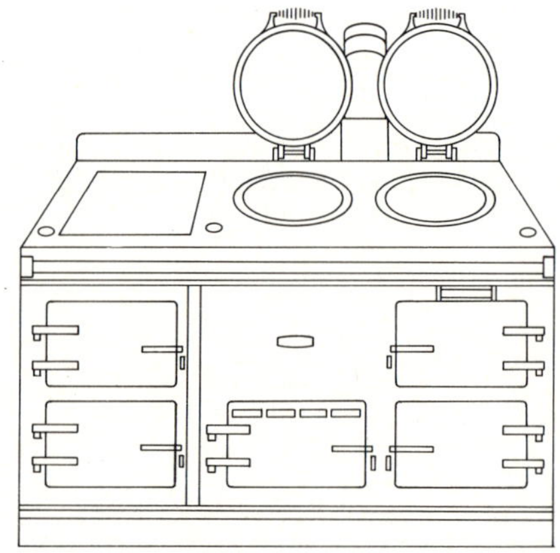

A real "heart-of-the-home" cooker that uses its stored-up indirect heat just like the old-fashioned bakers' oven. Modern ones run on solid fuel, oil or gas. Model: Aga.

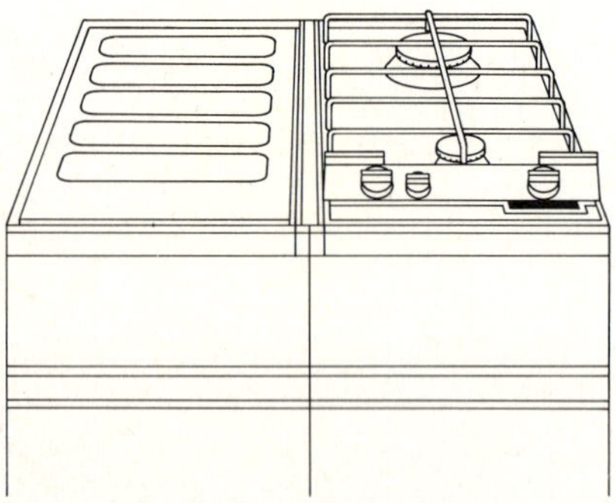

Units from a modular system are all the same size and can be added to at will. Here a two-burner cook-top lines up next to a stainless-steel pan stand. Model: Balay.

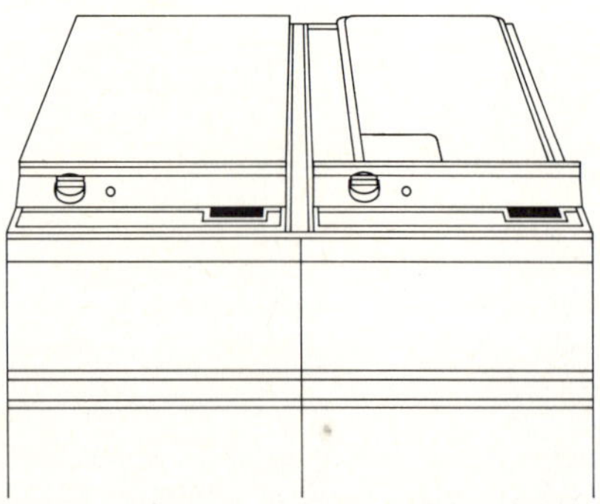

Side by side, a pair of electric grill plates form a combination from the modular system. One has a stainless-steel cover, which provides extra work-space. Model: Balay.

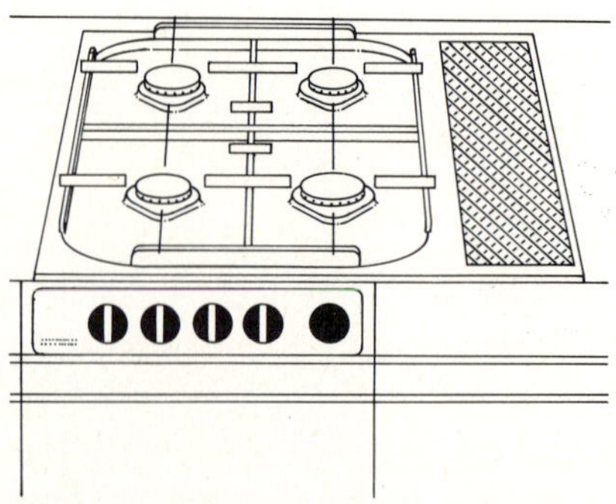

Stainless-steel gas cook-top with fail-safe ignition and four burners. There is a useful built-in parking lot for pots on the right. Model: Miele KM15.

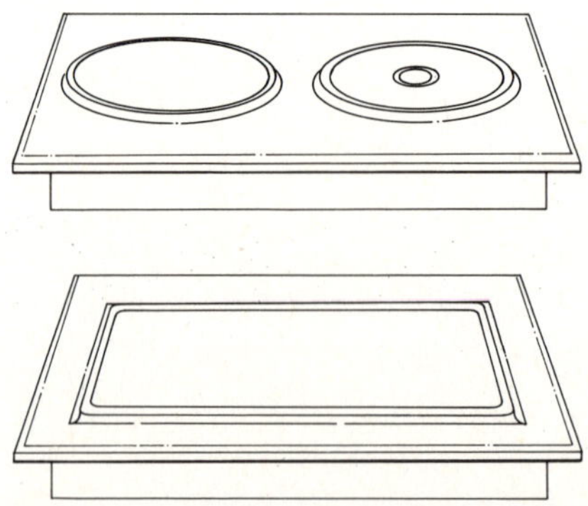

Design your own built-in cooking centre with a combination of rings and grill plates that are all built to a standard size. Model: Neff Domino range.

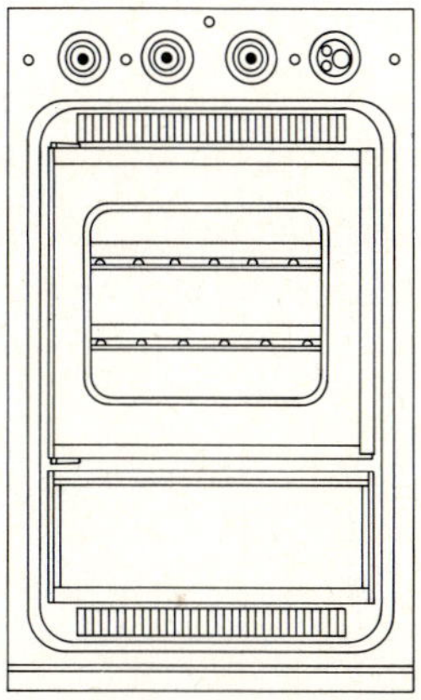

Double electric oven incorporates a huge grill that can sizzle up to 24 pieces of chicken at once. The fan convector oven ensures an even heat. Model: Belling Formula.

An electric fan convection oven that can be built in to a high-level housing unit or slotted beneath a work-top with an inset matching cook-top. Model: Philips AKB 203.

Full-size electric oven made to fit in a line of base units under an inset cook-top. It has a large grill within the oven and digital automatic timing device. Model: Herd Bosch.

Electric built-in oven with a self-cleaning programme, an exhaust duct, an integral roasting thermometer and a choice of door colours. Model: Thermador MSC 18.

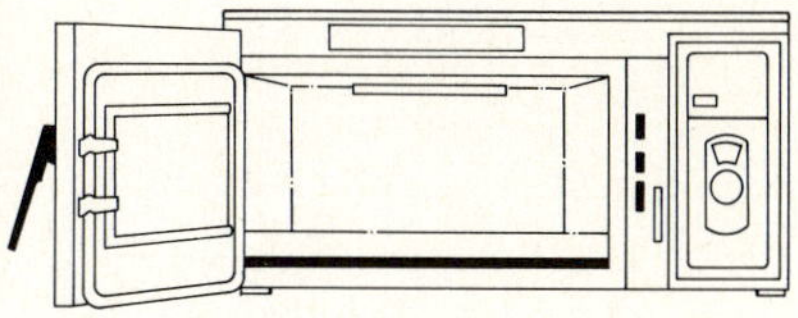

A microwave oven with a browning element so that food looks as well cooked as it is. Stainless-steel interior discourages dirt build-up. Model: Thermador MC17.

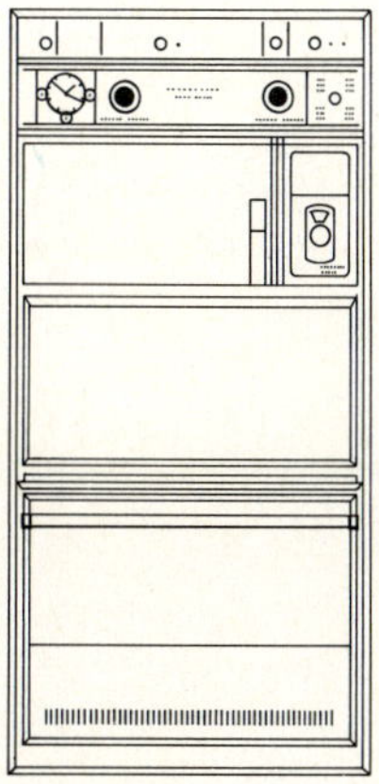

Combination microwave and self-cleaning electric oven. The microwave has three heat settings for cooking or defrosting. Model: Thermador MTR 27.

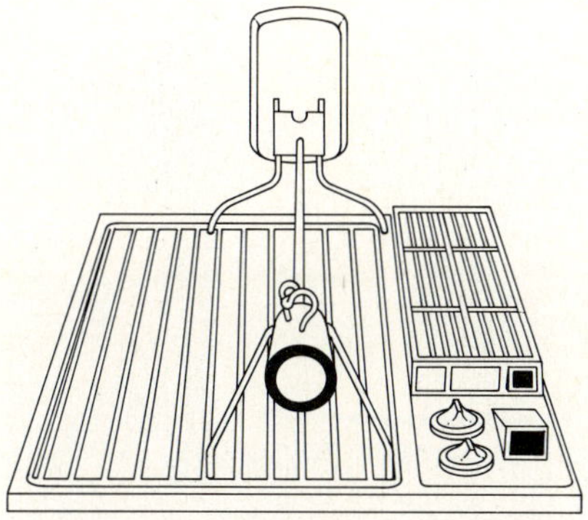

A grill range with a unique and effective built-in ventilation system and a rôtisserie attachment. Model: Jenn-Air Deluxe Grill.

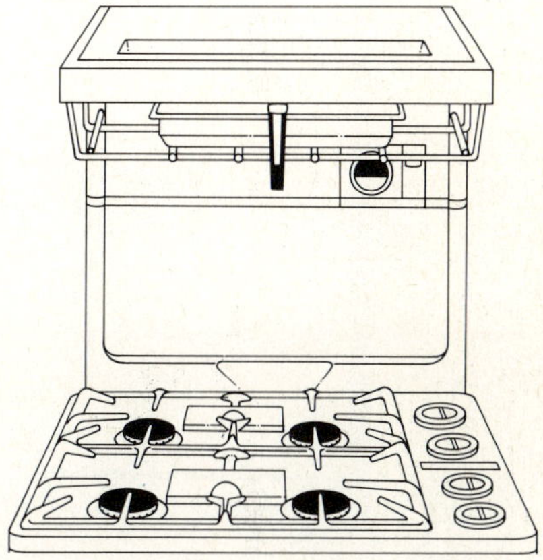

Gas cook-top with eye-level grill and backplate. The top of the grill canopy doubles as a useful plate warmer. Model: Moffat 2000.

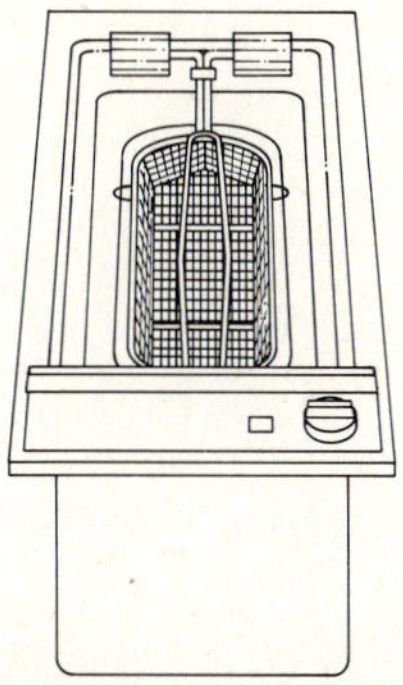

If your family is fond of french fries, it could be worth installing a built-in fryer. Domestic models are just scaled down versions of catering equipment. Model: Neff Domino range.

Electric cook-top of brushed chrome has four high-speed radiant rings with spillage trays under for easy cleaning. The splashback is made of black glass. Model: Moffat Slimline.

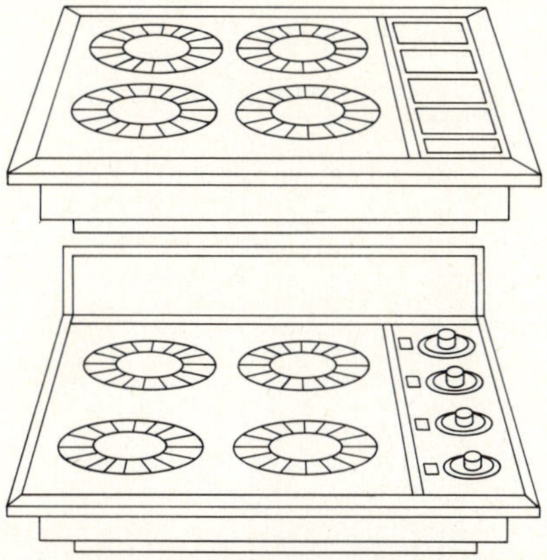

The cleanest way to cook is on a ceramic glass sheet with no nooks and crannies to harbour dirt. Heating elements are placed beneath the circular patterns. Model: Moffat.

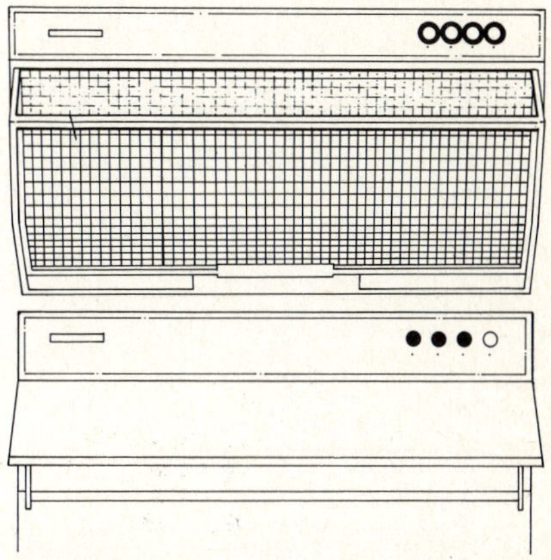

Cooker hoods can be used either to circulate or extract air. Both operations pass the air through a cleansing charcoal filter. Model: Miele.

Refrigerators and freezers

Choosing the right refrigerator for your household is mainly a matter of deciding on the capacity you will require, though there are a few details you should bear in mind as well. Check that the door opens the right way, that the shelving is adjustable, that defrosting is simple and that there is plenty of space for tall bottles and not too much devoted to egg racks and compartments whose purpose is shrouded in mystery.

As for freezers, the basic choice is between the chest type (efficient, but bulky and hard to find things in) and the upright variety (compact, but more expensive to run as heat is admitted every time the door is opened).

Refrigerator and matching upright freezer are built into a wood-framed room divider (left).

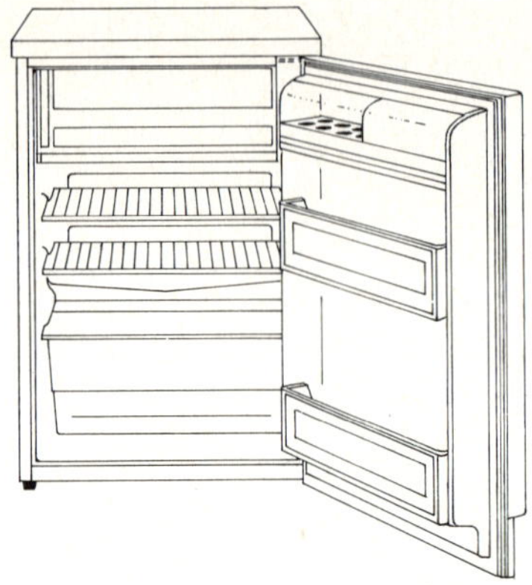

Compact refrigerator ideal for a small family or a weekend cottage. It has plenty of room in the door for bottles and a three-star frozen-food compartment. Model: Philips

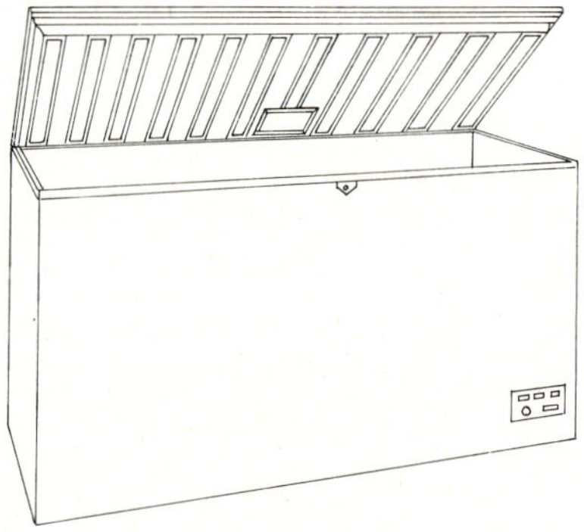

One of the largest domestic chest freezers has a capacity of 541 litres (19.1 cu ft). Its bulk perhaps makes it more suitable for the outhouse than the kitchen. Model: LEC

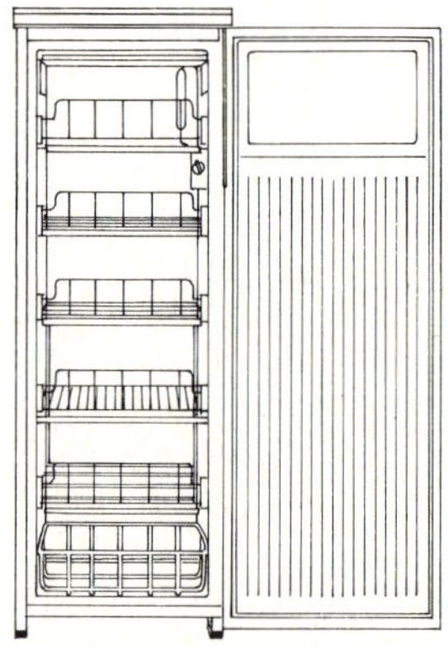

The tall, slim shape of the upright freezer is ideal if you have nowhere but the kitchen to keep it. This model has a capacity of 206 litres (7.3 cu ft). Model: Tricity

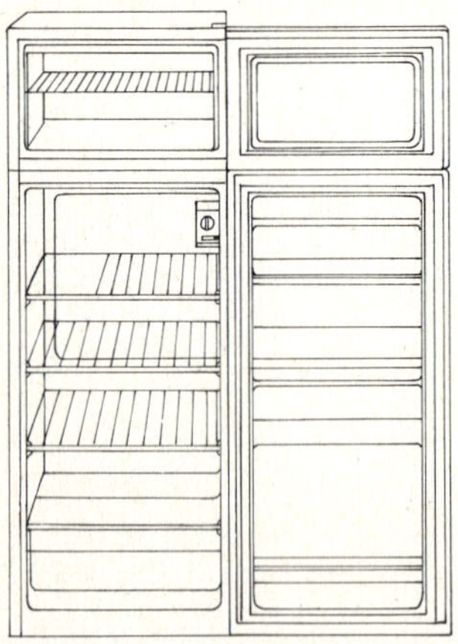

A fridge/freezer combination gives you ample refrigerator space and freezing capacity in one compact unit that saves on floor space. Model: Hoover

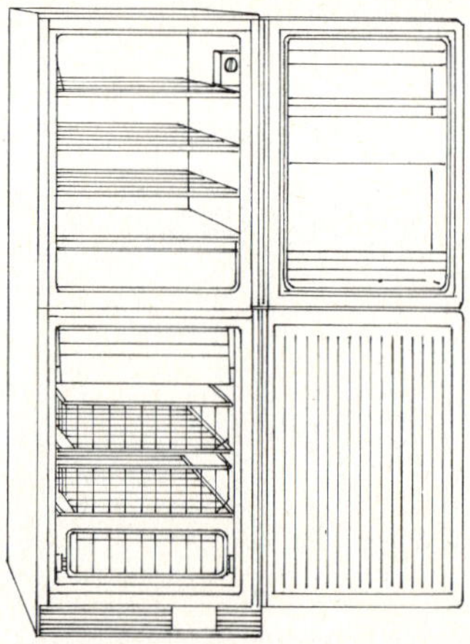

This half-and-half model gives you more freezer space at the expense of the refrigerator. Your cooking habits will dictate the proportion right for you. Model: Hoover

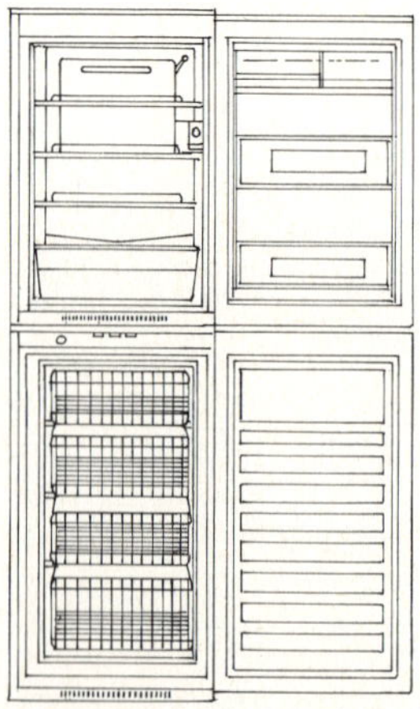

Another half-and-half combination, but built up from two separate units. The door frames accept panels of laminate so the whole set-up can be disguised. Model: Philips

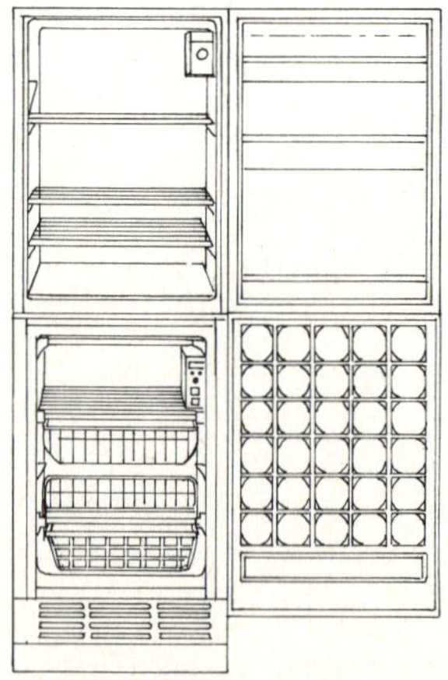

Family-sized fridge/freezer. Sections should operate independently for the best results. A choice is usually offered between left- and right-opening doors. Model: Electrolux

Mini-refrigerator for a home bar lacks a frozen-food compartment but makes up to three trays of ice (for boats or caravans choose a similar model run off bottled gas). Model: Philips

Tall, thin refrigerator with a lot of space for bottles. Adjustable shelves are a boon when you want to chill a whole gâteau or a tureen of summer soup. Model: LEC

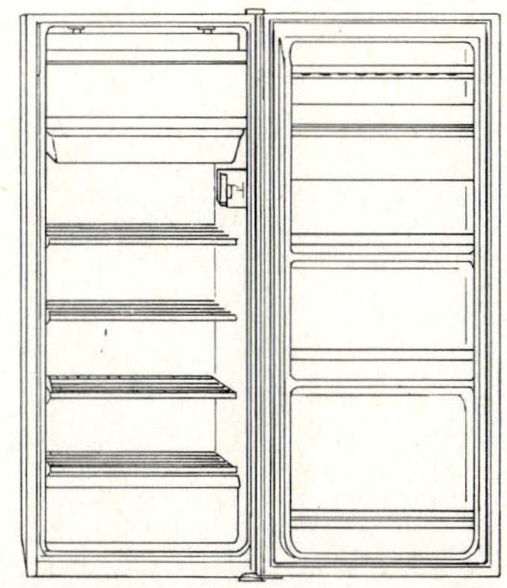

A big refrigerator with plenty of shelf space. Tall bottles that do not fit in the door can stick their necks through a hinged section in the top shelf. Model: Hoover

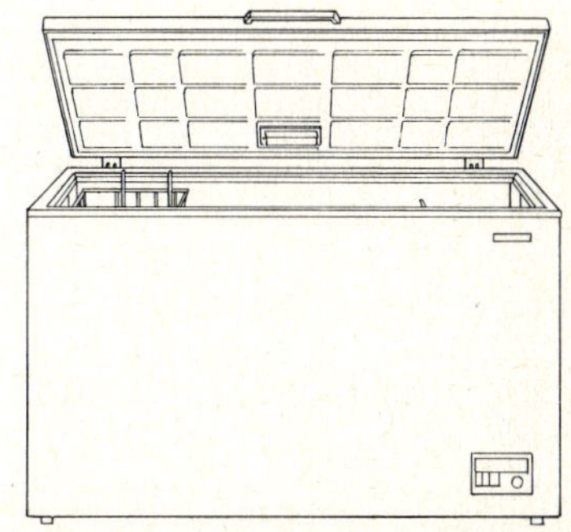

If you intend to go into freezing in a big way, choose a big chest freezer and keep it in the garage or utility room. This freezer has a 396-litre (14-cu ft) capacity. Model: Tricity

This compact freezer has an 84-litre (3-cu ft) capacity, which makes it quite adequate for a small family, and it has the added advantage of fitting under the work-top. Model: Tricity

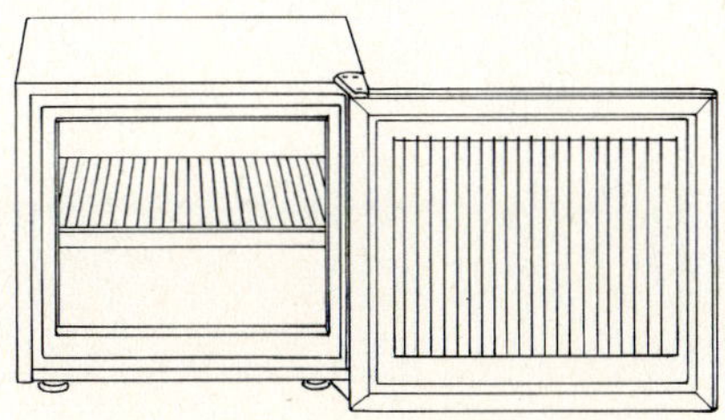

Tiny freezer only 49 cm (19 in) high, with a 50-litre (1.75-cu ft) capacity, will sit happily on top of a fridge or on the work-surface. Model: Hoover

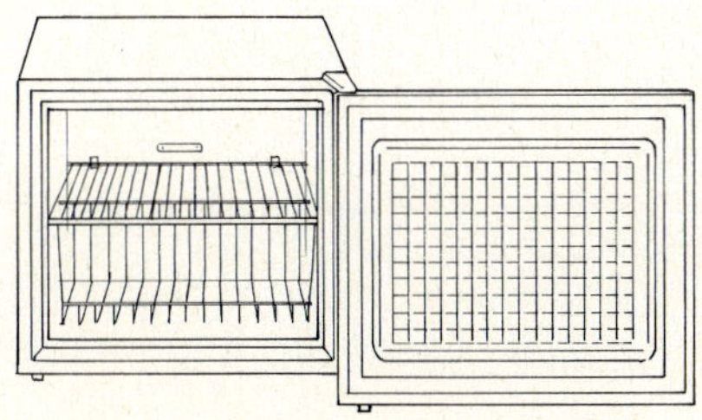

A small freezer is the answer for the small kitchen, and it is a practical choice if you just want to stock up for the week rather than freeze garden produce. Model: Philips

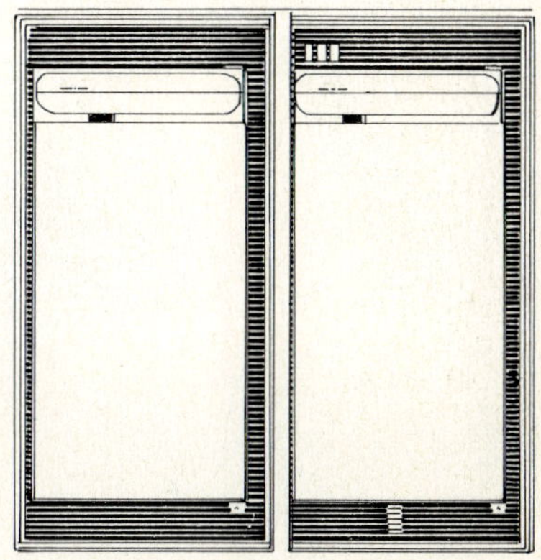

Refrigerator and freezer for the streamlined kitchen. Built-in models do save bending and stretching, and are adequate for the average family. Model: Tricity

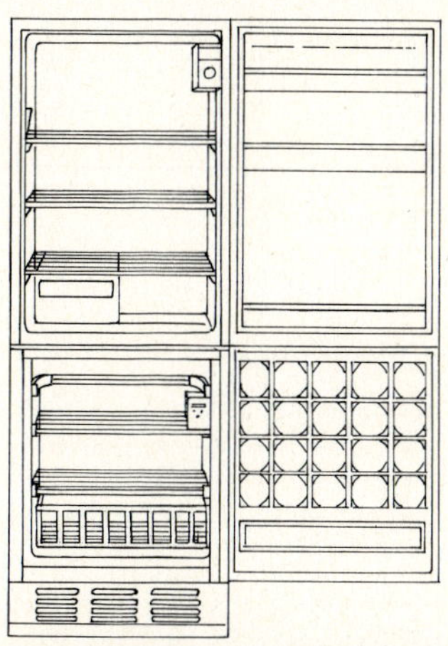

Compact combination that's more fridge than freezer. Gas fridge/freezers are also available; the advantages of gas are silence and that there are no moving parts to go wrong.

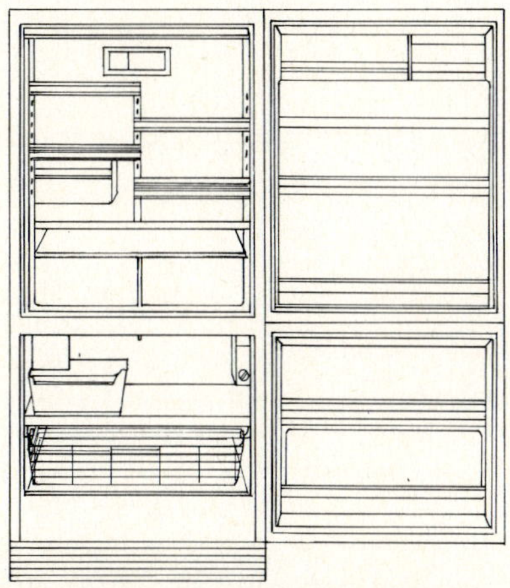

A wide fridge/freezer with plenty of extras, such as ice-maker, humidity control and convertible doors, which can be changed from left to right. Model: Amana

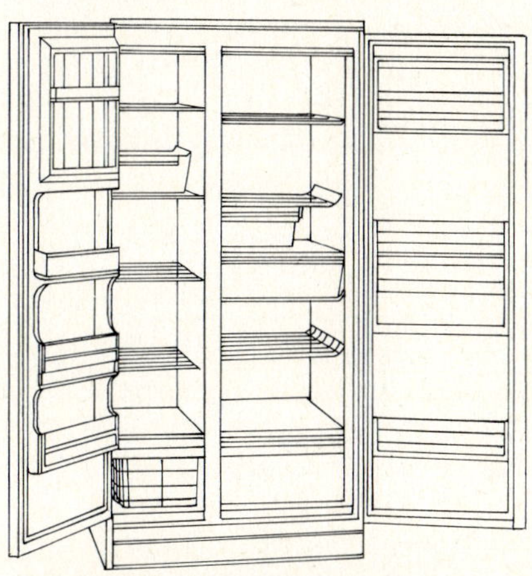

Massive two-door fridge/freezer for large families and big kitchens. It has a high humidity compartment, which will keep vegetables for up to three weeks. Model: Amana

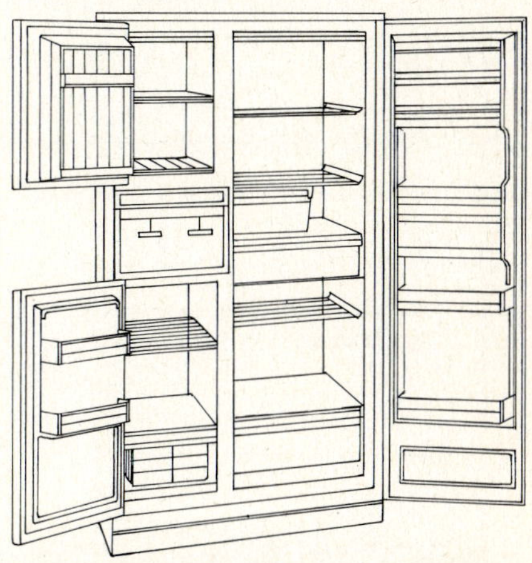

Three-door model with a separate compartment for dispensing chilled water and ice. Frozen food most in demand goes in the smaller freezer, bulk supplies below. Model: Amana

Sinks and taps

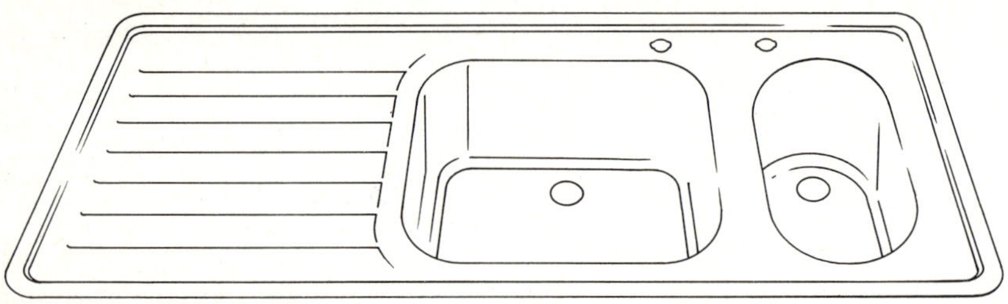

Single stainless-steel sink and oval waste bowl keep rubbish and dishes apart.
Model: TRF Plant 17/4818/SR

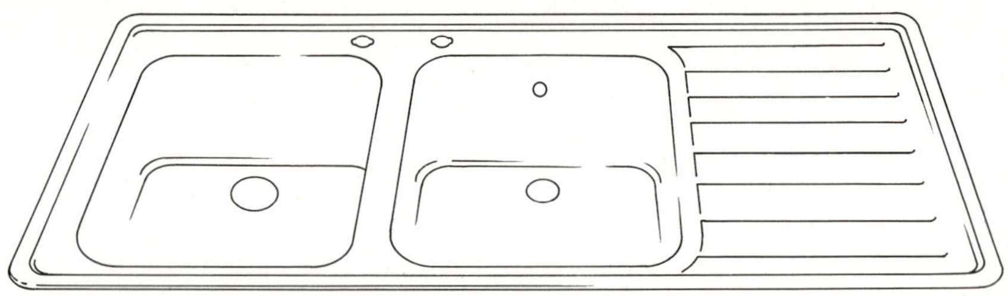

Double-bowled sink and drainer for washing the dishes from left to right.
Model: TRF Plant 17/5418/SR

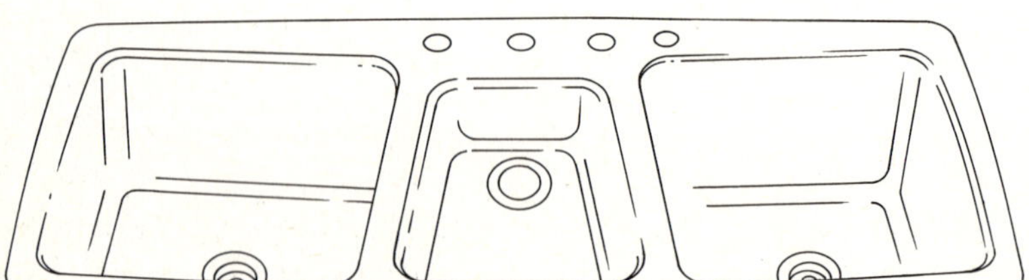

Enamelled cast-iron sink—will not scratch, stain, dent, chip or cause any clatter.
Model: Kohler Trieste K-5914

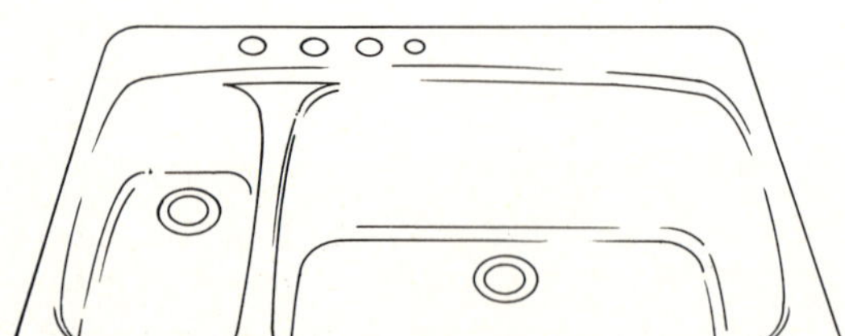

Colourful enamelled cast-iron sink with deep bowl for dishes and shallow one for waste.
Model: Kohler Lakefield K 5924

The kitchen sink is no longer a symbol of drudgery when it is created in glossy, enamelled steel or acrylic and its efficiency multiplied by several bowls and a generous expanse of drainer. For doing the dishes, a double-bowled sink is advisable, since it allows you to soak pans while washing glasses, or to clean the dishes in hot, soapy water in one bowl before rinsing them in the other. The treble sink, even more efficient, includes an extra bowl for the waste disposer, so that rubbish and dishes never coincide and spoons are not sucked into the teeth of the machine.

A separate sink is useful for vegetable preparation. The high tap and deep bowl leave plenty of space for the washing (left).

Washing-up is as painless as possible (far left) with a treble sink to separate waste, rinsing, soaking and vegetable preparation.

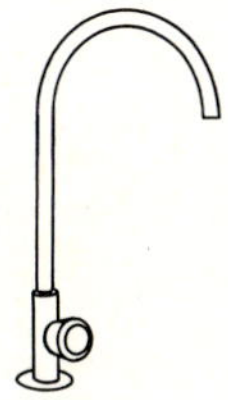

Tall, spindly laboratory-type taps are at a convenient height for washing vegetables, dishes, or your hair.

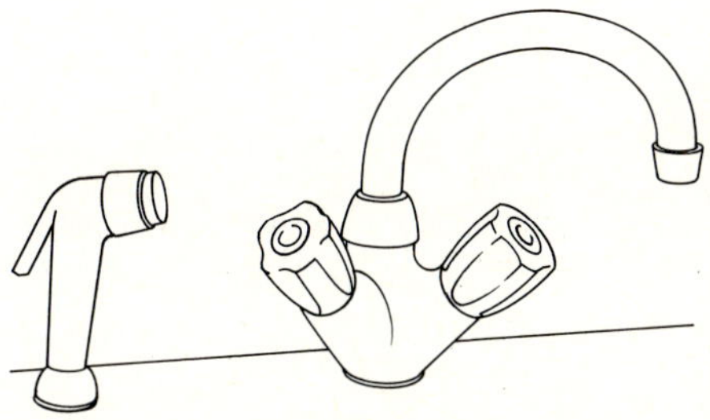

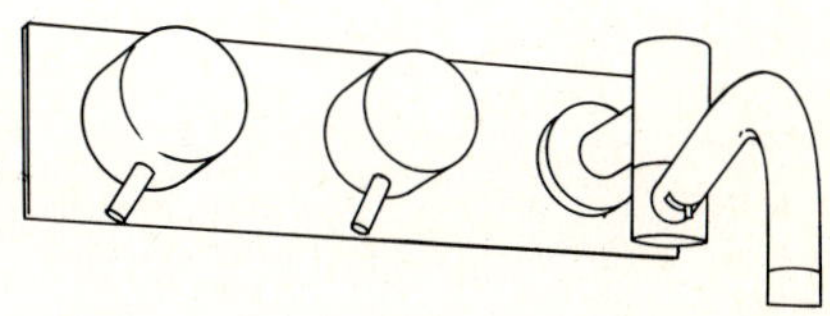

Distinguished wall-mounted mixer taps made of highly polished brass.
Model: Vola 633

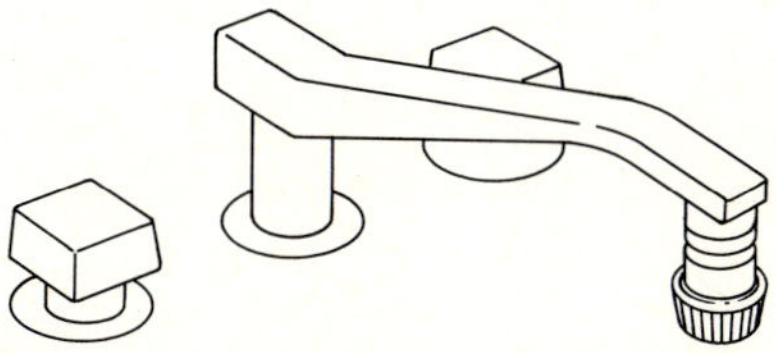

Chunky, swivel mixer tap with an automatic flow control valve to save water.
Model: Kohler Alterna.

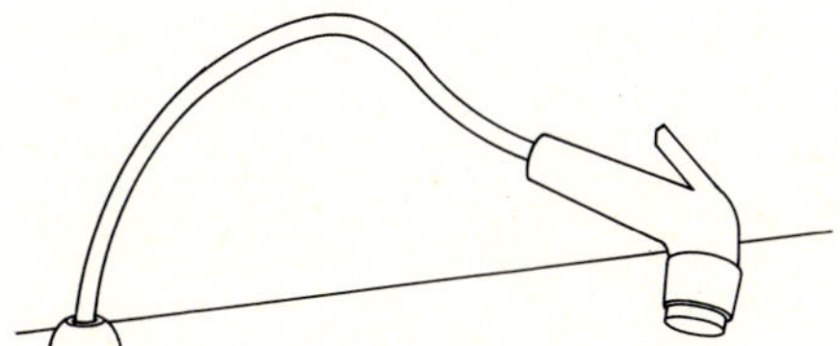

Pull-out spray is a useful addition to the mixer tap for rinsing with very hot water.
Model: Barking Brassware Biflo

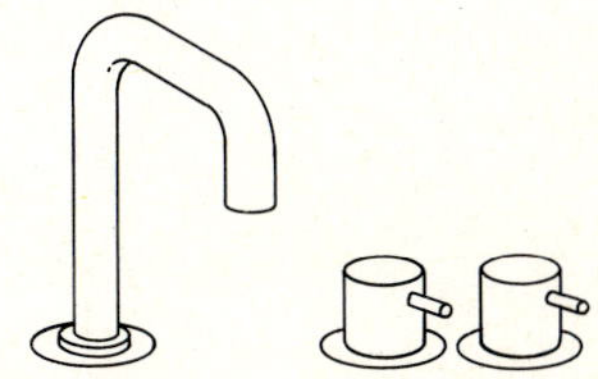

Danish-designed swivel mixer tap, stove enamelled in fifteen brilliant colours.
Model: Vola KV2

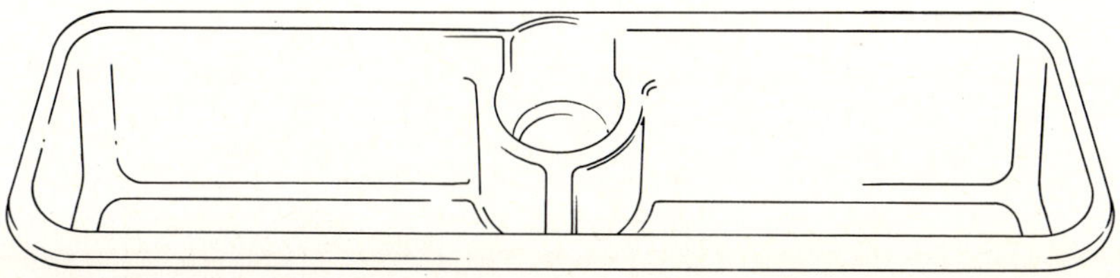

For clutter-free washing-up, a white, ceramic double-bowled sink with a separate chute for disposing of food waste.

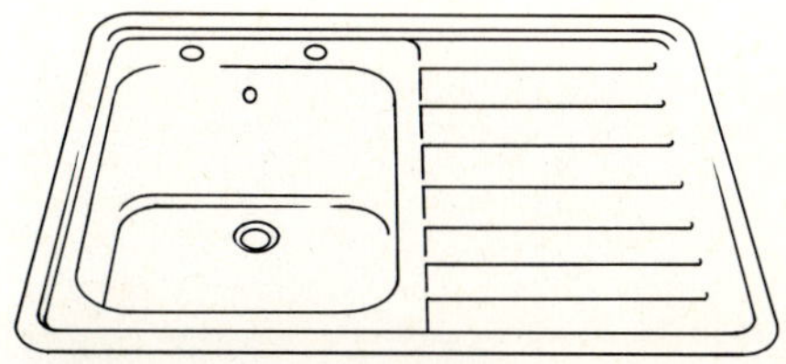

The basic system for those who have a dishwasher or who don't use many dishes.
Model: TRF Plant 17/3618/SR

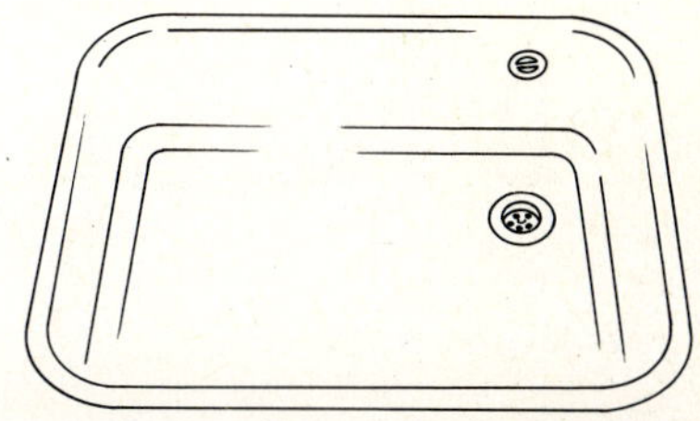

Enamelled steel bowl. A sink minus drainer can easily be built into existing work-tops.
Model: Berglen 100

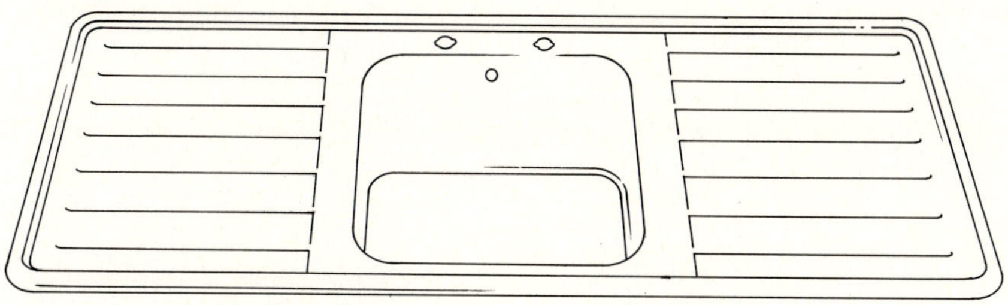

Stainless-steel double drainer—one side makes a heat-resistant resting place for hot pots.
Model: TRF Plant 17/5418/SR

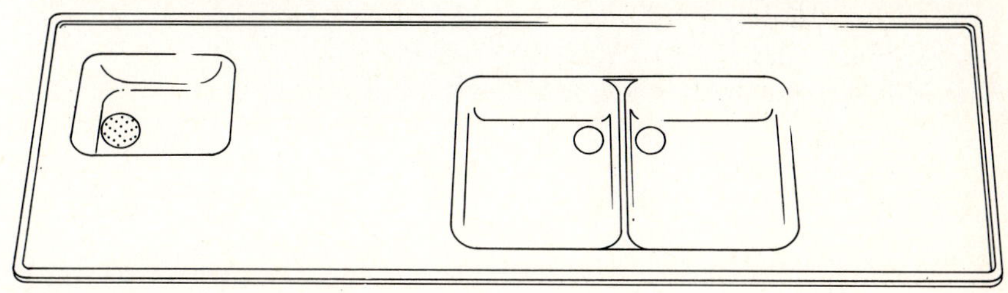

Double bowl and slop sink surrounded by flat expanse of stainless-steel drainer.
Model: Anderson S/34

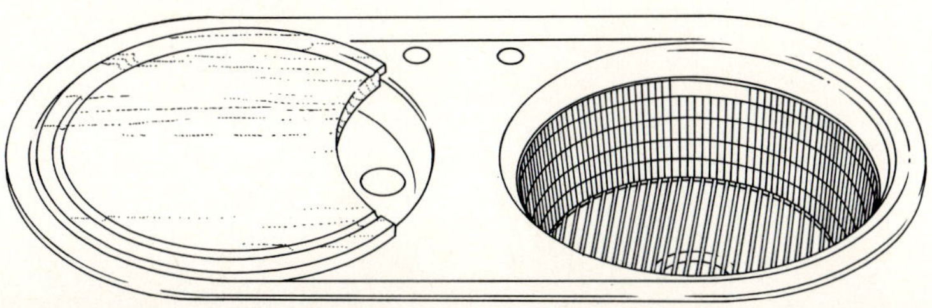

Enamelled steel bowls with chopping board and draining basket.

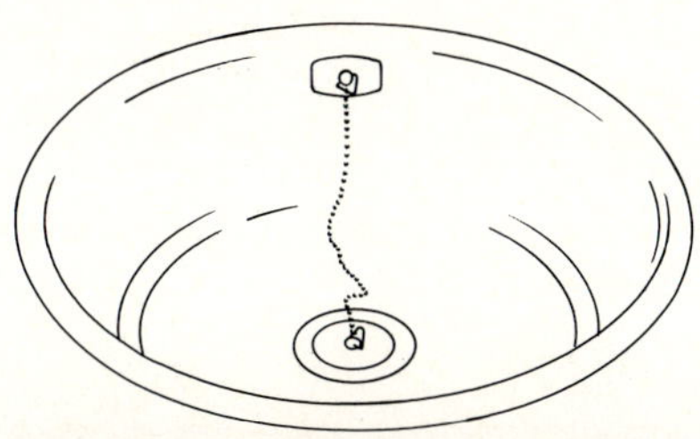

Washing-up bowl-type sink made of vitrified enamel in eleven radiant colours.
Model: Vendôme

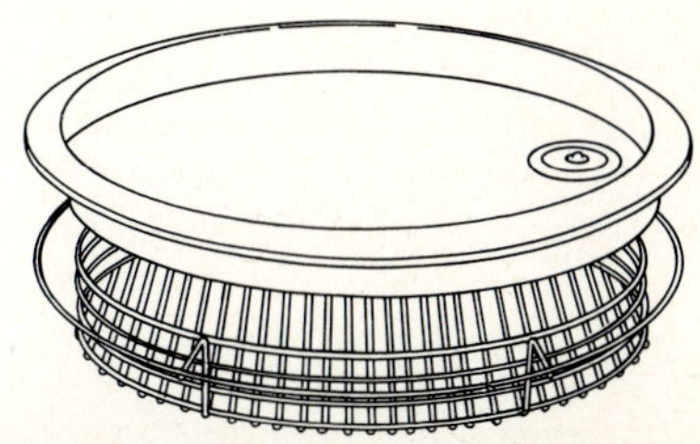

Vendôme's sink accessories include a sorting rack for draining dishes and a plastic-covered wire draining basket for vegetables.

Dishwashers and laundry machines

Machines that wash and dry dirty plates or dirty clothes really do remove a lot of drudgery from the day-to-day round of kitchen chores—but you must ensure that the type of machine you choose is suited to your needs as well as your budget, otherwise it could turn out to be worse than useless. There is no point, for instance, in snapping up a bargain dishwasher that is too small to take your large dinner plates or long-stemmed glasses. Machines do go wrong, so it makes sense to check that the manufacturers of the model you have in mind can offer prompt servicing facilities in your neighbourhood. Here is a cross-section of the different types of machine available.

A front-loading Miele dishwasher (left) conveniently built in next to the sink.

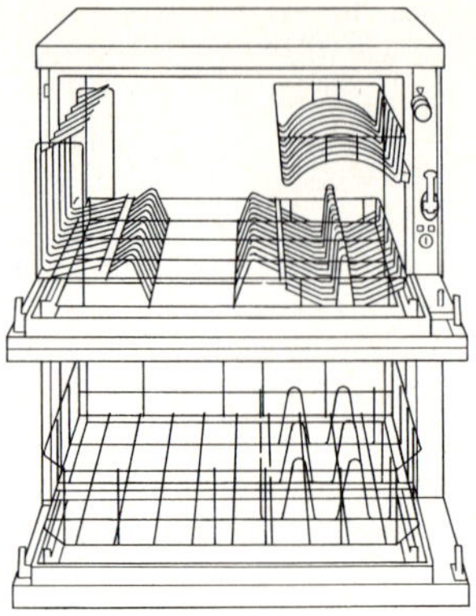

A dual-action dishwasher—delicate water jets in the upper compartment for plates and glasses—fiercer jets in the lower half for pans.
Model: Candy D190 Silent.

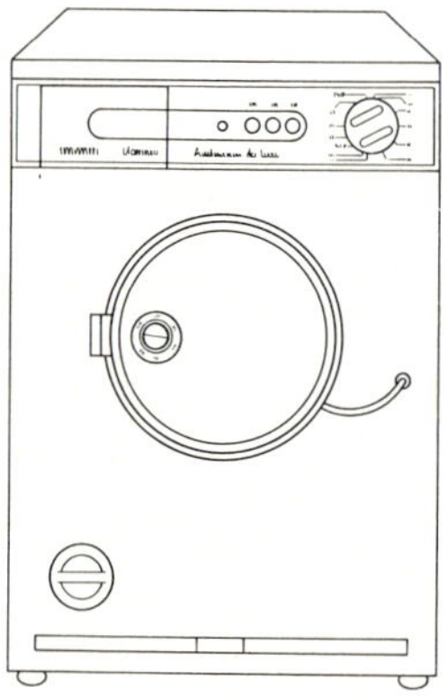

Fully automatic combination machine has a hot-air drier mounted in the door and eleven programmes to cater for any type of fabric.
Model: Colston Commodore.

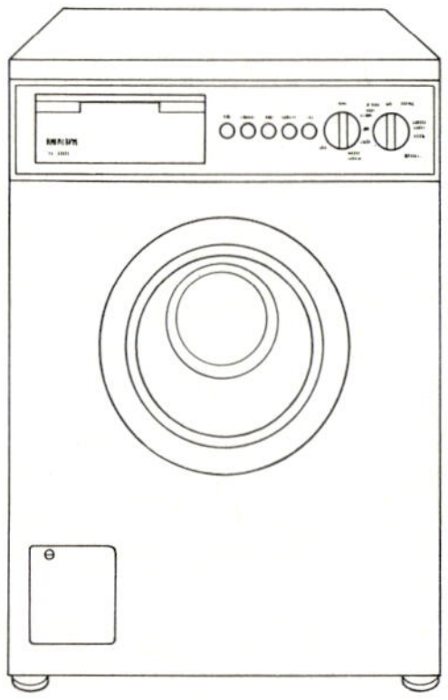

Front-loading automatics have many advantages. They can be stacked under a drier or slotted under a work-surface to save space.
Model: Miele W422.

Fully automatic tumble-drier with a variable heat setting. Blows cold at the end of drying time to prevent creasing.
Model: Bendix 7414.

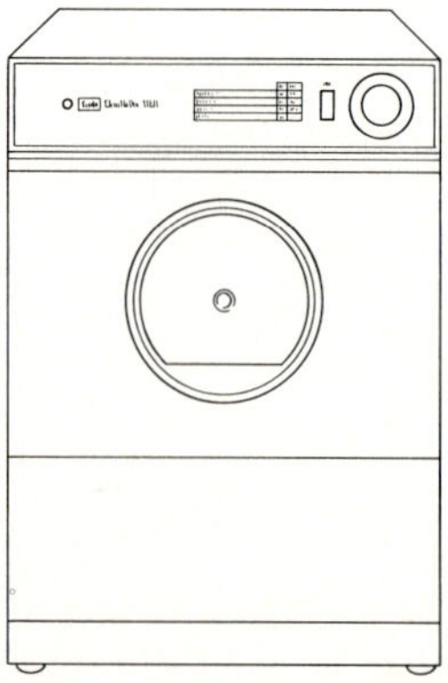

Automatic tumble-drier, with electronic moisture-content measurement, features a reverse-action drum to prevent creasing.
Model: Creda TD400RS.

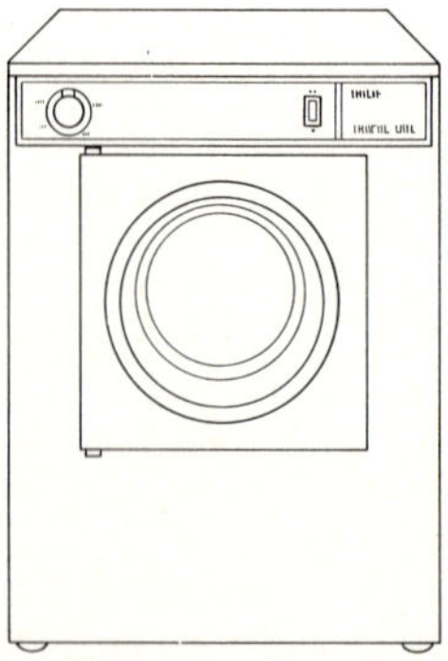

Tiny tumble-drier that takes a 2.7-kg (6-lb) load, has a venting kit as an optional extra and two heat settings.
Model: Philips 002.

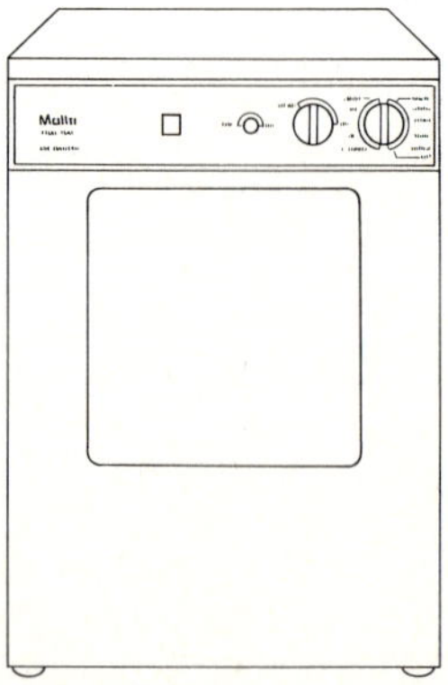

The condenser-drier requires no venting as the water vapour is recirculated and thus dissipated within the machine.
Model: Miele T337K.

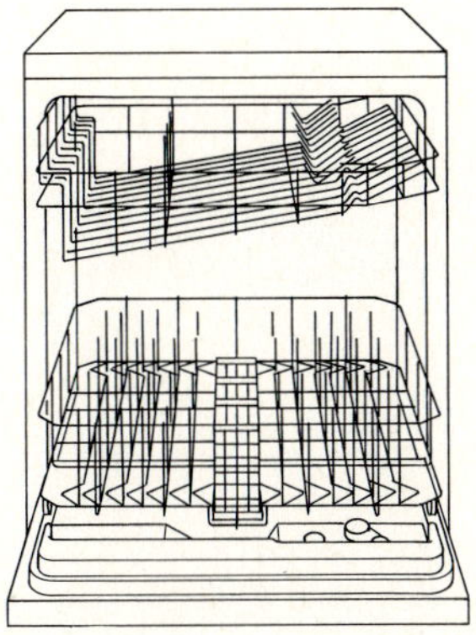

This large dishwasher will take up to twelve place settings, is fully automatic and has seven programmes.
Model: Philips 2000M.

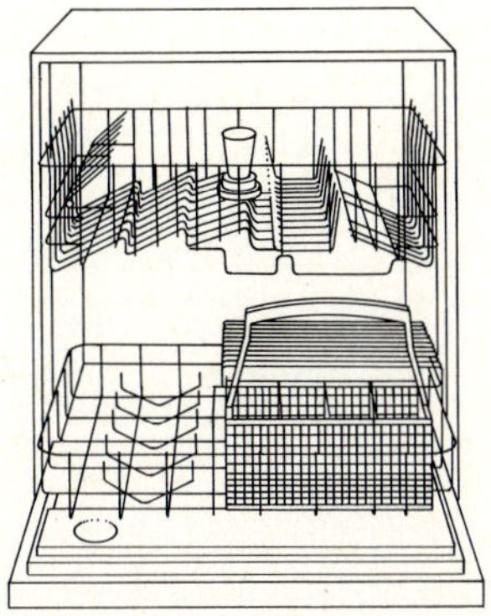

A dishwasher specifically designed to fit under a work-top. A face panel of any material can be slid into the door frame.
Model: Miele G505.

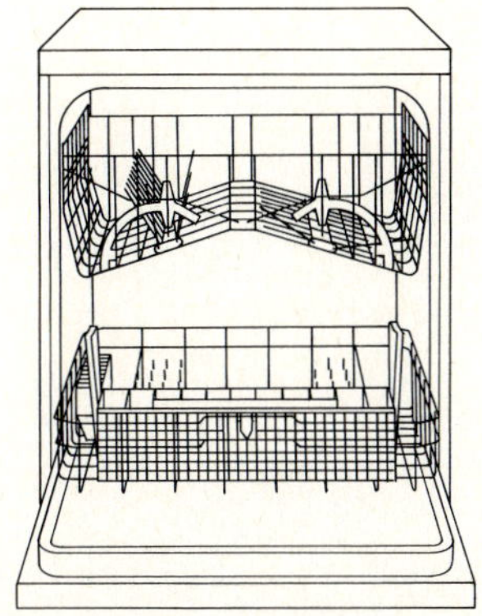

A family-sized dishwasher with adjustable racks for easy loading and a choice of seven cycles, including a soaking programme for pans.
Model: Hobart Kitchen Aid.

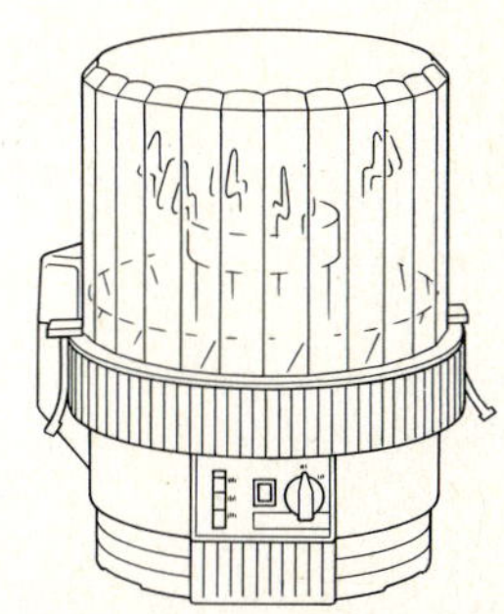

A mini-dishwasher that stands on the draining-board. It is compact and light-weight and needs expensive plumbing.
Model: Lylybet portable.

A top-loading machine, only 400 mm ($15\frac{3}{4}$ in) wide; yet it has seven basic programmes and takes a full 4-kg (9-lb) load.
Model: Philips AWB 101.

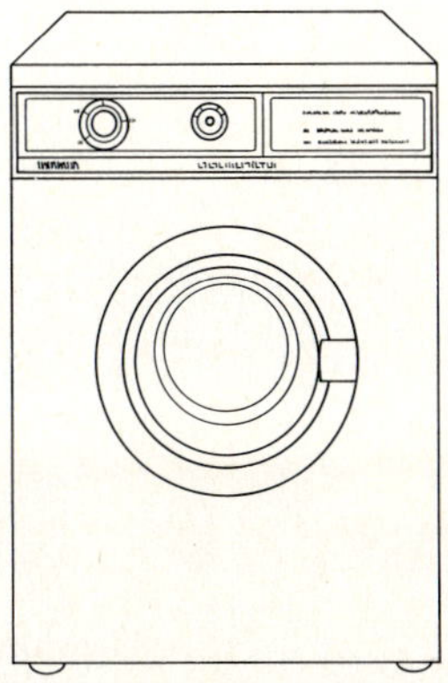

A simple front-loading automatic with few complications is perhaps the best investment. This one has five basic programmes.
Model: Philips AAC 740.

A good twin-tub washes clothes thoroughly and allows you to carry on washing while you rinse and spin. This one will rinse automatically.
Model: Hoovermatic.

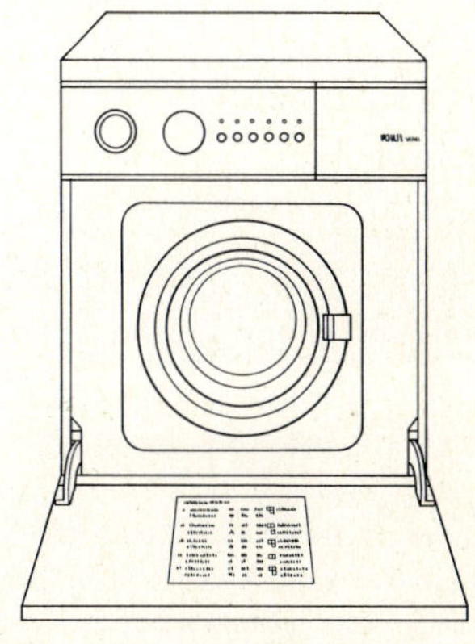

An automatic front-loader that takes a bigger than average load yet is made to standard kitchen unit dimensions.
Model: Bosch V500.

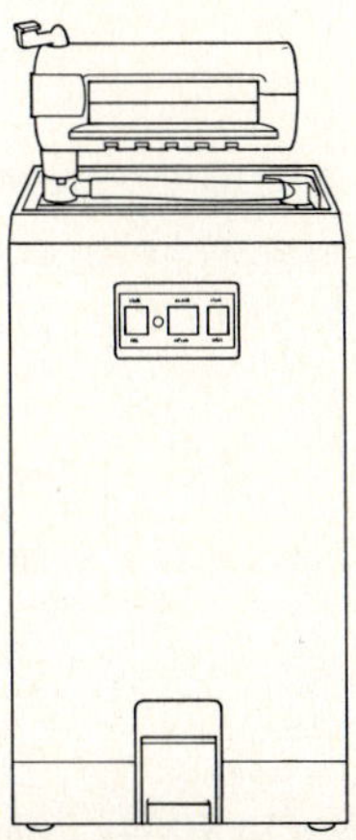

A single-tub machine washes a full load in about four minutes. For rinsing and drying, it can be linked to a spin-drier with a special attachment.
Model: Hoover W7002 with power wringer.

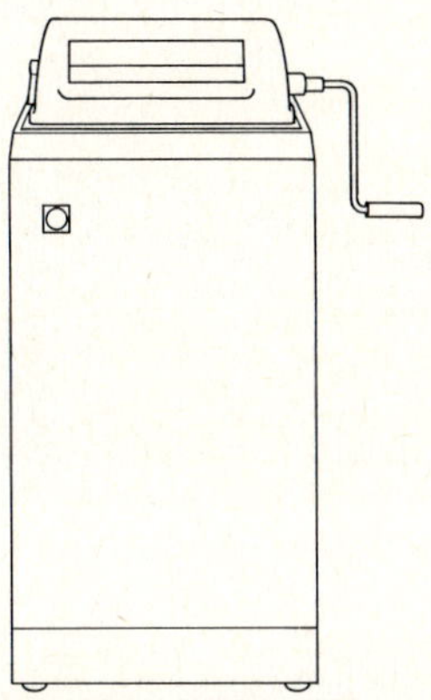

A single-tub machine with a hand wringer to squeeze clothes dry is probably one of the cheapest possible options for washday.
Model: Hoover 3104E.

A spin-drier will spin most clothes ironing dry in four minutes, and is a lot cheaper to run than a hot-air drier.
Model: Creda Debonair Autopump Spin-drier.

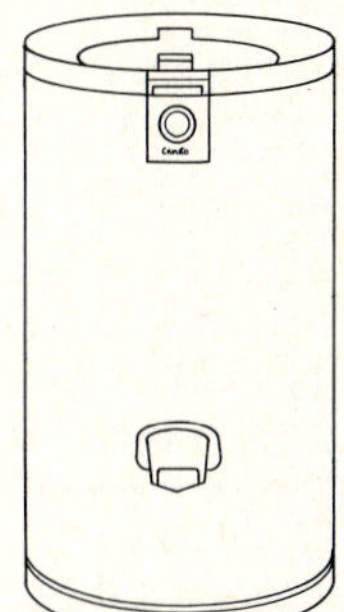

The pump type of spin-drier drains excess water straight into the sink, whereas the gravity type needs a bowl.
Model: Creda Debonair Gravity Spin-drier.

Kitchen units

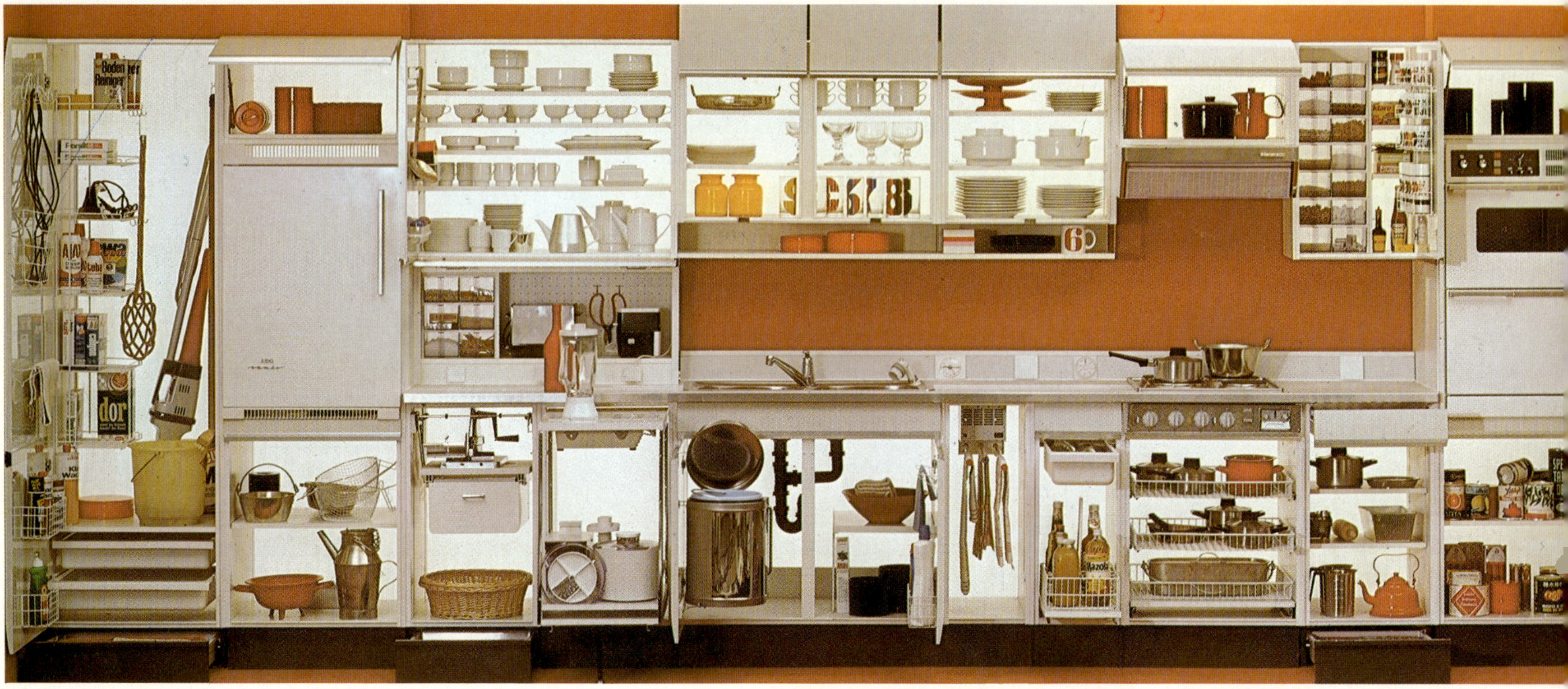

A well-designed kitchen-unit system should organize your kitchen storage for you. Adjustable shelving, sensible cupboards, pull-out racks and baskets provide a logical place for everything. Once you can see what you've got, there is less danger of running out of essential stores or discovering, at the back of an inaccessible shelf, an infuriating cache of half-used jars of stale cinnamon.

In choosing a storage system for the kitchen, do not be influenced by good looks alone. Check before you buy that the system is flexible enough to suit your particular requirements, and sufficiently well made to be efficient. If you are starting off in a small way and intend to add to the line-up of units as space and money become available, it is advisable to choose a popular range of units that will be available for many years.

Look carefully at the insides of drawers and cupboards—plastic-coated ones are much easier to clean. Make sure that all shelves are adjustable, otherwise you will waste space (a tin of tuna doesn't need the same headroom as a packet of breakfast cereal). Check that catches, handles and pull-out mechanisms are solid and simple and that wall-cupboard doors don't scalp you as you open them.

Plastic-coated wire baskets (right), a practical unit for the laundry area.

Inside these smart SieMatic units (above), drawers, shelves and wire baskets slide smoothly on adjustable tracking fitted with rollers. This system offers more than 450 fitments ranging from a purpose-built broom cupboard to a swing-out electric shoe polisher with three automatic shoe polish dispensers.

Danish kitchen furniture with eye-catching handle details (above and right) has a base unit with sensible shallow drawers that double up as trays. The cupboard doors are veneered with oak; the colourful handles are of practical ABS plastics. The overall effect disproves the notion that a row of cupboard doors must necessarily be dull and clinical.

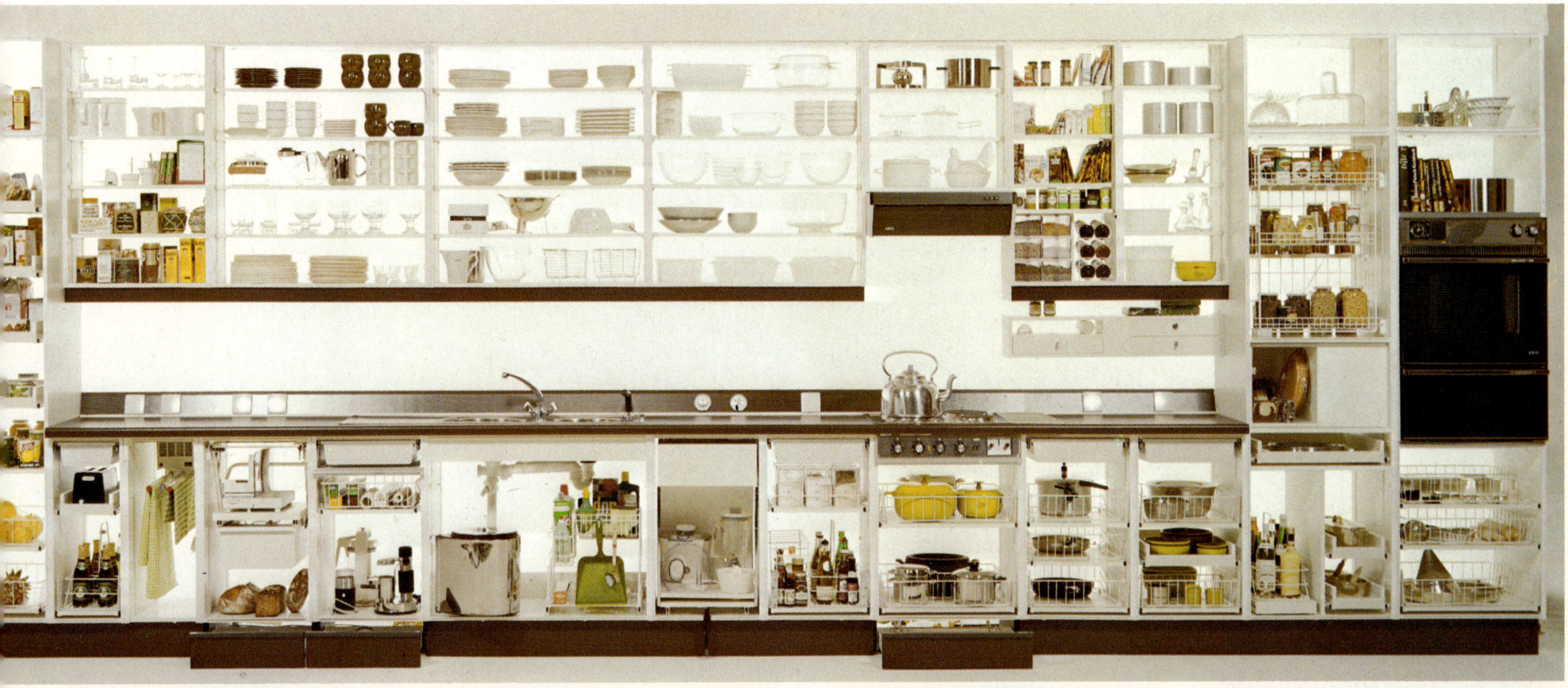

Every shelf (above) is fully adjustable, even the pull-out ones, which have a rim to prevent the contents from falling off.

Pull-out chopping board (left), strong enough to withstand heavy-handed axemen.

Kitchen units

Kitchen units are generally made to standard sizes. Until recently, the standard depth (the front-to-back measurement) of work-tops was 1 ft 9 in or 534 mm. This proved too narrow for many appliances, and with metrication the opportunity was taken to increase the depth to 600 mm. (2ft). The cupboards under the work-top, however, are often still made to the old dimensions, which allow room for plumbing behind the cupboards, while the work-top still meets the wall.

The increment of width for kitchen units is usually 600 mm, and as this is the same as the work-top depth there should be no geometrical problems at corners. A run of units along a wall is a different matter—the chances are a thousand to one against the length of a room being an exact multiple of 600 mm, so there will still be a problem of fit. Manufacturers deal with this problem in two ways—some increase their range to include units 300 mm (12 in), 400 mm (1 ft 4 in) and 500 mm (1 ft 8 in) wide, so with a bit of juggling the cupboards can be made to fit within 100 mm (but be careful—doors of different widths can play havoc with the general look of the kitchen). Some units are supplied with a separate work-top that is deliberately longer than it needs to be so it can be cut exactly to fit by the builder. Any odd space under the work-top can be used for a dishcloth rack or a space for trays.

Units on similar modules are made for wall cupboards and full-height cupboards. More comprehensive ranges include special housings for ovens, dishwashers, refrigerators and so on. Self-assembly units in kit form save money for the do-it-yourself enthusiast, and overcome the problem of getting the unit up stairways that would defeat the assembled product.

Materials and finishes

Most units are made with melamine work-tops and a polyester finish elsewhere. As these are among the most serviceable finishes, and since polyester can only be properly applied under factory conditions, manufactured units tend to be more popular than those run up by the local carpenter. For those who prefer materials that are kinder to the touch and softer to the eye, some manufacturers produce timber units. Beware of the machine-made, hand-crafted look complete with thin veneers laid to simulate boards, however, it is the genuine look and feel of wood that is the attractive thing about the old farm kitchen.

An advantage of the cheapest units, made of white wood, is that they can be painted and re-painted in hundreds of bright colours—with polyester-finished units, you are stuck with the colour for life.

The stained wood island unit (above) has a breakfast bar set at table height so there is no need to balance on a precarious bar stool while imbibing your early morning coffee.

A range of sophisticated pine units from Germany (above and left) that also satisfies nostalgic yearnings for rusticity. The solid wooden doors hide a multiplicity of modern gadgetry. A refrigerator is concealed in the full-height cupboards; even the oven door is boarded up.

Smart units with elegant contoured edges (above) come packed flat in boxes to assemble yourself. White, so easy to live with, is always a safe colour choice.

A simple, cheap and basic kitchen (right) marries the warm look of pine with the practical wipe-clean finish of the polyester painted panels. A good notion for busy young-marrieds.

A pastry-making trolley (above) slides discreetly into the line-up when not required.

The Habitat country kitchen (left) is simply and sturdily made of solid pine. Base units are wall hung, which is a blessing for the taller- or shorter-than-average cook.

itchen units

Counterbalanced up-and-over doors are the most convenient for wall cupboards.

Dishcloths have a place of their own on slide-out drying racks.

A pull-out extension at table height that becomes inconspicuous when not in use.

Where breakfast space is at a premium, folding tables and chairs, though frequently unattractive, are indispensable. This set (above) is prettier than most.

A length of hanging track with slide-in hooks, brackets and tiny perspex shelves runs the length of the work-top (left). Covered sockets provide for the low-voltage gadgetry.

This divided kitchen cutlery drawer has a lift-out, wipe-clean plastic insert. Keep silverware in a separate, lined drawer.

A complication that's probably more trouble than it's worth—a combined fold-down bread bin and slicer unit.

Plastic-coated wire trays slide back and forth independently of one another, so the contents of the drawer are always visible.

Deep aluminium roasting tins are made to do double duty as slide-out storage trays—ideal for heavy, bulky root vegetables.

A very solid table with a neat, white-tiled top (above) folds down from a distinguished line-up of full-height cupboards.

Useful gadgets are more useful when you can find them. Blender centre (right) organizes the mixer and all its bulky attachments.

Deep drawer for storing tall bottles. For low-level storage, drawers are much more accessible than shelves.

Swivelling semicircular wire trays make good use of the often wasted space in a corner, though drawers within cupboards can be inconvenient.

The most convenient base units have a separate drawer above the cupboard door, so items in constant use are quickly to hand.

Another way to capitalize on corners—a simple arc that pivots to shut but can just as easily be left open—providing the shelves are tidy.

Problem kitchens

It's not difficult to plan an efficient kitchen in a good-sized room with four true walls, one door and a window—but not all rooms are like that. Ergonomic dimensions and efficient, logical work centres seem laughably remote when such theories are applied to a tiny triangle with bumpy walls, uneven floors and four doors opening into it. If this sounds like your problem, don't despair. Rules were ever made to be bent, if not broken, and the ingenuity you will be forced to employ to make the room workable might transform a nightmarish hovel into the most interesting room in the house.

You may, on the other hand, have inherited a perfectly efficient kitchen that offends solely on the grounds of dullness, and the problem then is how to make it your kitchen, reflecting your character and tastes. I think you will find no kitchen problem is incapable of solution if you tackle those awkward corners and boring vistas with a spirit of adventure and an open mind.

The most awkward kitchen

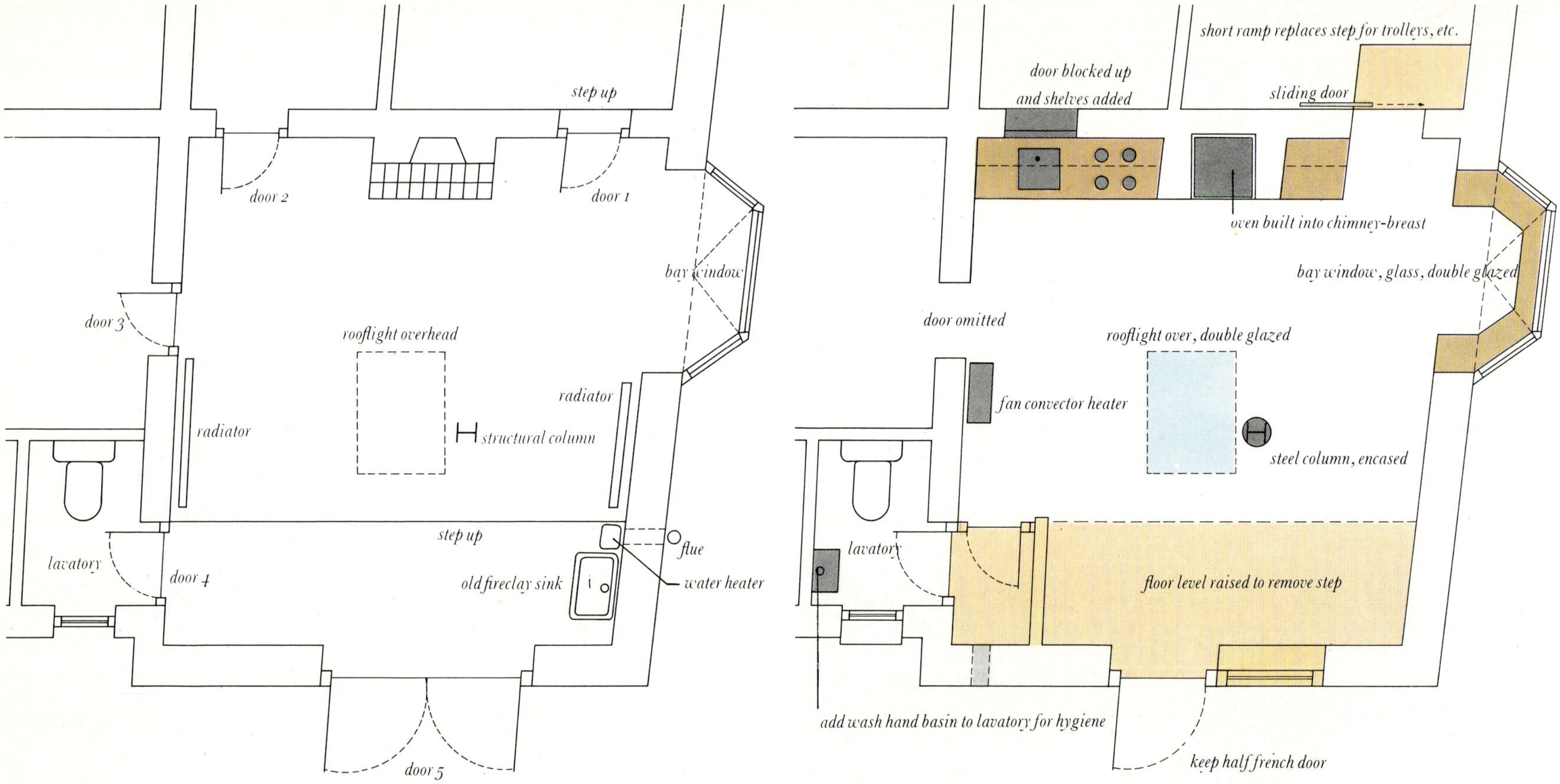

The nightmare room illustrated above shows some of the awful problems you might inherit when moving house, and how, by taking a long, cool look at the situation before making changes, you can achieve some approach to your dream kitchen after all.

Floor levels

If there are changes of floor level that seriously interfere with the kitchen layout, the lower level can be raised to the higher, although check first that the existing floor structure is suitable. If this is done, remember that any doors opening off or into the old lower level will have to be changed, and possibly windows too. Skirtings will have to be moved up, as well as low wall electric sockets or radiators.

Dropping the floor level rather than raising it is likely to be more expensive since the damp-proof course in the wall may have to be altered, pipework re-routed, electric cables reorganized, earth excavated, wall plaster extended and other structural details taken into consideration and modified where necessary. Single steps at doorways (e.g. at door 1) are dangerous anywhere in a building. At the entrance to a kitchen, where there is likely to be frequent movement by people carrying trays of food, they are even more to be avoided. If possible the floor should be revised so it is level through the opening. A fairly cheap alternative would be to build a short ramp, which would allow trolleys to be wheeled easily through the door.

Doorways

It may well be that some of the doors in the room are actually unnecessary for efficient movement about the house. If this is so, remove one or two and block up the openings with brick and plaster, or timber and plaster (e.g. at door 2). Shut off the openings on the far, non-kitchen, side, leaving a recess into which shelves can be fixed. Alternatively you can leave the doorways open, so long as they don't directly lead into rooms in which you wish to maintain some degree of privacy. You might easily gain some extra space if you refix a door to swing the other way, but remember that the lock must also be changed. Sliding doors are a good idea, but the gaps around them sometimes cause draught and sound-proofing problems. Another drawback is the amount of valuable space they occupy when slid open against the wall.

If the kitchen adjoins a sitting-room, help to exclude cooking smells, steam and noise by fitting a spring to the door so that it closes after you. Should noise exclusion be especially important, sound-proofing can be increased by adding a sheet of hardwood to one or both sides of the door, or by hanging a door curtain. In either case the door should fit snugly into the frame.

If you buy a house in which the lavatory has direct access to the kitchen (e.g. at door 4), you may find that the building society and the local health authority will combine in insisting that you provide a lobby space between kitchen and lavatory, with two separate doors. The lobby space must also be ventilated by means of an air brick or ventilator. This requirement can cause considerable problems, and it may well prove cheaper to take out the lavatory.

Double doors opening on to a terrace (e.g. at door 5) are handy for meals outside, but can take up valuable wall space. It might be better instead to have only one door and block off the other half, up to say 1000 mm (3 ft 4 in), and fit a window above.

Windows

As everyone knows, a bay window is a delightful spot in which to place a circular dining table; fitted seats with storage space under make it particularly welcome in the kitchen. Perhaps, more unusually, you might turn it into an interesting work-area by positioning the work-tops and units in the bay—and possibly the sink units might

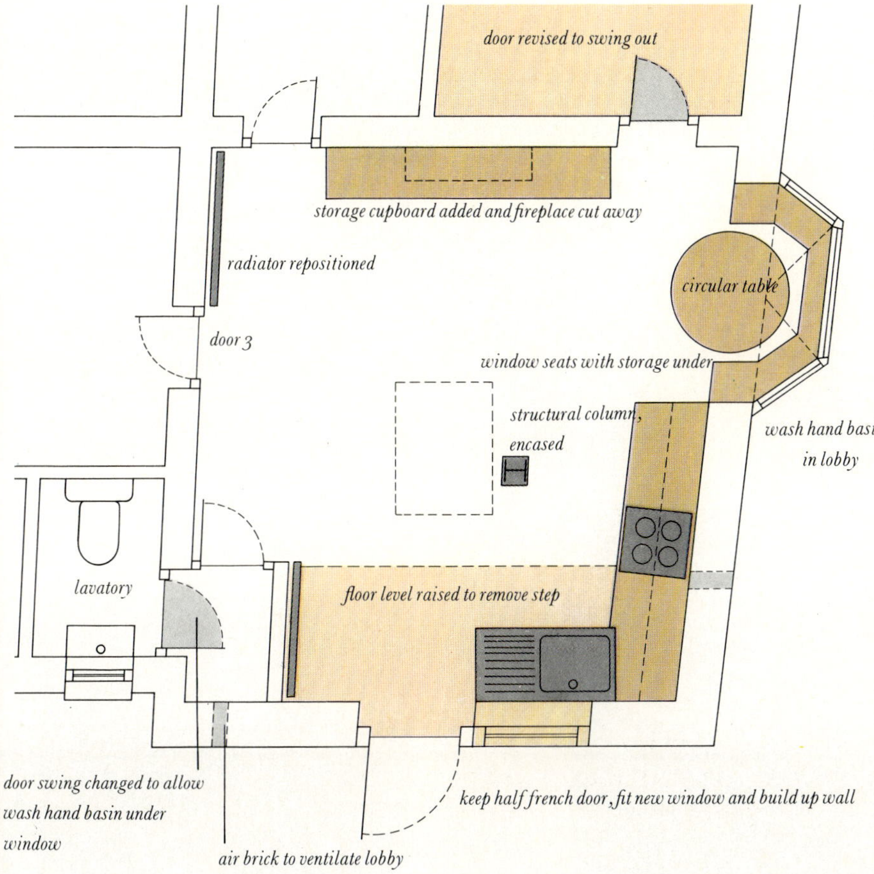

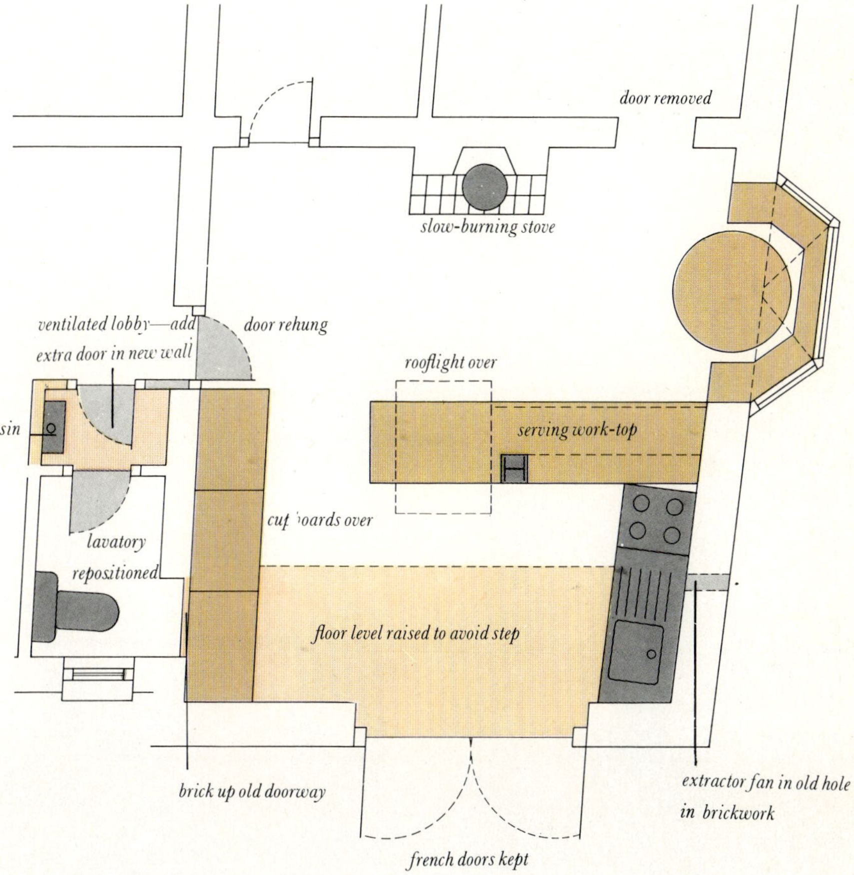

fit as well. Condensation may cause problems where steam and heat are near glass, but double glazing will reduce this and help to keep the room warm.

Chimney stacks

If a continuous flat wall is really badly needed, e.g. for a range of standard wall units, the chimney stack can be demolished and the brickwork made good before plastering. However, it is likely that you will need to dismantle more than just the chimney-breast as the whole stack may rise several storeys above the room being converted and have to be taken down as well. It is therefore probably cheaper to leave the stack alone and just to hollow out the chimney-breast to take a cupboard, built-in oven, heating boiler or a stove.

The old flue could be used as an extract duct for a fan, although this is not a particularly efficient way of extracting air. The opening should be shut off at the bottom by a register plate to prevent dirt dropping down, but there should be a ventilating grille in the plate.

You could also level off the old hearth of the fireplace until it is even with the main floor. Later, it can be covered with the same flooring material as the rest of the kitchen.

Structural columns

Instead of trying to eliminate columns by changing the main roof structure, it would be more economical to integrate any columns into the kitchen design—to make something decorative from a structural necessity.

Rooflights

Overhead lighting can add a pleasant atmosphere to a room. However, in a kitchen, great care should be taken to avoid condensation because this will drip as it forms on the underside of a rooflight glass. It could spoil your furniture or flooring, so double glaze the glass in the rooflight or add a flat laylight below.

Ventilating fans need to be fitted high up in a kitchen and the rooflight may prove an ideal place to do this.

Radiators

It is feasible to modify existing radiators and their pipework to suit your new kitchen plan. However, if there is a shortage of space, new, more compact radiators might be more suitable, or even long, narrow radiators fitted vertically to save wall space at low level. Yet another choice is fan convector radiators, which give off more heat than their size suggests.

Sinks and water heaters

The old sink will probably be connected to the drainage via a waste pipe and gulley. Therefore, it is advisable for the waste drainage from a new sink to be placed in the same area of the kitchen. The sink can of course be positioned so that a new drain connection is made, though it must be related to the extant drainage system.

Again it is quite satisfactory to connect new gas cooking equipment to existing gas-supply pipework. An old water heater flue outlet could be kept as a ventilator or enlarged for a fan outlet.

Irregular walls

Not all walls meet each other at neat right angles in the corner. Irregular walls may add charm to the room, but they do present problems when trying to make an accurate line-up of units. This can be solved by using special work-tops that are cut or scribed to both walls, the units below being placed against only one of them. Alternatively, corners out of square can be avoided by stopping the units short and leaving a space in the corner.

Similar problems are caused by walls that are slightly out of the vertical. Horizontal battens of unequal thickness fixed to the back of the units, top and bottom, will correct any inaccuracies and allow the fixed units to hang true.

A tight squeeze

It is fairly simple to devise a workable plan for a large kitchen, as little mistakes and awkwardnesses can be circumnavigated and, in time, accepted. In a tiny kitchen, however, every inch of space has to work for its living, and little errors, like a cupboard door opening the wrong way or an awkwardly placed tap, become magnified out of all proportion.

The main problem is getting the basic equipment into a restricted space. Obviously room must be found for a sink, a cooker and a refrigerator—but do they necessarily have to be of standard size? A single-bowl sink should be sufficient, perhaps with a chopping board that fits into it when it is not being used for washing up. Instead of a full-scale stove consider a two-burner cook-top and a small, wall-mounted oven. Install a tiny refrigerator, and if it proves insufficient place a larger fridge/freezer, for long-term supplies, in the hall or the garage. Sort out all the items, such as tinned foods and seldom-used pans and containers, that could be kept outside the kitchen, so saving valuable space. The restricted amount of floor space means that you will be using the walls wherever possible. You can pile more on to shelves, racks and hooks than would ever fit into a neat line of wall cupboards. The ceiling, too, can be exploited—a framework suspended overhead will provide additional space for hanging things. A window takes up a lot of wall space, and that, too, could be done away with in the name of extra storage space as long as there is an alternative source of light—a rooflight or a glazed door—and a source of ventilation, preferably a good extractor system ducted to the outside.

Mini-kitchens

There is a variety of instant kitchens-in-cupboards on the market that generally consist of a base unit with two electric rings, a tiny sink/draining-board on top and, below, a small fridge and some storage shelves. These units can be as small as 600 mm (2 ft) deep, 1000 mm (3 ft $3\frac{1}{2}$ in) long and 900 mm (3 ft) high. All they need in the way of services are a couple of power sockets, a water supply and a waste pipe. Such units were never intended to replace a full-scale kitchen, but they are perfectly adequate for offices or beach huts.

This kitchen (above) has benefited from a little judicious juggling of windows to make room for a wall-mounted oven.

What do you do with a long, thin room that has unsightly walls and an uneven floor? The answer (left) was to build a simple kitchen inside a "skin" of new walls raised on a low dais. Only the clutter under the work-tops is hidden from the dining area.

An intelligent use of wall-space in an open-plan New York apartment (right).

When you are short of space, you might make do with a kitchen on the landing (above)—but check with the local authorities first.

That awkward little space under the stairs is recruited to expand the hallway into a perfectly acceptable kitchen (below).

Space-saving ideas

Even large kitchens suffer from a lack of work-space. A pull-out board is always useful but it must be solid and stable (above).

The fold-away wood and laminate breakfast-table is a real space-saver (left) —but don't lean your elbows too heavily on it.

If there is no room for the refrigerator in the kitchen, put it in the hall instead—subtly disguised, of course (left).

A mobile mini-kitchen (above) needs only a power socket to plug into. This makes bed-side breakfasting a reality.

In the cleverly exploited corner (below) a hinged screen-type door folds back, allowing access to the cupboard under the sink.

An ingenious system of box-like shelves and a table that practically lays itself (above). An idea easily copied by the home handyman.

Doing it on the cheap

If your problems are more financial than spatial it is not necessary to resort to a camp fire and a blackened cauldron. The secondhand market and the want ads are a fruitful source of kitchen equipment and furniture, and sales are a culinary bargain-hunter's paradise. Standard units, sinks, cookers of all kinds, refrigerators, utensils and flooring are always obtainable somewhere at a reduced price. Furniture not habitually connected with the kitchen can be happily adapted. A medley of low cupboards can be made to harmonize if a continuous work-top is placed over them, a bookcase fixed above a counter-top makes a marvellous dresser and curtains hide a multitude of ill-assorted yet useful boxes. Plastic milk crates and orange boxes, scaffolding poles and planks supported by piles of bricks, old marble washstands, industrial shelving and office furniture all earn their place in the budget kitchen.

The shelf kitchen

Using one of the proprietary metal wall channel systems and its associated brackets, a whole kitchen can be wall-hung like shelves, using extra-long brackets to support the work-top. A shelf kitchen is a practical solution for rented accommodation, because all the shelves would inevitably be adjustable and the whole kitchen could be dismantled and refixed if required. The work-top, which could be made from a standard door—plastic-laminated if funds will allow—must be very securely fixed to its supporting brackets, because it must be rigid if a sink bowl is to be let into it, or the waste pipe will get damaged. If there is risk of movement, flexible pipework must be used. Taps should be mounted on the wall to keep them rigidly fixed. The shelves could be anything from simple planks to prefinished shelves coated with plastic laminate or a wood veneer. Standard drawer sets or wire baskets with runners are available from hardware shops and can be usefully fixed underneath a work-top. A cheap wall unit, balanced on one of the shelves and securely fixed to the wall at the back, would keep pots and plates free from dust.

The advantages of the shelf kitchen is that it can grow as funds become available—more shelves of different widths can be added as long as the wall standards chosen at the beginning are long enough and sufficiently secure to take the load.

The cupboard kitchen

If it becomes necessary to hide your simple kitchen from the critical eyes of guests, then curtains or roller blinds are the cheapest solution, but from the safety point of view the fabrics used should be fire-proofed. If the whole run of shelves and units sits neatly in an alcove or takes up an entire wall, it could be treated in the manner of a wardrobe and closed off completely with sliding doors.

The cheapest island

A pleasant island kitchen can be constructed using scaffolding posts to suspend shelving and electrical outlets above a back-to-back arrangement of standard units. An island unit is ideal in a large room where the walls are uneven, and as long as the sink can be connected to a waste pipe, and the wiring can be brought through the floor or the ceiling, it should be feasible.

A confident carpenter made these mobile units that disappear behind the venetian blinds (above).

A DIY work-top of solid pine (below). The wide overlapping flange of the inset sink will hide any ragged edges made by the inexpert carpenter.

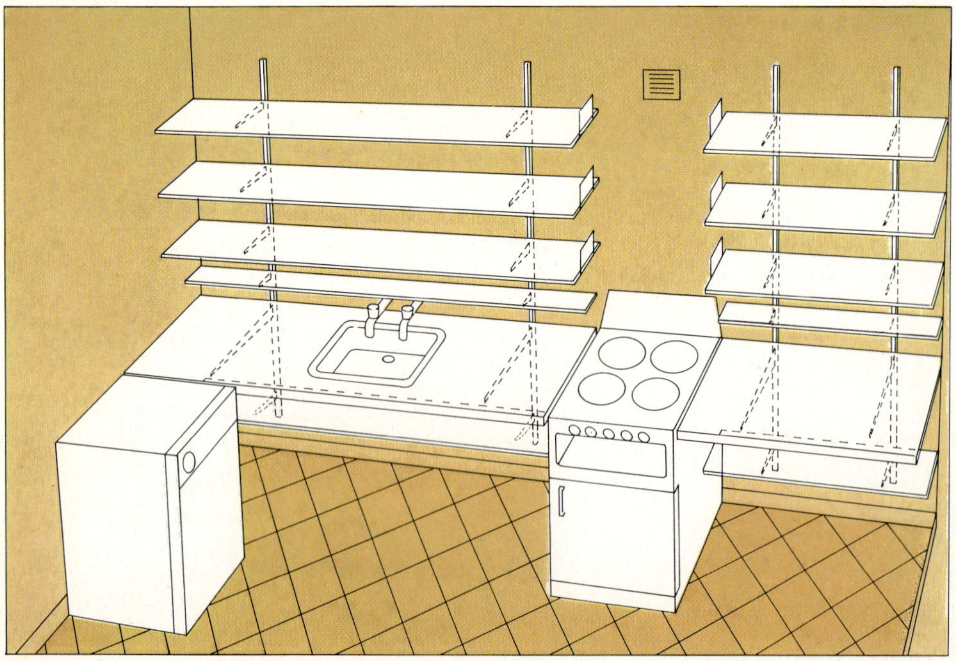

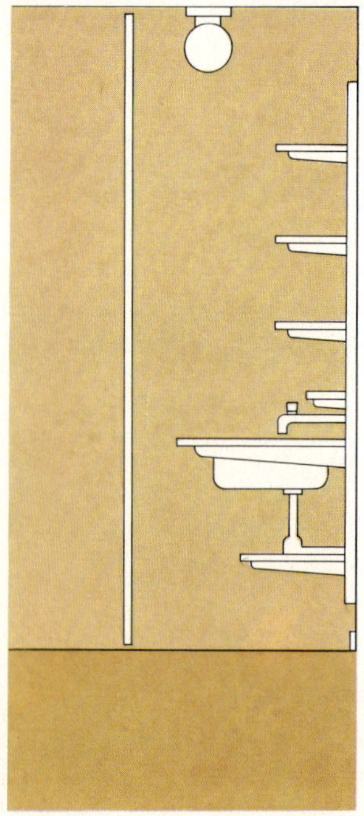

The shelf kitchen (left) consists of a few simple components:
2 standard doors (Formica faced) 1981 mm (6 ft 6 in) x 686 mm (2 ft 3 in). One door has been cut to fit.
8 planks 225 mm (9 in) wide. Four planks 1981 mm (6 ft 6 in) long, the remaining four cut to fit. On either side of the cooker, three shelves are fitted above the work-top and one below.
2 planks 125 mm (5 in) wide, one 1981 mm (6 ft 6 in) long, the other cut to fit
4 metal wall standards
8 pairs 200-mm (8-in) brackets
2 pairs 100-mm (4-in) brackets
6 bookends
1 inset sink bowl and trap
1 pair taps
1 second-hand cooker
1 second-hand refrigerator

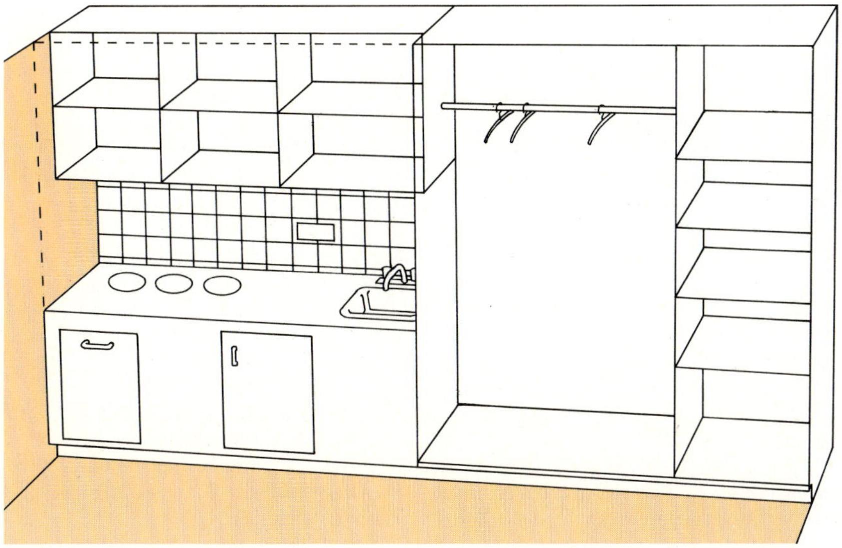

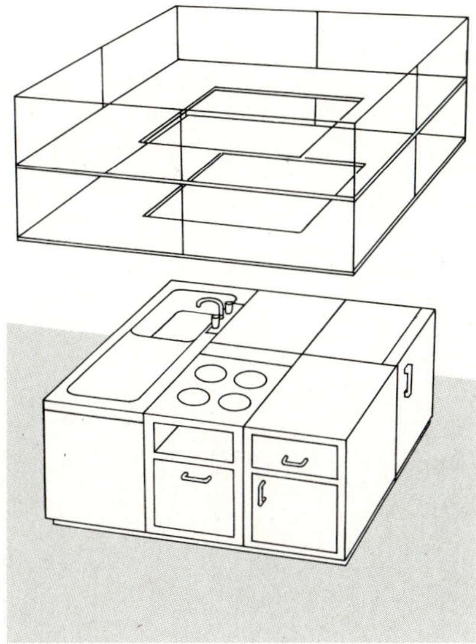

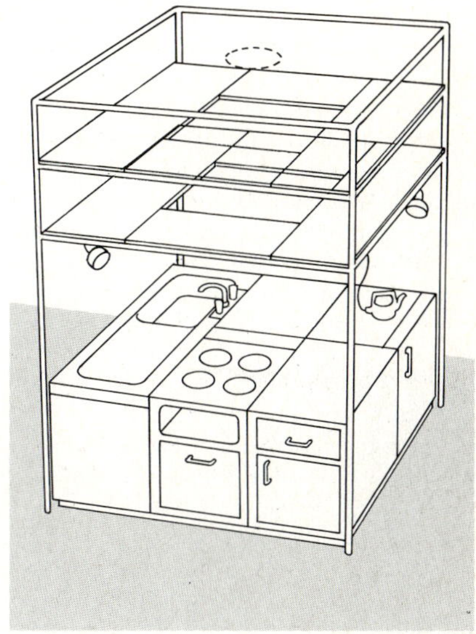

A small, simple and cheap kitchen in a cupboard takes up one wall of a studio apartment and incorporates clothes storage (above).

A tiny kitchen in a corner cupboard assembled from standard units and DIY shelving (below). A folding door conceals it completely.

Island kitchens are not the prerogative of the rich— all you need is space to move around. In the diagram (above) and the photograph (below) storage shelves are suspended from the ceiling on simple metal brackets. Water supplies and waste pipes can be buried under the floor at little extra cost, and electrical wiring and ventilation ducts can be run through the ceiling just as easily as within the walls.

A simple island unit (above) consists of standard units placed back to back. A scaffolding framework with posts at each corner supports shelves and racking above. Electric points are fixed to the underside of the shelves and clip-on lights are fixed to the posts.
An L-shaped work-top could be made to cover the refrigerator and the base units to give a continuous work surface.

Glossing over the problem

How do you stamp your own personality on a kitchen inherited from the previous occupant of your home? Ripping out a row of units just because you don't like the colour is both wasteful and unnecessary.

Timber cupboards can easily be repainted, or the existing paint or varnish can be removed with paint stripper or burnt off with a blow torch. Then sand down the bare wood and seal it with a clear polyurethane varnish to bring out the natural colour.

Revamping a polyester finish on a factory-made unit is not quite so easy—though not impossible. The shiny surface must be roughened before there is any chance of the new paint adhering to the plastic backing. The success of the job depends on the care taken in the preparation—everything must be scrupulously clean, for even the smallest particle of dust will ruin the final effect. Ensure your brush is very clean, and use a gloss or satin gloss paint, preferably of a thixotropic (non-drip) variety.

You could try self-adhesive, washable PVC on the door fronts, but you are likely to have difficulty trimming the material on the edges of the doors in a way that will prevent peeling. A small timber or aluminium batten glued all around would overcome this problem.

If none of these do-it-yourself solutions appeal, then remove the cupboard doors completely and treat the shell of the units as open shelving. Alternatively, you can buy doors in another colour, should the kitchen units you have inherited still be in production. If they are, and you don't have as many complete units as you'd like, then it is often possible to add to them. One slight snag to this is that many manufacturers of standard units do not make the same design for long and it may prove impossible to get more of the same units in the right colour. It would then be better to concentrate on filling the available spaces with contrasting furniture such as narrow shelving, antique dressers or marble-topped tables.

Changing the surroundings

Where the units themselves are tolerable, make your impression on the room by changing the floor, walls and ceiling. You might, for instance, transform the room with a dramatic pattern on the floor. This can modify the kitchen's apparent size and atmosphere in one operation. Similarly, the change from a strong pattern to something plain or simple is equally effective.

Existing wall tiles can be removed with determination and a sharp chisel, and a new coat of paint, paper, tiles or pine boarding will all help to change the character of the kitchen.

The ceiling is also a potential player in the transformation scene. Paint, paper,

A bold coat of blue lifts this small kitchen (left) out of the doldrums. A new work-top bypasses a charming, old-fashioned cupboard.

Once upon a time this was a bright, white room with pine units (above). The new owners achieved a cosier ambience with paper and paint.

lower or raise part or all of it, and the room will be dramatically altered.

Light and colour

Exciting effects can also be achieved by revising the lighting. Spotlights in the room will dramatize your favourite possessions and recessed lights with dimmer switches around the eating area will promote an air of cosy intimacy. If cash is short, then a new lamp shade and a coloured bulb is much better than nothing.

The cheapest and most effective method of transforming somebody else's kitchen into your own is to change its colour. The room will begin to reflect your personality when you apply your colour choice to walls, doors, window frames, units and even the exposed pipework. Dynamic use of colour makes a gloomy room bright and cheerful, and changes a jazzy muddle to cool and sophisticated charm.

A face-lift for a clinical white kitchen (above). The base cupboards have gone and the walls have come out in a rash of green gingham.

More dash than cash (above). A wallpapered sink unit, a home-made adjustable table and dish-towel curtains star in a triumph of invention.

Acres of plain white plaster and tiles proved a fruitful canvas for the artistic owners of this farmhouse kitchen in Zalipie, Poland (above).

A large refrigerator, disguised with a smart coat of brown paint and a bowl of dried flowers, blends unobtrusively with the background (above).

An assortment of cookers are tidied up with a tiled work-surface (below). Base cupboards are decorated with strips of dowelling.

Kitchens of character

It is certainly important to design a kitchen so that it functions well—but this ideal should not be allowed to squeeze out every vestige of character. Few will gasp in amazement at the efficiency of your cooking centre, but many will be amused or charmed by the inventive touches that represent your own contribution to the personality of your kitchen.

The owners of the homes in this chapter share the lively conviction that kitchens should say more about the personalities of the people who work in them than can be expressed by yards of laminated plastic and stainless steel. Since they hail from widely differing backgrounds—from an artists' colony in California to London's House of Commons—their ideas are very different. You may not agree with any of them; they certainly would not agree with each other. But whether their ideas delight or grate upon you, the point is that they offer a challenge, a base of inspiration from which your own decorative imaginings can take wing.

Conversions

Home is a railway carriage (above and left). The kitchen makes ingenious use of a cramped space with an overabundance of windows. Even the crockery on the shelves is highlighted by a cheery glow from the garden.

Idiosyncratic clutter in a kitchen that was once a conservatory (below and right). There is nowhere to put a wall cupboard, so narrow shelves follow the line of the glazing bars.

In this converted country railway station the ticket office has been transformed into a kitchen (above).

A marble slab for rolling out pastry is let into the table top (left).

The solid splendour of this Victorian gothic station obviates the need for further architectural embellishments (below).

The personal touch

Precisely purpose-built, ensuring that everything gets returned to its allotted place on the sculptured shelving unit (right).

The zebra stripes and the hand-blown light bulbs (below) serve no grand purpose except to give pleasure to the owner.

The personality of the owner—a painter—is given free rein in the kitchen of this old San Francisco warehouse (above).

An elaborate coffee bar complete with espresso machine is conjured up in a bright corner of a French kitchen (right).

Clement Freud, gourmet, wit, Liberal MP and TV personality, pictured (above) in his North London kitchen, built to his own design in a glass and cedarwood extension.

A curved housing unit adds an individualistic touch to the brace of fridges against the far wall. The extractor hood over the cook-top is given the same treatment (left).

One man's nightmare of a dust-trap is another man's attractive pile of kitchen pots, pans, plants and clutter (below).

Idiosyncratic kitchens

John Prizeman designed these sculptural all-in-one freestanding units that encapsulate every kitchen feature (above and left). They need only to be plugged in and plumbed up to the water supply to provide a compact kitchen anywhere—the ultimate, though at the moment somewhat expensive, answer to single-room living. The setting chosen for the robot, however, is not considered typical.

Toile de Nîmes *once made Mr Levi's fortune in cowboy country. Now denim is* haute couture *and has even found its way on to the front panels of these kitchen cabinets (left).*

A lot of imagination and a couple of pots of paint have imposed a positive and cheerful personality on what was a rather dull line-up of standard units (above).

A colour-matched line-up of vivid kitchen units and equipment (left) is the principal decorative feature of this otherwise rather bleak New York apartment.

The Persian carpets and antique furniture have overrun the confines of the living area and captured the kitchen. Easy-clean plastics have backed right up to the sink. (above).

Idiosyncratic kitchens

An extravagant joke at the expense of English Gothic, the kitchen (below) has adopted the trappings of church architecture. The 16th-century rood screen, salvaged from a derelict church in Leeds, now enshrines the culinary chancel (detail above).

Sam's Kitchen (right) is not the greasy diner its name suggests, although finely carved pillars (detail above) conceal canned food. An extraordinary blend of Victorian Gothic and Islamic design, the kitchen was made for the eponymous Sam by designer Johnny Grey.

The chef imitates the chef d'oeuvre, painted on the door of his Parisian kitchen (above).

Trompe-l'oeil decoration may not deceive the eye but it's a fertile source of visual wit.

A movable feast

"Nothing helps scenery like ham and eggs," said Mark Twain.

Today, we take meals in trains, boats and planes for granted and rarely give a second thought to how the food has arrived on our plates. The kitchen is as mobile as we are. Even our most forward-looking transport includes magnificent catering aids able to dispense unexceptional meals with the minimum of fuss.

An outdoor meal is different—a romantic interlude in our humdrum lives. The smell of woodsmoke curling into the air, the glow of charcoal embers under a steak, a forkful of freshly caught trout by a grass-banked stream, these are what we treasure. But to arrive at these age-old pleasures we now employ all manner of advanced equipment, undreamed of in the days when food fell to the huntsman's spear. A nostalgic taste of the simple life is our quest; the hiss of a gas canister, the turn of a battery motor our means. Do we gain or lose by them?

A movable feast

Travelling through time

The first great European travellers, the restless Vikings, rode the sea in ships that carried canvas tents to pitch on land. Stretched over wooden supports, these tents were as spacious as marquees. Their lives were by no means so uncomfortable as has been depicted. Viking burial sites have disclosed plenty of kitchen equipment: vast cauldrons of bronze and iron, iron kettles and pothooks, wooden trenchers, cups, plates, dishes, ladles, even a kitchen stool. As for food, apart from beef and mutton bones the burial sites have also revealed grains of wheat in an oak chest, cress seeds, nuts and traces of two species of wild apple.

At sea, the Vikings ate salted fish or boiled their meat over braziers installed in the tiny covered area in the stern. Similar cooking methods were followed by other mariners for many centuries after. But always there was the spectre of scurvy, caused by the near impossibility of storing green vegetables on a long voyage. The cause and cure of scurvy were discovered in the eighteenth century, when, due in part to the efforts of the great explorer and "seaman's seaman" Captain Cook, the juice of lemons or limes became part of the standard daily ration of the Royal Navy.

Among other delicacies created to enliven the monotony of shipboard fare were the smoked hams and clotted cream taken by West Country emigrants to the New World, and the ketchups that "will keep for twenty years" devised by the stoic wives of sea captains bound for the Indies.

By the end of the nineteenth century, however, trans-ocean travellers, at least in the first class, were able to enjoy most of the comforts offered by hotels on land. But in that over-fed era there also lived young men of sterner stuff who were still able to appreciate the simpler joys of holidaying in a small boat on the Thames. For riverside chefs, Jerome K. Jerome outlined the advantages of a methylated spirit stove over paraffin models: "You get methylated pie and methylated cake. But methylated spirit is more wholesome when taken into the system in large quantities than paraffin oil"—advice that has never been improved upon.

But of all travellers on land, probably the most experienced were the armies of Europe that roamed down the centuries, occasionally fighting one another, but obsessed always with the problem of extracting a living from the countryside. Thus Napoleon, past master of the art and leader of armies that marched on their stomachs, was able to make do at the conclusion of the Battle of Marengo with a chicken and a few crayfish culled from the devastated neighbourhood, so immortalising the struggle in the minds of gourmets as well as historians.

It was another Frenchman, Alexis Benoit Soyer, a serious inventor with a showman streak, who transformed the British army's catering. As a young man, he worked in the kitchens of several great French houses before coming to England, where eventually he became chef de cuisine at the Reform Club in London. The club lived up to its name, for, in 1841, it permitted him to install his own patented gas stoves. But Mr Soyer also had a social conscience; in 1847, when the Irish potato famine was at its fearsome height, he set up temporary soup kitchens in Dublin. On his return to London, Soyer instructed ladies in the art of making "cheap soup for the hungry poors", and wrote a cookery book.

This dashing machine brought a gourmet touch to French military catering in 1892 (above). The cook maintained an even oven temperature by rotating the wheel on top.

A few years later, following the outbreak of the Crimean War, he abandoned a not-too-successful career as a restaurateur, and, together with a secretary and several subordinate chefs, set off for the battlefront.

Conditions in the Crimea were appalling. Visiting the base camp at Balaclava with Florence Nightingale, Soyer found that men returning from thirty-six hours in the trenches in bitter weather, had nothing to eat but raw salt pork. The great cauldrons in which the meat ration was cooked in the hospitals at Scutari and Constantinople were as disgusting as the meals they produced. Meat was jammed in the cauldrons so tightly that some of it didn't get boiled at all. Orderlies would mark off large portions for themselves with anything that came to hand . . . a bayonet, a pair of candle snuffers. Almost as bad was the waste; the water in which the meat was boiled was thrown away instead of being retained to make a nourishing soup.

Soyer set to work. He reorganized the hospital kitchens and made the food palatable, revamped the soldiers' diet so that they received meat at least three times a week and appointed himself as chef of the Fourth Division, wandering up and down the lines in his own patent cooking wagon. This was so successful that it later became standard equipment throughout the Army.

Going native in Madagascar with the traditional—and efficient—clay oven (left).

A cook-sergeant's ingenuity helps to make First World War fare more palatable (below).

Master chef Alexis Soyer (foreground, above) awaits the general's verdict on his field kitchen designed to improve the lot of British troops in the Crimean War of 1853-6.

Sixty years on—in the First World War—Soyer's machine was still standard equipment (below), helping to alleviate the monotony of bully beef and tinned stew.

Cookery below zero. Sir Ernest Shackleton and his heroic companions of the 1914-16 Antarctic expedition make the best of their two-year enforced sojourn on the ice floes (above).

Mobile restaurants, set up at night in the streets or car parks of Singapore (below), providing cheap, colourful and exciting meals for citizens and tourists alike.

Travelling through time

In Britain, the coming of the railways presented problems undreamed of by the engineers who built them.

"When actually on a carriage or railway journey it is unwise to make large meals," warned a doctor in 1875. "They are sure to be swallowed in a hurried manner and in a state of heat and excitement very unfavourable to digestion. The best way is to make no meal at all until the journey is over, but to carry a supply of cold provisions, bread, eggs, chickens, game sandwiches, Cornish pasties, almonds, oranges, captain's biscuits, water, and sound red wine or cold tea, sufficient to stay the appetites of the party, and let a small quantity be taken every two hours."

Until The Desert Song *revolutionized Bedouin custom, Arab gentlemen in a hurry preferred to lunch in transit—and alone (above).*

Travellers on American railroads were not so faint-hearted, however. There, the trains were graced with elaborate kitchens kitted out with all manner of appliances. Hot and cold meats, pyramids of oysters, pâtés, pies and soups were displayed on a counter in the bar next to the kitchen. This notion was quickly superseded by the separate restaurant car, ornate with carved mahogany, plush and marble-topped dining-tables.

Victorians may have fussed about their constitutions but they were not timid about travel. The Grand Tour, which rounded off the education of many an eighteenth-century English gentleman, was replaced in the nineteenth-century by a travel explosion largely created by Thomas Cook, pioneer of the package tour. But there were other Victorian travellers who scorned this and roamed far beyond the paths trodden by Mr Cook.

A particularly doughty traveller was Francis Galton, a cousin of Charles Darwin. His *Art of Travel*, published in 1872, contains many useful tips: to quench the thirst, he suggests either stripping off the clothes and spreading them out to make the most of a rain shower, or dipping into the contents of an animal's paunch. He is equally helpful to those intending to sleep under the stars. Bivouacking, rather than tenting, had Galton's vote. The latter he considered too close to civilization, and there was always the risk of marauders, who might creep up at night and spear the traveller through the canvas.

But on the whole, he got on well with the natives: "A frank, joking, but determined manner, joined with an air of showing more confidence in the good faith of the natives than you really feel, is best," he advised. "On arrival at an encampment, the natives commonly run away in fright. If you are hungry, go boldly into their huts, take just what you want, and leave fully adequate payment. It is absurd to be over-scrupulous in these cases."

Other pioneers met the challenge of the wild with more self-reliance. American settlers learned how to scoop trout out of a brook with a frying-pan and cooked their meals outdoors in cast-iron Dutch ovens buried in hot coals. Cowhands on the Western Plains cooked over an open fire and drove their cattle across the prairie accompanied by a chuck-wagon carrying bacon and beans, pots and pans and the cook who, if the ballads are to be believed, was famed more for his fists than his cuisine.

The haybox, used by nineteenth-century British farm workers to carry hot food to the fields, came back into favour during both World Wars, but the principle that food partially cooked would continue cooking in a well-insulated box had long been known.

The Polynesians cooked meat wrapped in banana leaves between heated stones in earth ovens, the Tahitians cooked fish wrapped in leaves in ashes, but barbecues as such have mistier origins. They were particularly fashionable in the southern states of America before the Civil War, when they figured at political gatherings; after the war the notion became popular in the North as well.

Caravan comes from a Persian word meaning a group of pilgrims or travellers The growth of sea routes ended the days of the great silk caravan route from China to the Mediterranean, but others remained in use until this century. Travelling at two or three miles an hour, for fourteen hours a day—or overnight if it was very hot—the long camel trains broke their journeys at caravanserais. Here were stables with rooms above, grouped around an open courtyard. Climbing out of the panniers in which they had travelled, passengers cooked a simple meal before retiring.

British gypsies at least have now shed their romantic trappings in favour of modern caravans, parked on a site. But many of their old cooking traditions linger on; pheasant or rabbit stew, for instance, cooked in an iron pot over an open fire and flavoured with wild garlic, thyme or juniper. Few, probably, still indulge in hedgehog baked in clay, but some of the older people still observe the old cooking taboos. A woman's skirt, for example, must never touch the pots or utensils.

Nineteenth-century wanderers expected a degree of comfort, however exotic their

Transporting the food was no problem in the Land of Cockaigne; *Peter Breughel's view of the medieval—earthly—Paradise (below).*

A pause for refreshment on a grouse moor in 1896. The headgear added considerably to the birds' enjoyment of the day (below).

surroundings. Those contemplating a shooting party in the forest of British Guiana were advised by an old Equatorial hand to include among their essentials tins of pressed food, bags of flour, jars of salt, butter, bottles of brandy and Holland gin with "its usual accompaniment of Angostura bitters with swizzle sticks".

Outdoor catering was, and is, an integral part of a day at the races. At the turn of the eighteenth century, fashionable Ascot picnics often greatly delayed the racing timetable and were the cause of innumerable accidents to racegoers. Coaches rolled out of London in the morning piled high with hampers of venison, fish and confectionery, later to be washed down with oceans of champagne or hock and seltzer.

Representatives of the Raj carried the decencies of black tie and silver forks to rain forest and coral strand. Lion, gnu and wildebeeste died inconsolate if they fell to a hand unsteadied by an impeccable martini.

Altogether, outdoor eating isn't what it used to be. In 1861, Mrs Beeton suggested the following picnic fare for "a party of 40 persons: A joint of cold roast beef, a joint of cold boiled beef, 2 ribs of lamb, 2 shoulders of lamb, 4 roast fowls, 2 roast ducks, 1 ham, 1 tongue, 2 veal-and-ham pies, 2 pigeon pies, 6 medium-sized lobsters, 1 piece of collared calf's head, 18 lettuces, 6 baskets of salad, 6 cucumbers."

A far cry from primitive man thrusting a few berries into his mouth, or indeed the modern astronaut dining off a pellet or two. The transport is always improving, but how about the food?

Let's drink to Yesterday—Henri Cartier-Bresson, whose brilliant camera was so shortly to be employed in recording the horrors of war, captured this evocative glimpse of a peaceful French family picnic on the Marne.

The discomfiture of Stout Parties and the English penchant for taking their pleasures sadly were favourite themes with Mr Punch (above).

Unchangeable and unchanging—top hats, champagne and Rolls-Royces—one meets all one's friends at Ascot (right).

Floating kitchens

It may be comforting to know that a simple portable stove has been tested and not found wanting half-way up Annapurna, or that a particular pack of dried stew apparently seemed most delicious in the Gobi, but most travellers who include their kitchens in their luggage are chiefly concerned with the illusion of home comfort. The dedicated mountaineer has his eyes on the summit; the weekend camper's reluctant helpmate on storage space for her fourth-best china. Similarly, while the round-the-world yachtsman—or woman—concentrates on what he or she can do without, the chief cook on a family voyage is more likely to be concerned with what she can get into the craft. Happily, nowadays, there are few items of kitchen equipment that won't travel.

Galleys

Many small boats are fitted with a standard, built-in galley and it is not possible to do more than make certain adaptations to it. But buyers of new boats in basic hull form have a chance not only to choose galley fittings but also to influence design. Whatever the size or type of boat certain principles hold true.

The sequence of preparing, cooking and finally serving food is the same as on land, the difference being that on water it may have to be accomplished in the teeth of a nor'-easter, and that while in motion one at least of the crew is bound to remain at the helm. For this reason, many sea-going cooks recommend siting the galley close to the cockpit so that a slopping mug of soup is easily handed to the person at the tiller, and storm warnings easily handed back. This location also enables the breeze to dispel cooking odours and cool the cook, a useful advantage so long as it doesn't also snatch at the burner flame.

When rough seas or cold weather demand the battening down of the cabin hatch and port-holes, other ventilation is vital. On larger boats an extractor hood leading to a vent is often fitted over the stove; on smaller craft a fan directly above the stove can substitute. But on all boats there should be at least one vent by the galley, cowled to exclude the elements.

The layout of galley equipment is based on safety and convenience. On large craft it is better arranged in a compact "U" or "L" shape than stretching out along one side of the boat so overtaxing the cook's legs.

Lighting is sometimes a problem on small boats: if excessively bright it may disturb the sleep of an exhausted crew who have just come off watch, and if too dim it may lead to physical or culinary accidents. Concealed lighting fitted under the lockers solves this problem and the lamps are less vulnerable to damage.

Non-slip flooring such as cork matting is a refinement for more sophisticated craft; non-slip shoes being considered sufficient on smaller boats. Attachments for webbing belts or safety harnesses for the cook are standard on ocean racers and even those who don't contemplate high-adventure may appreciate a bulkhead grab rail.

Galleys on canal boats and river cruisers often incorporate static stoves. But for any vessel venturing into salt water, gimballed stoves are the only answer. Oven doors should drop down rather than open sidewards and cook- and table-tops should be surrounded by fiddles (guard rails) to prevent pans and plates sliding off. Some stoves have additional guards around the burners themselves.

Of the cooking fuels available, bottled gas is probably the most versatile; paraffin burners give excellent heat, but tend to smell; and electric rings make a heavy demand on your batteries. Sir Francis Chichester, on his round-the-world voyage, used a paraffin stove equipped with two silent burners and a self-cleaning device, but less proficient sailors find the familiarity of the gas flame comforting. Bottled-gas cookers for nautical use come in all sizes from a noble two-burner plus oven and grill down to a humble portable on which to boil an egg or a kettle. For safety reasons, fuel tanks should be stored outside the galley itself, though as close to the cooker as is feasible to lessen the risk of pipe leaks.

Space for food preparation can be doubled with clever sliding or folding work-surfaces over the sink, for example. Work-

Setting the stove next to the cockpit hatch helps cooking smells depart and the cook-top guard rail stops pans doing likewise (left).

Motor cruisers moving in smooth waters can ship sophisticated galley equipment (above)—but leave room for the fire extinguisher too.

tops should be washable and fitted with fiddles. The corners should be rounded; these are less painful to knock against.

Storage lockers must be accessible and be fitted with stout catches to prevent their contents showering into the cabin each time the boat meets a large wave. Doors should have hooks and eyes rather than magnetic latches and drawers be of the lift-and-pull variety. Fiddles again make sense for shelves. Floor lockers that open from the top can be divided into vertical compartments (ideal for beer cans) or fitted with trays or wire baskets. This type of locker often has a padded top and doubles as a seat.

Electric refrigerators are usually confined to craft whose batteries and chargers are capable of coping with such luxuries as well as providing the power for more essential tasks. Gas refrigerators depend on a flame staying alight in all conditions. But if you do install a refrigerator, make sure it is heavily insulated and opens from the top. Top-opening models retain the cold better and the same sudden lurch that sends the contents of an ill-secured locker spilling out can have a similarly disastrous effect on a front-opening refrigerator.

The alternative to a refrigerator is an ice-box, either built in or portable. This is, of course, dependent on shore facilities to refreeze ice-packs or to supply ice, not always available on a long haul. Farther down the scale there is a simple box-like cooler made of porous cement, which depends on water evaporation to lower the inside temperature.

Garbage pails should be of the pedal variety and be fitted with carrying handles. Check, too, that the lids fit tightly enough to contain odours and prevent spillage.

Include a fire extinguisher in the list of essentials and make sure it is ready to hand for emergencies. Finally, if the weather looks rough don't scorn to cook in oilskins: better a fevered brow than a burnt arm.

This trim houseboat (above and below) boasts plenty of home comforts as well as the grandeur of a fine wooden floor. The spotlight above the galley adds intimacy to evening cooking.

The floating homes of Hong Kong's boat people in Aberdeen harbour create a colourful virtue out of necessity (below). Long custom makes maximum use of a very limited space.

Caravans and camping

Caravans—or trailers in the United States—are either mobile towed homes or all-in-one motor caravans. The latter range from roomy, purpose-built edifices to small converted vans. Variations on the theme include trailer homes, canvas annexes and the demountable—an independent caravan body behind a pick-up or van cab. This last notion, new in Britain, is a familiar sight on US highways.

The standard caravan kitchen, if there is such a thing, usually includes a sink, oven, grill, double-ring cook-top, refrigerator or ice-box, storage cupboards and a table and seats. Luxury vehicles (generally more comfortable on European autoroutes and American highways than in British lanes) possess air-conditioning, hot and cold piped water, extractor fans and so on. Minimal equipment in a converted light van may be no more than a table and cook-top, and the cooking has to be performed seated, kneeling or even standing out of doors. There is no point in aiming at gracious living in this kind of setting, but much can be done to brighten up the production-line blandness of larger caravan kitchens, and those planning their own conversions can at least make sure they don't aim for impossible heights.

Colour is most important, but attempts to simulate a house interior with wood veneers and a jolly splash of chintz often seem incongruous. Too much brilliance eventually palls, too little shows up the lack of space only too clearly. One way of relieving the claustrophobic house-in-a-hutch appearance is to introduce a different colour into the kitchen area.

Curtains are probably best kept uniform throughout—and not in a hurtful print that clashes with the (hopefully) wonderful countryside outside the window. Flat surfaces, however, cry out for some imaginative handling. Painting the ceiling an unusual shade or making work-tops, cupboard and drawer fronts a bold colour are all feasible, but the easiest of all to juggle with is the floor. Carpets aren't particularly practical in caravans, but they are more attractive and kinder to the feet than vinyl and a doormat. A compromise—the caravanner's burden— would be to carpet the sleeping area and introduce a different texture and colour into the kitchen area with a vinyl floor.

Another factor that dominates caravan living is the problem of keeping them clean. Housework doesn't automatically become minimal in cramped conditions, indeed it is often exacerbated. Dirty table-tops or work-surfaces and greasy cookers will swiftly convert a gleaming home-on-wheels into a slum.

A combined sink-and-cooker unit in stainless steel stands up well to constant use and isn't too hard to care for. (This is an improvement on the plastic sinks popular a few years ago that often became singed by pots overhanging the edge of the cooker.) Anyone relying on a small portable single- or double-burner stove should again go for stainless steel, or the easiest to clean of all—the type with a vitreous enamel base.

Extra work-tops can fold or slide out of the way when not in use, but in home conversions try to eliminate chasms between units as these would act as a harbour for dropped food or dirt. Corners that would be hard to clean and protruding edges should be rounded off.

In motor caravans where headroom is limited, sinks and cookers may have to be installed at a low level. Tables, which should have a heat-resistant surface, often turn into bed supports at night.

Storage is limited, particularly in towed caravans, where too much weight high up can overbalance them. Cupboard catches need to be efficient and an arrangement of moulded compartments rather than rigid shelving inside cuts down on breakage and travel rattle.

Battery-operated fluorescent lighting has now largely replaced bottled gas lights in motor caravans. Fluorescent lighting is bright so should be sited in a way that will illuminate the stove without dazzling the cook. But on the whole, motor caravanners are better off with gas-operated equipment—particularly in wet weather—unless they are convinced beyond all doubt that their wiring is perfectly sound. Other caravanners may install electrical equipment if they plan to use their vehicles at sites with plug-in mains, or if their caravan is sufficiently luxurious to possess its own generator, but without these facilities usage is very curtailed. An electrically operated 12-volt absorption-type refrigerator, for example, will only run for half an hour or so when the vehicle's engine is off.

The better insulated the vehicle the less likelihood there is of condensation. However, adequate ventilation is very important, especially at night when the oxygen has been consumed by the stove and the sleeping family.

A fire extinguisher should also be included in the list of equipment, and any curtains near cookers trimmed to fall far short of danger. Fitting wire gauze across rooflights and vents at night is a good idea when heading into mosquito country.

A fisherman is a fine camping accessory, but, when fish are shy, standby stores cooked on the single-burner stove (above) save the day.

A combined sink, stove and storage unit are attractive as well as practical in the limited confines of a caravan (above).

Camping kitchens

The most comprehensive kitchen for campers is the roof-rack type that wraps an acrylic sink with tap, a shelf and storage locker, a laminated work-top, a stainless-steel cooker and grill, a cutlery drawer and six large containers into one streamlined package. These containers can be used to carry the water supply or for storing food or other items during the journey, then double as seats at the destination. Billed as the world's first roof-rack unit able to provide running water, there is still room to pack a table and five-berth tent inside its folds.

Apart from this sort of device, however, campers have little to do with kitchens; they generally prefer equipment more in tune with the great outdoors.

Camping equipment

The cooker is the make or break element in camp catering and the choice is wide. It is claimed that it was the inviolable British passion for toast at breakfast that first spurred manufacturers to add a grill to some of their stoves. Since the grill can be used for more exciting foods than bread its inclusion is to be welcomed.

Simple one-burner stoves are really only for hikers or solitary campers content with the barest essentials, though of course they may also appeal to larger parties as an auxiliary cooker. The two-burner is the most usual choice in Europe, but in North America three-burners are also sold.

Stoves run on bottled gas outsell other models for reasons of economy, safety and ease of maintenance. Methylated spirit can be expensive, paraffin needs to be preheated and can be difficult to obtain and petrol is dangerous. A large container of gas lasts a two-burner cooker in average use for about three to four weeks.

Automatic ignition now gives press-button action, and design features such as better-shaped grids to secure all manner of pans are improving performance. The most important criteria, though, are still how easy the stove is to clean and transport, how effective its simmer controls are and how it will stand up to winter storage.

Lids protect the burners while travelling, and act as windshields or splashbacks when opened up. On some models they turn the stove into a creditable if garish copy of a briefcase. Enamelled or stainless-steel stoves are both easy to clean and keep in good condition when out of use.

High-pressure stoves fit directly on to gas canisters or the larger containers; low-pressure stoves are connected to the canister with a hose and are fitted with regulators. Low-pressure models have the edge for cooking because the flame is more constant, especially in variable weather conditions.

But for both high- and low-pressure appliances it is vital that the safety rules should be followed. Always fit new containers in the open air or somewhere very well ventilated, away from any form of fire or flame. Never unscrew a container while any gas remains inside; never apply lubricants to any part of an appliance.

Check hoses and sealing washers frequently for leaks; never leave a lit stove unattended or allow it to be looked after by children.

More rugged campers may by this time be wondering nostalgically what has happened to the old-fashioned camp fire reeking of woodsmoke. True, the camp fire avoids the expense and fuss of manufactured appliances, but opportunities to practise this most delightful form of open-air cooking are now severely curtailed by law, at least in Europe.

Perhaps of greater moment to the average camper is the weight problem. Hikers and cyclists must obviously keep their equipment to a minimum, but car-borne campers can achieve a certain degree of luxury. Portable kitchen units in the form of lightweight, shelved stands, for example, are extremely practical. Made of stainless steel or aluminium with their own windshields, these units provide shelves and warming racks—sometimes even enclosed cupboards. This is the best means of raising the stove to a more convenient and safer height than ground level. Here, too, is storage space. Specially designed stakes can be purchased to secure the unit legs firmly into the ground, however uneven it may be.

Tables and chairs may not accord with the gypsy image, but they do deter the local insect population and prevent a certain stiffness in the joints. Campers' stools that pack flat into a light folding table are easily transported; some camp tables even include zipped storage space underneath.

Even a portable refrigerator, cumbersome on tour, makes sense for people spending a holiday in one place as well as for those who demand ice in their drinks wherever they may be. Similarly, portable ice-boxes are ideal for short trips but useless when the proposed expedition takes the camper far from anywhere he can refreeze his ice-packs. However, for those who do travel with an ice-box, remember to place the packs at the top or in the middle rather than the bottom of the box, so that the cold can work down. And if buying a refrigerator go for a model that works either off mains electricity, a car battery or bottled gas. A one-cubic-foot-capacity refrigerator will run for about twelve days on a single large gas canister. But don't forget you'll need a water carrier of heavy-duty polythene that collapses flat as well.

Cooking pans and tableware have come a long way since the days of billycans and plastic plates. Nests of non-stick saucepans whose lids double as poachers and whose handles remove to turn them into serving dishes have now been developed to a point where their non-stick qualities are said to be proof even against metal cutlery.

Melamine tableware, manufactured in many bright colours, is stain-resistant and virtually indestructible. Transparent plastic tankards or beakers made of methacrylate are a quite convincing, shatterproof substitute for glass.

These are the campers' essentials. But there are in addition many extras available, ranging from orange globe lights and collapsible toasters to plastic egg boxes, all designed to bring solace to those who prefer the outdoors tempered by home comforts.

Picnic equipment

The ideal picnic combines the best of two worlds: a lazy outdoor meal in idyllic surroundings with the prospect of a return to civilization in the not-too-distant future. The average picnic usually provides a fleeting glimpse of the ideal, but, such are the vagaries of climate and other natural hazards, it is sometimes only the amiability of the guests that rescues the occasion from disaster. But providing that the guests are indeed amiable, the weather perfect and the picnic site chosen with care, what else can contribute to success?

Attractive food, for one thing. A packet of dull sandwiches washed down with a mug of warm white wine does not add up to the stylish repast that first set the imagination on fire. Picnic hampers may contain a range of prettily matched equipment, but they too often fail to provide enough room for food. A few extra carriers are necessary. The range of rigid air-tight containers is so wide there's little excuse nowadays for squashed provisions. But the most successful containers are the wide-mouthed vacuum jars and insulated bags. Using these, chilled or hot food will guarantee picnic bliss to a degree undreamed of by the sandwich-maker.

The same insulated bag keeps wine chilled far better than any flowing stream without risking broken bottles. Other exotic contraptions for transporting drink are not always so efficient.

Salad ingredients travel better separately, but require a bowl to toss them in. There are picnic sets available that include a salad bowl with two sizes of melamine plates, a flask, four beakers and plastic-handled stainless-steel cutlery. Whether to go for this sort of thing or stick to earthenware crockery is a matter of personal taste. Certainly, such items as plastic cutlery which couldn't cut a slice of meat without snapping are much better left at home. But perhaps the most heinous crime perpetrated in the name of picnics was the introduction of a contrivance designed like an aircraft snack holder to clip on to the car seat.

Camp catering on a large scale becomes less of a bunfight when a table and chairs are included in equipment (right).

Smokers

Home-smoked foods are growing in popularity and the smaller smokers can easily be carried on a picnic or taken along on a fishing holiday. Some barbecues, too, double as smokers with the addition of a smoking tray and hood. Wood chips or sawdust of non-resinous woods—oak is particularly delightful—are the best fuel for these and the small portable smokers.

Large smokers are available for those whose catch runs to forty trout.

Patio grills

One of the most sophsticated forms of mobile equipment is the infra-red grill that works off bottled gas. Based on an idea of a French aircraft designer, it is constructed of die-cast aluminium with Teflon-coated cooking surfaces. These cookers recycle their own heat and perform all manner of tasks. Food may be grilled or broiled, spit roasted or gratinéed and it is even possible, with the hood closed, to bake a cake. There are two independently controlled burners and the whole thing folds up like an attaché case for travelling, though it is probably better left semi-permanently in the patio.

A movable feast

Barbecues

The Great Outdoors: some food, some wine and a fireside seat! Even the simplest barbecue captures the magic (above).

The ancient art of cooking over hot charcoal has been almost smothered by the sophisticated battery of barbecues now available. Nowadays, some barbecues have more refinements than the indoor kitchen stove. In the rush to incorporate the latest mechanical knick-knacks the prime virtues of barbecuing—simplicity plus the magnificent aroma and taste of charcoal-grilled meat—have been brushed aside. American electrically and gas-operated models which, like saunas, use lava rock as a heating medium are light-years away from glowing campfire embers.

Before buying a barbecue, decide exactly what you want from it. Will it be used for simple family meals or more sophisticated entertaining? Where are you going to use it? Would you prefer a compact portable model or something custom-built in the garden or patio?

The smallest, cheapest barbecue is the throwaway type, an inexpensive, self-contained pack of heavy foil tray, fuel and wire grid. All that is needed to start it is a match. This will cook two large steaks or three chops or several sausages. It burns for two hours, so it may be possible to use it again before it is thrown away.

At the other end of the scale there is the combined barbecue and table, a fairly formidable item of garden furniture. There can be problems with these, however: the tiled table around the barbecue box is pretty and useful, but a certain amount of gymnastics is required to reach the food cooking in the centre. A barbecue this size is also a nuisance to store and transport. If left out during the winter, even under a tarpaulin, frost may crack the tiles.

In between these two extremes barbecues come in myriad guises and shapes. The popular Japanese-style hibachi or cast-iron fire boxes are hard-wearing and available in several sizes, as are other excellent barbecues in cast aluminium, sheet metal or a combination of both.

Portable barbecues

Some light, compact barbecues on the market are specifically designed for easy transport in the car. Others, which either stand on their own feet or detach to become a table-top model, are useful for those who have more homes than gardens. Flat, rectangular barbecues pack more easily into the back of the car than dish-shaped ones, but the human porter bent on a picnic is most likely to be pleased by the version that folds into its own light case.

Table-top barbecues

These are ideal for town-dwellers with only a tiny patio or balcony. They can be placed on a stone seat, on a small table, on the ground, or even on a wide window sill. They may also be considered by those who have no outside facilities at all, since they can be used indoors, in the hearth or in the kitchen. Barbecuing needn't only be a summer pastime. The cook who has visions of being forced outdoors on a chilly evening to warm his hands over the glowing coals while the rest of the family wait snugly inside to be fed, might well consider a table-top model a satisfactory investment. Some of these have roasting spits, others are more basic.

Barbecuing on the terrace takes the travel out of serving a meal outdoors. The barbecue can be a portable model (above) or a permanent fixture, an essential part of the terrace design (below), positioned where the smoke won't drive everyone back into the house.

Standing barbecues

Bulbous-shaped like the driers in a hairdresser's, resting on tripods or a trolley, free-standing barbecues start to look like some weird garden sculptures. Racks for implements and other accessories may be fitted and many now have motors for turning the spit. If not, it is possible to buy separate motors. As well as a choice of grid heights for grilling, some models offer a choice of spit-roasting positions. Barbecues that tilt so that the spit turns in front of, rather than over, the fire box cut out the problem of fat flaring into the burning coals. Fit a pan to catch the fat and juices for basting. On other barbecues the fire box is constructed so that both grilling and spit-roasting can be carried out at the same time.

Party grills

These wagons are more like mini-restaurants than barbecues. Chopping boards, preparation surfaces, racks for warming plates, compartments to keep food hot, wine racks and a glittering range of tools are arrayed to delight the heart of the charcoal fanatic. Certainly such a contraption will intrigue your guests; it is, however, a mite extravagant for just sizzling up a few sausages. But do not

One way of keeping guests and smoke apart is to build a chimney over the grill (above). A smaller barbecue can be used here too.

The barbecue you build yourself may be a stylish work of art or a rough-and-ready composition echoing its surroundings (above).

The grandest barbecues are kitchens in themselves, with plenty of room (above) to display the food, the utensils . . . the wok.

The washing up won't go away, but it needn't be carried far (below).

despair; there are a number of models with two or more grills that work independently, so that only one need be employed when the company is reduced.

Made-to-measure barbecues
Really dedicated barbecue addicts often prefer a permanent grill, either built on to the terrace or recessed into an existing garden or patio wall. If do-it-yourself plans baffle your own constructive talents, get a builder to run it up for you . . . but do remember that the idea is that you should be eating in the midst of nature's joys rather than a massive complex of cooking gear. In other words, let the barbecue complement your garden rather than become its commanding feature.

Lighting-up time
Charcoal is ideal for barbecuing because it is slow burning and generates intense heat. Loose lump charcoal gives off more smoke than briquettes (thereby imparting more of a charcoal tang to food and cook) and is easier to light. However, briquettes burn longer. Or you can make your own charcoal by burning woods such as ash, oak and birch. If the barbecue doubles as a smoker as some now do, oak is very pleasant.

Remember to site your barbecue in accordance with the prevailing wind so that those to be fed aren't going to be smoked themselves. When the fire is well established (i.e. the charcoal is glowing by night or grey in daylight—after about 30-45 minutes), the damper control should be closed.

If you line the barbecue fire box with foil, shiny side up, it will reflect more heat and make the clearing-up operation simpler. It's a good idea, too, to keep a few old coals in the foil lining for use in damping down a too-fierce barbecue next time round. Using a special barbecuing base-fuel underneath the charcoal is another refinement; it isn't really necessary, but it does allow more air to circulate, so promoting a better fire. Light the charcoal with fire lighters, wood shavings, special barbecue lighting paste, briquettes or methylated spirit. Never use petrol, paraffin, oil or any form of grease, which are both dangerous and damaging to the flavour of the food. Put out the fire by covering it with the extinguishing tray, if there is one, or damping it with old charcoal, sand or a very fine water spray. The coals can then be tipped into a bucket of water and dried for reuse; water must never be poured on to the coals though, for it will crack the barbecue.

Purists demand nothing more of food cooked outdoors than that it should have a delightful flavour of wood smoke. But the more sophisticated barbecuing equipment becomes, the more aficionados develop their own ethos. There is a great debate over whether the food should be basted beforehand with oil or whether this causes burning. Common sense soon settles the matter: food that is to be spit-roasted, with the exception of kebabs, usually requires longer cooking. Therefore, basting beforehand is advisable to help seal in the juices and prevent dryness. Food for grilling, such as steaks, chops, sausages, fish, and small portions of poultry, will not require basting if it contains a certain amount of fat and is cooked quickly. Even purists, however, appreciate a mouthful of tender meat between the cinders, so prebaste anything that looks very dry. Marinading in spices, herbs and oil tenderizes cheaper cuts and gives additional flavour; so does adding herbs or aromatic woods such as bay, juniper, hickory and fruitwoods to the fire while cooking is in progress. Meat grilled over grapevine prunings produces a most memorable meal. If you wish to baste a spit-roast again during cooking, brush rather than pour on the oil.

Delicate foods like fish can be barbecued in foil with some butter and herbs. But if you plan to grill them over the open fire, a double-sided wire fish holder prevents fall-out when turning them over. These holders come in various sizes and shapes, but for sturdier meats they seem much less important than a pair of tongs for manipulating each individual piece.

Potatoes and sweetcorn cook well in foil, and a crisp salad is always the perfect accompaniment to barbecue food. If you wish to cook other vegetables over the fire as well use long-handled saucepans; long-handled salt and pepper shakers are also advisable for painless seasoning. Oven gloves or barbecue mitts and a protective apron complete the ensemble.

But if all this seems like too much hard work for what originally set out to be a cook's soft option, remember you can build a perfectly satisfactory barbecue yourself with just a few bricks and a metal grill. Arrange the bricks into four walls, leaving gaps near the bottom for the wind to whistle through and encourage the fire. Then lay some chicken wire or a metal grid across the walls above the top of the fire and top up with another course of bricks to act as a windshield. It couldn't be simpler.

CEREALS
ATORA

Stocking up

Food can never be filed away in a drawer and forgotten. Coming home after shopping, every item from mackerel to mustard must be distributed to various depots around the kitchen, each designed to keep different foods in peak condition.

Though ancient preservation methods such as salting, drying or smoking foods have never entirely been abandoned—and in a new wave of enthusiasm even modern housewives are practising these arts to help fill their store cupboards—it is the refrigerator and freezer that today do most of the work in making perishable items last longer.

However, they don't solve every problem. All food has a maximum storage life and some food simply can't be frozen. So the argument for including the old-fashioned larder or pantry in the up-to-date kitchen is just as valid as it was a hundred years ago.

Stocking up

From brine cask to freezer bag

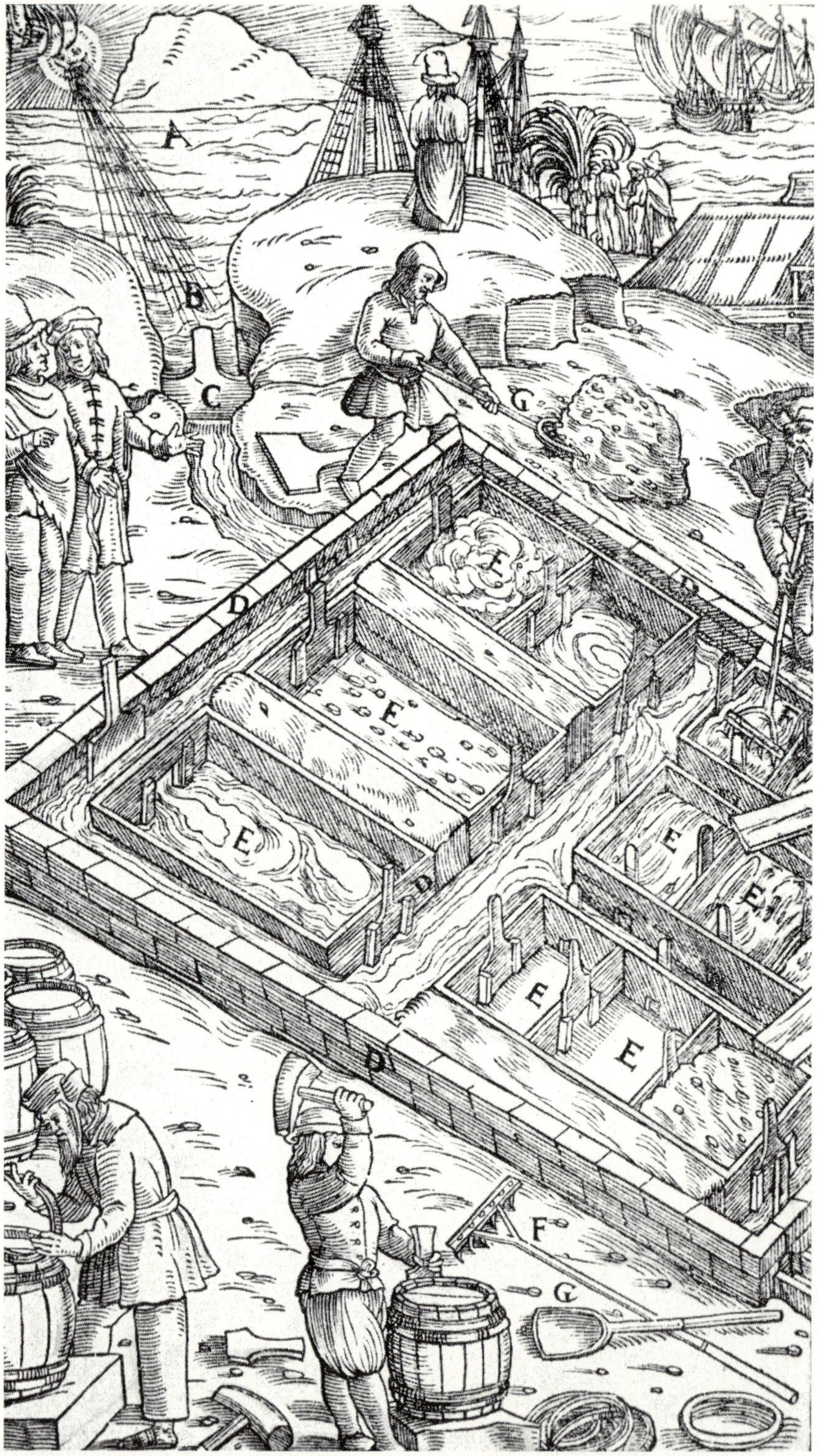

Medieval households placed salt, sugar and seasonings in ship-shaped nefs on the table in front of the lord of the manor. A French model of 1482 hides the salt in the stern (left).

Sea water diverted from a nearby sluice was transformed into salt by evaporation in a 16th-century salt garden (above). The salt was then put into casks to be sold.

If ice hadn't occurred naturally in the world, how soon would man have invented it? Its usefulness has long been known: an ice-house in China dates back to the eighth century BC. Today ice is still our major aid in preserving food, but it wasn't until the eighteenth century that it was produced artificially.

Other early methods of preservation were sometimes eccentric. The cookery book of a Roman writer, Apicius, suggested that birds will not spoil so quickly if drawn and then boiled in their feathers. And fresh grapes, he wrote, should be stored in rainwater reduced by two-thirds in a receptacle treated with pitch and sealed with gypsum, and kept out of the sun. More commonly, the Greeks and Romans, as well as later generations, supplemented their diet with dried, smoked or salted foods when fresh materials were scarce.

The most precious items to be carefully stored in medieval times were the luxury spices. Used in quantities we would now regard as prodigious, they flavoured bland gruels or indifferent wine and disguised the saltiness or even putridity of meat and fish. They were locked away in what was known as the wardrobe, where dried fruits, sugar and almonds were also stored. The locks deterred both thieves and poisoners. Sugar came in fourteen-pound cones, scented with violet, rose or cinnamon. Salt was kept dry near the fire in wooden boxes or drawers. At meal times salt, sugar and seasonings were placed in a nef, a ship-shaped vessel, in front of the lord of the manor. Tables for lesser members of the household were placed at right angles to the lord's own and were thus "below the salt".

A rich medieval baron would usually carry his knife with him. Other eating utensils were kept in chests. Spoon racks and wall cupboards for cutlery appeared later. Forks weren't generally used in Britain until the seventeenth century.

One of the earliest food-storage cupboards was the livery, in common use in Elizabethan times. Mounted on legs or hung on the wall, servants carried the "livery"—bread, wine or beer—up to the sleeping-rooms at night. Ventilation holes in the wood kept the snack fresh.

The term "dresser" was derived from the dresser board used for preparing food. When these were joined to cupboards the dresser resulted. The first fifteenth-century dressers, also known as court cupboards, were used for displaying drinking cups, and the number of shelves depended on rank.

The introduction of china rather than pewter plates in the seventeenth century boosted the popularity of dressers. They gradually became more elaborate. Despite regional variations—the traditional Welsh dresser, for example, had drawers rather than a lower cupboard— the major change of doors, fitted over the upper shelves, didn't occur until the nineteenth century.

Other practical furniture for storage included the ingenious seventeenth-century table-chair. This was a legged box surmounted by a work-top. When the top was swung back the box became the chair, the top the chair-back.

Most households, however, still relied on the traditional barrels, tubs and earthenware crocks for storing food. A fashionable seventeenth-century London house might devote a special room with shelves and drawers to storage, but in the country a honeycomb of cellars, pantries, larders, smoke-houses, cheese-rooms, and butteries eased congestion.

Dressers followed various styles. The traditional Welsh dresser (below) has lower drawers instead of cupboards.

Noble families kept drinking cups in court cupboards like this Elizabethan one at Melford Hall, Suffolk (below).

Table-chairs were a popular and highly functional 17th-century innovation. The one shown below is at Cotehele House, Cornwall.

From brine cask to freezer bag

The Industrial Revolution in Britain created huge urban sprawls that stretched the old methods of food distribution to their utmost. There were few shops and only the most primitive means of storing food; in general, merchants and artisans alike bought fresh food daily from street vendors.

In the country, improved animal husbandry meant that households depended less on salted or dried meat. The great houses in the eighteenth and nineteenth centuries stored fresh meat in ice-houses built in the grounds. These deep, domed, brick structures were entered along a tunnel via a series of thick wooden doors. The ice, hacked from local ponds or transported by cart from chillier regions, was stacked on shelves around the walls of the underground chamber.

Immigrants to the New World also stored food in ice hacked from rivers: they protected the ice in sawdust and placed it in wooden cages, high off the ground, in which the meat was preserved. Ice later became one of the first American exports, but initially most immigrants had still to hang, salt or smoke much of their meat. Barrels of beef or pork, cider and apples, and bins of root vegetables were kept in the cellars, and dried fruit hung from the rafters.

These traditional ways of preserving food were slow to die out. Until the beginning of this century the labyrinth of rooms used for food preparation and storage remained a feature of larger country households.

In fact, the latter part of the Victorian era was flush with inventions that were eventually to transform household habits, though housewives themselves were often slow to welcome them. The principle of canning was alighted on by a Frenchman, Nicolas Appert, in 1809, though the original containers were of glass. Twenty years later food in tin cans was in commercial production in America, and tinned meat was on display at London's Great Exhibition of 1851. It was cheap, but not an instant hit: perhaps because the world had to wait so long for the simple can opener to be invented. Shopkeepers, by means of an elaborate cutting mechanism, had to open the cans themselves in the customer's presence. Screw-top jars were not patented until 1858; before this housewives sealed their preserves with a bladder or a wax-dipped cloth.

Frozen meat first reached Britain in 1880—almost by chance. A consignment of chilled meat, dispatched from Australia in one of the newly invented refrigerator ships, froze en route. Very soon, frozen meat was being shipped to worldwide markets.

The twentieth century brought even more radical change. The distant ice-house and the cumbersome ice-box gave way to the compact refrigerator: after the First World War these gradually became less of a novelty. After the Second World War kitchen designers and manufacturers concentrated on convenience with built-in storage units and time-saving products. The frozen ready-cooked TV dinner and the microwave oven seemed poised to take over; but then a reaction set in. Once more, kitchen shelves are filling up with home-prepared pickles and bottled fruit, preserved in the traditional way. One hopes that their place alongside factory-packaged food will remain secure for a long time.

The 18th-century street vendor (above) walked twenty miles a day to bring morning-picked vegetables to the London housewife.

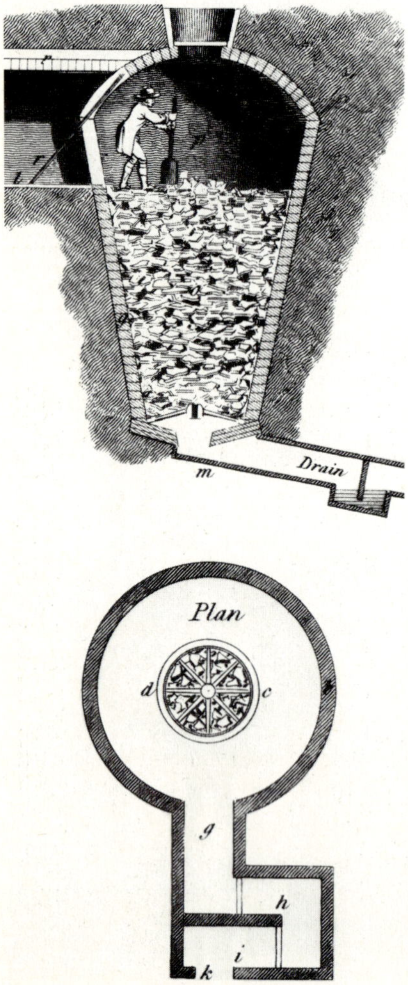

By the 18th century, the ice-house (left) had become a standard feature of the grander country estate. Ice, hacked from winter lakes, and stacked in a deep pit beneath the house, kept meat fresh all summer long. Below is the 200-year-old ice-house at Hatchlands, England.

Queen Victoria's Christmas dinner could strain even the vast resources of Windsor Castle's larder (below) to their utmost.

Horse-drawn ice-carts (above) carrying supplies for the home ice-chest were once a familiar sight in cities. Earlier, carts were drawn by oxen.

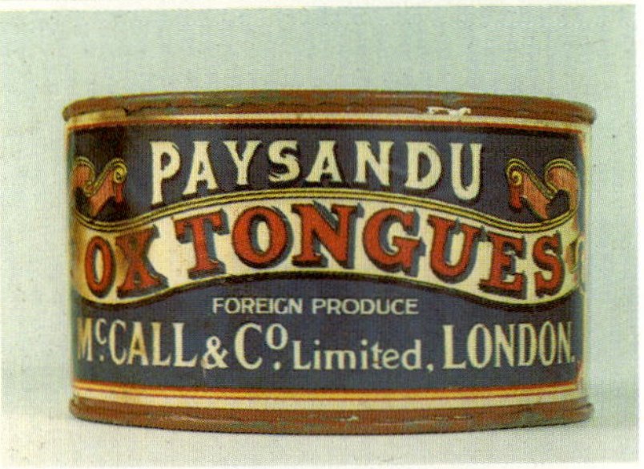

The invention of the tin can (above) provided 19th-century households with a whole new array of preserved foods. Unfortunately, the can antedated the can opener by some fifty years.

This early German zinc-lined refrigerator (below) was kept cool by daily doses of ice poured through a hatch in the central compartment. The tap provided iced water.

Chilled drinks for vicarage lawns and ice-cream for empire-builders were produced by alarming machines like this (above).

Chilling and freezing

Some early models of a refrigeration machine tempted housewives at the end of the nineteenth century, but they were such a rarity even in 1920 that many cookery books did not mention them. The process of deep-freezing foods was developed in the twenties, but a home deep-freeze only became widespread in England from the early 1960s.

Refrigerators

A refrigerator is designed to store perishable food at a steady temperature of 2 to 7°C (35° to 40°F). It inhibits the action of enzymes, but can't halt them entirely. The frozen-food compartment keeps pre-frozen food frozen, but that is all. In Britain there are standard star markings to define the storage life of frozen foods:

Star	Temperature	Storage Life
1 (*)	– 6°C (21°F)	1 week
2 (**)	–12°C (10°F)	1 month
3 (***)	–18°C (0°F)	3 months

A special marking (in effect a fourth star) indicates that the temperature in the compartment is sufficiently low to freeze unfrozen food.

To get the best from a refrigerator don't pack it too tightly—air must circulate—and only place in it food already cooled to room temperature. Warm foods cause condensation. Wrap those which tend to dry out, such as cheese or meat, in foil or polythene. Nowadays it is safe to cover and keep most open cans in the fridge; however, opened cans of fruit, fruit juices and evaporated milk should always be emptied into a container.

Soups and desserts to be chilled or mousses, which require setting, should be placed in the coldest area—nearest the ice-making apparatus. This leaves the lower shelves and salad bin free for green vegetables and fruit (always wrap onions, garlic, melon and fish and other foods with a strong aroma). A drip tray underneath thawing meat is essential.

Refrigerators should be defrosted about once a fortnight (in more venerable machines perhaps once a week) or when the ice is about $\frac{1}{4}$ in thick. No machine can operate efficiently under a thick blanket of "snow". When thawed, clean the interior with a cloth wrung in a solution of bicarbonate of soda (1 teaspoon in a pint of warm water); dry before switching on.

Freezers

Designed to maintain a temperature of –18°C (0°F), a freezer completely halts the action of enzymes or bacteria. But it is not magic. What comes out is only as good as what is put in. If the food is not fresh or of good quality to begin with, there's little point in freezing it. Fish, particularly, should come straight from the hook or out of the net. The faster the food is frozen, the better it will taste later on—if the process is prolonged, its cell structure may be damaged by large ice crystals forming.

One of the main attractions of a freezer is that foods can be bought more economically in bulk. However, unless the purchase of whole carcasses of meat is strictly controlled, there will be no room in the freezer for other foods. Each cubic foot takes between 40 and 48 kg (25 and 30 lb) of frozen produce. The freezer operates best when it is about two-thirds full. This allows room to freeze additional items. About 10 per cent of the freezer capacity can be frozen at any one time.

There is a wide range of wrapping materials on the market for every need. Waxed cartons, plastic containers, heavy-duty polythene bags and foil containers come in many sizes. Freezer burn or deterioration occur only if the wrapping is not completely water-proof and airtight. It is vital to remove as much air as possible from the package before freezing: for small items suck it out with a straw; place larger ones in a bowl of cold water to force the air out, then seal immediately, clamping loose carton lids with freezer tape. Joints of meat, poultry with protruding bones or individual stock or dog bones should be masked with foil to avoid piercing other packs. When re-using freezer wraps remember they should be thoroughly clean and smell-free.

Scientific tests show that blanching preserves colour and flavour, helps retain vitamin C and kills micro-organisms. However, even if unblanched frozen vegetables show no visible deterioration, they won't be quite the same. Mushrooms and potatoes are the exceptions: sauté mushrooms in butter, or freeze them raw; cook potatoes almost completely.

Fresh fruit can be frozen raw or in sugar or syrup. Lemons freeze well either whole or sliced. Bread, pastry, cakes, butter, double cream and cheese freeze successfully. Left-over slivers of cooked meat can be stored in gravy or in sandwiches—most sandwiches freeze well, except those with a filling of egg, banana, salad or tomato. Even stock and fresh herbs can be frozen in ice-cube trays. Ice-cream won't last forever—and leave out mayonnaise, hard-boiled eggs and jellies.

The diagram (right) suggests how to pack a refrigerator/freezer for maximum efficiency.

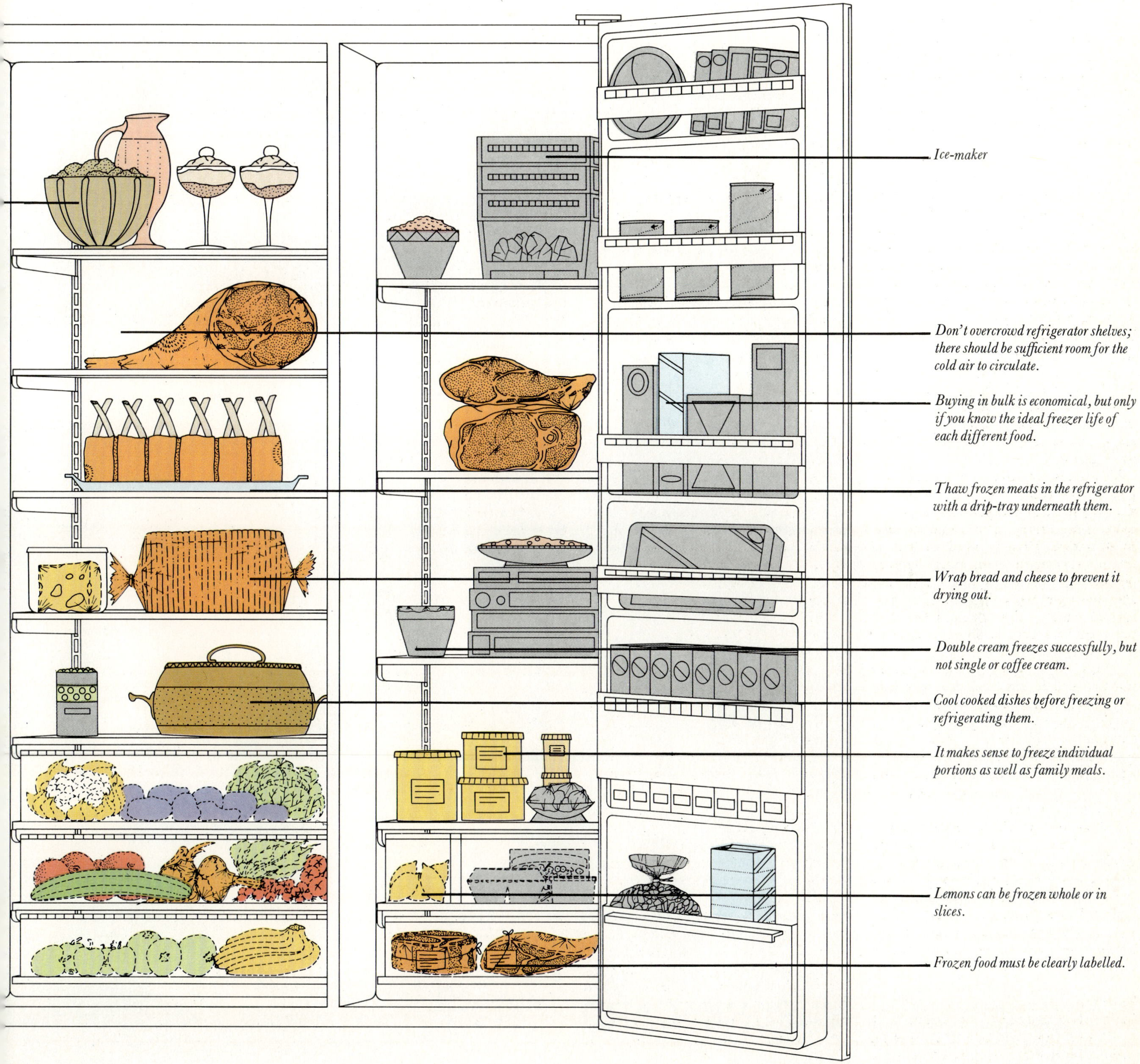
Ice-maker
Don't overcrowd refrigerator shelves; there should be sufficient room for the cold air to circulate.
Buying in bulk is economical, but only if you know the ideal freezer life of each different food.
Thaw frozen meats in the refrigerator with a drip-tray underneath them.
Wrap bread and cheese to prevent it drying out.
Double cream freezes successfully, but not single or coffee cream.
Cool cooked dishes before freezing or refrigerating them.
It makes sense to freeze individual portions as well as family meals.
Lemons can be frozen whole or in slices.
Frozen food must be clearly labelled.

Stocking up

Where to store what

The great heaps of artichokes, leeks and carrots that spill picturesquely on to the tiled kitchen floors in seventeenth-century Dutch and Flemish still-life paintings could have been placed there by housewives who knew their onions. Fresh vegetables need air circulating around them, and those stored in the kitchen rather than in the crisper section of the fridge must be at the lowest, coolest level in the room, stored in racks of wire mesh or in coarsely woven baskets. Potatoes need a cool, dark place because light encourages them to turn green and to sprout.

Eggs cook better and the shells will not crack if kept at room temperature. Place a rack holding the next half-dozen eggs near a work-top, and store the rest of them in the fridge.

Fats should be stored in a cool dark place and during use should always be kept out of sunlight. It is satisfactory to freeze fats, but they are best stored in a refrigerator and better still if used when absolutely fresh. If not kept in good storage conditions they will deteriorate.

To speed up meal preparation, ingredients such as flour, sugar, oil, vinegar, herbs, spices, tea and coffee should be stored so that they are readily accessible. Salt can be kept in a wide-mouthed jar close to the cooker for last-minute seasoning.

Whether to take dry goods from their packets to store in jars is a question of personal taste. Packets take up less space, but glass jars (which should be tightly stoppered) give a decorative touch to shelves and one can tell at a glance which ones need refilling. Storage tins, however attractive their design, must be checked to make sure they are truly airtight — the shelf life of many products depends on the exclusion of air. But even in airtight storage, flavours can fade. Don't expect dried herbs, for example, to last for years. Eventually they will lose both their kick and their colour. The pungency of ground spices is also prey to time. Whole spices keep best, but the entire contents of the spice rack should be renewed every year. Canned foods such as meat, fish, vegetables and soups can be stored for up to two years provided they are in a dry place. Flour keeps well for up to six months; after that the raising agent in the self-raising flour might not be so active.

Now that so much bread and cake comes with additives and coated wrappers to retain moisture, their storage requirements have changed. Big earthenware crocks with close-fitting lids were designed to prevent baker's loaves from drying out; but they only encourage mould in wrapped bread. Since it is hardly practical to unwrap a wrapped loaf, especially if it is sliced, storage should be provided for both types — well ventilated for mass-produced bread and moisture preserving for baker's loaves.

Unopened packets and bulk purchases, cans and jams should be kept fairly cool. If they are too warm, jams, whatever the fruit that went into their making, will turn thick and sugary. A dry, well-ventilated cupboard (insect-free and mouse-proof) is best. Beware of storing soaps and detergents in the same cupboard as foodstuffs as their smell is all-pervasive.

A larder with shelves of tile, slate or marble has become something of a luxury, but it is still ideal for storing cheese, cooked meat and desserts that don't need chilling, and for home-made chutneys and preserves that are in current use. Game such as venison is also best kept in the larder.

Store vegetables according to the painting (above) by 17th-century artist Frans Snyders. There's no need to have them rolling around the floor, but they should be kept in a dark, airy place.

Labels that are both decorative and descriptive (below). Glassware is arranged against the window as a translucent contrast to enamel and earthenware.

Gaudy packaging need not be shut away. Stored on open shelves (above) it is a colourful foil to the adjacent array of design-conscious storage jars.

Food always looks good behind glass. The airtight jars with ground-glass stoppers preserve the pungency of herbs and spices (top).

Eggs respond better to baking and whipping and are less likely to crack in boiling water if they are stored at room temperature (above).

Stocking up

Storage check list

Storage life for fresh meat and fish

Fresh meat	Freezer —18°C (0°F)	Refrigerator 2-7°C (35-45°F)
Joints: Beef	8 months	3-5 days
Lamb	6 months	3-5 days
Pork	6 months	3-5 days
Minced meat	3 months	1-2 days
Kidney, liver, etc.	3 months	1-2 days
Bacon	2-3 months	7-10 days
Sausages	2 months	1-2 days
Poultry	6-8 months	2-3 days
Game	6-8 months	2-3 days
Chops	3 months	3-5 days
Steaks	3 months	3-5 days
Stewing meat	3 months	3-5 days
Fresh fish		
Oily fish: mackerel, salmon, herring	2-3 months	1-2 days
White fish: plaice, sole, cod	6 months	1-2 days
Shellfish	1 month	1 day

Similar cuts of meat, such as chops, cutlets and steaks, can be packed together in the same bag, separated by double layers of heavy-duty polythene or foil dividers.

Cook lobsters and crabs before freezing and shell oysters, clams and scallops.

Fish off the fishmonger's slab may be several days old; only fish caught that day should be frozen.

Pet food may contain more harmful bacteria than meat intended for human consumption. Be wary of freezing or refrigerating it.

Recommended thawing times for frozen meat and fish

	In the refrigerator	At room temperature
Joints under 3 lb	3-4 hours per lb	1-2 hours per lb
Joints 3 lb and over	4-7 hours per lb	2-3 hours per lb
Thick cuts of meat	5-6 hours	2-4 hours
Poultry	2 hours per lb	1 hour per lb
Fish	8 hours per lb	4 hours per lb

Fish must be covered and slowly thawed in the refrigerator.

Thawing in the refrigerator is recommended when time allows.

In emergencies only, thaw by immersing in cool (not warm) water in a watertight wrapping.

Cook thawed foods as soon as possible.

Cooking from the frozen state

May be cooked frozen	Must be thawed first
All beef joints on the bone	All boneless joints
All lamb joints on the bone	All boiling joints
Pork joints weighing 4 lb or more	Pork joints on the bone under 4 lb
Chops, steaks, stewing meat	Poultry
Shrimps and prawns	Most fish

Boiling meat from the frozen state can result in weight loss and poor flavour.

Unthawed fish must be cooked at a lower temperature and for far longer than normal, which is likely to kill the delicate flavour.

Roasting times for frozen meat on the bone

At 180°C (350°F) or Gas Mark 4

Joints under 4 lb	
Beef	30 minutes per lb plus 30 minutes
Lamb	35 minutes per lb plus 35 minutes
Joints 4-6 lb	
Beef	35 minutes per lb plus 35 minutes
Lamb	40 minutes per lb plus 40 minutes
Pork	45 minutes per lb plus 45 minutes
Joints over 6 lb	As above or longer, needs testing

Bone is an excellent heat conductor, but roasting frozen meat takes longer. If using a meat thermometer to check that it is properly cooked do not let the thermometer point touch the bone.

Cold storage life of the basics

	Freezer —18°C (0°F)	Refrigerator 2-7°C (35-45°F)
Butter	4-6 months	1 month
Cheese	4-5 months	1 month
Cream cheese	2-3 months	1 week
Fruit and fruit juices	8-12 months	2-3 days
Vegetables	8-12 months	3-5 days
Bread, buns, rolls	6 months	—
Un-iced cakes	3-4 months	—
Baked pies	6 months	1 day
Unbaked pies	1-2 months	1 day
Cooked meat dishes	1-2 months	3-4 days
Pâté	2 months	2-3 days
Sauces	2 months	2-3 days
Mayonnaise	—	3 months
Egg whites or egg yolks	8-12 months	2-3 days
Cooked ham	3-4 months	7-10 days
Sandwiches	4-6 weeks	—
Steamed puddings	1 year	—
Fresh yeast	1 month	3 weeks

Cupboard storage life

Dried fruits	6 months	Icing sugar	1 year
Most canned fruits	1-2 years	Instant coffee	1 year
Canned prunes and rhubarb	9 months	Drinking chocolate, cocoa	1 year
Dried or skimmed milk	9-12 months	Canned fruit juices	1 year
Canned milk puddings	1 year	Packet soups	1 year
Jellies	9-12 months	Canned soups	2 years
Jams and marmalades	1-2 years	Dried peas, beans, lentils	6-12 months
Cake mixes	9 months	Canned vegetables	2 years
Pastry mixes	6 months	Rice, pasta	1 year
Biscuits	3-12 months	Canned pasta foods in sauce	2 years
Flour	6 months	Canned meat	Up to 5 years
Cornflour, custard powder	1 year	Canned meat meals	2 years
Sugar	Up to 5 years	Canned fish in oil	Up to 5 years
		Canned fish in sauce	1 year

A "bloom" on chocolate doesn't necessarily mean it is uneatable, it is merely the fat coming to the surface.

Salted butter will keep better than unsalted when not refrigerated.

Ceilings and walls both play roles in this imaginative use of a small storage area (right).

Stocking up

The complete larder

There is a strong case to be made for adding a larder to the kitchen. If space permits it is a most valuable ally. Housewives of old wouldn't have been without one. Now we have refrigerators and freezers, but their functions are not strictly comparable. Larders have virtues of their own.

Much food continues to mature and improve after it has been picked, killed or prepared, and a refrigerator is usually not the right place for it to do this. Also, some food has such a pungent aroma that it influences the flavour of its neighbours if kept in close proximity. There are many things, such as fruit and vegetables, that, except in the hottest weather, do not need to be kept in a refrigerator, but are equally not best kept in the warm atmosphere of the kitchen itself. This is where the traditional tiled larder is so useful.

Location

The ideal larder is an integral part of the kitchen. A long trudge to select supplies is likely to prove exasperating.

There is, however, a more important consideration: the larder should always, in the northern hemisphere, be attached to the north wall, the coolest wall of your house. This wall must be pierced for the coolest possible flow of fresh air to enter the larder. If your existing kitchen has no north wall and you need a larder, you may have to settle for some other situation, but never place it against a south-facing wall unless it is extremely well insulated. Achieving the correct atmospheric conditions inside the larder is comparatively easy in temperate countries like Britain. In countries where the climate reaches extremes, as it does in parts of the United States, air conditioning could be considered to maintain an even coolness. In the Middle East they build wind towers to feed down a draught to the storage-room, but a carefully placed extractor fan may do the trick by pulling a stream of air across the shelves. Even in hot countries or during a blazing summer in temperate countries the temperature tends to drop a little at night, so any storage-room lined with materials that keep cool is an advantage. Don't keep the fridge in the larder unless it has its own sealed duct to the outside, as it gives off quite a lot of heat.

The jam-packed larder (left), with a cold marble slab and a north-facing window, opens triptych-like on to the kitchen.

Adjustable shelves (above) accommodate long-term supplies of food and drink. Coarse mesh over open windows keeps intruders at bay.

Once a gloomy passageway, the invaluable larder (below) is built between the thick brick walls of a kitchen and a garage.

Construction

For those who are about to build a house or construct a kitchen from scratch, I have designed a larder that I suspect will never be built as it is shown, but whose general principles can be usefully incorporated in any adaptation that is appropriate to the particular circumstances you find in your own kitchen.

Walls must be well insulated so that the coolness is kept in and the warmth of the kitchen easily kept out. Brick or block, if the construction of the floor will stand it, is best. On the outside north wall airbricks at the top and bottom, with fine gauze covers to keep out all forms of insect life, provide the necessary airflow. The door, too, must be well insulated and close fitting.

The interior of the larder should ideally be lined with glazed tiles, and the shelves constructed of slate, marble or stone, all of which retain coolness. Happily, there is something very attractive and appetizing about food stored against this clean-cut, natural-looking background.

Uses

Many things can be stored in the larder to advantage and the more generously proportioned it is, the more will probably be found to fill it. Its simplest function is providing overnight storage for cooked food such as the remains of joints, poultry or pies, which in winter, certainly, you won't want to resume eating chilled from the refrigerator. In summer, when the larder temperature is unavoidably higher, it is probably advisable to store cooked meat or fish in the refrigerator, but fruit pies can certainly survive a night in the open. Cover all cooked food in the larder. The air is full of harmful micro-organisms and despite the wire gauze over the wall vents to keep out insects, only a genius manages to avoid the occasional flying beast entering surreptitiously when the larder door has been opened.

Fresh food that can be stored in the larder includes vegetables and fruit, game (hung correctly, of course), sausages and salamis, strings of onions and garlic, and cheese. The larder is the ideal compromise for storing cheese when some in the family like their Camembert upright, others prefer it running away. It also provides a satisfactory alternative to chocolates melting around the house in summer, and cut flowers, too, appreciate a cool atmosphere overnight. Bottles of milk, for which there is no room in the fridge, can be covered with an inverted terracotta bowl. This catches the moisture in the air, which in turn cools the outside of the bottle.

Jars of honey and home-made jams are natural larder storage items, as are bottled fruits and home-made chutneys and pickles. Home-made lemon curd should keep six weeks in a cool larder. It keeps double the time in a refrigerator, but who needs several jars taking up valuable space. So divide up the batch instead.

The generous size of most larders makes them useful for storing large items like bread bins or bargain cans of best olive oil brought back as a holiday souvenir. And those who economize by buying in bulk soon run out of conventional cupboards; who wants to clamber up to the loft for another can of anchovies? Packets of pasta that are an awkward length can also find a place in the larder, and if decanted into airtight bins even dry packaged goods like flour can be kept there. Rarely used pots and pans, such as preserving pans, can easily be tucked into an obscure corner either on the floor or on the larder shelves.

When the fridge is packed in summer, there's probably room in the larder, too, for extra bottles of soft drinks, mixer drinks and cans of fruit juice, which come in sizes that challenge cupboard shelves.

A larder should be a chilly cell with thick walls and cold surfaces. Keep it cool by following the guidelines below.

Storing wine

A cellarful of fine vintage wines, bin after bin of dusty bottles, contains a more rarefied air of mystique than almost any other aspect of the good life. Yet the storage of wine is really quite simple.

The cellar itself is generally omitted from modern houses, and the cool, dark, brick-floored underground vault, so indispensable to our ancestors, is now available only to those living in old houses or to those with a friendly wine merchant. For the rest of us some substitute has to be found.

In fact, a cupboard will serve perfectly well. All that wine requires is a constant temperature, darkness and an absence of vibration. The cupboard under the stairs may not be ideal, since it is often stuffy, must double as a receptacle for brooms and bicycles, and suffers from the overhead pounding of feet all day. An ordinary kitchen cupboard is really much better. The difficulty of achieving the coolness traditionally associated with wine storage in a centrally heated kitchen is actually far less important than the avoidance of extreme temperature changes. No wine will stand boiling or freezing, but it can be kept anywhere between 7° and 21°C (45° and 70°F) without undue damage. In high temperatures wine tends to mature more quickly and there is the danger of seepage around the cork—but if coolness is difficult to provide, a steady warmth is fine.

Inside the cupboard, a wood or metal rack is the most practical arrangement. Sturdy cardboard delivery boxes turned on their sides may substitute unless damp will cause them to collapse. Wine can simply be stacked horizontally in piles, though removing a bottle might be tricky.

Wine is stored on its side to keep the cork wet. This prevents the cork drying out and shrinking, leading to the admission of air, which causes the wine to turn sour—a problem first brought to the attention of the trade by Louis Pasteur.

Laying down château- or domaine-bottled wine until it reaches perfect maturity is a highly rewarding investment, but even cheap red wine may benefit from six months' to a year's home storage. All wines kept longer than a week or two still need to be stored horizontally.

Decanting—the art of pouring wine into a decanter to remove the sediment—should not be restricted only to fine, old wines. Some lusty young wines benefit from standing twenty-four hours in a decanter, whereas an hour makes all the difference to others. Generally, the more full-bodied the wine, the longer it needs.

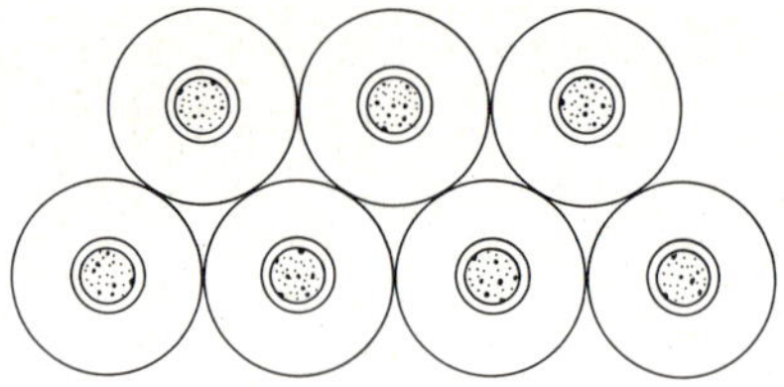

Wine is always stored horizontally, label on top, to prevent the cork from drying and shrinking, and thus letting in air.

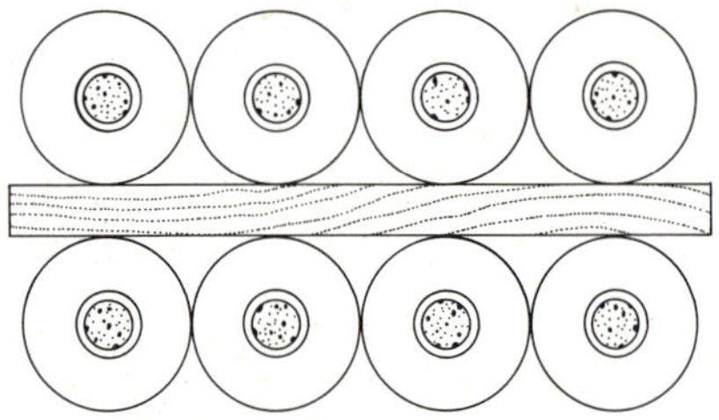

Laths between the rows enable one bottle to be removed from the bottom of the pile without disturbing the rest.

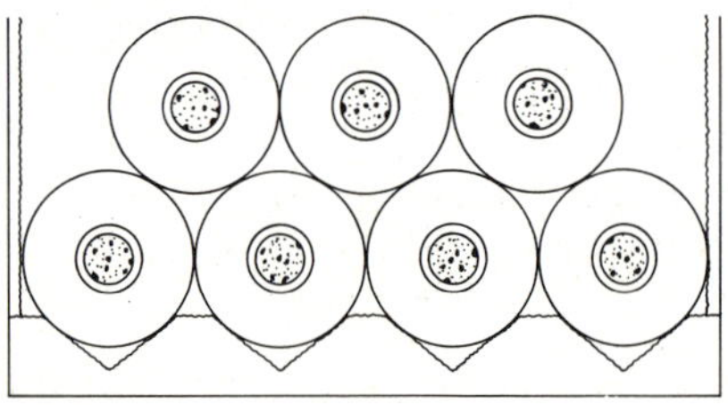

Porous concrete trays are a cool form of storage—above all else wine needs to be kept at a constant temperature.

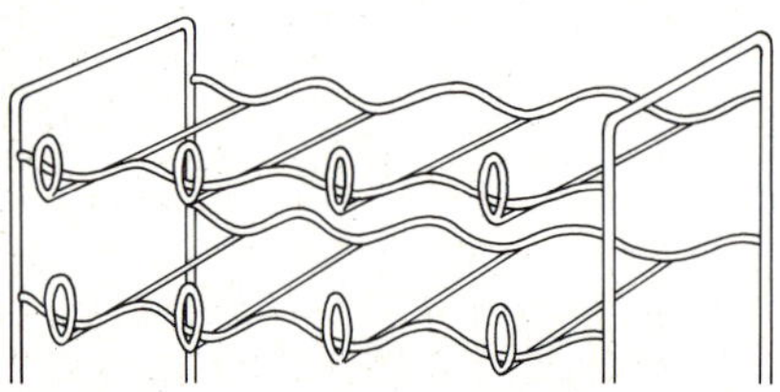

A simple wire rack that is very slightly tilted quickly converts an ordinary cupboard into a proper wine "cellar".

This form of plastic rack contains up to twelve bottles. The holes are wide enough for all except champagne bottles.

Fine wines grow old gracefully in a cool climate (above). Providing protection against light and vibration, the traditional brick-floored cellar is the ideal resting place.

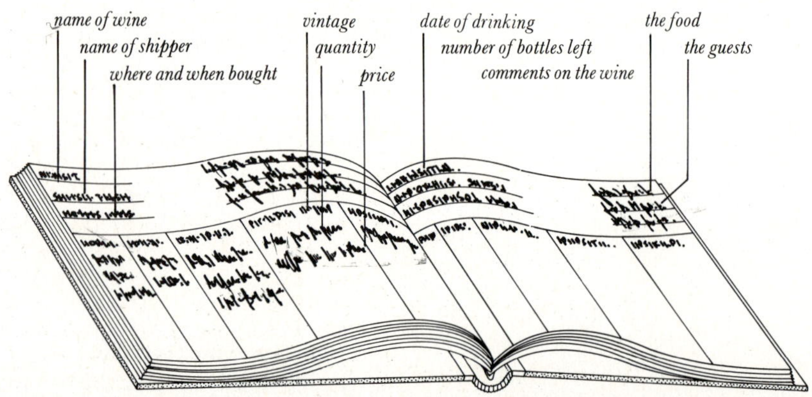

A personal cellar book is essential for anyone seriously investing in wine; those whose motives are more self-indulgent may also like a record of their hobby's ups and downs.

Thermostatic temperature controls keep the line-up of wines in these remarkable kitchen drawers in tip-top condition (above).

Memories are made of this . . . crate ends above the bins are a decorative reminder of wines that once stayed here (below).

Wine crates themselves can be pressed into service to make storage bins that have all been carefully labelled (above).

Even wines kept for only a short while need to be stored horizontally in order to get the very best out of them (above).

Wine, food and cookery books are gathered together to make an attractive work-area-cum-library for the bon viveur (below).

Finishing touches

When you are satisfied that your kitchen works well and your equipment is stored in the right place, then is the time to look around and decide how you can make the room an even more pleasant place to be in, and how it may reflect your own personality.

If you have beautiful pots and pans, you will probably want to keep them on display rather than hidden away in cupboards; they will immediately add character to the kitchen, as will serving dishes, pretty china, glass, or indeed any of the utensils that are used in the preparation and serving of food.

Then the materials you use, big bowls of eggs, baskets of vegetables and fruit, pasta and beans in jars, spices and herbs in phials, home-made jams and preserves in glass jars with hand-written, blue-bordered labels, all contribute to the comfort and charm of the room.

Don't stop there; instead, add your own ideas to make the kitchen your room and nobody else's. Don't forget a vase of fresh flowers, some green herbs and other simple touches that help make the room a happy place to be in. Remember—it's the details that people notice first.

Displaying your batterie de cuisine

Convenience. Efficiency. Safety. These are the keys to arranging the batterie de cuisine. Only when the basics have been considered is it time to turn to their display. Priorities vary: one cook gathers together equipment even before lighting the oven; another follows a recipe step by step, reaching for utensils only when needed.

Study each wall and counter-top, even the ceiling and extractor hood. They are all potential "pictures". By making a group of small items form a still life the eye will be forced to stop and stare. Always keep in mind the relation of each to the other in form, texture and colour.

Antique and modern utensils look good when massed together. Try complements and contrasts: shiny articles look good against dull backgrounds and soft ones against hard; a dark surface enhances copper and stainless steel and a pastel wall makes a perfect foil for white china. Light sources can be turned to definite advantage. Sieves and other see-through utensils hung across a bar near a window create interesting shadows, as does a single object set on a counter directly underneath the light.

The mingled textures of glass, copper and enamel against a black wall look glamorous in the cooking area (right).

Enhance the status of the kitchen-in-the-corner with a few cheap and cheerful utensils (below). Glowing spice jars and condiments in array boost a new cook's self-confidence.

Diversity is decorative. Sieves, sifters and whisks, hung on meat hooks from latticework (below) make an intriguing display. Eggs are safely stored but readily available in the egg-shaped rack.

When the stove is in the centre of the kitchen (above right), all four sides of the extractor hood are used for hanging equipment—a good way to save cupboard space for other items.

A cluster of kitchen gadgets (right) enhances a cream-coloured wall. The hanging display is both attractive and positioned conveniently for the cook to reach everything with ease.

Collections

A deceptive array (above) of wooden pears, waxen tarts and china berries with a porcelain-lidded pot disguised as a pile of plates.

A non-culinary collection of baskets, butterflies and shells keeps the mind off the dull business of washing up (left).

Glass shelving (left) shows collections off to advantage. These antique apothecaries' jars and bottles are not only for decoration; they also make splendid storage jars for herbs and spices.

An obsolete kitchen range (above) now plays host to a variety of charming Victorian jugs, ewers, bowls, mugs, plates and vases massed together on the hearth and hung from a mantel rail.

A wine connoisseur (above) displays her taste. Labels are stuck on with a waterproof adhesive, then sealed with polyurethane varnish.

A collection of traditional ceramic colanders displayed to good effect in an old farmhouse kitchen (below).

Collections

A meticulous arrangement of incongruous objects (above) is a bizarre, colourful contrast to the cupboard, full of strictly practical pots and pans.

A delight to the francophile, the pinboard (below) is neatly arranged with a collection of enamel signs from façades of French houses.

A jumble of photographs and drawings (above) is conveniently confined to pinboards and contrasts with the neat work-top below.

Edwardian nostalgia (below) unites spice jars and a frieze of old postcards. The horizontal arrangement echoes the drawers below.

A few china plates, perhaps holiday souvenirs, built into a collection (right) to decorate a wall where furniture would block the way.

Decoration details

A collection of cookery books kept safely by the kitchen door, away from grease, steam, and sticky fingers (above).

A lovely clutter of kitchen utensils, old advertisements and enamel bins add charm and character but need dusting (below).

An appropriate kitcheny collection of white china toast racks (above) displayed to good effect on a lacquered cane wall shelf.

A decorative facelift for the price of a pot of paint (below). If you don't have faith in your artistic talents, use a stencil kit.

Hand embroidered cloth and a tiled sink (above)—simple rustic decoration to enhance a sunny farmhouse kitchen.

A hanging shelf that exploits the interesting shapes of traditional kitchen utensils and glass storage jars (above).

A pleasing patchwork of old tiles (right) picked up from antique shops and demolition sites. As the tiles are acquired, they are stuck on top of clinical plain white tiles.

Finishing touches

Plants in pots

Once the kitchen has been efficiently designed for cooking, it can be decoratively disguised as a greenhouse, a potting shed, a bower or a tropical forest. Distributed among china displays or along shelves and window sills, plants make a fresh, green contrast to chrome and Formica and are perfect antidotes to drab corners. Greenery belongs naturally in a farmhouse kitchen, but it will look equally well standing out against more clinical surroundings.

Almost any house plant will grow in the kitchen, but it must be in the right location, with an appropriate amount of warmth, light and moisture. Nearly all commercially grown plants come complete with directions for their care. These must be carefully followed. A sun-loving Poinsettia *(Euphorbia pulcherrima)* will shrivel atop a dark cupboard; Cinerarias *(Senecio cruentus)* need moisture and will not survive next to the stove, and Christmas Fern *(Polystichum acrostichioides)* scorches in strong sunlight. Some plants are fairly tough; Parlour Ivy *(Philodendron scandens)*, Swiss Cheese Plant *(Monstera deliciosa)* and Speedy Jenny *(Tradescantia fluminensis)* accept the rougher existence of excessive heat, draughts and gas fumes. Plants must not hamper the activity in a small kitchen. Nothing is more irritating than to knock over the greenery while reaching for a pan. A solution is a canopy of hanging baskets, overflowing with trailing plants such as Geraniums *(Pelargoniums)* and Black-eyed Susans *(Thunbergia alata)* which can complement a dangling display of kitchen equipment. Small plants such as cacti, ferns and African Violets *(Saintpaulia ionantha)* are another solution in a cramped space and look even more attractive en masse. Succulents, which like the sun in a south window, are particularly striking grouped together.

The bigger the plant the better it looks if there is plenty of space around it. Big kitchens can accommodate jungles of contrasting foliage—agglomerations of greenery in which blades of palms, dark, waxy lobes of *Monstera deliciosa*, the slender Weeping Fig *(Ficus benjamina)* and floppy Dumb Cane *(Dieffenbachia picta)* all jostle for position in the light.

The graceful Ficus benjamina *(above right) is set against a bamboo shade background to prevent a kitchen from looking merely functional.*

Spear-like palm leaves (right) echo the linear design of the background screen while counteracting its starkness.

Don't always put plants in conventional pots. Cacti (above) make a succulent casserole.

Water-lilies and rushes make an exotic water-garden (above) in a "tropical" kitchen.

An attractive display of plants (below) turns the kitchen sink into a conservatory.

An indoor herb garden

Fortunate is the cook who is able to give a dish instant aromatic subtlety by plucking fresh herbs from an indoor kitchen garden. To the purist, dried herbs are no substitute for fresh. To the romantic, a row of identical storage jars is less interesting than feathery tufts of dill and fennel, spiky branches of rosemary and curly leaves of parsley, sprouting from pots or a window-box.

Although it may appear to be banked high with a tangle of different species, a window-box should contain separate pots, so that each can be revolved to give the plants equal light on all sides. Any herb that will grow in the garden will thrive indoors if placed in sunlight, preferably in a south-facing window. Although most varieties smell sweet only when pinched, some will respond to heat by releasing their spicy fragrance. Rosemary, delicious with roast lamb, can also be grown merely for the pine-scented, Mediterranean aroma that it gives off in front of a hot window or in a sunny garden.

Watering depends upon weather, or room temperature, and the thirst of each particular herb. Most like to be kept moist, but none will survive in perpetually sodden soil. The pots must have drainage holes, covered with bits of broken pottery to prevent soil loss. When roots begin to straggle through the holes the plant is ready for transplanting to a larger pot.

The healthiest plants have the best of indoor and outdoor worlds, and the kitchen herb garden should be moved outside when the weather is warm. Too great a contrast between outdoor and indoor temperature is fatal, but all herbs benefit from being placed outside on sunny days. The perfect arrangement for this double life is a wide ledge on the outside of the window so that they can be seen and tended from within.

Sage, basil, thyme, mint, chives and marjoram thrive in the circular bowl (above), which is easily rotated to give them all equal light.

When the window (top left) is swung open, the hanging pots go with it—an ingenious way of giving them sun and fresh air.

A sunny, south-facing window sill, the ideal place to grow indoor herbs, supports pots of fennel, basil and parsley (left).

In this attractive and useful display (right), rosemary flourishes in the brown dish and parsley in the blue pot. The strawberry jar harbours sage at the top and rue below.

Rosemary (Rosmarinus officinalis) *Perennial. Needs full sun and well-drained soil. Goes well with lamb.*

Winter savory (Satureja montana) *Perennial. Needs full sun and well-drained soil. Good with beans.*

Tarragon (Artemisia dracunculus) *Perennial. Needs full sun and dryish soil. Good with roast chicken.*

Chives (Allium schoenoprasum) *Perennial. Needs semi-shade and rich, wet soil. Good in salads.*

Sweet marjoram (Origanum majorana) *Annual. Needs sun and well drained soil. For soups and stews.*

Mint (Mentha spicata)
Perennial. Likes wet soil. For cooking vegetables or making sauce.

Chervil (Anthriscus cerefolium)
Annual. Needs semi-shade and moist soil. Good in egg dishes, sauces, salads.

Thyme (Thymus vulgaris)
Perennial. Needs well-drained soil. For meats and stuffings.

Sage (Salvia officinalis) *Perennial. Needs full sun and dryish soil. For stuffings and cheese.*

Dill (Peucedanum graveolens)
Annual. Needs dryish, sunny conditions. For fish and pickles.

Basil (Ocimum basilicum)
Annual. Needs full sun and dryish, rich soil. For egg or tomato dishes.

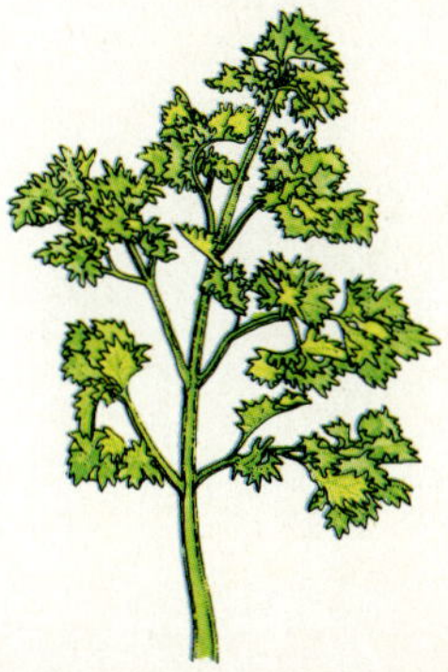

Parsley (Carum petroselinum)
Biennial. Needs half shade and moist soil. For sauce and butter.

ROMEO Y JULIETA
Romeo No. 1
BARTON

The Conran kitchens

I have always loved kitchens ever since I started cooking. Cooking for me is much more than preparing a meal—it becomes a very important part of the day's activity in my household right from the moment that we start to discuss, usually just after breakfast, what we are going to cook for lunch and dinner. We consider who is going to be at those meals and what they would like; what is coming to its prime in the vegetable garden and what we may find in the market. We scan cookbooks for inspiration, turning over ideas and suggestions—and then return from the butcher and fishmonger with purchases that turn all the plans upside-down because something unexpected and delicious has turned up.

Then the pleasure of the kitchen really starts. Unpacking and laying the purchases out on plates, in bowls and in baskets—the food looks too good to eat. Intense industry begins; cutting, scraping, peeling, chopping; favourite knives, thick pans, pottery bowls that are just right, all add to the sensual pleasures of the cooking process.

The kitchen itself almost becomes part of me as I move around using it, knowing exactly where everything is and how it works, cursing inadequacies and bad planning, and vowing that if I ever design another kitchen I'll get it right next time.

While the whole pleasurable business goes on, I chat to my friends, whom I encourage to help in some of the duller chores with a glass of cool white wine.

A house in the country

A view of the kitchen through the door from the vegetable garden (above).

The tiled cooking section with central island unit seen (left) from the eating area, with its huge oak table and original oak flooring.

The kitchen in my house in the country is designed to work in many different ways. It is the house where my family lives so it has to work as a family kitchen, feeding as many as sixteen children and adults at a time. I have an office in this house and frequently use it for business meetings, so I want to be able to entertain my colleagues. It must also work as a test kitchen for my wife, who is a food writer, a journalist and authoress of several cookbooks. Finally, in the Habitat shops we sell a large variety of cooking utensils and we frequently want to give them a trial by fire before we put them in our range.

But the most important thing about the kitchen is that it should be a friendly and happy room, the sort of place where friends and family want to be and where we want to work.

Before we bought our house it had been a small school and the present kitchen was the assembly-room, hung with photographs of boys in cricket gear. Previously it had been a grand country-house and the kitchen had been the billiard-room.

We chose to make this particular room into the kitchen because it has direct access to the vegetable garden, we could build a larder in the north-facing corner, and there

Relaxation is easy in a basket chair by the open woodfire surrounded by log baskets of various shapes and sizes (above).

Rug in front of the deep-blue oil-fired stove (above) adds a touch of comfort for the cook to otherwise strictly functional surroundings. The huge windows run the entire length of the kitchen.

are fireplaces at each end. Four huge windows with window seats facing east (sun at breakfast, but not too hot at lunch) overlook marvellous views of the Berkshire countryside. It is a large room 11 m x 15 m (35 ft x 50 ft) and has a beautiful oak floor. With all these natural advantages it would have been difficult not to have made a super kitchen.

Some of the things we wanted to achieve with this kitchen we had never been able to do before, and others were repeats of past successes. We had never been able to have an island kitchen unit. This is an idea I had from working in restaurant kitchens, and in our room it acts as a natural and successful barrier between the eating and cooking areas. The huge aluminium hood provides excellent extraction, with ducting connecting it to the outside, and is a good place to hang pans, skillets and colanders, so that they are always to hand. Best of all it's a concentrated light fitting, with four sealed bulkhead units that throw the light downwards, exactly where it is needed most.

We had never had a separate scullery before, and this really is a great luxury because the dirty pans and dishes can be piled up out of the way while we are eating. The open shelves are very practical and dishes can be stacked easily and quickly without wrestling with sliding or opening doors: also when laying up the table it is so easy to see the dishes and glasses you need quickly. But it can be a disadvantage if things on the shelves aren't used fairly regularly, as they may get rather dusty.

The larder is probably the most useful adjunct that any kitchen can have, and it is extremely sad that its modern equivalents, the refrigerator and the deep-freeze, really don't replace all the many functions that the larder of old achieved. Much food, particularly game and meat, improves in its uncooked state if it is kept in the correct condition for a period. Most cheese is damaged by refrigeration, but perhaps one of the worst faults of the refrigerator is that food in such close proximity picks up the flavour of its neighbours. The larder's main advantage is that it removes from the kitchen all food that can deteriorate and from the refrigerator all food that doesn't benefit from being there.

But the greatest pleasure of the larder is to see, displayed on cool slate shelves, all your supplies and preserves, jams and pickles, and hanging hams and game birds—the hoarding instinct in us is given material gratification. However, beware of magpie children seduced by those shelves of sweet comestibles as they search for the jars of damson jam.

Bright chrome covers of the stove (above) reflect utensils lying on the teak work-surface in front. Far left are the fridge and vegetable sinks.

Anybody can construct a larder if they have a north-facing exterior wall. It is necessary to pierce this wall to achieve an airflow from outside and it is important to build walls and doors on the inside that properly insulate the larder from the warmth of the kitchen. Interior surfaces should be able to retain the coolness of night air, so shelves made of slate, stone or marble are best. Walls should be of brick or stone which can be surfaced with glazed ceramic tiles. The larder is conveniently near the back door, so shopping can be deposited directly on the shelves.

Lights from the huge aluminium extraction hood shine directly on to the cooking and preparation area. Pots, pans and bunches of onions and herbs hang overhead, always ready for use (above).

A house in the country

Decorative plates and bowls (above) are attractively displayed on open shelving; the rounded wooden shelf conceals drawers.

Charcoal or wood grill (below) is built into the chimney-breast. The patterned and plain ceramic tiles are easy to clean.

One of the things that we tried to avoid in the kitchen was closed cupboards. We do have cupboards under the sink for the compost bucket and the rubbish bucket, some cupboards next to the refrigerator for all the tinware, most of which is infrequently used, and cupboards the other side of the charcoal grill for farinaceous products that could deteriorate in the slightly damp coolness of the larder. But apart from this everything is on display—easy to get at and decorative to look at.

The Aga stove, in this case oil fired, but also available in gas or solid fuel, dominates our cooking arrangements. This excellent cooking device, invented in Sweden by Dr Gustav Dalen in 1929, is manufactured in Britain. It remains ready for use twenty-four hours a day, 365 days a year. In the winter its warm presence is an important part of kitchen life. After cold forays into the vegetable garden it's comforting to warm your hands and your bottom against it. Dishcloths are always dry because they get hung over the rail; this is a good place to hang damp clothes, and the coolest oven can even be used to dry saturated shoes.

Our model has four ovens of various heats from fast-roast and bake to one that is invaluable for warming plates. Aga fanatics will tell you of marvellous stews that they have made by leaving the casserole all night in the slowest oven. On the top under the handsome chrome covers are two steel plates, one hot enough to simmer, one for fast boiling and frying. There is also a flat aluminium plate for serving dishes, which warms them up just enough to ensure that food always arrives hot on the table.

Steak and other meats can be grilled directly on the top of the hottest steel plate, an idea I culled from a restaurant kitchen. Toast is made by putting the slices of bread in a wire rack and sandwiching it between the cover and the hot top.

We have an auxiliary cooker in the form of four Scholtes electric hot-plates and, although they are not in constant use, they are very helpful when we have large numbers of guests or complicated meals.

Our other cooking arrangement is the charcoal or wood grill built into the chimney-breast at the kitchen end of the room. Although this is by no means an essential, it is a nice addition, because nothing tastes better than wood-grilled meat or fish.

We have a large refrigerator and a small deep-freeze outside the kitchen. We dislike deep-freezing as a regular practice, because nothing tastes as good once it's been frozen and de-frozen as it does when it's fresh, and also because it can ruin the pleasure of the seasonality of food. The taste of the first fresh pea in June is an enormous pleasure, but only if you haven't been eating them constantly throughout the year. Despite this we have to admit that the freezer has its uses, especially when the garden over-produces tomatoes and broad beans and we are threatened with pounds and pounds going to waste — also it is invaluable for ice-cream or chilling a bottle of white wine rather rapidly. Best of all it keeps Aquavit, Framboise and Poire Williamene in the marvellous condition that enables them to be poured like freezing syrup into small liqueur glasses.

Our refrigerator is nothing like as heavily used as it would be if we didn't have a larder. It produces ice cubes, but I wish I had one of those marvellous American fridges that produces them automatically. We also put in it milk, cream, fruit juices and anything else that we want to keep chilled.

One of the greatest benefits of living in an old house are the cellars; ours are huge and stretch under most of the house. We store apples and potatoes there, and grow winter salad in peat. We have a barrel of beer in one cellar, which had been expressly designed for that purpose with a raised floor and a drain in the lower level. But the greatest treat is the properly designed wine cellars with their cool brick-built vaulted bins.

The squirrel instinct that gets pleasure from the well-stocked larder is equally satisfied by reviewing a few dozen bottles of wine laid out in the cellar. Few people these days can afford the capital to lay down extensive cellars of fine wine, but even if wine remains in your cellar for only a short period it will benefit by being kept at the correct temperature and in the correct position.

The other most important consideration in any kitchen is the finish of the surfaces, and it is always a battle between cleanliness and durability and sympathetic mellowness.

As I said, one of the bonuses of the room we converted was the beautiful oak floor, which was ideal for the eating end of the kitchen but not very satisfactory in the cooking and washing areas. So we cut back the oak boards and installed rectangular ceramic tiles at this end of the kitchen, and also extended them into the larder and

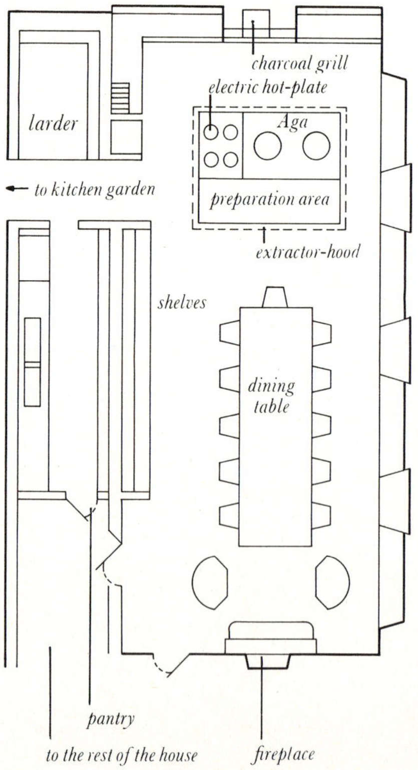

Plan of the Conrans' kitchen (above).

scullery. They are hard on the feet, but they clean easily and will last for hundreds of years. We also made a tile skirting around all the units so the paint or timber isn't damaged when mopped down. A concession to the cook is a rather nice but threadbare rug behind the cooker. It helps the feet and although it gets rather grubby it can be washed easily — the cats like it too!

On the big central cooking and storage island every surface is covered with 10-cm (4-in) square white-glazed ceramic tiles. They are extremely durable if well laid, and if one gets damaged it is not too difficult to replace. The same finish, but this time with a pattern, covers the back wall of the kitchen surrounding the charcoal grill and behind the vegetable preparation sink. Again, they are practical and durable; because they are ceramic tiles they have an association with traditional kitchens which makes them feel right.

The work-surfaces around the vegetable sinks and on the other side of the grill and the large slab behind the cookers are solid teak. The same wood has also been used for the draining-board in the scullery. Teak is a very good wood for these purposes—it is extremely hard, and has a natural oiliness, which can be easily rejuvenated if the surface does dry out a bit and because of this does not take up the stains that other paler woods can suffer. But most important it's very stable and can cope with dampness and heat without flying into a tantrum and warping and splitting.

The ceiling is tongued-and-grooved pine boards with a rather traditional half-round detail at the joints. It is painted glossy cream and is about two feet lower than the original ceiling to allow for the ducting from the ventilation hood and the recessed lights over the table. It insulates the room above from the heat and noise of the kitchen below. It also, in my opinion, improves the proportions of the kitchen.

The glazed white ceramic sinks (above), which are aesthetically pleasing, have a convenient deep hole between them for draining kitchen scraps.

Continuous tops and shelves in the scullery (left) are for stacking dishes ready for the dishwasher, and then easily reached for laying the table. The entrance to the larder is at the end of the room.

The Conrans' model larder (above) has both wood and slate shelves. Root vegetables are stored correctly near the ventilation holes, and the jams and fruits are cool and dry nearer the ceiling.

A house in the country

The oil-fired stove is a marvellous deep-blue vitreous enamel, which ties up with the blue in the tiles on the back wall. Apart from this there is very little colour in the kitchen other than the colour of natural materials—the teak tops, the oak floor and table, and shelves and drawers of the shelf unit. All the walls, windows and doors are painted a pale cream.

The huge oak table was made for us by Michael Wickham, who owns a workshop in Coleshill, Wiltshire, from the beams of a sixteenth-century barn, so this, coupled with its traditional design, makes many people believe that it is rather ancient. Around the table we have an ever-changing selection of rush-bottomed English country chairs—some painted, some plain—changing because it is difficult to get them re-rushed, and they are often worm-eaten and therefore break under the weight of heavy diners.

There are a few other small things that are important about our kitchen/living-room . . . the canary, very old, who sings particularly loudly after a large lunch, when many people have raised their voices to be heard above the hubbub . . . the cats, who catch the mice and who love the warm stove at one end of the room and the basket chair at the other . . . small greenhouses that are warmed by the radiators under the window seats and used in the spring for propagating seedlings . . . the wood fire and great Chinese baskets full of logs—the smell of woodsmoke and the comfort of a blazing fire . . . the display of dishes and pots, which are perhaps more decorative than useful, but are useful in their decorativeness . . . the pictures of food, and particularly that strange casting of a basket of trout on a plate. All these things add up to a comfortable and practical room that is a pleasure to work in and a pleasure to eat in. It is, literally, a living room.

Properly designed wine cellars (above), with their cool brick-vaulted bins, form part of the extensive underground space at Barton Court. The bottles are stored at the correct temperature and position to ensure maximum benefit to the wine.

Concealed wooden drawers (left) house clean dishcloths below bowls of fruit and a rack of eggs.

Miniature greenhouses sit on several of the broad window sills above the warm radiators (right) where seedlings are propagated in spring.

The Conran kitchens

A London home

This imposing house, designed and built in 1815 by Decimus Burton, was part of Nash's grand plan for Regent's Park.

When we found this house it had not been lived in for seven years and was very damp and dilapidated. The kitchen had not been touched since the early part of the century and was dominated by a huge cooker and a giant central-heating boiler that hissed and spluttered in one corner when turned on.

The cooker had to go, but economy forced us to keep the boiler. We hid this in a louvered cupboard and grew to love its presence rather like an old grandmother sitting by the fireside. We bought two cheap standard gas cookers and put them side by side: luckily there was a chimney flue on this wall, so we opened it up and put a stainless-steel grille over the opening—this proved to be a most efficient form of extraction, the pull from the chimney sucking away all cooking fumes.

A beautiful curved dresser was in the wrong position because of boxing in the boiler, but it was carefully and successfully moved along the wall. This is a marvellous backdrop for the kitchen and invaluable for storage. Our other inheritance was a larder with slate shelves and tiled walls. It is a bit damp as it's built under the garden and has no through ventilation, but it's still a larder.

By the side of the cookers there is a work-surface covered in white melamine—not perfect, but reasonably durable and hygienic. Then there is that paragon of sinks, the Willow. It is of white-glazed ceramic with two bowls, but between the two bowls is a 15-cm (6-in) diameter round hole 25 cm (10 in) deep with a drain at the bottom. Into this hole should go a removable stainless steel basket (plastic now, alas!) so that tea leaves, coffee grounds and kitchen scraps can be poured into this magic hole and all the water will drain away leaving damp garbage for dumping straight into the bin. It speeds the washing-up process enormously. You might ask why not use a waste-disposal unit, which grinds up the rubbish straight into the drains, but I've never liked the idea of providing the sewer rats with all that pre-digested food—also I value organic kitchen waste as compost. To the right of the sink there is a dishwasher under a teak draining-board.

The wall behind the cookers and sink is lined with hexagonal ceramic tiles. A deep shelf unit shields strip lights, to illuminate the work-surfaces and provide a convenient place for large pans.

On the other side of the kitchen is a row of Habitat pine kitchen units with open pine shelves above and shielded light strips on their underside. In the middle of the room a 2-m x 1-m (6-ft x 3-ft) ash table seats eight people for meals. The floor is covered with slightly marbled plastic tiles, not ideal but economical, and the ceiling is covered with white-painted tongued-and-grooved boarding to cover an octopus of pipes and to allow five recessed lights to be positioned over the table.

Although the result looks quite glamorous, and as a kitchen it certainly works very well indeed, it really is an example of making the best of what you find and simply and economically complementing it.

Mellow but efficient lighting (above), recessed over the central table and under deep shelves, makes a pleasing atmosphere.

The louvered cupboard (right) successfully hides the giant central-heating boiler.

Country cottages

Many years ago we found a dilapidated farm cottage at the end of a beautiful unspoiled village in East Anglia. It was on the edge of a small stream, which ran parallel to the village High Street, shaded by a huge chestnut tree and under the lee of a great hill with an old windmill on the top of it. But it had almost come to the end of its life and if we hadn't found it, and rebuilt it, it would have become completely derelict.

The kitchen, which was originally a shed built of flint and slate, had been attached to the cottage proper, but had been used for making baskets from the willow trees that grew along the edges of the stream. We connected the room to the rest of the house by making an eight-foot-wide opening through the main adjoining wall. This could be closed off by a sliding panel.

The kitchen itself was simple. The floor was dark-brown quarry tiles; the ceiling, which followed the shape of the room, was lined in pine tongued-and-grooved boards; a panel of the same material shielded a row of tungsten strip lights, which gave a warm mellow light in the room but was strong enough to illuminate the work-surface well. We built a larder in the north-facing corner, where we also put the refrigerator, but with an extra vent to the outside so the hot air

The simple kitchen furniture is ideally suited to their indoor/outdoor life (above).

Fortunate in having a country market and a well-stocked river near their Dordogne home, the Conrans need little storage space (left).

coming from it didn't interfere with the coolness of the larder.

I designed the kitchen units, which were made at my factory, and placed them along one wall with a stainless-steel sink built into one of the units. The cupboards were pine with white-painted sliding doors and white melamine tops. This system has the advantage that it can be mounted on the wall at exactly the level required. This is useful for tall or short people or for aligning them with existing equipment. I also think that they look nice and unpretentious today, so many years after they were designed.

The other simple piece of furniture is the plain, scrubbed pine table surrounded by some lovely bentwood armchairs.

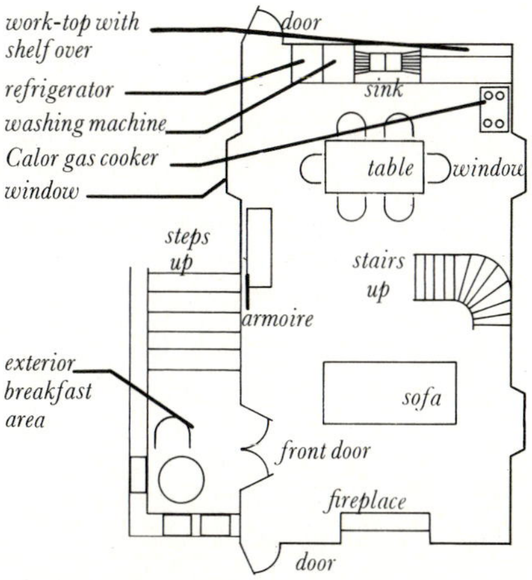

The Dordogne kitchen layout (above).

The Conrans are able to bake their own bread and cook in the great fireplace of their Habitat-furnished Dordogne kitchen (above).

Just outside the kitchen door is a small brick-paved patio beneath a roof of vines supported on wires. It is a perfect place for breakfast, lunch and supper on warm days.

It's a comfortable room, always making it a pleasure to arrive there late on a Friday night after a hard week's work in the city; you can feel the tension seeping away.

My home in France

This is a very simple house built on a rock directly overlooking the huge Dordogne River. When we found the house in this perfect, green, uninhabited valley, it had not been lived in for many years and did not appear to have a proper kitchen—most extraordinary for a French house.

We wanted to use the house in the simplest way possible, arriving with cars full of children and friends and getting the house into action immediately, so we decided to strip out all the partitions and make one large room in which we would both cook and sit. We also wanted the cheapest and most basic kitchen possible, so we made one long counter-top of solid oak—the sink, washing machine and refrigerator at one end, and the Calor gas cooker at the other. Open shelves under the work-top take the rubbish bins, baskets full of vegetables and the large pans, and the shelf over the sink and work-top has a concealed tungsten strip light housed in its depth. Large glass jars and pots to hold dry goods, spices and herbs sit on top of the shelf.

A walnut armoire holds all the china and glass and tins and packets, but there is no great storage problem because most of the food is bought from the market on the day that it will be eaten.

The kitchen table is positioned between two windows to take advantage of the beautiful views over the river and over a green meadow, where sheep graze surrounded by walnut trees.

Because the kitchen table doubles as the dining-table, food comes directly from the cooker to the table, and a breeze that always seems to blow, even on the hottest days, obligingly removes all cooking smells and keeps us cool.

It's not very difficult to design a simple kitchen for a holiday house, especially in France. This one works very well, was extremely easy and cheap to build, and is a civilized component of a large multi-purpose living-room.

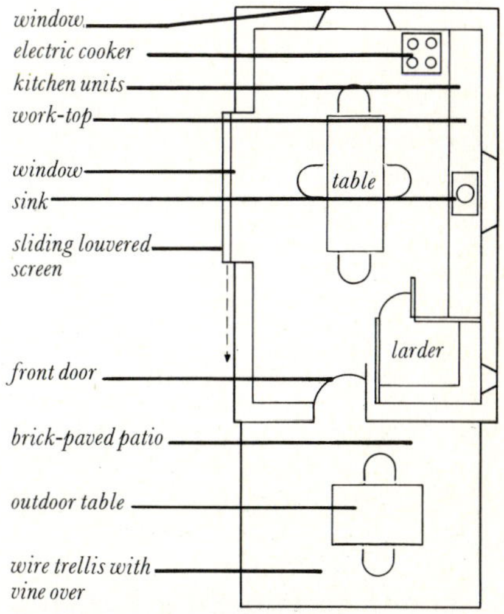

Plan of the Suffolk kitchen (above).

Easy-to-clean quarry tiles and a minimum of equipment keep the kitchen work-load down (below) in the Conrans' Suffolk cottage—a welcome retreat after the busy week.

The Conran kitchens

Neal Street Restaurant

I started up this restaurant back in 1972 with two partners. We opened it because we were interested in food and two of us had been professionally involved in designing and operating restaurants in the past. With the rebirth of Covent Garden we sensed a marvellous opportunity to create the kind of restaurant that we and our friends would enjoy. We might even make some money.

I have been involved in the restaurant business since 1955, when I worked as a washer-up and vegetable boy in an elegant Parisian restaurant. I then opened several small, simple, cheap restaurants in London with a partner. We called them the Soup Kitchens, because they served four different kinds of soup in addition to French bread and butter, cheddar cheese, apple tart and cream and espresso coffee. In their day they were quite a revolution. I then opened another restaurant called The Orrery in Chelsea. It had a delightful stone-flagged courtyard, huge plane trees and a barbecue—one of the few places to eat out-of-doors in London at that time.

When we found the site in Neal Street, Covent Garden, which is actually part of, but independent from, our design offices, it seemed the perfect place to create another restaurant.

Our patrons arrive through the upstairs entrance and pass a long white marble-topped counter laden with a selection of salads and cold hors d'oeuvre, which are replenished from the large teak-faced refrigerator behind it.

The walls are cream-painted brick, left much as they were when it was a vegetable warehouse. Downstairs is the bar, wine cellar and kitchen.

I learned from my French restaurant experience that a kitchen must be compact. If there are huge distances to walk, then the chefs become inefficient and consequently the customers cannot be served quickly.

This kitchen is very simple. Two large catering gas cookers are placed at either end of the central island; sandwiched between them are a charcoal grill and an electric deep-fryer. Fixed above these on the central column is a salamander, or gas-fired grill. Over the entire top is a very efficient extraction system, really one of the most vital ingredients of a restaurant kitchen. There are powerful lights in the hood directed on to the cookers, another essential in a good kitchen.

Around the tiled walls of the room is a work-surface finished in white melamine with a teak edge, under which are a cupboard, shelves and a large refrigerator for the ingredients that the chef wants quickly to hand.

Well-lit cooking units are grouped around a central column (below), leaving walls free for preparation. About 200 meals a day are cooked to order in this kitchen.

There is a cold-room for stocks of fish, meat and vegetables and also a room for washing up and vegetable preparation.

In front of the cooking island is a large stainless-steel cupboard, which is partly a bain-marie (a bath of hot water in which containers holding various sauces and soups are kept warm). Underneath is a hot cupboard for plates and dishes, the top of which is a hot surface for dishing up food to go in the lift to the restaurant above.

The plan is simple, the design ungimmicky, the materials hard-wearing and the equipment robust. All of these I believe are the elements that combine to make a good restaurant kitchen or, for that matter, a good domestic kitchen.

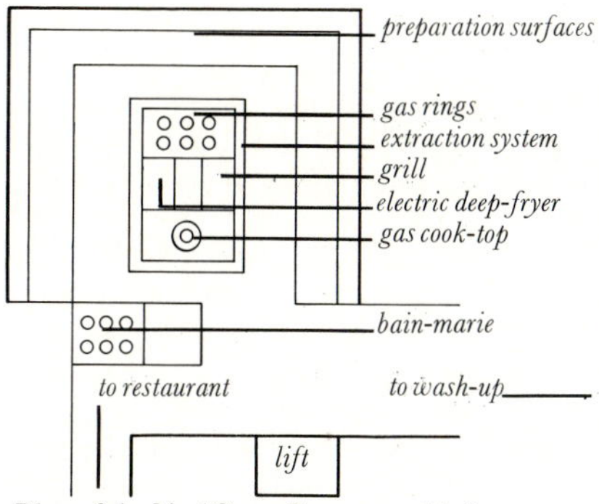

Plan of the Neal Street Restaurant kitchen.

The hot cupboard (below) keeps dishes warm. The far section is a bain-marie for sauces.

Terence Conran (above) in the kitchen of the restaurant with Head Chef Santiago Gonzalez and Manager Charles Campbell.

The restaurant, once a vegetable warehouse, has retained its original brick walls (below). The marble-topped counter is used as a servery.

The Conran kitchens

My office kitchen

When I was consigned to a basement which had been part of an old banana warehouse in the vegetable market area of London, I was determined to make it as comfortable as possible. I use my office for conferences during the day, and I sometimes spend the night there. I wanted a large amount of space that would include a private shower and lavatory, and a kitchen that could be used to cook occasional breakfasts as well as informal relaxing lunches for my clients. We have other uses for the kitchen, too. It provides the background for many of the photographs taken for the Habitat catalogues, and is a setting for displaying the domestic products designed in the Conran Associates' office.

The kitchen is painted cream rather than white to fit in with the rest of the office decoration. It becomes part of the main room by opening up two large louvered doors, or alternatively the doors can be closed for preparing a meal while a meeting takes place in the main room.

The white-tiled top units go around the three sides of the alcove and under them are simple white melamine-faced cupboards, which open with touch catches. There are some pine drawers inside the cupboards for cutlery and small cooking utensils. There is a small electric hob, a stainless-steel sink and a tiled shelf at eye-level; the floor tiles, which are also used throughout the office, form a plinth for the units.

The large 2.4-metre (8-ft) diameter conference table is also used for serving meals. I find the whole problem of serving food in an office fascinating. Either it is done in a grand manner or it is squalid, with the meal cooked over a grubby gas ring. The final indignity seems to me to be a row of automatic drink dispensers, purveyors of noxious liquids, which manage to make tea taste of coffee, coffee of chocolate and chocolate of chicken soup!

In this small, basic kitchen it is at least possible to produce a simple meal attractively and efficiently.

Elegant louvered doors (below) conceal a kitchen. This area of the room is used for eating or working, although the two often go together.

The circular table enables everyone to be heard during a business lunch (below). The wall poster sets the theme but the table setting is informal.

The white pillar (above) divides the desk from the conference-cum-dining area. Having a dual-purpose table helps promote the room's uncluttered appearance. Efficient air conditioning helps you to forget you are in a windowless basement office.

Under the stove (above) a pine drawer holds cutlery and there is storage space for food, all neatly out of sight behind a cupboard door.

Pots and serving trays are the only bright colours against the all-white of the built-in units (below). It is designed for efficiency without fuss.

Batterie de cuisine

You will never find a good craftsman who uses second-rate tools; equally a good cook cannot work well with thin pans and blunt knives.

Apart from the functional necessity of good-quality equipment, the aesthetic pleasure that the best cookware brings to the process of food preparation is very important—imagine a fine coq au vin cooking in a gaudy and overdecorated enamel casserole, a delicious terrine in a jokey shaped pottery dish or a fresh green salad in an orange plastic bowl.

There is a certain affinity between good food and natural materials and simple shapes. This is not to say that a little decoration doesn't occasionally contribute charm and style, but it should always be a gentle embellishment, and never dominate or confuse the purpose of the utensil.

Whilst most of the best kitchen tools have been tried, tested and refined in kitchens over the last century, occasionally some new piece of equipment comes on to the market that really does do the job better than its predecessor.

This chapter surveys the best equipment on the market today, although few cooks could possibly need all that is shown on these pages. You should only add to your collection when you feel convinced that you really need to; there is nothing more tiresome than drawers and cupboards full of gadgets that are never used.

Knives and cleavers

Cutting and chopping

Swift, deft slicing depends upon finely balanced, razor-sharp knives. Carbon-steel knives have the edge over stainless ones which, although bright and hard wearing, cannot be sharpened to the keenness of their flexible, stainable rivals. All knives should be sharpened on a steel after use—a really sharp blade brushed across a tomato should split the skin by its mere weight. Blades must be firmly riveted to the handles; wooden handles give a firm grip, but, unlike plastic ones, must not be placed in the dishwasher. Carbon-steel knives should be washed by hand and stored, like stainless ones, in a rack where they cannot be blunted by other utensils. The extent of a knife batterie depends upon individual needs, but basic to most kitchens are a couple of cook's knives for general chopping, a paring knife for vegetables and a carving knife. All cutting jobs can be done with knives, but some may be done more easily with gadgets. Knife virtuosity takes practice. Meanwhile, gadgets help.

Stainless-steel fork for barbecues and bonfire parties. The long handle keeps you away from the flames.

Steel for sharpening knives—should be held at a 20-degree angle to the blade.

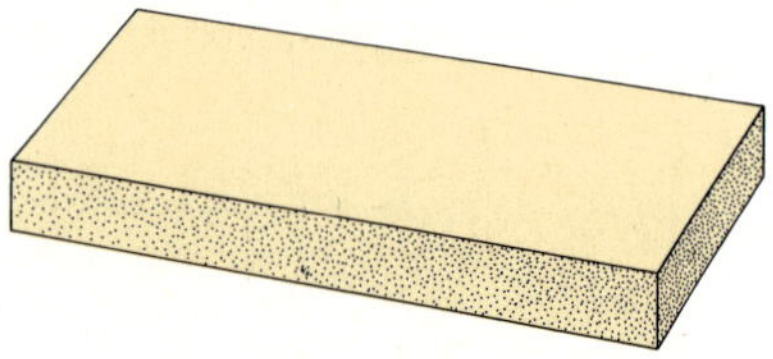

Rough on one side and smooth on the other, carborundum stones are cheap, traditional knife sharpeners. The knife should be drawn across the coarse side first at a 20-degree angle. Use the smooth side for the final, fine edge.

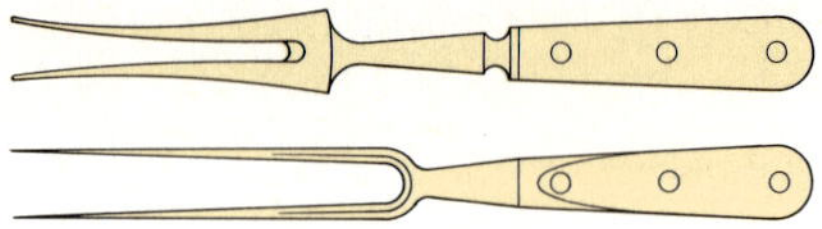

Stainless-steel carving forks, shapely and traditional, or straight, for steadying the meat when cutting fine slices..

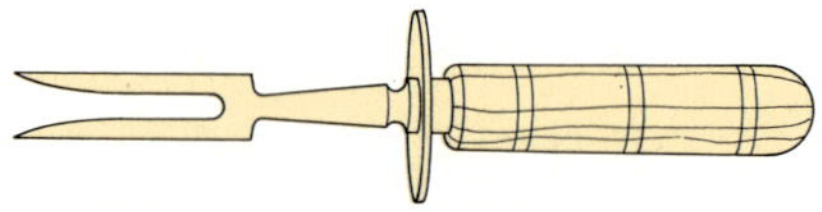

Stainless-steel carving fork with guard and a sturdy beech handle.

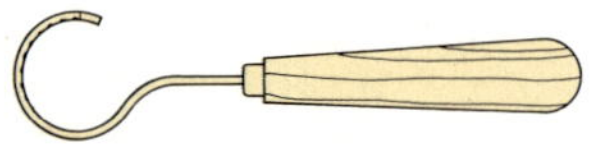

Butter curler. The hook scrapes a ribbed curl from the surface of a cold butterpat.

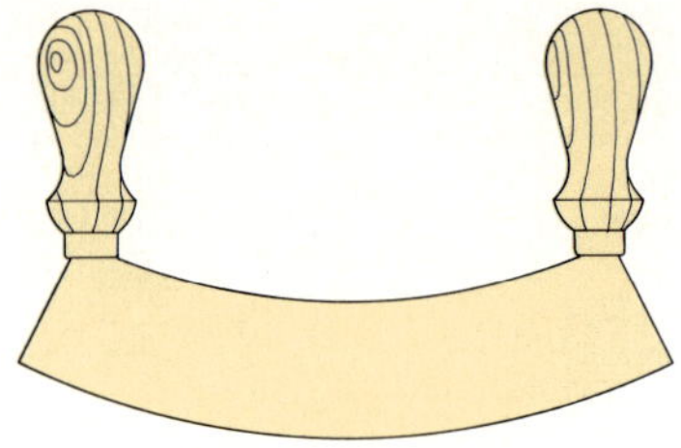

The mezzaluna, a double-handled chopper with stainless-steel blade; demolishes vegetables and meat as it is rocked backwards and forwards.

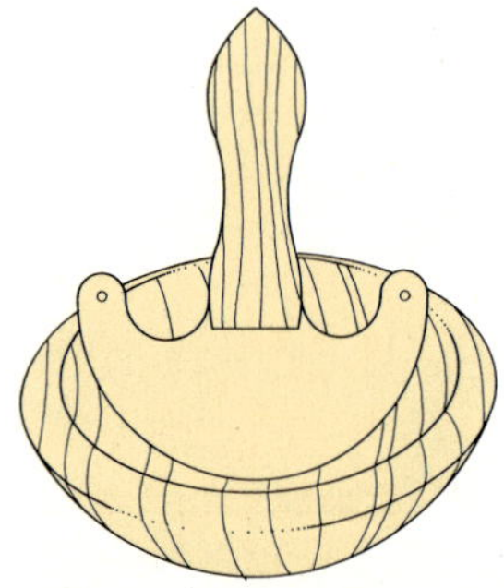

A crescent-shaped blade, curved to fit its wooden bowl, for quick, thorough chopping of herbs, garlic, parsley and shallots.

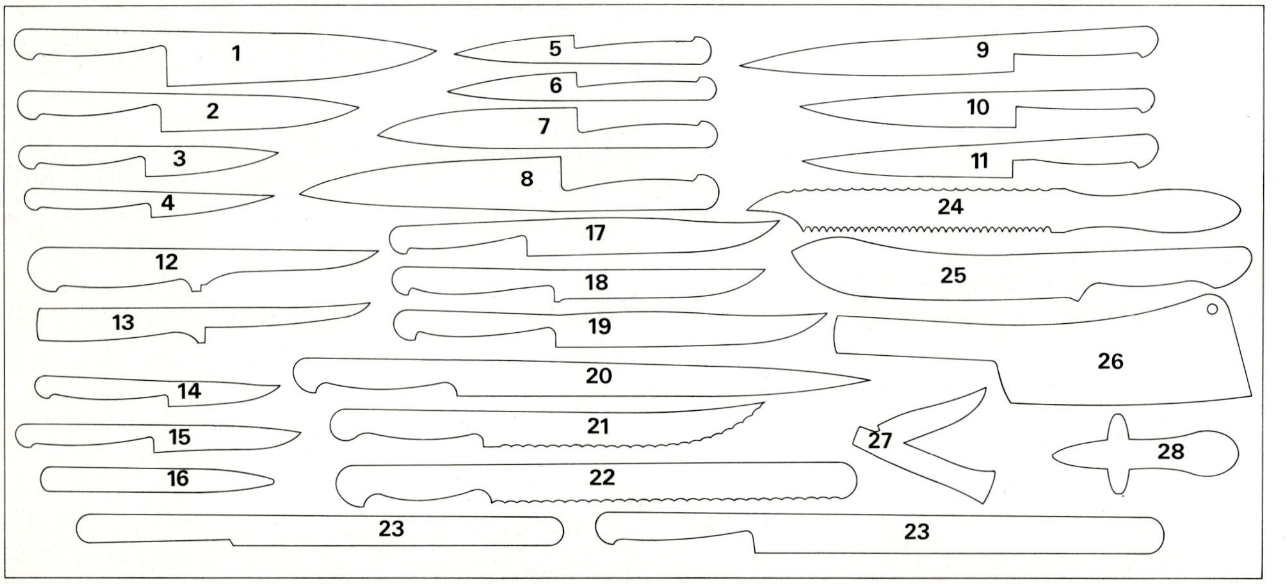

1-4 *Sabatier cook's knives in stainless steel.*
5-8 *Sabatier cook's knives in carbon steel. Two excellent sets of French knives for quick, confident chopping and slicing. Blades are 3 in, 4 in, 6 in, and 8 in.*
9-10 *Sabatier carbon-steel filleting knives, 6-in and 8-in blades, which are slim and supple for slicing raw meats and fish.*
11 *Sabatier stainless-steel filleting knife, 6-in blade.*
12 *Sabatier carbon-steel boning knife with a stiff 5-in blade.*
13 *Victorinox stainless-steel boning knife, 5-in blade.*
14 *Joseph Elliott, Sheffield stainless-steel paring knife, 3-in blade.*
15 *Joseph Elliott, Sheffield stainless-steel tomato knife, 4-in blade.*
16 *French stainless-steel serrated grapefruit knife bends into the fruit.*
17 *Sabatier stainless-steel carving knife, 8-in blade.*
18-19 *Joseph Elliott, Sheffield stainless-steel carving knives, 6-in and 8-in blades.*
20 *Gustav Emil Ern carbon-steel carving knife, 12-in blade.*
21 *Gonch Gironde stainless-steel bread knife, 8-in serrated blade.*
22 *Gustav Emil Ern stainless-steel ham slicer with 10-in fluted blade.*
23 *Gustav Emil Ern carbon-steel ham slicer with plain blade.*
24 *German stainless-steel deep-freeze knife with an 8-in blade—a gnasher for cutting through hard-frozen food.*
25 *Gustav Emil Ern stainless-steel butcher's knife, 8-in blade.*
26 *Sabatier stainless-steel meat cleaver. A heavy 7-in blade for splitting bones.*
27 *Stainless-steel folding picnic knife, $3\frac{1}{2}$-in blade.*
28 *Stainless-steel oyster knife, $1\frac{1}{4}$-in blade.*

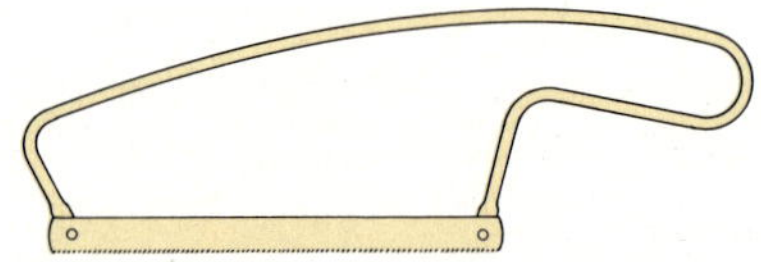

Stainless-steel kitchen saw for domestic butchery. Easily bisects the most obstinate bone.

Flexible, stainless-steel spatula for turning omelettes, lifting slices of pie and spreading soft mixtures.

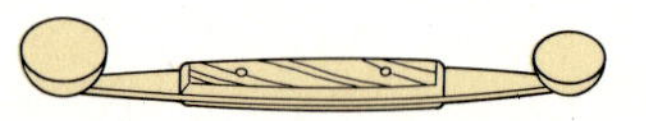

Double-ended melon baller, also for scooping decorative spheres from vegetables and suitably firm fruits.

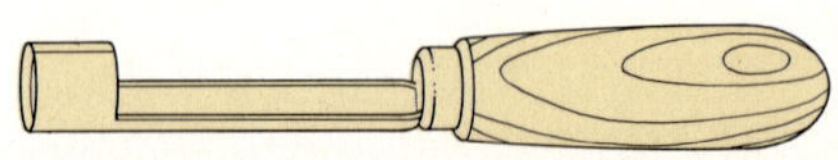

Apple corer. To be aimed at the top of the apples, pushed through and then withdrawn with the core in its trough.

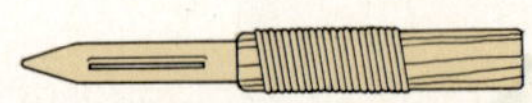

Potato peeler, quicker than a paring knife for stripping the skins of most vegetables.

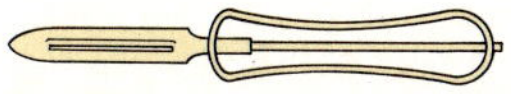

Swivel-action peeler rotates according to different surfaces and cuts either way with its double-edged blade.

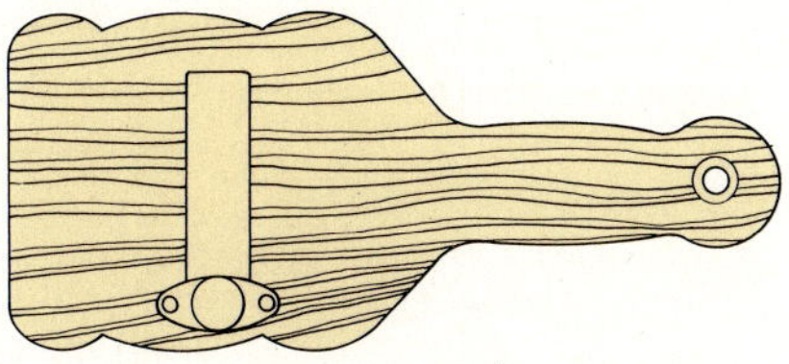

A truffle slicer will slice less exalted foods like cheese and chocolate. The adjustable blade carves different thicknesses.

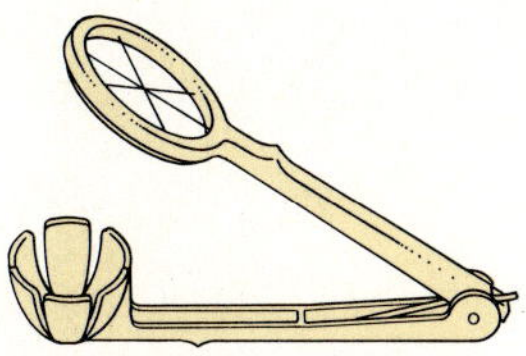

Aluminium egg-wedger. Wire cutter splits a hard-boiled egg into six segments.

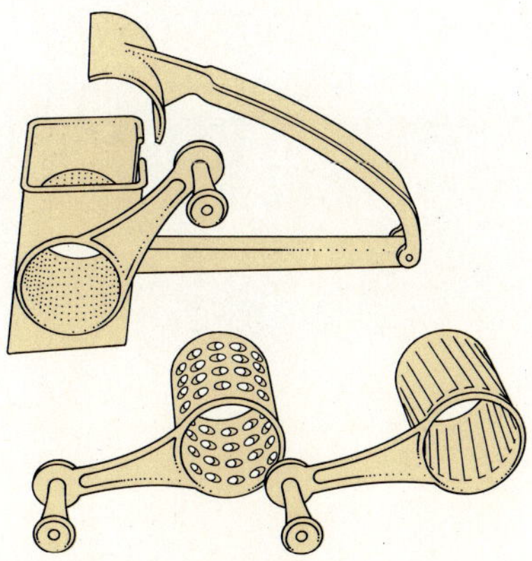

Plastic mouli-grater with alternative metal attachments for coarse or fine grating of cheese, chocolate, nuts and carrots.

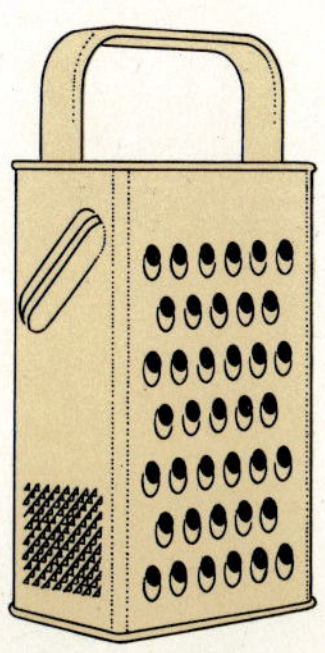

Box grater, with three kinds of perforations and a sharp slit for slicing vegetables.

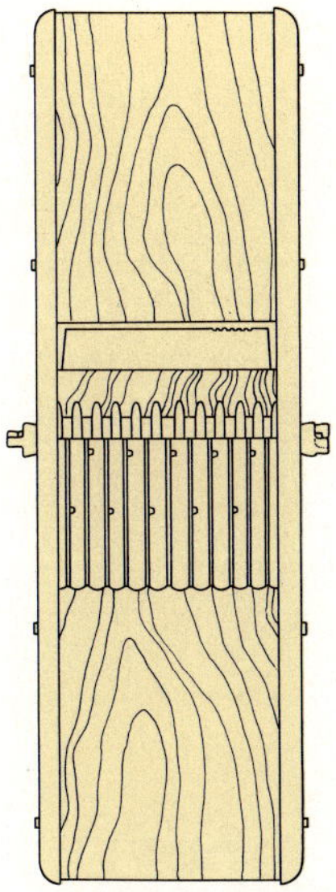

The mandoline, a wooden board with adjustable steel cutters for slicing and shredding.

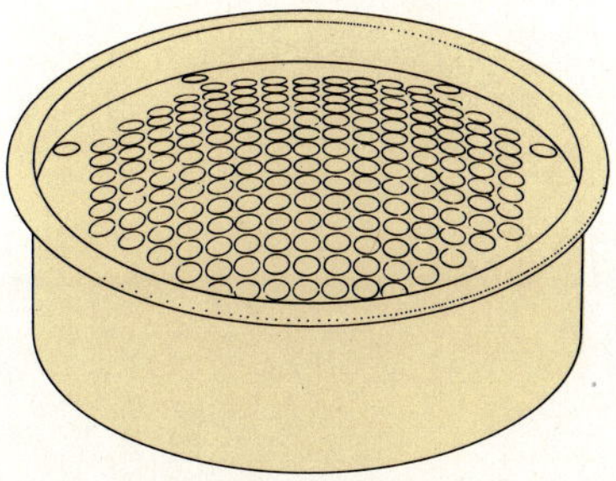

Stainless-steel cheese grater with a bowl below to hold piles of shredded Cheddar.

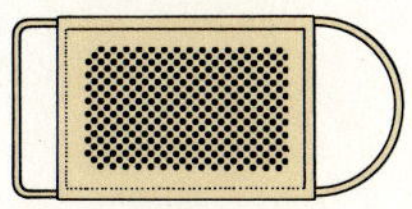

Little nutmeg grater has fine perforations and a box for the nutmegs.

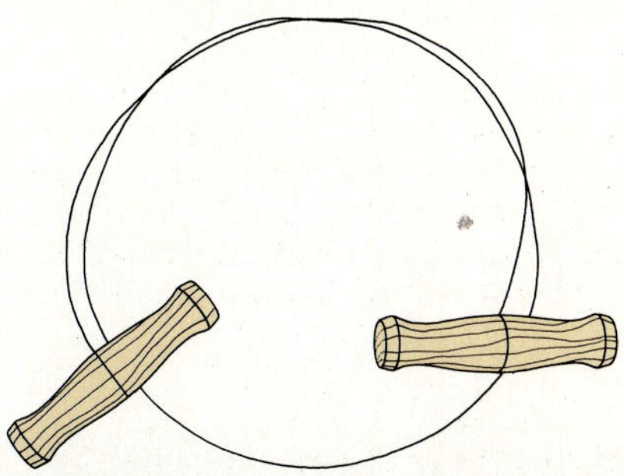

Traditional cheese wire will slit the hardest or crumbliest of cheeses. Hold the wire taut with its wooden handles and draw it through a Cheddar or a Cheshire.

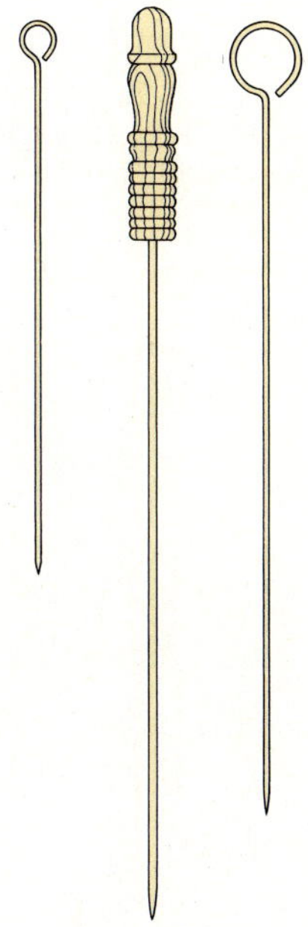

A selection of skewers. The wooden-handled Oriental skewer is ideal for kebabs.

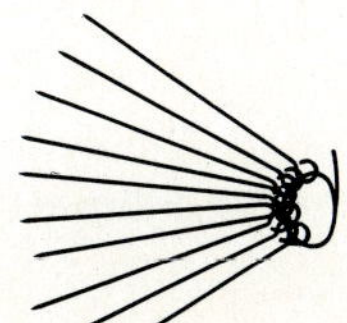

Set of ten stainless-steel poultry pins, useful for fixing loose wings and untidy pieces of meat, before putting the bird in the oven.

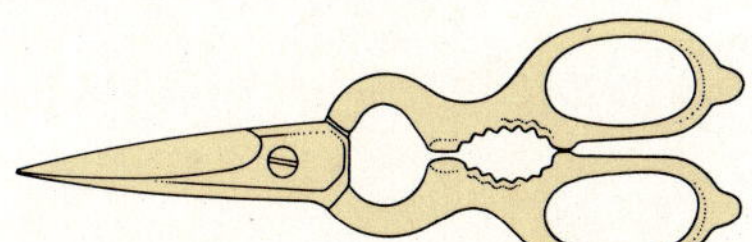

Tough kitchen scissors which can be dismantled for cleaning. The central ring is a most efficient nutcracker.

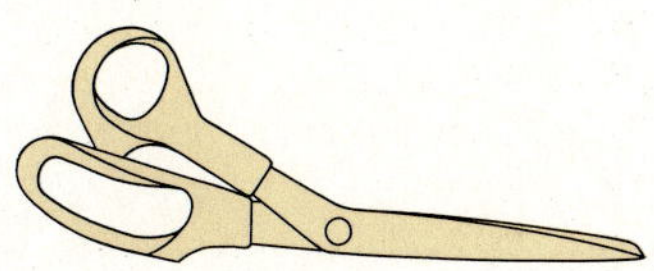

Right- and left-handed kitchen scissors, light and very comfortable to use.

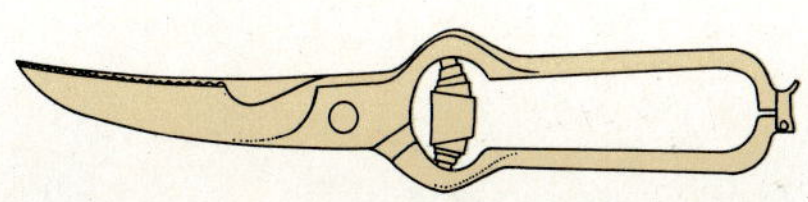

Spring-action shears for clipping through poultry joints.

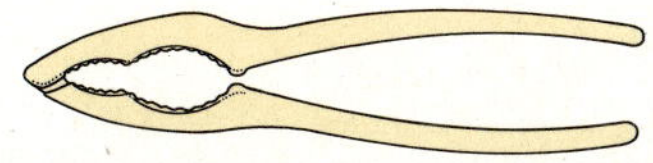

A sure and painless way to crack nuts or lobster claws.

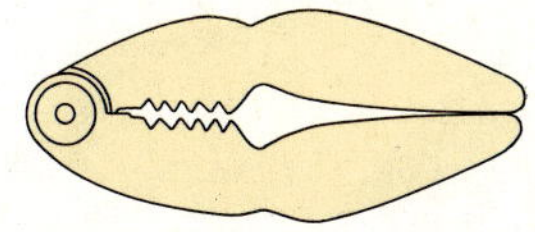

For cracking crab and lobster claws in the kitchen or at the table.

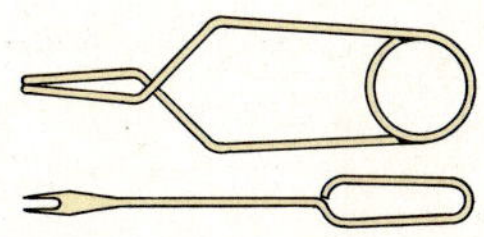

Snail tongs and spike for grasping the shell and spearing the flesh.

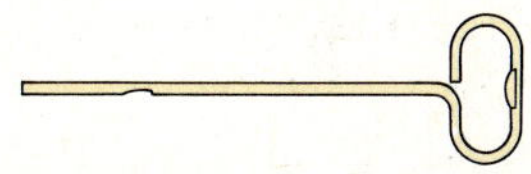

A giant replacement for missing openers on sardine tins, will wind back the lid of any sized can.

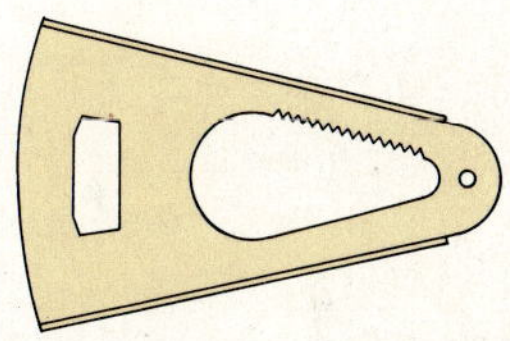

Bright enamelled-steel screw-top jar and bottle opener with can piercer.

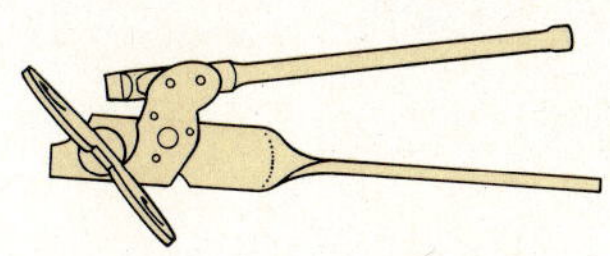

Can and bottle opener in one.

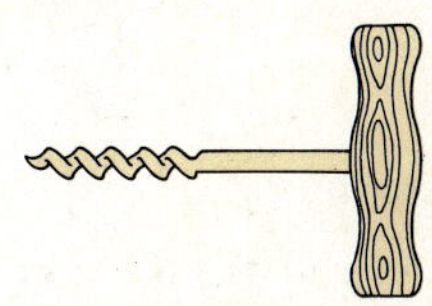

Simple steel corkscrew with wooden handle.

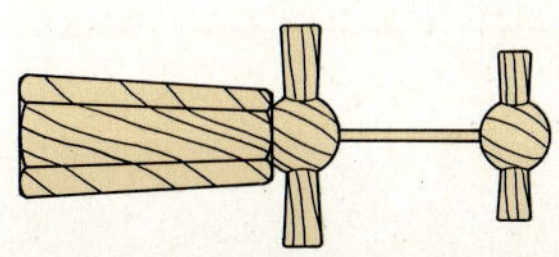

Boxwood corkscrew that fits over the cork. Screw in the top handle and twist out the cork with the bottom one.

Mixing and measuring

Preparing ingredients is often the most energetic stage of cooking. With well-designed tools waiting in the right places it can be creative fun; with inferior ones, badly maintained and inconveniently arranged it becomes a battle, a muddle and a chore. It's worth knowing where not to economize—buy good-quality tools—spoons that don't split for example, chopping boards that don't warp and mincers which do more than merely mush. It's also well worth recognizing that some irresistibly attractive gadgets do not answer one's actual needs and appear less attractive as they gather dust. Well-chosen, hard-wearing utensils are the means to rapid, confident and precise preparation.

1 *Avery Precision Scales weigh up to 2 lb (1 kg) in metric and Imperial.*
2 *Compact, attractive Terraillon scales in brilliant plastic. Five-pound ($2\frac{1}{2}$-kg) capacity weight in metric and Imperial.*
3 *Clear polypropylene measuring jugs. 1-pint (575-ml) or 2-pint (1100-ml) capacity.*
4 *Toughened glass measuring jugs. 1 pint (0.5 litre) and $\frac{1}{2}$ pint (0.3 litre).*
5 *Set of bright plastic measuring spoons—$\frac{1}{4}$ teaspoon to 1 tablespoon.*

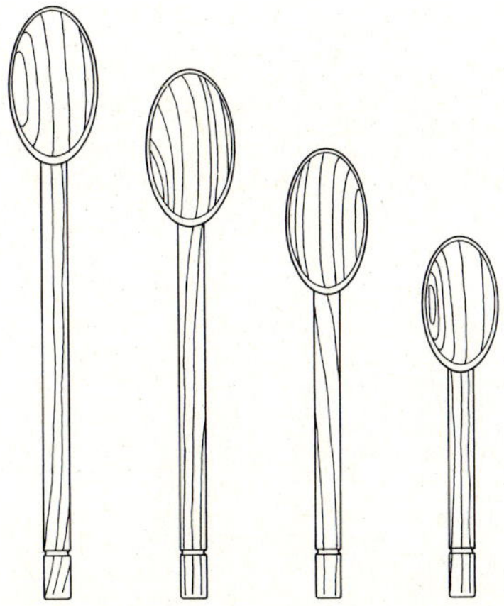

Selection of boxwood spoons, hard and well-seasoned enough not to split and splinter. Wood absorbs flavours, so the curry spoon should be kept away from the custard.

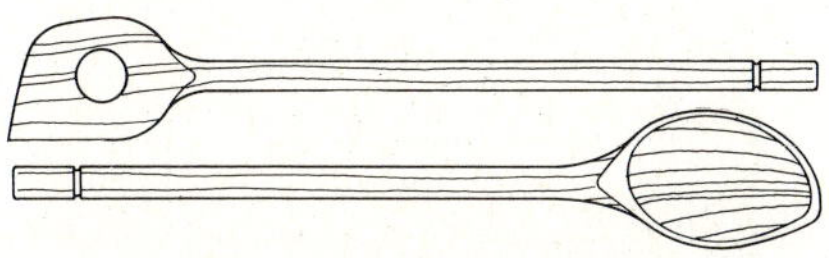

Beechwood spoons with pointed edges for scraping round the corners of pans. The one with a hole is for blending batter.

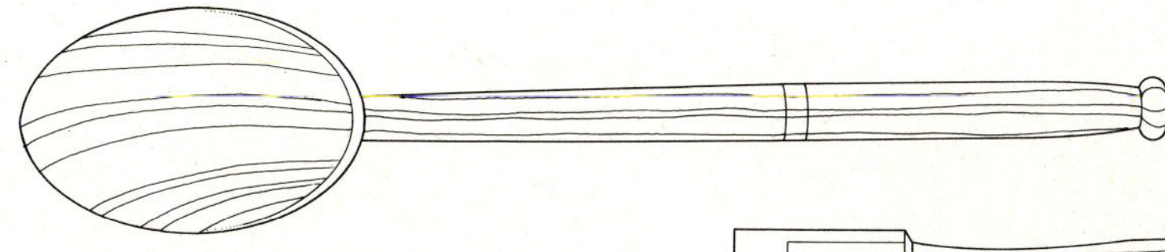

Large beechwood kitchen spoon for stirring large, deep vats of liquid.

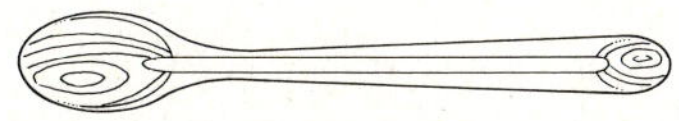

Olivewood tasting spoon. Liquid flows from one end to the other, cooling on the way.

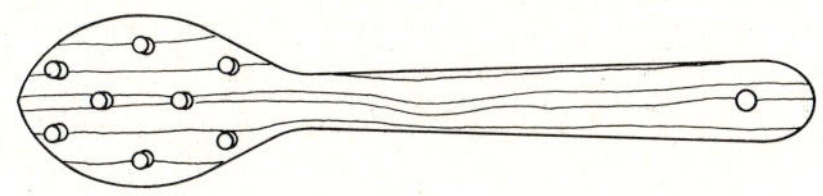

Beechwood spaghetti spoon. Threads of slippery pasta get caught in the holes.

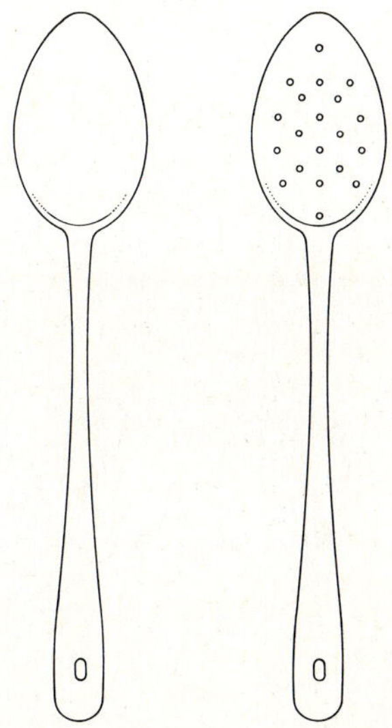

Stainless-steel basting spoons, one with small perforations for holding back crisp pieces of loose meat.

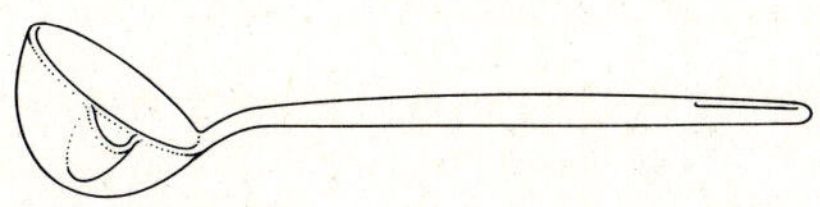

Aluminium ladle for straining off fat which rises to the surface and pours over the lip.

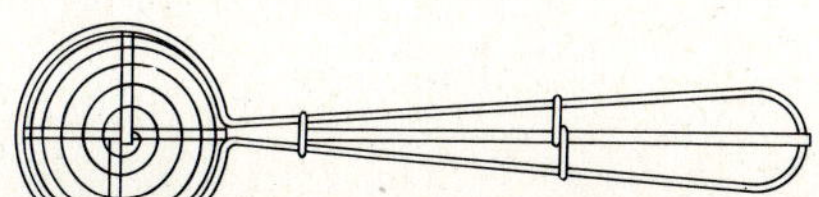

Wire mesh ladle for removing crisp chips from deep fat.

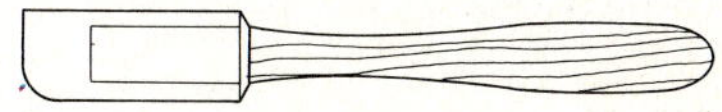

Last-lik kitchen spatula with a rubber paddle, scrapes every trace of mixture from mixing bowls and blender goblets.

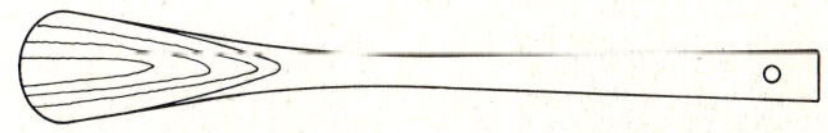

Boxwood spatula. The flat surface makes it better than a spoon for scraping sticky lumps of sauce back into the pan.

Little sieve for tea leaves, coffee grounds or for straining corked wine.

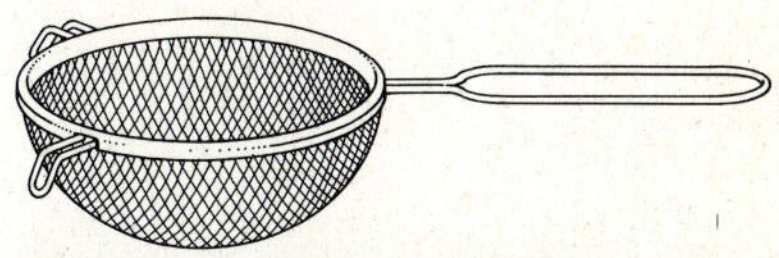

Tinned mesh wire sieve, strong enough for masking and puréeing cooked fruit and vegetables as well as for straining liquid.

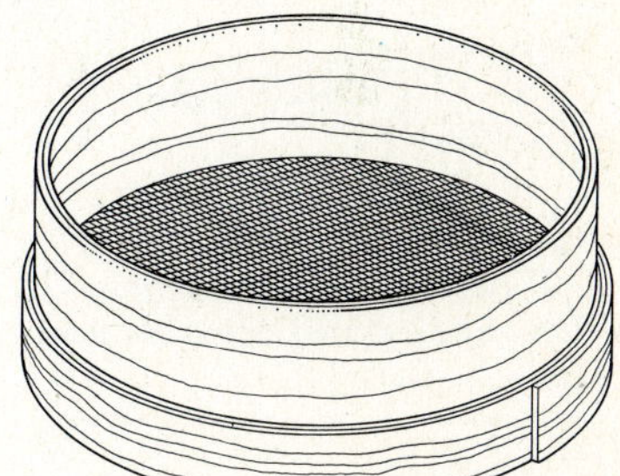

Cook's sieve, tight as a drum for sifting mounds of flour or mushing large amounts of cooked fruit and vegetables.

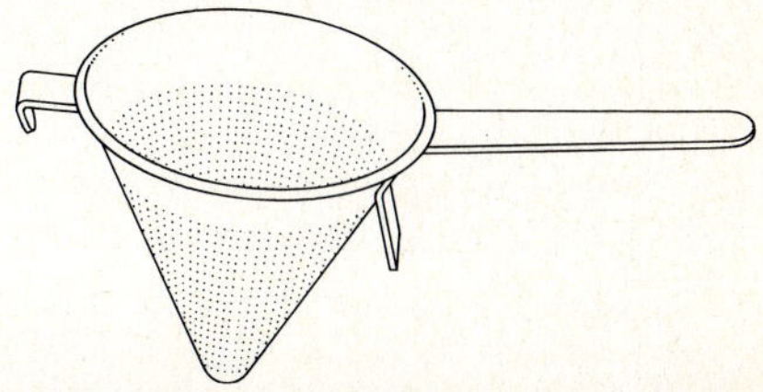

Stainless-steel chinois or sieve used for straining stocks and sauces. The conical shape controls the flow of liquids.

Mixing and measuring

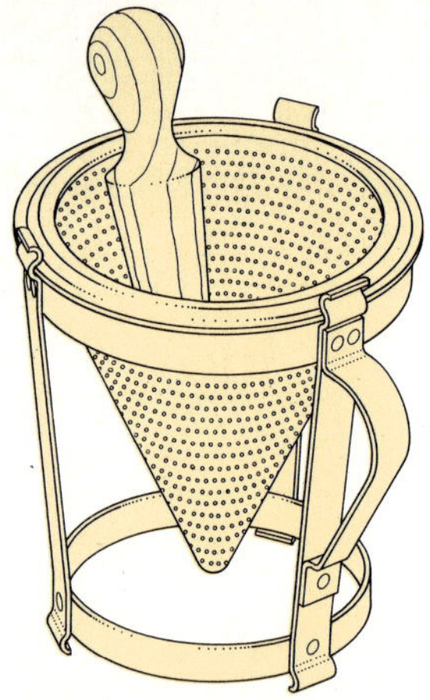

Tin-plated chinois with its own stand. It is sturdy enough to resist the pressure of the pointed pestle, which pushes food through its perforated cone. Produces medium-textured purées.

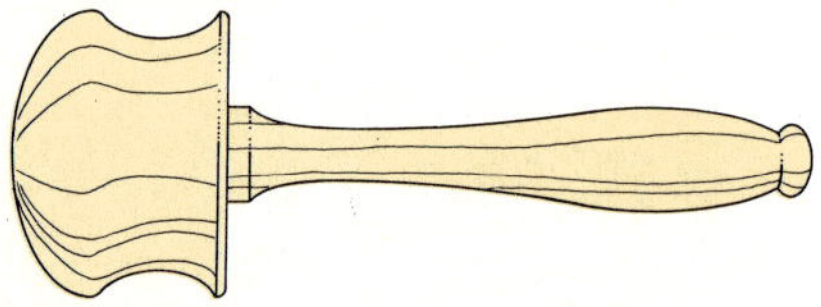

French champignon made of polished beechwood. The "mushroom" pusher works against the coarse mesh of a sieve and pulverizes soft fruit and vegetables.

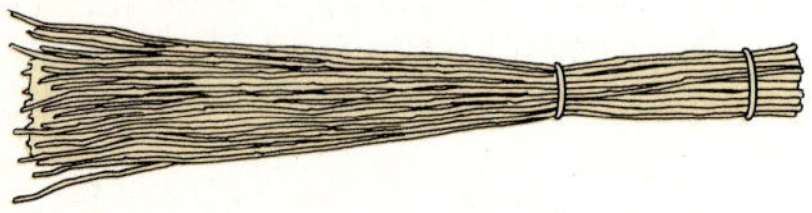

Birch whisk, a primitive but effective way to blend. The stiff twigs make sauces glossy, they never scratch the surface of the pan and are easy to rinse clean.

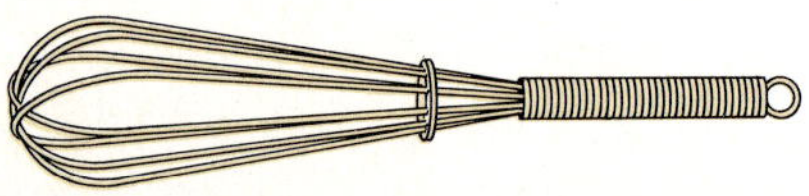

Light wire whisk with coiled wire handle, for beating batter and turning egg whites into airy foam.

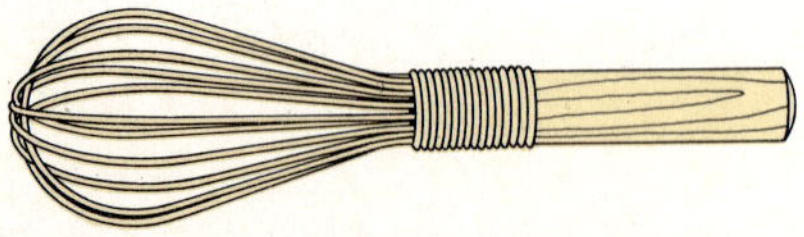

Balloon whisk—a bulbous cage of wires quickly and easily beats the most voluminous mounds of egg white, especially when used with an untinned copper bowl.

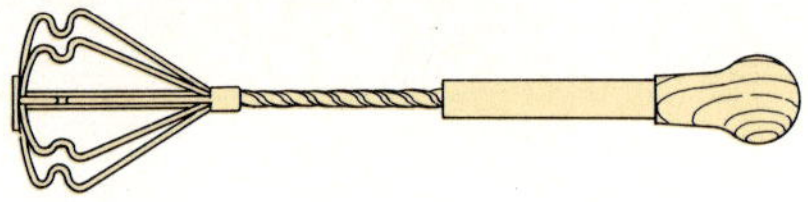

Spinning top whisk whips a dollop of cream or froths a milkshake.

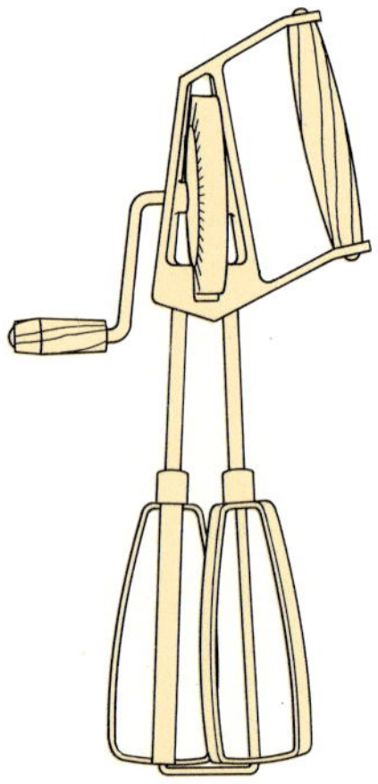

Rotary whisk with stainless-steel blades, an effortless way to aerate egg whites and stiffen double cream.

Wire basket for swinging the salad dry—but you need plenty of space.

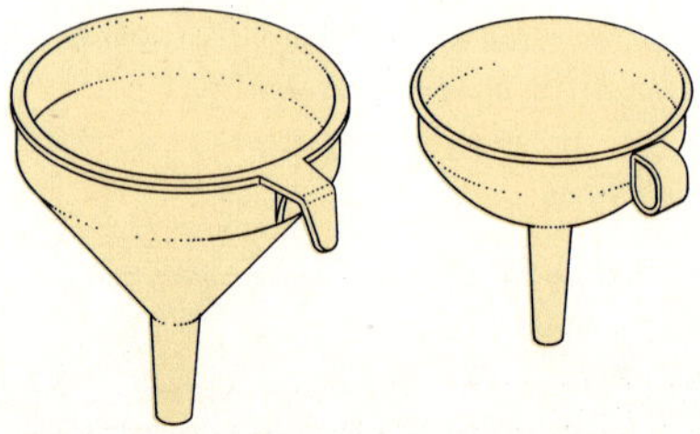

Polythene and stainless-steel kitchen funnels.

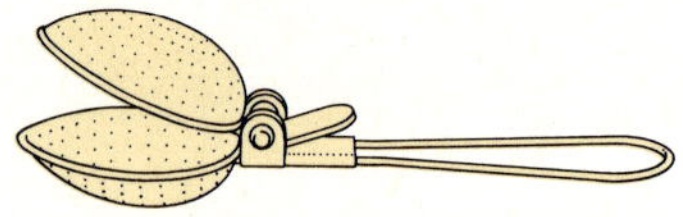

For the single cup of tea, a chromium-plated infuser to hold the tea leaves.

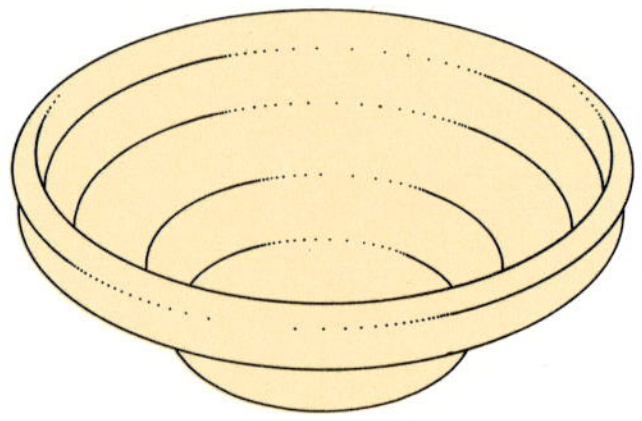

Glazed ceramic egg separator. The white flops through the slit, the yolk slides to the bottom of the bowl.

Thick beech chopping board mellows as it matures if it is nourished with olive oil.

Striped chopping board made of alternating walnut and ash and stabilized by rubber feet.

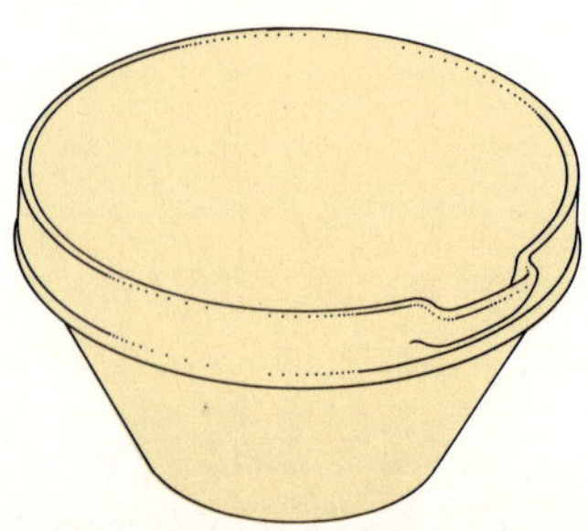

For accurate pouring, a stoneware mixing bowl with a lip.

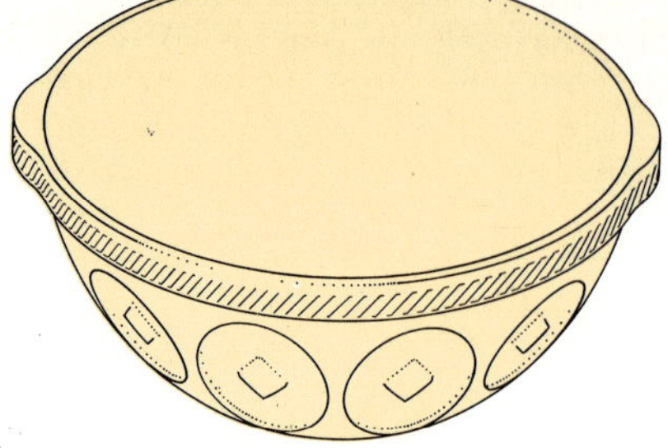

Traditional English mixing bowl in glazed, buff and white ceramic. A flattened surface on its side allows it to be held steady at a tilt—a convenient angle for beating.

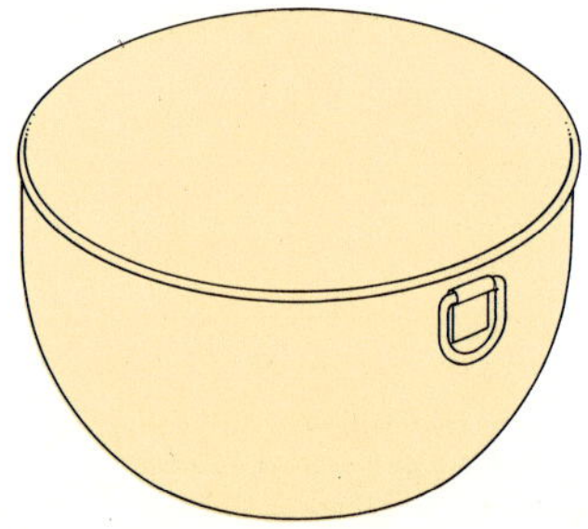

Stainless-steel mixing bowl, pristine, shiny and indestructible. Use with a wooden spoon for quieter whipping and whisking.

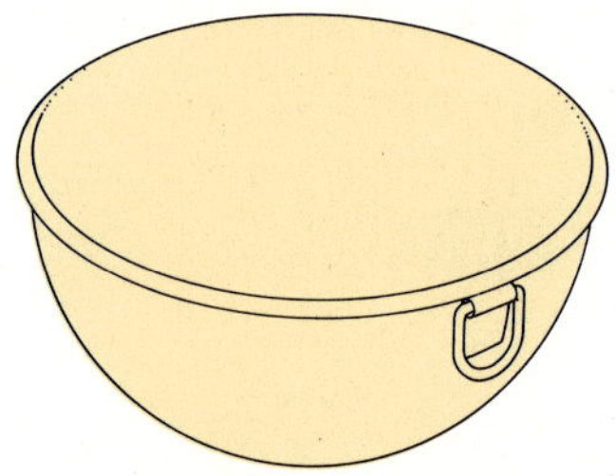

Untinned copper egg bowl. The ideal vessel to use with a balloon whisk for whipping billows of egg white.

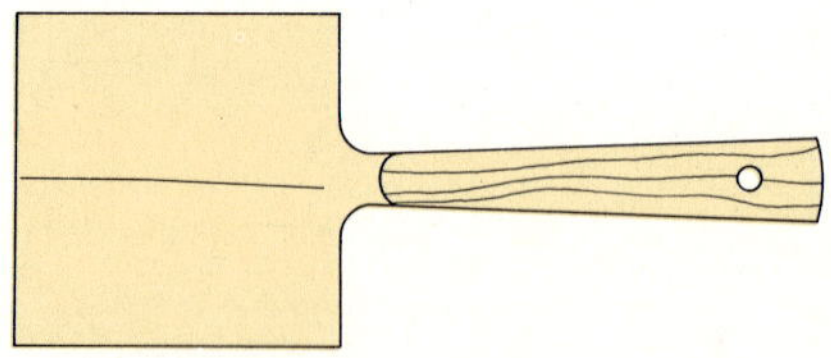

Hefty carbon-steel pounder with razor edges for flattening meat and then trimming it.

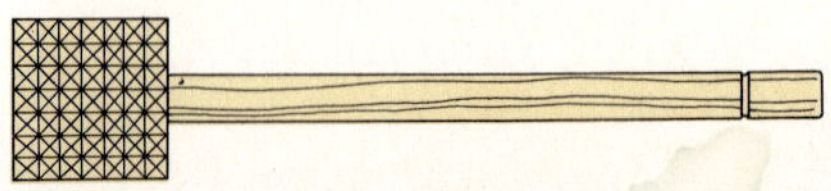

Beechwood hammer. Notched sides tenderize tough meat, smooth ones slap it flat.

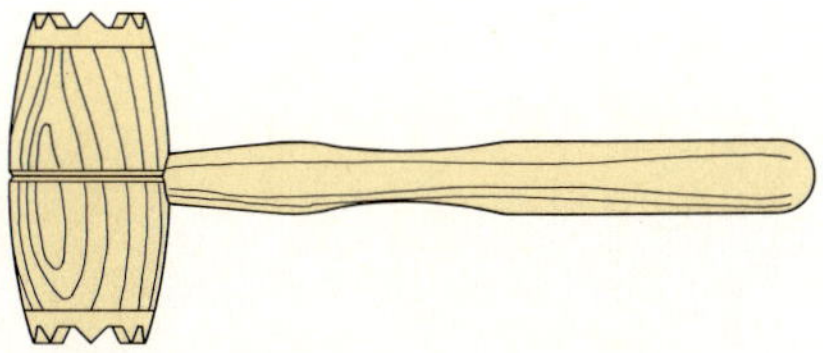

Varnished sycamore meat pounder with metal notches from which the remnants can easily be extracted.

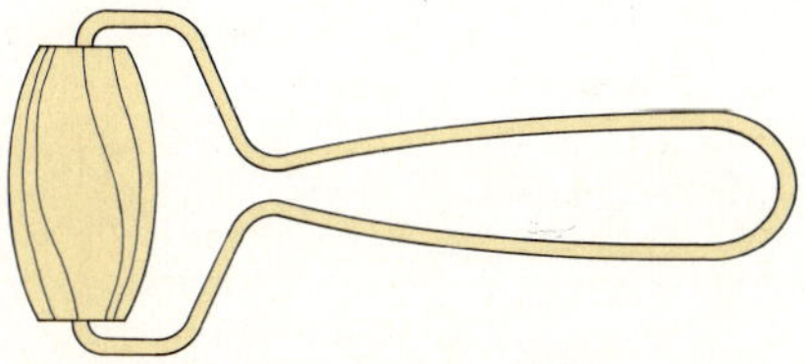

Fruit and vegetable press with a wooden roller for wheeling around the sieve.

Pestle and mortar, in hard, pure white porcelain. The end of the pestle is unglazed to grind with greater friction.

Olivewood pestle and mortar with a deep bowl to prevent spillage. Ideal for seeds and spices, moister mixtures will gradually seep into the wood.

Citrus squeezer. The inner dome is for lemons; its clear plastic cover for oranges.

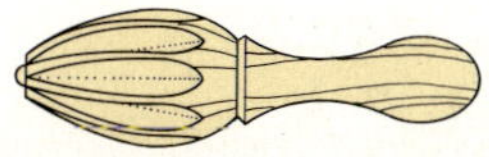

Traditional English beechwood squeezer, for screwing the juice out of half lemons.

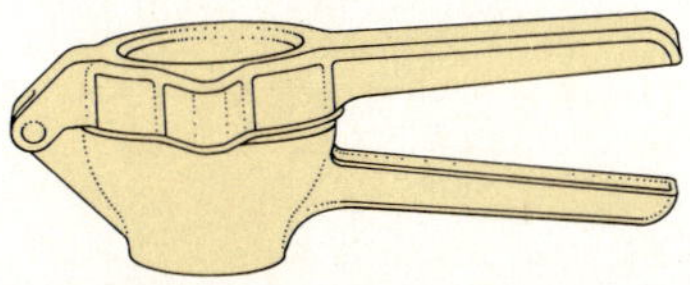

Aluminium squeezer clamps down on lemons and oranges and extracts oil from the skins as well as juice from the flesh.

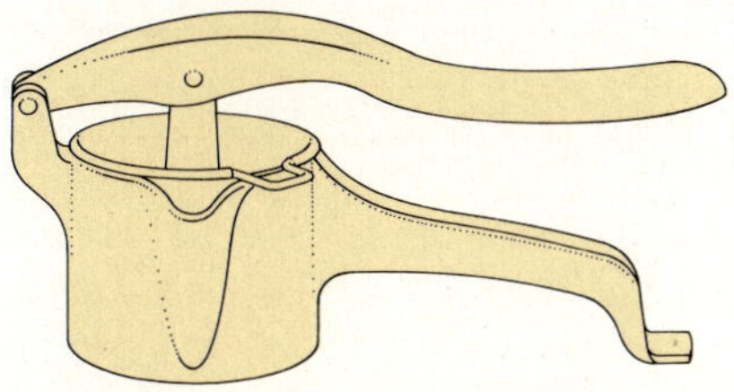

Simplex juice press will encompass a half-grapefruit.

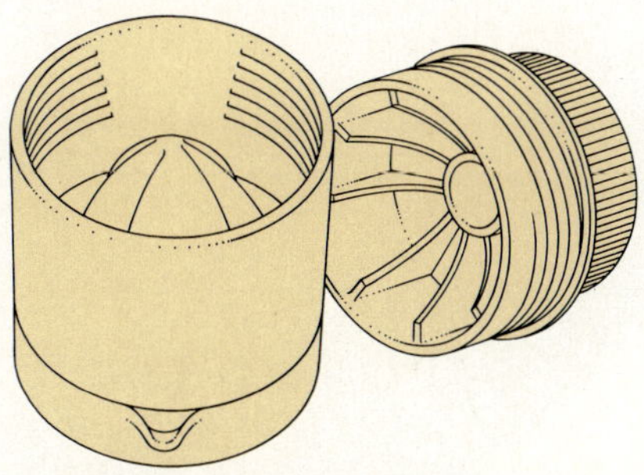

Plastic lemon squeezer with a lid to help you screw down the fruit.

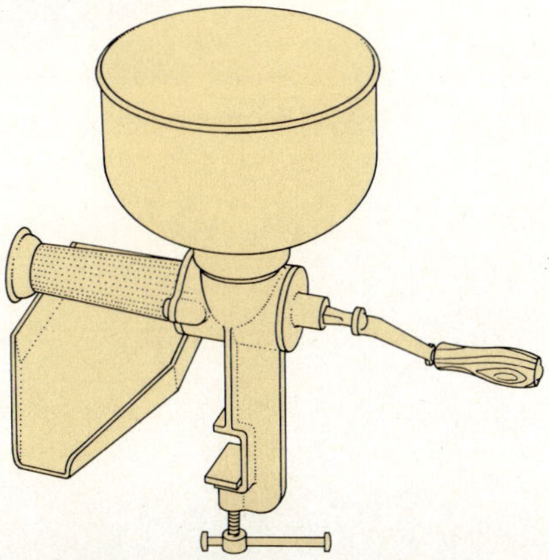

Tomato juicer and pulper. Smooth juice streams into the chute and skins are expelled through the end of the cone.

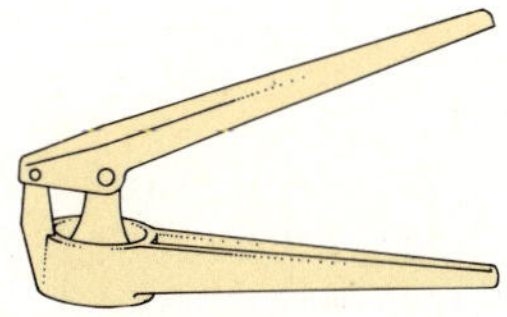

Susi garlic press. The aluminium "foot" squashes both peeled and unpeeled cloves.

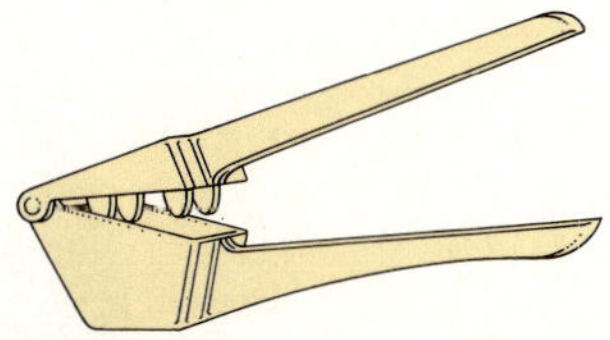

Aluminium ice-crusher with teeth that smash cubes into splinters.

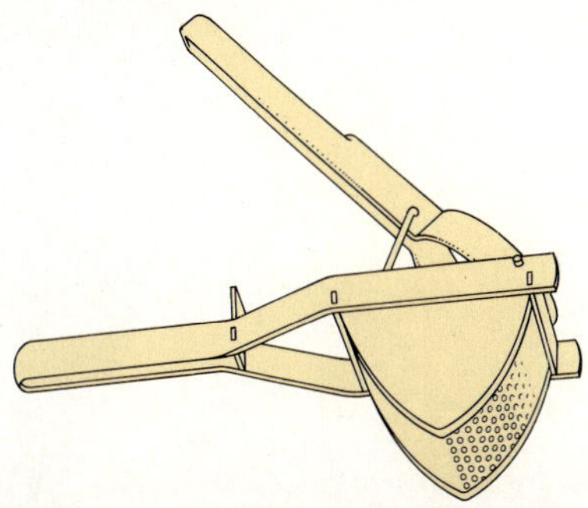

Potato ricer squeezes boiled potatoes into a smooth mash.

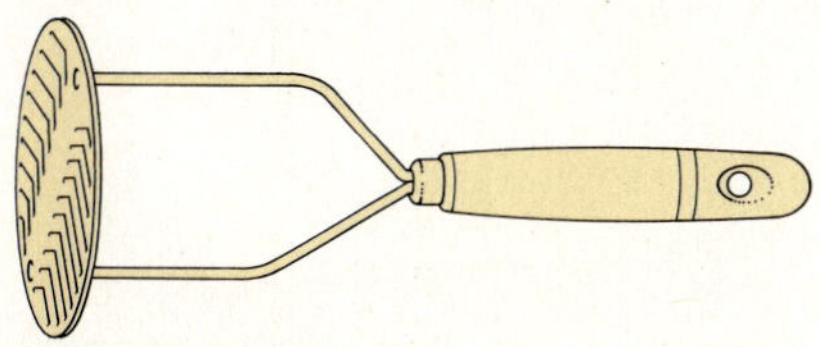

Chrome-plated Skyline potato masher squashes lumps as it is pumped up and down.

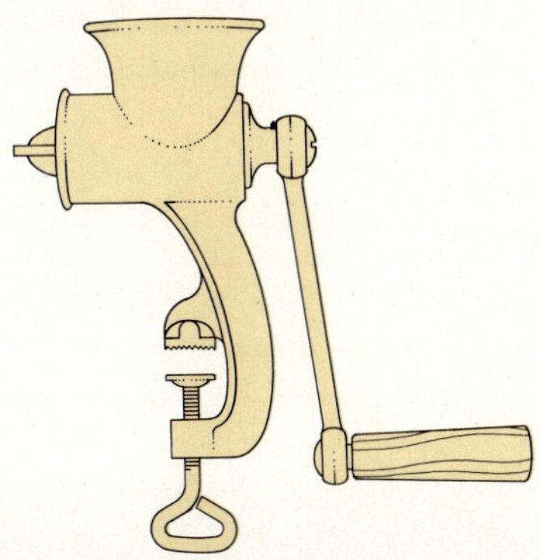

Spong meat mincer made of heavy iron. Clamps on to the table and won't budge as you grind up the gristle and muscle.

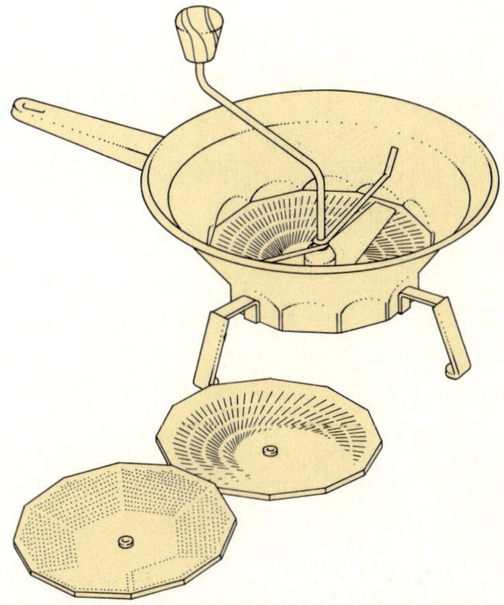

Mouli-Legumes fruit and vegetable mincer with alternative metal discs. The texture of the purée depends upon fine, medium or coarse perforations on the metal discs.

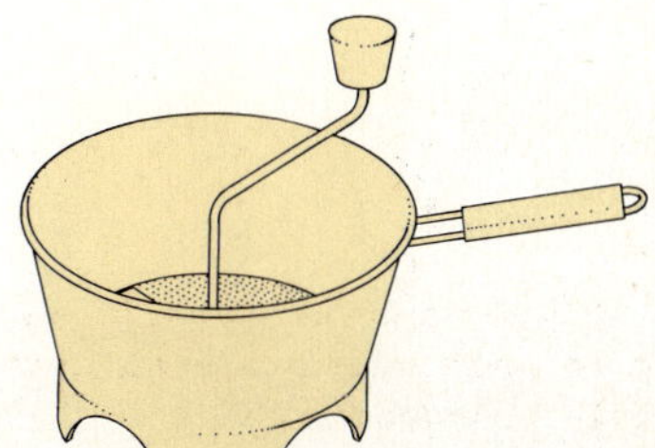

Mouli babyfood mincer, like the adult version, but a more economical way to mash smaller quantities.

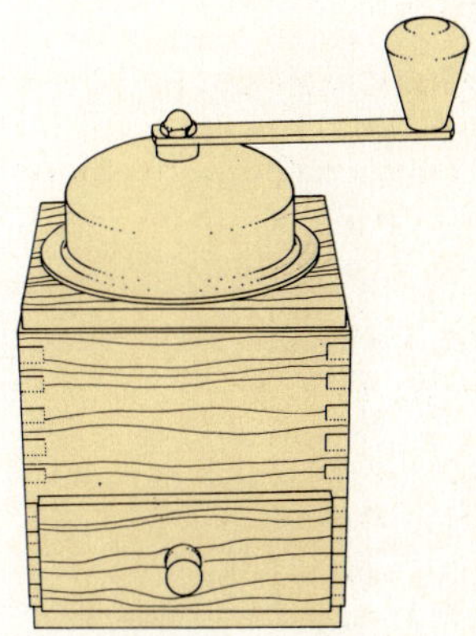

Classic wooden coffee mill with an adjustable grinder. The drawer holds four ounces.

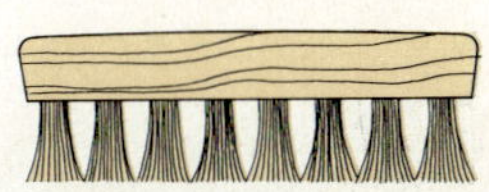

Wooden brush with nylon bristles for scrubbing potatoes, turnips and swedes.

Serving and presentation

Batterie de cuisine

Serving and presentation

Successful presentation can easily be kept simple. Good food is attractive enough not to need the enhancement of cut glass and fancy dishes. Simply designed, good looking bowls, jugs and moulds are easy to clean and neither formal nor informal. They fit in with all kinds of eating.

(Previous page). Food looks delectable against white. The porcelain pot is a perfect background to a dark-brown consommé.

Enamel coffee jug for the simple jug method. Throw in the ground coffee and add boiling water, then stir and wait.

Traditional French filter pot, recommended by Brillat-Savarin in the 18th century, is still an excellent coffee-maker.

La Cafetière, a quick way to make good coffee: sink the grounds with the plunger after brewing for six minutes.

Melitta coffee pot and filter. To avoid cool coffee stand the pot on an asbestos mat over a weak flame. Use finely ground coffee.

Melitta plastic filter; line with paper and balance it on the coffee cup.

One-cup coffee maker, an aluminium perforated basket with an inner lid to hold down grounds as you pour on the water.

The Ibrik, a long-handled little saucepan for making Turkish coffee.

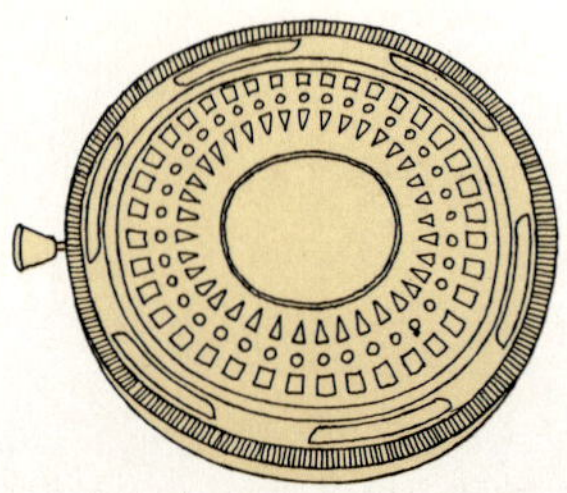

Stainless-steel food warmer, heated by candles.

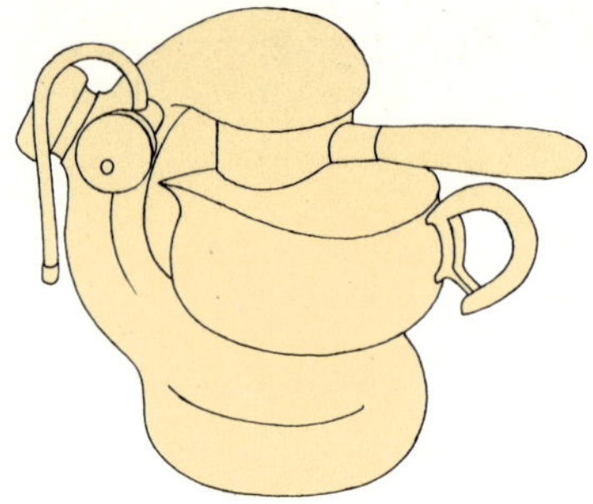

Shining, tubular stainless-steel coffee machine which builds up steam for espresso and capuccino.

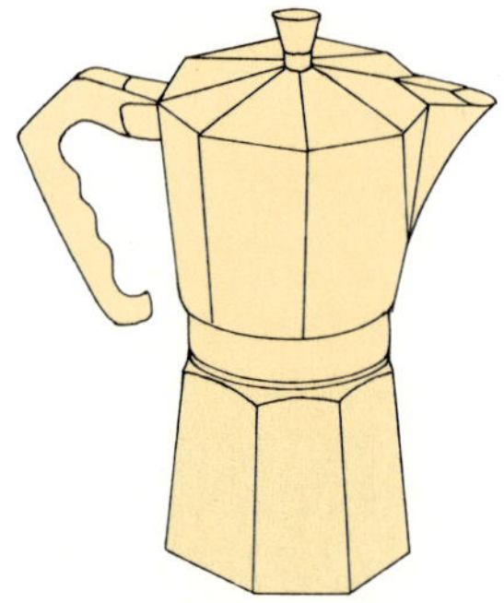

Espresso maker, a three-piece octagonal pot that holds the water in the bottom and the grounds in the middle. Water is forced through to make coffee at the top.

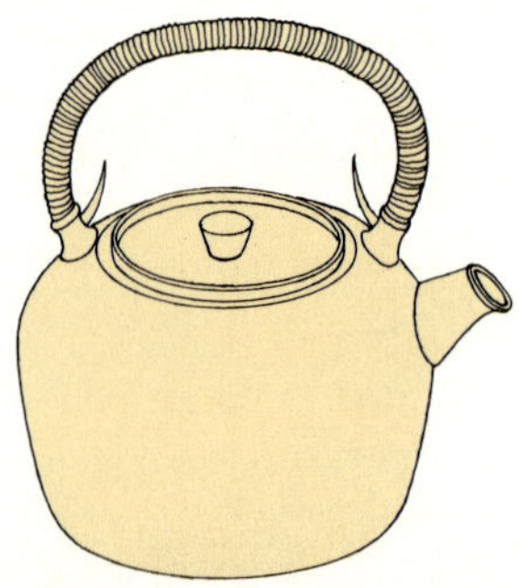

Dansk teapot made of brown-glazed porcelain. A short, squat pot which sits firmly on its broad base. Keeps tea drinkably hot for a long time.

Old-fashioned brown teapot for cosy English teas. Traditional and cheap.

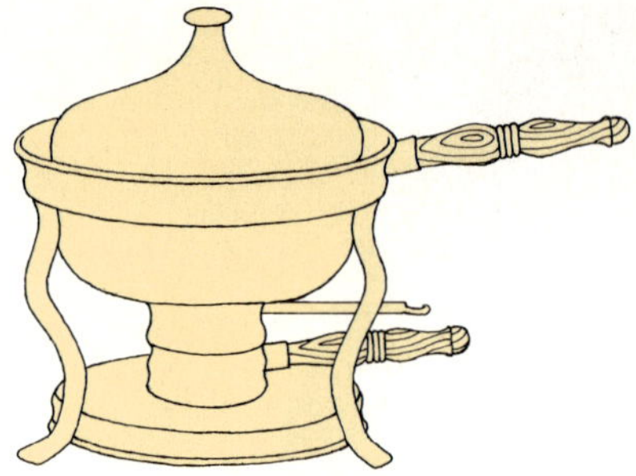

Copper chafing dish for cooking at the table, or keeping food hot.

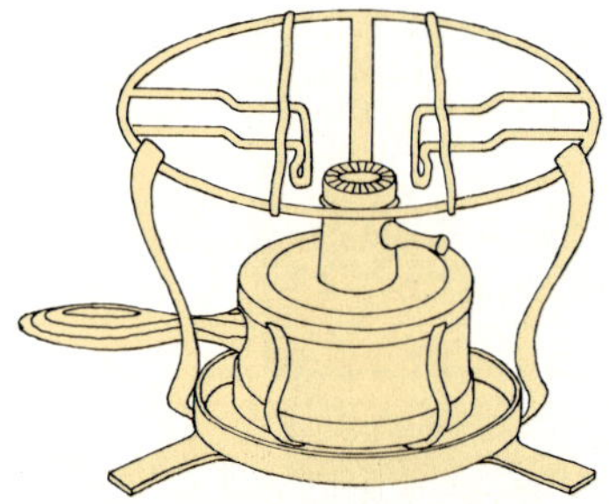

Alcohol burner for flamboyant chefs who perform at table.

Gourmet pot set made for the bubbling oriental fondue of meat slivers and vegetables.

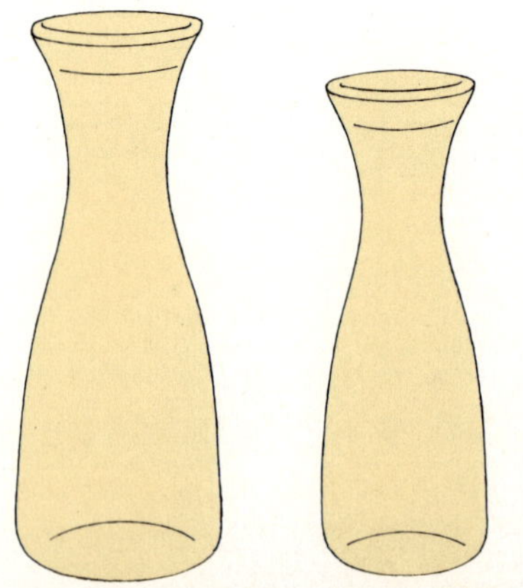

Clear glass carafes, with flared necks for easy decanting, show off the true colours of wine. Even cheap wines improve with decanting.

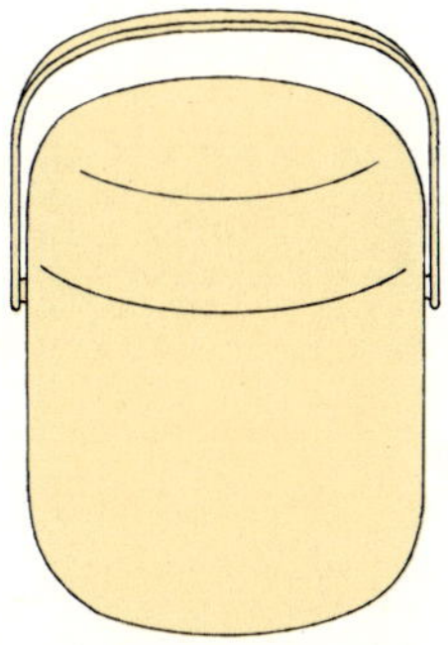

Simple, stainless-steel ice bucket, for hocks, champagne—and ice packs.

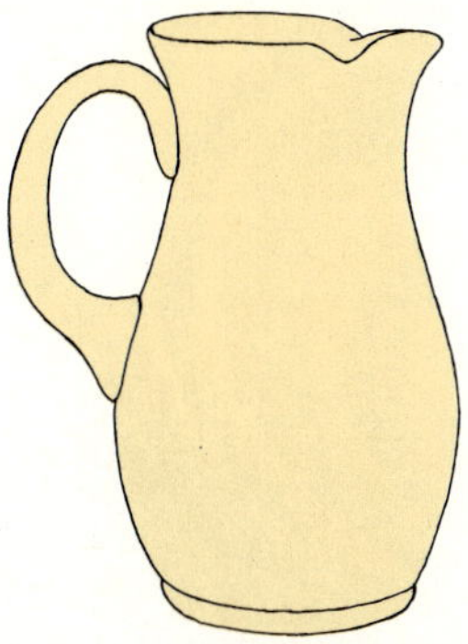

Glass water jug with a fluted lip to hold back the ice cubes.

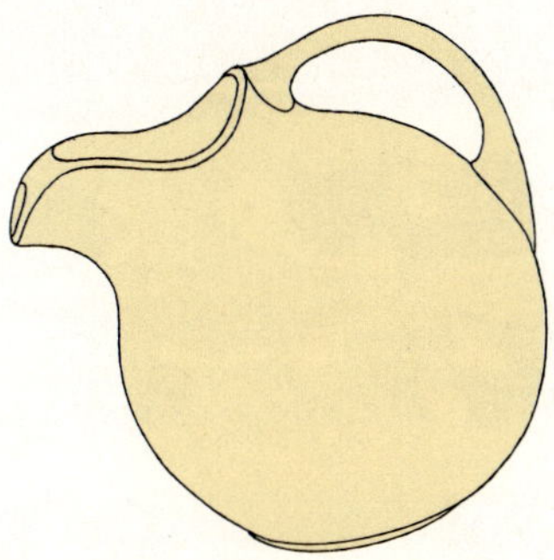

Ball jug; a china globe with a spout to prevent ice cubes falling out.

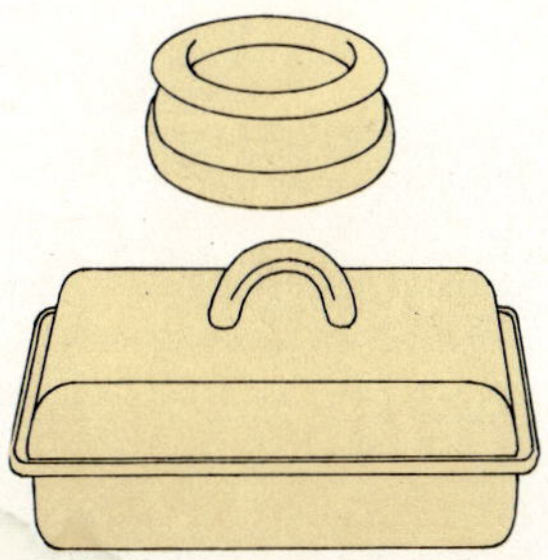

Stone pot for a small portion of butter; white china dish for half a pound.

Milk jug and creamer made of dazzling white china.

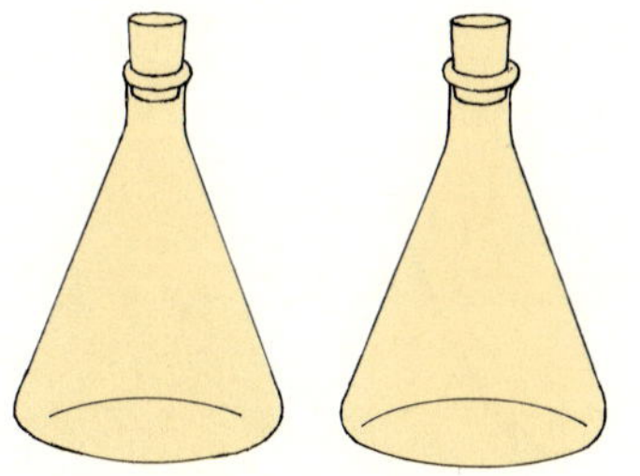

Cork-stoppered, laboratorial glass flasks for oil and vinegar.

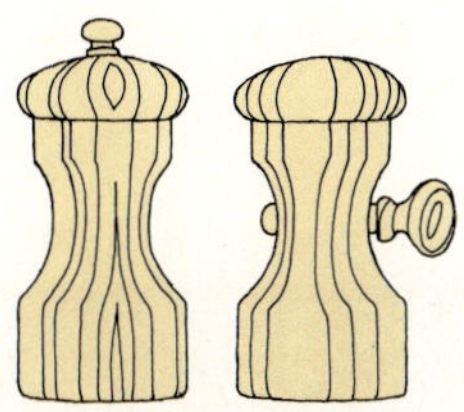

Olivewood salt and pepper grinders.

Pot and spatula for mustard.

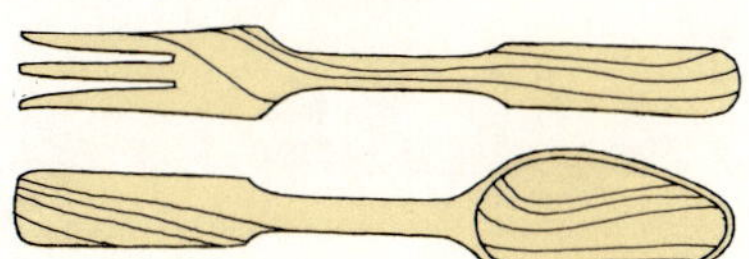

Beechwood salad servers.

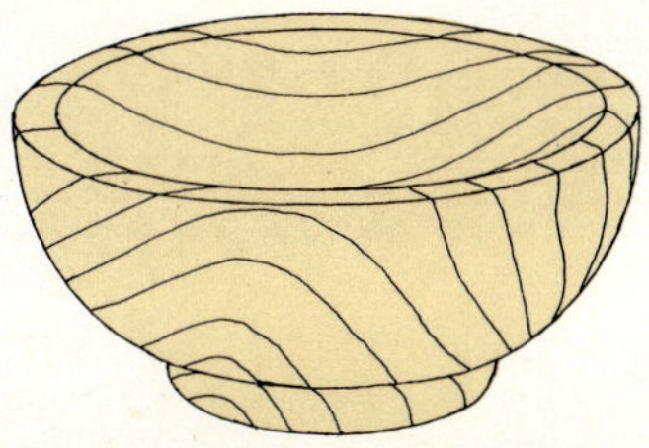

Elmwood salad bowl, not to be washed in hot water. Wipe it after use and nourish the wood with oil.

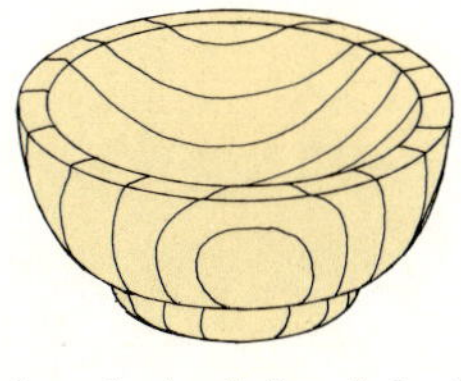

Individual wooden bowls for salads, rice and macrobiotic fans.

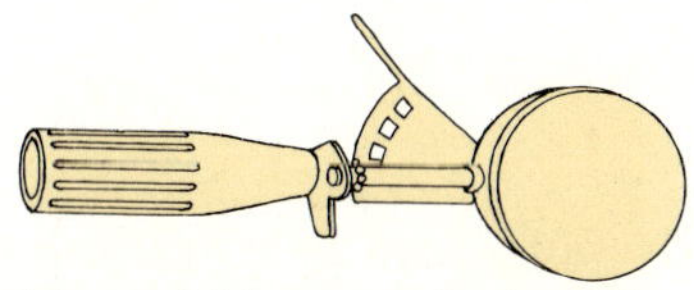

Stainless-steel Atlas scoop makes domes of ice-cream. Press the lever and the cutter carves out a perfect hemisphere.

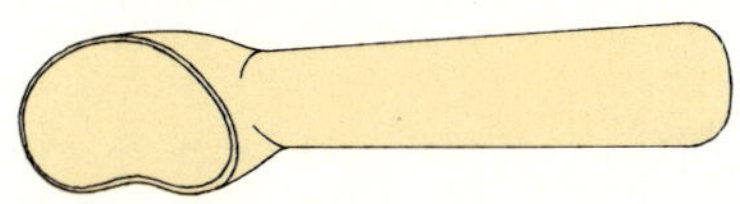

Scooping rock-hard ice-cream is easier with the Zerrol dipper, a warm spoon filled with antifreeze.

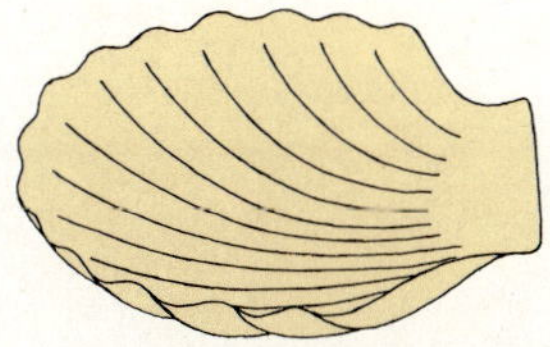

Porcelain scallop shell, a pretty white dish for gratinéed seafood which goes in the oven and under the grill.

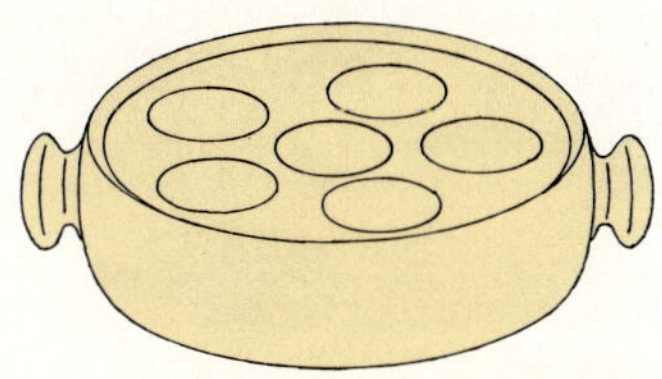

Escargot dish. Deep sockets hold shelled snails in the buttery sauce.

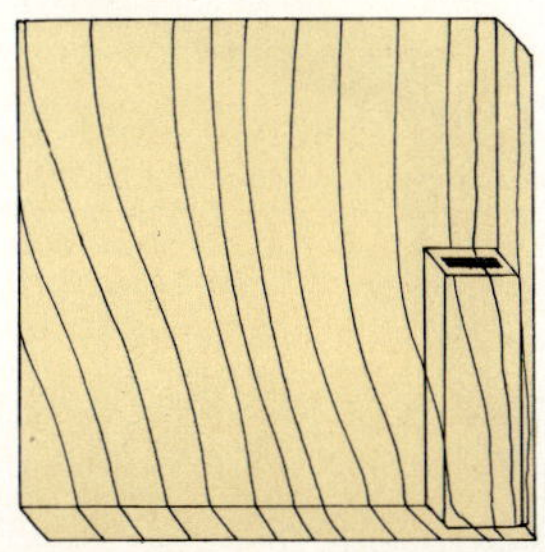

A slab of hardwood makes a good cheeseboard. The cheese knife goes in the side slit.

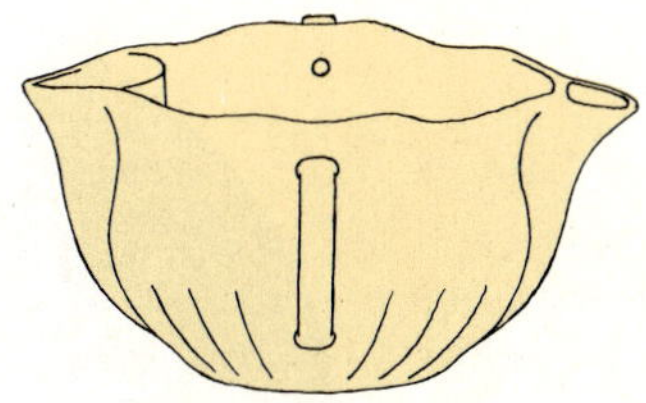

Gras-maigre gravy boat with two spouts for syphoning off the floating fat or the submerged juices.

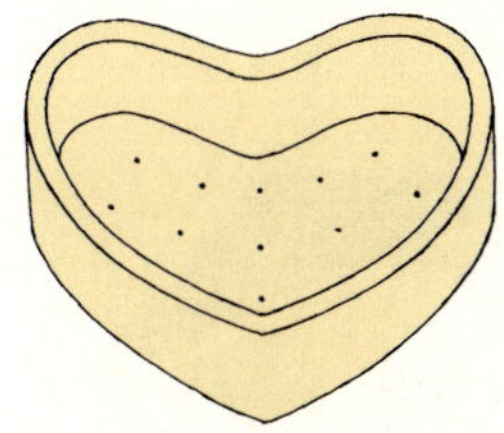

Porcelain heart for moulding the sweet cream-cheeses called cœurs à la crème.

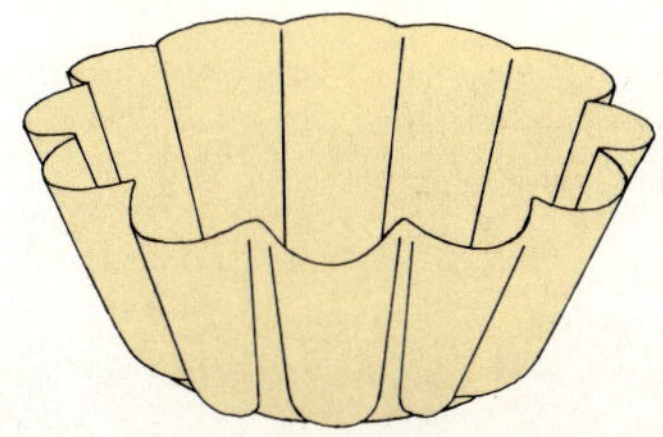

Aluminium mould for fluted gâteaux, creams and jellies.

Tinned steel ice-cream mould, adds a touch of baroque to an ordinary block.

Lightweight pine tray.

Baking

The life of the house once revolved about baking day. The tantalizing aroma, as the week's loaves, the pies and the cakes slowly gilded in the oven, would summon adults and children alike in expectant homage to the kitchen.

Though this weekly ceremony is now sadly neglected, baking still ranks high among kitchen skills. The apple pie, the rich fruit cake crammed with currants, the soigné soufflé that sends shivers down the novice's spine—all gladden us as much as ever. And even more delightfully, more and more people are rediscovering the joys of baking and eating their own bread.

Baking equipment hasn't changed much in principle, but pans, trays, dishes and tins are now made in materials that clean easily and don't stick. And refinements, such as removable bases, help the humblest home baker to experiment successfully.

1 *Glazed porcelain soufflé dishes*
2 *A shell-shaped bun sheet adds a touch of glamour to teatime entertaining.*
3 *Tins with removable bases and expanding spring-clip rims make cheesecakes manageable.*
4 *Individual rum baba moulds.*
5 *Plain bun sheet.*
6 *Pastry cutters.*

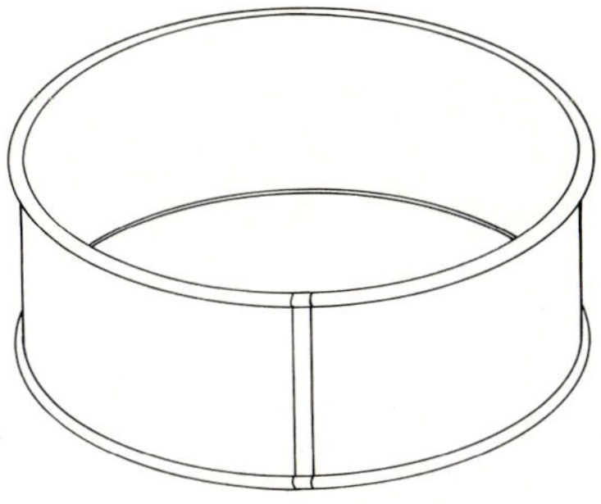

Large, round cake tin. Deep enough to bake a split-layer cake when oven space for separate sandwich tins is impossible.

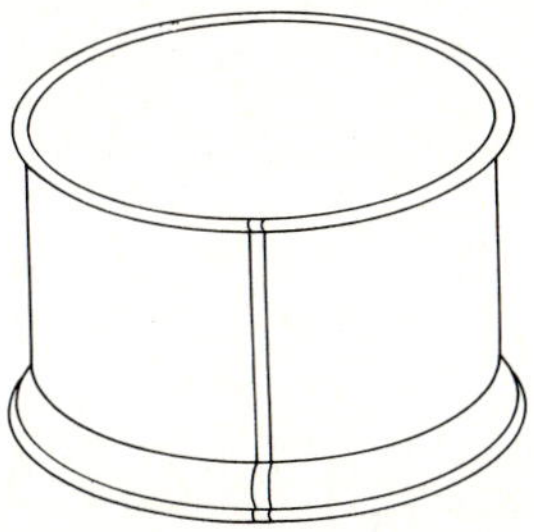

Deep, round cake tin with a loose, double base that both prevents cakes burning and makes them easier to remove when cooked.

Large, square cake tin, ideal for rich fruit cakes. Made of good quality tin-plate.

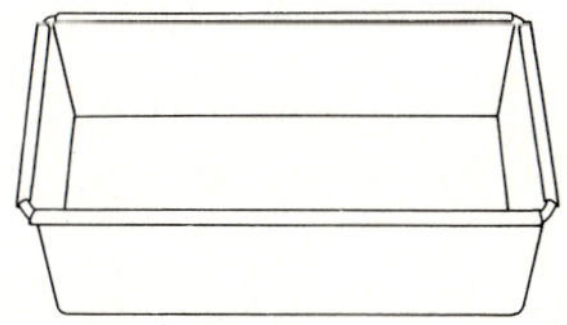

Square cake tin suitable for gingerbread, brownies or cakes iced on top.

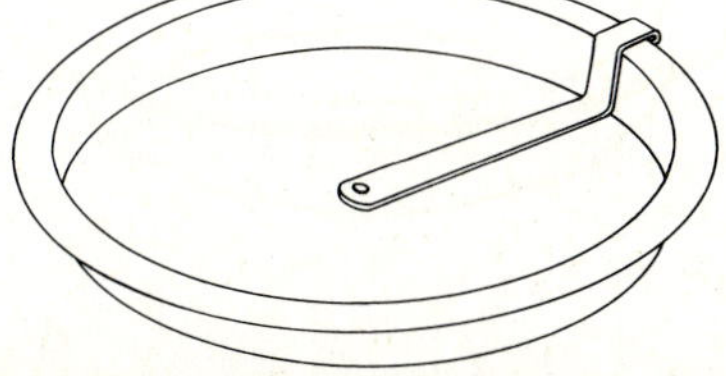

Sandwich tin with sliding lever ensures detachable sponges.

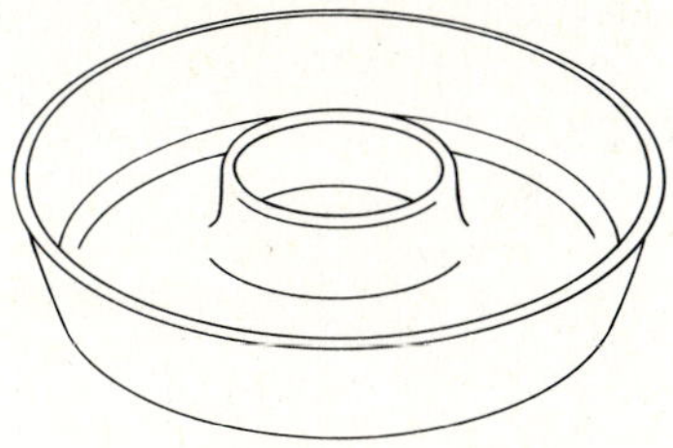

Aluminium savarin mould makes family-size rum babas. Also a good shape for cakes, puddings or cold savoury mousses.

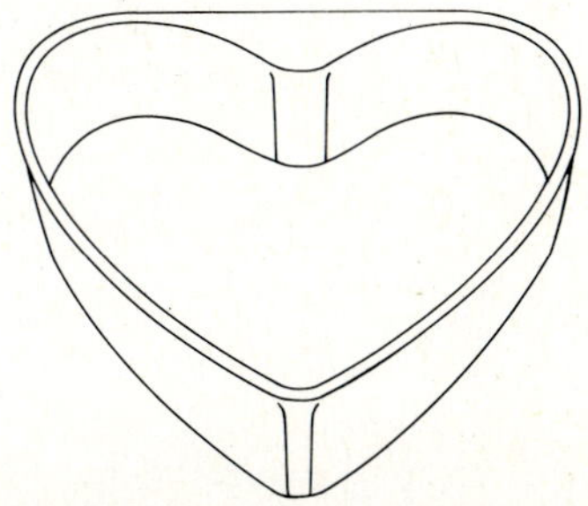

Heart-shaped cake tin turns St Valentine's Day and other sentimental occasions into a suitably romantic feast.

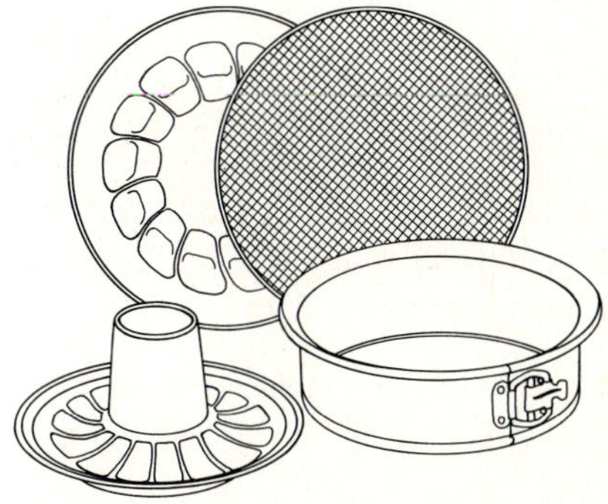

Three-in-one spring-form tin with spring-apart sides has a trio of separate bases for baking a variety of cakes.

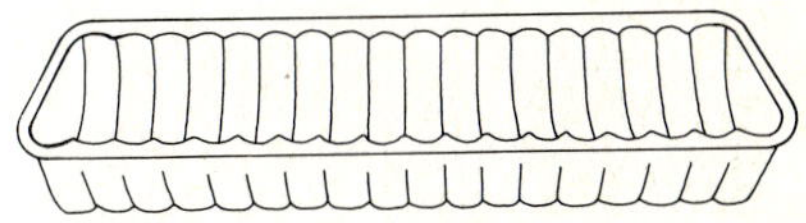

Ribbed cake tin with curved sides gives Yuletide logs or plain gingerbread and other teabreads some surface interest.

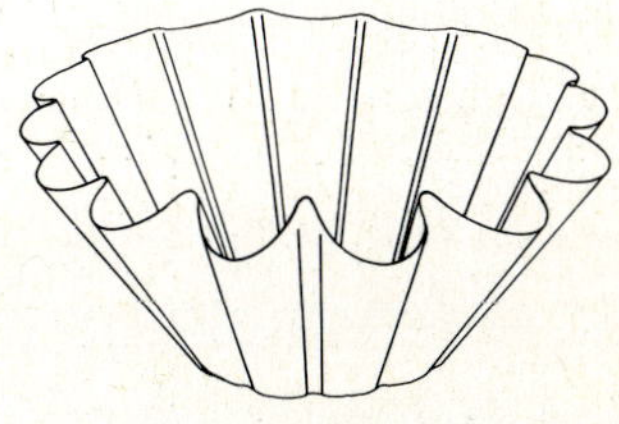

Aluminium brioche tin transmits the heat quickly to produce a crusty surface without drying out the dough.

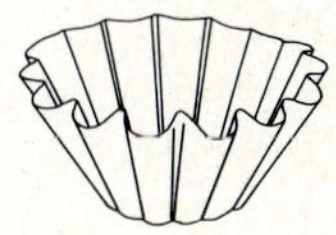

Individual brioche tin. Can also be used as a jelly mould.

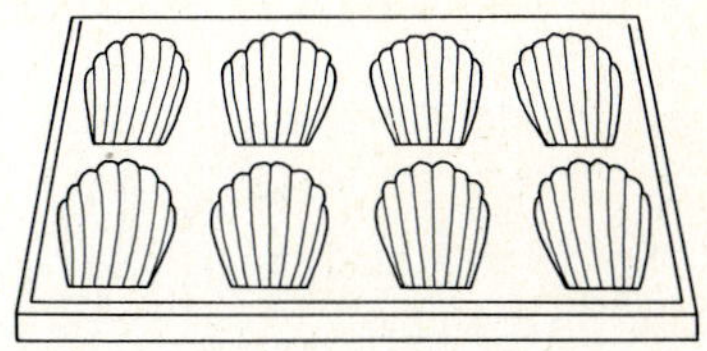

Patterned madeleine sheet makes a dozen small, light sponge cakes.

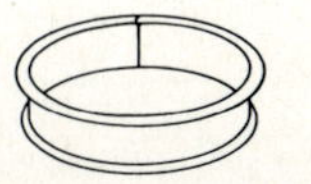

Muffin ring. Could be used for other confections such as buns, rolls or babas.

Baking

Stainless-steel baking pan. Useful for batter and other puddings or baking fruit.

Heavy aluminium shallow pan with 1-in raised sides for perfect Swiss rolls.

Square flan form for an alternative shape to savoury quiches or sweet flans.

Rectangular tinned biscuit tray for plain or fancy shapes.

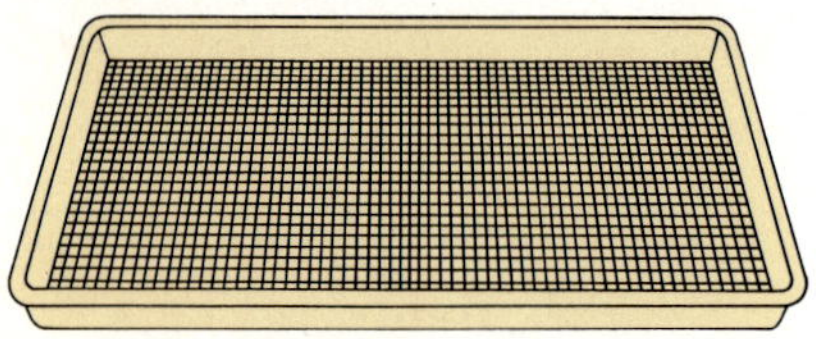

Perforated sheet for buns or rolls allows air to reach all surfaces during baking, then doubles as a cooling tray.

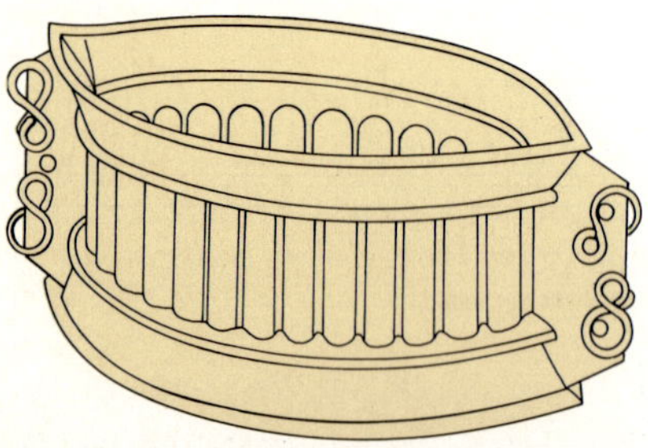

Tinned oval pie mould with removable sides allows a chunky game pie or pâté en croute to be shaped attractively.

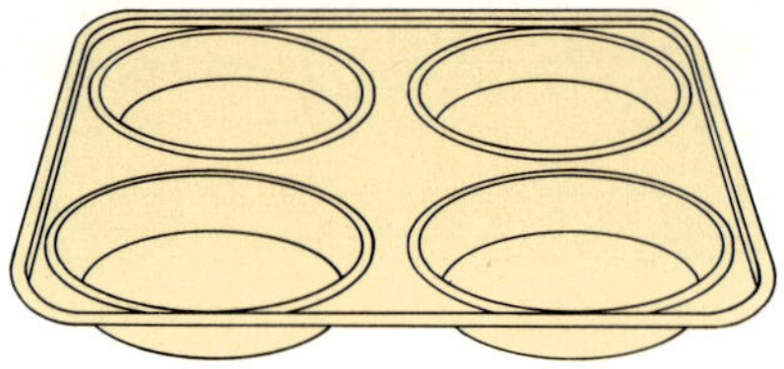

Yorkshire pudding tin provides four big portions of the beefeater's favourite batter pudding accompaniment.

Enamelled pie tin with a wide rim gives a good edge to latticed or double-crust pies.

Traditional English pottery pie dish. An oval dish with a wide lip gives good support to well-filled fruit or meat pies.

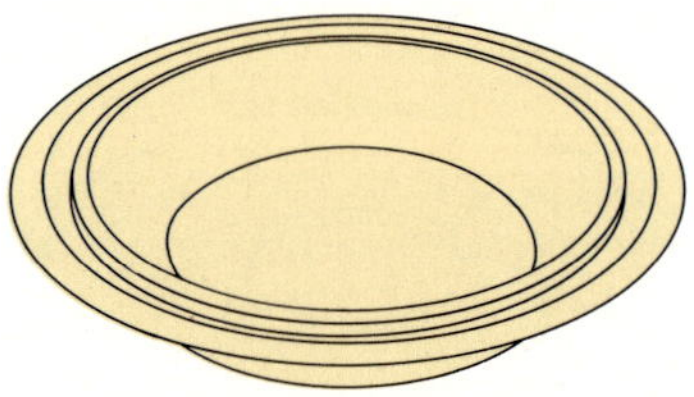

Stainless-steel pie pan with a wide, troughed rim prevents juices spilling out of the dish and spoiling the oven floor.

Rosewood-handled palette knife with blade of forged Sheffield steel, invaluable for easing out cooked flans, smoothing uncooked batter and icing cakes.

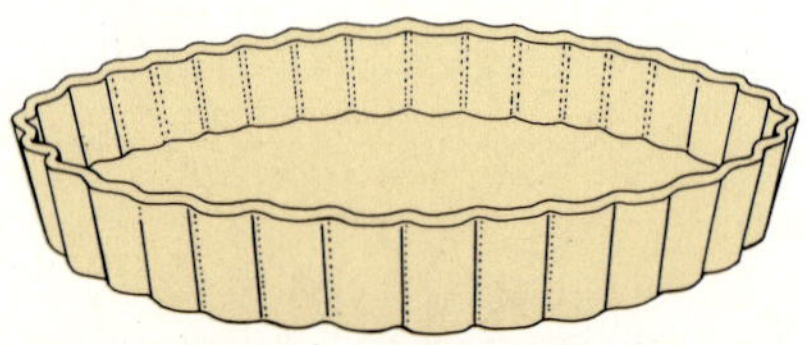

Oval crinkled flan dish in white ceramic is the perfect foil for both savoury and glazed fruit flans, and looks good on the table.

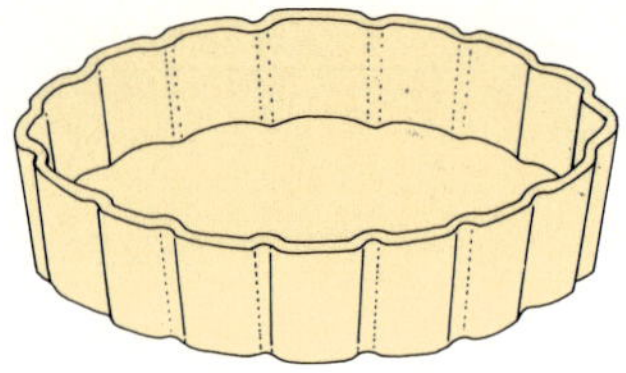

Deep, round crinkled dish for quiches, crème brulée or similar sweet delights that are taken straight from oven to table.

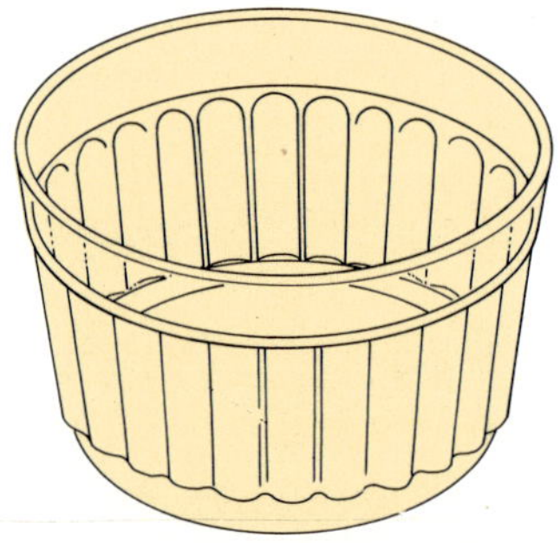

A touch of glass turns a soufflé into a visual triumph: hand-blown dish has fluted sides, but its plain lip is easy to grasp.

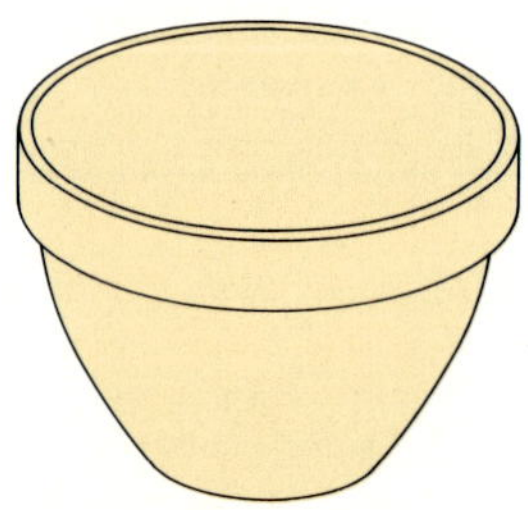

Stoneware pudding basin with dark-brown rim and interior, dull buff exterior. Perfect for rice puddings and custards.

Tinned dariole moulds for castle puddings or individual baked custards.

Pyrex loaf pan turns out crusty loaves. Glass cleans easily and conducts the heat well for even baking.

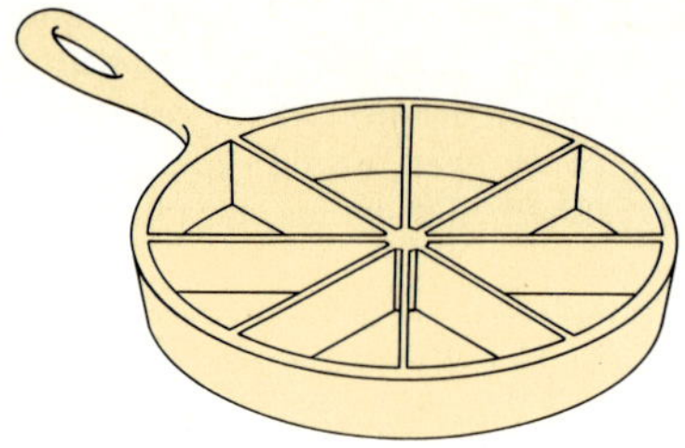

Heavy cast-iron skillet is the classic pan for corn bread, here divided into compartments for wedge-shaped slices.

Hinged rin with drop-down sides enables bread or pâtés to emerge unscathed.

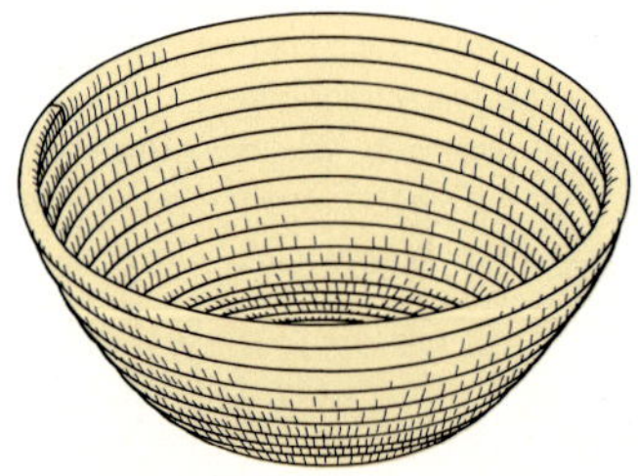

Banneton for raising bread. The reed basket imprints a pattern on rising dough, giving loaves attractive rustic contours.

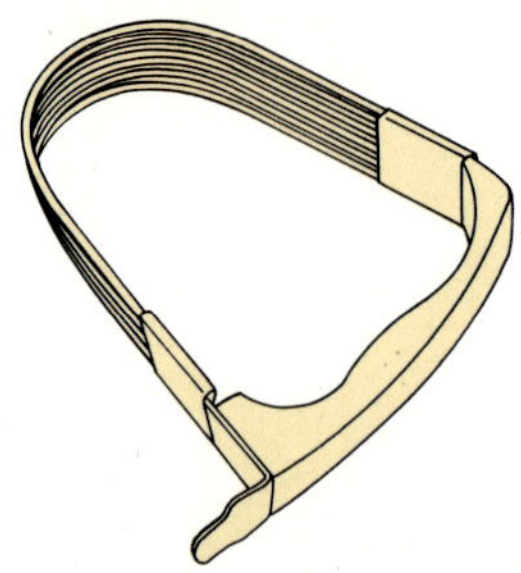

Plastic-handled pastry blender with stainless-steel wires scoops up stray flakes in the mixing bowl and amalgamates the dough.

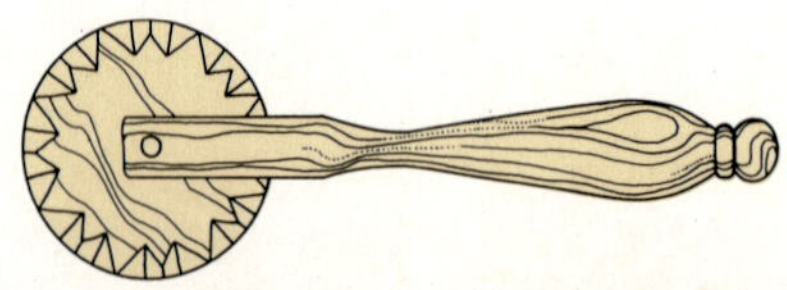

Boxwood pastry wheel gives a neat crimped edge, especially to lattice strips, and is also helpful for trimming ravioli.

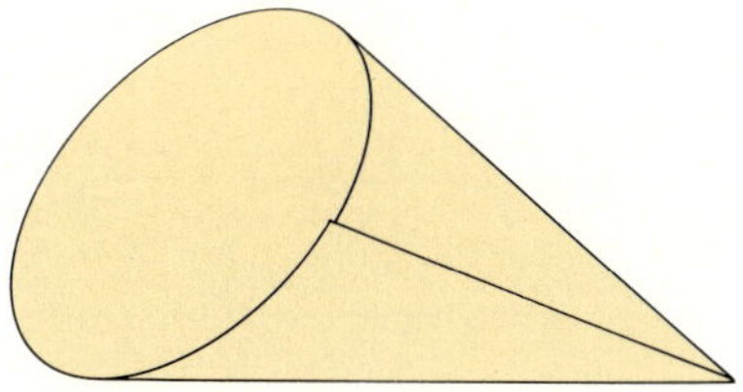

Tinned steel cornet mould. Shapes up pastry for cream horns, ham or salmon cornucopias for the buffet table.

Perforated flour dredgers. Handled beer-stein shape is made of lightweight tinplate; straight sifter has a wire mesh top and may also be used for sugar.

Chromium-plated icing set includes six nozzles and a syringe to cover cakes with a variety of fancy frostings.

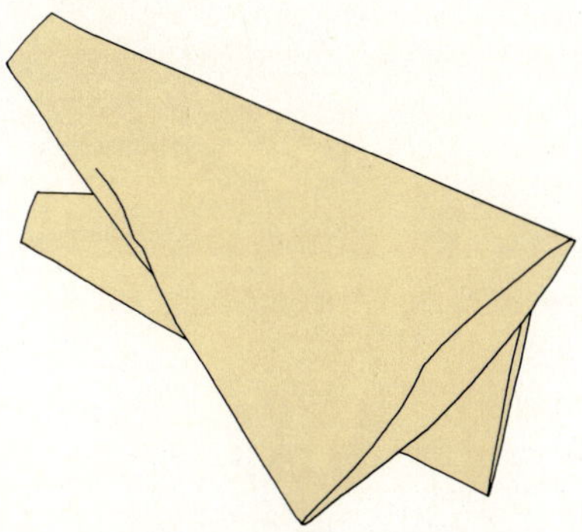

Nylon pastry bag for squeezing out dough responds to the slightest pressure. Dries quickly after washing.

Pastry brush with natural bristles and a wooden handle brings a gleam to pies.

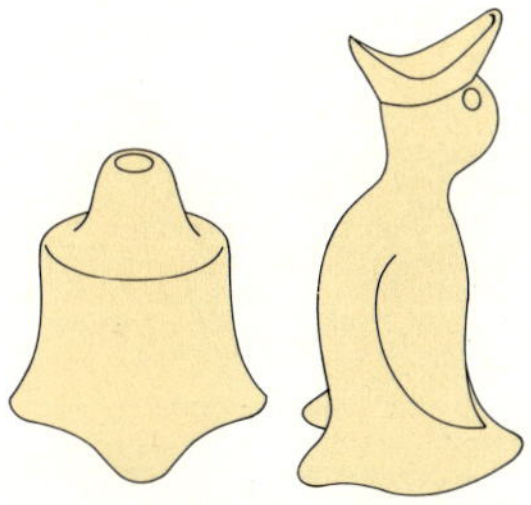

Pie funnels. A support for pastry lids during baking to prevent them becoming soggy; the singing blackbird ushers out steam through its wide open beak.

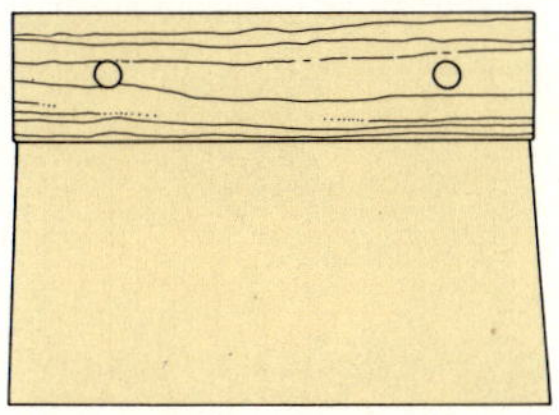

Wood-handled dough scraper in stainless steel helps keep pastry or bread dough in one piece during kneading, then makes a clean sweep of the sticky bits left on the board.

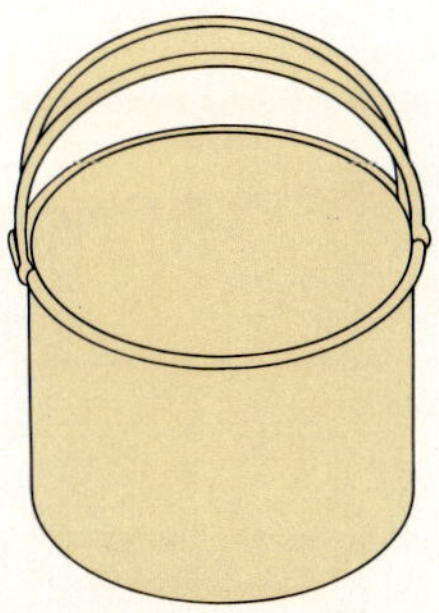

Biscuit cutter with an arched handle for plain rounds comes in two sizes.

Fancy-shaped cutters form gingerbread men, animal shapes and other children's favourites.

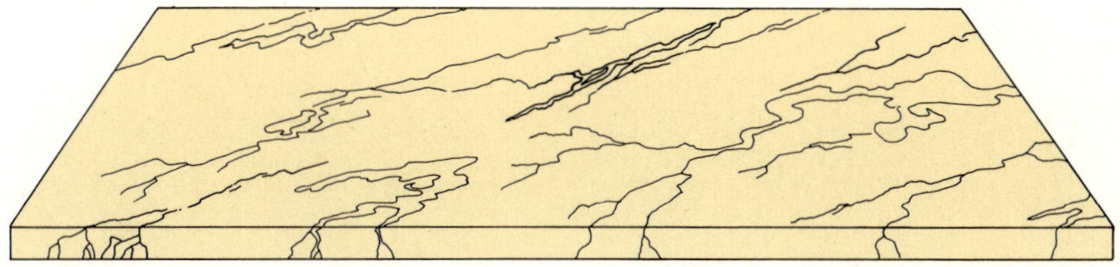

Finest pastry board of all is the marble slab. Its cool surface never absorbs fats; its good looks always delight.

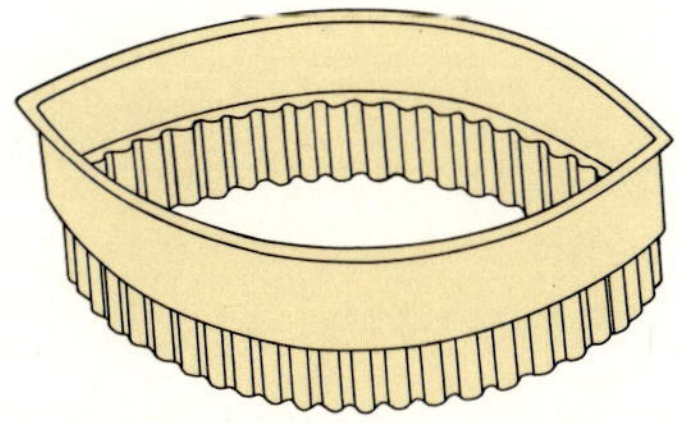

Oval cutter of heavy tinned steel makes a clean job of slicing through puff pastry for immaculate vol-au-vents.

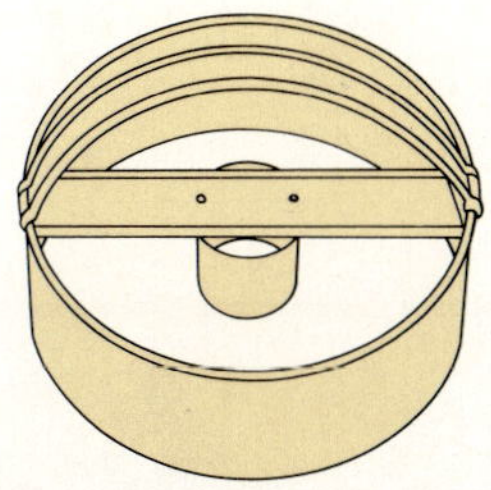

Sturdy doughnut cutter with a small inner ring gives more doughnut than hole.

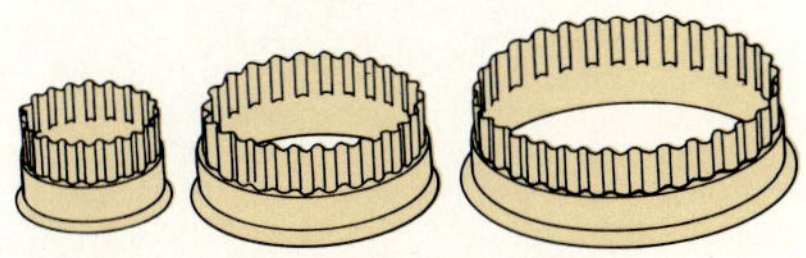

Set of three round crinkled pastry cutters for tartlets or small pies.

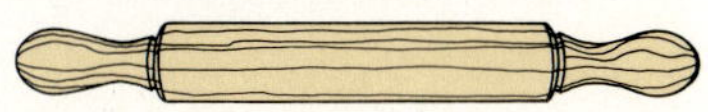

Polished beechwood rolling pin smooths out pastry without wearing it down.

China rolling pin is filled with iced water to keep pastry cool and manageable.

Straight, heavy rolling pin sometimes preferred by professional bakers, but there is a knack to wielding them well.

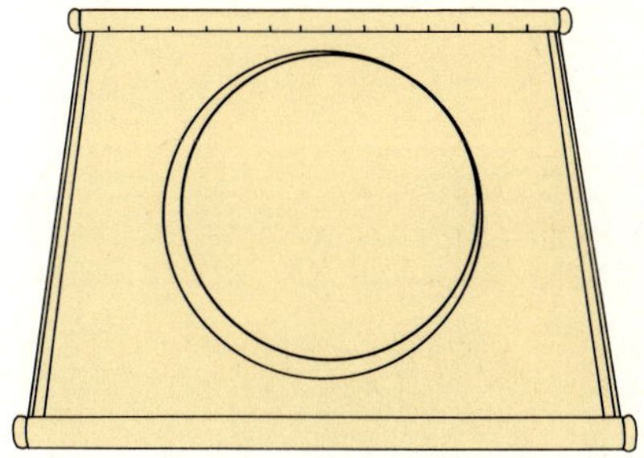

Roll-up canvas pastry cloth in a weighted frame makes a good substitute board after it has been well floured.

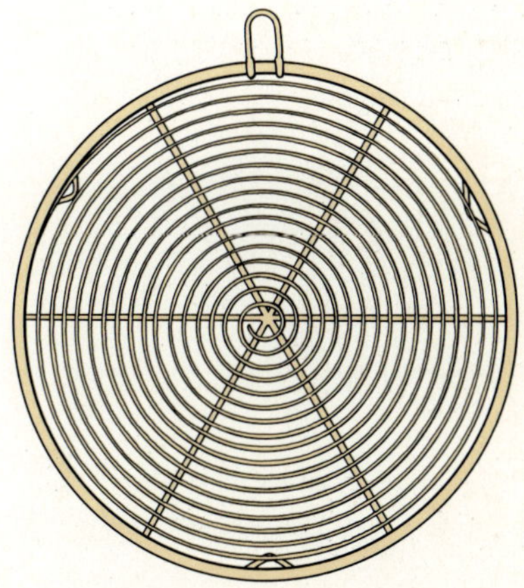

Wire cake rack specially designed for large, circular cakes. For small or square cakes an oblong rack is best.

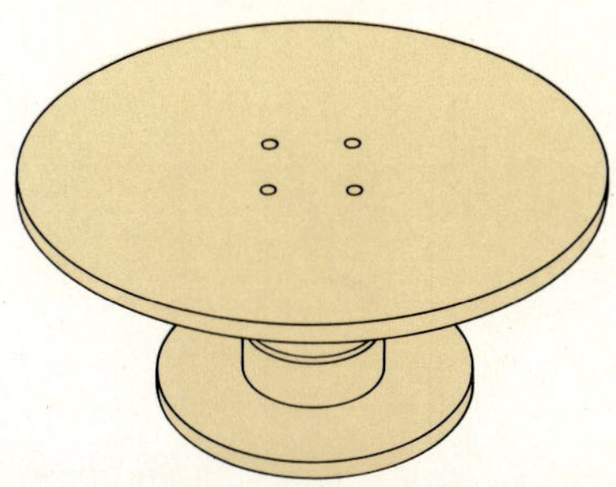

Revolving icing stand in cast-iron. One hand slowly turns the cake while the other applies the trimmings. This makes icing a cake all over a much easier operation.

Roasting and casseroling

Roasting and casseroling

Casseroles, or cocottes, are versatile vessels used for roasting, baking, boiling, braising and stewing. A selection of shapes is desirable, but if you can only buy one choose an oval rather than a round one. This will take ducks and joints as well as risottos, stews and soups. The base of a casserole should be heavy enough to prevent tipping and the lid snug-fitting to trap the moisture. The casserole should be a good conductor, made of material that will transmit heat evenly through the contents. Enamelled ironware fits the bill perfectly; it heats up evenly and will safely go in the oven or on top of the stove. Glazed earthenware is also successful as a heat transmitter and retainer, but it must be used with caution over direct heat. Its rough brown surface makes stews look doubly nourishing; but be careful of cracks and faults in the pottery, where stale flavours and dirt collect.

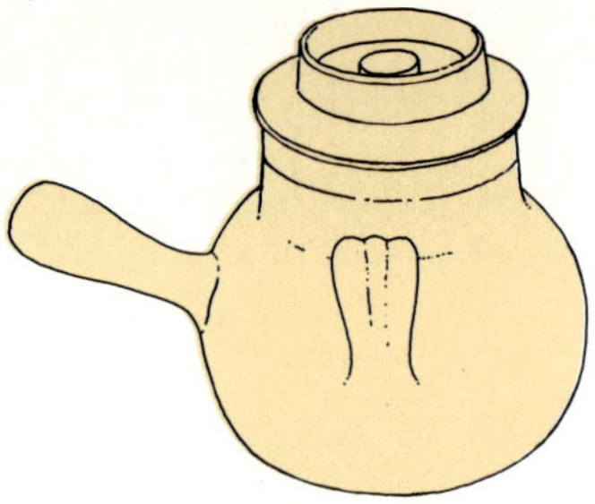

Earthenware daubière for cooking slow stews. The narrow neck keeps in the goodness while the daube bubbles.

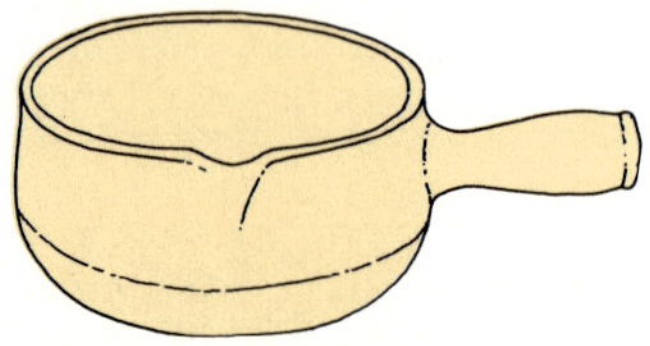

Earthenware poêlon, a round Provençal pot for ratatouilles and stews.

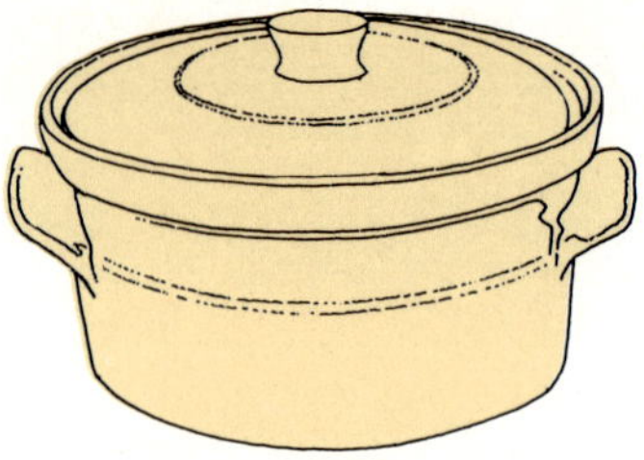

Earthenware casserole for country cooking.

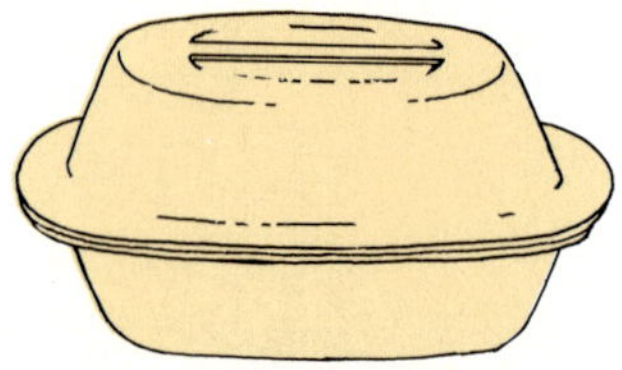

The Schlemmertopf cooks food in its own fat. Wet the clay halves and braise a bird or a rolled roast between them.

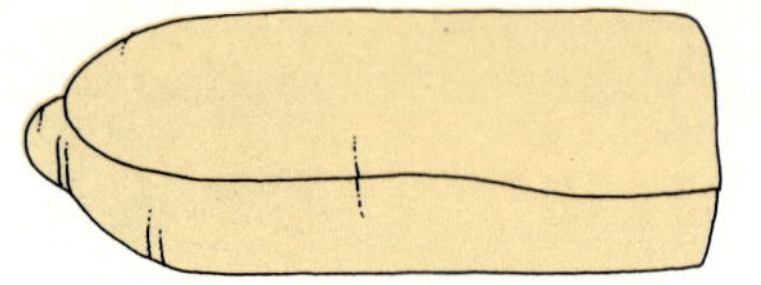

Fish brick, an elongated version of the chicken brick, for baking a cod or a mackerel in its own juices.

Mock pâté en croûte made of pastry-coloured porcelain are mallard's-head handle. Different lids were available to match the different ingredients.

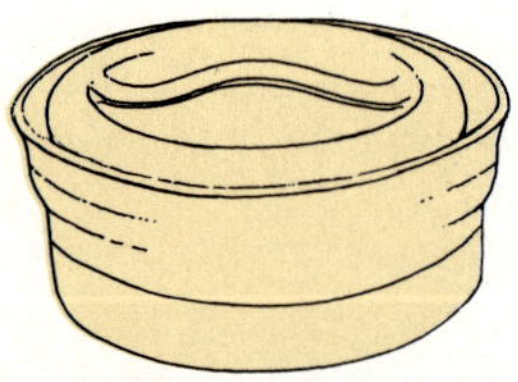

Dark, lustrous oval terrine, made of brown glazed earthenware.

Le Creuset's "volcanic" orange cast-iron terrine bakes easy-to-slice oblong pâtés.

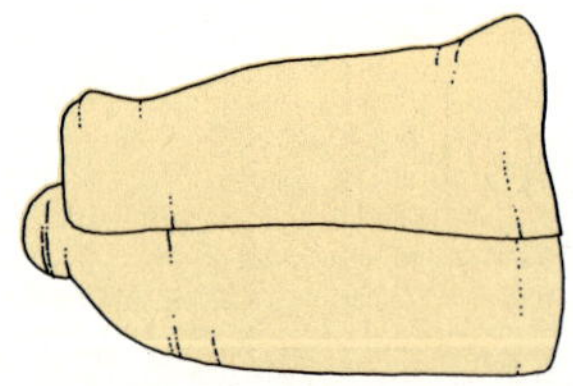

Chicken brick, an earthenware roaster, encloses a whole bird and holds in all its juices while cooking it very evenly.

Deep brown pot perfect for heavy stews or bean mélanges.

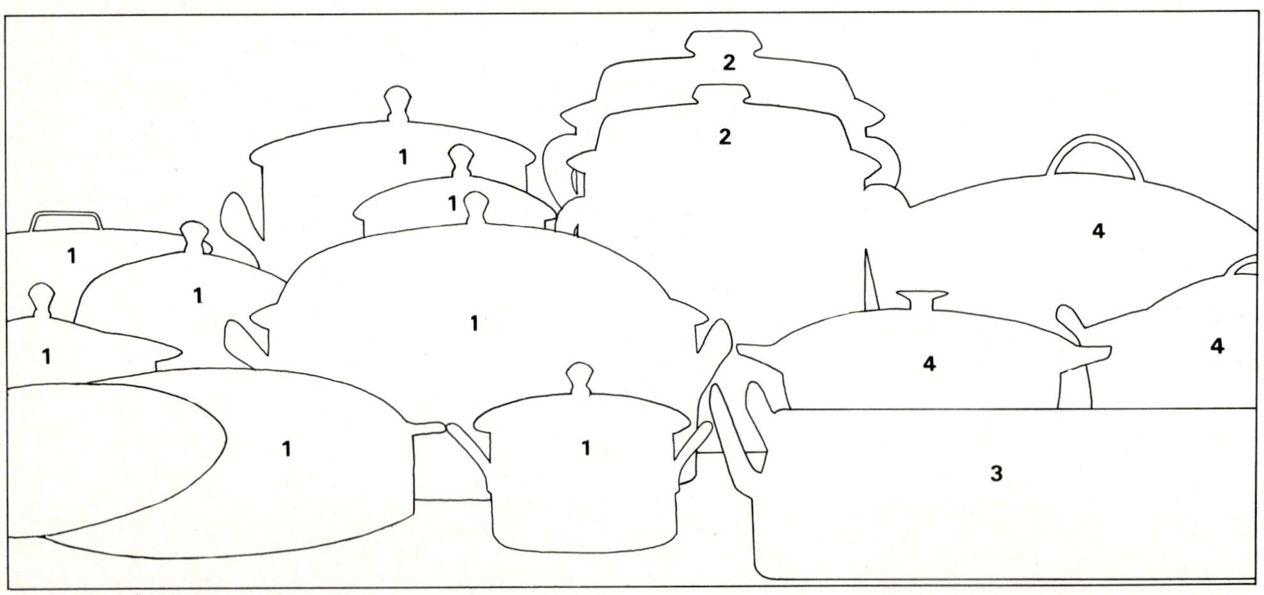

1 *Copper casseroles, which are available in a large number of shapes and sizes, heat up and cool down in a flash and transmit heat exceptionally evenly. To keep them gleaming, polish with salt and vinegar or salt and lemon juice.*

2 *Deep earthenware marmites for stocks and stews. Height means minimum evaporation during slow cooking.*

3 *Tournus heavy-duty, aluminium roasting pan with sturdy handles that are easy to grip.*

4 *Le Creuset cocottes made of vitreous enamelled cast-iron are ideal for casseroling and for a wide range of other cooking purposes as well. Their white enamelled linings are easy to clean and cannot contaminate the contents.*

The Paderno stainless-steel casserole is a gleaming contrast to homely earthenware. The rim acts as a handle.

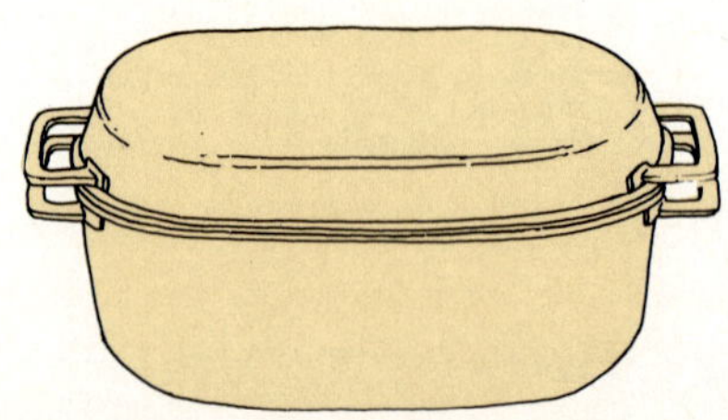

Heavy cast-iron pan shuts tightly with a clang and is a capacious casserole for whole chickens and pot roasts.

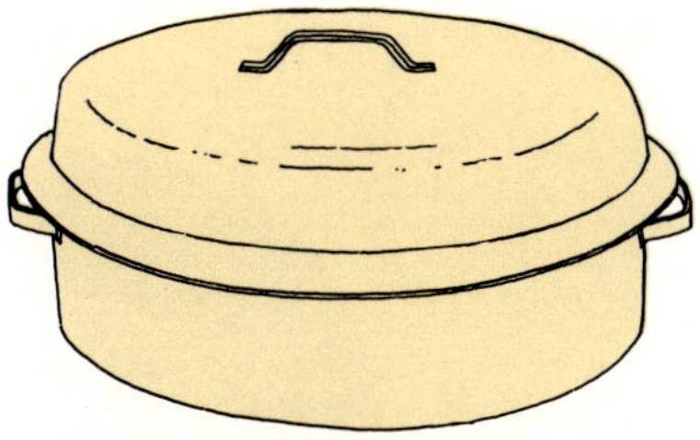

Covered roaster, a deep pan that creates an oven within the oven and magnifies the heat.

Magnalite oval roaster, a bright, domed pan sold in many sizes to encompass vast turkeys or little chickens.

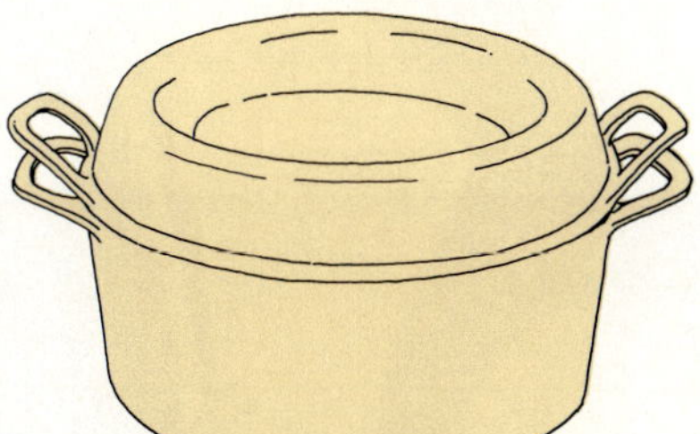

Doufeu, a self-basting pot roaster or braising pan. The dip in the lid is filled with cold water, which encourages condensation within and conserves the natural juices.

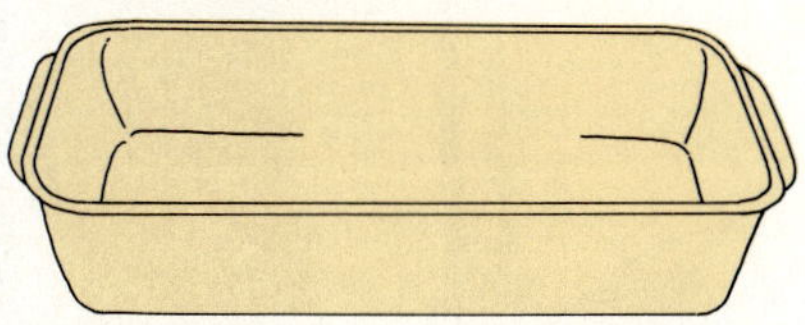

Le Creuset cast-iron oven dish, flame-coloured with a white lining. An attractive dish for steak-and-kidney pie, lasagne, moussaka and all kinds of gratins.

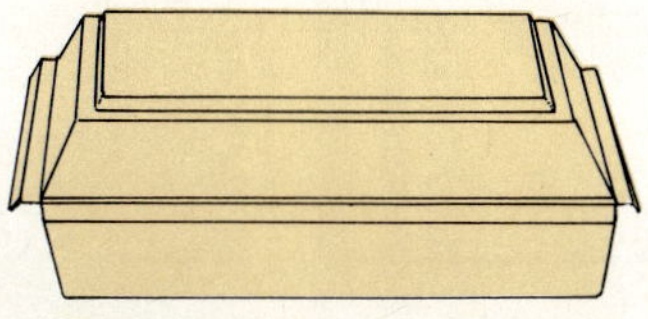

Tinned chop roaster; the lid traps the heat and keeps the meat juicy.

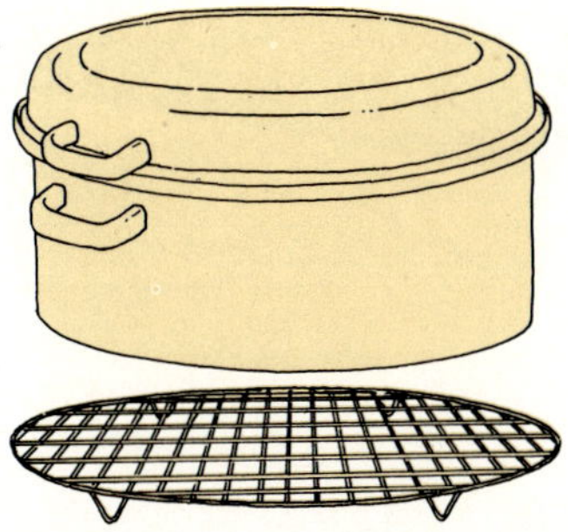

Black-enamelled oval roaster with a rack to stop meat from sticking to the bottom.

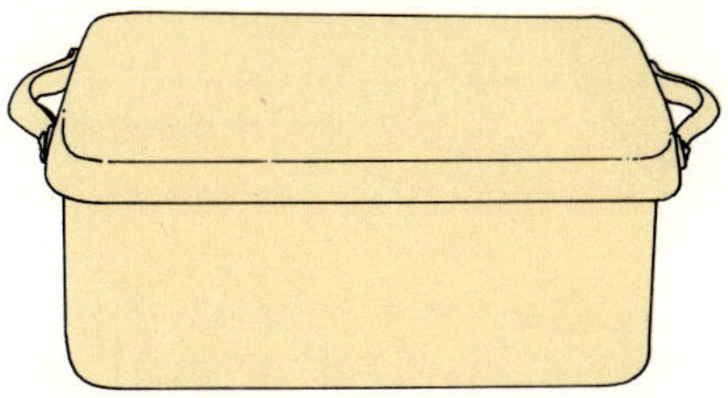

Deep roaster, an aluminium box with a cover to seal in the vapours.

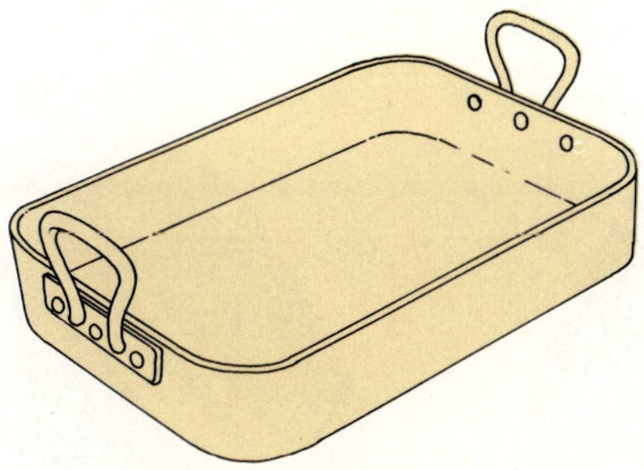

French aluminium roaster with safe, strong handles.

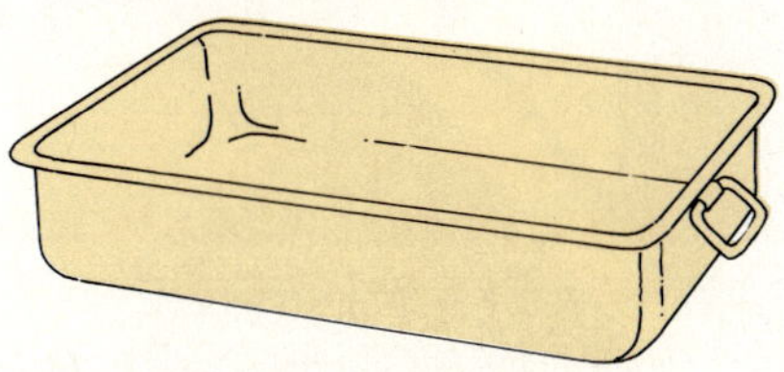

Small Paderno stainless-steel roaster for a compact joint. Open-rolled edges make it smooth to clean.

Oval copper braising pan, glows warmly and transmits heat with unequalled speed.

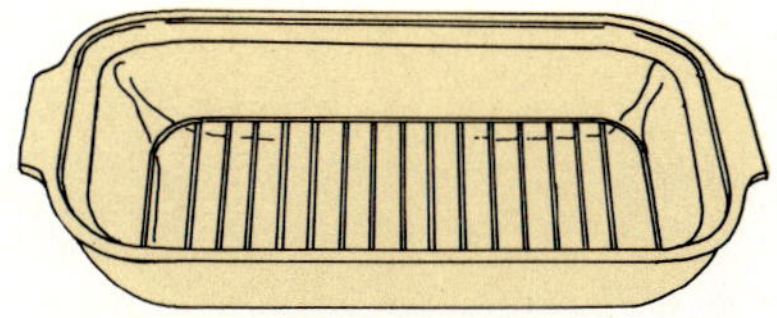

Stainless-steel roasting pan with a rack to raise the meat above its crackling fat.

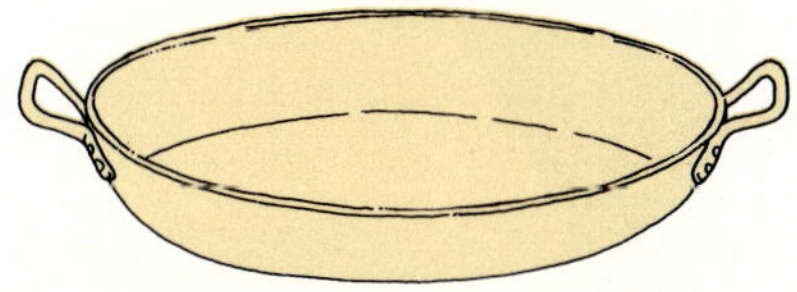

Copper roasting dish with iron handles, an excellent conductor of heat.

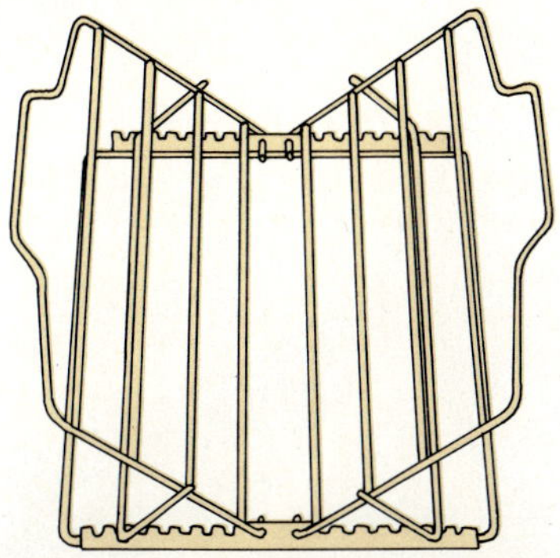

Adjustable roasting rack accommodates bulky turkeys or baby chickens and prevents meat from sitting in its own fat.

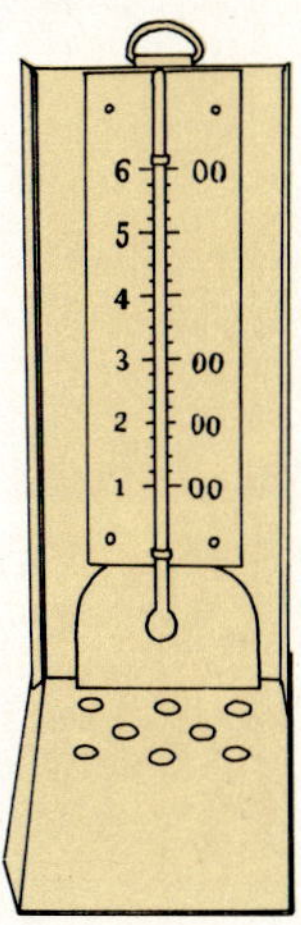

Oven thermometer in a protective steel case, which unfolds to form a stand.

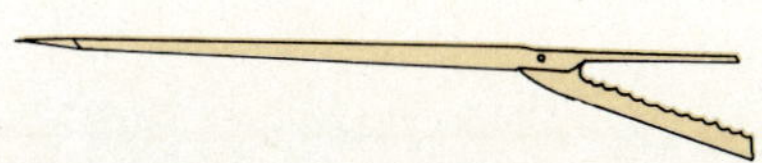

Italian larding needle for threading succulent strips of fat through lean meat.

Wooden 8-in (203-mm) long skewer for pinning up a chicken cavity.

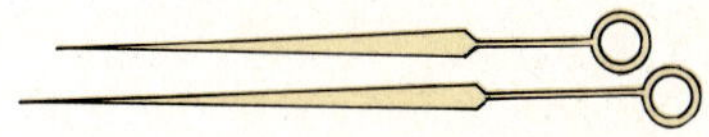

Stainless steel skewers, $6\frac{1}{2}$ in and $8\frac{1}{2}$ in (165 mm and 215 mm) long. Flat-sided prongs give them a firmer hold on the meat.

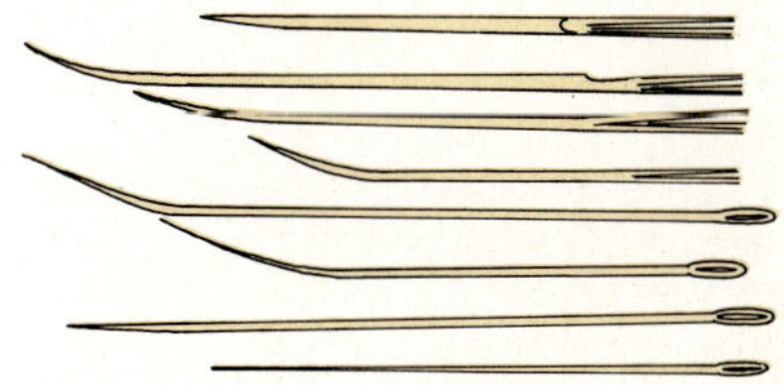

Set of butcher's needles, four for larding and four for stitching up cavities and flaps or skin.

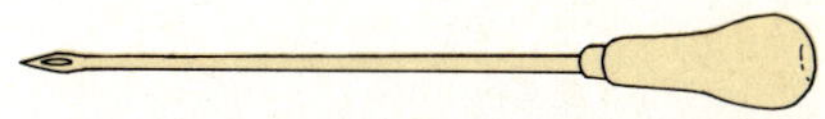

Butcher's needle. Poke it through the meat, thread the needle and draw back the twine.

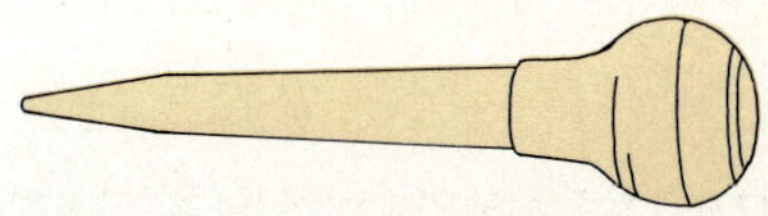

Bulb baster squirts fat over the joints to keep them moist. The tough rubber bulb is attached to an unbreakable aluminium tube.

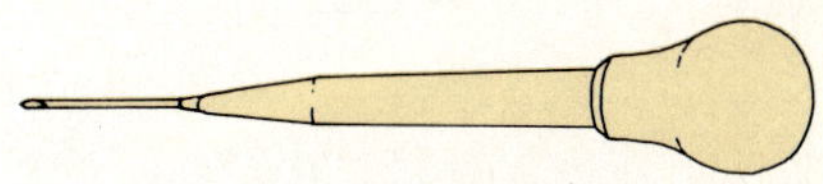

Bulb baster with a needle for injecting the heart of a roast with pan juice or marinade.

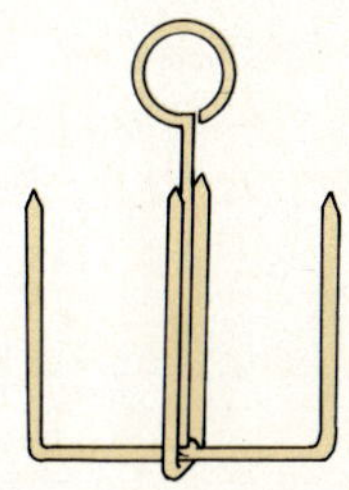

Baked potatoes cook more quickly on the hot spikes of this metal stand.

Salamander, a blistering iron to make golden-brown toppings. Heat up the disc in a burner and pass it over cheese and breadcrumbs.

Batterie de cuisine

Gadgets

Gadgets

Gadgets are controversial additions to the kitchen. Some people despise them, others collect them compulsively and the majority become attached to a few. This assortment combines specialized machinery for those who love egg wedging or ice-cream churning with devices basic to good cooking, such as timers, and thermometers, and neat, cheap tools that cut out unnecessary drudgery and stop you wasting hours over your olives or runner beans.

Home-made pasta dangles from an Excelsa noodle machine (see pp. 308-309), which rolls dough and cuts it in innumerable ways.

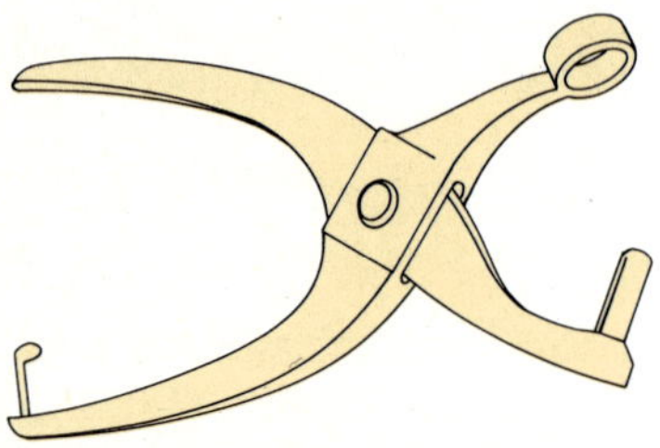

Nickled-steel pitter that punches the stones out of cherries and olives.

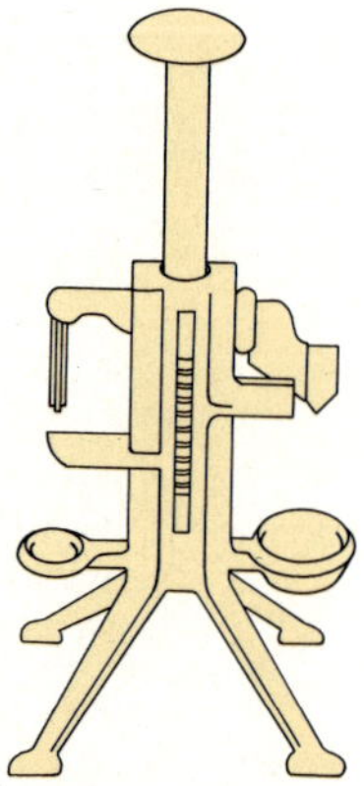

Cast aluminium pitter. Slam down the knob to stone and slice plums on one side and stone olives and cherries on the other.

Traditional egg timer with three minutes' worth of pink sand.

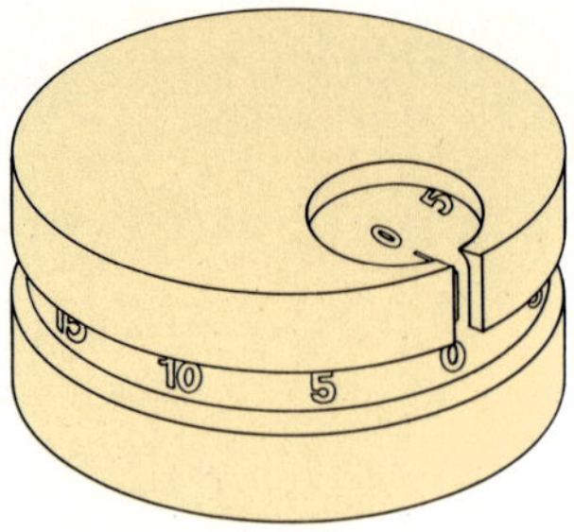

Terraillon timer, runs on clockwork and burrs when time is up.

Tiny stainless-steel thermometer gives an instant, accurate reading on anything from ice-cream to roast pork.

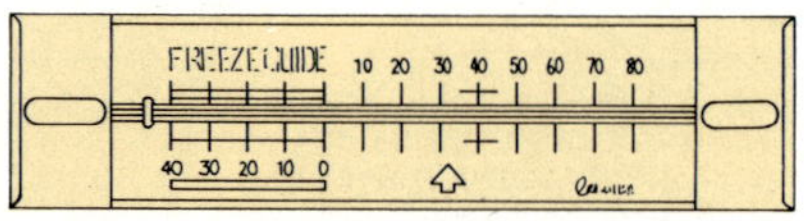

Stainless-steel thermometer for the freezer.

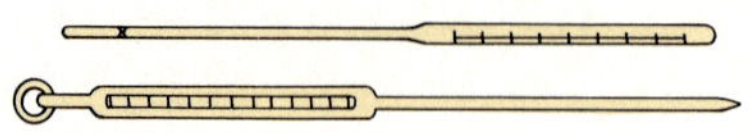

Set of thermometers for meat, dough and fat. They all fit into the case, shown in the lower drawing, which protects them in the food and in the kitchen drawer.

Salometer, essential in preserving, tests the salty strength of brines.

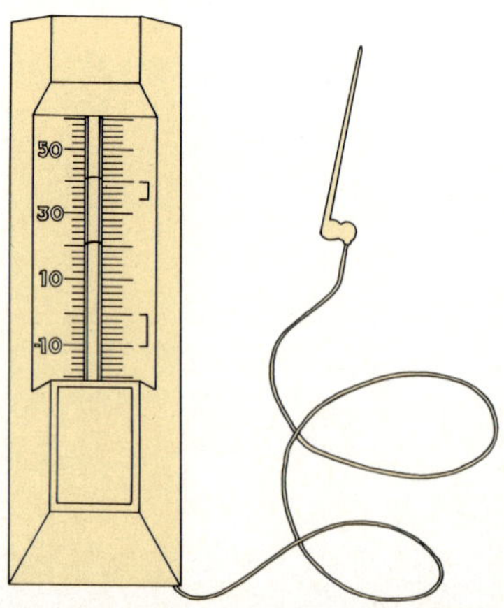

Inside/outside freezer thermometer. You won't have to lose cool air by opening the freezer door to investigate temperature.

Instant thermometer, takes temperatures in Fahrenheit and centigrade.

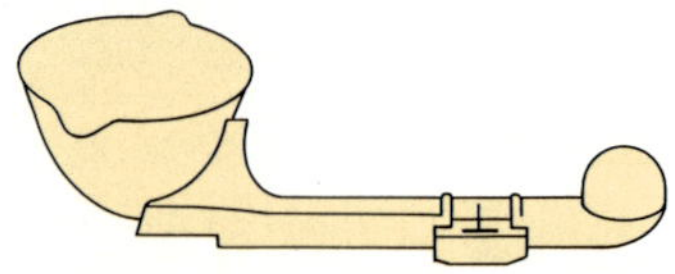

Dr Oetker Balance Scoop. German scales that work like a miniature see-saw.

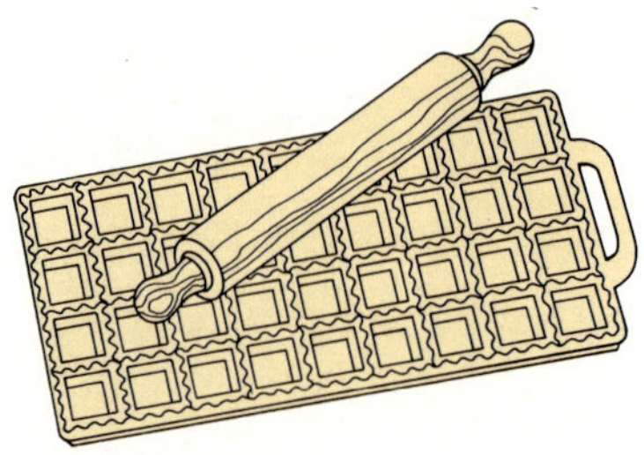

Aluminium mould and wooden roller make neatly serrated ravioli squares.

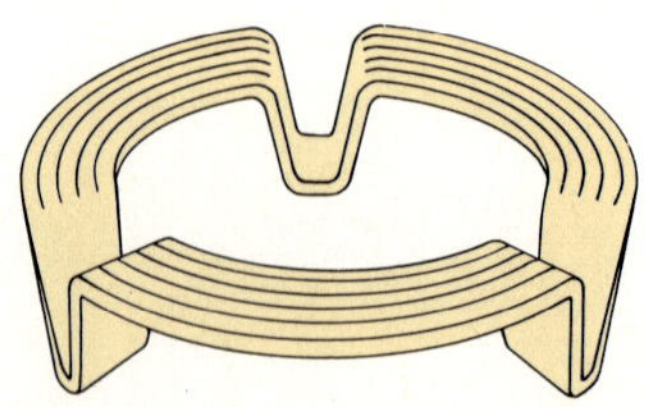

Metal trivet to support a sauce in a bain marie of warm water.

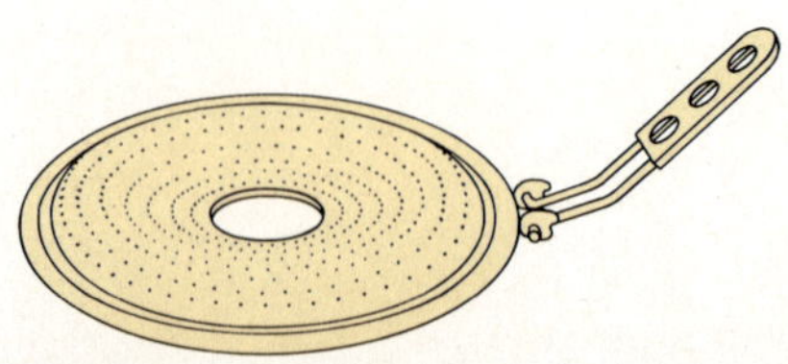

Heat-diffuser mat protects pans from direct heat. Ideal for slow simmering.

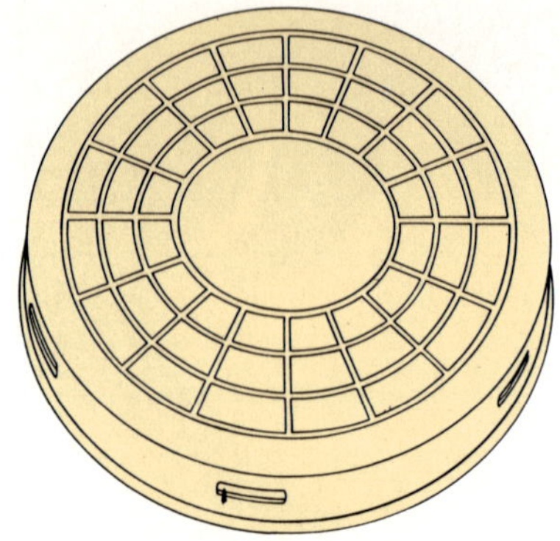

Flame Tamer stands between the burner and the pan. Protects frail vessels from fierce heat and prevents food burning.

Asbestos heat-diffusing mat spreads heat evenly beneath slowly simmering pans.

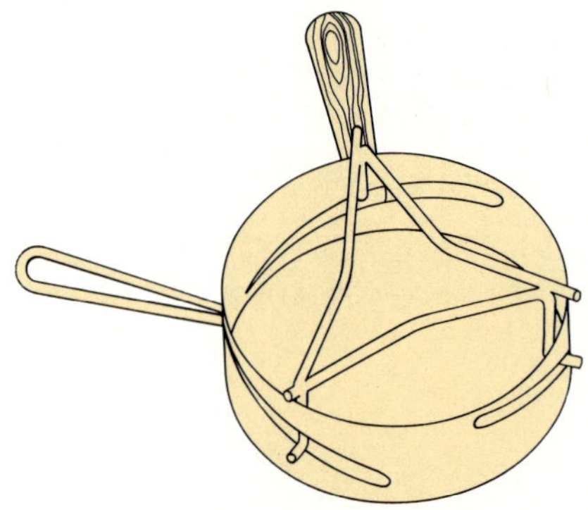

Cuidox or gentle cooker, a French device to raise pans above the flame and prevent porcelain cracking or sauces scorching.

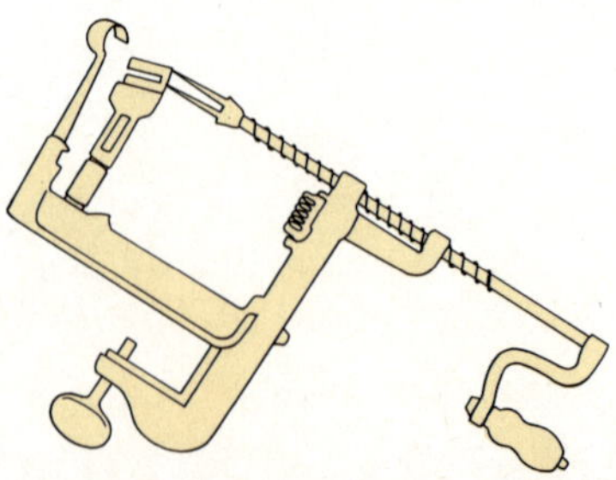

Apple gadget that works best on fresh, crisp fruit. Impale the apple and turn the handle. The fruit is peeled by the blade and cored and sliced by the hook.

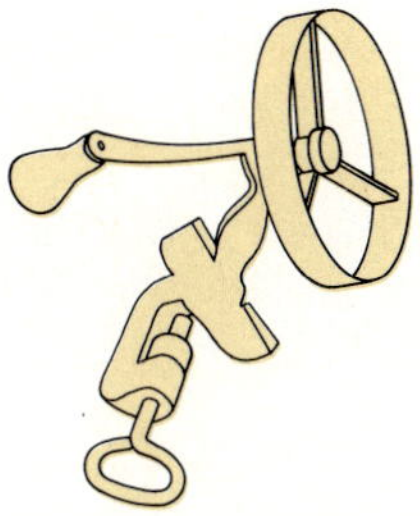

Cast-iron bean slicer with a slit for stripping off the strings.

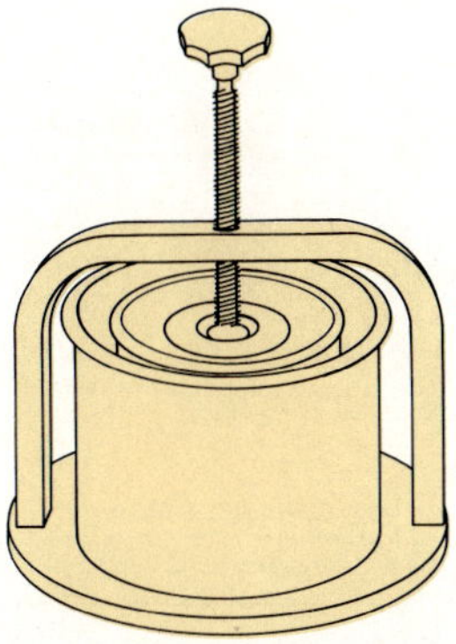

Meat press that refashions a boiled joint into an aspic-coated loaf. Put meat and broth into one of the buckets, screw down the lid and refrigerate until jellied.

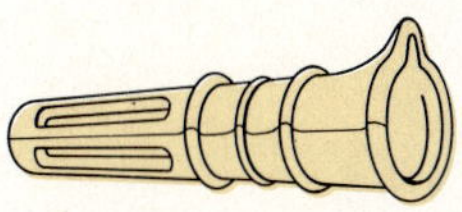

Tiny citrus squeezer that extracts a few useful drops of lemon to sharpen up a sauce. Screw it into the fruit and leave it there until it's needed again.

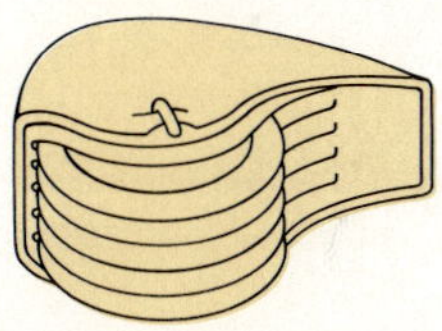

Schneidboy rotary food slicer. Wheel it over meat, herbs and vegetables.

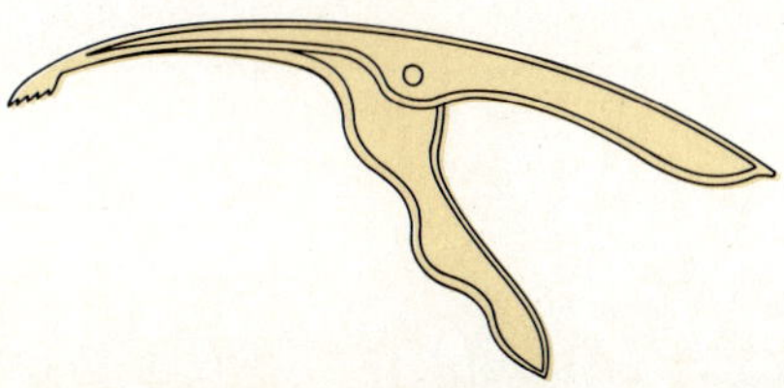

Stainless-steel Shrimpmaster with plastic handle. Insert the tip under the shell and nudge out the flesh by squeezing the levers.

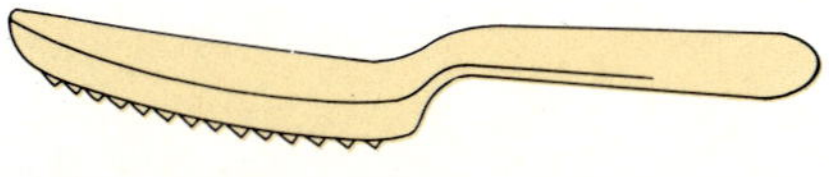

Remove fish scales by stroking fish from the tail upwards with the teeth of this stainless-steel knife.

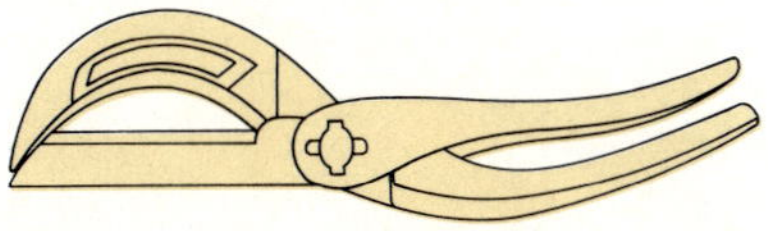

Clam opener. Split the clams over a bowl to save their juices.

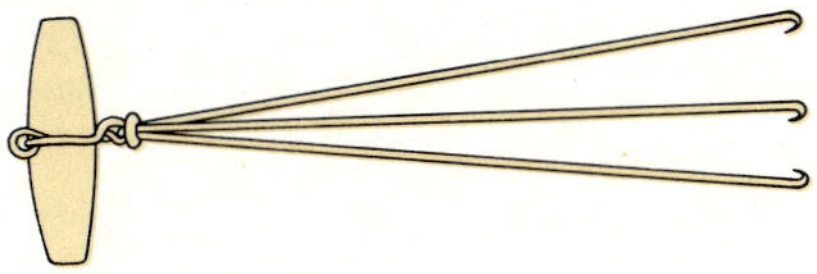

Cork retriever. Hooks catch the floating cork; plastic ring squeezes the wires together while you pull it out.

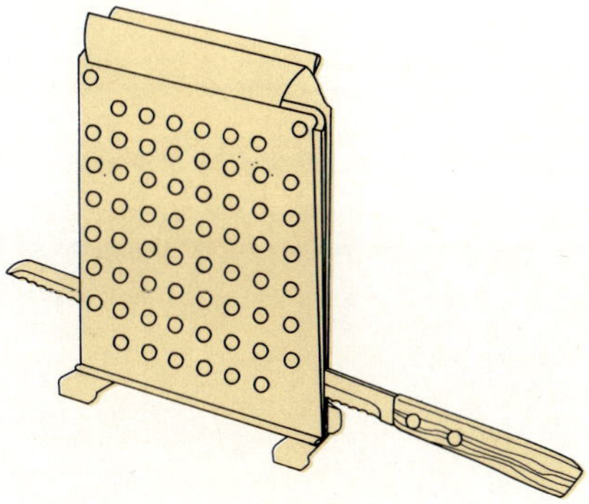

Slice-a-slice for dieters. Make slimmer sandwiches with this stainless-steel gadget that slices sliced bread in half.

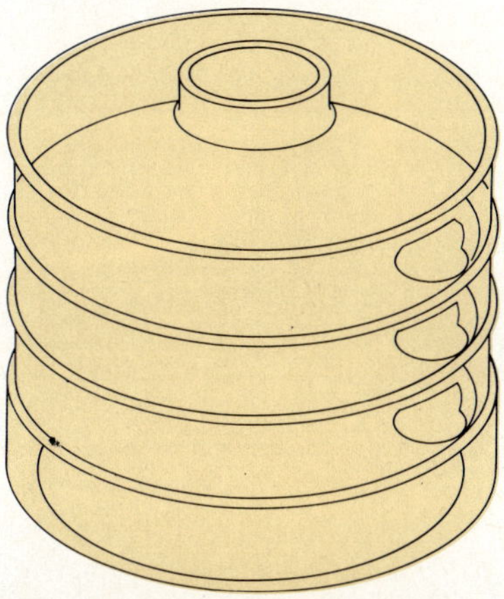

Watch mustard or bean shoots grow in a Bio-Snacky Sprouter, a 4-tier plastic device that raises little crops quickly.

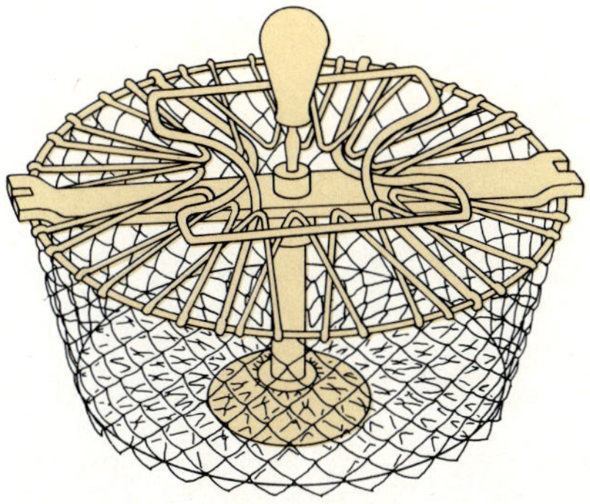

Salad spin-drier. Suction pads hold it still while pusher whirls the basket round like a spinning-top.

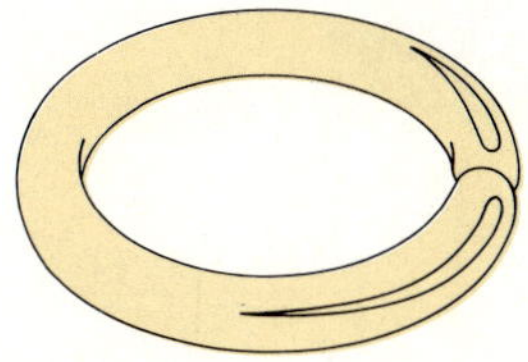

Toughened glass milk saver rattles the pan before the foam starts to swell.

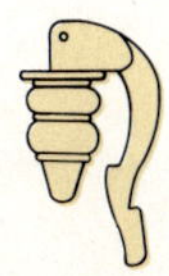

Expanding stopper fits any bottle neck.

Egg pricker. A hole at each end will stop an egg cracking in boiling water.

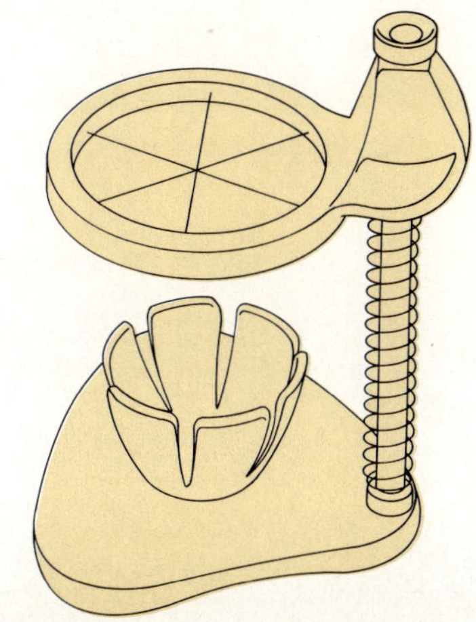

The perfect egg wedger. Slippery boiled eggs are held steady and split into six.

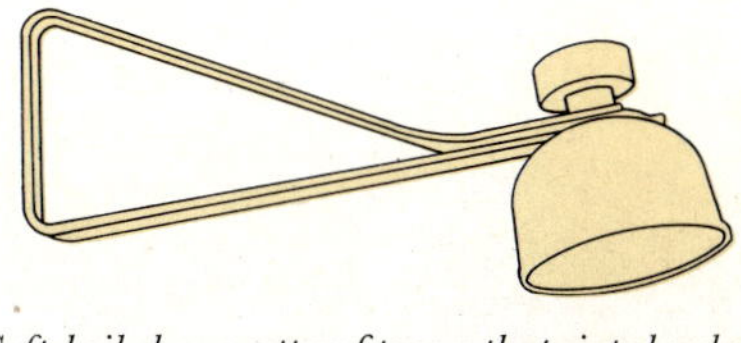

Soft-boiled-egg cutter; fits over the pointed end of the egg. Pull the spring-loaded knob twice to decapitate.

Rubber ice-tray; bend it and the ice-cubes pop out, one at a time if necessary.

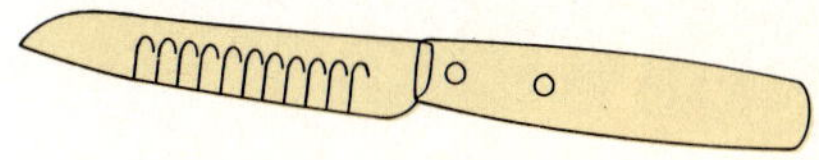

Garnishing knife. Fluted stainless-steel blade makes a pretty pattern as it cuts.

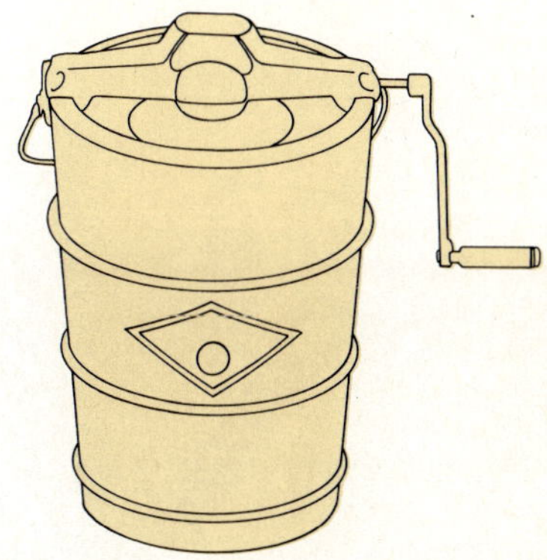

Hand-cranked ice-cream freezer for energetic traditionalists. The crank operates paddles that thicken the cream as they turn.

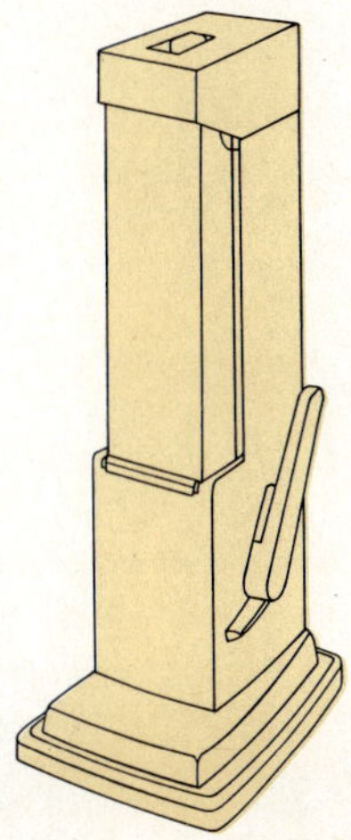

Kenwood Sodastream for cheap, fizzy drinks.

Boiling and steaming

Pots and pans should be substantial. Flimsy ones heat up unevenly, scorch their contents and are easily knocked over. Tinned copper pans are the best conductors of heat, but they are expensive and need vigorous polishing to keep their looks and regular re-tinning to protect food from toxicity. Enamelled cast-iron ware is excellent, especially for slow cooking. It absorbs heat gradually, spreads it evenly and retains it. Lined with glossy enamel, it is swift to clean and won't discolour food. Porcelain is pretty and fragile, stainless steel and aluminium less pretty but very tough. Although stainless steel looks impeccable, it is a poor conductor of heat and is often given a thick aluminium or copper base for successful results. Aluminium pans are good heat conductors if they have heavy bases, but they taint white wine, egg yolks, or food left in them overnight.

1 *Aluminium kettle for poaching a whole fish.*
2 *Aluminium asparagus steamer with adjustable inner tray.*
3,4 *Deep and shallow aluminium stewpans.*
5 *Aluminium bain-marie pan, for conserving the texture and temperature of sauces.*
6 *Thick-based aluminium saucepan.*
7 *Aluminium stockpot, narrow to retain juices.*

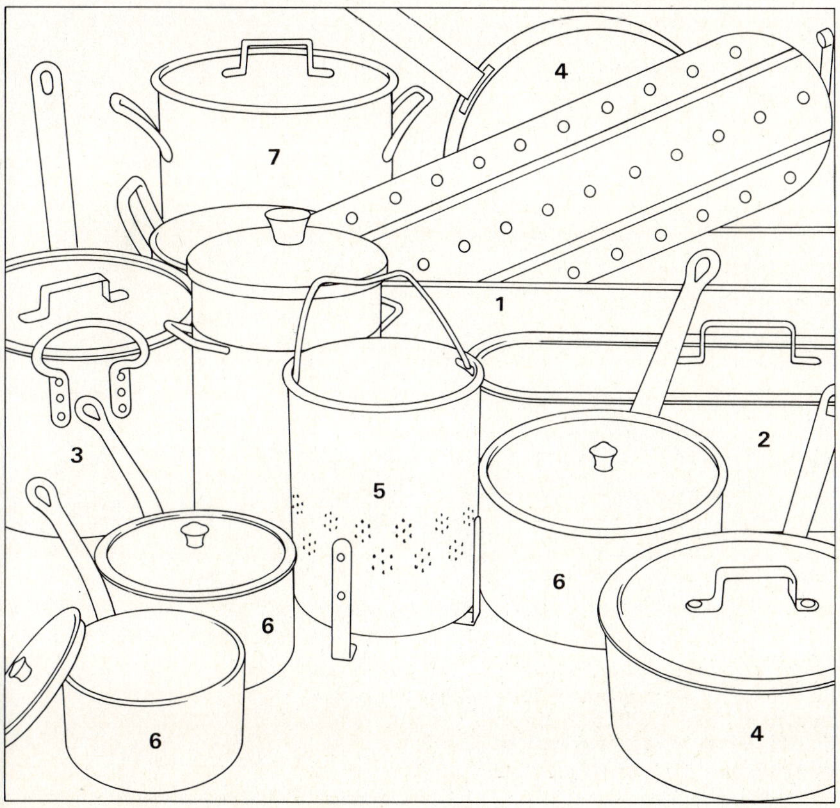

Extra-heavy tinned copper saucepan, transmits even heat in an instant.

Stainless-steel saucepan with a mild-steel base to spread heat evenly and rapidly.

Hammered aluminium saucepan, strong, thick and light weight.

Rough and ready aluminium pan with a pouring lip. Not thick enough for tricky sauces, but adequate for heating milk or boiling eggs.

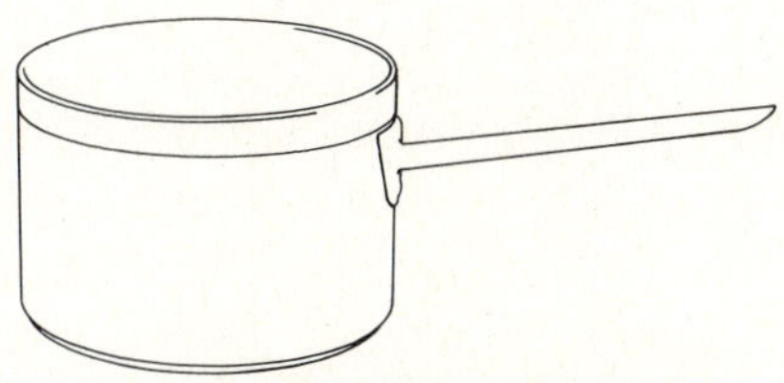

Extra heavy stainless-steel Paderno saucepan, with an aluminium bottom to conduct heat efficiently.

Leu Creuset cast-iron casserole. It is a modern equivalent of the traditional poêlon, an all-purpose earthenware dish used by French country cooks.

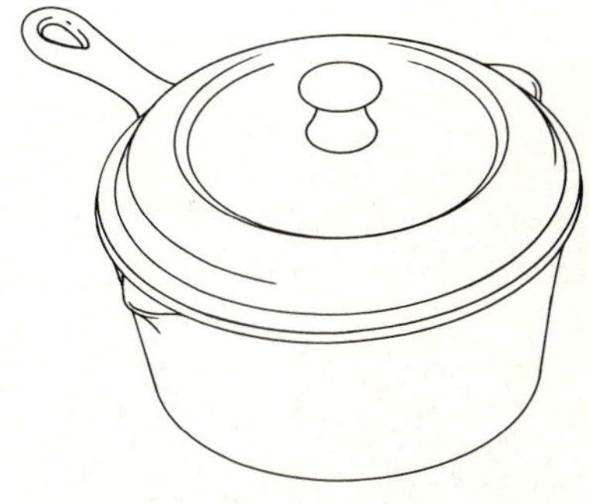

Le Creuset lipped saucepan, made of thick cast iron, heats slowly and evenly. Pure white enamelled interior wipes clean in a trice and will not contaminate foods left in it overnight.

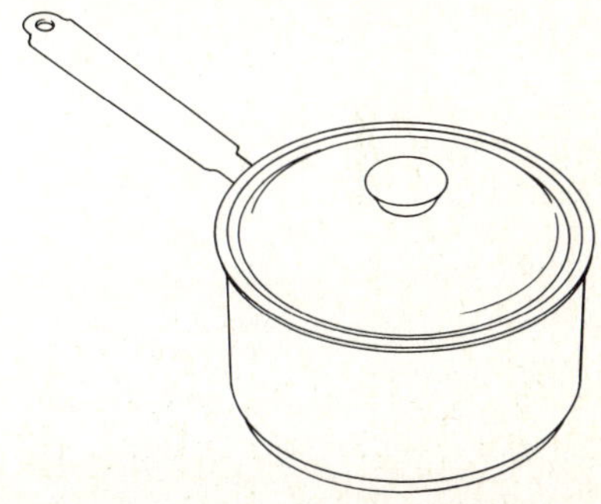

Cuisinarts pristine, stainless-steel saucepan with aluminium-clad base for good conductivity.

Double-purpose stainless-steel saucepan with an aluminium bottom. The shining tub splits into two independent pans.

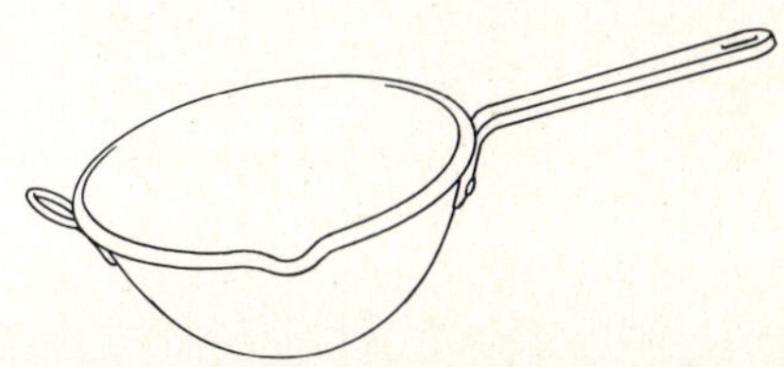

Untinned copper zabaglione pan for beating up the frothy, alcoholic custard over a deep saucepan of boiling water.

Boiling and steaming

Enamel double boiler, easy to clean but easily chipped. Handles soon heat up so grip them with an oven glove.

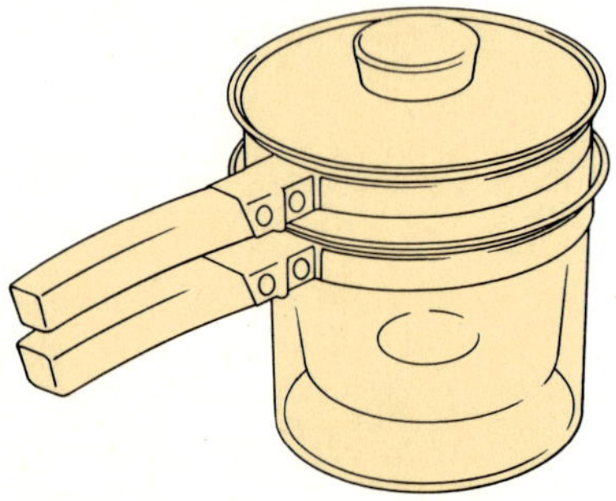

Pyrex glass double boiler for keeping an eye on the changing temperature of the water or the state of a sauce.

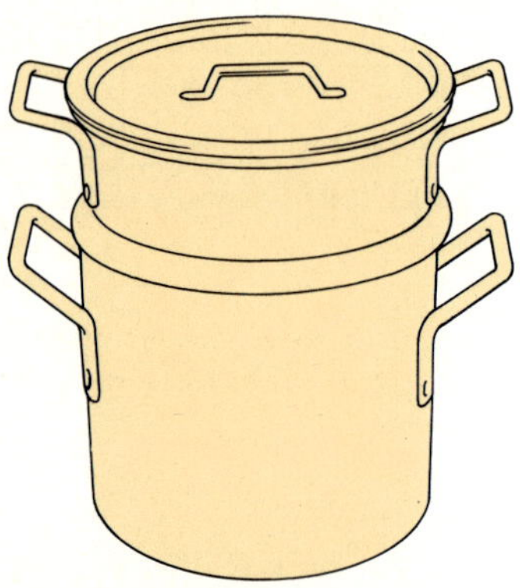

Aluminium double boiler, not for small families, detaches to make two stockpots.

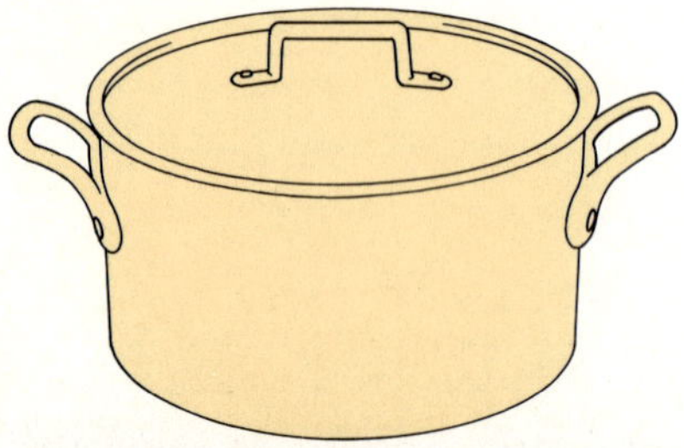

Tournus aluminium stewpot and casserole. Not suitable for solid-fuel cookers.

Steel marmite, a stock or stewpot, which is narrow to restrict evaporation and tall to contain layers of different ingredients.

High, narrow stainless-steel stockpot.

Heavy-gauge aluminium stockpot or stewpot, with inner wire basket for steaming and lifting solid foods out of their liquids.

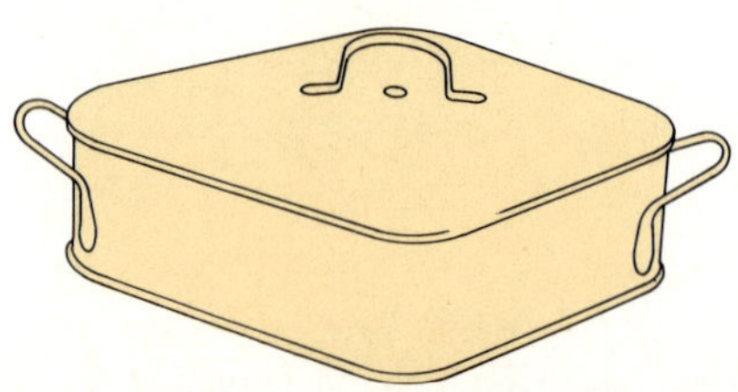

Tinned steel poacher with removable rack. A luxury designed to cook the luxurious, diamond-shaped turbot.

Aluminium seafood cooker, holds stacks of clams and mussels. Lid fits tightly enough to cook them in very little water.

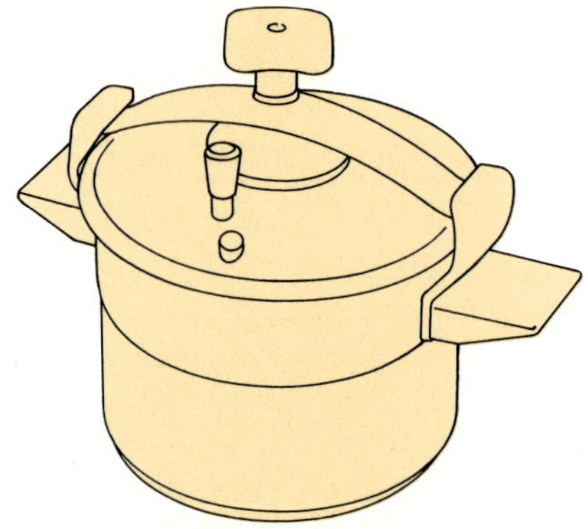

A safe, smart-looking aluminium pressure cooker for cutting cooking time in half.

Big mug or small saucepan. Pours neatly over the stainless-steel rim.

Traditional French country milk jug for the stove and then the breakfast table. Holes in the lid prevent milk boiling over.

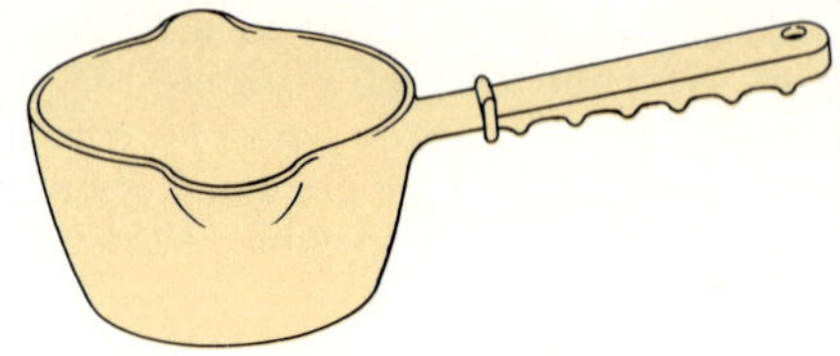

Double-lipped aluminium milk pan with ridged plastic handle for firm gripping and steady pouring.

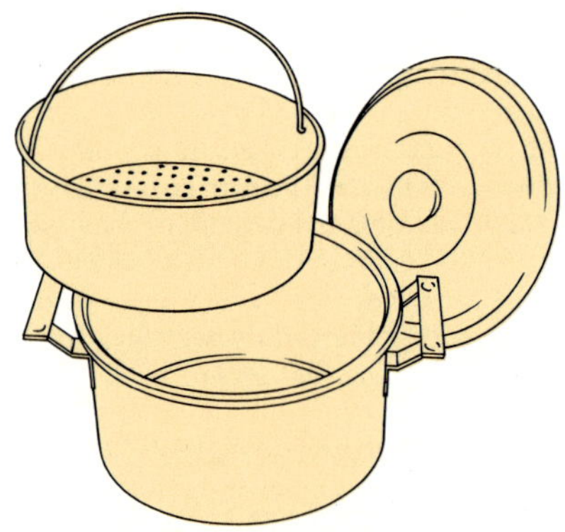

Heavy Cuisinarts steamer for fine-flavoured, firm-textured vegetables. The bottom pot is useful on its own, the perforated pan doubles up as a colander when needed.

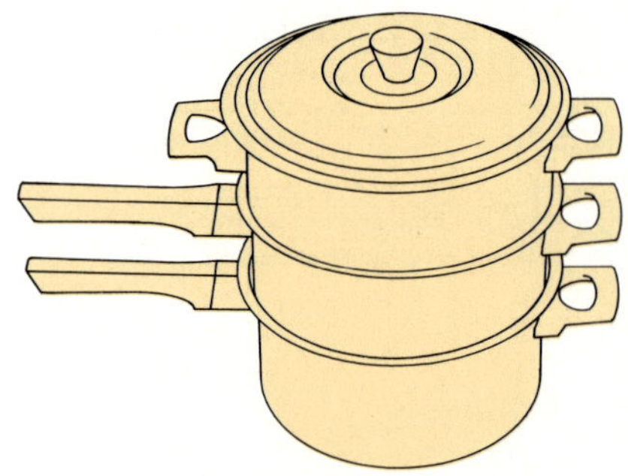

Thrifty three-in-one steamer made of gleaming stainless steel. Bottom pan is also used independently, lid fits all tiers.

Double-decker kettle for steaming hams.

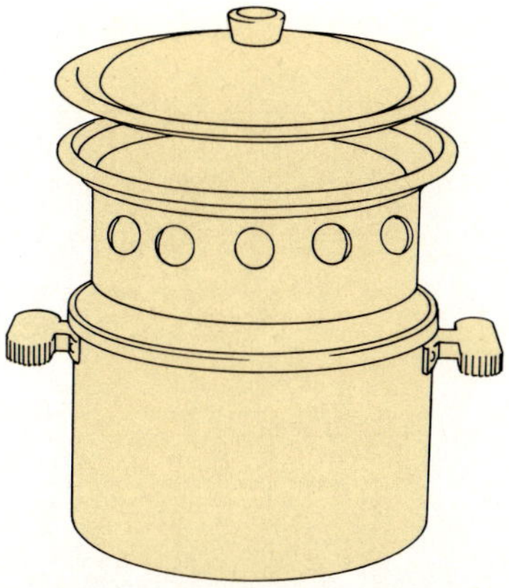

Bungalow cooker with holes in the upper part of the steaming pan so that juices do not drain into the boiling water.

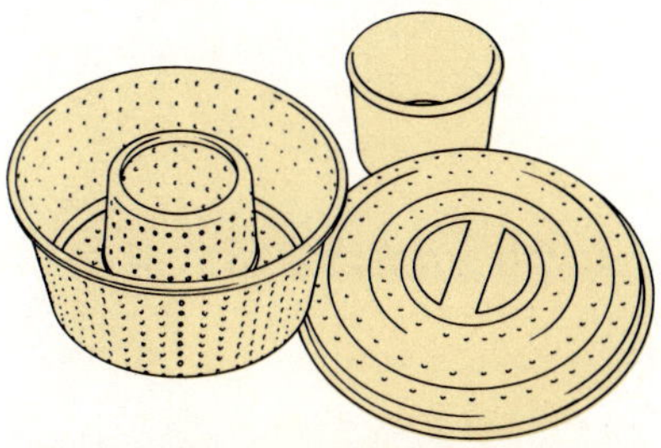

Steamer mould for cooking rice in a ring.

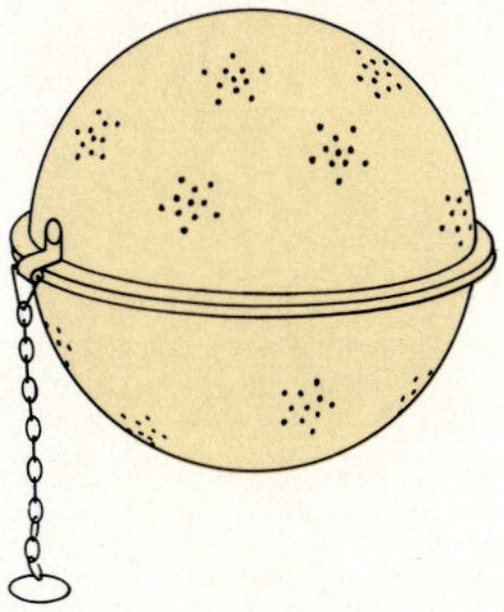

Ball for steaming rice, hooks on to the pan and hangs above the water.

Collapsible wire steaming basket.

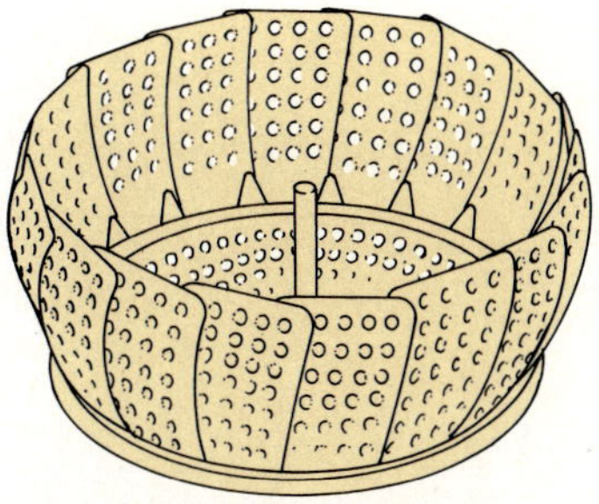

Norwegian vegetable steamer. Perforated "petals" fan out to fit different pan diameters.

Enamelled steel steamer.

North African double steamer for making couscous, grain steamed in the perforated bowl over stewed meat and vegetables.

Called a poacher, this pan is strictly a steamer because the eggs are cooked over the boiling water rather than in it.

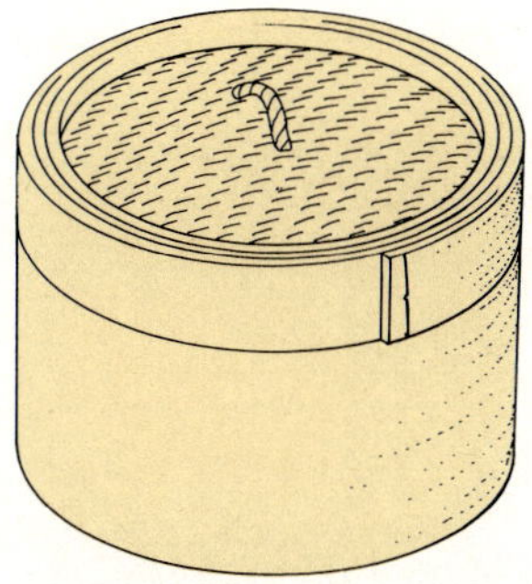

Chinese steamers, an economical and delightful way of cooking three things at once over a wok-full of boiling water.

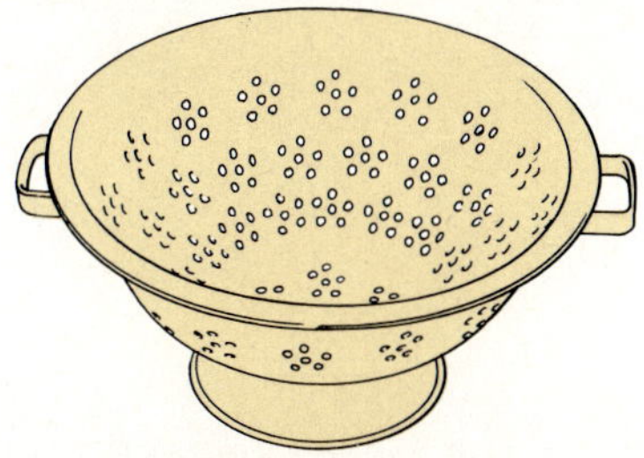

White-enamelled colander; with a lid on top and a saucepan below it makes a steamer.

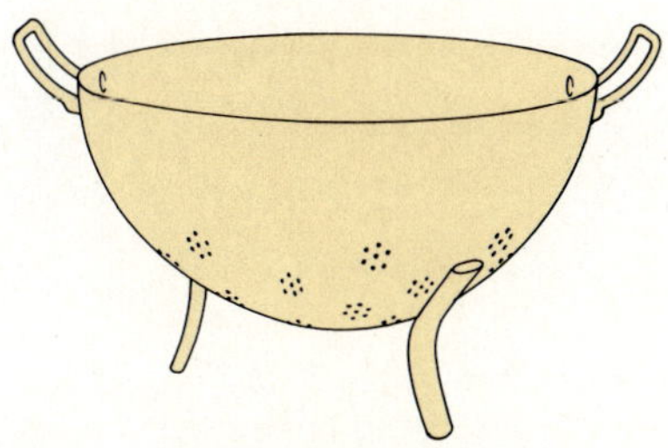

Capacious French colander on sturdy legs.

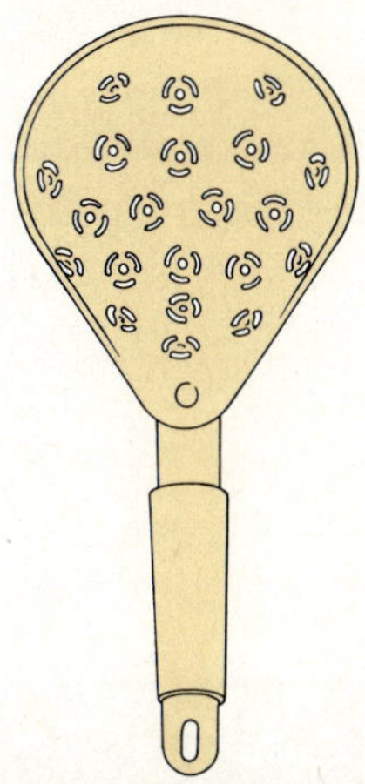

Stainless-steel spaghetti scoop with a pretty pattern of perforations. Only the smallest pasta shapes escape.

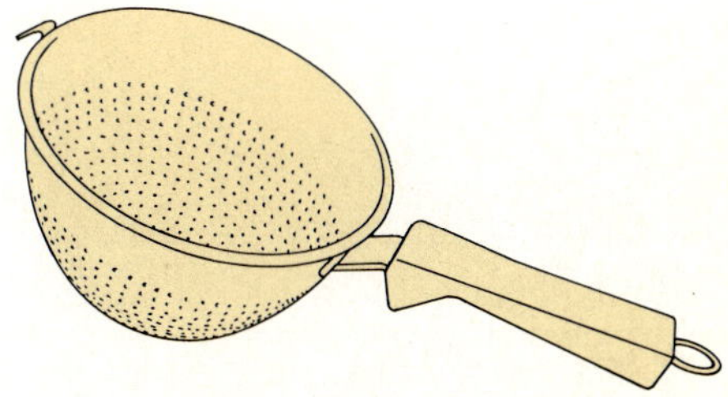

Small scoop with stainless-steel bowl, a cross between a spoon and a strainer.

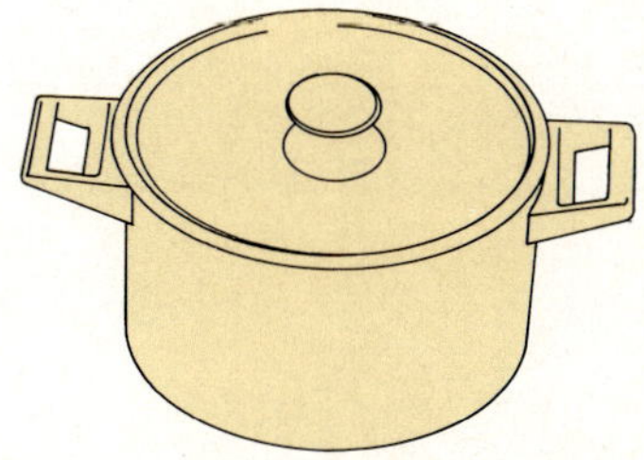

Multi-purpose aluminium pot, equipped with wire basket and tripod, stews, fries, steams and boils.

Brightly coloured enamel kettle with white interior. Be careful of the hot handle and the pot, which swings as you pour.

Stainless-steel kettle with a rigid handle that won't tilt the scalding contents of the pot on to your pouring hand.

Frying and grilling

Instead of using one old frying-pan for everything from bubble and squeak to crêpes suzette, it's worth buying a selection of pans for different jobs—choose round and oval heavy-bottomed frying-pans for general use, then consider an iron-handled skillet which will go in the oven, a straight-sided sauteuse for jerking and tossing food in butter and a pan reserved for omelettes. For crêpes and omelettes buy pans which are heavy enough to absorb and retain high heat, and smoothly curved and shallow for the dexterous manoeuvres of swishing a wash of batter or beaten egg around before flicking the pancakes or omelettes over and out. Iron and steel pans must be treated with care or they will rust; season them with a lick of oil and a rubbing of salt. After use clean them by wiping out with kitchen paper rather than by soaking in hot, soapy water, as detergents and abrasives will destroy the build-up of oil that acts as a natural non-stick surface.

The wok or Chinese cooking vessel, designed for swift movement over high heat, rests for an instant on its metal stand (left).

Old man of the stove, a hefty iron skillet which will go in the oven or on the top, but reacts too slowly for volatile sauces.

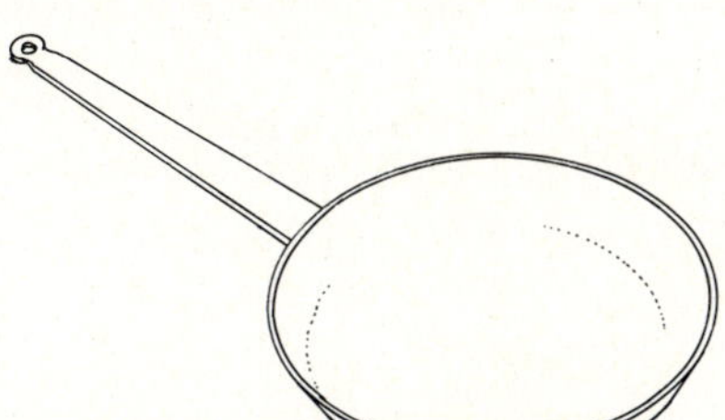

Black iron frying-pan; heat it up gently and wipe its oily surface clean with salt and kitchen paper. Never wash in soapy water.

Black iron frying-pan. Clean it with paper and salt, not soap and water.

Oval frying-pan made of black iron, a good shape for sautéing fish and browning roasts. Season it with oil and salt before using for the first time, and thereafter wipe clean with kitchen paper.

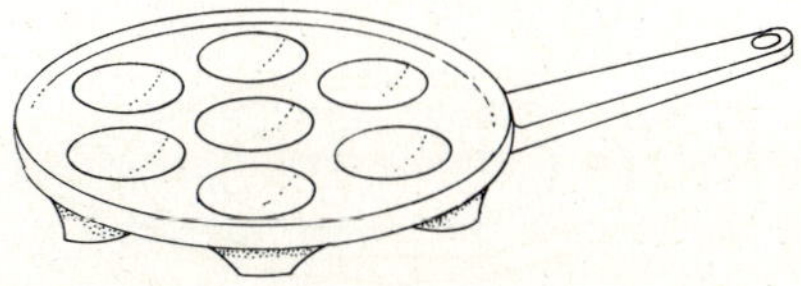

As used by ancient Romans and modern Scandinavians; a pan to make puffy, golden Danish dumplings.

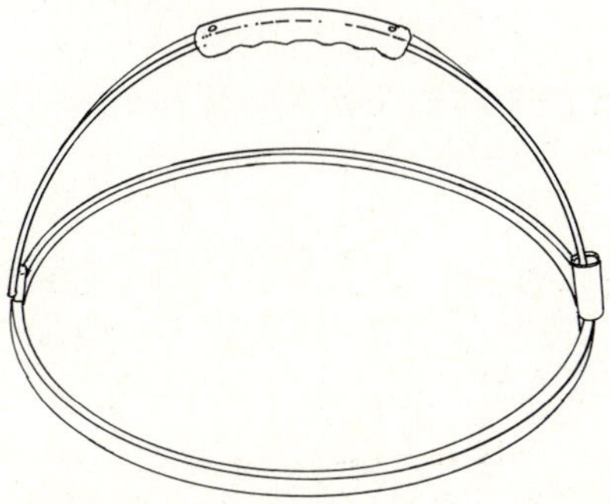

Traditional griddle for drop scones and griddle cakes.

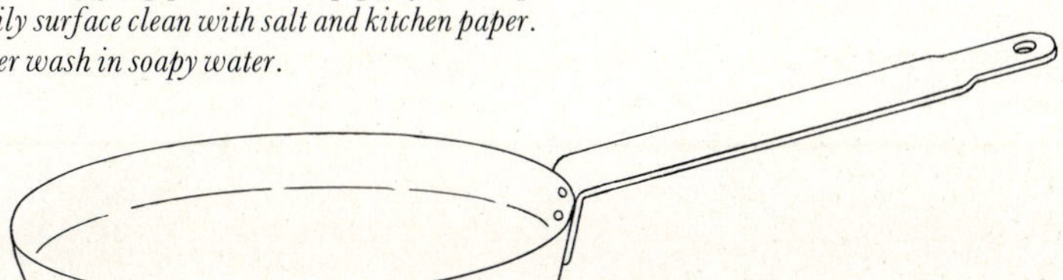

Black iron, oval fish pan for frying whole plaice and soles.

Thick soapstone griddle absorbs heat rapidly and sears in a flash.

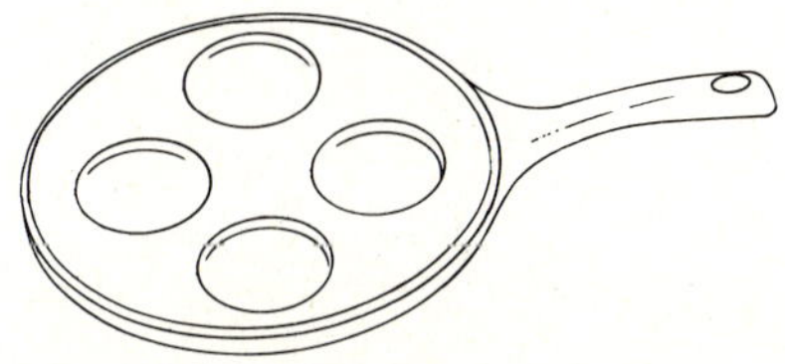

Frying-pan for round fried eggs. Grease the sockets before dropping them in.

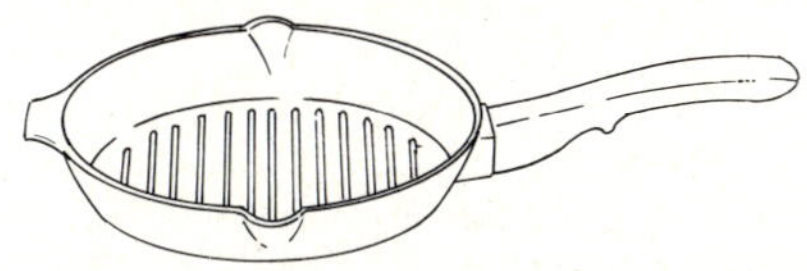

Hefty, black iron frying-pan with ridges to keep the meats out of the fat.

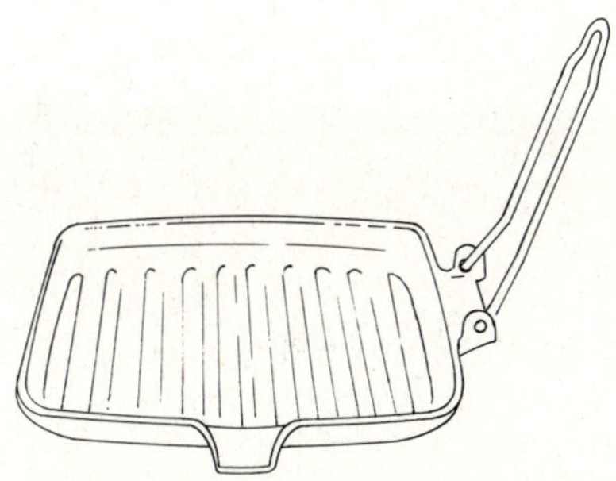

Le Creuset monogrill, a ridged cast-iron square for searing steaks and chops.

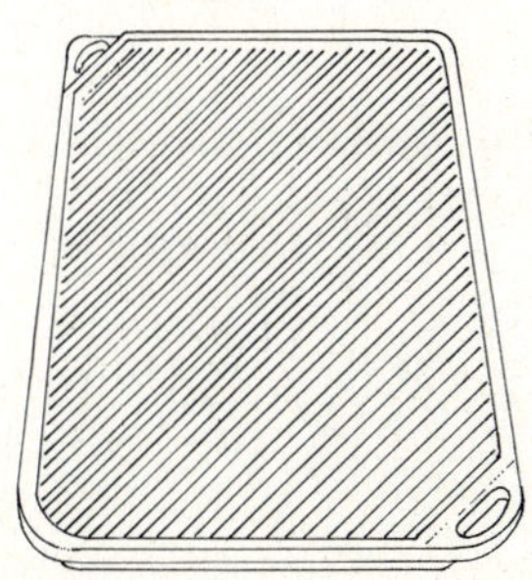

Cast iron, oblong grill plate, long enough for a line-up of sizzling steaks.

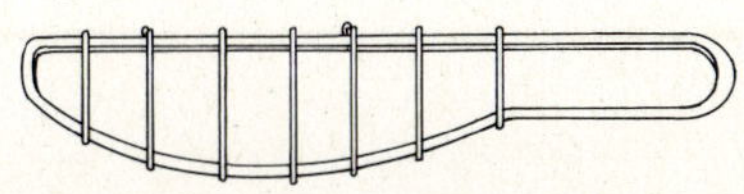

Wire jaws to clasp a small fish over the fire. Protect your hand with a mitten.

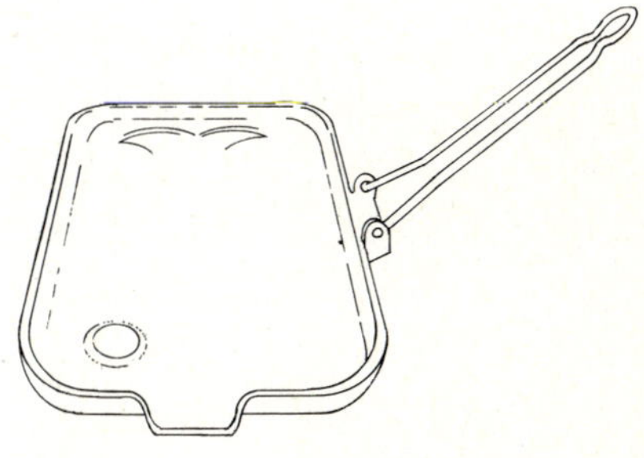

Cast-iron fish grill, to go under the heat, not on top of it. Slash fish on both sides or they will curl up in the cooking.

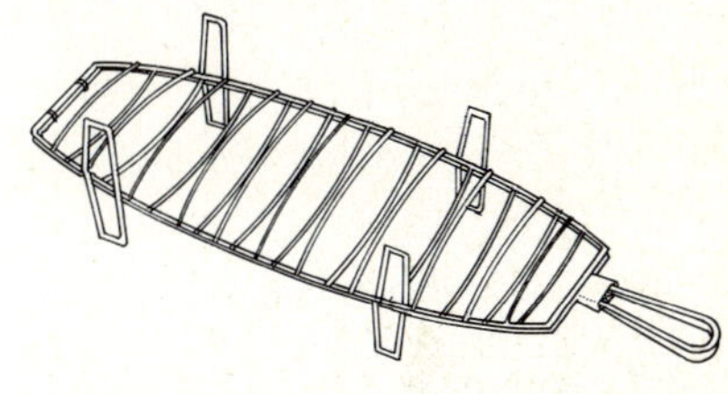

Tinned steel fish grill stands in the coals and holds the fragile flesh intact. Grease the wires before laying down your fish.

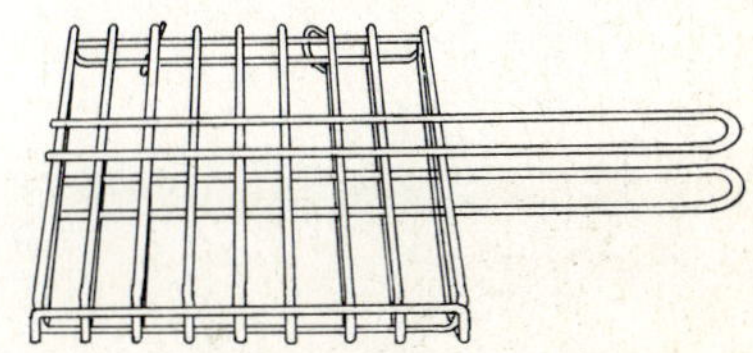

Wire griller grid for barbecue.

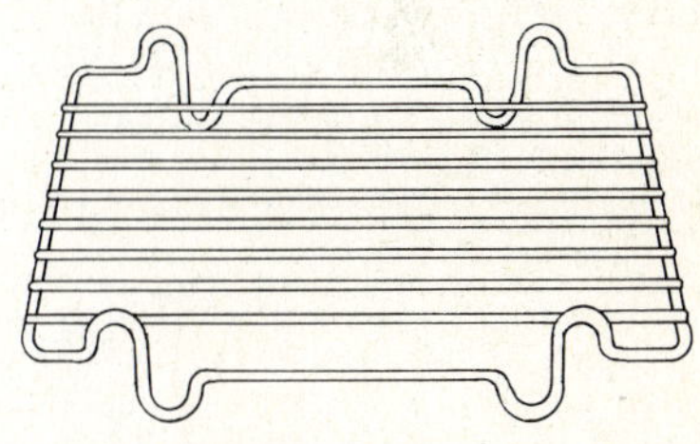

Tinned wire meat stand.

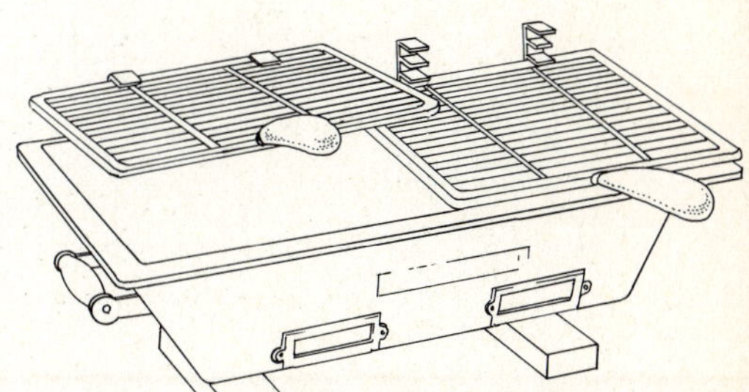

Hibachi grill; cast-iron trough holds the burning charcoal, and meats lie on the adjustable, wood-handled grid-iron.

Frying and grilling

Aluminium sauteuse, a wide and straight-sided pan for tossing and shaking food in butter.

French aluminium sauteuse hammered into dimples for extra strength.

Aluminium sauté pan with steeply curved, tinned metal handle, which keeps cool and feels comfortable.

Copper sauté pan, excellent for fast frying and browning.

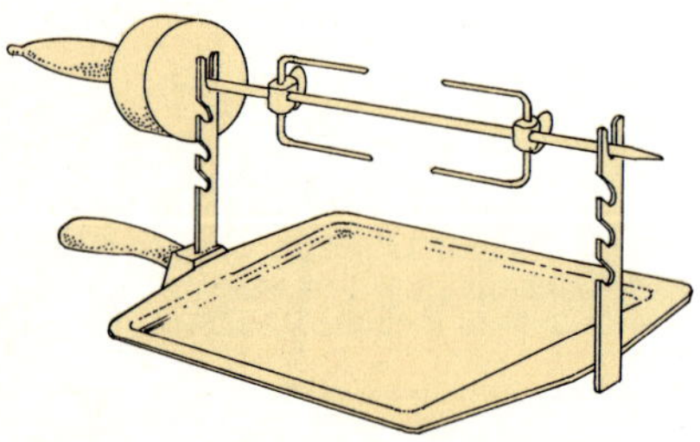

Chickens and joints are done to a turn on the Cocambroche Four rôtisserie. The rotating roast, powered by clockwork, is cooked by a side fire while drippings fall into the pan.

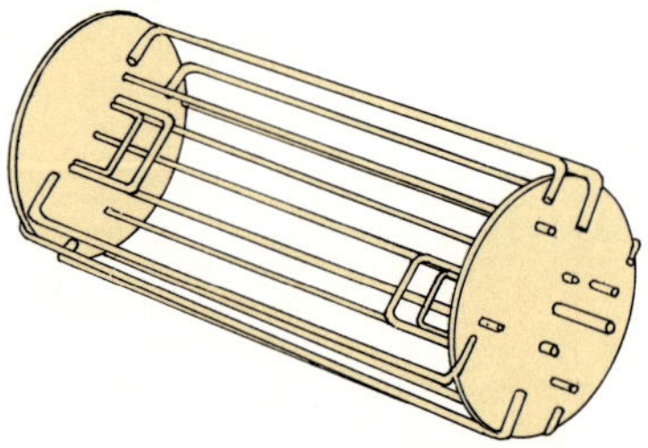

Cocambroche tambour, an adjustable wire cage that hooks on to the Cocambroche rôtisserie and holds slim burgers and large roasts that won't fit on to the spit.

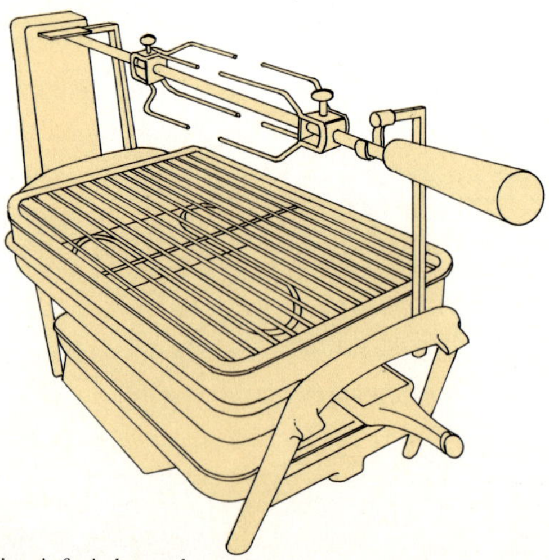

Smokeless, spatter-free rôtisserie for indoor and outdoor barbecues.

Copper gratin pan, a beautiful, shallow oval, lined with impregnable stainless steel—an expensive but worthwhile investment.

Copper flambé pan, deep enough for food and sauce to be whirled around.

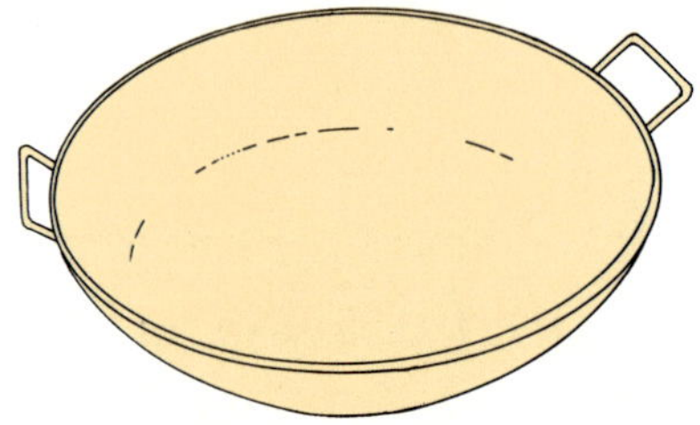

Cuisinarts stainless-steel gratin pan, mirror-finish with thick aluminium-sandwich base for possible stove-top use.

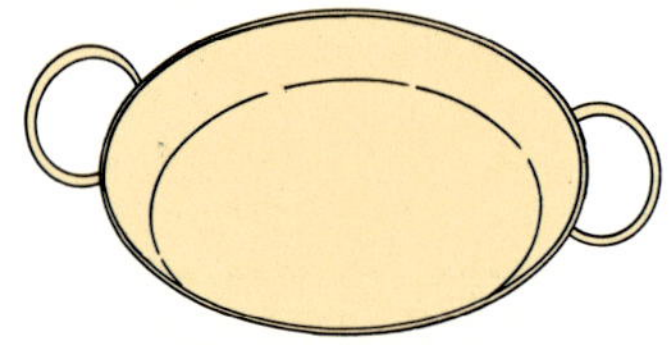

Aluminium paella pan, also useful for risottos and currys.

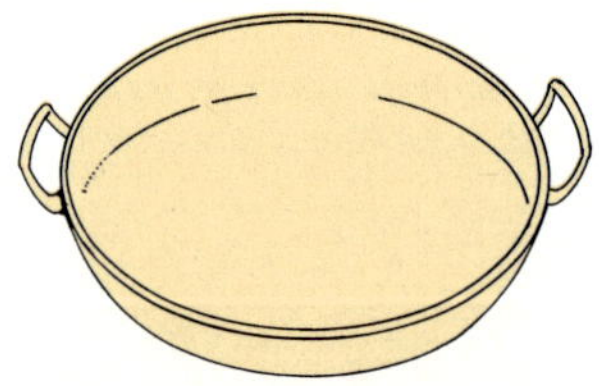

Copper dish with "ears", the perfect shape for a gratin of sizzling eggs and cream.

Highly polished aluminium pan reflects the flawless omelette.

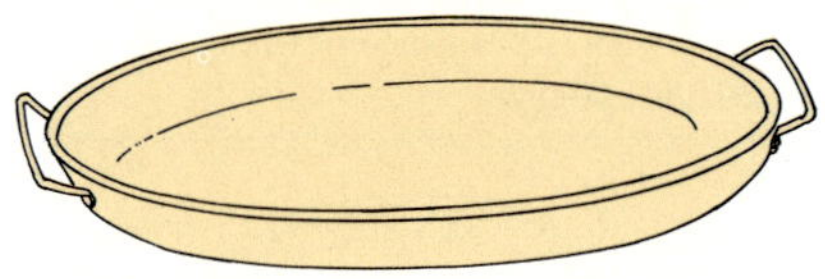

Oval copper dish, a superb pan for presenting a golden gratin.

Copper omelette pan, traditionally smooth and curved for deft manoeuvres.

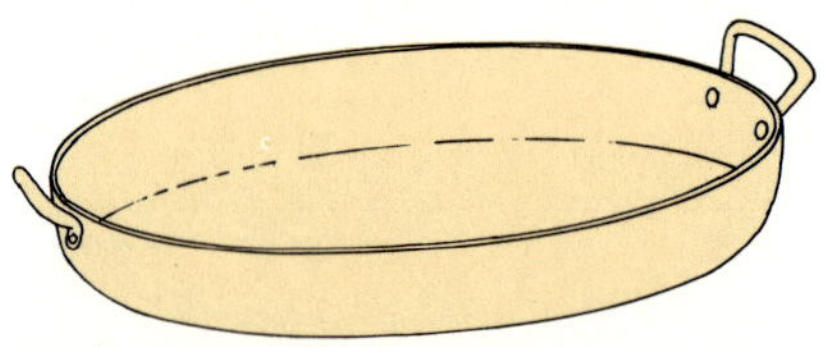

Oval aluminium gratin dish designed for brief exposure to intense heat. A shining item to set on the table.

Iron crêpe pan, shallow and manipulable for swilling round batter and flicking over the pancakes.

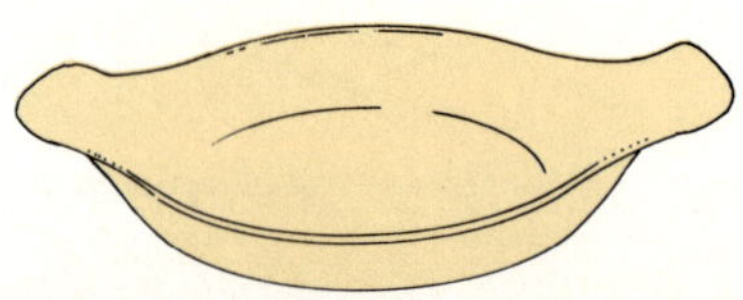

French porcelain gratin dish surrounds a sauce with classical elegance.

Turner with bevelled edges for lifting up the most papery crêpes.

Le Creuset crêpe pan. Its matt-black, cast-iron surface is suitably smooth for peeling off the pancakes.

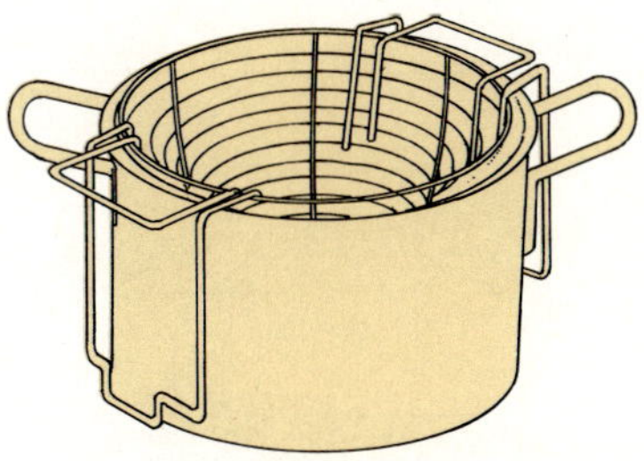

Stainless-steel chip fryer. The depth of the pan guards against spluttering fat.

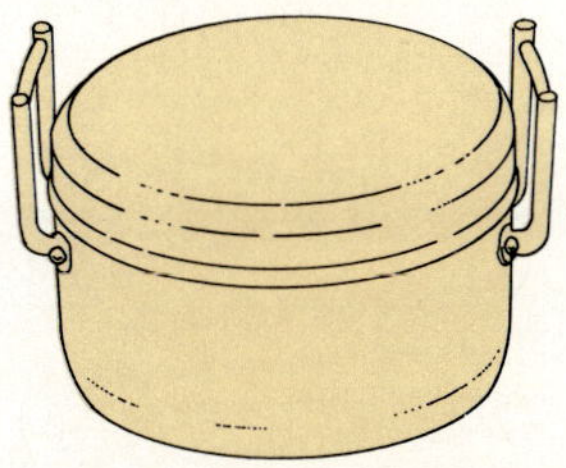

Aluminium bassine, a classic French fryer which heats up rapidly. The lid is used between fry-ups to seal in the recycled oil.

Iron fryer, with handles to support the basket while the chips drain.

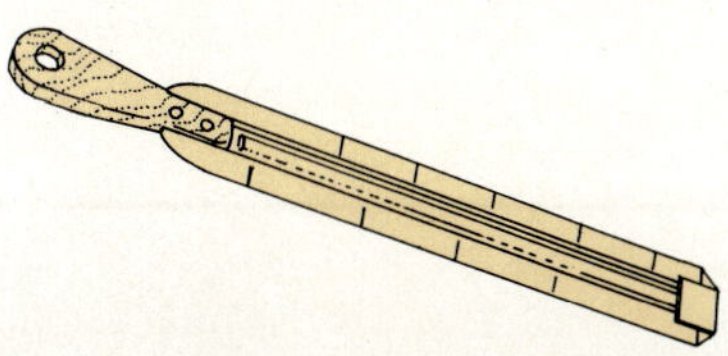

Deep frying thermometer that clips on to the side of the pan.

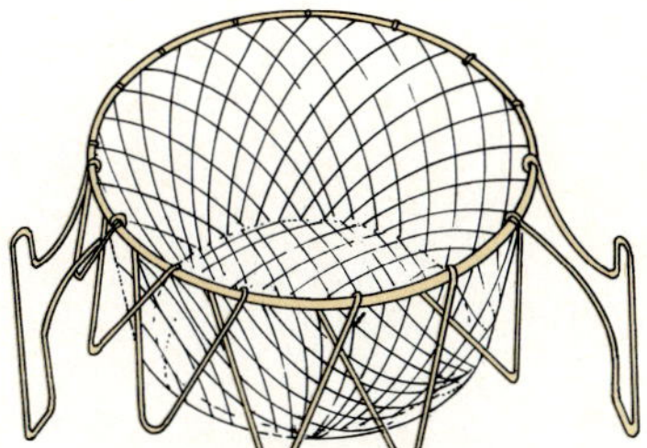

Collapsible wire basket for deep frying or whirling the salad dry.

Le Creuset chicken fryer, a staunch cast-iron pot with a domed lid. Its matt black lining "seizes" and browns the meat.

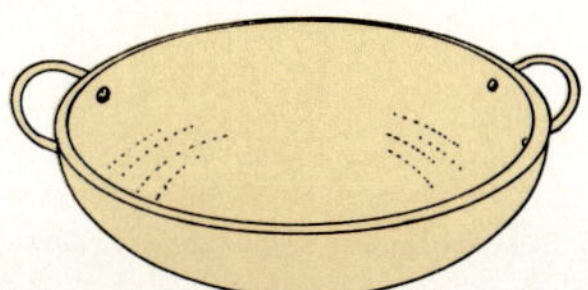

Double-handled copper wok, designed for quick stir-frying. Its bowl-shaped bottom is balanced over gas or electric rings on a metal wok stand.

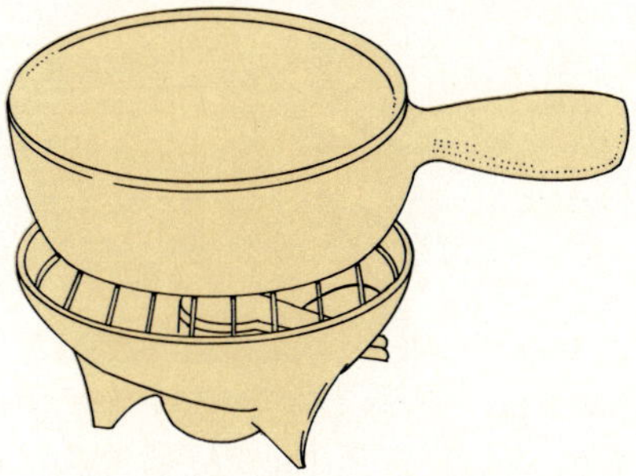

Le Creuset fondue set. The cheese bubbles without curdling in the thick-set pot.

Bellied pot for meat fondues. Plump shape stops splatter.

Cast-iron waffle iron presses the batter into a rosette of hearts.

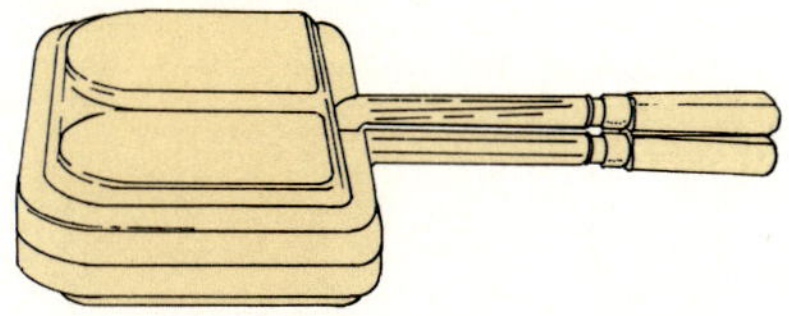

Double sandwich toaster.

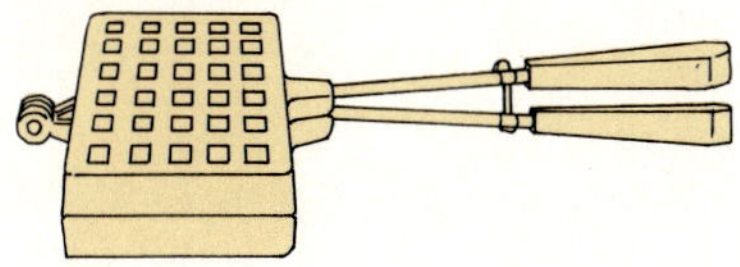

French aluminium waffle iron for crisp, chequered waffles.

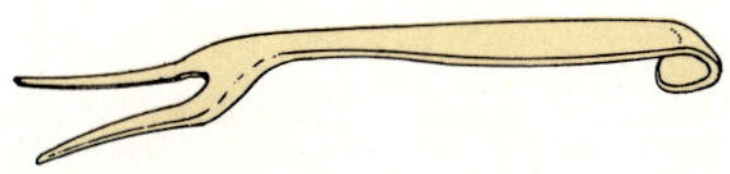

Aluminium pot fork. The long twirled prongs hold chunks of meat securely.

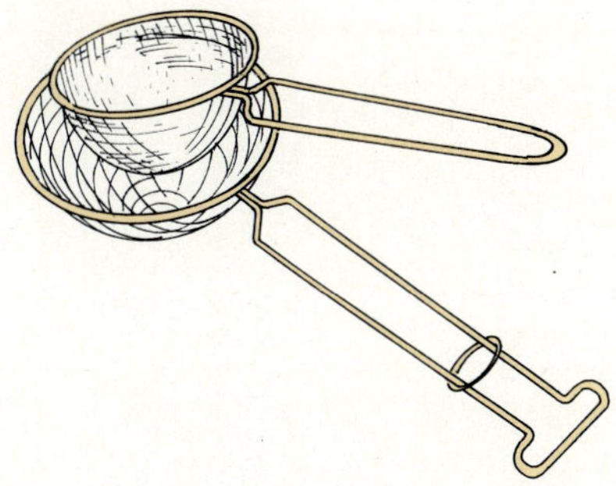

Bird's-nest maker. Clamp the wire baskets together over cooked noodles or a slice of bread and fry until the starch is a crisp hollow.

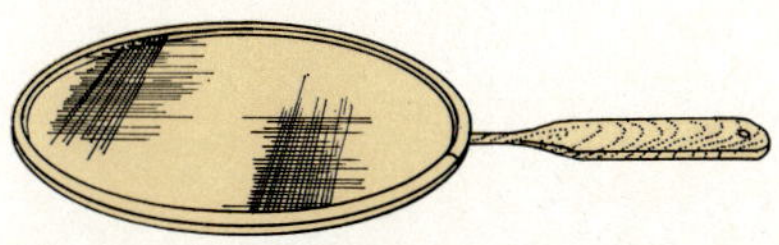

Anti-splash guard, a wire-mesh bat that covers frying-pans and sauté pans.

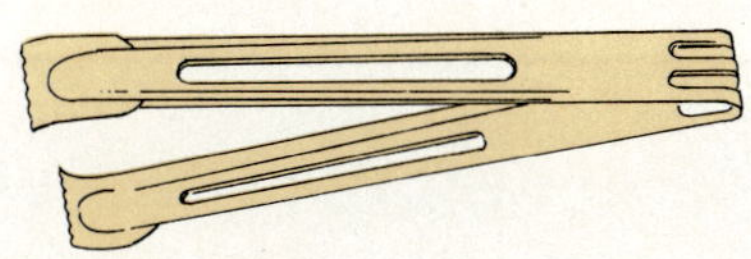

Spring action aluminium food tongs.

Deep-bowled skimmer, a German ladle for catching dumplings or chips. Its foot-long handle keeps the simmering broth or crackling oil at a safe distance.

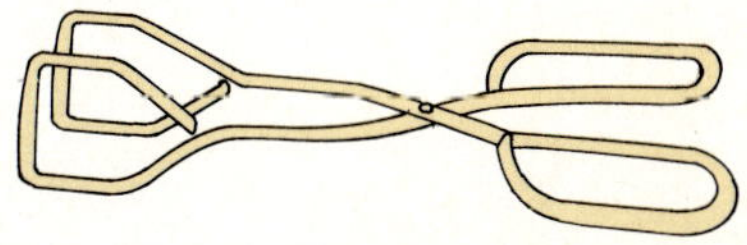

Scissor action stainless-steel tongs grip without piercing.

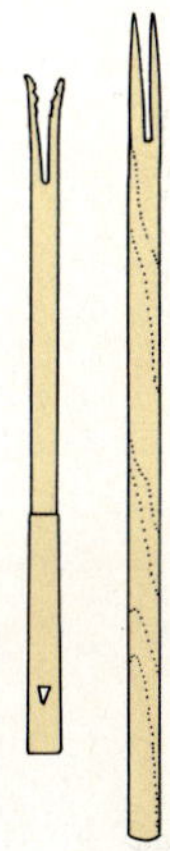

Wooden and stainless-steel forks for dunking bread cubes in cheese fondue.

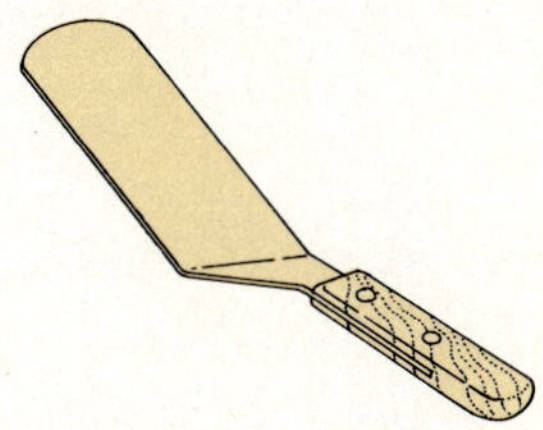

Flexible spatula for sliding between the pancake and the pan.

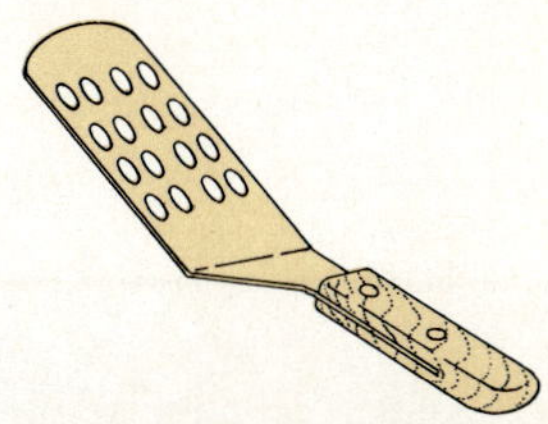

Slotted spatula for flipping and folding pancakes and retrieving fried potatoes.

Cooking for keeps

Cooking for keeps

Home-made jams and marmalade, bottled fruits and chutneys are resuming their traditional pride of place in the store cupboard. Essential for jam-making is a good-quality preserving pan with a heavy base. An aluminium or stainless steel pan is ideal; so is copper, but not for making pickles or chutney, because it would react adversely with the vinegar. Using a sugar thermometer to gauge whether setting point has been reached is quicker and truer than the traditional method of testing a spoonful of jam on a cold saucer.

Another home industry growing in popularity is wine and beer-making. For this you will need some specialist equipment, such as fermentation vessels, glass airlocks, syphon tubing, funnels and sediment filters, but other items like a boiling pan, sieves, scales, measuring jugs, bottles and corks are probably already on your shelves.

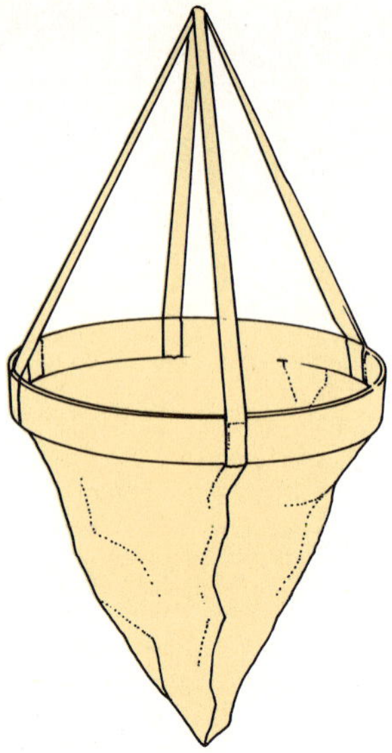

Jelly bag in flannel has a wooden rim and looped suspension to hold it aloft while pulp juices drip through.

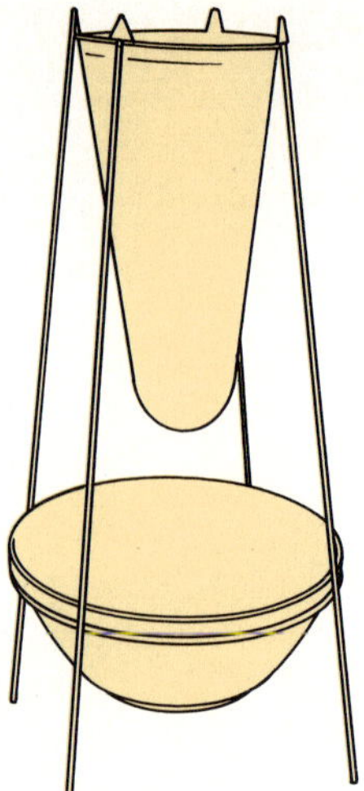

Jelly bag of heavy felt has its own galvanized steel stand with room for a basin below.

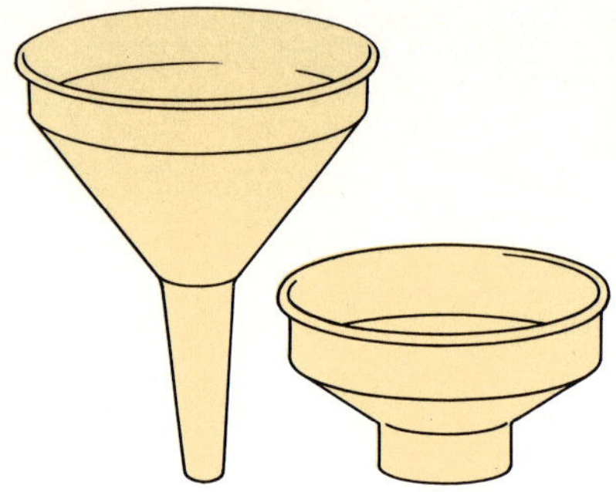

A clear polythene kitchen funnel eases liquids into narrow-necked bottles without spillage and an aluminium jam-potting funnel smoothes the passage of preserves.

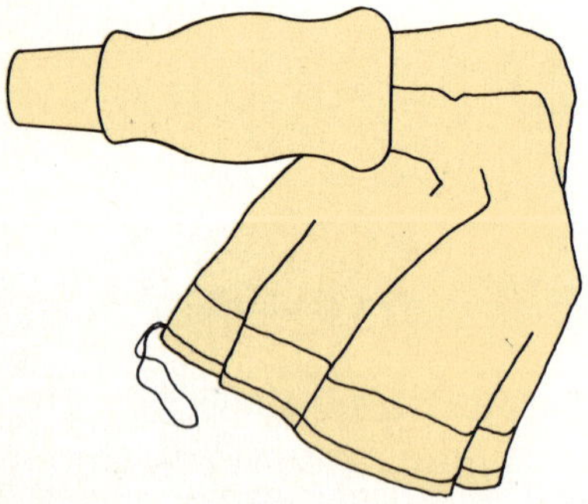

White nylon fruit-squeezing bag forces soft fruit into a smooth purée, syrup or jelly. The forcing ring is of wood.

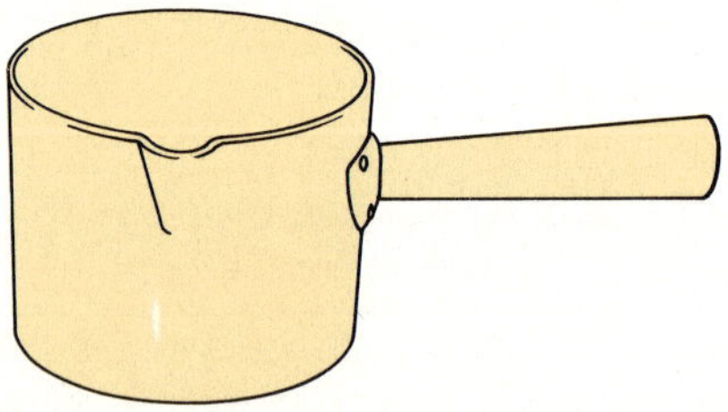

Smart sugar-boiling pan in copper, ideal for caramels and other high-temperature work: the unlined copper will not intereact harmfully with boiling sugar.

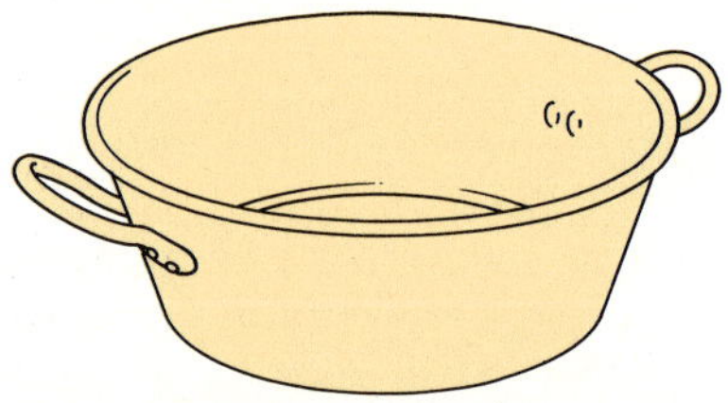

This high-grade aluminium preserving pan with a ground base is tough but comparatively light. Aluminium conducts heat well, so the simmering fruit cooks consistently.

Green glass adds colour to shelves: fruit juice bottle has a secure spring-clip stopper; airtight preserving jar boasts strong metal clips and a rubber seal. Spare seals can be bought separately.

1 *Bottled fruit provides a pleasant reminder of summer all year round.*
Preserving jars of strengthened glass with strong metal clips are perfect for bottling.
2 *Rubber sealing rings inside preserving jar lids ensure an airtight fit.*
3 *The best preserving pans are wide in shape to allow rapid evaporation while simmering the fruit, and have a heavy base to prevent jam burning during boiling.*
4 *A jam thermometer cuts out guesswork in telling whether setting point is near.*

The ubiquitous jam jar. Two sizes, with polythene covers.

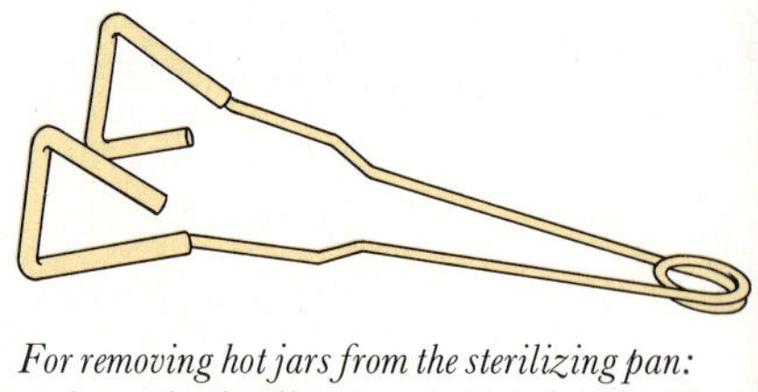

For removing hot jars from the sterilizing pan: spring action bottling tongs in plated steel with rubber tips.

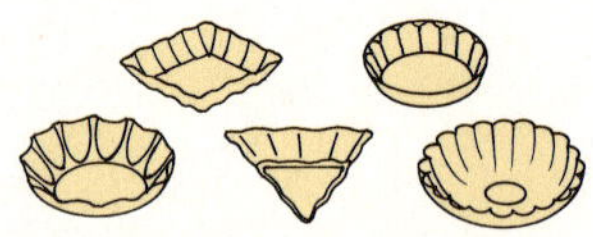

Chocolate moulds for a variety of home-made petits fours. This set of five gives a variety of shapes.

Tempting sweets are given distinctive shapes in rubber fondant moulds. This one (below) makes 75 melting mouthfuls.

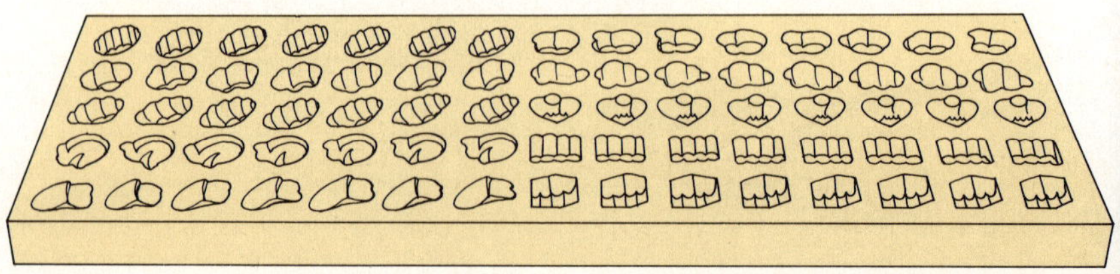

Cellophane discs to cover preserves with a protective film.

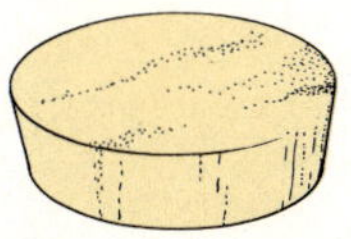

Cork bung. Comes in many sizes, is airtight, odourless and long-lasting.

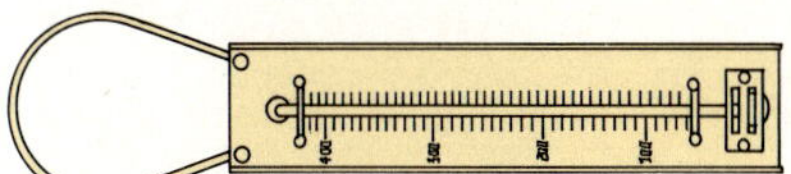

Brass sugar thermometer. Registers 60°-420°F. Wipes out guesswork in jam- or candy-making.

Aluminium fish smoker used with oak sawdust, fired by methylated spirit. Also good for pork, lamb, sausages.

Plastic dustbin with lock-on lid for beer or wine-making. Best used for short-term storage or the initial stages. High-density polythene won't impart a plastic flavour to the fermenting brew. The usual capacity of these bins is from 5 to 10 gallons.

Glass demijohns suitable for both secondary fermentation and maturing the vintage. They hold $\frac{1}{2}$ *to 4 gallons.*

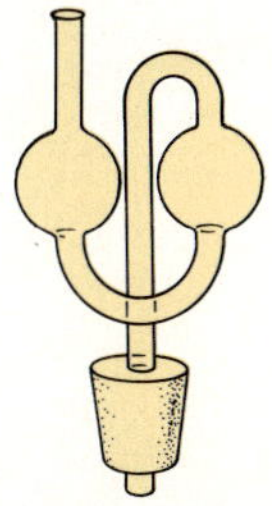

Glass airlock. Fits into cork bung. When partly filled with water, fruit flies and air are kept out, but gases formed during the fermentation process can escape.

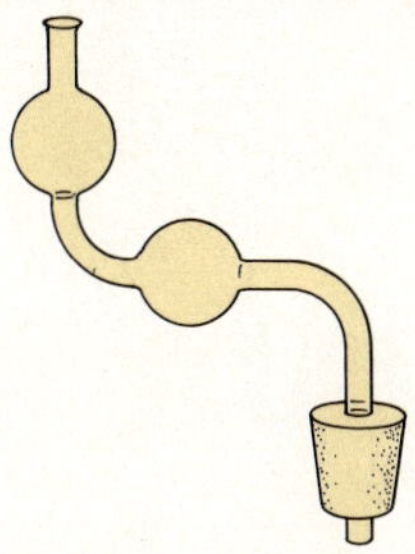

Another type of airlock.

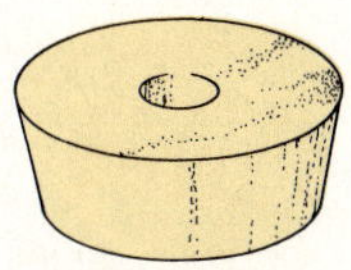

Cork bung with a hole to take the airlock. Using rubber bungs would result in the wine gaining an unwelcome flavour.

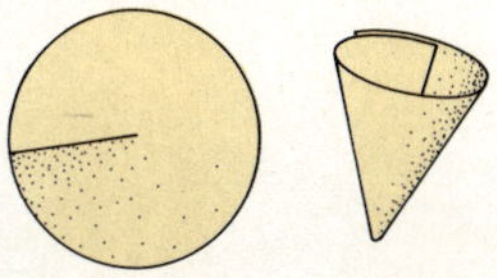

Filter pads. Used with a funnel during bottling to help remove sediment.

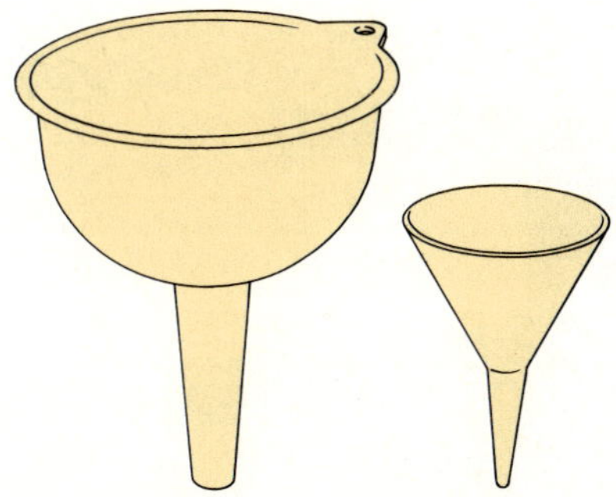

Large polythene funnel for pouring thick fruit pulps or transferring wine and beer into new containers; small funnel for filtering or decanting wine.

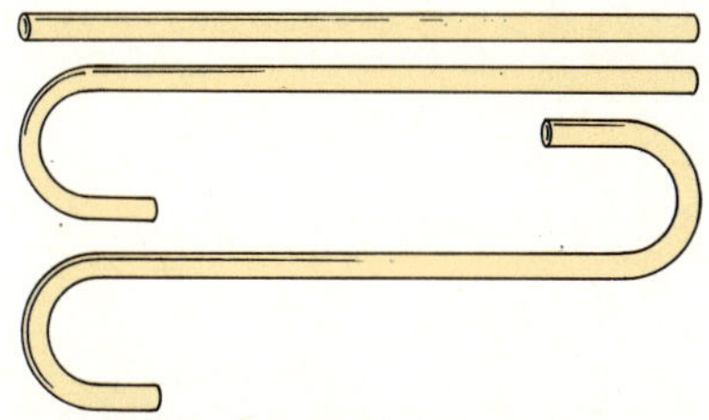

Glass tubing for racking wine. Tubing with curved ends prevents sediment being drawn up from the bottom of a container.

Rubber tubing is used to syphon wine or beer from bucket to demijohn and then into bottles.

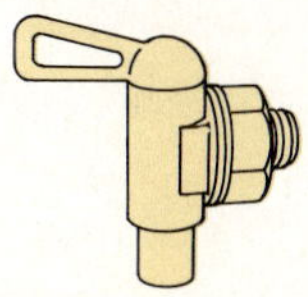

A syphon tap fits on to rubber tubing to control the flow.

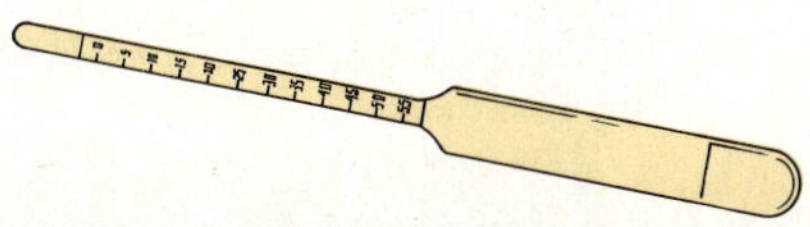

Hydrometer. Measures the sugar content or gravity of liquids. The specific gravity of a liquid is an accurate guide to what degree of fermentation it has reached.

Wine and beer bottles. Wine bottles are traditionally made of tinted glass except those for some sweet white wines and rosés. Beer bottles are extra strong to withstand the often considerable build-up of gas during storing. Label all brews when bottling them.

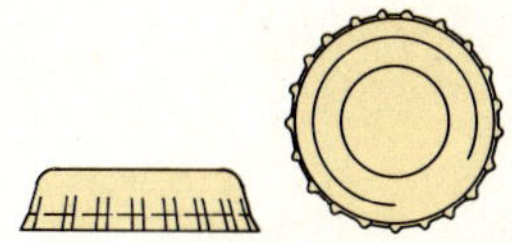

Crown corks with a metal flange for capping beer bottles.

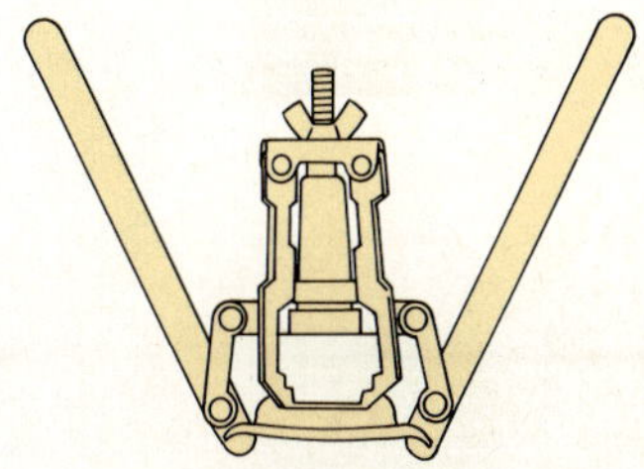

Crown corker. This model gives the tight seal necessary for highly gaseous beers.

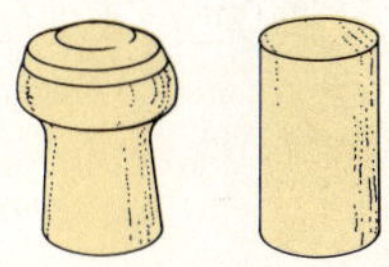

Flanged wine corks are for sparkling wine, straight-sided ones for still wine.

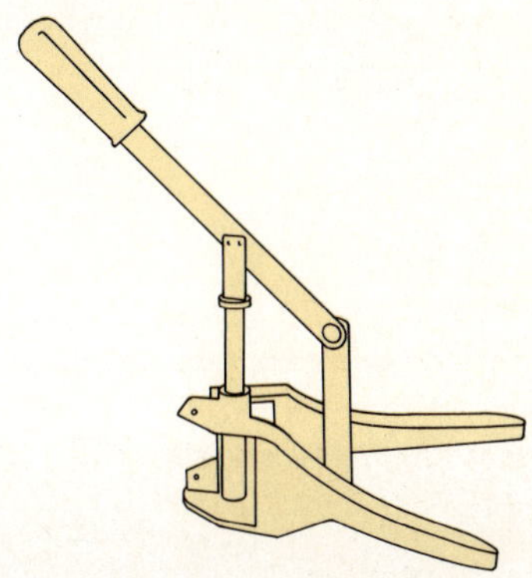

Hand corker of steel and aluminium with a plastic handle drives home wine corks.

Electrical gadgetry

Mechanical aids in the kitchen can be time-saving, and they are therefore invaluable to a busy cook. They are also likely to encourage the naturally timid to try out a greater variety of recipes—and thus open up a whole new aspect of cooking.

If you are starting from scratch you might well consider purchasing a multipurpose appliance—some of which aim to be the ultimate kitchen accessory. But they all have some imperfections and they are of course more liable to go wrong as their mechanism is so complicated. Therefore you may be better off with a few specialized gadgets that perform each function to perfection. One final word of warning: no electrical parts must ever be immersed in water when an electrical gadget is washed.

1 *Kenwood mincer with medium and coarse blades.*
2 *Kenwood Chef blender attachment.*
3 *Braun Kitchen Machine coffee mill attachment.*
4 *Kenwood Chef egg whisk.*
5 *Kenwood Chef Model A901 with stainless-steel bowl.*
6 *Kenwood Chef accessories: slice drum (left); shredder drum (right).*
7 *Kenwood Chef beater.*
8 *Braun Kitchen Machine accessories: slicing and shredding blades.*
9 *Kenwood Chef juice extractor attachment.*

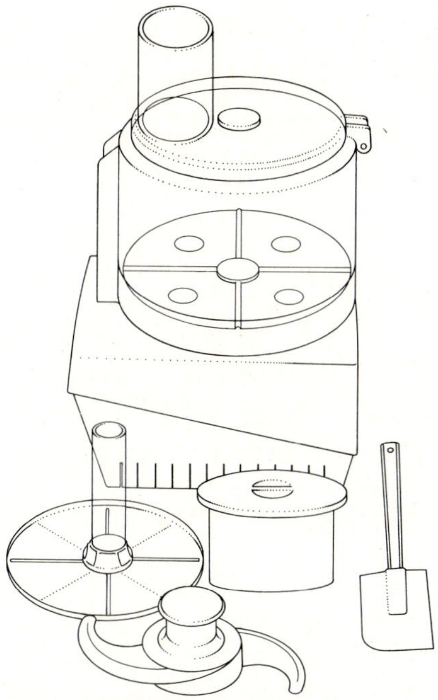

Magimix, or Cuisinarts food processor, has a distinctive oval chimney. It is an indispensable kitchen aid, which processes food by means of its double-bladed multipurpose knife, slicing disc, shredding disc and plastic mixing blade. The space-saving base is under 200 mm (8 in) square.

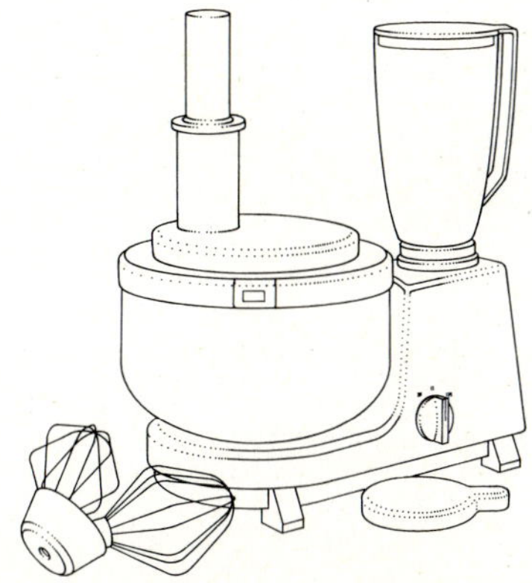

Bosch Magic Mixer—near perfection for performance, adaptability and compactness. Its beaters are attached to the bottom of the mixing bowl.

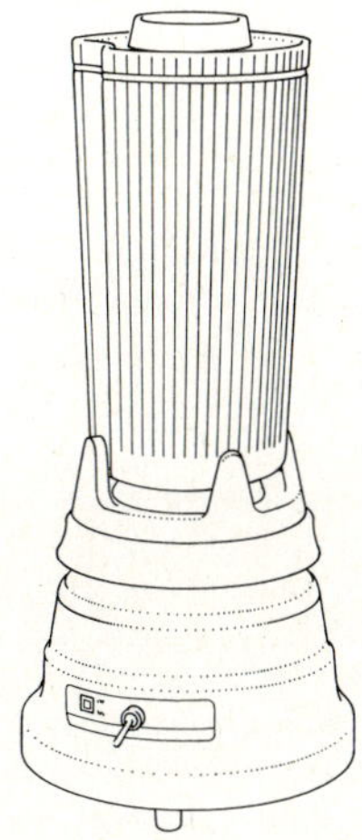

This Waring single-speed blender is simple, sturdy and excellent value for money. The blades are set fairly low so small quantities can also be liquified.

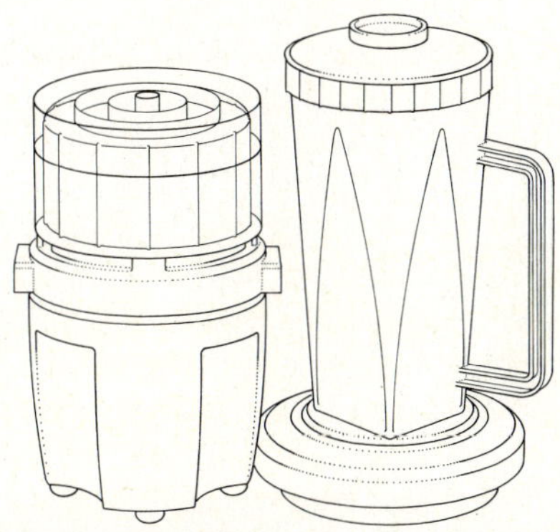

Moulinette chopper/blender, a versatile and powerful pulverizer for meat, cheese and vegetables. Its large capacity blender attachment will liquidize soups in seconds.

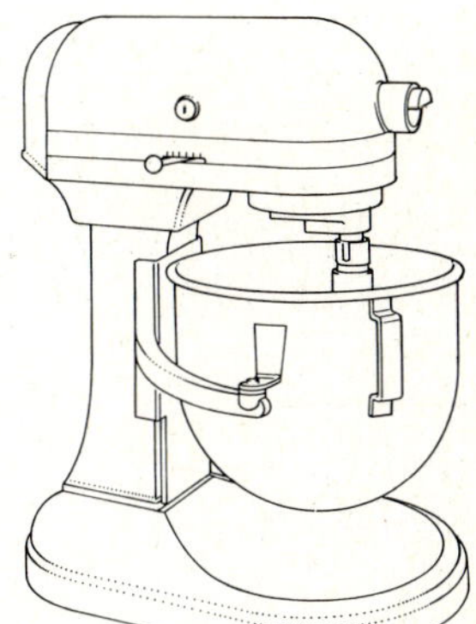

KitchenAid K-5A electric mixer is made in solid steel to last a lifetime. A powerful ten-speed motor drives this mixer which beats, mixes, whips and kneads in superlative style. Unlined copper beating bowls available.

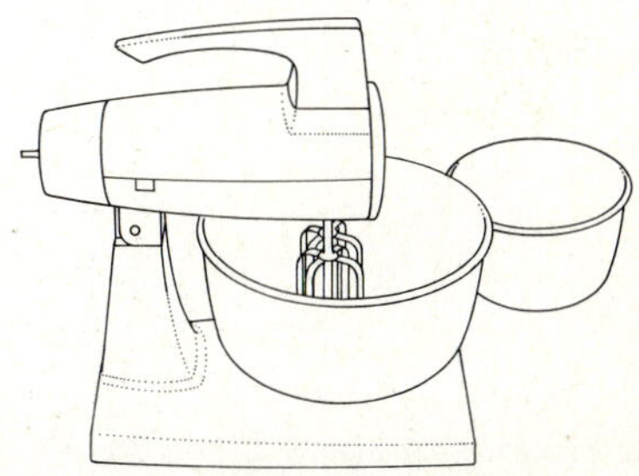

Sunbeam Mixmaster mixes, beats and whips through a range of twelve speeds.

Farberware hand mixer—easily and conveniently controlled in a one-handed operation.

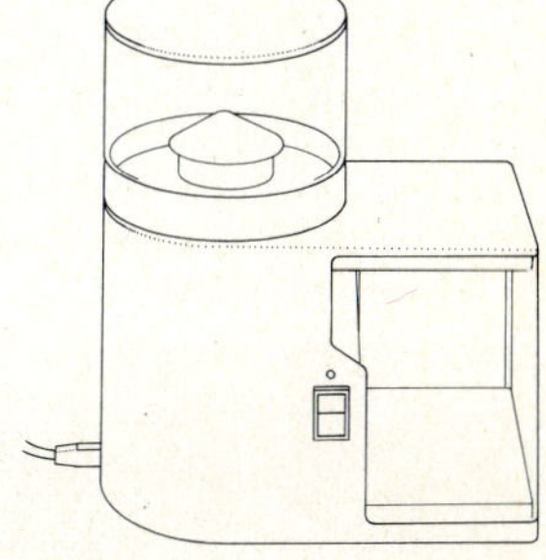

This Braun coffee mill is neat and compact.

Batterie de cuisine

Electrical gadgetry

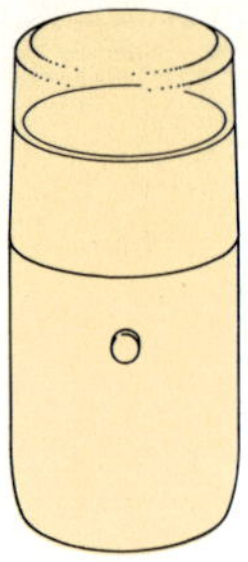

Single-speed Braun coffee mill with push-button on-off switch.

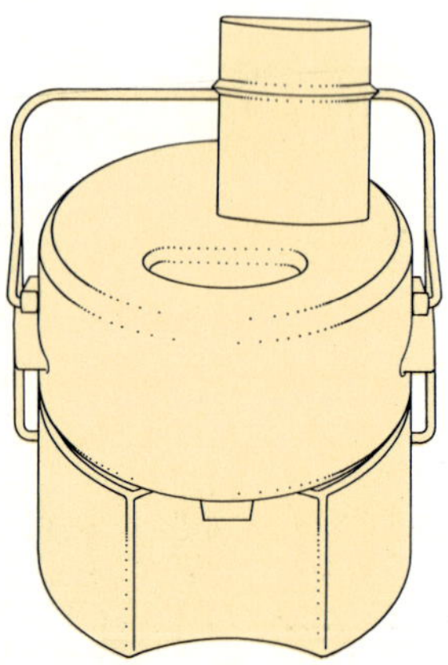

Braun vegetable and fruit juice extractor—compact to store, convenient to carry and quick to pulverize.

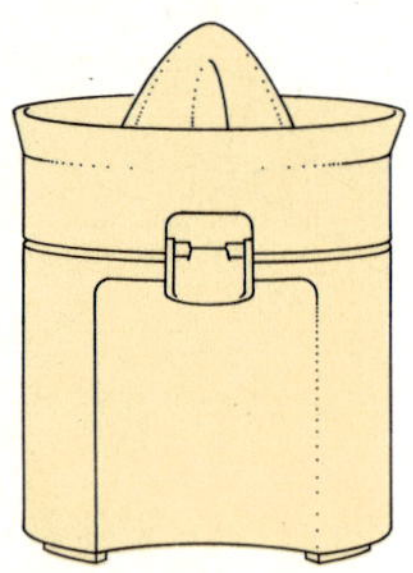

Braun Citromatic Juicer for quick refreshing drinks.

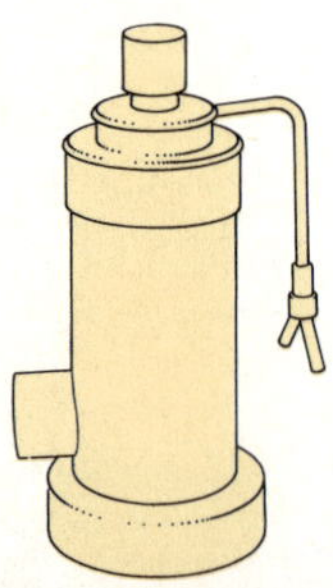

A marvellous miniature espresso coffee-maker which is fool-proof, even for novices.

Europiccola espresso machine for brewing up mouth-watering ristretto and capuccino coffee. Its small capacity ensures you get a fresh cup of espresso every time.

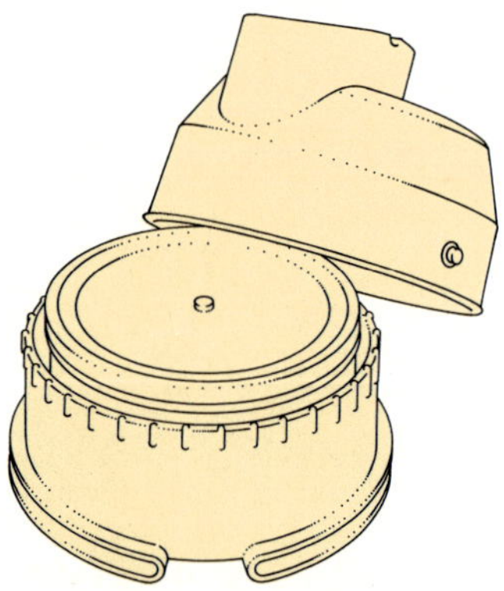

Salton ice-cream machine. This 200-mm (8-in) high unit fits neatly in the freezer and makes wonderfully textured ice-cream, without churning or mixing rock salts and ice.

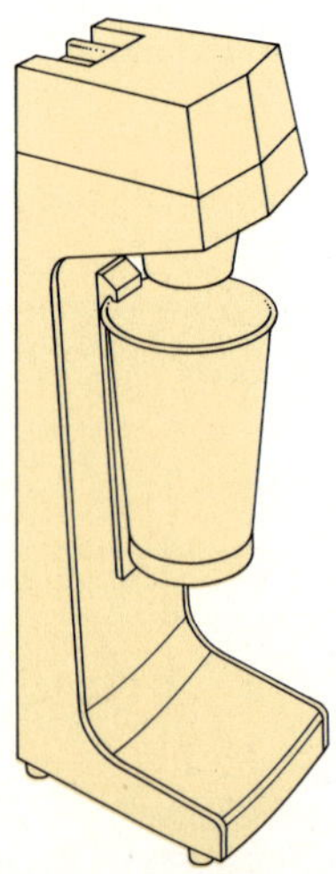

Milkshake-maker with single mixing spindle for making up to a quart of frothing malty summer drinks.

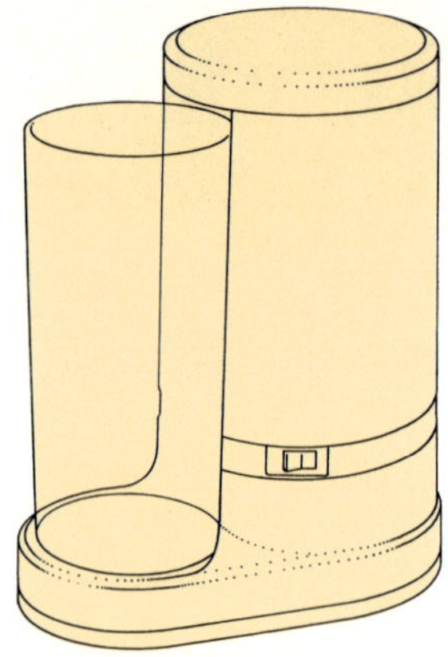

Watermate filters water and removes all impurities, both chemical and mineral—ideal for those with a discerning palate.

Salton yogurt-maker thermostatically controls the culture as it grows into creamy yogurt.

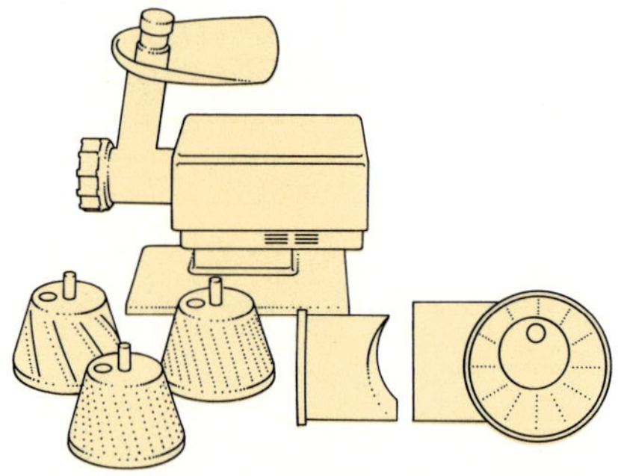

Moulinex's powerful mincer with coarse and fine cutters, a citrus press and interchangeable cones that grate, slice and shred.

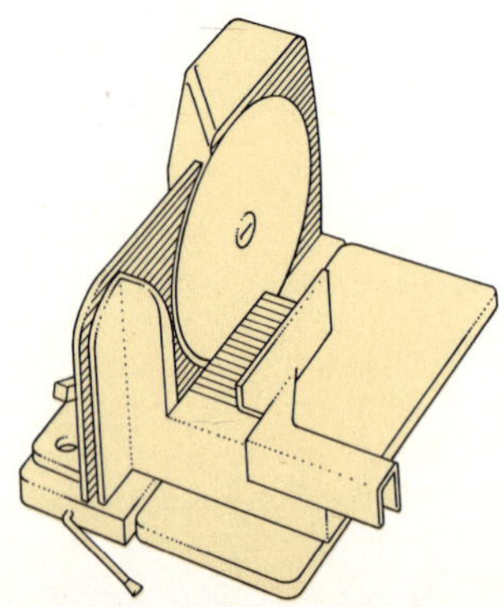

Slicing machine with well-designed hand guard to protect the operator.

Electric kettles for speedy boiling anywhere round the house.

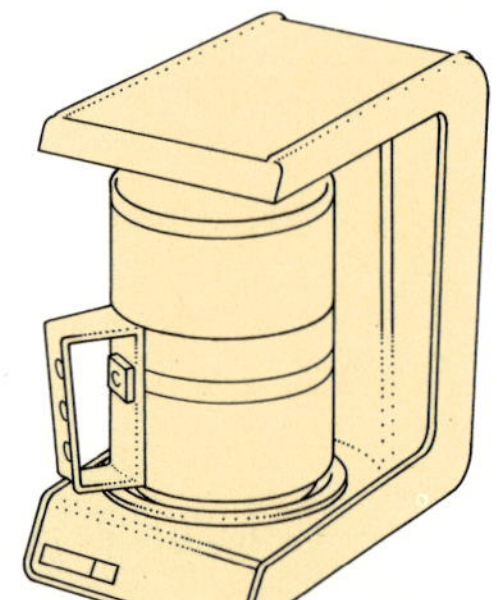

Moulinex filter coffee-maker with thermostatically-controlled hotplate to keep hot that welcome extra cup.

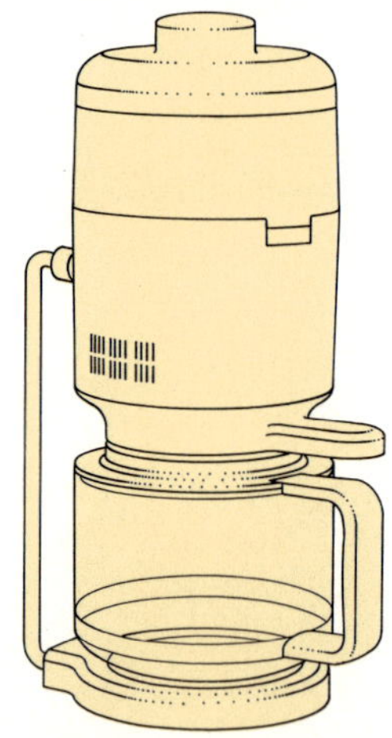

Braun filter coffee-maker is vertically sealed so all the richness and flavour is retained as the water flows directly on to the coffee in the heatproof container.

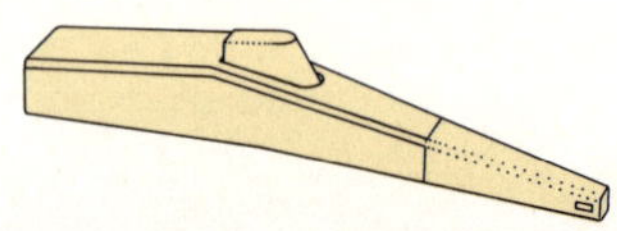

The matchless electric sparker for gas appliances without their own lighter.

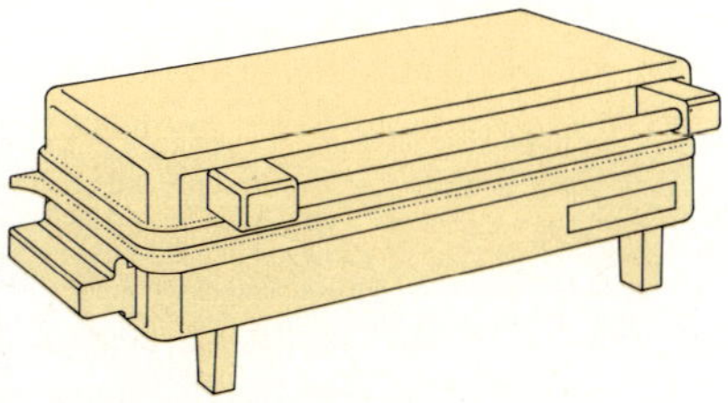

Infra-red grills quickly seal in natural juices and delicious flavours. They are quick, safe, easy-to-use and energy saving.

Prestige slow cooker for low temperatures. The stoneware pot, which lifts out of the casing, is also a serving dish.

Well-insulated electric roaster/mini oven with an excellent range of temperatures. Bed-sitter inhabitants can cook a whole meal in its ovenproof, lidded glass dishes.

Waffle iron with handy thermostat for temperature control and cast-aluminium grids.

Heavy cast aluminium Farberware griddle conveys safe, fast heat to steaks and hamburgers.

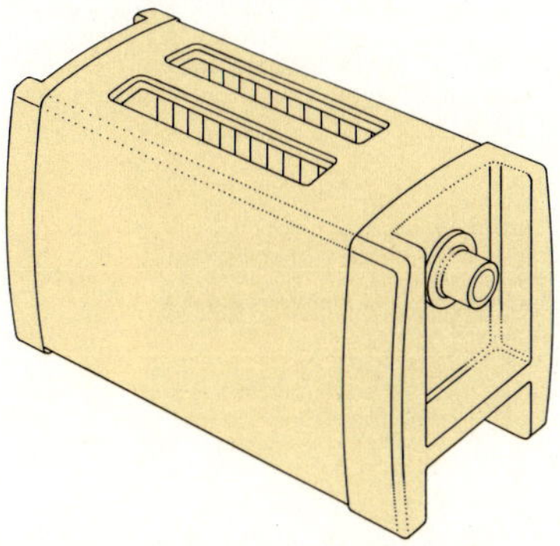

Pop-up toaster with variable shades of brown.

GE Toast-R-Oven for even top browning, versatile toasting, adaptable baking and quickly heated frozen dinners.

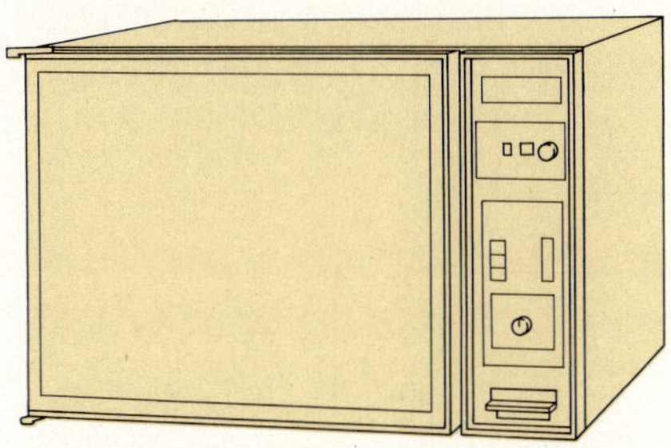

Litton microwave oven has a flexible range of cooking speeds and an easy-to-read timer on the front to count every precious cooking second.

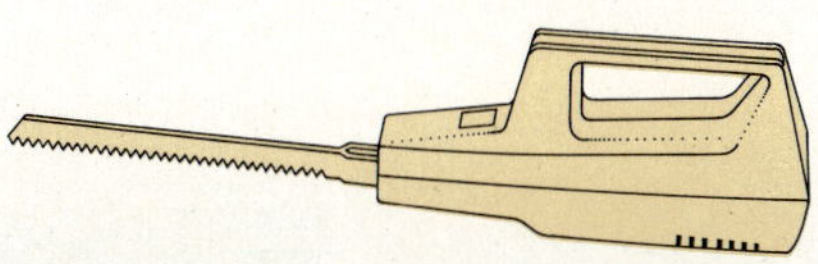

Electric knives effortlessly ease their way through difficult joints and frozen foods.

Farber counter-top convection oven with constantly circulating hot air rapidly produces a meal that is browned and appetizing.

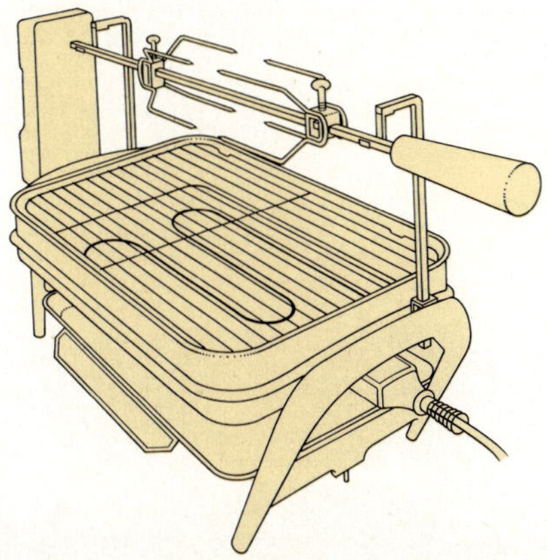

Farber broiler/rôtisserie for use inside the house and out of doors.

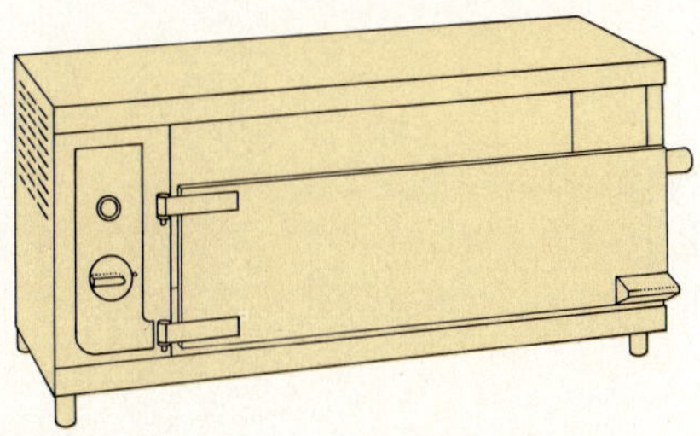

Rôtisseries grill or spit-roast quick snacks, party kebabs or complete chickens automatically, evenly and cleanly.

Salton hot tray with adjustable temperature control and circular "hot spot" to keep beverages slightly hotter than the other food.

Automatic egg cooker for up to eight perfectly boiled eggs every breakfast or four poached eggs for a quick snack.

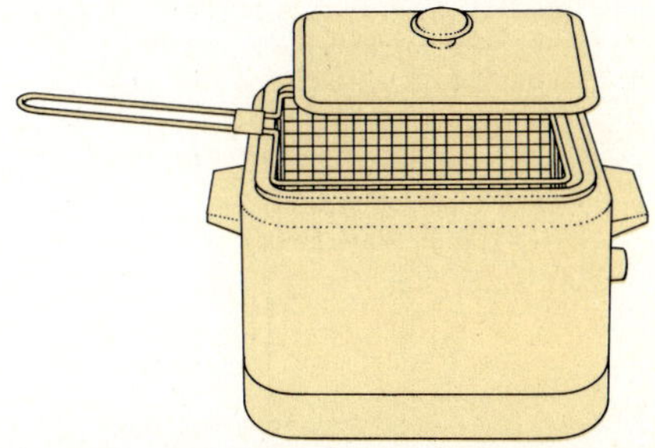

Nesco deep fryer quickly recovers to its correct frying temperature when food is added, thereby ensuring a successful fry-up.

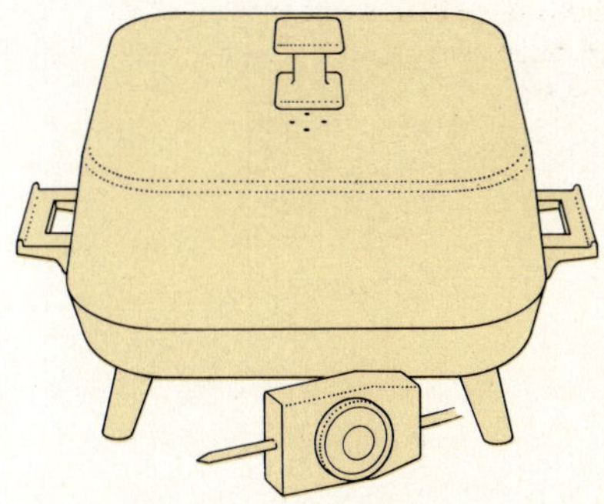

Sunbeam Frypan can also braise, stew, roast, bake, boil and even steam. An excellent alternative to a conventional cooker and much more economic to run.

Time-All will start cooking your dinner while you're on the homebound train, or switch on the percolator for your early-morning coffee.

Bins, jars and racks

Intelligent storage saves time spent searching for the right utensils and money spent replacing the mouldy food which has been kept at the wrong temperature. Cool suits most foods but surprisingly, refrigeration can be a mistake. It kills the flavour of cheese, hastens the decline of root vegetables, makes eggs fragile in boiling water and less responsive to the whisk. Wine should be kept at an even temperature in a dark place; though a wine rack looks attractive it may be better kept out of the limelight.

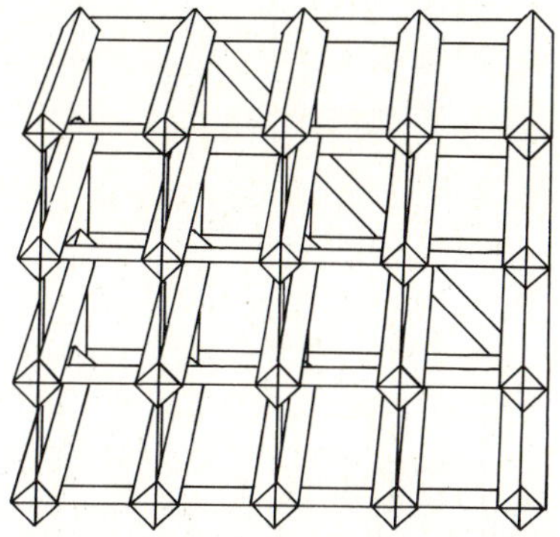

Sturdy grid of wood and metal (above left) cradles twelve wine bottles. Keep it dark at a temperature of 60-65 degrees.

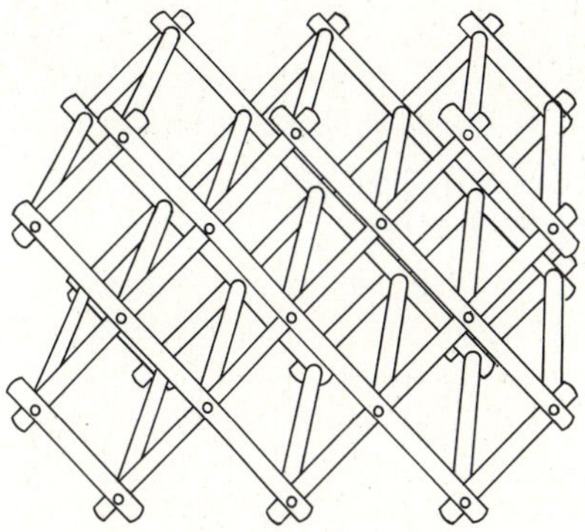

Wooden wine rack, folds flat or expands concertina fashion.

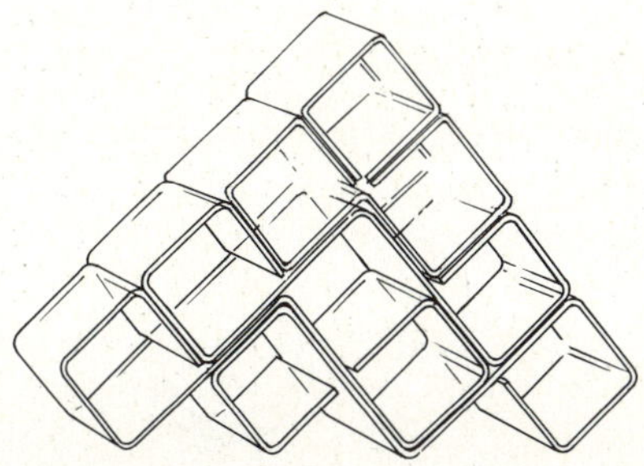

Perspex wine rack. The cellular system of cubes can expand indefinitely.

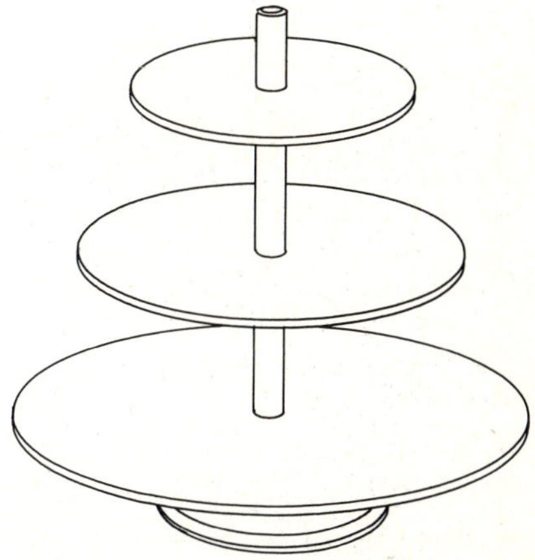

Lazy Susan, a revolving wooden stand, enables indolent breakfasters to reach the marmalade without stretching.

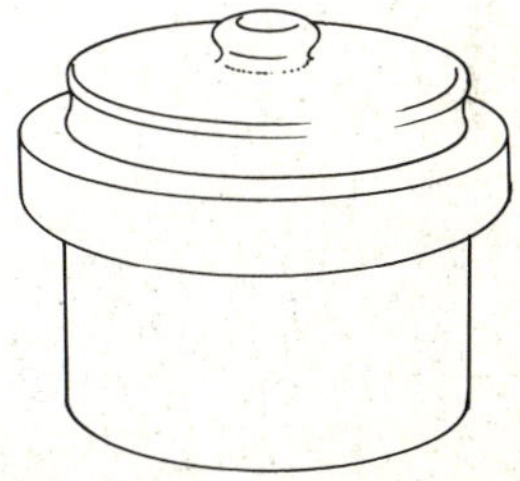

Earthenware butter cooler keeps the contents fresh and firm without becoming refrigerator-hard.

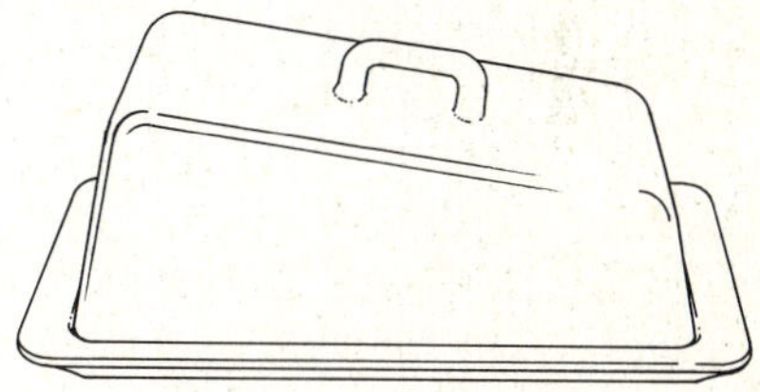

Traditional china cheese dish perfectly fits over a wedge of Cheddar or Stilton. To keep the cheese firm and to prevent it sweating, stand the dish in a cool place.

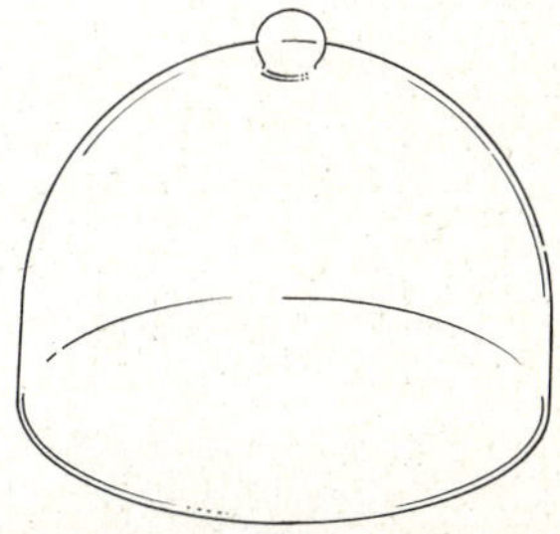

Cheeses look handsome under the glass cheese dome; if they're not in such good condition you can tell at a glance.

Bins, jars and racks

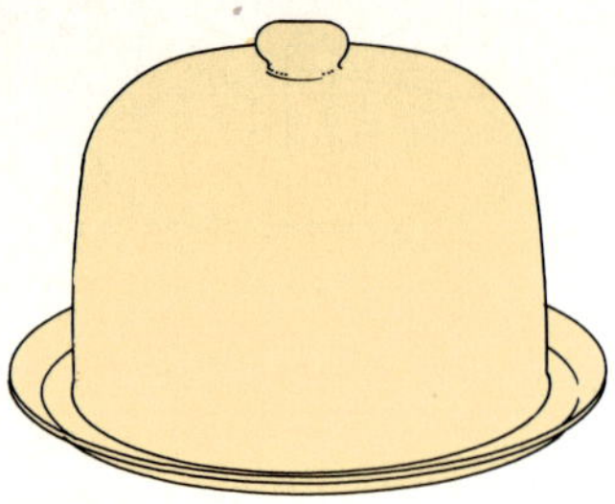

Traditional porcelain cheese cover encloses a whole Stilton.

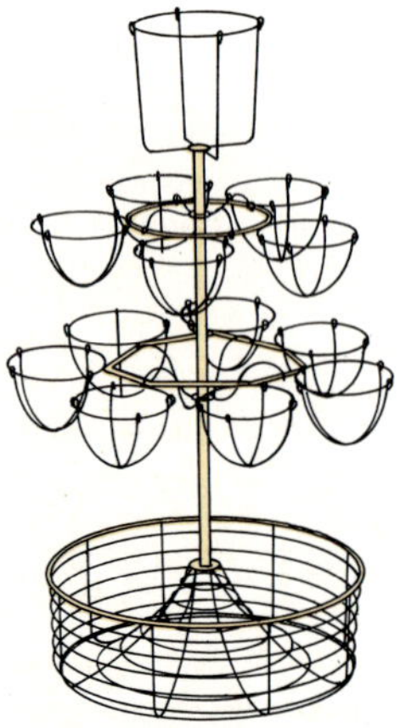

Skeletal egg tree made of tinned wire.

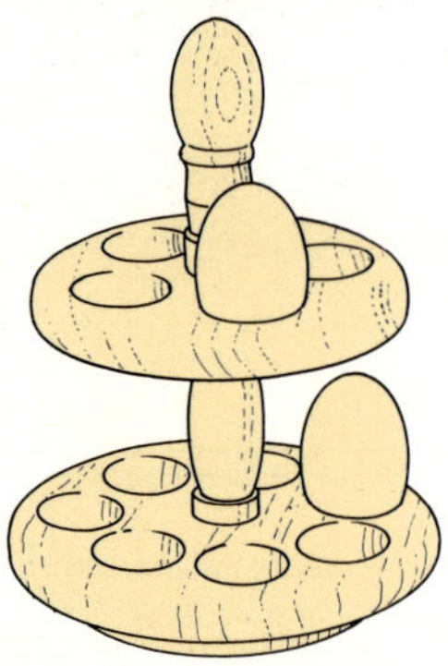

Elm and beech egg-stand holds a dozen; the apex egg is of wood.

Bulbous wire basket for storing eggs or swinging salads.

Egg-shaped egg board. The beechwood oval is a pretty background to brown and white shells.

Small wire bulb for keeping garlic fresh.

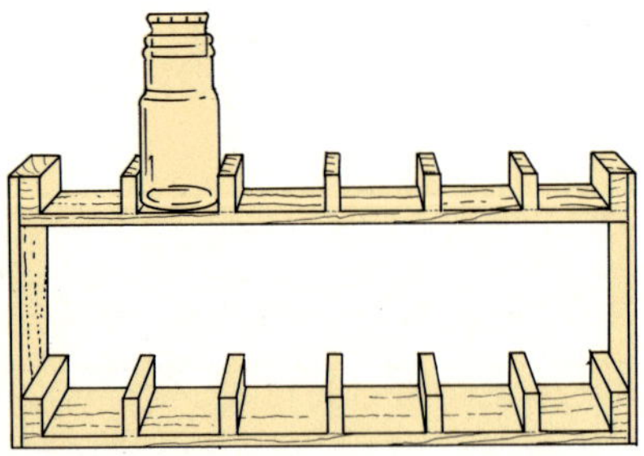

Double tier spice rack. Beechwood slots take the small stoppered glass jars.

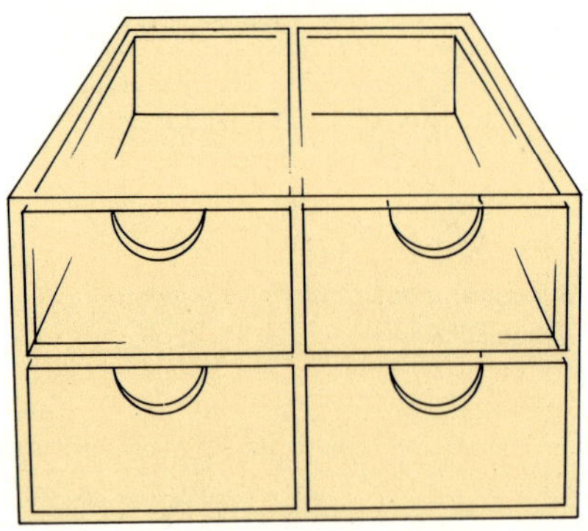

Perspex chest of drawers shows off a coloured collection of spices.

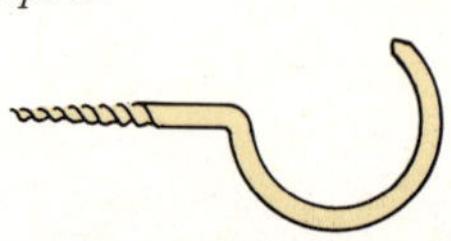

Pot hook for the farmhouse look. Screw a row into the shelf and hang teacups from them.

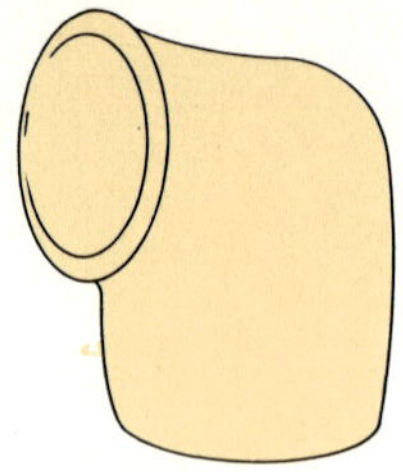

Stone salt pot with a big mouth for a quick handful.

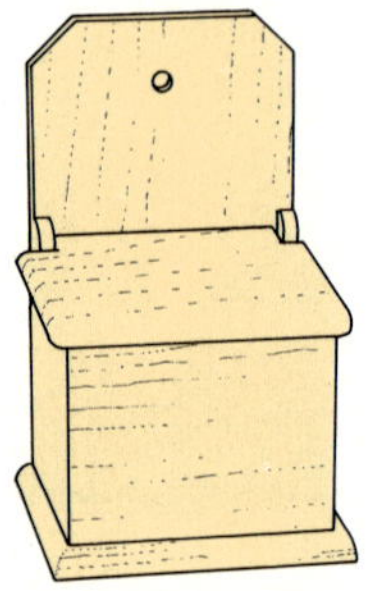

Bird box without a hole; an attractive wooden salt container to hang by the cooktop.

Spaghetti is awkward to store without a tall, stoppered jar.

Glazed earthenware jar for potted goose and pork. Good, too, for dripping or lard.

Big plywood "hatboxes", stencilled or blank for dry foods.

Storage jars with ground glass stoppers keep spices pungent and herbs sweet.

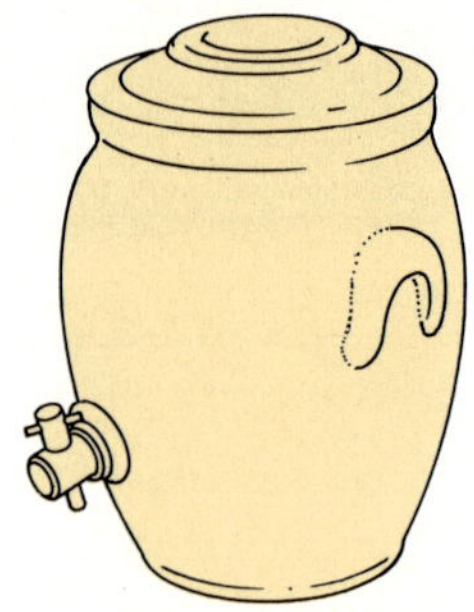

Stout stone vinegar jar.

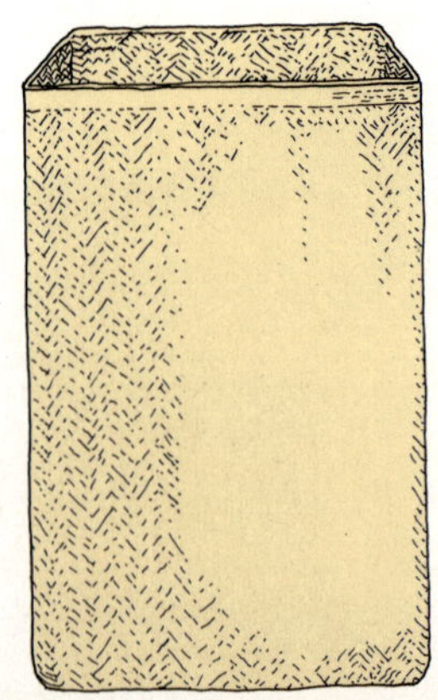

Tall wicker basket for an armful of French loaves.

Capacious bread crock keeps crusty loaves fresh—though it's unsuitable for wrapped bread.

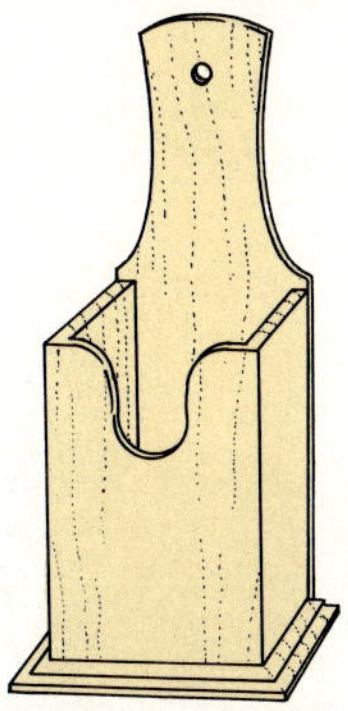

Pine box for spoons and spatulas.

Earthenware jar for tools you want close to hand.

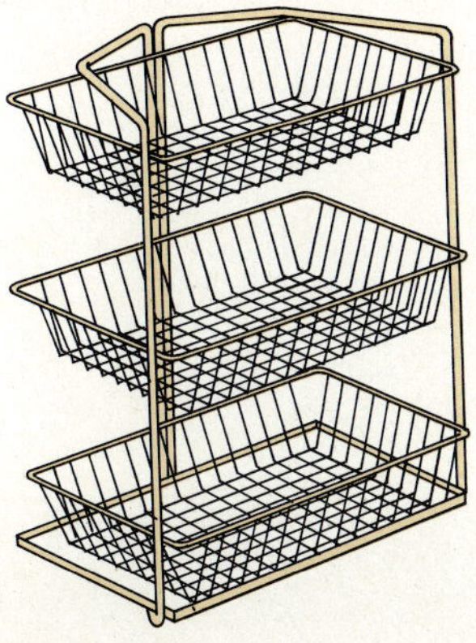

Wicker vegetable basket adds a rural touch to supermarket produce.

Wicker vegetable basket adds a rural touch to supermarket produce.

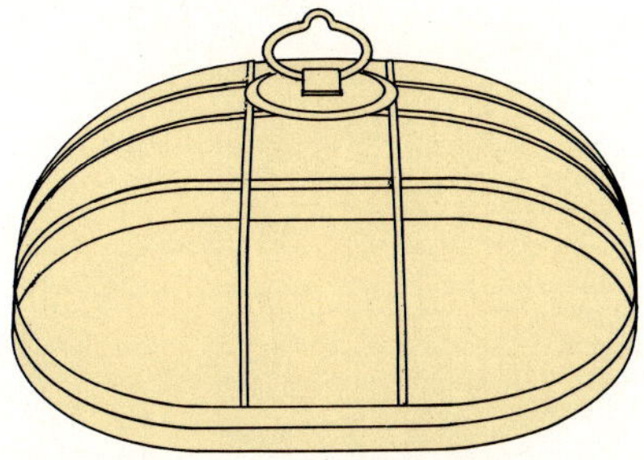

Traditional mesh cover keeps flies off meat.

Refrigerator pots protect flavours from each other.

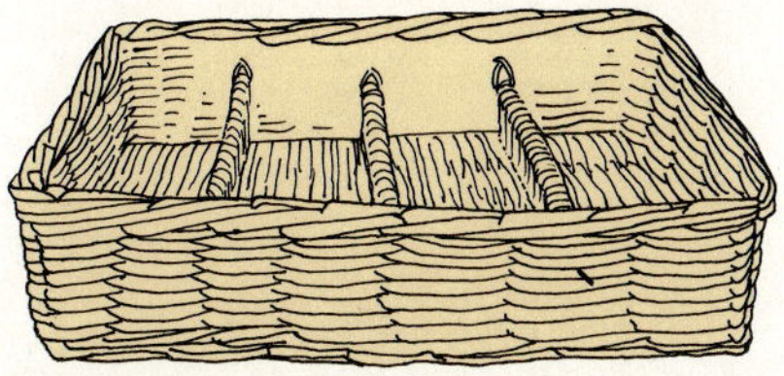

White willow cutlery basket.

Beech cutlery box with a red baize lining.

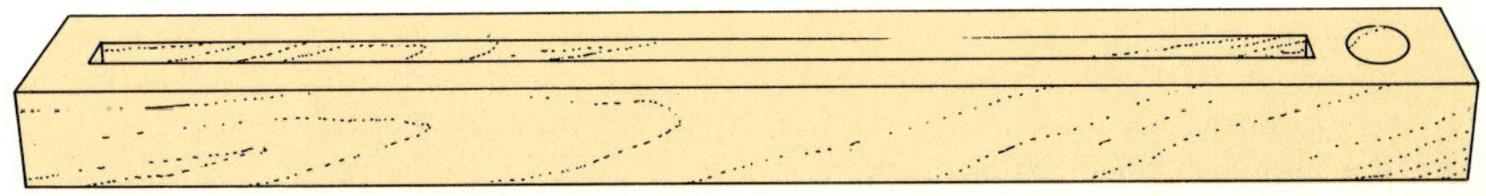

Wooden knife rack with a long slot for the blades and a hole for the sharpening steel.

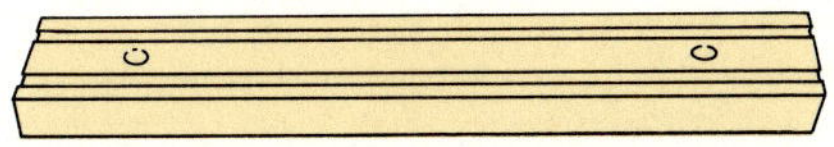

Magnabar knife rack. Double magnets grip the blades.

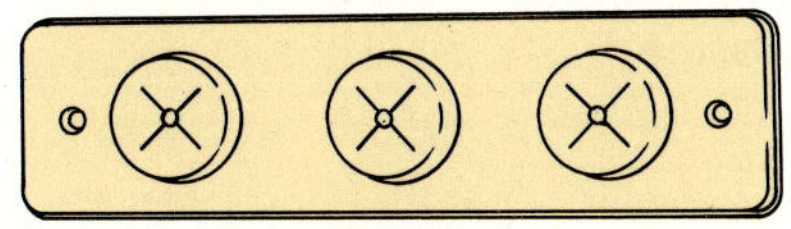

Tea towel holder with rubber grippers. Hang it out of sight and near at hand.

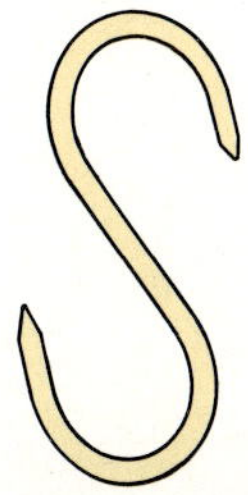

You don't need a carcass to make use of butchers' hooks. Range them along a rail to hang up pots, pans and strings of onions.

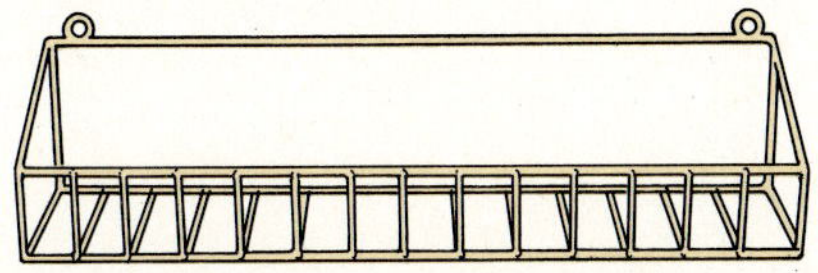

Little rack made of white, plastic-coated wire—useful for spice jars.

Traditional wicker picnic hamper for good summers and a general storage trunk when the weather is not so hot.

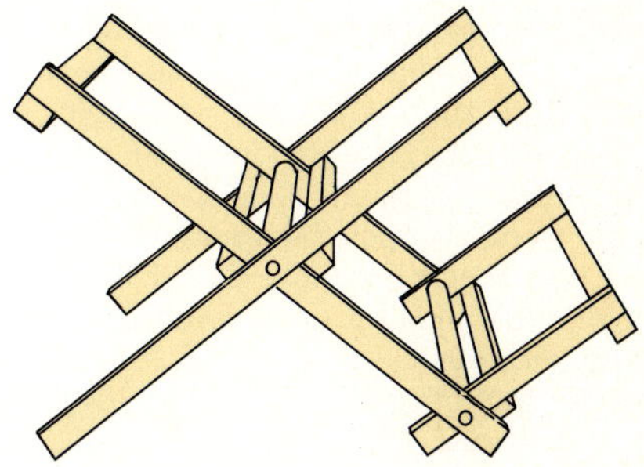

Wooden draining rack folds up like a deck chair for easy, compact storage.

Unless you appreciate the stains of meals gone by, use a perspex cookery book stand to keep the food off the page.

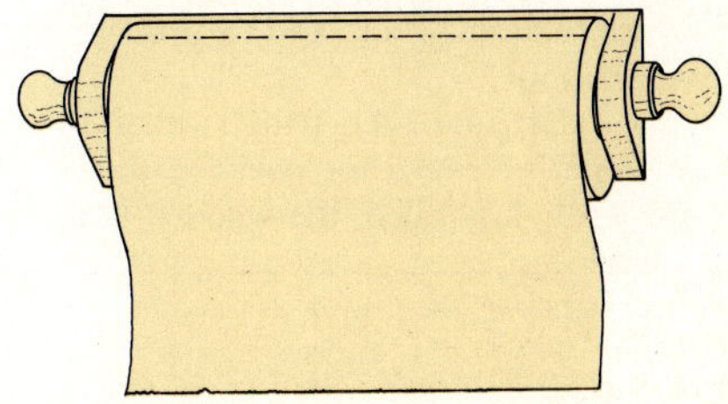

Beechwood holder keeps kitchen roll at the ready.

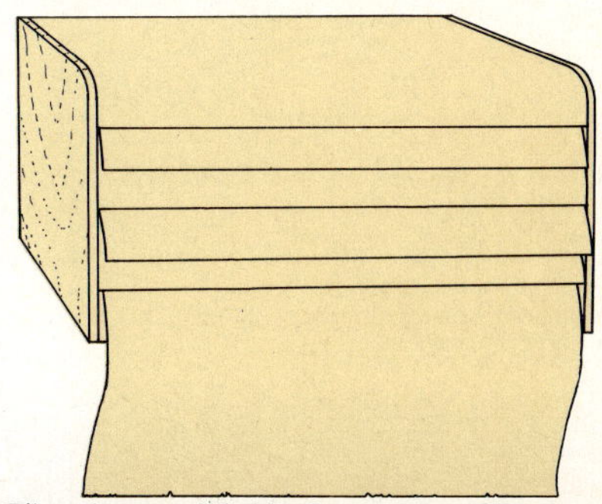

Three-in-one roll holder for snapping off kitchen foil, polythene bags and kitchen paper. Fix it to a wall near the stove.

Basic batterie de cuisine

This seems to me the ideal basic collection of cooking equipment for somebody starting up house. Most of the tools come from the Habitat collection and are well made and reasonably priced. With care all these products should last you for life and make your cooking time a pleasure.

The cook's knives are of good quality and if looked after will serve you well; a sharpening steel has been included to keep them razor sharp. Wooden spoons and a solid wood chopping board are essentials, the board being quite nice enough to bring to the table and the spoons can duplicate as salad servers.

The beautiful red-and-white-enamelled cast-iron casserole and the gratin dish are perfect for cooking, because the thickness of the iron spreads the heat. They are also handsome enough to bring to the table so that food can be served sizzling hot. The Mouli-legume with its three grades of sieve is extremely useful for soups and purées and the finest mashed potatoes, but I am sad that the manufacturer has decided to make the body in orange plastic. The potato peeler takes off the minimum of potato skin; and the glass lemon squeezer separates the pips from the juice and really does extract every drop.

The white china soufflé dish and cocottes have many other uses as well as being perfect for their original purpose. One of the main characteristics of good kitchen-ware is that it can make the transition from kitchen to dining-room and be perfectly at home in both.

Look after your kitchen tools well. If they are properly cleaned and polished, the steel pans left lightly oiled, the wooden boards and spoons scrubbed and dried after use, they will all improve with age and become a part of your enjoyment of cooking.

1 *three cook's knives—carbon steel 75 mm (3 in) long, 126 mm (5 in) long, 202 mm (8 in) long; to be used as a carving knife.*
2 *palette knife*
3 *carving fork*
4 *sharpening steel*
5 *selection of wooden spoons*
6 *rolling pin*
7 *chopping board*
8 *can opener*
9 *corkscrew*
10 *potato peeler*
11 *whisk*
12 *ladle*
13 *skewers*
14 *measuring jug*
15 *scales with Imperial and metric weights*
16 *lemon squeezer*
17 *grater and slicer*
18 *hand-held sieve or strainer*
19 *soufflé dish*
20 *several cocottes*
21 *two pudding or mixing basins*
22 *large mixing bowl*
23 *pie dish*
24 *steel frying-pan*
25 *steel omelette pan*
26 *three saucepans*
27 *cast-iron casserole*
28 *cast-iron gratin dish*
29 *colander*
30 *roasting tin*
31 *flan tin with loose bottom*
32 *cake tin*
33 *glass storage jars*
34 *Mouli-legumes*

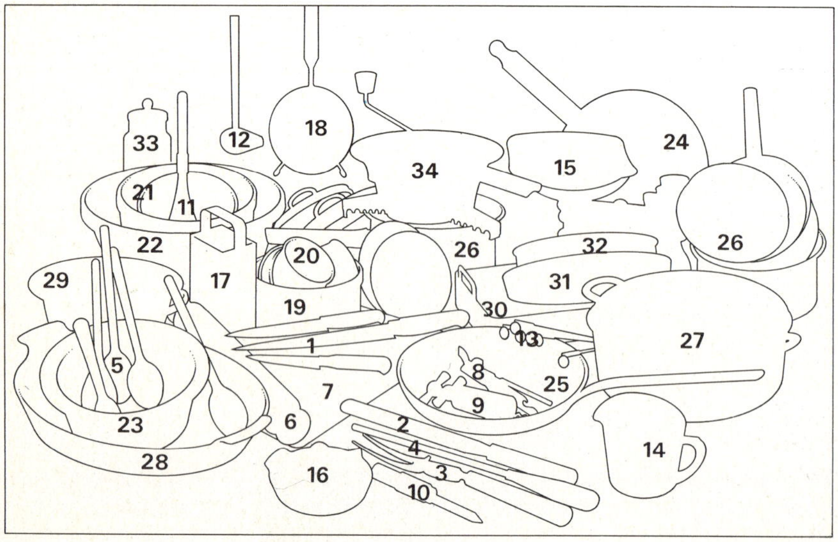

NAME
ADDRESS
TELEPHONE NUMBER
NAME
ADDRESS

Useful addresses

Creating a kitchen is a highly individual affair. Having studied the various styles, having viewed their merits from every angle and examined the equipment in detail, the exciting possibilities of this most useful room are still a little bewildering. How to begin? Practical advice and illustrated examples aren't the entire story: knowing where to find the essential machines and useful gadgets, the right furniture or the most appropriate decorating materials is just as important as knowing exactly what you want to buy.

The following list of useful addresses, though by no means comprehensive, may help you in your quest. It tells you of the exhibitions where manufacturers' ranges can be compared; the associations that offer consumer advice; the shops and manufacturers who stock or make specialized equipment; the organizations that will help with repairs. With these addresses in front of you, the path towards the kitchen you most desire should be much smoother.

Useful addresses

Terence Conran, who has compiled this book, also runs the Habitat chain of stores in the United Kingdom, France and Belgium and Conran's in the United States. Many of the things illustrated in these pages can be found in the stores, so we give you a list of their addresses:

United Kingdom

Birmingham
41-43 New Street Shopping Centre

Bolton
9-13 Knowsley Street

Bournemouth
Parkway House, Avenue Road

Brighton
11 Churchill Square
Western Road

Bristol
Clifton Heights, Triangle West

Bromley
12 Westmoreland Place

Cardiff
14 Wharton Street

Cheltenham
108-110 The Promenade

Coventry
63-64 Hertford Street

Croydon
1111-1114 Whitgift Centre

Glasgow
140-160 Bothwell Street

Guildford
4-6 North Street

Kingston upon Thames
14-16 Eden Walk

Leicester
13 Belgrave Gate
Haymarket Centre

Liverpool
17-21 Dawson's Way
St John's Centre

London
206-222 King's Road, SW3

London
156-158 Tottenham Court Road W1

London
The Conran Shop,
77-79 Fulham Rd, SW3

Manchester
14 Dalton Street

Manchester
Southmoor Road
Wythenshawe, M23 9DS

Newcastle upon Tyne
Eldon Square Shopping Centre

Northampton
The Grosvenor Centre

Nottingham
144-147 Victoria Centre

Romford
38-42 Market Place

Wallingford
Hithercroft Road

Watford
18 Queen's Road

York
26 High Ousegate

France

Paris
Centre Commercial de la Tour Maine-Montparnasse
11 rue de l'Arrivée,
Boîte Cidex 1001

Paris
35 avenue de Wagram

Orgeval
La Maison Blanche, RN13

Montpellier
Centre Commercial
Le Polygone Cidex 0109

Belgium

Bruxelles 1000
6 Place de la Monnaie

United States

New York, NY
Conran's at the Market in the Citicorp Center,
3rd Avenue, Lexington and 54th

General

Accent on Information Inc., Gillum Rd and High Drive, PO Box 700, Bloomington, IL 61701, is a non-profit organization serving disabled persons by collecting and disseminating specialized information. Services are available through *Accent on Living*, a quarterly magazine; Accent on Information, a computerized retrieval system; and Accent Special Publications.

Acoustical & Board Products Assoc., 205 W Touhy Ave, Park Ridge, IL 60068. (Manufacturers representing major US producers of acoustical ceiling materials, hardboard and insulation board.)

American Council on Consumer Interests, 162 Stanley Hall, University of Missouri, Columbia, MO 65201, disseminates information on consumer problems and promotes better consumer education.

American Gas Association, 1515 Wilson Blvd, Arlington, VA 22209.

American Institute of Architects, 1735 New York Ave NW, Washington DC 20006.

American Institute of Kitchen Dealers, 114 Main St, Hackettstown, NJ 07840, publishes an annual directory of certified kitchen designers and another of accredited member kitchen specialists.

American Plywood Association, Tacoma, WA 98401.

Association of Home Appliance Manufacturers, 20 N Wacker Dr., Chicago, IL 60606, publishes annual directories of certified appliances.

Architectural Aluminum Manufacturers Association, 410 N Michigan Ave, Chicago, IL 60611 (window and curtain-wall manufacturers).

Consumer Federation of America, 1012 14th St NW, Suite 901, Washington DC 20005, promotes the rights of consumers by stimulating and providing increased consumer information, and by analyzing consumer issues and publishing the results of their researches in a monthly magazine.

Consumer Protection Center, 2000 H St NW, Washington DC 20006, gives consumers with complaints appropriate referals to federal, state and local sources, where problems can quickly be solved.

Consumers Educ. & Protective Assoc. International, 6048 Ogontz Ave, Philadelphia, PA 19141, educates the consumer to combat fraud and other unscrupulous business activities, and to strengthen the consumers' interests.

Consumers' Research, Bowerstown Rd, Washington, NJ 07882, is a non-profit service reporting laboratory tests on a wide range of goods for consumers. Maintains extensive library, including over 20,000 file folders and a large pamphlet collection and publishes a monthly magazine.

Consumers Union of United States, 256 Washington St, Mount Vernon, NY 10550, tests, rates and reports on competing brands of appliances, food products, household equipment, etc. Publishes monthly Consumer Reports, including Annual Buying Guide Issue in December. Also publishes special reports on particular fields of consumer interest, such as health, family planning.

Cultured Marble Institute, 230 N Michigan Ave, Chicago, IL 60601, will give information to the public about the uses of cultured marble and its advantages.

The Electrification Council, 90 Park Ave, New York, NY 10016.

Gas Appliance Manufacturers Assoc., 1901 N Fort Myer Dr., Arlington, VA 22209 (manufacturers of residential gas appliances and equipment).

International Association of Electrical Inspectors, 802 Busse Hwy, Park Ridge, IL 60068, promotes the use of electrical wiring and equipment in compliance with National Electric Code. Publishes annual membership directory.

National Electrical Manufacturers Assoc., 115 E 44th St, New York, NY 10017, publishes material on wiring, installation of equipment, lighting and standards.

National Home Improvement Council, 11 E 44th St, New York, NY 10017, includes manufacturers of building products, lenders, utilities, associations, dealers and contractors. Conducts educational and promotional programs to encourage modernizing of homes.

National Housewares Manufacturers Assoc., 1130 Merchandise Mart, Chicago, IL 60654 (manufacturers of housewares and small appliances).

National Institute for Consumer Justice, Administrative Conference of the US, 726 Jackson Place NW, Washington DC 20506, facilitates the remedy of grievances and provides legal recourse for the consumer.

National Woodwork Manufacturers Assoc., 400 W Madison St, Chicago, IL 60606, publishes information on proper care and finishing of windows, sashes, doors and frames, and issues folders on modular standards.

Showrooms

Los Angeles Home Furnishings Mart, Los Angeles, CA. (Permanent exhibit center for manufacturers in the home furnishings industry.)

New York Home Furnishings Market, 205 Lexington Ave, New York, NY 10016. (Permanent showrooms for furniture, lamps, fabrics, outdoor furniture, mirrors and draperies.)

Exhibitions

Atlanta Home Furnishings Market, Peachtree Center, Peachtree, GA. (Twice annually in January and July; fourteen floors of exhibit space covering furniture, floor covering, decorative accessories, guild lines, lamps, mirrors and picture lines.)

Florida Furniture Mart. (Twice annually in March and August; home furnishings, furniture, floor covering, wall covering, lighting and decorative accessories.)

Home Furnishings Market Week, San Francisco, CA. (Annually in January; largest combined display of Eastern and Western manufacturers of furniture, floor coverings and decorative accessories.)

National Home Center/Home Improvement Congress and Expo. (Annually in March; trade show to retain home center/home improvement markets of all items in home improvement field.)

National Housewares Expo, Chicago, IL. (Annually in January; world's largest display of housewares and small electrical appliances.)

New Haven Home Show, New Haven, CT. (Annually in May; comprehensive display of new products and services designed for better living in our energy-shortage economy. Emphasis on home decorating and furnishings.)

New England Home Show, Boston, MA. (Annually in March; displays of home furnishings, housewares and gardens.)

Appliances, major

Major Appliance Consumer Action Panel, 20 N Wacker Dr., Chicago, IL 60606, receives comments and complaints from appliance owners, studies industry practices and advises industry of ways to improve its service to customers. Also reports to consumers about how to get the best performance from their appliances. Individual complaints are forwarded to a senior executive of the manufacturer of the product involved.

National Appliance & Radio-TV Dealers' Association, 318 W Randolph St, Chicago, IL 60606, also deals with stoves, refrigerators, washers and irons.

Ranges, Ovens, Cook-tops

Admiral Corp., 1701 E Woodfield Rd, Schaumberg, IL 60172.

Amana Refrigeration Inc., Amana, IA 52204.

Athens Stove Works, 202 Hicks, PO Box 10, Athens, TN 37303.

Brown Stove Works Inc., 1422 Caroline Ave NE, Cleveland, TN 37311.

Caloric Corp., Topton, PA 19526.

Chambers Corp., Old Taylor Rd, Oxford, MS 38655.

Defiance International Ltd, 87–71 Lefferts Blvd, Richmond Hill, NY 11418.

Distinctive Appliances Inc., 8826 Lankershim Blvd, Sun Valley, CA 91352.

Edison, 1 Edison Center, Box 1111, Chattanooga, TN 37401.

Farberware, 100 Electra Lane, Yonkers, NY 10704.

Frigidaire Division, GMC, 300 Taylor St, Dayton, OH 45442.

Gaffers & Sattler Inc., 4851 S Alameda St, Los Angeles, CA 90058.

General Electric Co., Appliance Division, Appliance Park, Louisville, KY 40225.

Gibson Appliance Corp., Gibson Appliance Center, 1401 Van Deinse Rd, Greenville, MI 48838.

Hardwick Stove Co., 240 Edwards SE, Cleveland, TN 37311.

Hotpoint Contract Sales, General Electric Company, Appliance Park, Louisville, KY 40225.

Husqvarna Inc., 151 New World Way S, Plainfield, NJ 07080.

Jenn-Air Corp., 3035 Shadeland Ave, Indianapolis, IN 46226.

Keller Columbus Div., Keller Industries Inc., 2999 Silver Drive, Columbus, OH 43224.

Kenmore, from Sears, Roebuck & Co., Sears Tower, Chicago, IL 60684.

Litton Microwave Cooking Products, 1405 Xenium Lane, Minneapolis, MN 55441.

Magic Chef Inc., 740 King Edward Avenue, Cleveland, TN 37311.

Modern Maid Division, McGraw-Edison Co., PO Box 1111, Chattanooga, TN 37401.

Monarch Kitchen Appliance Co., 715 N Spring St, Beaver Dam, WI 53196.

O'Keefe & Merritt Co., Tappan Park, Mansfield, OH 44901.

Optimus-Princess Inc., 12423 E Florence Ave, PO Box 3448, Sante Fe Springs, CA 90670.

Orbon Industries Inc., PO Box 585, Belleville, IL 62222.

Phillips-Buttorff Corp., PO 1129, Nashville, TN 37202.

Princess Mfg Corp., 741 S Fremont Ave, Alhambra, CA 91803.

Roper Corp., 1905 W Court St, Kankakee, IL 60901.

Royal Chef Div., Gray & Dudley Co., 2300 Clifton Rd, Nashville, TN 37209.

Ryan Mfg Co., Norwich, CT 06360.

Sunray Stove Co., Div. Glenwood Range Co., 435 Park Ave, Delaware, OH 43015.

Tappan Co., Tappan Park, PO Box 606, Mansfield, OH 44901.

Thermador, Div. of Norris Industries, 5119 District Blvd, Los Angeles, CA 90040.

Welbilt Corp., Welbilt Sq., Maspeth, NY 11378.

Whirlpool Corp., Administrative Center, Benton Harbor, MI 49022.

White-Westinghouse Corp., 930 Ft Duquesne Blvd., Pittsburgh, PA 15222.

Microwave Ovens

Admiral Corp., 1701 E Woodfield Rd, Schaumberg, IL 60172.

Amana Refrigeration Inc., Amana, IA 52204.

Caloric Corp., Topton, PA 19562.

Defiance International Ltd, 87–71 Lafferts Blvd, Richmond Hill, NY 11418.

Distinctive Appliances Inc., 8826 Lankershim Blvd, Sun Valley, CA 91352.

Edison, 1 Edison Center, Box 1111, Chattanooga, TN 37401.

Frigidaire Division, GMC, 300 Taylor St, Dayton, OH 45442.

Gaffers & Sattler Inc., 4851 S Alameda St, Los Angeles, CA 90058.

General Electric Co., Appliance Division, Appliance Park, Louisville, KY 40225.

Hardwick Stove Co., 240 Edward St, Cleveland, TN 37311.

Hobart Corporation, Troy, OH 45374.

Husqvarna Inc., 151 New World Way S, Plainfield, NJ 07080.

Litton Microwave Cooking Products, 1405 Xenium Lane, Minneapolis, MN 55441.

Magic Chef Inc., 740 King Edward Ave, Cleveland, TN 37311.

Modern Maid Division, PO Box 1111, Chattanooga, TN 37401.

O'Keefe & Merritt Co., Tappan Park, Mansfield, OH 44901.

Orbon Industries Inc., PO Box 585, Belleville, IL 62222.

Panasonic, One Panasonic Way, Secaucus, NJ 07094.

Roper Corp., 1905 W Court St, Kankakee, IL 60901.

Sanyo Electric Inc., Appliance Div., 51 Joseph St, Moonachie, NJ 07074.

Sharp Electronics Corp., 10 Keystone Pl., Paramus, NJ 07652.

Tappan Co., Tappan Park, PO Box 606, Mansfield, OH 44901.

Thermador, Div. of Norris Industries, 5119 District Blvd, Los Angeles, CA 90040.

Welbilt Corp, Welbilt Sq., Maspeth, NY 11378.

Whirlpool Corp., Administrative Center, Benton Harbor, MI 49022.

White-Westinghouse Corp., 930 Ft Duquesne Blvd, Pittsburgh, PA 15222.

Barbecues, Indoor, Built-in

Bakers Pride Oven Co., 1641 E 233rd St, Bronx, NY 10466.

Broan Mfg Co. Inc., 926 West State St, Hartford, WI 53027.

Chicago Combustion Corp., 616 Hardwick St, Belvidere, NJ 07823.

Distinctive Appliances Inc., 8826 Lankershim Blvd., Sun Valley, CA 91352.

Edison, One Edison Center, Box 1111, Chattanooga, TN 37401.

Goodwin of California Inc., 1075 Second St, Berkeley, CA 94710.

Jenn-Air Corp., 3035 Shadeland Ave, Indianapolis, IN 46226.

Kich-N-Vent, Home Metal Products Co., 750 Central Expressway, Plano, TX 75074.

Mobex Corp., 4100 W Commonwealth, Fullerton, CA 92633.

Modern Maid, Div. McGraw-Edison Co., PO Box 1111, Chattanooga, TN 37401.

Swanson Mfg Co., 607 S Washington St, Owosso, MI 48867.

Thermador, Div. of Norris Industries, 5119 District Blvd, Los Angeles, CA 90040.

Waste King, Div. Norris Industries, 5119 District Blvd, Los Angeles, CA 90040.

Useful addresses

Refrigerators and freezers

Acme National Refrigerator Co., 19–26 Hazen St, Astoria, NY 11105.

Admiral Corp., 1701 E Woodfield Rd, Schaumberg, IL 60172.

Amana Refrigeration Inc., Amana, IA 52204.

Cervitor Kitchens Inc., 1500–1516 Santa Anita, El Monte, CA 91733.

Cryogenic Technology Inc., Kelvin Park, 266 Second Ave, Waltham, MA 02154, for gas refrigerators.

Danby USA Appliance Corp., 133–50 41st Ave, Flushing, NY 11355.

Davis Products Co. Inc., 111 Beeson St, Dowagiac, MI 49047.

Douglas Crestlyn International Inc., 1241 East Lake Dr., Ft Lauderdale, FL 33316.

Frigidaire Division, GMC, 300 Taylor St, Dayton, OH 45402

Gaffers & Sattler Inc., 245 N Vineland, City of Industry, CA 91744.

General Electric Co., Appliance Div., Appliance Park, Louisville, KY 40225.

Gibson Appliance Corp., Gibson Appliance Center, 1401 Van Deinse Rd, Greenville, MI 48838.

Goodwin of California Inc., 1075 Second St, Berkeley, CA 94710.

Hoover Co., 101 E Maple St, North Canton, OH 44720.

Hotpoint Contract Sales, General Electric Co., Appliance Park, Louisville, KY 40225.

Husqvarna Inc., 151 New World Way S, Plainfield, NJ 07080.

Kelvinator Appliance Co., 4248 Kalamazoo SE, Grand Rapids, MI 49508.

Kenmore, from Sears, Roebuck & Co., Sears Tower, Chicago, IL 60684.

King Refrigerator Corp., 76–02 Woodhaven Blvd, Glendale, NY 11227.

Magic Chef Inc., 740 King Edward Ave, Cleveland, TN 37311.

Monarch Kitchen Appliance Co., 715 N Spring St, Beaver Dam, WI 53916.

O'Keefe & Merritt Co., Tappan Park, Mansfield, OH 44901.

Orbon Industries Inc., PO Box 585, Belleville, IL 62222.

Sanyo Electrical Inc., Appliance Div., 51 Joseph St, Moonachie, NJ 07074.

Sharp Electronics Corp., 10 Keystone Place, Paramus, NJ 07652.

Springer-Penguin Inc., 11 Brookdale Pl., Mt Vernon, NY 10550.

Sub-Zero Freezer Co. Inc., PO Box 4130, Madison, WI 53711.

Tappan Co., Tappan Park, PO Box 606, Mansfield, OH 44901.

Thermolator Co., Van Dorn Co., 5611 Progress Rd, Indianapolis, IN 46241, for gas refrigerators.

U-Line Corp., 8900 N 55 St, Box 23220, Milwaukee, WI 53223.

United Refrigerator Co., PO Box 247, Hudson, WI 54016, for two temperature portable refrigerators.

Whirlpool Corp., Administrative Center, Benton Harbor, MI 49022.

White-Westinghouse Corp., 930 Ft Duquesne Blvd, Pittsburgh, PA 15222.

Dishwashers

Admiral Corp., 1701 E Woodfield Rd, Schaumberg, IL 60172.

Caloric Corp., Topton, PA 19562.

Chambers Corp., Old Taylor Rd, Oxford, MS 38655.

Edison, One Edison Center, Box 1111, Chattanooga, TN 37401.

Frigidaire Division, 300 Taylor St, Dayton, OH 45442.

Gaffers & Sattler Inc., 4851 S Alameda St, Los Angeles, CA 90058.

General Electric Co., Appliance Div., Appliance Park, Louisville, KY 40225.

Gibson Appliances Corp., Gibson Appliance Center, 1401 Van Deinse Rd, Greenville, MI 48838.

Hotpoint Contract Sales, General Electric Co., Appliance Park, Louisville, KY 40225.

Husqvarna Inc., 151 New World Way S, Plainfield, NJ 07080.

Kelvinator Appliance Co., 4248 Kalamazoo SE, Grand Rapids, MI 49508.

Kenmore, from Sears, Roebuck & Co., Sears Tower, Chicago, IL 60684.

KitchenAid, Hobart Corporation, Troy, OH 45374.

Magic Chef Inc., 740 King Edward Ave, Cleveland, TN 37311.

Manville Mfg Corp., 342 Rockwell Ave, Pontiac, MI 48053.

The Maytag Co., 403 N 4th, Newton, IA 50208.

Modern Maid, Div. McGraw-Edison Co., PO Box 1111, Chattanooga, TN 37401.

Norge Co., 410 E Maple St, Herrin, IL 62948.

O'Keefe & Merritt Co., Tappan Park, Mansfield, OH 44901.

Orbon Industries Inc., PO Box 585, Belleville, IL 62222.

Roper Corp., 1905 W Court St, Kenkakee, IL 60901.

Royal Chef Div., Gray & Dudley Co., 2300 Clifton Rd, Nashville, TN 37209.

Tappan Co., Tappan Park, PO Box 606, Mansfield, OH 44901.

Waste King, Div. Norris Industries, 5119 District Blvd, Los Angeles, CA 90040.

Whirlpool Corp., Administrative Center, Benton Harbor, MI 49022.

White-Westinghouse Corp., 930 Ft Duquesne Blvd, Pittsburgh, PA 15222.

Washing machines and dryers

Antar Industries Inc., 350 Fifth Avenue, New York, NY 10001.

Aqua Power Washer, Bowles Fluidics Corp., 9347 Fraser Ave, Silver Spring, MD 20910.

Blackstone Corp., 1088 Allen St, Jamestown, NJ 14701.

Centrex Corp., 750 Western Ave, Findlay, OH 45840.

Dexter Co., 709 Depot Ave, Fairfield, IA 52556.

Eden Sales & Service Co., 700 W North St, Springfield, OH 45504.

Frigidaire Division, Dept 2361, Dayton, OH 45401.

General Cold Corp., Empire State Bldg, New York, NY 10001.

The Hoover Co., 101 E Maple St, Canton, OH 44720.

Hotpoint Contract Sales, General Electric Co., Appliance Park, Louisville, KY 40225.

Hoyt Manufacturing Corp., 100 Forge Rd, Westport, MA 02790.

Kenmore, from Sears, Roebuck & Co., Sears Tower, Chicago, IL 60684.

Maytag Co., Newton, IA 50208.

Modern Maid Div., PO Box 1111, Chattanooga, TN 37401.

Orbon Industries Inc., PO Box 585, Belleville, IL 62222.

Rival Mfg Co., 36th & Bennington, Kansas City, MO 64129.

Sanyo Electric Inc., Appliance Div., 51 Joseph St, Moonachie, MJ 07074.

Space Mates, from White-Westinghouse, PO Box 44168, Columbus, OH 43204.

Speed Queen Div., McGraw-Edison Co., Ripon, WI 54971.

Whirlpool Corp., Administrative Center, Benton Harbor, MI 49022.

White-Westinghouse Corp., 930 Ft Duquesne Blvd, Pittsburgh, PA 15222.

Appliances, small

Braun North America, 55 Cambridge Parkway, Cambridge, MA 02142 (electric coffee mills, juice extractors).

Cuisinarts Inc., PO Box 353, Greenwich, CT 06830 (food mixers).

Dyneck Corp., 160 Irving Ave, Port Chester, NY 10573 (watermates).

Farberware, Div. of LCA Corp., 100 Electra Lane, Yonkers, NY 10704 (hand mixers, griddles, waffle irons, broiler-rôtisseries).

H. Freidman & Sons, 16 Cooper Sq., New York, NY 10003 (milkshake mixers).

General Electric Co., Housewares Div., 1285 Boston Ave, Bridgeport, CT 06610 (Toast-R-Ovens).

International Register Co., 4700 West Montrose Ave, Chicago, IL 60641 (Time-All clocks).

KitchenAid, Hobart Corp., Troy, OH 45374 (choppers, coffee mills, cutter mixers, dicers, food cutters, food mixers, etc.).

R. McMullan & Associates, Pineview Drive, Wexford, PA 15090 (electric slicers).

Magic Mill, Div. of Stratford Squire International, 235 West 2nd St, Salt Lake City, UT 84101 (food mixers).

Moulinex, from Mouli Manufacturing Co., 1 Montgomery St, Belleville, NJ 07109 (electric knife sharpeners, meat grinders, coffee makers, rôtisseries, chopper/blenders).

Nesco, from The Hoover Co., 101 E Maple St, Canton, OH 44720 (toasters, irons, electric fry pans, roasters).

Nutone Scoville, Madison &

Red Bank Rds, Cincinnati, OH 45227 (blenders, mixers, shredder-slicers, meat grinders, can openers, ice crushers, fruit juicers, knife sharpeners, power posts and power units).

Oster, from Freitag-Fuller Inc., 41 Richmondville Ave, Westport, CT 06880 (automatic egg cookers).

Ramsey Imports, PO Box 277, Ramsey, NJ 07446 (Espresso makers).

Rival Mfg Co., 36th & Bennington, Kansas City, MO 64129 (electric can openers, electric blenders, meat grinders, electric knives, home food slicers).

Ronson Corp., 1 Ronson Rd, Ogletown, DE 19702 (Food-matic mixes, blends, slices, shreds, grinds, grates, squeezes, crushes, etc.).

Salton Inc., 1260 Zerega Ave, Bronx, NY 10462 (ice-cream machines, peanut butter machines, yoghurt makers, hot plates and heated trolleys).

Sunbeam Corp., 5400 West Roosevelt Rd, Chicago, IL 60650 (food mixers, fry pans).

Waring Products, Div. of Dynamics Corp. of America, Rte 44, New Hartford, CT 06057 (blenders).

Food warming equipment

Edison, One Edison Center, Box 1111, Chattanooga, TN 37401.

Husqvarna Inc., 151 New World Way S, Plainfield, NJ 07080.

Merco Products Inc., 1298 Bethel Dr., Eugene, OR 97402.

Modern Maid, PO Box 1111, Chattanooga, TN 37401.

Salton Inc., 1260 Zerega Ave, Bronx, NY 10462.

Thermador, Div. of Norris Industries, 5119 District Blvd, Los Angeles, CA 90040.

Details

National Association of Mirror Manufacturers, 1225 19th St NW, Room 807, Washington DC 20036.

National Curtain, Drapery & Allied Products Association, c/o Penn Affiliates Inc., Mgrs, 271 North Avenue, New Rochelle, NY 10801.

Southern Woodwork Association, c/o John Bondurant, PO Box 192, Athens, GA 30601. (Manufacturers of special and made-to-order architectural woodwork for moldings, millwork, doors and windows.)

Doors

Concord Products Co., 1951 Broadway, Camden, NJ 08104.

Cornell-Newton Inc., 9399 Wilshire Blvd, Beverly Hills, CA 90210.

Creative Woodworking Co. Inc., 1370 Ralph Ave, Brooklyn, NY 11236.

Crown Decorating Products Mfg Corp., 150 E 57th St, Los Angeles, CA 90011.

Customwood Mfg Co., 4840 Pan American Freeway, Albuquerque, NM 87125.

Del Mar Co., 7130 Fenwick Lane, Westminster, CA 92683.

Entol Industries Inc., 6300 NW 74 Ave, Miami, FL 33166.

Forms & Surfaces Inc., PO Box 5215, Santa Barbara, CA 93108.

Gargoyles Ltd, 512 S Third St, Philadelphia, PA 19147.

Gayeski Furniture Coordinates, Div. Gayeski & Sons, 263 S River St, Hackensack, NJ 07601.

Georgia Pacific Corp., 900 SW Fifth, Portland, OR 97204.

Interwall Systems, Div. Interior Products Graph Inc., 850 Third Ave, New York, NY 10022.

Knipp & Co. Inc., 3401 S Hanover St, Baltimore, MD 21225.

La Cour-Denno Associates, 964 Third Ave, New York, NY 10022.

Louisiana-Pacific, 1300 SW Fifth Ave, Portland, OR 97201.

Louverdrape Inc., 1100 Colorado Ave, Santa Monica, CA 90401.

Marlite Commercial Products, Div. Masonite Corp., Main St, Dover, OH 44622.

Modern Partitions, Div. Trendway Corp., PO Box 728, Holland, MI 49423.

Modernfold, Div. American-Standard Inc., PO Box 310, New Castle, IN 47362.

Pinecrest Inc., 2118 Blaisdell Ave S, Minneapolis, MN 55404.

Simpson Timber Co., 900 Fourth Ave, Seattle, WA 98164.

Stanwood Corp., 711 N Broadway, Stanley, WI 54768.

Tropicraft of San Francisco, 568 Howard, San Francisco, CA 94105.

US Plywood, Div. Champion Int., 1 Landmark Tower, Stamford, CT 06921.

Vaughan Walls Inc., 11681 San Vicente Blvd, Los Angeles, CA 90049.

Walker & Zanger Inc., 179 Summerfield St, Scarsdale, NY 10583.

Whittlewood Corp., PO Box 26208, Albuquerque, NM 87125.

Wood Art Inc., 153 E 57 St, New York, NY 10022.

Woodwork Corp. of America, 1432 W 21st St, Chicago, IL 60608.

Door furniture

All Habitat shops

Acme Metal Goods Mfg Co., 2 Orange St, Newark, NJ 07102.

American Tack & Hardware Co., 25 Robert Pitt Dr, Monsey, NY 10952.

Hancock-Gross, 401 N 21st St, Philadelphia, PA 19103.

Jiffy Enterprises Inc., 3100 T Admiral Wilson Blvd, Pennsauken, NJ 08109.

Kirsch Co., 309 North Prospect St, Sturgis, MI 49091 (knobs in brass, chrome or antique white finishes).

Knape & Vogt Mfg Co., 2700 Oak Industrial Drive, Grand Rapids, MI 49505.

Leigh Products Inc., Coopersville, MI 49404.

Stanley Drapery Hardware, Judd Square, Wallingford, CT 06492.

Floor repair equipment

H. B. Fuller Co., 315 S Hicks Rd, Palatine, IL 60067 (ceramic tile adhesives).

San-Tek, 114 N Third St, Minneapolis, MN 55401 (vinyl repair film).

Vinylife Inc., 2628 Pearl Rd, Medina, OH 44256 (vinyl repair equipment).

Locks

Amerock Corp., 4000 Auburn St, Rockford, IL 61101.

Dexter Locks from Kysor Industrial Corp., 1601 Madison Ave SE, Grand Rapids, MI 49507.

Eaton Corp., Yale Marketing Dept, PO Box 25288, Charlotte, NC 28212.

Kwikset Locks, Emhart Corp., 516 E Santa Ana St, Anaheim, CA 92803.

Leigh Products Inc., Glade Street at Larch, Coopersville, MI 49409.

Little Home Products, 6843 Valjean Ave, Van Nuys, CA 91406.

Schacht Rubber Mfg Co., 238 Polk St, Huntington, IN 46750.

Vanderbilt Products Inc., 585 Dean St, Brooklyn, NY 11238.

Waterbury Lock & Speciality Co., 203 Broad St, Milford, CT 06460.

Paints, varnishes, enamels

Evans Products Co., Paint Div., Box 4098, Roanoke, VA 24015 (latex finish paints).

The Flecto Co., Box 12955, Oakland, CA 94608 (gloss finishes for wood, metal and ceramics).

Frisch & Co., 88 E 11th St, Paterson, NJ 07524.

Glidden-Durkee, Div. of SCM Corp., 900 Union Commerce Bldg, Cleveland, OH 44115.

Ideal Aerosols Inc., 6925 Tujunga Ave, North Hollywood, CA 91609 (spray enamels, lacquers, candy flake metallic color, vinyl spray, epoxy spray paint, fluorescent spray paints).

Magicolor Paint Co., 1191 S Wheeling Rd, Wheeling, IL 60090.

Minwax Co., Clifton, NJ 07014 (scratch-resistant finishes for wood furniture, floors and units).

Red Devil Paints and Chemicals, 30 N West St, Mount Vernon, NY 10550.

Schulte Paints, 627–45 East Holly Ave, St Louis, MO 63147.

Tobias Paint Mfg Co., 7515 Northfield Rd, Cleveland, OH 44146.

United Coatings Inc., 3050 N Rockwell, Chicago, IL 60618 (latex).

White-Westinghouse Electric Corp., Industrial Materials Div., Manor Rd, Manor, PA 11665.

Wonder Color Inc., 15160 Keswick St, Van Nuys, CA 91405 (spray paints, latex gloss enamels).

Equipment for special purposes

Compact kitchens

Acme National Refrigerator Co., 19–26 Hazen St, Astoria, NY 11105.

Cervitor Kitchens Inc., 1500 Santa Anita Ave S, El Monte, CA 91733.

Cornwall Corp., 500 Harrison Ave, Boston, MA 02118 (tabletop stoves).

Useful addresses

Davis Products Co., 111 Beeson St, PO Box 360, Dowagiac, MI 49047.

Douglas Crestlyn International Inc., 1241 East Lake Dr, Ft Lauderdale, FL 33316.

Dwyer Products Corp., Calumet Ave, Michigan City, IN 46360.

Ewing Kitchen Designers, 2425 McKinney Ave, Dallas, TX 75201.

King Refrigerator Corp., 76–02 Woodhaven Blvd, Glendale, NY 11227.

KitchenAid Div., Hobart Corp., Troy, OH 45374.

Kord Manufacturing Co. Inc., 4510 White Plains Rd, Bronx, NY 10470 (tabletop stoves).

Norcold Inc., PO Box 180, Sidney, OH 45365.

Don Roberts Sales Co., 231 Ferris Ave, White Plains, NY 10603.

Flooring

All Habitat shops (rugs, mats, carpets, natural wood floors, cork tiles, vinyl).

Carpet & Rug Industry, Consumer Action Panel, Box 1568, Dalton, GA 30720, acts as arbitrator for consumer complaints relating to the products and services of the carpet and rug industry; also provides information to assist consumers with their purchase of carpet and rugs.

Carpet & Rug Institute, PO Box 2048, Dalton, GA 30720, publishes books dealing with carpet maintenance.

Congoleum Industries Inc., 195 Belgrove Dr, Kearny, NJ 07032 (cork, linoleum, felt base, asphalt tile, vinyl, vinyl asbestos solid, foam vinyl).

Maple Flooring Manufacturers Assoc., 424 Washington Ave, Oshkosh, WI 54901, publishes pamphlets on installation and finishing of hardwood flooring.

National Oak Flooring Manufacturers Assoc., 814 Sterick Building, Memphis, TN 38103, publishes a guide to oak floors, and a hardwood flooring handbook.

Resilient Tile Institute, 26 Washington St, East Orange, NJ 07017 (manufacturers of asphalt tile or vinyl asbestos tile).

Wood & Synthetic Flooring Institute, The Breeder Co., 1201 Waukegan Rd, Glenview, IL 60025.

Kitchen carpets

Congoleum Industries Inc., 195 Belgrove Dr, Kearny, NJ 07032.

Crown Industries, Div. of Ludlow Corp., 2100 Commerce Dr., Fremont, OH 43420.

Lees Carpets, Valley Forge Corporate Center, King of Prussia, PA 19406.

Mohawk Carpet, 919 Third Avenue, New York, NY 10022.

Monarch Carpet Mills, 5025 New Peachtree Rd, Chamblee, GA 30341.

Ozite Corp., 1755 Butterfield Rd, Libertyville, IL 60048.

Viking Carpets Inc., 10 West 33rd St, New York, NY 10001.

Kitchen mats

Ace Industries Inc., 9517 Avenue J, Brooklyn, NY 11236.

Akro Corp., 1212 7th St SW, Canton, OH 44709.

Crown Industries, Div. of Ludlow Corp., 2100 Commerce Dr., Fremont, OH 43420.

Globe-Superior Div., 9401 Blue Grass Rd, Philadelphia, PA 19114.

Royal Rubber & Mfg Co., 5951 E Firestone, South Gate, CA 90280.

Linos, vinyl and vinyl asbestos

Amtico Flooring Div., American Biltrite Inc., Amtico Square, Trenton, NJ 08607.

Armstrong Cork Co., Liberty & Charlotte, Lancaster, PA 17604.

Congoleum Industries Inc., 195 Belgrove Dr., Kearny, NJ 07032.

GAF Corporation, Floor Products Division, 140 W 51st St, New York, NY 10020.

Goodyear Tire Co., Flooring Dept, 1210 Massillon Rd, Akron, OH 44305.

Kentiles Floors Inc., Brooklyn, NY 11215.

Mannington Mills Inc., Salem, NJ 08079 (sheeting only).

National Floor Products Co. Inc., PO Box 354-A, Florence, AL 35630.

Parkwood Laminates Inc., Industrial Ave, Lowell, MA 01853.

Uvalde Rock Asphalt Co., Frost National Bank, San Antonio, TX 78205.

Cork

Arco Chemical Co., Div. Atlanta Richfield Co., 1500 Market St, Philadelphia, PA 19101.

C.I.D. Associates Inc., PO Box 10, Allison Park, PA 15101.

Cork Plus Inc., 135–43 Front St, Bridgeport, PA 19405.

Cork Products Co. Inc., 250 Park Ave S, New York, NY 10003.

Dependable Cork Co. Inc., Jefferson Crossing, Morristown, NJ 07960.

Dippel, Vogler & Sharkey Co. Inc., 515 Madison Ave, New York, NY 10022.

Dodge Cork Co., PO Box 989, Lancaster, PA 17604.

Expanko Cork Co., PO Box 384, West Chester, PA 19380.

Flexco, Div. Textile Rubber, PO Box 553, Tuscubia, AL 35674.

Lawton Carpet, 62–33 Woodhaven Blvd, Rego Park, NY 11374.

Manton Cork Corp., 27 Benson Lane, Merrick, NY 11566.

Starck Carpet Co., 979 Third Ave, New York, NY 10022.

Walker & Zanger Inc., 179 Summerfield St, Scarsdale, NY 10583.

Tiles

Agency Tile Inc., 499 Old Nyack Tpk, Spring Valley, NY 10977.

American Olean Tile Co., 1000 Cannon Ave, Lansdale, PA 19446.

Amsterdam Corp., 950 Third Ave, New York, NY 10022.

Architectural Products, Interpace Corp., 2901 Los Feliz Blvd, Los Angeles, CA 90039.

Briare Co. Inc., 964 Third Ave, New York, NY 10022.

County Floors Inc., 300 E 61 St, New York, NY 10021.

Designers Tile International, 6812 SW 81st St, Miami, FL 33143.

H. & R. Johnson Inc., State Highway 35, Keyport, NJ 07735.

Latco Products, 3371 Glendale Blvd, Los Angeles, CA 90039.

Ludowici Celadon Co., 111 E Wacker Dr., IL 60601.

Metro Mosaics & Metro Flor, 137 Commercial St, Plainview, NY 11803.

Mid-State Tile Co., PO Box 627, Lexington, NC 27292.

Nassau Flooring, 242 Drexel Ave, Westbury, NY 11590.

Raventos International Corp., 150 Fifth Ave, New York, NY 10011.

Signature Floors Inc., 979 Third Ave, New York, NY 10022.

Sikes Corp., PO Box 447, Lakeland, FL 33801.

Structural Stoneware Inc., PO Box 119, Minerva, OH 45638.

3M Co., 3M Center, St Paul, MN 55101.

US Ceramic Tile Co., 1375 Raff Rd NW, Canton, OH 44710.

Wenczel Tile Corp., Klag Ave, PO Box 5308, Trenton, NJ 08678.

Wood

E. S. Adkins & Co., Salisbury, MD 21801 (yellow pine).

Aetna Plywood Inc., 1733 N Elston Ave, Chicago, IL 60622.

Arkansas Oak Flooring Co., Pine Buff, AR 71601.

Babcock Lumber Co., 2220 Palmer St, Pittsburgh, PA 15218 (maple & oak).

E. L. Bruce Co. Inc., PO Box 16902, Memphis, TN 38116 (oak, walnut, beech, pecan).

Chromalloy American Corp., 641 Lexington Ave, New York, NY 10022 (hardwood maple, oak, etc.).

Connor Forest Industries, PO Box 847, Wausau, WI 54401 (maple, birch).

Harris Hardwood Co. Inc., Roanoke, VA 24015 (oak, hard maple, beech, cherry, walnut, teak).

Harris Mfg Co., Greenway at Walnut St, Johnson City, TN 37601 (oak, maple, beech and colonial plank).

J. E. Higgins Lumber Co., 99 Bay Shore Blvd, PO Box 3161, San Francisco, CA 94119 (hardwood).

International Paper Co., Long-Bell Div., PO Box 579, Longview, WA 98632 (oak, composite).

Memphis Hardwood Flooring Co., 1551 Thomas, Memphis, TN 38107 (oak).

Miller & Co. Inc., Selma, AL 36701 (oak).

R. C. Owen Co., Lafayette Rd, Hopkinsville, KY 42240 (oak, beech, maple, walnut strip and plank).

Parkwood Laminates Inc., Industrial Ave, Lowell, MA 01853 (hardwood).

Potlatch Corp., Southern Div., Wood Products Group, Warren, AR 71671 (shortleaf pine).

Radiation Technology Inc., 1 Lake Denmark Rd, Rockaway, NJ 07866 (hardwood, ash, oak, maple).

Riverside Millwork Co. Inc., 77 Merrimack St, Penacook, NH 03301 (hardwood).

Shepard & Morse Lumber Co., Riverside Office Park, Box 600, Weston, MA 02193 (hardwood).

Thomson Oak Flooring, Rte 1, Box 37, Thomson, GA 30824 (oak).

Tibbals Flooring Co., PO Drawer A, Oneida, TN 37841 (parquet flooring with and without self-adhesive backing).

Wood-Mosaic Corp., PO Box 21159, Louisville, KY 40221 (hardwood speciality & parquetry walnut, teak).

Woodcraft Industries, 302 Cass Ave, Mount Clemens, MI 48043 (portable wood flooring, oak and teak. Aluminum border trim & sections).

Marble

Agency Tile Inc., 499 Old Nyack Tpk, Spring Valley, NY 10977.

Amsterdam Corp., 950 Third Ave, New York, NY 10022.

Continental Creative Sales Inc., 279 Marshall St, Paterson, NJ 07503.

Designers Tile International, 6812 SW 81 St, Miami, FL 33143.

Elon Inc., 964 Third Avenue, New York, NY 10022.

Fritz Chemical Co., PO Box 17087, Dallas, TX 75217.

Georgia Marble Co., 2575 Cumberland Pkwy NW, Atlanta, GA 30339.

Harmony Carpet Corp., 979 Third Ave, New York, NY 10022.

Italian Marble Industries, 228 Park Ave S, New York, NY 10003.

Lawton Carpet, 62–33 Woodhaven Blvd, Rego Park, NY 11374.

Puccio Collection, 232 E 59th St, New York, NY 10022.

3M Co., 3M Center, St Paul, MN 55101.

VIP Fine Marble Inc., 210 Lawrence Ave, Staten Island, NY 10310.

Vermont Marble Co., 61 Main St, Proctor, VT 05765.

Walker & Zanger Inc., 179 Summerfield St, Scarsdale, NY 10583.

Terrazzo

American Marble Mosaic Co., 6302 St Augustine, Houston, TX 77021.

Universal Protective Coatings, 123–29 Jordan St, San Rafael, CA 94901.

Zanin & Son Inc., 1927 Park Ave, Weehawken, NJ 07087.

Industrial

Arco Chemical Co., 1500 Market St, Philadelphia, PA 19101 (plastic oak).

Duracote Corp., 358 N Diamond St, Ravenna, OH 44266 (synthetic resin coated fiberglass).

Dur-a-Flex Inc., 100 Meadow St, Hartford, CT 06114 (epoxy).

Flecto Co. Inc., 1000–02 45th St, Oakland, CA 94608 (seamless plastic – acrylic).

H. Koch & Sons, Div. of Gulf & Western Industries Inc., 5410 E La Palma Ave, Anaheim, CA 92807 (molded non-slip fiberglass).

Kompolite, 2515 Newbold Ave, Bronx, NY 10462.

Melflex Products Co., Div. of A.A. Imperial Corp., 811 Moe Dr, Akron, OH 44310 (rubber).

Reliance Floors Corp., 4131 T. Bergen Tpke, North Bergen, NJ 07047 (designers, formulators and installers of epoxy floors).

Furniture

All Habitat shops (for tables, chairs, dressers, stools).

Furniture Industry Consumer Action Panel, PO Box 951, High Point, NC 27262, provides a third party mechanism for resolving complaints involving manufacturing defects in, quality of, and service for furniture.

Arnoldware-Rogers Inc., PO Box 790, Panama City, FL 32401.

Atlas Co., Div. of Kimberly Rose, 2211 N Elston Ave, Chicago, IL 60614.

Chaircraft Inc., Box 2627, Hickory, NC 28601.

James David, 128 Weldon Parkway, Maryland Heights, MO 63043 (trolleys and tables)

Door Store, 3140 17 St NW, Washington, DC 20007 (folding chairs and bentwood chairs).

Erie Seating Co., 691 North Sangamon St, Chicago, IL 60622.

Ever-Ready Appliance Mfg Co., 5727 W Park, St Louis, MO 63110.

Futura Industries Corp., Boise, ID 83702.

Geofre Products, 195 Chrystie St, New York, NY 10002.

Gotham Industries, 2660 N Clybourn, Chicago, IL 60614.

Harry Levitz Co. Inc., 230 Fifth Ave, 1150 Broadway, New York, NY 10001.

Loroman Co. Inc., 230 Fifth Ave, New York, NY 10001.

Paul J. Safina Co. Inc., 1–9 Portal St, Brooklyn, NY 11233.

Salmanson Co., 18 Market St, Union City, PA 16438.

Samsonite Corp, 11200 E 45th Ave, Denver, CO 80217 (folding furniture and vinyl upholstered chairs).

Shamrock Industries Inc., 1010 Lyndale Ave N, Minneapolis, MN 55411.

Stendig Inc., 410 E 62 St, New York, NY 10021.

Syroco, Div. Dart Industries Inc., Syracuse, NY 13201.

Unitron, 12824 South Cerise Ave, Hawthorne, CA 90250.

Dining nooks

Ableart Upholstery Co. Inc., 206 E Jericho Tpke, Mineola, NY 11501.

Din-A-Co., 500 S Hicks Rd, Palatine, IL 60067.

Kitchen Nooks Inc., 2575 Park Rd, Hallandale, FL 33009.

Northern Kitchens, Rib Lake, WI 54470.

Sheridan Upholstering & Mfg Co., 2036 Center Ave, Pittsburgh, PA 15219.

Style Trend Dining Nooks, B. L. Brinkley Co., 24710 Westmoreland Dr., Farmington, MI 48024.

Syroco, Industrial & Contract Div., Syracuse, NY 13201.

Tri-Art Breakfast Nooks, 500 Sunrise Hwy, Rockville Center, NY 11570.

Heating

Better Heating-Cooling Council, 35 Russo Place, Berkeley Heights, NJ 07922, publishes a booklet that explains heating systems including solar heat.

Blueray Systems, 375 North Broadway, Jericho, NY 11753 (oil-fired heating systems).

Edwards Engineering Corp., 101 Alexander Ave, Pompton Plains, NJ 07444 (gas or oil-fired heating systems).

General Electric Co., Major Appliance Group, Appliance Park, Louisville, KY 40225 (electric, gas and oil systems).

Lennox Industries, Box 250, Marshalltown, IA 50158 (solar and conventional systems working on gas, oil, propane or electricity).

The Singer Co., Climate Control Div., 1300 Federal Blvd, Carteret, NJ 07008 (space-saving gas, electric or oil-fired systems).

A. O. Smith Corp., Box 28, Kankakee, IL 60901 (insulated electric water heaters).

The Trake Co., 3600 Pammel Creek Rd, La Crosse, WI 54601 (gas, oil or electrical systems).

Weil-McLain Co., Michigan City, IN 46360 (hot water, warm air and electric resistance systems).

Westinghouse Electric Corp., Central Residential Air Conditioning Div., 5005 Interstate Dr. N, Norman, OK 73069.

The Williamson Co., 3500 Madison Rd, Cincinnati, OH 45209 (gas, electric or oil-fired systems).

Solar heating

Allen Associates, 2594 Leghorn St, Mountain View, CA 94023.

Champion House Builders, Solar Furnace Division, 5573 E North St, Dryden, MI 48428 (their solar heating system operates with conventional systems via thermostatic control).

Florida Conservation Foundation, 935 Orange Ave, Winter Park, FL 32789, provides a basic guide to solar energy.

Garden Way Laboratories, Box 66, Charlotte, VT 05445.

Kalwall Corp., Solar Components Division, Box 237, Manchester, NH 03105.

Oak Ridge Solar Engineering, Box 3016, Oak Ridge, TN 37830.

PPG Industries, One Gateway Center, Pittsburgh, PA 15222.

Raypak, 3111 Agoura Rd, Westlake Village, CA 91359.

Solarcell Corp., 1455 NE 57th St, Ft Lauderdale, FL 33334 (water heating only).

State Industries, PO Box 307, Ashland City, TN 37015 (water heating systems only).

Lighting

American Home Lighting Institute, 230 N Michigan Ave, Chicago, IL 60601 (manufacturers, distributors and retailers of residential light fixtures; trains lighting consultants).

Fluorescent Lighting Association, 101 Park Avenue, New York, NY 10017, seeks to educate the public about this form of lighting.

Incandescent Lamp Manufacturers Assoc., 760 S 13th St, Newark, NJ 07103 (small independent lamp manufacturers).

Useful addresses

Lamp & Shade Institute of America, 15 E 26th St, New York, NY 10010 (manufacturers of portable electric lamps and lamp shades).

Manufacturers of Illumination Products, 158–11 Jewel Ave, Rm 307, Jamaica, NY 11365 (manufacturers of lamps and lighting equipment).

New York Lamp & Shade Manufacturers Assoc., 15 E 26th St, New York, NY 10010.

Incandescent

All Habitat shops.

Duro-Test Corporation, 2321 Kennedy Blvd, North Bergen, NJ 07047.

Gem Electric Mfg Co. Inc., 390 Vanderbilt Motor Pkwy, Hauppauge, NY 11787.

General Electric Co., Nela Park, Cleveland, OH 44112.

GTE Sylvania Inc., 1 Stamford Forum, Stamford, CT 06904.

House of Rand, 681 Main St, Belleville, NJ 07109.

L. Mendelson Co., Furlong, PA 18925.

North American Philips Lighting Corp., Bank St, Hightstown, NJ 08520.

Panasonic Special Products Div., 200 Park Ave, Pan Am Bldg, New York, NY 10017.

Softlite Inc., Box 343, Orange, NJ 07051.

Teledyne Big Beam, 292 E Prairie St, Crystal Lake, IL 60014.

Thomas Industries Inc., 207 E Broadway, Louisville, KY 40202.

Union Electric Products Co., 124 Washington Ave, Brooklyn, NY 11205.

White-Westinghouse Electric Corp., Interior Lighting Division, US Hwy 61 S, PO Box 824, Vicksburg, MO 39181.

Fluorescent

Cable Electric Products Inc., 234 Daboll St, Providence, RI 02907.

Crown Creative Industries, Donohoe Rd, PO Box 578, Greensburg, PA 15601.

General Electric Co., Nela Park, Cleveland, OH 44112.

GTE Sylvania Inc., 1 Stamford Forum, Stamford, CT 06904.

House of Rand, 681 Main St, Belleville, NJ 07109

North American Philips Lighting Corp., Bank St, Hightstown, NJ 08520.

Panasonic Special Products Div., 200 Park Ave, Pan Am Bldg, New York, NY 10017.

Prestigeline, Div. Weiman Co., 5 Inez Drive, Brentwood, NY 11717.

Swivelier Co., 33 Rte 304, Nanuet, NY 10954.

Teledyne Big Beam, 292 E Prairie St, Crystal Lake, IL 60014.

Union Electric Products Co., 124 Washington Ave, Brooklyn, NY 11205.

Undercounter

Duray Fluorescent Mfg Co., 5645 N Ravenswood Ave, Chicago, IL 60660.

Kosman Lighting Equipment Co., 2201 Third St, San Francisco, CA 94107.

Fittings and switches

All Habitat shops.

Air King Corp., 3065 N Rockwell, Chicago, IL 60618.

Bell Electric Co., 2600 W 50th, Chicago, IL 60632.

Cable Electric Products Inc., 234 Daboll St, Providence, RI 02907.

E & B Mfg Co., 29604 King Rd, Romulus, MI 48174.

Gem Electric Mfg Co. Inc., 390 Vanderbilt Motor Pkwy, Hauppauge, NY 11787.

General Electric Co., Wiring Devices, Nela Park, Cleveland, OH 44112.

House of Rand, 681 Main St, Belleville, NJ 07109.

Lakewood Engineering & Mfg Co., 212 N Carpenter, Chicago, IL 60607.

Leviton Mfg Co. Inc., 59–25 Little Neck Pkwy, Little Neck, NY 11362.

Lightolier Inc., 346 Claremont Ave, Jersey City, NJ 07305.

Newell Co. Inc., 916 Arcade Ave, Freeport, IL 61032.

Nutone Housing Products, Madison and Red Bank Roads, Cincinnati, OH 45227.

Perfect-line Mfg Corp., 80 E Gates Ave, Lindenhurst, NY 11757.

Prestigeline, Div. of Weiman Co., 5 Inez Dr., Brentwood, NY 11717.

M. H. Rhodes Inc., 97 Thompson Rd, Avon, CT 06001.

Sunray Lighting Co., 4228 Sepulveda Blvd, Culver City, CA 90230.

Teledyne Big Beam, 292 E Prairie St, Crystal Lake, IL 60014.

Trine Mfg Corp., Div. Square D Co., 1430 Ferris Place, Bronx, NY 10461.

Union Electric Products Corp., 124 Washington Ave, Brooklyn, NY 11205.

Waxman Industries, 24455 Aurora Rd, Bedford Heights, OH 44146.

Sinks

Stainless steel and pressed steel

All Habitat shops.

Active Tool & Mfg Co., 888 Clairponte, Detroit, MI 48215.

Aetna Plumbing Industries Inc., 266 Eisenhower Lane, Lombard, IL 60148.

AMA Enterprise Corp., 444 Hempstead Tpke, West Hempstead, NY 11552.

American Standard Inc., PO Box 2003, New Brunswick, NJ 08903.

Atlanta Roll Forming Corp., 50–05 98th St, Corona, NY 11368.

Bradford White Corp., 100 Main St, Middleville, MI 49333.

Brass-Craft Mfg Co., 700 Fisher Bldg, Detroit, MI 48202.

Briggs, Box 22622, Tampa, FL 33622.

BW Plumbing Products Corp., 201 E Fifth St, Mansfield, OH 44901.

Caloric Corp., Topton, PA 19562.

Challenge Stamping & Porcelain Co., Cornelia St, Grand Haven, MI 49417.

Consumer Products, PO Box 171231, Memphis, TN 38117.

Crown-National Co., 266 Eisenhower Lane, Lombard, IL 60148.

Davis Products Co., 111 Beeson St, PO Box 360, Dowagiac, MI 49047.

Defiance International Ltd., 87–71 Lefferts Blvd, Richmond Hill, NY 11418.

Delta Faucet Co., PO Box 31, Greensburg, IN 47240.

Dwyer Products Corp., Calumet & Grand Sts, Michigan City, IN 46360.

Elkay Manufacturing Co., 2700 S 17th Ave, Broadview, IL 60153.

Federal Stainless Sink, Unarco Industries, PO Box 429, Paris, IL 61944.

Gerber Plumbing Fixtures Corp., 4656 W Touhy Ave, Chicago, IL 60646.

Halsey Taylor Co., 1554 Thomas Rd, S.E., Warren, OH 44481.

Ingram-Richardson Inc., State Road, 28 W Frankfort, IN 46041.

Jensen-Thorsen Corp., 301 Interstate Rd, Addison, IL 60101.

Just Manufacturing Co., 9233 King St, Franklin Park, IL 60131.

Kohler Co., Kohler, WI 53044.

Lawndale Industries Inc., Box 1408, Aurora, IL 60507.

Legion Stainless Sink Corp., 21–07 40 Ave, Long Island City, NY 11101.

Life Time Sinks and Faucets, Div. Consumer Products, PO Box 171231, Memphis, TN 38117.

Manesco Inc., 151 Haven Ave, Port Washington, NY 11050.

Moen, Div. Stanadyne, 377 Woodland Ave, Elyria, OH 44035.

Neptune Lifetime Suites, 1801 W 1912 St, Broadview, IL 60153.

Peerless-Mayer Inc., Div. Frigitemp Corp., 401 Hunts Point Ave, Bronx, NY 10474.

Peerless Pottery, 917 N St Joseph, Evansville, IN 47712.

Plumb Shop, Div. Brass Craft, 700 Fisher Bldg, Detroit, MI 48202.

Polar Ware Co., 4900 Lake Shore Rd, Sheboygan, WI 53081.

The Revere Sink Corp., 44 Coffin Ave, New Bedford, MA 02746.

Robinson Export-Import Corp., 6732 Industrial Rd, Springfield, VA 22151.

Royal Chief Div., Gray & Dudley Co., 2300 Clifton Rd, Nashville, TN 37209.

Ryan Mfg Co., 675 W Thames St, Norwich, CT 06360.

Stainless Steel Sink Inc., 300 Fay Ave, PO Box 296, Addison, IL 60101.

The Sterling Sink Co., 123 Forbes Rd, PO Box 2334, Gastonia, NC 28052.

Superior Stainless Steel Products Inc., Box 2203, Gastonia, NC 28052.

Unarco Home Products Div., Unarco Industries, PO Box 429, Paris, IL 61944.

Vance Industries Inc., 7401 W Wilson, Chicago, IL 60656.

Verson Home Products, PO Box 15828, Dallas, TX 75215.

Zeigler-Harris Corp., PO Box 1110, San Fernando, CA 91341.

Enameled

Federal Stainless Sink, Unarco Industries, PO Box 429, Paris, IL 61944.

Ingram-Richardson Inc., State Road, 28 W Frankfort, IN 46041.

Kohler Co., High Street, Kohler, WI 53044 (triple compartment sinks).

Molded plastic

Acorn Marble Co., 2077 Easy St, Walled Lake, MI 48088.

Arundale Inc., 1173 Reco Ave, St Louis, MO 63126.

Barko Industries Inc., 2409 Georgetown Rd, Danville, IL 61832.

Bemis Mfg Co., 300 Mill St, Sheboygan Falls, WI 53085.

Borg-Warner Corp., Plumbing Products Div., 201 E Fifth St, Mansfield, OH 44901.

Bradley Corp., Faucet & Special Products Div., PO Box 348, Menomonee Falls, WI 53051.

BW Plumbing Products Corp., 201 E Fifth St, Mansfield, OH 44901.

Cerilean Products, 1904 N Kenmore, South Bend, IN 46628.

Chemcraft Inc., 1520 Adams St, Elkhart, IN 46514.

Continental Assoc. Industries, 660 W Billinis, Salt Lake City, UT 84115.

Crest Mfg Corp., 130 S Calverton Rd, Baltimore, MD 21223.

E. I. Dupont De Nemours & Co., Tatnall Bldg, Products Information Section, Wilmington, DE 19898.

Formco Inc., 7745 School Rd, Cincinnati, OH 45242.

General Bathroom Products Corp., 2201 Touhy Ave, Elk Grove, IL 6007.

Kinzee Industries Inc., 259 Second St, Saddle Brook, NJ 07662.

L & M Cultured Marble Co., 6433 W 99th St, Chicago Ridge, IL 60415.

Lawndale Industries Inc., Box 1408, Aurora, IL 60507.

Lusterock International, 4125 Richmond Ave, Houston, TX 77027.

Marble Industries Inc., Houston, TX 77007.

Marbletek Corp., 44 Lochdale Rd, Roslindale, MA 02131.

Moellering Industries, 2819 Massachusetts Ave, Cincinnati, OH 45225.

Molded Marble Products, Div. Lippert Corp., PO Box 219, Menomonee Falls, WI 53051.

Orbit International Inc., GPO Box 3327, San Juan, PR 00936.

Powers-Fiat Corp., Div. of Powers Regulator Co., 3400 Oakton St, Skokie, IL 60076.

Romarco Corp. PO Drawer 218, Morgantown, NC 28655.

Rynone Industries Inc., Waverly Permaform Div., PO Box 389 Waverly, NY 14892.

Town Craft Vanities, 15–32 127 St, College Point, NY 11356.

United States Gypsum Co., 101 S Wacker Dr., Chicago, IL 60606.

Williams, Div. Leigh Products, 1536 Grant St, Elkhart, IN 46514.

Faucets

AMA Enterprise Corp., 444 Hempstead Tpke, West Hempstead, NY 11552.

American Brass Mfg Co., 5000 Superior Ave, Cleveland, OH 44103.

Bradley Corp., Faucet & Special Products Div., PO Box 348, Menomonee Falls, WI 53051.

Brass Decor, 5629 Bellaire Blvd, Houston, TX 77036.

Building Components Div., Rockwell International, PO Box 798, Morgantown, WV 26505.

Burlington Brass Works, Burlington, WI 53105.

BW Plumbing Products Corp., 201 E Fifth Street, Mansfield, OH 44901.

Chicago Faucet Co., 2100 S Nuclear Dr., Des Plaines, IL 60018.

Chicago Specialty Mfg Co., 7500 Linder, Skokie, IL 60076.

Consumer Products, PO Box 171231, Memphis, TN 38117.

Crane Co., 300 Park Ave, New York, NY 10022.

Defiance International Ltd, 87–71 Lefferts Blvd, Richmond Hill, NY 11418.

Delta Faucet Co., PO Box 31, Greensburg, IN 47240.

Eljer Plumbingware Div., Wallace-Murray Corp., 3 Gateway Center, Pittsburgh, PA 15222.

Elkay Manufacturing Co., 2700 S 17th Ave, Broadview, IL 60153.

Faucet-Queens Inc., 1741 W Belmont Ave, Chicago, IL 60657.

Gerber Plumbing Fixtures Corp., 4656 W Touhy Ave., Chicago, IL 60646.

Grohe, Div. of Flygt Corp., 1591 Elmhurst Rd, Elk Grove Village, IL 60007.

Hancock-Gross Inc., 401 N 21st St, Philadelphia, PA 19130.

Indiana Brass Co. Inc., Box 367, Frankfort, IN 46041.

Just Manufacturing Co., 9233 King St, Franklin Park, IL 60131.

Kohler Co., Kohler, WI 53044.

Life Time Sinks & Faucets, Div. Consumer Products, PO Box 171231, Memphis, TN 38117.

Manesco Inc., 151 Haven Ave, Port Washington, NY 11050.

Manville Mfg Corp., 342 Rockwell Ave, Pontiac, MI 48053.

Melard Mfg Corp., 153 Linden St, Passaic, NJ 07055.

Michigan Brass Co., 500 S Water St, Grand Haven, MI 49417.

Milwaukee Faucets Inc., 4250 N 124 St, Milwaukee, WI 53222.

Moen, Div. Stanadyne, 377 Woodland Ave, Elyria, OH 44035.

Peerless Faucet Co., Box 31, Greensburg, IN 47240.

Peerless Pottery, 917 N St Joseph, Evansville, IN 47712.

Price Pfister, 13500 Paxton St, Pacoima, CA 91331.

Robinson Export-Import Corp., 6732 Industrial Rd, Springfield, VA 22151.

Royal Brass Mfg Co., 1420 E 43 St, Cleveland, OH 44103.

Speakman Co., PO Box 191, Wilmington, DE 19899.

Streamway Products Div., Scott & Fetzer Co., Sharon Dr, Westlake, OH 44145.

Ultraflo Corp., 4515 S Columbus Ave, PO Box 2294, Sandusky, OH 44870.

Unarco Home Products Div., Unarco Industries, PO Box 429, Paris, IL 61944.

Union Brass & Metal Mfg, 501 W Lawson Ave, St Paul, MN 55117.

US Caster Corp., 9999 W 75 St, Shawnee Mission, KY 66204.

Universal-Rundle Corp., PO Box 960, New Castle, PA 16103.

Valley Faucet & Eastman Central D, Divs of US Brass Corp., PO Box 37, Plano, TX 75074.

Waterbury Pressed Metal Co., 419 Brookside Rd, Waterbury, CT 06708.

Waste disposers

Admiral Corp. 1701 E Woodfield Rd, Schaumberg, IL 60172.

Caloric Corp., Topton, PA 19562.

Chambers Corp., Subsidiary of Rangaire Corp., Old Taylor Rd, Oxford, MS 38655.

Cyclone Industries, 5500 W 102 St, Los Angeles, CA 90045.

Defiance International Ltd., 87–71 Lefferts Blvd, Richmond Hill, NY 11418.

Gaffers & Sattler Inc., 4851 S Alameda St, Los Angeles, CA 90058.

General Electric Co., Bldg 4, Rm 256, Appliance Park, Louisville, KY 40225.

Hotpoint Contract Sales, General Electric Company, Appliance Park, Louisville, KY 40225.

In-Sink-Erator, Div. Emerson Electric Co, 4700 21 St, Racine, WI 53406.

KitchenAid Div., Hobart Corp., Troy, OH 45374.

Magic Chef Inc., 740 King Edward Ave, Cleveland, TN 37311.

The Maytag Co., Newton, IA 50208.

Modern Maid, PO Box 1111, Chattanooga, TN 37401.

National Disposal Div., Hobart Corp., Troy, OH 45374.

O'Keefe & Merritt Co., Tappan Park, Mansfield, OH 44901.

Roper Corp., 1905 W Court St, Kankakee, IL 60901.

Royal Chef Div., Gray & Dudley Co., 2300 Clifton Rd, Nashville, TN 37209.

Tappan Appliance Division, Tappan Park, Mansfield, OH 44901.

U-Line Corp., 8900 N 55th St, Box 23220, Milwaukee, WI 53223.

Waste King, Div. Norris Industries, 5119 District Blvd, Los Angeles, CA 90040.

Whirlaway Co., A Tappan Div., 4240 E La Palma, Anaheim, CA 92803.

Whirlpool Corp., Administrative Center, Benton Harbor, MI 49022.

Trash compactors

Amana Refrigeration Inc., Amana, IA 52203.

Broan Mfg Co. Inc., 926 W State St, Hartford, WI 53027.

Caloric Corp., Topton, PA 19562.

Cabinet Component Co., 5201 SW Westgate, Rm 102, Portland, OR 97221.

Frigidaire Div., GMC, 300 Taylor St, Dayton, OH 45442.

Gaffers & Sattler Inc., 4851 S

Useful addresses

Alameda St, Los Angeles, CA 90058.
General Electric Co., Appliance Park, Louisville, KY 40225.
Gibson Appliance Corp., Gibson Appliance Center, Greenville, MI 48838.
Hotpoint Contract Sales, General Electric Co., Appliance Park, Louisville, KY 40225.
In-Sink-Erator, Div. Emerson Electric Co., 4700 21 St, Racine, WI 53406.
Kelvinator Appliance Co., 4248 Kalamazoo SE, Grand Rapids, MI 49508.
Kenmore from Sears, Roebuck & Co., Sears Tower, Chicago, IL 60684.
KitchenAid, Hobart Corporation, Troy, OH 45374.
Magic Chef Inc., 740 King Edward Ave, Cleveland, TN 37311.
Modern Maid, PO Box 1111, Chattanooga, TN 37401.
O'Keefe & Merritt Co., Tappan Park, Mansfield, OH 44901.
Roper Corp., 1905 W Court St, Kankakee, IL 60901.
Tappan Appliance Div., Tappan Park, Mansfield, OH 44901.
Tony Team Inc., 6701 110th St, Minneapolis, MN 55438.
Whirl-a-Way Co., 4240 E La Palma, Anaheim, CA 92806.
Whirlpool Corp., Administrative Center, Benton Harbor, MI 49022.

Storage

Cabinets, stock units

All Habitat shops.
Acme Cabinet Mfg Corp., 909 Highway 37, Toms River, NJ 08753.
Adelphi Kitchens, 3000 Penn Ave, West Lawn, PA 19609.
Alabama Metal Products Co. Inc., PO Box 608, Rosedale, MS 38769.
American Cabinet Corp., PO Box 1326, Dublin, GA 31021.
American Forest Products Corp., 2740 Hyde St., PO Box 3498, San Francisco, CA 94119.
Bloch Industries Inc., 130 Commerce Dr., Rochester, NY 14623.
Boise Cascade, Kitchen Cabinet Div., PO Box 514, Berryville, VA 22611.
Boro Wood Products Co. Inc., Bennettsville, SC 29512.
BPI Inc., 2701 Fairview Rd, Zeeland, MI 49464.
Brammer Mfg Co., 1701 Rockingham Rd, Davenport, IA 52808.
Brandom Mfg Corp. of Texas, PO Box 636, Keene, TX 76059.
Buell Cabinet Co. Inc., 600 N Franklin, Fort Scott, KS 66701.
Builders Supply Co. Inc., 5701 S 72 St, Omaha, NB 68127.
Cabinets by Caldwell Inc., 6621 Clarksville Hwy, Joelton, TN 37080.
Caravelle Wood Products Inc., 3333 East End Ave, South Chicago Heights, IL 60411.
Carroll Industries Inc., Box 510, Conway, NH 03818.
Champion Wood Products, 1301 Watt, Jeffersonville, IN 47130.
Colgan Inc., 620 Maria St, Kenner, LA 70062.
Connor Forest Industries, PO Box 847, Wausau, WI 54401.
Continental Kitchens Inc., Bldg 26, Spokane Industrial Park, Spokane, WA 99216.
Craft Maid Custom Kitchens Inc., PO Box 4026, Reading, PA 19606.
Creative Cabinets Inc., 3215 N Pan Am Expsy, San Antonio, TX 78220.
Crown Kitchen Cabinet Corp., 9200 Atlantic Ave, Ozone Park, NY 11416.
Custom Furniture & Cabinets, Rte 5, Box 892, Post Falls, ID 83854.
Custom Wood Products Inc., Box 4072, Roanoke, VA 24015.
Daralco Inc., 3201 Brighton Blvd, Denver, CO 80216.
Del-Mar Cabinets, Div. Triangle Pacific Cabinet Corp., 15 Linkwood Rd NW, Atlanta, GA 30311.
Del-Wood Kitchens Inc., R.D. 3, Hanover, PA 17331.
Dewils Industries Inc., 6307 NE 127th Ave, Vancouver, WA 98662.
Diamond Industries, Div. of Medford Corp., PO Box 1008, 550 SE Mill St, Grants Pass, OR 97526.
Dura Craft Kitchens, A Div. of L & M Mfg Co., 110 W Oak St, Gillespie, IL 62033.
Dura Maid Industries Inc., Architectural Material Center, 101 Park Ave, New York, NY 10017.
E & E Enterprises Inc., 912 W Cedar, Cedar Hill, TX 75104.
Evans Cabinet Corp., PO Box 548, Dublin, GA 31021.
Excel Wood Products Co. Inc., PO Box 819, Lakewood, NJ 08701.
Farina Kitchens, 145 Union St, Holbrook, MA 02343.
Fillip Metal Cabinet Co., 701 N Albany St, Chicago, IL 60612.
Francisco Cabinet Corp., 1525 Illinois St, Des Moines, IA 50314.
Frey Cabinet Co., 510 S Main St, Pittsburgh, PA 15220.
Gamma Cabinet Mfg Co., Richard Mine Rd, Wharton, NJ 07885.
Grandview Products Inc., Box 874, Parsons, KS 67357.
Haas Cabinet Co. Inc., 615 W Utica, Sellersburg, IN 47172.
Hager Mfg Co., 1512–32 N Front St, Mankato, MN 56001.
Hansa International Inc., 10 Kearney Rd, Needham, MA 02194.
Home Crest Corp., PO Box 595, Eisenhower Dr. E, Goshen, IN 46526.
Howell Woodwork Inc., 520 James St, Lakewood, NJ 08701.
Imperial Cabinet Co. Inc., PO Box 427, Gaston, IN 47342.
IXL Furniture Co., Div. of Westinghouse, Elizabeth City, NC 27909.
Jeffrey Steel Products, 1345 Halsey St, Brooklyn, NY 11227.
Kapri Kitchens, Div. of Cordal Inc., Dallastown, PA 17313.
Keller Kitchen Cabinets Southern Corp., State Rd 44, Box 1089, Deland, FL 32720.
Kemper, Div. of The Tappan Co., 701 S North St, Richmond, IN 47374.
KinZee Industries Inc., 259 Second St, Saddle Brook, NJ 07662.
Kitchen Beauty, Cabinets by Kabinart Corp., PO Box 7156, Nashville, TN 37210.
Kitchen Contractors Inc., 2413 Elizabeth St, Seagoville, TX 75159.
Kitchen Kompact Inc., KK Plaza, Jeffersonville, IN 47130.
Lawrence Cabinets Inc., 1401 Cattleman Rd, Sarasota, FL 33580.
Lewis Les-Care Kitchens, No. 1 Les-Care Dr., Waterbury, CT 06705.
Long-Bell Div., International Paper Co., Box 579, Longview, WA 98632.
Lucci, from Cabinet Systems Inc., 3 Belle Ave, Lewistown, PA 17044.
M & W Products Co. Inc., 1667 Penfield Rd, Rochester, NY 14625.
N. J. MacDonald & Sons Inc., PO Box 365, West Bridgewater, MS 02379.
Major Line Products Co. Inc., 402 Tyler St, Hoquiam, WA 98550.
Marvel Metal Products Co., 3843 W 43 St, Chicago, IL 60632.
Maracini & Sons Inc., 1409 Stephenson Ave, Iron Mt, MI 49801.
Markus Cabinet Mfg Co., 601 S Clinton, Aviston, IL 62216.
Marsh Furniture Co., PO Box 870, High Point, NC 27261.
Maryland Maid Kitchens, Div. of Colonial Hardwood Flooring Inc., 227 E Washington St, Hagerstown, MD 21740.
Mastercraft Inc., 6175 E 39th Ave, Denver, CO 60207.
Medallion Kitchens Inc., 810 1st St S, Hopkins, MN 55343.
Merillat Industries Inc., 2075 W Beecher Rd, Adrian, MI 49221.
Mid-Continent Millwork Inc., Mid-Continent Bldg, 372 St Peter St, St Paul, MN 55102.
Modesign Inc., 36–10 13th St, Long Island City, NY 11106.
Mother Hubbard's Cupboards, 1835 Dual Hwy, Hagerstown, MD 21740.
Murray Export Industries, PO Box 686, Westfield, NJ 07090.
North American Cabinet Corp., 701 South Grove, Marshall, TX 76570.
North Valley Plastics Inc., 4650 Caterpillar Rd, Redding, CA 96001.
Northern Kitchens, Rib Lake, WI 54470.
Olde Towne Cupboards Corp., Souderton, PA 18964.
Olympia Sales Co., 1537 South 700 West, Salt Lake City, UT 84104.
Orbit International Inc., GPO Box 3327, San Juan, PR 00936.
The Overton Co., PO Box 848, Kenly, NC 27542.
Peerless-Mayer Inc., Div. Frigitemp Corp., 401 Hunts Point Ave, Bronx, NY 10474.
Plastic Top Co., Div. Dar Tile, PO Box 3509, Albuquerque, NM 87110.
Prestige Cabinet Corporation of America, 29 Rider Place, Freeport, NY 11520.
Prestige Products Inc., PO Box 314, Twin Rivers Industrial Park, Neodasha, KS 66757.
Quinco Kitchens Inc., 3709 Dodds Ave, Chattanooga, TN 37407.
Regal Wood Products Inc., 8600 NW South River Dr., Miami, FL 33166.

Reliance Hardwood & Dimension Co., Box 18041, Minneapolis, MN 55418.
Riviera Products, Div. of Evans Products Co., 1960 Seneca Rd, St Paul, MN 55122.
Rosebud Mfg Co. Inc., Madison, SD 75042.
Royal Cabinet Mfg Co., 10515 Harper Ave, Detroit, MI 48213.
H. J. Scheirich Co., PO Box 21037, Louisville, KY 40221.
Schrock Bros Mfg Co. Inc., 217 S Oak St, Arthur, IL 61911.
Serway Brothers Inc., 916 Erie Blvd West, Rome, NY 13440.
Skaret's Cabinets Inc., PO Box 172, Mound, MI 55364.
Southeastern Cabinet Co., PO Box 889, Dothan, AL 36301.
Springfield Cabinet Works Inc., 932 Dayton Ave, Springfield, OH 45506.
Superior Wood Work Inc., 7157 Dale Rd, El Paso, TX 79915.
Triangle Pacific Cabinet Corp., 4255 LBJ Freeway, Dallas, TX 75234.
Trimline Cabinet Div., Mouldings Inc., PO Box 858, Marion, VA 24354.
United Cabinet Div., Beatrice Foods Co., Aristokraft Square, PO Box 420, Jasper, IN 47546.
US Laminates, 1429 Park St, PO Box 960, Hartford, CT 06101.
Ute Fabricating, Box 128, Fort Duchesne, UT 84026.
Valley Kitchens Inc., 123 W Main St, Lebanon, OH 45036.
Vaughan & Sons, PO Box 17258, San Antonio, TX 78285.
Waldorf Kitchens, Box 578, MD 20601.
Wayneco Inc., 800 Hanover Rd, York, PA 17404.
Well-Bilt Products Inc., 5561 NW 36th Ave, Miami, FL 33142.
Wellborn Cabinet Inc., Route No. 1, Ashland, AL 36251.
Western Cabinet & Millwork, 11801 NE 116th, Kirkland, WA 98033.
Westwood Products Inc., 560 21 St SE, PO Box 12245, Salem, OR 97309.
White-Meyer Wood Products Inc., 141st & Route 45, Orland Park, IL 60462.
Wilson Cabinet Co., PO Box 489, Port Clinton, OH 43452.
Woodstock Mfg Corp., 1605 Baltimore, Kansas City, MO 64108.
Yorktowne, Div. of The Wickes Corp., PO Box 231, Red Lion, PA 17356.

Cabinets, custom units

Alderform Laminated Products, Division of Alderman Interior Systems, 4511 W Buffalo Ave, Tampa, FL 33614.
Allmilmo Corp., 122 Clinton Rd, Fairfield, NJ 07006.
American Cabinet Corp., PO Box 1326, Dublin, GA 31021.
American Wood Shop Inc., 711 Center Point Rd NE, Cedar Rapids, IA 52402.
Ampco Products Inc., 7795 W 20 Ave, Hialeah, FL 33014.
Bilt-in Wood Products Co., 3500 Clipper Rd, Baltimore, MD 21211.
Birchcraft Kitchens, 1612 Thorn St, Reading, PA 19601.
Bonarrigo Homecraft Inc., PO Box 333, Moscow, PA 18444.
Boro Industries Inc., PO Box 11558, Fort Worth, TX 76109.
Boro Kitchen Cabinets, 56–06 Cooper Ave, Brooklyn, NY 11227.
Boro Wood Products Co. Inc., Bennettsville, SC 29512.
BPI Inc., 2701 Fairview Rd, Zeeland, MI 49464.
Brandom Mfg Corp. of Texas, PO Box 636, Keene, TX 76059.
Capri Kitchens, 17 Murray St, Plymouth, MA 02360.
Cardinal Kitchens Inc., 410 Fourth Ave, Brooklyn, NY 11215.
Henry M. Carr Inc., 1150 Vermont St, Frankfort, IN 46041.
Century Wood Products Inc., Box 783–924 E Park St, Olathe, KS 66061.
Champion Wood Products, 1301 Watt, Jeffersonville, IN 47130.
Chandlers Plywood Products Inc., 3716 Waverly Rd, Huntington, WV 25704.
Charlotte Wood Products, 202 Pearl St, Charlotte, MI 48813.
Christian Brothers Inc., RD No. 1, Box 202, Montoursville, PA 17754.
Contemporary Systems Inc., 10 Kearney Rd, Needham, MA 02194.
Coppes Inc., 401 E Market St, Nappanee, IN 46550.
Craft Maid Custom Kitchens Inc., PO Box 4026, Reading, PA 19606.
Crown Kitchen Cabinet Corp., 9200 Atlantic Ave, Ozone Park, NY 11416.
Custom Furniture & Cabinets, Rte 5, Box 892, Post Falls, ID 83854.
Custom Hall Inc., PO Box 689, Fairfield, CT 06430.
Custom Maid Cabinets Inc., 2131 W 117 St, Cleveland, OH 44111.
Dayton Showcase Co., 2601 W Dorothy Lane, Dayton, OH 45439.
Del-Wood Kitchens Inc., RD 3, Hanover, PA 17331.
Dewils Industries Inc., 6307 NE 127th Ave, Vancouver, WA 98662.
Dudley Cabinets Inc., 1312 Main St, Millis, MA 02054.
Dura Craft Kitchens, A Div. of L & M Mfg Co., 110 W Oak St, Gillespie, IL 62033.
Dura Maid Industries Inc., Architectural Material Center, 101 Park Ave, New York, NY.
Dura Supreme Inc., 10800 County Rd 15, Minneapolis, MN 55441.
E & E Enterprises Inc., 912 W Cedar, Cedar Hill, TX 75104.
Evans Cabinet Corp., PO Box 548, Dublin, GA 31021.
Farina Kitchens, 145 Union St, Holbrook, MA 02343.
Fillip Metal Cabinet Co., 701 N Albany St, Chicago, IL 60612.
Forward Products Inc., Main St, Evans City, PA 16033.
Frey Cabinet Co., 510 S Main St, Pittsburgh, PA 15220.
Gamma Cabinet Mfg Co., Richard Mine Rd, Wharton, NJ 07885.
Gleason Kitchen Inc., Rocky Glen Industrial Park, Moosic R.D. No. 2, Avoca, PA 18641.
Hager Mfg Co., 1512–32 N Front St, Mankato, MN 56001.
Heritage Cabinets Inc., 348 Broad St, Fitchburg, MA 01420.
Herrmann & Safranek, 4005 El Camino Real, Atascadero, CA 93422.
Holiday Kitchen Cabinets Inc., 19021 Florida, Roseville, MI 48066.
Howell Woodwork Inc., 520 James St, Lakewood, NJ 08701.
Imperial Cabinet Co. Inc., PO Box 427, Gaston, IN 47342.
Jeffrey Steel Products, 1345 Halsey St, Brooklyn, NY 11227.
J-Wood Inc., Rte 322, Box 367, Milroy, PA 17063.
Kapri Kitchens, Div. of Cordal Inc., Dallastown, PA 17313.
Kinzee Industries Inc., 259 Second St, Saddle Brook, NJ 07662.
Kitchen Concepts Inc., 3601 Princeton NE, Albuquerque, NM 87107.
Kitchen Mart Inc., 7815 National Turnpike, Louisville, KY 40214.
Kountry Kraft Kitchens Inc., Newmanstown, PA 17073.
Chris J. Krogh Inc., 164 Milton Ave, Alpharetta, GA 30201.
Krown Kitchens Inc., Leola, PA 17504.
L-Co Cabinet Corp., PO Box 490, Shamokin, PA 17872.
Laminite Plastics Corp., 2800 Peterson Ave, Chicago, IL 60659.
Lawrence Cabinets Inc., 1401 Cattleman Rd, Sarasota, FL 33580.
Lewis Les-Care Kitchens, No. 1 Les-Care Dr., Waterbury, CT 06705.
Lucci, from Cabinet Systems Inc., 3 Belle Ave, Lewistown, PA 17044.
M & W Products Co. Inc., 1667 Penfield Rd, Rochester, NY 14625.
N. J. MacDonald & Sons Inc., PO Box 365, Pleasant St, West Bridgewater, MA 02379.
Macor Manufacturing Corp., 7482 Dixie Highway, Bridgeport, MI 48722.
Major Line Products Co. Inc., 402 Tyler St, PO Box 478, Hoquiam, WA 98550.
Mallis Wood Products Inc., 115–10 Dunkirk St, St Albans, NY 11412.
Markus Cabinet Mfg Co., 601 S Clinton, Aviston, IL 62216.
MarVell Kitchens Inc., 1150 Wyoming Ave, Wyoming, PA 18644.
Micamade, Lafayette Rd, Medina, OH 44256.
Miceli Cabinet Corp., 501 Washington Ave, Carlstadt, NJ 07072.
Miller Maid Cabinets Inc., 4805 Hardegon Rd, Indianapolis, IN 46227.
Modern Cabinet Corp., 106 Pearl St, Mt Vernon, NY 10550.
Modesign Inc., 36–10 13th St, Long Island City, NY 11106.
Morr-Craft Products Inc., 1414 Spring Garden Ave, Pittsburgh, PA 15212.
Mother Hubbard's Cupboards, 1835 Dual Hwy, Hagerstown, MD 21740.
Mutschler, Div. Triangle Pacific Corp., 302 S Madison St, Nappanee, IN 46550.
N.I.N.E. Inc., National

Useful addresses

Industries New Enterprise, Midway Industrial Park, Odenton, MD 21113.
North Valley Plastics Inc., 4650 Caterpillar Rd, Redding, CA 96001.
Northern Kitchens, Rib Lake, WI 54470.
A. L. Novak Co., 2700 W Belmont Ave, Chicago, IL 60618.
Olde Towne Cupboards Corp., Souderton, PA 18964.
Orbit International Inc., GPO Box 3327, San Juan, PR 00936.
Pennville Custom Cabinets, Div. Commercial Electric Co., 600 E Votaw St, Portland, IN 47371.
Pioneer Craftsman Inc., 333 N 3rd St, Reading, PA 19601.
Poggenpohl/USA, 222 Cedar Lane, Teaneck, NJ 07666.
Prestige Cabinet Corporation of America, 29 Rider Place, Freeport, NY 11520.
Presto Kitchens & Baths, 8805 SW 132 St, Miami, FL 33176.
Quaker Maid Kitchens, Div. of The Tappan Co., Leesport, PA 19533.
Quality Custom Kitchens Inc., 295 E Main St, Leola, PA 17540.
Quinco Kitchens Inc., 3709 Dodds Ave, Chattanooga, TN 37407.
Ralsco Inc., 389 Warren Ave, Brockton, MA 02401.
Regal Cabinet Inc., 315 Holland Sylvania, Toledo, OH 43615.
Regal Wood Products Inc., 8600 NW South River Dr., Miami, FL 33166.
Rene Products, 8600 Harrison Pike, Cleves, OH 45002.
Rich-Craft Custom Kitchens, 141 W Penn Ave, Robesonia, PA 19551.
Rich-Maid Kitchens Inc., Box 38, Wernersville, PA 19565.
Riviera Products, Div. of Evans Products Co., 1960 Seneca Rd, St Paul, MN 55122.
Rosebud Mfg Co. Inc., Madison, SD 57042.
Roseline Products Inc., 120 Schmitt Blvd, Farmingdale, NY 11735.
Royal Cabinet Mfg Co., 10515 Harper Ave, Detroit, MI 48213.
Rutt Custom Kitchens Div., Route 23, Goodville, PA 17528.
St Charles Mfg Co., 1611 E Main St, St Charles, IL 60174.
Scio Cabinet Co. Inc., PO Box 526, Fowler Ave, Scio, OH 43988.
Leo H. Scott Cabinets Inc., Ferrum, VA 24088.
Serway Brothers Inc., 916 Erie Blvd West, Rome, NY 13440.
Skaret's Cabinets Inc., PO Box 172, Mound, MI 55364.
Southeastern Cabinet Co., PO Box 889, Dothan, AL 36301.
Style Trend Mfg, 2370 Henry St, Muskegon, MI 49441.
Stylecraft-Kitchens Inc., Box 258, Blue Ball, PA 17506.
Stylewood, Div. of Thompson Industries Inc., 2601 Waterview Ave, Baltimore, MD 21230.
Sunearth Cabinetworks, Spring House Village Center, Spring House, PA 19477.
Sunshine Kitchens Inc., 16111 NW 13 Ave, Miami, FL 33169.
Superior Wood Work Inc., 7157 Dale Rd, El Paso, TX 79915.
Tailored Kitchens Co. Inc., 380 Ninth St, Jersey City, NJ 07302.
Tarantino Bros Inc., 17614 St Clair Ave, Cleveland, OH 44110.
Top Shop, 1035 Frances Ave, Billings, MT 59101.
Town Craft Vanities, 15–32 127 St, College Point, NY 11356.
Trimline Cabinet Div., Mouldings Inc., PO Box 858, Marion, VA 24354.
Tuscaloosa Woodworkers, Route No. 1, Duncanville, AL 35456.
Ute Fabricating, Box 128, Fort Duchesne, UT 84026.
Valley Cabinet Mfg Inc., 4361 Jetway Court, North Highlands, CA 95660.
Waldorf Kitchens, Box 578, Waldorf, MD 20601.
Well-Bilt Products Inc., 5561 NW 36th Ave, Miami, FL 33142.
Western Cabinet & Millwork, 11801 NE 116th, Kirkland, WA 98033.
Whitehall Industries Inc., Whitehall Bldg, East Rockaway, NY 11518.
Wilson Cabinet Co., PO Box 489, Port Clinton, OH 43452.
Wilson Custom Kitchens, South Feazel St, Harrisburg, IL 62946.
Wood-Hu Kitchens Inc., 343 Manley St, W Bridgewater, MA 02379.
Wood-Mode Cabinetry, Kreamer, Snyder County, PA 17833.
Wood Products Co., PO Box 15146, Sacramento, CA 95813.

Cabinets, knock-down units

American Cabinet Corp., PO Box 1326, Dublin, GA 31021.
Belwood, Div. US Industries Inc., Ackerman, MS 39735.
BPI Inc., 2701 Fairview Rd, Zeeland, MI 49464.
Continental Kitchens Inc., Bldg 26, Spokane Industrial Park, Spokane, WA 99216.
Crown Kitchen Cabinet Corp., 9200 Atlantic Ave, Ozone Park, NY 11416.
Diamond Industries, Div. of Medford Corp., PO Box 1008, 550 SE Mill St, Grants Pass, OR 97526.
Homewood Industries Inc., 17641 S Ashland Ave, Homewood, IL 60430.
Laminite Plastics Corp., 2800 Peterson Ave, Chicago, IL 60659.
Major Line Products Co. Inc., 402 Tyler St, PO Box 478, Hoquiam, WA 98550.
Modern Cabinet Corp., 106 Pearl St, Mt Vernon, NY 10550.
Murray Export Industries, PO Box 686, Westfield, NJ 07090.
Orbit International Inc., GPO Box 3327, San Juan, PR 00936.
Plywood Components Inc., 6523 NE Old Salem Rd, Albany, OR 97321.
Presto Kitchens & Baths, 8805 SW 132 St, Miami, FL 33176.
Projection Products, PO Box 909, Newton, NC 28658.
Town Craft Vanities, 15–32 127 St, College Point, NY 11356.
V-T Industries Inc., 1000 Industrial Park, Holstein, IA 51025.
Waldorf Kitchens, Box 578, Waldorf, MD 20601.
Well-Bilt Products Inc., 5561 NW 36th Ave, Miami, FL 33142.
Western Cabinet & Millwork, 11801 NE 116th, Kirkland, WA 98033.
Westwood Products Inc., 560 21 St SE, PO Box 12245, Salem, OR 97309.

Ventilation

Home Ventilating Institute, 230 N Michigan Ave, Chicago, IL 60601, provides information on proper home ventilation to consumers, architects, builders and contractors.

Window fans, electric

Frigid Inc., Thermoware Electric Corp., 1250 Rockaway Ave, Brooklyn, NY 11236.
The Hoover Co., 101 E Maple St, Canton, OH 44720.
Hunter Div., Robbins & Myers Inc., 2500 Frisco Ave, Memphis, TN 38114.
Lakewood Engineering & Mfg Co., 212 N Carpenter, Chicago, IL 60607.
Lasko Metal Products Inc., 300 Confederate Dr., Franklin, TN 37064.
Leigh Products Inc., Glade St at Larch, Coopersville, MI 49404.
W. B. Marvin Mfg Co., Urbana, OH 43078.
Manning-Bowman, Div. McGraw Edison Co., Parkade Plaza, Columbia, MO 53233.
Nautilus Industries, 926 State St, Hertford, WI 53027.
Panasonic Special Products Div., 200 Park Ave, Pan Am Bldg, New York, NY 10017.
Patton Electric Co., 11401 Bluffton Rd, Fort Wayne, IN 46809.
Sanyo Electric Inc., 51 Joseph St, Moonachie, NJ 07074.
Superior Electric Products Corp., Nash Rd, Cape Girardeau, MO 63701.
Toastmaster, Div. McGraw-Edison Co., Parkade Plaza-601 W, Columbia, MO 65201.
Vernco Corp. of Tennessee, 1804 22nd St, Columbus, IN 47201.

Ventilating hoods

Admiral Corp., 1701 E Woodfield Rd, Schaumberg, IL 60172.
Aubrey Mfg Inc., 6709 Main St, Union, IL 60180.
Broan Mfg Co. Inc., 926 W State St, Hartford, WI 53027.
Brown Stove Works Inc., 1422 Caroline Ave NE, Cleveland, TN 37311.
Caloric Corp., Topton, PA 19562.
Chambers Corp., Subsidiary of Rangaire Corp., Old Taylor Rd, Oxford, MS 38655.
Defiance International Ltd, 87–71 Lefferts Blvd, Richmond Hill, NY 11418.
Distinctive Appliances Inc., 8826 Lankershim Blvd, Sun Valley, CA 91352.
Emerson Electric Co., Rittenhouse/Pryne Div., 475 Quaker

Meeting House Rd, Honeoye Falls, NY 14472.
Fasco Industries Inc., Consumer Products Div., 810 Gillespie St, Fayetteville, NC 28302.
Fashion-Craft Products Inc., PO Box 168, Nappanee, IN 46550.
Gaffers & Sattler Inc., 4851 S Alameda St, Los Angeles, CA 90058.
General Electric Co., Bldg 4, Rm 256, Appliance Park, Louisville, KY 40225.
Goodwin of California Inc., 1075 Second St, Berkeley, CA 94710.
H & G Range Hoods, 167–11 69th Ave, Flushing, NY 11365.
Hardwick Stove Co., 240 Edwards SE, Cleveland, TN 37311.
Hotpoint Contract Sales, General Electric Company, Appliance Park, Louisville, KY 40225.
Kich-N-Vent, Home Metal Products Co., 750 Central Expsy, Plano, TX 75074.
Magic Chef Inc., 740 King Edward Ave, Cleveland, TN 37311.
Miami-Carey, A Jim Walter Co., 203 Garver Rd, Monroe, OH 45050.
Modern Maid, PO Box 1111, Chattanooga, TN 37401.
Monarch Kitchen Appliance Co., 715 N Spring St, Beaver Dam, WI 53916.
Monk Hood, 128 Industrial Rd, Addison, IL 60101.
National Industries Inc., Box 293, Industrial Park, Ocala, FL 32670.
NuTone Div., Scovill Mfg Co., Madison & Red Bank Rds, Cincinnati, OH 45227.
O'Keefe & Merritt Co., Tappan Park, Mansfield, OH 44901.
Orbon Industries Inc., PO Box 585, Belleville, IL 62222.
PM Range Hoods Corp., 43 Florida St, Farmingdale, NY 11735.
Rangaire Corp., Home Products Div., Box 177, Cleburne, TX 76031.
Roper Corp., 1905 W Court St, Kankakee, IL 60901.
Royal Chef Div., Gray & Dudley Co., 2300 Clifton Rd, Nashville, TN 37209.
Stewart Mfg Co., 320 E St Joseph St, Indianapolis, IN 46202.
Stovent Manufacturers, 8225 Scyene Rd, Dallas, TX 75227.
Swanson Mfg Co., 607 S Washington St, Owosso, MI 48867.
Tappan Appliance Division, Tappan Park, Mansfield, OH 44901.
Thermador, Div. of Norris Industries, 5119 District Blvd, Los Angeles, CA 90040.
Universal Metal Industries, 1441 S 26 Pl., Phoenix, AZ 85034.
Valley Products Co., 750 Carver Ave, Westwood, NJ 07675.
Vent-A-Hood Co., PO Box 426, Richardson, TX 75080.
Ventrola Mfg, 501 S Chestnut, Owosso, MI 48867.
Weiss Hardware & Mfg Co. Inc., 169 Bowery, New York, NY 10002.
Welbilt Corp., Welbilt Square, Maspeth, NY 11378.
Whirlpool Corp., Administrative Center, Benton Harbor, MI 49022.
White-Westinghouse Corp., 930 Ft. Duquesne Blvd, Pittsburgh, PA 15222.
Williams, Div. Leigh Products, 1536 Grant St, Elkhart, IN 46514.
Wood-Mode Cabinetry, Kreamer, Snyder County, PA 17833.
Zenith Metal Products Corp., 723 Secane Ave, Primos, PA 19018.

Air conditioning

Frigidaire Division, Dept 2361, Dayton, OH 45401.
Gaffers & Sattler Inc., 4851 S Alameda, Los Angeles, CA 90058.
Jenn-Air Corp., 3035 North Shadeland Ave, Indianapolis, IN 46226.
Kenmore, from Sears, Roebuck & Co., Sears Tower, Chicago, IL 60684.
Westinghouse Electric Corp., Room Air Conditioning Division, Rte 27 & Vineyard Rd, Edison, NY 08817.

Walls

All Habitat shops (for glazed ceramic tiles, cork, hessian wall coverings, wallpapers, paints).
National Decorating Products Association, 9334 Dielman Ind. Dr, St Louis, MO 63132 (distributors and retailers of paint, wallpaper and other decorating products).
Painting & Decorating Contractors of America, 7223 Lee Hwy, Falls Church, VA 22046.
Tile Council of America, PO Box 326, Princeton, NJ 08540 (manufacturers of domestic ceramic tiles for floors and walls).
Wallcovering Manufacturers Association, 1099 Wall St W, Lyndhurst, NJ 07071 (publishes pamphlets and other material on hanging wallcoverings and the proper care of wallcoverings).
Boyd Architectural Wallcoverings, 333 N Baldwin Pk Blvd, City of Industry, CA 91746 (cork, fabrics, felt, foil, metal, vinyl, wood veneers).
Four Walls Inc., 160 E 56 St, New York, NY 10022 (cork, fabrics, felt, foil, vinyl).
Richard E. Thibaut Inc., 204 E 58 St, New York, NY 10022 (cork, fabrics, felt, foil, vinyl, wood veneers).

Ceramic tiles

Agency Tile, 499 Old Nyack Tpk, Spring Valley, NY 10977.
American Olean Tile Co., 2340 Cannon Ave, Lansdale, PA 19446.
Architectural Products, Interspace Corp., 2901 Los Feliz Blvd, Los Angeles, CA 90039.
Auffray & Co., 146 E 46 St, New York, NY 10022.
Bemis Co. Inc., Bemis Mill Div., S Missouri St, Bemis, TN 38314.
Continental Creative Sales Inc., 279 Marshall St, Paterson, NJ 07503.
Country Floors Inc., 300 E 61 St, New York, NY 10021.
Design-Technics Ceramics Inc., 160 E 56 St, New York, NY 10022.
Designers Tile International, 6812 SW 81 St, Miami, FL 33143.
Elon Inc., 964 Third Ave, New York, NY 10022.
Forms & Surfaces Inc., PO Box 5215, Santa Barbara, CA 93108.
Gerber Industries Inc., 1510 Fairview Ave, St Louis, MO 63132.
Otto Gerdau Co., 82 Wall St, New York, NY 10005.
Hastings Tile, 964 Third Ave, New York, NY 10022.
Homecraft Marketing Inc., 208 Russell Place, Hackensack, NJ 07601.
Jim Hurt of Texas, PO Box 531, McAllen, TX 78501.
Interspace Corp., c/o Architectural Products Sales, 2901 Los Feliz Blvd, Los Angeles, CA 90039.
H. & J. Johnson Inc., State Highway 35, Keyport, NJ 07735.
Latco Products, 3371 Glendale Blvd, Los Angeles, CA 90039.
Lawton Carpet, 62–33 Woodhaven Blvd, Rego Park, NY 11374.
Ludowici Celadon Co., 111 E Wacker Dr., Chicago, IL 60601.
Metal Dimensions, Div. Miller Industries, 16295 NW 13 Ave, Miami, FL 33169.
Metro Mosaics & Metro Flor, 137 Commercial St, Plainview, NY 11803.
Michigan Brick, Corunna, MI 48817.
Mid-State Tile Co., PO Box 627, Lexington, NC 27292.
Miraplas Tile Co., 980 Parsons Ave, Columbus, OH 43206.
Mosaic Tile Co., 834 Richwood Rd, PO Box 999, Florence, AL 35630.
National Gypsum Co., 325 Delware Ave, Buffalo, NY 14202.
P & S Sales, Rydal West, Jenkintown, PA 19046.
Raventos International Corp., 150 Fifth Ave, New York, NY 10011.
Robertson-American Corp., S Pennsylvania Ave, Morrisville, PA 19067.
Sikes Corp., PO Box 447, Lakeland, FL 33802.
Stark Ceramics Inc., PO Box 8880, Canton, OH 44711.
Structural Stoneware Inc., PO Box 119, Minerva, OH 44657.
Summitville Tiles, Summitville, OH 43962.
Trimourti India Inc., 42 W 58 St, New York, NY 10019.
US Ceramic Tile Co., 1375 Raff Rd SW, Canton, OH 44710.
Walker & Zanger Inc., 179 Summerfield St, Scarsdale, NY 10583.

Cork

Armstrong Cork Co., Liberty & Charlotte Sts, Lancaster, PA 17604.
Bayberry Handprints Inc., Far Reach Trail, Putnam Valley, NY 10579.
Brewster Corp., 50 River St, Old Saybrook, CT 06475.
L. E. Carpenter & Co., 170 N Main St, Wharton, NJ 07885.
Cartier Mills Inc., Div. David & Dash, 2445 N Miami Ave, Miami, FL 33137.
Ronald Charles Associates, 3900 N Miami Ave, Miami, FL 33127.
Claridge Products & Eqpt

Useful addresses

Inc., Harrison, AR 72601.

Cohama Decorative Fabrics, United Merchants & Mfrs, 214 Madison Ave, New York, NY 10016.

Cork Plus Inc., 135–143 Front St, Bridgeport, PA 19405.

Cork Products Co. Inc., 250 Park Ave S, New York, NY 10003.

Crown Wallcovering Corp., 979 Third Ave, New York, NY 10022.

Decro-Wall, 375 Executive Blvd, Emsford, NY 10523.

Dippel, Vogler & Sharkey Co. Inc., 515 Madison Ave, New York, NY 10022.

Dodge Cork Co., 19 Laurel St, PO Box 989. Lancaster, PA 17604.

Durawall Inc., 10 Market St, Kenilworth, NJ 07033.

Expanko Cork Co., PO Box 384, West Chester, PA 19380.

Gilford Inc., 250 Park Ave S, New York, NY 10003.

S. M. Hexter Co., 2800 Superior Ave, Cleveland, OH 44114.

L. Jones & Co. Inc., 155 E 56 St, New York, NY 10022.

Katzenbach & Warren Inc., 155 E 56 St, New York, NY 10022.

Laminating Services Inc., 4700 Robards Ln, Louisville, KY 40218.

Laue Wallcovering Inc., 201 E 56 St, New York, NY 10022.

J. M. Lynne Co. Inc., 149 Sullivan Ln, Westbury, NY 11590.

Manton Cork Corp., 27 Benson Ln, Merrick, NY 11566.

Bob Mitchell Designs, 8535 Warner Dr., Culver City, CA 90230.

Pageant Wallpaper Co., 979 Third Ave, New York, NY 10022.

C. W. Stockwell Inc., 320 N Madison Ave, Los Angeles, CA 90004.

Russ Stonier Inc., 50 S Mannheim Hillside, IL 60162.

Vaughan Walls Inc., 11681 San Vicente Blvd, Los Angeles, CA 90049.

Warner Co., 108 S Desplaines St, Chicago, IL 60606.

Wicander Enterprises Inc., 4 Front St, Exeter, NH 03833.

Metal tiles

The October Co. Inc., 51 Ferry St, Easthampton, MA 01027.

Vikon Tile Corp., 130 N Taylor St, Washington, NJ 07882.

Mirror tiles

Binswanger Mirror Co., 1355 Lynnfield Rd, Memphis, TN 38117.

Continental Creative Sales Inc., 279 Marshall St, Paterson, NJ 07503.

Hoyne Industries Inc., 1058 E 230 St, Carson, CA 90745.

Latco Products, 3371 Glendale Blvd, Los Angeles, CA 90039.

Lombardo Associates Inc., 411 E John St, Lindenhurst, NY 11757.

National Products Inc., 900 Baxter Ave, Louisville, KY 40204.

Walker & Zanger Inc., 179 Summerfield St, Scarsdale, NY 10583.

Plastic tiles

Lusterrock International, 4125 Richmond Ave, Houston, TX 77027.

Meakins McKinnon Inc., 378 Niagara St, Lockport, NY 14094.

Miraplas Tile Co., 980 Parsons Ave, Columbus, OH 43206.

Romarco Corp., PO Drawer 218, Morganton, NC 28655.

Vinyl wall coverings

Adams Leathers & Vinyls Inc., 50 Amor Ave, Carlstadt, NJ 07072.

Barclay Fabrics Co. Inc., 7120 Airport Hwy, Box 650, Pennsauken, NJ 08101.

Bayberry Handprints Inc., Far Reach Trail, Putnam Valley, NY 10579.

B. Berger Co., 1608 E 24 St, Cleveland, OH 44114.

Birge-Reed Forest Products Inc., 390 Niagara St, Buffalo, NY 14240.

Brewster Corp., 50 River St, Old Saybrook, CT 06475.

Carnegie Fabrics Inc., 15 E 22 St, New York, NY 10010.

L. E. Carpenter & Co., 170 N Main St, Wharton, NJ 07885.

Cartier Mills Inc., Div. David & Dash, 2445 N Miami Ave, Miami, FL 33137.

China Seas Inc., 149 E 72 St, New York, NY 10021.

Christopher Prints, 134 Sand Park Rd, Cedar Grove, NJ 07009.

Coating Products, 580 Sylvan Ave, Englewood Cliffs, NJ 07632.

Cohama Decorative Fabrics, United Merchant & Mfrs, 214 Madison Ave, New York, NY 10016.

Columbus Coated Fabrics, 1280 N Grant Ave, Columbus, OH 43216.

Commercial Plastics International Ltd, Wallcovering Div., 807 Haddon Ave, Haddonfield, NJ 08033.

Construction Specialties Inc., PO Box 380, Muncy, PA 17756.

Crown Wallcovering Corp., 979 Third Ave, New York, NY 10022.

David & Dash Inc., 2445 N Miami Ave, Miami, FL 33137.

Deco/Gard Products, PO Box 400, Muncy, PA 17756.

Decorative Arts Wallcovering Inc., 2200 W Greenleaf, Evanston, IL 60202.

Decorators Walk, 171 E 56 St, New York, NY 10022.

Decro-Wall, 375 Executive Blvd, Ernsford, NY 10523.

Jack Denst Designs Inc., 7355 S Exchange Ave, Chicago, IL 60649.

Durawall Inc., 10 Market St, Kenilworth, NJ 07033.

Facade Papers Inc., 7618 Spafford Rd, Cleveland, OH 44105.

Flo-tech Corp., 2 Lee Blvd, Frazer, PA 19355.

Formica Corp., 120 E Fourth St, Cincinnati, OH 45202.

Franciscan Fabrics Inc., 938 Harrison St, San Francisco, CA 94107.

Gilford Inc., 250 Park Ave S, New York, NY 10003.

B. F. Goodrich, General Products Co., 500 Main St, Akron, OH 44318.

Grace Wallcoverings, Div. W. R. Grace & Co., 1255-A Lynnfield Rd, Memphis, TN 38138.

S. M. Hexter Co., 2800 Superior Ave, Cleveland, OH 44114.

ICI United States Inc., Concord Pke & New Murphy Rd, Wilmington, DE 19899.

Imperial Wallcoverings, 23645 Mercantile Rd, Cleveland, OH 44122.

J. Josephson Inc., 35 Empire Blvd, South Hackensack, NJ 07606.

Paul Kaiser Associates Inc., 4100 N Miami Ave, Miami, FL 33127.

Kaiser Gypsum Co. Inc., Kaiser Center, 300 Lakeside Dr., Oakland, CA 94666.

Katzenbach & Warren Inc., 155 E 56 St, New York, NY 10022.

Knight Bros Inc., 12401 Euclid Ave, Cleveland, OH 44106.

Laminated Services Inc., 201 E 4700 Robards Ln, Louisville, KY 40218.

Laue Wallcovering Inc., 201 E 56 St, New York, NY 10022.

J. M. Lynne Co. Inc., 149 Sullivan Ln, Westbury, NY 11590.

McCanless Custom Fabrics Inc., PO Box 1447, Salisbury, NC 28144.

Marlite Commercial Products, Div. Masonite Corp., Harger & Main Sts, Dover, OH 44622.

Bob Mitchell Designs, 8535 Warner Dr., Culver City, CA 90230.

Moderncote, An American Standard Co., PO Box 685, New Castle, IN 47362.

Northeastern Wallcoverings, 292 Summer St, Boston, MA 02210.

Pageant Wallpaper Co., 979 Third Ave, New York, NY 10022.

Pallette Prints Inc., PO Box 12526, Philadelphia, PA 19151.

Ronald Charles Associates, 3900 N Miami Ave, Miami, FL 33127.

Stamford Wall Paper Co. Inc., 153 Greenwich Ave, Stamford, CT 06904.

Standard Coated Products, Formica Products, 120 E Fourth St, Cincinnati, OH 45202.

Stauffer Chemical Co., Plastics Div., Westport, CT 06880.

C. W. Stockwell Inc., 320 N Madison Ave, Los Angeles, CA 90004.

Thomas Strahan Co., Wall covering Div. National Gypsum Co., Heard & Maple, Chelsea, MA 02150.

Tenneco Chemicals, Polymers & Plastics Div., 300 Needham St, Newton Upper Falls, MA 02164.

US Gypsum Co., 101 S Wacker Dr., Chicago, IL 60606.

United DeSoto, 3101 S Kedzie Ave, Chicago, IL 60623.

Albert Van Luit & Co., 4000 Chevy Chase Dr., Los Angeles, CA 90039.

Vaughan Walls Inc., 11681 San Vicente Blvd, Los Angeles, CA 90049.

Wall Trends International, PO Box 10, 17 Mileed Way, Avenel, NJ 07001.

Warner Co., 108 S Desplaines St, Chicago, IL 60606.

Winfield Design Associate Inc., 2690 Harrison St, San Francisco, CA 94110.

Zina Studios Inc., 85 Purdy Ave, Port Chester, NY 10573.

Wall panels

Abitibi, 3250 W Big Beaver Rd, Troy, MI 48084.

Allied Plywood Corp., Box 56, Boston, MA 02129.

American Forest Products Corp., 2740 Hyde St, PO Box 3498, San Francisco, CA 94119.

Bangkok Industries, 1900–10 S 20th St, Philadelphia, PA 19145.

Barclay Industries Inc., 65 Industrial Rd, Lodi, NJ 07644.

Bradley Plywood Corp., PO Box 1408, Savannah, GA 31402.

Champion Building Products, Champion International Corp., 1 Landmark Square, Stamford, CT 06921.

DG Shelter Products, Hearin Division, PO Box 25448, Portland, OR 97225.

Dimensional Plastics Corp., 1065 E 26 St, Hialeah, FL 33013.

Distco Laminating Inc., 4934 Starr SE, Grand Rapids, MI 49506.

Evans Products Co., PO Box E, Corvallis, OR 97330.

Fiberesin Plastics Div., US Gypsum Co., Box 88, Oconomowoc, WI 53066.

Formica Corp., 120 E Fourth St, Cincinnati, OH 45202.

Foster Grant Co., 217 Hamilton St, Leominster, MA 01453.

Funder America Inc., Bethel Church Rd, Mocksville, NC 27028.

Georgia Pacific Corp., 900 SW 5th Ave, Portland, OR 97204.

Gold Bond Building Products, Gold Bond Bldg, 327 Delaware Ave, Buffalo, NY 14202.

Kemlite Corp., 101 N Republic Ave, Joliet, IL 60434.

Laminite Plastics Corp., 2800 Peterson Ave, Chicago, IL 60659.

Lancaster Diversified Industries Inc., 102 Chester St, Lancaster, PA 17602.

Mann & Parker Lumber Co., Box 18, Constitution Ave, New Freedom, PA 17349.

Marlite Division, Masonite Corp., Dover, OH 44622.

Masonite Corp., 29 N Wacker, Chicago, IL 60606.

North Pacific Lumber Co., Engineered Panel & Component Div., 1505 SE Gideon, PO Box 3915, Portland, OR 97208.

Paeco Inc., 500 Market St, Perth Amboy, NJ 08861.

Pan-Pacific Overseas, 2 Park Ave, New York, NY 10016.

Pavco Industries Inc., PO Box 612, Pascagoula, MS 39567.

Permabond Industries Inc., 25784 Borg Rd, Elkhart, IN 46514.

Plastic Products Co., 1609 Union Ave, Baltimore, MD 21211.

Ply-Germ Industries Inc., 919 Third Ave, New York, NY 10022.

Plywood Components Inc., 6523 NE Old Salem Rd, Albany, OR 97321.

Polyplastex United Inc., 870 Springfield Rd, Union, NJ 07083.

Premier Trading Co., 1505 SE Gideon, PO Box 4204, Portland, OR 97208.

REO Industries Inc., 633 3rd St NW, Massillon, OH 44646.

Resotech Corp., PO Box 304, Watertown, NY 13601.

Rex Plastics Inc., PO Box 948, Thomasville, NC 27360.

Robinson Export-Import Corp., 6732 Industrial Rd, Springfield, VA 22151.

Roseburg Lumber Co., Box 1088, Roseburg, OR 97470.

Simeone National Corp., 2300 Commonwealth Ave, North Chicago, IL 60064.

The Mark Thomas Co., 6443 SW Beaverton-Hillsdale Hwy, Portland, OR 97221.

United States Gypsum Co., 101 S Wacker Dr., Chicago, IL 60606.

US Plywood, 1 Landmark Sq., Stamford, CT 06921.

Welsh Panel, Box 1218, Longview, WA 98632.

Westchester Venetian Marble, South Buckhout St, Irvington on Hudson, NY 10533.

Ralph Wilson Plastics Co., (Wilson Art), 600 General Bruce Dr., Temple, TX 76501.

Wood Mosaic Corp., PO Box 21159, Louisville, KY 40221.

Folding doors

American Door Co. Inc., PO Box 626, 2424 Home St, Mishawaka, IN 46544.

Bifolds, from E. A. Nord Co., PO Box 1187, Everett, WA 98206.

Clopay Corp., 1215 Clopay Sq., Cincinnati, OH 45214.

Foster Grant Co., 217 Hamilton St, Leominster, MA 01453.

Grosfillex Inc., 843 N 9th St, Reading, PA 19604.

Kaywood Div. of Joanna Western Mills Co., PO Box 307, Benton Harbor, MI 49022

Kirkead Industries Inc., 5860 N Pulaski Rd, Chicago, IL 60646.

Lustre Line Products Co., Richmond & Norris St, Philadelphia, PA 19125.

National Industries Inc., Box 293, Industrial Park, Ocala, FL 32670.

Paeco Inc., 500 Market St, Perth Amboy, NJ 08861.

Panelfold Doors Inc., 10700 NW 36 Ave, Miami, FL 33167.

Pella Windows & Doors, 100 Main St, Pella, IO 50219.

Premier Trading Co., 1505 SE Gideon, PO Box 4204, Portland, OR 97208.

Western Laminates Inc., 3827 Lake St, Omaha, NB 68111.

Wing Industries Inc., PO Box 38347, Dallas, TX 75238.

Woodford-Marco Mfg Co., Box 346, Forest Grove, OR 97116.

Windows

Venetian Blind Council, PO Box 670, East Orange, NJ 07018.

Window Shade Manufacturers Assoc., Executive Plaza, 1211 W 22nd St, Oak Brook, IL 60521 (prime manufacturers of cloth window shades and window shade rollers).

Andersen Corp., Bayport, MN 55003.

Caradco Window & Door Div., Scovill Mfg Co., 1098 Jackson St, Dubuque, IA 52001.

Camden Glass & Metals Co., 111 Marlton Ave, Camden, NJ 08105.

Chromalloy-American Corp., 641 Lexington Ave, New York, NY 10022.

O'Fallon Lumber & Supply Inc., 126 West Elm St, O'Fallon, MO 63366.

Pella Windows & Doors, 100 Main St, Pella, IA 50219.

Scranton Plate Glass Co., 1101 Penn Ave, Scranton, PA 18509.

Southern Cross Lumber & Millwork Co., 143 Brown Rd, Hazelwood, MO 63042.

United Plate Glass Co., 127 Anderson St, Pittsburgh, PA 15212.

Utica Glass Co., 725 Varick St, Utica, NY 13502.

Shades and blinds

All Habitat shops.

Breneman Inc., 1133 Sycamore St, Cincinnati, OH 45210.

C-Mor Co., 7 Jewell St, Garfield, NJ 07026.

Clopay Corp., 1215 Clopay Sq., Cincinnati, OH 45214.

Graber Co., Graber Plaza, Middleton, WI 53562.

Import Specialists Inc., 82 Wall St, New York, NY 10005.

Newell Co. Inc., 916 S Arcade Ave, Freeport, IL 61032.

One Touch of Glamour Inc., 6130 N Broadway, Chicago, IL 60660.

Unitron, 12824 S Cerise Ave, Hawthorne, CA 90250.

Work-tops

The Diller Corp., 6126 Madison Ct, Morton Grove, IL 60053.

E. I. Dupont De Nemours & Co., Tatnall Bldg Products Info. Section, Wilmington, DE 19898 (corian).

Dura-Beauty, Consoweld Corp., 700 Durabeauty Lane, Wisconsin Rapids, WI 54494.

Fabricon Products (Lamin Art), 6430 E Slanson Ave, Los Angeles, CA 90040.

Fibresin Plastics, Div. US Gypsum, Box 88, Oconomowac, WI 53066.

Formica Corporation, 120 E Fourth St, Cincinnati, OH 45202.

Micarta, from Westinghouse Electric Corp., Hoover St, Hampton, SC 29924.

Nevamar, Div. Exxon Chemical Corp., Telegraph Rd, Odenton, MD 21113.

Parkwood, 1350 S Second St, Coschocton, OH 43812.

Pioneer Plastics Corp., Pionite Rd, Auburn, ME 04210.

Textolite, from General Electric Co., 1350 S Second St, Coschocton, OH 43812.

Wilson Art, 600 General Bruce Dr., Temple, TX 76501.

Butcher's wooden blocks

Butcherblock, LDC, 1864 Massachusetts Ave, Cambridge, MA 02140.

H & W Products Inc., 1200 Summer St, Stamford, CT 06905.

Valley Wood Products Inc., R.D., Sugarloaf, PA 18249.

The Kitchen Book cannot claim personal knowledge of all the addresses given above, but it is hoped that they will be useful. All enquiries should be directed to the relevant manufacturer and not to the author or the publishers.
All information is correct at the time of going to press, but, owing to the vagaries of economic life, the editors cannot guarantee its continuing accuracy.

Metrication

The metric system is based upon the distance of ten million metres between the North Pole and the Equator, and was devised by French scientists at the end of the eighteenth century as a logical alternative to calculations based on the weight of a grain of wheat or the length of a king's arm. It has been adopted internationally as a standard method of measurement, although Britain, most of the Commonwealth countries and the United States are still in the throes of "going metric" and forsaking the old Imperial and US systems.

The four basic metric measures are:
metres (for lengths)
litres (for liquids)
grammes (for solids)
degrees centigrade (for temperatures)

Metric weights and measures are decimal systems—that is, they are calculated in units of ten. Divisions of the main units are tenths, hundredths, thousandths, etc., which are formed by adding the prefixes: deci (one-tenth), centi (one-hundredth), milli (one-thousandth), kilo (one thousand), hecto (one hundred) and deca (ten).

10 millimetres (mm) = 1 centimetre (cm)
10 centimetres = 1 decimetre (dm)
10 decimetres = 1 metre (m)
10 metres = 1 dekametre (dk)
10 dekametres = 1 hectometre (hm)
10 hectometres = 1 kilometre (km)

Comparing metric and Imperial measures
A metre is about 3 ft 3 in
Ten centimetres are about 4 in
One centimetre is about $2/5$ in
One millimetre is about $1/25$ in
28 grams = 1 oz
1 kg is about 2lb
1 litre = $1\frac{3}{4}$ pints
$\frac{1}{2}$ litre = 18 fl oz = about $\frac{1}{2}$ pint
10 sq cm = 1 sq in

To convert centimetres into inches, or vice versa, use the ruler below. Switching from one system to another involves the problem of exact conversion. Confronted with a metric measurement it is difficult to know whether it is a simple ready reckoner conversion from the old Imperial figure or if it is the result of rounding up or down to a new metric measurement. Look at a selection of 1 lb jars of jam whose weights are printed in metric and Imperial. You are likely to find that the metric equivalent of 1 lb is variously described as 450, 454 or 455 grammes. After metrication many products stay the same size as before—the traditional fifty-two-inch-wide fabric is faithfully converted into its exact metric equivalent of 132 cm. In other instances, however, the metric measurement is a reduction or an enlargement to the nearest round figure. For example, the 35-inch-high kitchen unit is more likely to be converted into the neat size of 900 mm rather than its accurate equivalent of 889 mm. This small adjustment of approximately half an inch can cause trouble, especially if you intend to put new washing machines or fridges under old work-tops or new units between existing fittings. For complete accuracy carry a metal ruler or consult your supplier. The conversion table below is designed to guide you through some of the changes you may find when choosing major items of kitchen furniture or decorating materials.

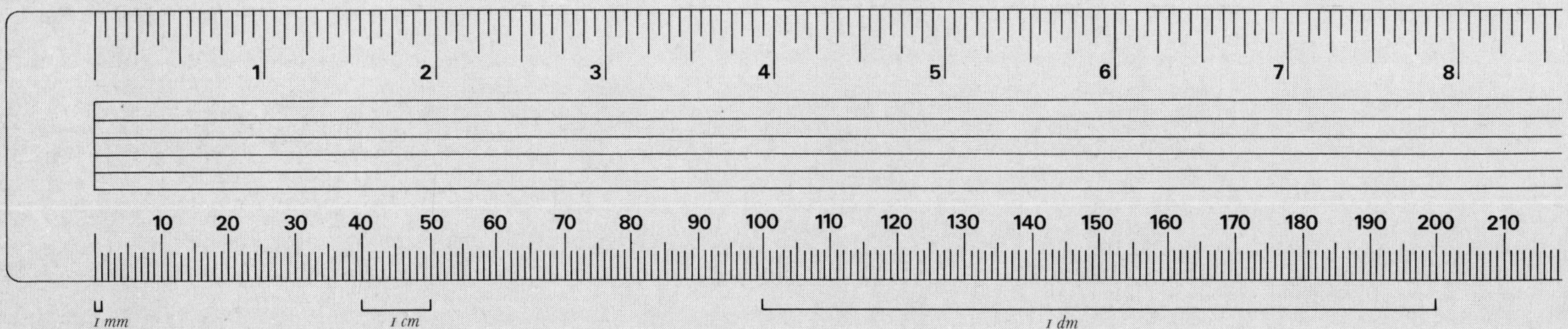

Conversion for the kitchen

Kitchen units	Width	Height	Depth	Width	Height	Depth
Base units	18, 24, 30, 36, 42, 54 in. (457, 610, 762, 914 mm, 1.07, 1.37 m)	36 in. (914 mm)	18, 21 in. (457, 533 mm)	400, 500, 600, 800, 1000 mm (16, 20, 23, 32, 40 in.)	900 mm (35 in.)	600 mm (23 in.)
Sink units	36, 42, 54, 63 in. (914 mm, 1.07, 1.37, 1.60 m)	36 in. (914 mm)	18, 21 in. (457, 533 mm)	1.2, 1.5, 1.8 m (47, 59, 71 in.)	900 mm (35 in.)	600 mm (23 in.)
Wall units	24, 30, 36, 42 in. (610, 762, 914 mm, 1.07m)	20 in. (508 mm)	10, 12 in. (254, 305 mm)	400, 500, 600, 800, 1000 mm (16, 20, 23, 32, 40 in.)	450 mm (18 in.)	300 mm (12 in.)
Building and decorating materials						
Wall tiles	$4\frac{1}{4}$ in., 6 in. (107, 152 mm)			100 mm (4 in.)		
Floor tiles	9 in., 12 in. (229, 305 mm)			300 mm ($11\frac{3}{4}$ in.)		
Sheet floorings	6 ft (1.83 m)			2.0 m (6 ft $6\frac{3}{4}$ in.)		
Paint	Already metric – see opposite			500 ml ($\frac{1}{2}$ litre) (about 1 pint) 1 litre (about 2 pints) $2\frac{1}{2}$ litres (over 4 pints) 5 litres (nearly 9 pints)		
Wallpaper	21 in. x 11 yds. (533 mm x 10 m)			533 mm x 10 m		

Weights, measures and cooking

American cookery books give measurements for most of their recipes by volume, a few by weight. The British and French give most of their measurements by weight, a few by volume. Each country, however, uses a different system of weights and measures. The Americans and British use many of the same terms—pounds, ounces, pints—but the quantities for liquid measures are different; the British fluid ounce is .96 of the American one. The metric system is now being adopted by Britain and America, but is still relatively unfamiliar. The conversion table below should help you move from one system to another, although the equivalents given are approximate only. For more exact equivalents in transposing from one system to another, use the conversion formulae on the right.

To convert	multiply	by
Ounces to grammes	ounces	28.35
Grammes to ounces	grammes	0.035
Litres to British quarts	litres	0.88
Litres to American quarts	litres	0.95
British quarts to litres	quarts	1.14
American quarts to litres	quarts	1.057
Inches to centimetres	inches	2.54
Centimetres to inches	centimetres	0.39

United States, British and metric recipe equivalents

Ingredient	United States	British	metric
Flour	1 tablespoon	¼ oz	10 g
	4 tablespoons	1 oz	25 g
	8 tablespoons	2 oz	50 g
	1 cup + 4 tablespoons	¼ pound	125 g
	4½ cups	1 pound	450 g
	¼ cup	1 oz	25 g
	½ cup	3 oz	75 g
	⅔ cup	4 oz	125 g
	1 cup	5 oz	150 g
Sugar	4 tablespoons	2 oz castor sugar	50 g
	8 tablespoons	¼ pound castor sugar	125 g
	1 cup + 3 tablespoons	½ pound castor sugar	225 g
	2⅓ cups	1 pound castor sugar	450 g
	¼ cup	2 oz	50 g
	½ cup	3 oz	75 g
	⅔ cup	4 oz	125 g
	1 cup	7 oz	200 g
Butter or fat	2 tablespoons	1 ounce	25 g
	¼ cup (4 tablespoons)	2 ounces	50 g
	½ cup (solidly packed)	¼ pound	125 g
	1 cup (solidly packed)	½ pound	225 g
	2 cups (solidly packed)	1 pound	450 g
Liquids	¼ cup	2 fl oz	0·0568 litre
	½ cup	4 fl oz	0·125 litre
	⅔ cup	5 fl oz	0·143 litre
	¾ cup	6 fl oz	0·166 litre
	1 cup	8 fl oz	0·25 litre
	2 cups	16 fl oz	0·5 litre
Rice	1 cup	5 oz	150 g

Index

D

E

Index

Index

L

MN

O

PQ

R

Index

S

T

UV

WYZ

Acknowledgements

The publishers wish to thank the following individuals and organizations for their assistance in the preparation of this book.

AEG-Telefunken (UK) Ltd, Slough, Berks; Mr Ahmed, The Ganges Restaurant, London; Ajimura Japanese Restaurant, London; Alno-UK Ltd, London; American Embassy, London; Amtico Ltd, London Showroom; W. S. Atkins Group Ltd, Epsom, Surrey; Belling & Co. Ltd, Enfield, Middx; Robert Bosch Ltd, Watford, Herts; Braun Electric (UK) Ltd, Sunbury-on-Thames, Middx; Patricia Braun, *Trade Associations & Professional Bodies of the UK* (Pergamon Press, Oxford); British Airways; British Gas; British Transport Hotels (Travellers-Fare); The Building Centre, London; Anthony Byers; Capital Hotel, London; Clifton Nurseries, London; Comera Cuisines Ltd, New Malden, Surrey; *Complete Home Catalog* (Bantam Books, New York); *Contract* (Gralla Publications, New York); Cordon Bleu Cookery School, London; Creda Electric Ltd, Stoke-on-Trent, Staffs; Ministry of Defence; Design Centre, London; Divertimenti Ltd, London; Electricity Council, London; English Ceramic Tile Co. Ltd, London; English Rose Kitchens Ltd, Warwick; Thomas Ford (Smithfield) Ltd, London; Johnny Grey; Grovewood Products Ltd, Tipton, W. Midlands; Hammoco Designs Ltd, Oxford; Harvey Nichols Ltd, London; Heidapal, Herford, Germany; Colin Hodson (Hodson Rivers Associates); Hoover Ltd, Greenford, Middx; Hygena Ltd, Liverpool; Inner London Education Authority; Intercontinental Cooking & Tableware Co. Ltd (ICTC), Sunbury-on-Thames, Middx; *Interior Design* (Whitney Communications Corp., New York); Robert Jackson and Co. Ltd, London; Leon Jaeggi & Son Ltd, London; Jenn-Air Corp., Indianapolis, Indiana, USA; Anthony Kirk, South London Consortium for Local Authority Building Research and Development; *Kitchen Business* (Gralla Publications, New York); Kitchen Consultants Ltd, Kenton, Middx; London Hilton; McDonald's Golden Arches Restaurant Ltd, London; Cilla & Sandy Mackay; Rory McKechnie, *Camping & Sporting Equipment News;* Main Gas Appliances Ltd, London; Donald C. Mallows; Marks & Spencer Ltd, London; Tony Mayes, Pindisports; David Mellor, London; Miele Co. Ltd, London; Móstoles Industrial, S.A., Madrid, Spain; Multyflex Kitchens Ltd, Llanelli, Dyfed; Hilary Nimmo; N.V. Philips Gloeilampenfabrieken, Eindhoven, Holland; Poggenpohl U.K. Ltd, New Malden, Surrey; Rentokil Ltd (Products Division), East Grinstead, W. Sussex; Royal Hospital Chelsea, London; Sans Souci Restaurant, London; Pat Scovell, Elizabeth David Ltd; Securit, São Paulo, Brazil; SieMatic U.K. Ltd, Ilford, Essex; Solent Ceramics, Southampton; Tectum Køkkenet, Copenhagen, Denmark; Thorn Domestic Appliances (Electrical) Ltd, Havant, Hants; Jack and Jane Tressider; Van den Berghs & Jurgens Ltd, Burgess Hill, Sussex.

Photographs

Photographs are listed from left to right in descending order. Abbreviations used are CC—Clive Corless, CP—Camera Press, RS—Roger Stowell, JS—Jessica Strang, EW—Elizabeth Whiting, MMC—Maison de Marie Claire, RG—Reanne Giovanni.

Front jacket EW/photo Tim Street Porter; Elliot Fine; Conran Ink/photo RS; RS; CC; Bill McLaughlin; EW/photo Jerry Tubby. **Inside flap** CC **Back jacket** RS **8/9** Claus Hansmann **10/11** Crown Copyright: reproduced by permission of the Department of the Environment; Claus Hansmann; C.M. Dixon; Museum of London; Scala **12/13** Michael Holford; John Bethell; Scala; Radio Times Hulton Picture Library; Mauro Pucciarelli; Compton Castle, a property of the National Trust/photo John Bethell **14/15** Scala; Claus Hansmann; Radio Times Hulton Picture Library; Ronan Picture Library; John Bethell; Saltram House, a property of the National Trust/photo John Bethell; Mario Pucciarelli **16/17** Angelo Hornak; Angelo Hornak; Western Americana Picture Library; Western Americana Picture Library **18/19** Mary Evans; Saltram House, a property of the National Trust/photo John Bethell; Ronan Picture Library; Ronan Picture Library; Mary Evans; Ronan Picture Library; Ronan Picture Library; Mary Evans; Mary Evans **20/21** Radio Times Hulton Picture Library; Radio Times Hulton Picture Library; Radio Times Hulton Picture Library; courtesy of the Electricity Council; Popperfoto; Mary Evans **22/23** RS; RS; RG; RG; RS; Kerstin Bernhard; CP/photo Cecil Beaton; RS; CC; CC; RG **24/25** all RS **26/27** all RS **28/29** all CC **30/31** all CC **32/33** all CC **34/35** all RS **36/37** both RS **38/39** all RG **40/41** CP/photo Cecil Beaton **42/43** all RS **44/45** RG; RG; Norman McGrath; Norman McGrath; RG **46/47** all RG **48/49** all RG **50/51** all RG except top far right, John W. Retallack **52/53** all RG **54/55** all RG **56/57** Angus McBean; RS; RS; RS; RS; RS; RS; Angus McBean **58/59** all RS **60/61** all CC **62/63** all Kerstin Bernhard **64/65** all Kerstin Bernhard **66/67** CC **68/69** Radio Times Hulton Picture Library; CC; CC; Snark International/photo Edouard Rousseau **70/71** Charles Wiesehahn; Ministry of Defence; RS; Daily Telegraph; CC; JS; British Airways **72/73** CC; JS; CC; CC; Daily Telegraph; JS; Mary Fisher/Colorific **74/75** CC; CC; CC; CC; RS; CC **76/77** CC **78/79** Ezra Stoller Associates; Norman McGrath/architects Tony & Ann Woolner; JS **80/81** Bill McLaughlin; James Mortimer **82/83** Susan Griggs/photo Michael Boys; EW/photo Lavinia press; Conran Ink/photo Jerry Tubby **84/85** MMC; Tim Street Porter; Bill McLaughlin; MMC **86/87** JS; Norman McGrath/design Charles Morris Mount **88/89** ZEFA; EW/photo Tim Street Porter; JS; Susan Griggs/photo Michael Boys; **90/91** CP; EW/photo Jerry Tubby; CP **92/93** Norman McGrath/architect William Ehrlich; ZEFA; CP; Alen MacWeeney/design Martin Lipsitt; CP **94/95** Norman McGrath/architect Patrick Scott; CP; Norman McGrath/architect Patrick Scott; Norman McGrath/architect Patrick Scott **96/97** original photo John Prizeman/Graham Kerr; jigsaw puzzle photo CC **98/99** EW/photo Tim Street Porter; MMC; JS **100/101** EW/photo Graham Henderson; Robert Perron; CP; PAF International **102/103** Robert Perron; EW/photo Michael Nicholson; EW/photo Steve Colby; EW/photo Spike Powell; CP; Bill McLaughlin; Robert Perron **104/105** MMC; EW/photo Michael Nicholson; EW/photo Michael Nicholson; JS; Norman McGrath/architect Henry Smith Miller **110/111** CP; CP; EW/photo Graham Henderson; CP; Michael Wickham **112/113** CP; JS; EW/photo Michael Nicholson; EW/photo Tim Street Porter; John Prizeman/SieMatic; Conran Ink/photo Jerry Tubby; MMC **114/115** Elliot Fine; CP; Elliot Fine; Bill McLaughlin; Jed Wilcox/design Lalli; Bill McLaughlin; architect Norman Jaffe AIA **118/119** CP **120/121** RS; CP **124/125** Susan Griggs/photo Michael Boys; Daily Telegraph; CC **126/127** John Prizeman/Boffi; Bill McLaughlin; Julius Shulman; Habitat Designs Ltd; EW/photo Jerry Tubby; EW/photo Tim Street Porter; EW/photo Tim Street Porter **128/129** Robert Perron/Alan Buchsbaum & Howard Korenstein of Design Coalition; Stockman & Manners Assoc; Robert Perron/design Armstrong Childs; Norman McGrath/design Stephen Leigh; Norman McGrath/Alan Buchsbaum & Howard Korenstein of Design Coalition **130/131** CC; EW/photo Jerry Tubby **132/133** Norman McGrath/Alan Buchsbaum & Howard Korenstein of Design Coalition; JS; Robert Perron/architect Don Watson; RG/design Laura Odell; Corian counter top material by courtesy of Du Pont; Transworld Feature Syndicate Inc; CP EW/photo Tim Street Porter; courtesy of Poggenpohl Ltd **134/135** RS; CP; courtesy of Miele Company Ltd; Nilson/Anthony Verlag; RG/design Laura Odell; RS; courtesy of Poggenpohl Ltd **136/137** Bill McLaughlin; courtesy of Elkay; Daily Telegraph; Norman McGrath/architect Don Mallow; Bill McLaughlin; RS **138/139** Elliot Fine/architect Albert Grossman; Rosie Hayter/design Johnny Grey; MMC; Elliot Fine **140/141** CP; Norman McGrath; Conran Ink/photo Rupert Watts; Conran Ink/photo Rupert Watts; Michael Wickham; JS **142/143** MMC: MMC: RG/designers & architects Kahn & Mallis Assoc; MMC; Conran Ink/photo Spike Powell; Transworld Feature Syndicate Inc; CP **144/145** courtesy of Móstoles Industrial S.A.; CP; CP; RG/design Laura Odell; CP; RG/design Laura Odell; design Martin Lipsitt **146/147** EW/photo Clive Helm; EW/photo Clive Helm; John Prizeman/Ideal Home; courtesy of Erbi-Nederland BV; EW/photo Clive Helm; CP; Corian counter top material by courtesy of Du Pont **148/149** EW/photo Tim Street Porter; EW/photo Michael Nicholson; EW/photo Jerry Tubby; JS; John Bethell; courtesy of Bulthaup/photo Rudolph Schmutz; Brecht-Einzig Ltd/architects Professors Hans Kammerer & Walter Belz; Brecht-Einzig Ltd/architect Alan Tye **150/151** Alen MacWeeney/design Martin Lipsitt; Conran Ink/photo Jerry Tubby; CP; courtesy of Nairn Cushionflor; ZEFA; courtesy of Amtico Flooring; Hedrich-Blessing/courtesy St Charles Manufacturing Co.; Roger Phillips, copyright Mitchell Beazley; Norman McGrath/architect Ulrich Franzen; Jed Wilcox/design Lalli; CC **152/153** CP; EW/photo Tim Street Porter; EW/photo Lavinia Press; MMC; courtesy of Vigers Stevens & Adams Ltd; MMC; Norman McGrath/architect Patrick Scott; Nilson/Anthony Verlag; Daily Telegraph; courtesy of Hygena QA; Ezra Stoller Associates; Elliot Fine; Susan Griggs/photo Michael Boys; MMC; Norman McGrath/design Charles Morris Mount; Roger Phillips, copyright Mitchell Beazley **154/155** Robert Perron/architects Armstrong/Childs; CP; courtesy of Poggenpohl Ltd; CC **156/157** JS; RS; ZEFA; Brecht-Einzig Ltd/architect Wilhelm Haug; MMC; MMC, Brecht-Einzig Ltd/design Jacqueline de Roemer; ZEFA; Serge Korniloff/design Emily & Sam Mann; MMC **158/159** EW/photo Jerry Tubby; EW/photo Tim Street Porter; MMC; Bill McLaughlin; Norman McGrath/architect Patrick Scott; RG; Robert Perron/architect Peter Samton **160/161** Robert Perron/architects Gunn & Meyerhoff; Robert Perron/architects Gunn & Meyerhoff; EW/photo Tim Street Porter; John Bethell; EW/photo Michael Nicholson; MMC; courtesy of Miele Company Ltd; CP **162/163** John Bethell; Colorific/Agence Top/decorated by Berthelot; ZEFA; Daily Telegraph; courtesy of Grovewood Products Ltd; CC; Zwietasch; Daily Telegraph; Nilson/Anthony Verlag **164/165** CC; CP; EW/photo Michael Nicholson; Ezra Stoller Associates; Daily Telegraph; EW/photo Michael Nicholson **166/167** EW/photo Tim Street Porter; Norman McGrath/design David Kenneth Spectre; Norman McGrath/ design Robert Shaw Superstructures; MMC; MMC; Bill McLaughlin; EW/photo Michael Nicholson **168/169** EW/photo Tim Street Porter **170/171** Bill McLaughlin; CC; EW/photo Lavinia Press; RG/design Laura Odell; courtesy of Westinghouse Corporation; EW/photo Jerry Tubby **172/173** RG/design Laura Odell; CP; EW/photo Spike Powell; Jed Wilcox/design Lalli; Ezra Stoller Associates MMC **174/175** Roger Phillips, copyright Mitchell Beazley; Robert Perron; JS; Brecht-Einzig Ltd/architect Stephen Yakeley; J.O. Bragstad; EW/photo Tim Street Porter; Elliot Fine/architect Carl Hribar **180/181** Mansell Collection/G.E.C.; courtesy of Westinghouse Corporation; RG/design Laura Odell; CP; EW/photo Jerry Tubby **182/183** RG; Lehtikuva Oy; JS; RG/design Laura Odell; JS; EW/photo Jerry Tubby **184/185** EW/photo Tim Street Porter; EW/photo Michael Nicholson; EW/photo Spike Powell; EW/photo Michael Nicholson; EW/photo Tim Street Porter; EW/photo Tim Street Porter; EW/photo Jerry Tubby; EW/photo Spike Powell; courtesy of Armstrong Floors **186/187** Brecht-Einzig Ltd/architect Peter Aldington; EW/photo Michael Nicholson; MMC; MMC; Brecht-Einzig Ltd/architect John Guest; CP; Serge Korniloff/design Emily and Sam Mann **188/189** Brecht-Einzig Ltd/architect Stephen Yakeley; JS; JS; EW/photo Spike Powell; EW/photo Michael Nicholson; MMC **192/193** John Ledger; courtesy of SieMatic U.K. Ltd; CP; EW/photo Michael Nicholson; RS; EW/photo Jerry Tubby; London Associates; CP; Bill McLaughlin **196/197** Daily Telegraph **198/199** Norman McGrath/design Myron Goldfinger; EW/photo Spike Powell **200/201** courtesy of Miele Company Ltd **202/203** courtesy of SieMatic U.K. Ltd; courtesy of Tectum Køkkenet; courtesy of Tectum Køkkenet; courtesy of Tectum Køkkenet; courtesy of SieMatic U.K. Ltd; courtesy of Tectum Køkkenet; courtesy of Tectum Køkkenet **204/205** courtesy of Heidapal; courtesy of Poggenpohl Ltd; courtesy of Heidapal; courtesy of Hygena QA; Habitat Designs Ltd; Habitat Designs Ltd; courtesy of SieMatic U.K. Ltd **206/207** courtesy of Heidapal; courtesy of Robert Bosch Ltd; courtesy of Hygena QA; courtesy of Securit; courtesy of SieMatic U.K. Ltd; courtesy of SieMatic U.K. Ltd; courtesy of Heidapal; CP; courtesy of Securit; EW/photo Tim Street Porter; courtesy of Securit; courtesy of Hygena QA; ZEFA; courtesy of SieMatic U.K. Ltd; courtesy of Securit **208/209** MMC **212/213** Charles Wiesehahn/architect Y. Weymouth/Redroof Design; MMC; RG/design Kahn & Mallis Assoc; EW/photo Michael Nicholson; Susan Griggs/photo Michael Boys **214/215** ZEFA; courtesy of Heidapal; MMC; Tommy Candler; CP; CP; CP **216/217** CP; MMC; CP; CP **218/219** EW/photo Clive Helm; Bill McLaughlin; CP; MMC; Picturepoint; JS; EW/photo Spike Powell **220/221** John Bulmer/design Angela Conner **222/223** JS; JS; JS; JS; Bill McLaughlin; Bill McLaughlin; Bill McLaughlin **224/225** Robert Perron/architect Turner Brooks; Robert Perron/architect Tom Platt; EW/photo Michael Nicholson; EW/photo Tim Street Porter; MMC; Bill McLaughlin; EW/photo Tim Street Porter **226/227** John Prizeman/LEB; John Prizeman; Norman McGrath/design John Fowler; courtesy of Grovewood Products Ltd; Smiley/architect Alan Buchsbaum; Bill McLaughlin **228/229** John Bulmer/design Angela Conner; John Bulmer/design Angela Conner; Rosie Hayter/design Johnny Grey; Rosie Hayter/design Johnny Grey; MMC **230/231** Susan Griggs/photo Adam Woolfitt **232/233** Siegfried Sammer; Mary Evans; Copyright Imperial War Museum/photo Angelo Hornak; Mary Evans; Copyright Imperial War Museum/photo Angelo Hornak; by permission of the Royal Geographical Society; ZEFA **234/235** Mary Evans; Scala; Mansell Collection; Punch; Henri Cartier-Bresson from Magnum/The John Hillelson Agency; Radio Times Hulton Picture Library; **236/237** John Watney/photo Jerry Young; courtesy of Hoseasons Holidays Ltd; Siegfried Sammer; JS; JS **238/239** British Tourist Authority; courtesy of Winnebago Industries Ltd; ZEFA **240/241** all CP except top left, Stockpile/photo R. Curtis **242/243** CC **244/245** Victoria & Albert Museum, Crown copyright; Mansell Collection; Melford Hall, a property of the National Trust/photo John Bethell; Cotehele House, a property of the National Trust/photo John Bethell; National Museum of Wales **246/247** Mansell Collection; Hatchlands, a property of the National Trust; Michael Holford/British Museum; Mansell Collection; Mansell Collection; Angelo Hornak; Angelo Hornak; Mansell Collection; Mary Evans **250/251** JS; Scala; Transworld Feature Syndicate Inc; courtesy of Hygena QA; EW/photo Graham Henderson **252/253** CP **254/255** Michael Wickham; CC; CP **256/257** EW/photo Jerry Tubby; RG; RS; Conran Ink/photo Rupert Watts; CC; Rosie Hayter/design Johnny Grey **258/259** EW/photo Michael Nicholson **260/261** CP; Nilson/Anthony Verlag; EW/photo Geoffrey Frosh; Robert Perron/architect Peter Hamilton; Robert Perron/architect Ted Long **262/263** Norman McGrath/architect Patrick Scott; RS; MMC; Christine Hanscomb; MMC; Bill McLaughlin **264/265** Nilson/Anthony Verlag; EW/photo Graham Henderson; EW/photo Michael Nicholson; EW/photo Lavinia Press; EW/photo Jerry Tubby **266/267** CC; CP; EW/photo Michael Nicholson; EW/photo Tim Street Porter; MMC; JS; Christine Hanscomb **268/269** courtesy of Grovewood Products Ltd; EW/photo Graham Henderson; Peter Wrigley; courtesy of Bulthaup/photo Rudolph Schmutz; CC **270/271** CP; EW/photo Michael Nicholson; Roger Phillips, copyright Mitchell Beazley; CC **272/273** CC **274/275** all Conran Ink/photo RS **276/277** all Conran Ink/photo RS **278/279** Conran Ink/photo RS; Conran Ink/photo RS; Conran Ink/photo RS; Susan Griggs/photo Michael Boys; Susan Griggs/photo Michael Boys **280/281** MMC; MMC; MMC; Conran Ink **282/283** all RS **284/285** both RS **286/335** all CC.

Most of these photographs come from photographic agencies and not from manufacturers so neither the author nor the publishers are able to give further information about them.

Artists:

Marilyn Bruce, Ray and Corinne Burrows, Terence Dalley/Artist Partners, Chris Gillings, Hayward and Martin Limited (Jim Reed, James Farrant), Kevin Maddison, Francis Morgan, Coral Mula, Alan Suttie, Paul Wrigley, Peter Wrigley.

Index: Bruce Leigh
Editorial assistance: Louise Bernbaum, Andrew Duncan, Nicola Hemingway, Alexandra Towle
Additional picture research: Jan Jones, Sue Pinkus

Services: JD Colour Studios Limited; Summit Photography; Negs; Hatton Colour